D0857024

The

Victoria Woodhull

Reader

Edited by Madeleine B. Stern

M & S Press

Weston, Massachusetts

1974

The Publisher wishes to thank Miriam Y. Holden for the gracious loan of much of the material by Victoria C. Woodhull reproduced in this volume.

Madeleine B. Stern (partner in the firm of Leona Rostenberg Rare Books in New York City) is the author of *The Life of Margaret Fuller, Louisa May Alcott, Purple Passage: The Life of Mrs. Frank Leslie, Imprints on History: Book Publishers and American Frontiers, We the Women: Career Firsts of Nineteenth-Century America, The Pantarch; A Biography of Stephen Pearl Andrews, Heads and Headlines: The Phrenological Fowlers.* She has edited O. S. Fowler's *A Home for All . . .* (1853), and Stephen Pearl Andrews' *The Primary Synopsis of Universology and Alwato* (1871). Miss Stern is co-author (with Leona Rostenberg) of *Old and Rare: Thirty Years in the Book Business* (1974).

Printed on long-life, acid-free paper.

TABLE OF CONTENTS

Biographical Introduction by Madeleine B. Stern

The literature published under the name of Victoria C. Woodhull is not only radical and sensational but frequently profound; it is also voluminous. Yet Victoria Woodhull was accused of being unable even to write her name. Her reputation was paradoxical, her character intriguing. She was a stockbroker who exposed the frauds of the stock market and at one time preached its abolition. She was a champion of free love who rocked the nation by publicizing a free love scandal. She was, it was said, a "heroic soul," "pure and true;" it was also said that she was either a prostitute or "married rather more extensively than most American matrons."

Whatever the differences of opinion, there is no doubt that—thanks in part to her extraordinary personality—she gave an impetus to the feminist movement during the 1870's. She enunciated advanced, often revolutionary doctrine on sociology, sex and eugenics, on political theory and economics. Gathered together, the theories she publicized form a microcosm of the country's vanguard thought on woman's rights and government, on labor and finance. The significance of the writings and lectures that bear her name entitles her to an impartial biographical analysis.

Victoria Woodhull's career was checkered, her early life reflecting the fluid society of the country. One of a family of ten, she was born in Homer, Ohio, in September 1838. Her father, Reuben Buckman Claflin, was described by some as an eminent lawyer descended from a ducal family, by others as a conniving fraud. Her mother, Roxanna Hummel Claflin, was characterized by admirers as a lady of royal German ancestry, by disparagers as a shrewish termagant born out of wedlock. Though much of their daughter's life remains similarly conjectural, there is no doubt that she was named after England's Queen.

The impecunious Claflin family embarked upon a nomadic life during the 1840's and 1850's. Traveling through Ohio and Illinois, Kansas and Missouri, they dispensed a so-called elixir of life and a cancer cure. Victoria, who had been subject to visions from her third year, made an attractive clairvoyant as she matured and, with her sister Tennessee, earned money as mesmerist, spiritualist and magnetic healer. By the time she was fifteen she had developed into a slight and sparkling creature, lithe and graceful, her features illumined by a variable, intriguing expression.

It was then, at the age of fifteen, that she met and married her first husband, Dr. Canning Woodhull, an incipient alcoholic, by whom she had two children. One, Byron, was an idiot whose extreme retardation aroused her subsequent interest in eugenics. The other, a daughter, Zula Maud, was to share some of her mother's interests and evince literary aspirations of her own. Besides raising her children, Victoria Woodhull served a turn in the California theater. By the time the Civil War had ended, her first marriage also approached a terminal stage. Now in her late twenties, Victoria Woodhull was becoming a fascinating femme fatale, while Canning Woodhull was fast becoming a confirmed alcoholic.

In St. Louis, Victoria met the virile, mustachioed Colonel James Harvey Blood, who had served with the Sixth Missouri Volunteers during the War. Spiritualist and reformer, he overflowed with outspoken views on the freedom of speech, of thought, and of press. In 1866, having divorced Dr. Woodhull, Victoria joined forces with Blood. Although their marriage record of July 14, 1866, signed in Montgomery County, Ohio, exists, it shows merely an "intention" rather than an actual "return" for marriage—a technicality that never seems to have bothered Victoria. While she continued to use the surname Woodhull, she certainly regarded herself as the Colonel's wife.

Together they traveled to Pittsburgh, where Victoria received, or believed she received, a visitation from the spirit of Demosthenes with whom she had been familiar since childhood. The orator's spirit wisely directed her to move her ménage to New York—a ukase which she promptly obeyed.

With her sister Tennessee, the Colonel's wife resumed her occupation as clairvoyant and magnetic healer. Victoria's most illustrious client was none other than Commodore Cornelius Vanderbilt, to whom she had been introduced by her father. Besides being a railway magnate and capitalist, the Commodore was a connoisseur of race horses and of women with magnetic healing powers. He took to Mrs. Woodhull with alacrity.

Victoria had come to New York at a time when miles of track were being laid to open up the West. Indeed the railroads were creating much of the country's wealth, and the stock exchange was principally a market for railroad securities. The Woodhull-Vanderbilt rapport at this time was fruitful. Grateful either for Victoria's healing touch or for the tips she dispensed during clairvoyant trances, the Commodore provided the sisters with entrée to Wall Street.

On February 4, 1870, the business of Woodhull, Claflin & Company was formally begun at 44 Broad Street, New York City. The first women stockbrokers in history had opened a new occupation for their sex, and

Victoria Woodhull's extraordinary career as financier, feminist and mouthpiece of reform had begun.

The reaction of the press was gratifying. The role of Colonel Blood as the "& Company" of the firm was relegated to insignificance, while the "Bewitching Brokers" and the "Fascinating Financiers" were headlined. Victoria especially attracted the Fourth Estate as, arrayed in a blue walking suit, her hair closely cropped, she bought and sold gold, government bonds, railway, mining and oil stocks and bonds. Radiating intelligence, intensity and magnetism, she learned as she operated, observing that there were railway frauds as well as railway profits, and that Wall Street was often the scene of sharp practice and false claims, watered stocks and bogus bonds. For a time her firm prospered and the entire family ensconced itself, along with a contingent of hangers-on, in a palatial mansion on 38th Street. The household included Victoria's children and her parents, her sister Tennessee, Colonel Blood and—a presence that raised eyebrows—the Colonel's predecessor, the returned Dr. Canning Woodhull, now ill and in need. The eccentric and erudite reformer-philosopher, Stephen Pearl Andrews, friend of Blood and champion of labor and woman's rights, resided in the Murray Hill mansion occasionally and there, against an opulent background, Victoria Woodhull played the role of salon leader, discussing with her entourage free trade and free soil, free thought and free love.

The relation between Victoria's brokerage activities and the feminist cause was apparent to Susan B. Anthony, who descended upon Broad Street to interview Victoria and wish her well. Victoria herself saw that relationship clearly. She had entered the business, she claimed, to prove woman's ability. While others argued about women's equality with men, she had dramatized it. "Women have every right," she stated. "All they need do is exercise them. . . . We are doing daily more for women's rights, by practically exercising the right to carry on our own business, than all the diatribes of papers and platform speeches will do in ten years." "Woman's ability to earn money," she continued, "is a better protection against the tyranny and brutality of men than her ability to vote."

Yet the vote, and woman's possible role in the political arena preoccupied her, and the "speculative daughter of Eve" was shortly metamorphosed into a "petticoat politician." Partly to prove that women could wield political power wisely and deserved the franchise, partly to indicate that even without the ballot there was no law preventing them from holding political office, partly to publicize the reform views of Andrews and Blood on labor, commerce and suffrage, and partly simply for love of the limelight, Victoria Woodhull determined to run for the Presidency of the United States.

With a letter, penned probably with the help of her mentors, Andrews and Blood, she threw her neat little jockey cap into the ring. Her announcement was carried by the *New York Herald* on April 2, 1870: "While others of my sex devoted themselves to a crusade against the laws that shackle the women of the country, I asserted my individual independence; . . . I therefore claim the right to speak for the unenfranchised women of the country, and . . . I now announce myself as a candidate for the Presidency." An editorial in the same issue graciously commented: "Women always take the part of each other, and if the women can be allowed to vote, Mrs. Woodhull may rely on rolling up the heaviest majority ever polled in this or any other nation. Her platform . . . is short, sharp, decisive, and has the true ring in it. Now for victory for Victoria in 1872!"

Victoria was not destined for victory in 1872; in fact, by the time of the election her campaign had disintegrated and she herself, as will be seen, was in prison, charged with transmitting obscene literature through the mails. Meantime, however, she stood upon a radical platform built by Andrews and Blood and reflecting their reform views. Woman should be free to vote, to work and to love as she wished. The worker should be freed from the "oppressive weight" which capital laid upon labor. The profit system should be replaced by a system of "equitable commerce" formulated by Andrews' friend, the first American anarchist, Josiah Warren, who stipulated that the price of any article of merchandise should be determined only by its cost plus the time spent in selling it. Thus no individual could profit at the expense of another. A new land system entitling everyone to a portion of the land; a new financial system eliminating usury; a new sexual system governed by mutual consent and devoid of government interference—were all planks in the Woodhull platform.

In order to publicize both her reform program and her candidacy, Victoria founded, with her sister Tennessee and her husband Colonel Blood, a remarkable paper. *Woodhull & Claflin's Weekly* ran from May 14, 1870 until June 10, 1876. During that time it not only puffed the candidacy of a woman for President but became the "most spectacular advocate of suffrage in the period." In addition, it opened its columns to frank discussions of prostitution and free love, marriage and divorce, currency reform and industrial justice, spiritualism, internationalism, equal pay for equal work, and new employments for women. It exposed many of the fraudulent practices of post-war America, from railway swindles to Congressional land jobbery, from the Wall Street machinations that Victoria had observed on Exchange to the insurance companies that hawked false policies. Its original motto, "Upward &

Onward," was transformed into "Progress, Free Thought, Untrammeled Lives." Colonel Blood as managing editor and Stephen Pearl Andrews as voluble contributor of radical disquisitions helped the *Weekly* live up to its lofty maxims.

Expediency and opportunism may have played some part initially in attracting the self-styled presidential candidate to the views championed in her *Weekly*, but there is little doubt that she came to subscribe to those views with conviction. For a time she allied herself with the International Workingmen's Association organized in 1864 by Karl Marx. Indeed, she became the dominant personality in its leading American Section, No. 12. Besides supporting the International's advocacy of the rights of labor, she endorsed, at lively meetings of Section 12, woman suffrage and free love. More concerned with establishing an eight-hour-day for the workingmen than with encouraging a single standard for the sexes, the parent organization castigated Section 12 as "sensation-loving spirits" who merely played with the labor movement, and by 1872 the Section was expelled from the IWA. Meantime, Victoria Woodhull's interest in Marxism had resulted in the first American publication of an English translation of the *Communist Manifesto* which appeared in *Woodhull & Claflin's Weekly* on December 30, 1871.

During this period of the early '70's, numerous articles, including a series on "The Tendencies of Government" in the *Herald*, were published with the byline of Victoria Woodhull, and many speeches bearing her name were printed. There is no doubt that some portions of them were ghosted by Blood and by Andrews. Those reformers could not have found a more convincing mouthpiece for their views. She was indeed a powerful instrument upon which to play the rousing marches of reform. Holding her manuscript in one hand, she would mount the platform of Apollo Hall or Cooper Institute and, arrayed in black with a single red rose on her dress, would pour forth revolutionary concepts on free love and woman suffrage, labor and capital, internationalism and finance. As a lecturer she was magnetic, prepossessing, effective.

One of Victoria Woodhull's most important lectures had been delivered before the House Judiciary Committee in the national capital in January 1871. Her address concerned a *Memorial* on woman suffrage presented to Congress in her name the month before. The *Memorial* stipulated that woman's right to vote was already guaranteed by the Fourteenth and Fifteenth Amendments and that all Congress need do was to see that that right be exercised. Although those Amendments had been adopted to insure the ballot to black citizens, Victoria interpreted them as applying to all citizens, black and white, male and female. In the simplest terms she syllogized that all citizens could vote; women were citizens; therefore women could vote. No further Amendment was required; the elective franchise already belonged to woman.

While the Majority report of the House Judiciary Committee denied Victoria's plea and refuted her interpretation of the Constitution, her argument and her personality deeply impressed the feminists, some of whom had attended her lecture. As Susan B. Anthony put it, Victoria Woodhull "came to Washington from Wall Street with a powerful argument and with lots of cash behind her." The National Woman Suffrage Association, which had been organized in 1869 by Elizabeth Cady Stanton and Susan B. Anthony, invited Victoria to repeat her argument at their third annual Washington convention of 1871. For a short time both Mrs. Stanton and Isabella Beecher Hooker seem to have regarded Victoria Woodhull as a likely standard-bearer for their cause.

On the other hand, the American Woman Suffrage Association, a rival Boston group organized in 1869 to secure action through the States rather than through Congress, looked down their noses at what they regarded an indiscreet choice of speaker whose reputation was not altogether above suspicion. Mrs. Stanton's reply to the Bostonians was firm: "When the men who make laws for us in Washington can stand forth and declare themselves pure and unspotted from all the sins mentioned in the Decalogue, then we will demand that every woman who makes a constitutional argument on our platform shall be as chaste as Diana."

A chaste Diana was a far cry from a Victoria Woodhull who advocated and, according to some, practiced free love. For all Mrs. Stanton's sensible attitude, the union between Victoria and the feminists was short-lived. While it lasted, however, Victoria had not only enlivened a National Suffrage convention but, with her powerful argument, raised the issue of the franchise to a question of constitutional law and so given momentum to the cause.

At the November '71 elections, Victoria Woodhull followed up her argument with an attempt to put it into practice. Leading a group of thirty-two women to the polls, she made a bold but unsuccessful effort to cast her ballot. Despite this failure she proceeded with her political campaign. In May 1872, the Equal Rights Party, organized for that purpose, formally nominated Victoria Woodhull as a candidate for the presidency of the United States. A Victoria League was formed to support her cause, and *Woodhull & Claflin's Weekly* blossomed forth as a campaign sheet.

While the *Weekly* elucidated the Woodhull platform on behalf of the rights of labor and the freedom of woman, free speech and free press, free land and free love, other papers found in the candidate's private life material for more sensational copy. The so-called "Claflin Scandal Case" was emblazoned in the news when Victoria's mother, Roxanna Claflin, lodged a court complaint against Colonel Blood, charging him with having threatened her life. In addition to this awkward "in-law" drama, word that Victoria's two husbands were occupying the same domicile at the same time had spread. Victoria's own sensational candor in such lectures as that on Social Freedom when she informed her audience proudly that she was a free lover; her close relationship with the free love champion, Stephen Pearl Andrews; her insistence that no individual lover could own any other whether married or unmarried— all contributed to the portrait of the "Famous Family of Free Lovers" dished up in the public prints. Thomas Nast was moved to take up his perceptive pen and produce for *Harper's Weekly* a cartoon of Victoria Woodhull as Mrs. Satan holding a placard inscribed: Be Saved by Free Love. In her novel, *My Wife and I*, Harriet Beecher Stowe introduced a character named Audacia Dangyereyes who bore striking and unappetizing resemblances to a caricatured Victoria Woodhull.

At this juncture the presidential candidate was informed by her acquaintance and co-worker Elizabeth Cady Stanton that Harriet Beecher Stowe's distinguished brother, Henry Ward Beecher, pastor of Brooklyn's Plymouth Church and pillar of society, was having an affair with a parishioner, the editor Theodore Tilton's dark-haired wife Elizabeth, mother of four. Victoria Woodhull endorsed Beecher's action which applied the free love concept; what she could not condone was the hypocritical secrecy with which he practiced in private the principles she preached in public. Moreover, Victoria had been chastised in the public papers for her candor; Beecher, above suspicion, had escaped any hint of scandal. It was a situation that called for correction since Victoria Woodhull had no intention of being made "the scapegoat of sacrifice."

Consequently, the November 2, 1872 issue of *Woodhull & Claflin's Weekly* (post-dated, in common practice) broke the news of "The Beecher-Tilton Scandal Case" in an article that sparked a national bonfire. The disclosure evoked a library of pamphlets and songs, poems and burlesques, caused trials, arrests and re-arrests and exposed a scandal that held the public interest for nearly three years. Eventually it culminated in the Tilton-Beecher Trial which lasted nearly six months in 1875 and consumed over 2,700 pages of printed testimony before it ended in a hung jury.

Meanwhile, Anthony Comstock, vice-hunter and guardian of public morality, supported by the Y.M.C.A., stepped into the picture, charging Victoria Woodhull and her sister with having transmitted obscene literature—namely, the November 2, 1872 issue of the *Weekly*—through the mails. As a result, their paper was temporarily suspended; unable to attend either to her brokerage business or her journal, much less to her political candidacy, Victoria lacked funds and was forced to give up the Murray Hill mansion; finally, she was incarcerated for four weeks without trial in Ludlow Street Jail. When, in November 1872, the nation went to the polls to return Grant to the White House, the woman candidate of the Equal Rights Party—a party that had failed to secure a place on the electoral ticket—spent Election Day in a prison cell.

Not even Anthony Comstock could clip for long the wings of the woman named after England's Queen. Victoria Woodhull still had other lives to lead. After her release on bail, the case was eventually dismissed, the judge ruling that the 1872 statute applied only to books, pamphlets and pictures, not to newspapers. Victoria revived her *Weekly* to publicize her prison experiences and to plead for penal reform. She undertook lecture tours to inform her audiences that the human body was the temple of God and sexual freedom the elixir of life. She still advertised the dictates of Stephen Pearl Andrews, holding by and large to his doctrine of individual sovereignty—the doctrine that every individual must be free to think, to work, to love as he wished, without government interference, provided only that in the exercise of those freedoms he did not interfere with the individual sovereignty of others. Victoria's newspaper was continued until 1876; her lectures in the States until 1877.

Then, in 1877, her erstwhile patron, Commodore Cornelius Vanderbilt, died, leaving the bulk of his enormous estate to his son William and comparatively minor bequests to his remaining progeny who promptly proceeded to contest the will. The Commodore's known propensity for clairvoyants in general and for female clairvoyants in particular would, it was understood, play some part in determining his soundness of mind or his lack of it. In order, therefore, to avoid summoning the female clairvoyant Victoria Woodhull to the witness stand, it was said that William H. Vanderbilt had offered her a sizable sum to leave her native shores.

At all events, leave them she did. After a visit to Canada, Victoria, with her children, her sister and her parents, but without the now discarded Colonel Blood, arrived in England. There she lectured in the provinces until, on an eventful evening in December 1877, she opened her London season at St. James's Hall with a speech on "The Human Body, the Temple of God." In the audience that night sat a thirty-six-year-old British banker who had not only heard of Victoria Woodhull but closely followed her American career. On the basis of what he had read, and on the basis of what he now saw electrifying the podium of St. James's Hall, he determined to marry the dynamic and fascinating woman who fearlessly discoursed on the Garden of Eden she had found in the human body.

A partner in one of the oldest firms in the City of London—Martin's Bank, older than the Bank of England—John Biddulph Martin, descended on his mother's side from Martha Washington, had much to offer the thirty-nine-year-old exotic from the States. His family, however, did not take kindly to his choice, and it took six years for them to acquiesce to the proposed union. It was not until October 31, 1883, that Victoria Woodhull became Victoria Woodhull Martin. The former mistress of Broad Street and Murray Hill gracefully assumed her new role as mistress of 17 Hyde Park Gate, South Kensington, and of the Martin manor house in Bredon's Norton near Tewkesbury.

Some of Mrs. Martin's time was spent in defending her new name from sporadically launched attacks. As Harriet Beecher Stowe's *My Wife and I* had once caricatured her with some venom, the distinguished novelist Henry James sketched in his *Siege of London* a putative portrait of Victoria as the social climber, Mrs. Headway, who "must have repudiated more husbands than she had married." Actually, Victoria never climbed so high on the social ladder as her sister Tennessee, who in 1885 married the merchant, Francis Cook, shortly thereafter becoming Lady Cook with full rights to a chateau in Portugal and to a great art collection in Richmond.

Nor did social climbing interest Victoria Martin as much as Henry James indicated. Rather, still engrossed in problems of economics, she pursued the study of finance with a guide more expert if less radical than Colonel Blood or Stephen Pearl Andrews. The partner in Martin's Bank now elucidated for her the intricacies of wealth and value, trade and production, which she discoursed upon in the pamphlets of her later days.

Despite her wealth and the opportunity it gave for idleness, Victoria Martin was no more idle than had been the once impecunious Victoria Woodhull. Still ardently clinging to her belief in the importance of woman's economic independence, she launched her own monthly in 1892. With her daughter Zula Maud as associate editor, and her husband as occasional contributor, Victoria continued *The Humanitarian* until 1901. It was aptly named, for she used the monthly as the organ for her own essays—produced without the aid of a Colonel Blood or a Stephen Pearl Andrews—on "all subjects appertaining to the well-being of humanity." Articles on woman suffrage and a humanitarian government that sought to combat the unequal distribution of wealth appeared in *The Humanitarian*, along with less erudite essays on palmistry, astrology and psychical research—subjects that still fascinated the erstwhile clairvoyant from Homer, Ohio.

In 1892 she made an attempt at a political come-back by campaigning again for the presidency of the United States, using the pages of the newly founded *Humanitarian* to announce her candidacy and visiting the United States in a futile attempt to stir up interest. Despite her continued desire for political action by women, she did not identify herself with the English suffrage movement. Her interest in the franchise seems to have been eclipsed by her interest in woman's economic independence, and by the turn of the century her relations with suffrage leaders on both sides of the ocean had, thanks no doubt to personality differences, cooled. Pamphlets on eugenics or "stirpiculture" as it was called, and the "rapid multiplication of the unfit" pauper classes flowed from her pen, reminding the public that Victoria Woodhull Martin was still deeply concerned with the welfare of the world community and was not unmindful of a possible population explosion.

After her husband's death in 1897, the wealthy widow Martin sold her London residence and moved to Bredon's Norton. She spent her declining but far from empty years in a variety of pursuits most of which pertained in one way or another to the work and the interests of women. She founded a Women's International Agricultural Club and, as the years passed and technology advanced, a Ladies' Automobile Club and the Women's Aerial League of England. She organized patriotic fund-raising campaigns during the First World War and—clairvoyant soon to be vindicated—offered a trophy for the first successful transatlantic aerial crossing.

Victoria Woodhull Martin did not die until June 10, 1927, three weeks after Lindbergh's flight to Paris. She had come a long way from the Homer, Ohio of 1838, to an ancestral manor at Bredon's Norton. In the course of her colorful, eventful life she had seen many of her purposes realized. Women had been granted the elective franchise for which the petticoat politician of Murray Hill had once fought. Capital had begun to make terms with labor. Internationalism had, with the establishment of the League of Nations, become more than a word. It would take nearly half a century until the freedom of sexual relations and the single standard for men and women would be accepted with some equanimity. Other aspects of the reform program she had enunciated were and still are unrealized: eugenics; the economic equality of men and women; the elevation of a woman to the presidency.

Despite the strong probability that some portions of her writings and speeches had been penned by others, Victoria Woodhull had publicized, in a convincing and dynamic manner the reform views they outlined. She had made an impact upon the feminist cause with her powerful constitutional argument. More important, perhaps, she had gone beyond the confines of the militant feminist suffrage movement. Her outspoken dicta on the freedom of sexual relations and on eugenics; her ability to elucidate programs of radical economic and political reform; her belief in and practice of woman's economic independence—all place her in the vanguard of the woman's movement. Notorious and sometimes suspect, paradoxical and upon occasion opportunistic, she was still a "fearless advocate of all nameable freedoms." An effective mouthpiece of reform, she takes a colorful place in the feminist movement whose sphere she boldly enlarged.

Victoria Claflin Woodhull Martin

WASHINGTON, D.C.—THE JUDICIARY COMMITTEE OF THE REPRESENTATIVES RECEIVING A DEPUTATION OF FEMALE SUFFRAGISTS, JANUARY 11TH, 1871. VICTORIA C. WOODHULL READING HER ARGUMENT IN FAVOR OF WOMAN'S VOTING ON THE BASIS OF THE 14TH AND 15TH CONSTITUTIONAL AMENDMENTS.

Victoria Woodhull Reading Her Argument on Woman Suffrage before the House Judiciary Committee

Victoria Woodhull Nominated for the Presidency of the United States

Victoria Woodhull's Campaign Button

A PROTEST FROM VICTORIA C. WOODHULL.

Victoria Woodhull's Attempt to Cast Her Ballot

"GET THEE BEHIND ME [MRS.] SATAN!"
(Victoria Woodhull cartooned by Thomas Nast in *Harper's Weekly* for
February 17, 1872)

Cartoon of Victoria Woodhull as Mrs. Satan by Thomas Nast

Part I

SOCIOLOGY

Introduction by Madeleine B. Stern

Implicit in Victoria Woodhull's philosophy was the principle of social freedom or free love. In the wake of free sexual relations, she believed, would emerge woman's equality with man and her true emancipation—a belief that placed her in the vanguard of the Women's Liberation movement. The institution of marriage, like that of slavery, would be abolished for in the world she envisioned it was obsolete.

Victoria was not alone in such opinions. The French social philosopher Fourier, who developed the doctrine of "attractive industry" for workers who selected the tasks they enjoyed, had also insisted upon an end to legalized marriage. Josiah Warren, the first American anarchist, opposed free love, but endorsed the concept of the sovereignty of the individual, who should be left free to do exactly as he wished provided he did not infringe upon the comparable freedom of other sovereign individuals. Victoria Woodhull's friend and editor, Stephen Pearl Andrews, author of *Love, Marriage, and Divorce*, believed in both individual sovereignty and free love and did not hesitate to fill the columns of *Woodhull & Claflin's Weekly* with his thoughts on those subjects. The Massachusetts pastor, Charles Wentworth Upham, opposed marital restrictions and endorsed free sexual relations. One of the numerous communities that dotted the eastern seaboard during the nineteenth century—that of John Humphrey Noyes in Oneida—was based upon a system of "complex marriages" that were impermanent and mutually acceptable to the participants. Most of those who upheld the free love principle—Victoria Woodhull included—accepted the authority of the phrenologists, those nineteenth-century scientists of the mind, who announced that amativeness was a "faculty" that could and should be developed in proper harmony with other phrenological faculties.

The free love cultists, however, were in the minority. By 1871, when Victoria Woodhull delivered her speech on THE PRINCIPLES OF SOCIAL FREEDOM, Dame Grundy had lined up its opponents—the militant moralists who guarded everyone's chastity but their own, a task force that included the distinguished *Tribune* editor, Horace Greeley, who believed in the sanctity and indissolubility of marriage; the "roundsman of the lord," Anthony Comstock, bracing himself to nose out obscenity for the purification of mankind; the eminent pastor of Brooklyn's Plymouth Church, Henry Ward Beecher, who, it was soon to be disclosed by Victoria Woodhull herself, did not practice what he preached.

Two crimes of passion had brought the issue of free love into the public prints and confirmed the general revulsion against any interference with the institution of marriage. In the Fair-Crittenden case, Mrs. Fair had violated the "sanctity" of marriage by murdering a married man, Crittenden, who, she believed (though he did not) belonged more to her than to his wife. A far more notable case, involving more colorful protagonists, was the Richardson-McFarland affair. In 1869, a confirmed drunkard, Daniel McFarland, shot his divorced wife's lover, the well-known journalist and war correspondent, Albert D. Richardson. Richardson married Abby Sage McFarland on his deathbed, and at the trial that followed, the murderer was acquitted to expressions of overwhelming popular applause.

Against such a background, on November 20, 1871, Victoria Woodhull delivered on the platform of New York City's Steinway Hall one of her most famous speeches, a speech on THE PRINCIPLES OF SOCIAL FREEDOM in which she announced: "Yes, I am a Free Lover. I have an *inalienable, constitutional* and *natural* right to love whom I may, to love as *long* or as *short* a period as I can; to *change* that love *every day* if I please, and with *that* right neither *you* nor any *law* you can frame have *any* right to interfere."

Government's legal function, Victoria explained, was not to grant rights but to protect the individual's inherent constitutional rights; a marriage contract was no more indissoluble than any other contract; women as well as men were entitled to the pursuit of happiness and to the sovereignty of their own individuality. It was a false modesty that shut off discussion of sex; it was the double standard that resulted in the sexual submission of women and the legalized prostitution that existed in marriage, a prostitution comparable with that which flourished on New York's notorious Greene Street. Social or sexual freedom, not to be confused with sexual debauchery, would eliminate both types of prostitution and join religious and political freedom in the millennium around the corner.

Not the millennium, however, but THE BEECHER-TILTON SCANDAL CASE followed Victoria's address. In a sense, her part in that case was a dramatic application of the philosophy she had enunciated at Steinway Hall. Having ascertained that the venerable pastor Henry Ward Beecher was having an affair with his parishioner, Theodore Tilton's wife Elizabeth, Victoria Woodhull revealed the situation in an article designed to explode like a "bomb-shell into the ranks of the moralistic social camp." Victoria found no fault with Beecher's actions, but rather with the false social institutions that impelled him to hypocrisy and secrecy. Thus she opened war against the Sunday-school morality of half-way reformers, of the pious and the sanctimonious who stood in the way of the social revolution she believed to be at hand.

Her article (*Woodhull & Claflin's Weekly*, November 2, 1872) did indeed explode like a bomb-shell, not only in the enemy camp but in her own. In November 1872, a year after her speech on Social Freedom, Victoria Woodhull was arrested by Anthony Comstock for transmitting obscene literature—namely her exposure of the Beecher-Tilton Scandal—through the mail; the issue containing the exposure was suppressed; and Victoria and her sister were imprisoned for four weeks without trial in New York's Ludlow Street Jail. Thus by her own experience as well as in her speech, THE NAKED TRUTH, she proved that sexual freedom involved freedom of the press. Not without cause, Victoria Woodhull regarded herself as a kind of willing martyr to the social revolution she felt imminent.

She regarded herself also as a teacher, an enlightener, one who could carry the means of birth control to women (TO WOMEN WHO HAVE AN INTEREST IN HUMANITY, PRESENT AND FUTURE) and sex education to pre-adolescents (TRIED AS BY FIRE). Although she adopted some of the more or less absurd notions of the pseudo-scientists of her day—astonishing ideas about pre-natal influence and the evils of unsuccessful attempted abortions—Victoria Woodhull did adumbrate a tentative scheme of planned parenthood. Legalized marriage, she contended, interfered with eugenics, a subject that—thanks to the birth of her own idiot son—interested her profoundly and personally. Proper sexual relations were essential for a science of proper generation or STIRPICULTURE. The best children were produced by the best physical men and women, provided love existed between them—a dubious tenet in which other students of sex, notably Moses Harman, publisher of the Kansas weekly, *Lucifer*, concurred. Thus without sexual freedom for women, scientific propagation was impossible. According to the terms of the sexual science she developed, the female should be the dominant power in sex relations, with the right of sexual determination. Over-population bothered her less among the educated than among the uneducated, and the "misfit" she designated in THE RAPID MULTIPLICATION OF THE UNFIT were the imbeciles and criminals, the paupers and drunkards, the opium addicts and the hereditary-diseased.

Despite many inconsistencies and absurdities, Victoria Woodhull did indeed help impel the social revolution. Equally important, she cleared the ground for open discussion of a subject tabooed by the prurient. As she put it in TRIED AS BY FIRE, "If I do nothing else I know that I have awakened investigation on this subject. If all I have said is error; if the truth lie in altogether different directions from those in which I point, out of the discussion now going on the truth will be evolved."

SOCIOLOGY

(1)

A Speech on the Principles of Social Freedom . . . 1871.

The speech was reprinted in *Woodhull & Claflin's Weekly* (Aug. 16, 1873, pp. 2-7, 11-15), as "the first distinct announcement of the doctrines upon which the new social order will be founded—perfect individual sexual freedom, to be regulated by education instead of law."

"And the Truth shall make you Free."

A SPEECH

ON

The Principles of Social Freedom,

DELIVERED IN

Steinway Hall, Monday, Nov. 20, 1871,

BY

VICTORIA C. WOODHULL,

To an audience of 3,000 people, to which hundreds found it impossible to obtain admission; which, in consideration of the dreuching rain of the evening, is the best; evidence of what subject lies nearest the hearts of the people.

New York:

WOODHULL, CLAFLIN & CO.,

PUBLISHERS, 44 BROAD STREET.

1871.

The Principles of Social Freedom.

―――――◆―――――

It has been said by a very wise person that there is a *trinity* in all things, the perfect *unity* of the trinity or a tri-unity being necessary to make a complete objective realization. Thus we have the theological Trinity: The Father, the Son and the Holy Ghost; or Cause, Effect and the Process of Evolution. Also the *political* Trinity: Freedom, Equality, Justice or *Individuality, Unity, Adjustment;* the first term of which is also resolvable into these parts, thus: Religious freedom, political freedom and social freedom, while Religion, Politics and Socialism are the Tri-unity of Humanity. There are also the beginning, the end and the intermediate space, time and motion, to all experiences of space, time and motion, and the diameter, circumference and area, or length, breadth and depth to all form.

Attention has been called to these scientific facts, for the purpose of showing that for any tri-unity to lack one of its terms is for it to be incomplete; and that in the order of natural evolution, if two terms exist, the third must also exist.

Religious freedom does, in a measure, exist in this country, but not yet perfectly; that is to say, a person is not entirely independent of public opinion regarding matters of conscience. Though since Political freedom has existed in theory, every person has the *right* to entertain any religious theory he or she may conceive to be true, and government can take no cognizance thereof—he is *only* amenable to *society*-despotism. The necessary corollary to Religious and Political freedom is Social freedom, which is the third term of the trinity; that is to say, if Religious and Political freedom exist, *perfected*, Social freedom is at that very moment guaranteed, since Social freedom is the fruit of that condition.

We find the principle of Individual freedom was quite dormant until it began to speak against the right of religious despots, to determine what views should be advocated regarding the relations of the creature to the Creator. Persons began to find ideas creeping into their souls at variance with the teachings of the clergy; which ideas became so *strongly* fixed that they were compelled to protest against Religious Despotism. Thus, in the sixteenth century, was begun the battle for Individual freedom. The claim that rulers had *no right* to control the consciences of the people was boldly made, and right nobly did the fight continue until the *absolute* right to individual opinion was wrung from the despots, and even the *common* people found themselves entitled to not only entertain but also to promulgate *any* belief or theory of which they could conceive.

With yielding the control over the *consciences* of individuals, the despots had no thought of giving up any right to their *persons.* But Religious freedom naturally led the people to question the right of this control, and in the eighteenth century a new protest found expression in the French Revolution, and it was baptized by a deluge of blood yielded by thousands of lives. But not until an enlightened people freed themselves from English tyranny was the right to self-government acknowledged in theory, and *not yet* even is it fully accorded in practice, as a legitimate result of that theory.

It may seem to be a *strange* proposition to make, that there is no such thing yet existent in the world as self-government, in its political aspects. But such is the fact. If self-government be the rule, every self must be its subject. If a person govern, not only *himself* but others, that is despotic government, and it matters not if that control be over one or over a thousand individuals, or over a nation; in *each* case it would be the *same* principle of power exerted outside of self and over others, and *this* is despotism, whether it is exercised by *one* person over his subjects, or by *twenty* persons over a nation, or by *one-half* the people of a nation over the other half thereof. There is no escaping the fact that the principle by which the *male* citizens of these United States assume to rule the *female* citizens is *not* that of self-government, but that of despotism; and so the fact is that poets have sung songs of freedom, and anthems of liberty have resounded for an empty shadow.

King George III. and his Parliament denied our forefathers the right to make their own laws ; they rebelled, and being successful, inaugurated this government. But men do not seem to comprehend that they are now pursuing toward *women* the *same* despotic course that King George pursued toward the American colonies.

But what is freedom? The press and our male governors are *very much* exercised about this question, since a certain set of resolutions were launched upon the public by Paulina Wright Davis at Apollo Hall, May 12, 1871. They are as follows :

Resolved, That the basis of order is freedom from bondage ; not, indeed, of such "order" as reigned in Warsaw, which grew out of the bondage ; but of such order as reigns in Heaven, which grows out of that developed manhood and womanhood in which each becomes "a law unto himself."

Resolved, That freedom is a principle, and that as such it may be trusted to ultimate in harmonious social results, as in America, it has resulted in harmonious and beneficent political results ; that it has not hitherto been adequately trusted in the social domain, and that the woman's movement means no less than the complete social as well as the political enfranchisement of mankind.

Resolved, That the evils, sufferings and disabilities of women, as well as of men, are social still more than they are political, and that a statement of woman's rights which ignores the right of self-ownership as the first of all rights is insufficient to meet the demand, and is ceasing to enlist the enthusiasm and even the common interest of the most intelligent portion of the community.

Resolved, That the principle of freedom is one principle, and not a collection of many different and unrelated principles ; that there is not at bottom one principle of freedom of conscience as in Protestantism, and another principle of freedom from slavery as in Abolitionism, another of freedom of locomotion as in our dispensing in America with the passport system of Europe, another of the freedom of the press as in Great Britain and America, and still another of social freedom at large ; but that freedom is one and indivisible ; and that slavery is so also ; that freedom and bondage or restriction is the alternative and the issue, alike, in every case ; and that if freedom is good in one case it is good in all ; that we in America have builded on freedom, politically, and that we cannot consistently recoil from that expansion of freedom which shall make it the basis of all our institutions ; and finally, that so far as we have trusted it, it has proved, in the main, safe and profitable.

Now, is there anything so terrible in the language of these resolutions as to threaten the foundations of society? They assert that every individual has a *better* right to herself or himself than any other person *can have.* No living soul, who does not desire to have control over, or ownership in, another person, can have any *valid* objecticn to *anything* expressed in these resolutions. Those who are not willing to give up control over others; who desire to *own* somebody beside themselves; who are constitutionally predisposed against self-government and the giving of the same freedom to others that they demand for themselves, will of course object to them, and such are the people with whom we shall have to contend in this new struggle for a greater liberty

Now, the individual *is* either self-owned and self-possessed or *is not* so self-possessed. If he be self-owned, he is so because he has an *inherent* right to self, which right cannot be delegated to any second person; a right—as the American Declaration of Independence has it—which is "inalienable." The individual must be responsible to self and God for his acts. If he be owned and possessed by some second person, then there is *no such thing* as individuality : and that for which the world has been striving these thousands of years is the merest myth.

But against this irrational, illogical, inconsequent and irreverent theory I boldly oppose the spirit of the age—that spirit which will *not* admit all civilization to be a failure, and all past experience to count for nothing; against that demagogism, I oppose the plain principle of freedom in its *fullest, purest, broadest, deepest* application and significance— the freedom which we see exemplified in the starry firmament, where whirl innumerable worlds, and never one of which is made to lose its individuality, but each performs its part in the grand economy of the universe, giving and receiving its natural repulsions and attractions; we also see it exemplified in every department of nature about us : in the sunbeam and the dewdrop; in the storm-cloud and the spring shower; in the driving snow and the congealing rain—all of which speak more eloquently than can human tongue of the heavenly *beauty, symmetry* and *purity* of the spirit of freedom which in them reigns untrammeled.

Our government is based upon the proposition that : All men and women are born free and equal and entitled to certain inalienable rights, among which are life, liberty and the *pursuit* of happiness. Now what we, who demand social freedom, ask, is simply that the government of this country shall be administered in accordance with the spirit of this proposition. *Nothing* more, *nothing* less. If that proposition mean *anything*, it means *just what* it says, without qualification, limitation or equivocation. It means that *every* person who comes into the world of outward existence is of *equal* right as an individual, and is free as an individual, and that he or she is entitled to pursue *happiness* in whatever direction he or she may choose. Now this is absolutely true of all men and all women. But just here the wise-acres stop and tell us that *everybody* must not pursue happiness in his or her own way; since to do so absolutely, would be to have no protection against the action of individuals. These good and well-meaning people only see *one-half* of what is involved in the proposition. They look at a single individual and for the time lose sight of all others. They do not take into their consideration that every other individual beside the one whom they contemplate is *equally* with him entitled to the *same* freedom; and that each is free within the area of his or her individual sphere; and *not* free within the sphere of any other individual whatever. They do not seem to recognize the fact that the moment one person gets out of *his* sphere into the sphere of *another*, that other must protect him or herself against such invasion of rights. They do not seem to be able to comprehend that the moment one person encroaches upon another person's rights he or she ceases to be a *free* man or woman and becomes a *despot*. To all such persons we assert: that it is *freedom* and *not* despotism which we advocate and demand; and we will as rigorously demand that individuals be restricted to *their* freedom as any person dare to demand; and as rigorously demand that people who are predisposed to be *tyrants* instead of free men or women shall, by the government, be so restrained as to make the exercise of their proclivities impossible.

If life, liberty and the pursuit of happiness are *inalienable* rights in the individual, and government is based upon that inalienability, then it *must follow* as a *legitimate* sequence that the *functions* of that government are to *guard* and *protect* the right to life, liberty and the pursuit of happiness, to the end that *every* person may have the most *perfect* exercise of them. And the most perfect exercise of such rights is *only* attained when every individual is not only fully *protected* in his rights, but also *strictly restrained* to the exercise of them within his *own* sphere, and *positively* prevented from proceeding beyond its limits, so as to encroach upon the sphere of another: unless that other first *agree* thereto.

From these generalizations certain specializations are deducible, by which all questions of rights must be determined :

1. Every living person has certain rights of which no law can rightfully deprive him.

2. Aggregates of persons form communities, who erect governments to secure regularity and order.

3. Order and harmony can alone be secured in a community where every individual of whom it is composed is fully protected in the exercise of all individual rights.

4. Any government which enacts laws to deprive individuals of the free exercise of their right to life, liberty and the pursuit of happiness is despotic, and such laws are not binding upon the people who protest against them, whether they be a majority or a minority.

5. When every individual is secure in the possession and exercise of all his rights, then every one is also secure from the interference of all other parties.

6. All inharmony and disorder arise from the attempts of individuals to interfere with the rights of other individuals, or from the protests of individuals against governments for depriving them of their inalienable rights.

These propositions are all self-evident, and must be accepted by every person who subscribes to our theory of government, based upon the sovereignty of the individual ; consequently any law in force which conflicts with any of them is not in accord with that theory and is therefore unconstitutional.

A fatal error into which most people fall, is, that rights are conceded to governments, while they are only possessed of the right to perform duties, as a further analysis will show :

In the absence of any arrangement by the members of a community to secure order, *each* individual is a law unto himself, so far as he is capable of maintaining it against all other individuals; but at the mercy of all such who are bent on conquest. Such a condition is anarchy.

But if in individual freedom the *whole* number of individuals unite to secure *equality* and protection to themselves, they thereby surrender *no* individual rights to the community, but they simply *invest* the community with the power to perform certain specified *duties*, which are set forth in the law of their combination. Hence a government erected by the people is invested, *not* with the *rights* of the people, but with the *duty* of *protecting* and maintaining their rights *intact;* and any government is a *failure* or a *success* just so far as it fails or succeeds in this duty; and these are the legitimate functions of government.

I have before said that every person has the right to, and can, determine for himself what he will do, even to taking the life of another. But it is *equally* true that the attacked person has the right to defend his life against such assault. If the person succeed in taking the life, he thereby demonstrates that he is a *tyrant* who is at all times liable to invade the right to life, and that every individual of the community is put in jeopardy by the freedom of this person. Hence it is the *duty* of the government to so restrict the freedom of this person as to make it *impossible* for him to ever again practice such tyranny. Here the duty of the community ceases. It has *no* right to take the life of the individual. That is his own, *inalienably* vested in him, both by *God* and the *Constitution.*

A person may also appropriate the property of another if he so choose, and there is no way to prevent it; but once having thus invaded the rights of another, the whole community is in danger from the propensity of this person. It is therefore the duty of government to so restrain the liberty of the person as to prevent him from invading the spheres of other persons in a manner against which he himself demands, and is entitled to, protection.

The same rule applies to that class of persons who have a propensity to steal or to destroy the character of others. This class of encroachers upon others' rights, in some senses, are *more* reprehensible than any other, save only those who invade the rights of life ; since for persons to be made to appear what they are not may, perhaps, be to place them in such relations with third persons as to destroy their means of pursuing happiness. Those who thus invade the pursuit of happiness by others, should be held to be the *worst* enemies of society ; proportionably worse than the common burglar or thief, as what they destroy is more valuable than is that which the burglar or thief can appropriate. For robbery there may be *some* excuse, since what is stolen may be required to contribute to actual needs; but that which the assassin of character appropriates does *neither* good to himself nor to *any one else*, and makes the loser poor indeed. Such persons are the worst enemies of society.

I have been thus explicit in the analysis of the principles of freedom in their application to the common affairs of life, because I desired, before approaching the main subject, to have it *well settled* as to what may justly be considered the rights of individuals ; or in other words what individual sovereignty implies.

It would be considered a very unjust and arbitrary, as well as an unwise thing, if the government of the United States were to pass a law compelling persons to adhere during life to everything they should to-day accept as their religion, their politics and their vocations. It would *manifestly* be a departure from the true functions of government. The apology for what I claim to be an invasion of the rights of the individual is found in the law to enforce contracts. While the enforcement of contracts in which *pecuniary* considerations are involved is a matter distinct and different from that of the enforcement of contracts involving the happiness of individuals, *even in them* the government has *no* legitimate right to interfere. The logical deduction of the right of two people to *make* a contract without consulting the government, or any third party, is the right of *either or both* of the parties to *withdraw* without consulting any third party, either in reference to its enforcement or as to damages.

As has been stated, such an arrangement is the result of the exercise of the right of two or more individuals to unite their rights, perfectly independent of every outside party. There is neither right nor duty beyond the uniting—the contracting—individuals. So neither can there be an appeal to a third party to settle any difference which may arise between such parties. All such contracts have their legitimate basis and security in the honor and purposes of the contracting parties. It seems to me that, admitting our theory of government, no proposition can be plainer than is this, notwithstanding the practice is entirely different. But I am now discussing the abstract principles of the rights of freedom, which no practice that may be in vogue must be permitted to deter us from following to legitimate conclusions.

In all general contracts, people have the protection of government in contracting for an hour, a *day*, a *week*, a *year*, a *decade, or* a life, and *neither* the government nor *any other third* party *or* person, or *aggregates* of persons ever *think* of making a scale of respectability, graduated by the length of time for which the contracts are made and maintained. *Least of all* does the government require that any of these contracts shall be entered into for life. Why should the social relations of the sexes be made subject to a different theory? All enacted laws that are for the purpose of perpetuating conditions which are themselves the results of evolution are so many obstructions in the path of progress; since if an effect attained to-day is made the ultimate, progress stops. "Thus far shalt thou go, and no farther," is *not* the adage of a progressive age like the present. Besides, there can be no general law made to determine what individual cases demand, since a variety of conditions cannot be subject to one and the same rule of operation. Here we arrive at the most important of all facts relating to human needs and experiences: That while every human being has a distinct individuality, and is entitled to all the rights of a sovereign over it, it is not taken into the consideration that *no* two of these individualities are made up of the self-same powers and experiences, and therefore cannot be governed by the *same* law to the *same* purposes.

I would recall the attention of all objecting egotists, Pharisees and would-be regulators of society to the true functions of government—to protect the complete exercise of individual rights, and what they are no living soul except the individual has any business to determine or to meddle with, in *any* way whatever, unless his own rights are first infringed.

If a person believe that a certain theory is a truth, and consequently the right thing to advocate and practice, but from its being unpopular or against established public opinion does not have the moral courage to advocate or practice it, *that* person is a *moral coward* and a *traitor* to his own conscience, which God gave for a guide and guard.

What I believe to be the truth I endeavor to practice, and, in advocating it, permit me to say I shall *speak* so *plainly* that *none* may complain that I did not make myself understood.

The world has come up to the present time through the outworking of religious, political, philosophical and scientific principles, and to-day we stand upon the *threshold* of *greater* discoveries in more *important* things than have ever interested the intellect of man. We have arrived where the very *foundation* of all that *has* been must be analyzed and understood—and this foundation is the relation of the sexes. These are the bases of society—the very last to secure attention, because the most comprehensive of subjects.

All other departments of inquiry which have their fountain in society have been formulated into *special* sciences, and made legitimate and popular subjects for investigation; but the science of *society itself* has been, and still is, held to be too sacred a thing for science to lay its rude hands upon. But of the relations of science to society we may say the same that has been said of the relations of science to religion: "That religion has always wanted to do good, and now science is going to tell it how to do it."

Over the sexual relations, marriages have endeavored to preserve sway and to hold the people in subjection to what has been considered a standard of moral purity. Whether this has been successful or not may be determined from the fact that there are *scores of thousands* of *women* who are denominated prostitutes, and who are supported by *hundreds of thousands* of *men* who should, for like reasons, also be denominated prostitutes, since what will change a woman into a prostitute must also necessarily change a man into the same.

This condition, called prostitution, seems to be the *great evil* at which religion and public morality hurl their *special* weapons of condemnation, as the sum total of all diabolism; since for a woman to be a prostitute is to deny her not only all Christian, but also all humanitarian rights.

But let us inquire into this matter, to see just what it is; not in the vulgar or popular, or even legal sense, but in a purely *scientific* and *truly moral* sense.

It must be remembered that we are seeking after truth for the *sake* of the truth, and in utter disregard of *everything* except the truth; that is to say, we are seeking for the truth, " let it be what it may and lead where it may." To illustrate, I would say the extremest thing possible. If blank materialism were true, it would be best for the world to know it.

If there be any who are not in harmony with this desire, then such have nothing to do with what I have to say, for it will be said regardless of antiquated forms or fossilized dogmas, but in the *simplest* and *least* offending language that I can choose.

If there is *anything* in the whole universe that should enlist the *earnest* attention of *everybody*, and their support and advocacy to secure it, it is that upon which the true welfare and happiness of everybody depends. Now to what more than to anything else do humanity owe their welfare and happiness? Most clearly to being born into earthly existence with a sound and perfect physical, mental and moral beginning of life, with no taint or disease attaching to them, either mentally, morally or physically. To *be so* born involves the harmony of conditions which will produce such results. *To have* such conditions involves the existence of such relations of the sexes as will in themselves produce them.

Now I will put the question direct. Are not these *eminently* proper subjects for inquiry and discussion, not in that manner of maudlin sentimentality in which it *has been* the habit, but in a *dignified, open, honest* and *fearless* way, in which subjects of so great importance should be inquired into and discussed?

An *exhaustive* treatment of these subjects would involve the inquiry what should be the *chief* end to be gained by entering into sexual relations. This I must simply answer by saying, "Good children, who will not need to be regenerated," and pass to the consideration of the relations themselves.

All the relations between the sexes that are recognized as *legitimate* are denominated marriage. *But of what does marriage consist?* This very pertinent question requires settlement before any real progress can be made as to what Social Freedom and Prostitution mean. It is admitted by everybody that marriage is a union of the opposites in sex, but is it a principle of nature outside of all law, or is it a law outside of all nature? Where is the point before reaching which it is not marriage, but having reached which it is marriage? Is it where two meet and realize that the love elements of their nature are harmonious, and that they blend into and make *one* purpose of life? or is it where a *soulless form* is pronounced over two who know *no* commingling of life's hopes?

Or are *both* these processes required—first, the marriage union *without* the law, to be afterward solemnized *by* the law? If *both* terms are required, does the marriage continue after the *first* departs? or if the *restrictions* of the law are removed and the *love* continues, does *marriage* continue? or if the law unite two who *hate* each other, is that marriage? Thus are presented all the possible aspects of the case.

The *courts* hold if the law solemnly pronounce two married, *that they are* married, whether love is present or not. But is this really such a marriage as this enlightened age should demand? No! It is a stupidly arbitrary law, which can find no analogies in nature. Nature proclaims in *broadest terms*, and all her subjects re-echo the same *grand* truth, that sexual unions, which result in reproduction, are marriage. And sex exists wherever there is reproduction.

By analogy, the same law ascends into the sphere of and applies among men and women ; for are not they a part and parcel of nature in which this law exists as a principle ? This law of nature by which men and women are united by love is God's marriage law, the enactments of men to the contrary notwithstanding. And the precise results of this marriage will be determined by the character of those united ; all the experiences evolved from the marriage being the legitimate sequences thereof.

Marriage must consist either of love or of law, since it *may* exist in form with either term absent; that is to say, people may be married by *law* and all love be lacking ; and they may also be married by *love* and lack all sanction of law. True marriage must in reality consist entirely either of law or love, since there can be *no* compromise between the law of nature and *statute* law by which the former shall yield to the latter.

Law cannot change what nature has already determined. Neither will love obey if law command. Law cannot compel two to love. It has nothing to do either *with* love or with its absence. Love is superior to all law, and so also is hate, indifference, disgust and all other human sentiments which are evoked in the relations of the sexes. It legitimately and logically follows, if *love* have *anything* to do with marriage, that *law* has *nothing* to do with it. And on the contrary, if *law* have anything to do with marriage, that *love* has nothing to do with it. And there is no escaping the deduction.

If the test of the rights of the individual be applied to determine which of these propositions is the true one, what will be the result?

Two persons, a male and a female, meet, and are drawn together by a *mutual* attraction—a *natural* feeling unconsciously arising within their natures of which *neither* has any control—which is denominated love. This is a matter that concerns *these two*, and *no* other living soul has *any human* right to say aye, yes or no, since it is a matter in which none except the two have any right to be involved, and from which it is the duty of these two to exclude every other person, since no one can love for another or determine why another loves.

If true, mutual, natural attraction be sufficiently strong to be the *dominant* power, then it decides marriage ; and if it be so decided, no law which may be in force can *any more* prevent the union than a *human* law could prevent the transformation of water into vapor, or the confluence of two streams ; and for *precisely* the same reasons: that it is a *natural* law which is obeyed ; which law is as *high above human law* as perfection is high above imperfection. They marry and obey this higher law than man can make—a law as old as the universe and as immortal as the elements, and for which there is no substitute.

They are sexually united, to be which is to be married by nature, and to be thus married is to be united by God. This marriage is performed without special mental volition upon the part of either, although the intellect *may* approve what the affections determine ; that is to say, they marry because they love, and they love because they can neither *prevent* nor *assist* it. Suppose after this marriage has continued an indefinite time, the *unity* between them departs, could they any more prevent it than they can prevent the love? It *came* without their bidding, may it not also *go* without their bidding? And if it go, does not the marriage cease, and should any third persons or parties, either as *individuals* or as *government*, attempt to compel the *continuance* of a unity wherein *none* of the elements of the union remain?

At no point in the process designated has there been *any* other than an exercise of the right of the two individuals to pursue happiness in their *own* way, *which* way has neither *crossed* nor interfered with *any one else's* right to the *same* pursuit ; therefore, there is *no* call for a law to change, modify, protect or punish this exercise. It must be concluded, then, if individuals have the Constitutional right to pursue happiness in their *own* way, that all compelling laws of marriage and divorce are despotic, being *remnants* of the barbaric ages in which they were originated, and *utterly unfitted* for an age so *advanced* upon that, and so *enlightened* in the general principles of freedom and equality, as is this.

It must be remembered that it is the sphere of government to perform the *duties* which are required of it by the people, and that it has, in itself, no rights to exercise. These belong *exclusively* to the people whom it represents. It is *one* of the rights of a citizen to have a voice in determining what the duties of government shall be, and also provide how that right may be exercised; but government should not *prohibit* any right.

To love is a right *higher* than Constitutions or laws. It is a right which Constitutions and laws can *neither give* nor take, and with which they have nothing whatever to do, since in its *very* nature it is forever independent of both Constitutions and laws, and exists—comes and goes—in *spite* of them. Governments might just as well assume to determine how people shall exercise their right to *think* or to say that they shall not think at all, as to assume to determine that they shall not love, or how they may love, or that they shall love.

The proper sphere of government in regard to the relations of the sexes, is to enact such laws as in the present conditions of society are necessary to *protect each* individual in the *free* exercise of his or her *right* to love, and also to protect each individual from the forced interference of *every other* person, that would compel him or her to submit to *any* action which is against their *wish* and *will.* If the law do this it fulfills its duty. If the law do not afford this protection, *and worse still,* if it *sanction* this *interference* with the rights of an individual, then it is *infamous* law and worthy only of the *old-time* despotism; since individual tyranny forms *no* part of the guarantee of, or the right to, individual freedom.

It is therefore a strictly legitimate conclusion that where there is *no* love as a basis of marriage there should be *no* marriage, and if that which was the *basis* of a marriage is taken away that the *marriage* also ceases from that time, statute laws to the contrary notwithstanding.

Such is the character of the law that permeates nature from simplest organic forms—units of nucleated protoplasm to the most complex aggregation thereof—the human form. Having determined that marriage consists of a union resulting from love, without any regard whatever to the sanction of law, and consequently that the sexual relations resulting therefrom are strictly legitimate and natural, it is a very simple matter to determine what part of the sexual relations which are maintained are prostitutions of the relations.

It is certain by this Higher Law, that marriages of convenience, and, still more, marriages characterized by mutual or partial repugnance, are adulterous. And it does not matter whether the repugnance arises before or subsequently to the marriage ceremony. Compulsion, whether of the law or of a false public opinion, is detestable, as an element even, in the regulation of the most tender and important of all human relations.

I do not care where it is that sexual commerce results from the dominant power of *one sex* over *the other*, compelling him or her to submission against the *instincts of love*, and where hate or disgust is present, whether it be in the gilded palaces of Fifth avenue or in the lowest purlieus of Greene street, *there* is prostitution, and *all* the law that a *thousand* State Assemblies may pass cannot make it otherwise.

I know whereof I speak ; I have seen the most *damning* misery resulting from legalized prostitution. Misery such as the most degraded of those against whom society has shut her doors never know. Thousands of poor, weak, unresisting wives are yearly murdered, who stand in spirit-life looking down upon the sickly, half made-up children left behind, imploring humanity for the sake of honor and virtue to look into this matter, to look into it to the very bottom, and bring out into the fair daylight all the blackened, sickening deformities that have so long been hidden by the screen of public opinion and a sham morality.

It does not matter how much it may still be attempted to *gloss* these things over and to *label* them sound and pure ; you, each and every one of you, *know* that what I say is truth, and if you question your own souls you *dare* not reply : it is not so. If these things to which I refer, but of which I shudder to think, are not abuses of the sexual relations, what are?

You may or may not think there is help for them, but I say Heaven help us if *such* barbarism cannot be cured.

I would not be understood to say that there are no good conditions in the present marriage state. By no means do I say this; on the contrary, a very large proportion of present social relations are .commendable—are as good as the present status of society makes possible. But what I *do* assert, and that most *positively*, is, that *all* which *is* good and commendable, now existing, would *continue* to exist if all marriage · laws were repealed to-morrow. Do you not perceive that law has nothing to do in continuing the relations which are based upon continuous love? These are not results of the law to which, perhaps, their subjects yielded a willing or unwilling obedience. Such relations exist in *spite* of the law; would have existed *had there been* no law, and would continue to exist were the law *annulled.*

It is not of the *good* there is in the present condition of marriage that I complain, but of the *ill*, nearly the *whole* of which is the *direct* result of the law which continues the relations in which it exists. It seems to be the general argument that if the law of marriage were annulled it would follow that *everybody* must necessarily separate, and that all *present family* relations would be sundered, and complete anarchy result therefrom. Now, whoever makes that argument either does so thoughtlessly or else he is dishonest; since if he make it after having given any consideration thereto, he must know it to be false. And if he have given it no consideration then is he no proper judge. I give it as my opinion, founded upon an extensive knowledge of, and intimate acquaintance with, married people, if marriage laws were repealed that less than a *fourth* of those now married would immediately separate, and that *one-half* of these would return to their allegiance *voluntarily* within *one* year; only those who, under every consideration of virtue and good, should be separate, would permanently remain separated. And objectors as well as I know it would be so. I assert that it is *false* to assume that chaos would result from the abrogation of marriage laws, and on the contrary affirm that *from that very hour* the chaos now existing would *begin* to turn into order and harmony. What then creates social disorder? Very clearly, the attempt to exercise powers over human rights which are not warrantable upon the hypothesis of the existence of human rights which are inalienable in, and sacred to, the individual.

It is true there is no *enacted* law compelling people to marry, and it is therefore *argued* that if they *do* marry they should always be compelled to abide thereby. But there is a law *higher* than any human enactments which does compel marriage—the law of nature—the law of God. There being this law in the constitution of humanity, which, operating freely, guarantees marriage, why should men enforce arbitrary rules and forms? These, though having no virtue in themselves, if not complied with by men and women, they in the meantime obeying the law of their nature, bring down upon them the condemnations of an interfering community. Should people, then, voluntarily entering legal marriage be held thereby "till death do them part?" Most *emphatically* NO, if the desire to do so do not remain. How can people who enter upon marriage in utter *ignorance* of that which is to render the union happy or miserable be able to say that they will always "love and live together." They may take these vows upon them in perfect good faith and repent of them in sackcloth and ashes within a twelve-month.

I think it will be generally conceded that without love there should be no marriage. In the constitution of things *nothing* can be more certain. This basic fact is fatal to the theory of marriage for life: since if love is what *determines* marriage, so, also, should it determine its continuance. If it be primarily right of men and women to take on the marriage relation of their own free will and accord, *so*, too, does it remain their right to determine *how* long it shall continue and when it shall cease. But to be respectable (?) people must comply with the law, and thousands do comply therewith, while in their hearts they protest against it as an unwarrantable interference and proscription of their rights. Marriage laws that would be consistent with the theory of individual rights would be such as would *regulate* these relations, such as regulate *all other* associations of people. They should only be obliged to file marriage articles, containing whatever provisions may be agreed upon, as to their personal rights, rights of property, of children, or whatever else they may deem proper for them to agree upon. And whatever these articles might be, they should in all cases be equally entitled to public respect and protection. Should separation afterward come, nothing more should be required than the simple filing of counter articles

There are hundreds of lawyers who subsist by inventing schemes by which people may *obtain* divorces, and the people *desiring* divorces resort to *all sorts* of tricks and crimes to get them. And *all this* exists because there are laws which would *compel* the *oneness* of those to whom *unity* is beyond the realm of possibility. There are another class of persons who, while virtually divorced, endeavor to maintain a respectable position in society, by *agreeing* to *disagree*, each following his and her individual ways, behind the cloak of legal marriage. Thus there are *hundreds* of men and women who to *external* appearances are husband and wife, but in reality are husband or wife to quite different persons.

If the conditions of society were completely analyzed, it would be found that *all* persons whom the law holds married against their wishes find *some* way to *evade* the law and to live the life they desire. Of what use, then, is the law except to make *hypocrites* and *pretenders* of a sham respectability?

But, exclaims a very fastidious person, then you would have all women become prostitutes! By *no means* would I have *any* woman become a prostitute. But if by nature women *are* so, *all* the *virtue* they possess being of the *legal* kind, and not that which should exist with or without law, *then* I say they will not become prostitutes because the law is repealed, since at heart they are already so. If there is no virtue, no honesty, no purity, no trust among women except as created by the *law*, I say heaven help our morality, for nothing human can help it.

It seems to me that no grosser insult could be offered to woman than to insinuate that she is honest and virtuous only because the law compels her to be so; and little do men and women realize the obloquy thus cast upon society, and still less do women realize what they admit of their sex by such assertions. I honor and worship that purity which exists in the soul of every noble man or woman, while I pity the woman who is virtuous simply because a law compels her.

But, says another objector, though the repeal of marriage laws might operate well enough in all those cases where a *mutual* love or hate would determine *continuous* marriage or *immediate* divorce, how can a third class of cases be justified, in which but *one* of the parties desire the separation, while the other clings to the unity?

I assume, in the first place, when there is not mutual love there is no union to continue and nothing to justify, and it has already been determined that, as marriage should have love as a basis, if love depart marriage also departs. But laying this aside, see if there can any real good or happiness possibly result from an enforced continuance of marriage upon the part of one party thereto. Let all persons take this question home to their own souls, and there determine if they could find happiness in holding unwilling hearts in bondage. It is *against* the *nature of things* that *any* satisfaction can result from such a state of things except it be the satisfaction of knowing that you have succeeded in virtually imprisoning the person whom you *profess* to love, and that would be demoniacal.

Again. It must be remembered that the individual affairs of two persons are not the subject of interference by any third party, and if one of them choose to separate, there is no power outside of the two which can rightly interfere to prevent. Beside, who is to determine whether there will be more happiness sacrificed by a *continuation* or a *separation.* If a person is *fully* determined to separate, it is proof positive that another feeling *stronger* than all his or her sentiments of duty determine it. And here, again, *who* but the individual is to determine which course will secure the most good? Suppose that a separation is desired because one of the two loves and is loved elsewhere. In this case, if the union be maintained by force, at least *two* of three, and, probably, *all three* persons will be made unhappy thereby; whereas if separation come and the other union be consummated, there will be but one, unhappy. So even here, if the greatest good of the greatest number is to rule, separation is not only legitimate, *but* desirable. In all other things except marriage it is always held to be the right thing to do to *break* a *bad bargain* or *promise* just as soon as possible, and I hold that of *all things* in which this rule should apply, it should *first* apply to marriages.

Now, let me ask, would it not rather be the *Christian* way, in such cases, to say to the disaffected party: "Since you no longer love me, go your way and be happy, and make those to whom you go happy also." I know of no higher, holier love than that described, and of no more beautiful expression of it than was given in the columns of the *Woman's Journal*, of Boston, whose conductors have felt called upon to endeavor to convince the people that it has no affiliation with those who hold to no more radical doctrine of Free Love than they proclaim as follows:

"The love that I cannot command is not mine; let me not disturb myself about it, nor attempt to filch it from its rightful owner. A heart that I supposed mine has drifted and gone. Shall I go in pursuit? Shall I forcibly capture the truant and transfix it with the barb of my selfish affections, pin it to the wall of my chamber? God forbid! Rather let me leave my doors and windows open, intent only on living so nobly that the best cannot fail to be drawn to me by an irresistible attraction."

To me it is impossible to frame words into sentences *more holy, pure* and true than are these. I would ever carry them in my soul as my guide and guard, feeling that in *living* by them happiness would certainly be mine. To the loving wife who mourns a lost heart, let me recommend them as a panacea. To the loving husband whose soul is desolate, let me offer these as words of healing balm. They will live in history, to make their writer the *loved* and *revered* of unborn generations.

The tenth commandment of the Decalogue says: "Thou shalt not covet thy neighbor's wife." And Jesus, in the beautiful parable of the Samaritan who fell among thieves, asks: "Who is thy neighbor?" and answers his own question in a way to lift the conception wholly out of the category of mere local proximity into a sublime spiritual conception. In other words, he spiritualizes the word and sublimates the morality of the commandment. In the same spirit I ask now, Who is *a wife?* And I answer, not the woman who, ignorant of her own feelings, or with lying lips, has promised, in hollow ceremonial, and before the law, to love, but *she who really loves most*, and *most truly*, the man who commands her affections, and who in turn loves her, with or without the ceremony of marriage; and the man who holds the heart of such a woman in such a relation is "thy *neighbor*," and *that woman is " thy neighbor's wife*" *meant in the commandment;* and who-soever, though he should have been a hundred times married to her by the law, shall claim, or *covet* even, the possession of that woman as against her true lover and husband in the spirit, sins against the commandment.

We know positively that Jesus would have answered in that way. He has defined for us "the neighbor," not in the paltry and common-place sense, but spiritually. He has said : "He that looketh on a woman to lust after her hath committed adultery with her already in his heart." So, therefore, he spiritualized the idea of adultery. In the kingdom of heaven, to be prayed for daily, to come on earth, there is to be no "marrying or giving in marriage;" that is to say, formally and legally ; but spiritual marriage must always exist, and had Jesus been called on to define a wife, can anybody doubt that he would, in the same spirit, the spiritualizing tendency and character of all his doctrine, have spiritualized the marriage relation as absolutely as he did the breach of it? that he would, in other words, have said in meaning precisely what I now say? And when Christian ministers are no longer afraid or ashamed *to be Christians* they will embrace this doctrine. Free Love will be an integral part of the religion of the future.

It can now be asked : What is the legitimate sequence of Social Freedom? To which I unhesitatingly reply: Free Love, or freedom of the affections. "And are you a Free Lover?" is the almost incredulous query.

I repeat a frequent reply : "I am; and I can honestly, in the fullness of my soul, raise my voice to my Maker, and thank Him that *I am*, and that I have had the strength and the devotion to truth to stand before this traducing and vilifying community in a manner representative of that which shall come with healing on its wings for the bruised hearts and crushed affections of humanity."

And to those who denounce me for this I reply : "Yes, I am a Free Lover. I have an *inalienable, constitutional* and *natural* right to love whom I may, to love as *long* or as *short* a period as I can ; to *change* that love *every day* if I please, and with *that* right neither *you* nor any *law* you can frame have *any* right to interfere. And I have the *further* right to demand a free and unrestricted exercise of that right, and it is *your duty* not only to *accord* it, but, as a community, to see that I am protected in it. I trust that I am fully understood, for I mean *just* that, and nothing less!

To speak thus plainly and pointedly is a *duty I owe* to myself. The press have stigmatized me to the world as an advocate, theoretically and practically, of the doctrine of Free Love, upon which they have placed their stamp of moral deformity; the vulgar and inconsequent definition which they hold makes the theory an abomination. And though this conclusion is a no more legitimate and reasonable one than that would be which should call the Golden Rule a general license to all sorts of debauch, since Free Love bears the *same* relations to the moral deformities of which it stands accused as does the Golden Rule to the Law of the Despot, yet it obtains among many intelligent people. But they claim, in the language of one of these exponents, that " Words belong to the people; they are the common property of the mob. Now the common use, among the mob, of the term Free Love, is a synonym for promiscuity." Against this absurd proposition I oppose the assertion that words *do not* belong to the mob, but to that which they represent. Words are the exponents and interpretations of ideas. If I use a word which exactly interprets and represents what I would be understood to mean, shall I go to the *mob* and *ask* of *them* what interpretation *they* choose to place upon it? If lexicographers, when they prepare their dictionaries, were to go to the mob for the rendition of words, what kind of language would we have?

I claim that freedom means *to be free*, let the mob claim to the contrary as strenuously as they may. And I claim that love means an exhibition of the affections, let the mob claim what they may. And therefore, in compounding these words into Free Love, I claim that united they mean, and should be used to convey, their united definitions, the mob to the contrary notwithstanding. And when the term Free Love finds a place in dictionaries, it will prove my claim to have been correct, and that the mob have not received the attention of the lexicographers, since it will not be set down to signify sexual debauchery, and that only, or in any governing sense.

It is not only usual but also just, when people adopt a new theory, or promulgate a new doctrine, that they give it a name significant of its character. There are, however, exceptional cases to be found in all ages. The Jews coined the name of Christians, and, with withering contempt, hurled it upon the early followers of Christ. It was the most opprobrious epithet they could invent to express their detestation of those humble but honest and brave people. That name has now come to be considered as a synonym of all that is good, true and beautiful in the highest departments of our natures, and is revered in all civilized nations.

In precisely the same manner the Pharisees of to-day, who hold themselves to be representative of all there is that is good and pure, as did the Pharisees of old, have coined the word Free-Love, and flung it upon all who believe not alone in Religious and Political Freedom, but in that larger Freedom, which includes both these, Social Freedom.

For my part, I am extremely obliged to our thoughtful Pharisaical neighbors for the kindness shown us in the invention of so appropriate a name. If there is a more beautiful word in the English language than *love*, that word is *freedom*, and that *these two* words, which, with us, attach or belong to *everything* that is pure and good, should have been *joined* by our enemies, and *handed* over to us *already* coined, is certainly a high consideration, for which we should never cease to be thankful. And when we shall be accused of all sorts of wickedness and vileness by our enemies, who in this have been so just, may I not hope that, remembering how much they have done for us, we may be able to say, "Father, forgive them, for they know not what they do," and to forgive them ourselves with our whole hearts.

Of the love that says: "Bless *me*, darling;" of the love so called, which is nothing but selfishness, the appropriation of another soul as the means of one's own happiness merely, there is abundance in the world; and the still more animal, the mere desire for temporary gratification, with little worthy the name of love, also abounds. Even these are best left free, since as evils they will thus be best cured; but of that celestial love which says: "Bless *you*, darling," and which strives continually to confer blessings; of that genuine love whose office it is to bless others or another, there cannot be too much in the world, and when it shall be fully understood that this is the love which we mean and commend there will be no objection to the term Free Love, and none to the thing signified.

We not only *accept* our name, but we contend that *none* other could so well signify the *real* character of that which it designates—to be free and to love. But our enemies must be reminded that the fact of the existence and advocacy of such a doctrine cannot immediately elevate to high condition the great number who have been kept in degradation and misery by previous false systems. They must *not expect* at this early day of the new doctrine, that all debauchery has been cleansed out of men and women. In the haunts where it retreats, the benign influence of its magic presence has not yet penetrated. They must *not expect* that brutish men and debased women have as yet been touched by its wand of hope, and that they have already obeyed the bidding to come up higher. They must *not expect* that ignorance and fleshly lust have already been lifted to the region of intellect and moral purity. They must *not expect* that Free Love, before it is more than barely announced to the world, can perform what Christianity in eighteen hundred years has failed to do.

They must *not expect any* of these things have already been accomplished, but I will *tell* you what they *may* expect. They may expect *more* good to result from the perfect freedom which we advocate in *one century* than has resulted in a hundred centuries from all other causes, since the results will be in exact proportion to the extended application of the freedom. We have a legitimate right to predicate such results, since *all* freedom that has been practiced in *all* ages of the world has been beneficial *just* in proportion to the extent of human nature it covered.

Will any of you dare to stand up and assert that Religious Freedom ever produced a *single bad* result? or that Political Freedom *ever* injured a *single* soul who embraced and practiced it? If you can do so, then you may legitimately assert that Social Freedom *may* also produce *equally* bad results, but you cannot do otherwise, and be either conscientious or honest.

It is *too late* in the age for intelligent people to cry out *thief*, unless they have first been robbed, and it is equally late for them to succeed in crying down *anything* as of the devil to which a name attaches that angels love. It may be very proper and legitimate, and withal perfectly consistent, for philosophers of the *Tribune* school to bundle all the murderers, robbers and rascals together, and hand them over to our camp, labeled as Free Lovers. We will only object that they ought to hand the whole of humanity over, good, bad and indifferent, and not assort its worst representatives.

My friends, you see this thing we call Freedom is a large word, implying a deal more than people have ever yet been able to recognize. It reaches out its all-embracing arms, and while encircling our good friends and neighbors, does not neglect to also include their less worthy brothers and sisters, every one of whom is just as much entitled to the use of his freedom as is either one of us.

But objectors tell us that freedom is a dangerous thing to have, and that they must be its conservators, dealing it out to such people, and upon such matters, as they shall appoint. Having coined our name, they straightway proceed to define it, and to give force to their definition, set about citing illustrations to prove not only their definition to be a true one, but also that its application is just.

Among the cases cited as evidences of the evil tendencies of Free Love are those of Richardson and Crittenden. The celebrated McFarland-Richardson case was heralded world-wide as a case of this sort. So far as Richardson and Mrs. McFarland were concerned, I have every reason to believe it was a genuine one, in so far as the preventing obstacles framed by the "conservators" would permit. But when they assert that the murder of Richardson by McFarland was the *legitimate result* of Free Love, then I deny it *in toto*. McFarland murdered Richardson because he believed that the law had sold Abby Sage *soul* and *body* to him, and, consequently, that he *owned* her, and that *no* other person had *any* right to her favor, and that she had *no* right to bestow her love upon any other person, unless *that ownership* was first satisfied. The murder of Richardson, then, is not chargeable to his love or her love, but to the fact of the supposed ownership, which right of possession the law of marriage conferred on McFarland.

If anything further is needed to make the refutation of that charge clear, I will give it by illustration. Suppose that a pagan should be converted to Christianity through the efforts of some Christian minister, and that the remaining pagans should *kill* that minister for what he had done, would the crime be chargeable upon the Christian religion? Will any of you make that assertion? If not, neither can you charge that the death of Richardson should be charged to Free Love. But a more *recent* case is a still *clearer* proof of the correctness of my position. Mrs. Fair killed Crittenden. Why? Because she believed in the spirit of the marriage law; that she had a *better right* to him than had Mrs. Crittenden, to whom the law had granted him; and rather than to give him up to her, to whom he evidently desired to go, and where, following his right to freedom, he *did* go, she killed him. Could a more *perfect* case of the *spirit* of the marriage law be formulated? Most assuredly, no!

Now, from the standpoint of marriage, reverse this case to that of Free Love, and see what would have been the result had all those parties been believers in and practicers of that theory. When Mr. Crittenden evinced a desire to return to Mrs. Crittenden, Mrs. Fair, in practicing the doctrine of Free Love, would have said, "I have no right to you, other than you freely give; you loved me and exercised your right of freedom in so doing. You now desire to return to Mrs. Crittenden, which is equally your right, and which I must respect. Go, and in peace, and my blessing shall follow, and if it can return you to happiness, then will you be happy."

Would not *that* have been the *better*, the *Christian* course, and would not every soul in the broad land capable of a noble impulse, and having knowledge of all the relevant facts, have *honored* Mrs. Fair for it? Instead of a murder, with the probability of another to complement it, would not *all* parties have been *happy* in having done right? Would not Mrs. Crittenden have even *loved* Mrs. Fair for such an example of nobility, and could she not *safely* have received her even into her own heart and home, and have been a *sister* to her, instead of the means of her conviction of murder?

I tell you, my friends and my foes, that you have taken hold of the *wrong* end of this business. You are shouldering upon Free Love the results that flow from precisely its antithesis, which is the spirit, if not the letter, of your marriage theory, which is slavery, and not freedom.

I have a better right to speak, as one having authority in this matter, than most of you have, since it has been my province to study it in all its various lights and shades. When I practiced clairvoyance, *hundreds*, aye thousands, of desolate, heart-broken men, as well as women, came to me for advice. And they were from all walks of life, from the humblest daily laborer to the haughtiest dame of wealth. The tales of horror, of wrongs inflicted and endured, which were poured into my ears, first awakened me to a realization of the hollowness and the rottenness of society, and compelled me to consider whether laws which were prolific of so *much* crime and misery as I found to exist should be continued; and to ask the question whether it were not *better* to let the bond go free. In time I was fully convinced that marriage laws were productive of precisely the *reverse* of that for which they are supposed to have been framed, and I came to recommend the grant of entire freedom to those who were complained of as inconstant; and the frank asking for it by those who desired it. My *invariable* advice was: "Withdraw lovingly, but completely, all claim and all complaint as an injured and deserted husband or wife. You need not perhaps disguise the fact that you suffer keenly from it, but take on yourself all the fault that you have not been able to command a more continuous love; that you have not proved to be *all* that you once seemed to be. Show magnanimity, and in order to *show* it, try to *feel* it. Cultivate that kind of love which loves the happiness and well-being of your partner *most*, his or her person next, and yourself last. Be kind to, and sympathize with, the new attraction rather than waspish and indignant. Know for a certainty that love *cannot* be clutched or gained by being *fought* for; while it is not *impossible* that it may be won back by the nobility of one's own deportment. If it cannot be, then it is gone forever, and you must make the best of it and reconcile yourself to it, and do the next best thing—you may perhaps continue to *hold on* to a slave, but you have *lost* a lover."

Some may indeed think if I can keep the *semblance* of a husband or wife, even if it be not a lover, *better still* that it be so. Such is not my philosophy or my faith, and for such I have no advice to give. I address myself to such as have *souls*, and whose souls are in question; if you belong to the other sort, take advice of a Tombs lawyer and not of me. I have seen a *few* instances of the most magnanimous action among the persons involved in a knot of love, and with the most angelic results. I believe that the love which goes forth to bless, and if it be to *surrender* in order to bless, is love in the *true* sense, and that it tends greatly to beget love, and that the love which is demanding, thinking only of self, is not love.

I have learned that the first *great* error most married people commit is in endeavoring to hide from each other the little irregularities into which all are liable to fall. *Nothing* is so conducive to continuous happiness as mutual confidence. In *whom*, if not in the husband or the wife, should one confide? Should they not be each other's *best* friends, *never* failing in time of anxiety, trouble and temptation to give disinterested and unselfish counsel? From such a perfect confidence as I would have men and women cultivate, it is *impossible* that bad or wrong should flow. On the contrary, it is the *only* condition in which love and happiness can go hand in hand. It is the *only* practice that can insure continuous respect, without which love withers and dies out. Can you not see that in mutual confidence and freedom the very *strongest* bonds of love are forged? It is more blessed to grant favors than to demand them, and the blessing is large and prolific of happiness, or small and insignificant in results, just in proportion as the favor granted is large or small. Tried by this rule, the greater the *blessing* or happiness you can confer on your partners, in which your own selfish feelings are not consulted, the greater the satisfaction that will redound to yourself. Think of this mode of adjusting your difficulties, and see what a clear way opens before you. There are none who have once felt the influence of a high order of love, so *callous*, but that they *intuitively* recognize the true grandeur and nobility of such a line of conduct. It must always be remembered that you can never do *right* until you are first free to do *wrong;* since the doing of a thing under *compulsion* is evidence *neither* of good nor bad intent; and if under compulsion, who shall decide what would be the substituted rule of action under full freedom?

In freedom *alone* is there safety and happiness, and when people learn this great fact, they will have just begun to know how to live. Instead then of being the destroying angel of the household, I would become the angel of purification to purge out all insincerity, all deception, all baseness and all vice, and to replace them by honor, confidence and truth.

I know very well that much of the *material* upon which the work must begin is very bad and far gone in decay. But I would have everybody perfectly free to do either right or wrong, according to the highest standard, and if there are those so unfortunate as not to know how to do that which can alone bring happiness, I would treat them as we treat those who are intellectually without culture— who are ignorant and illiterate. There are none so ignorant but they may be taught. So, too, are there none so unfortunate in their understanding of the true and high relation of the sexes as not to be amenable to the right kind of instruction. First of all, however, the would-be teachers of humanity must become truly Christian, meek and lowly in spirit, forgiving and kind in action, and ever ready to do as did Christ to the Magdalen. We are not so greatly different from what the accusing multitude were in that time. But Christians, forgetting the teaching of Christ, condemn and say, "Go on in your sin." Christians must learn to claim *nothing* for themselves that they are unwilling to accord others. They must remember that *all* people endeavor, so far as lies in their power, and so far as it is possible for them to judge, to exercise their human right, or determine what their action shall be, that will bring them most happiness; and instead of being *condemned* and *cast out* of society therefor, they should be *protected* therein, so long as others' rights are not infringed upon. We think they do not do the *best* thing; it is our duty to endeavor to *show* them the better and the higher, and to induce them to walk therein. But because a person chooses to perform an act that *we* think a *bad* one, we have no right to put the brand of excommunication upon him. It is our Christian and brotherly duty to persuade him instead that it is more to his good to do something better next time, at the same time, however, assuring him he only did what he had a right to do.

If our sisters who inhabit Greene street and other filthy localities *choose* to remain in debauch, and if our brothers *choose* to visit them there, they are only exercising the *same* right that we exercise in remaining away, and we have no *more right* to abuse and condemn *them* for exercising their rights that way, than they have to abuse and condemn us for exercising our rights our way. But we have a *duty*, and that is by our love, kindness and sympathy to endeavor to prevail upon them to desert those ways which we feel are so damaging to all that is high and pure and true in the relations of the sexes.

If these are the *stray sheep* from the fold of truth and purity, should we not go out and gather them in, rather than remain within the fold and hold the door shut, lest they should enter in and defile the fold? Nay, my friends, we have only an assumed right to thus sit in judgment over our unfortunate sisters, which is the same right of which men have made use to prevent women from participation in government.

The sin of all time has been the exercise of assumed powers. This is the essence of tyranny. Liberty is a great lesson to learn. It is a great step to vindicate our own freedom. It is more, far more, to learn to leave others free, and free to do just what we perhaps may deem wholly wrong. We must recognize that others have consciences and judgment and rights as well as we, and religiously abstain from the effort to make them better by the use of any means to which we have no right to resort, and to which we cannot resort without abridging the great doctrine, the charter of all our liberties, the doctrine of Human Rights.

But the public press, either in real or affected ignorance of what they speak, denounce Free Love as the justification of, and apologist for, all manner and kind of sexual debauchery, and thus, instead of being the *teachers* of the people, as they *should* be, are the power which inculcates falsehood and wrong. The teachings of Christ, whom so many now profess to imitate, were *direct* and simple upon this point. He was not too good to acknowledge all men as brothers and all women as sisters; it mattered not whether they were highly advanced in knowledge and morals, or if they were of low intellectual and moral culture.

It is seriously to be doubted if any of Christ's disciples, or men equally as good as were they, could gain fellowship in *any* of your Fifth avenue church palaces, since they were nothing more than the *humblest* of fishermen, of no social or mental standing. Nevertheless, they were *quite* good enough for *Christ* to associate with, and *fit* to be appointed by Him to be "fishers of men." The Church seems to have forgotten that good *does* sometimes come out of the Nazareths of the world, and that wisdom *may* fall from the mouths of "babes and sucklings." Quite *too much* of the old pharisaical spirit exists in society to-day to warrant its members' claims, that they are the representatives and followers of Christ. For they are the I-am-holier-than-thou kind of people, who affect to, and to a great extent do, prescribe the standards of public opinion, and who ostracise *everybody* who will not bow to their mandates

Talk of Freedom, of equality, of justice! I tell you there is scarcely a *thought* put in practice that is *worthy* to be the offspring of those noble words. The *veriest systems of despotism* still reign in *all* matters pertaining to social life. Caste stands as boldly out in this country as it does in political life in the kingdoms of Europe.

It is true that we are obliged to accept the situation *just as it is.* If we accord freedom to all persons we must expect them to make their own best use thereof, and, as I have already said, must protect them in such use until they learn to put it to better uses. But in our predication we must be consistent, and now ask who among you would be *worse* men and women were *all* social laws repealed?

Would you *necessarily* dissolve your present relations, *desert* your dependent husbands—for there are even some of them—and wives and children simply because you have the *right* so to do? You are all trying to deceive yourselves about this matter. Let me ask of husbands if they think there would be fifty thousand women of the town supported by them if their wives were ambitious to have an *equal* number of men of the town to support, and for the same purposes? I tell you, nay! It is because men are held *innocent* of this support, and all the vengeance is visited upon the *victims*, that they have come to have an immunity in their practices.

Until women come to hold men to equal account as they do the women with whom they consort; or until they regard these women as just as respectable as the men who support them, society will remain in its present scale of moral excellence. A man who is well known to have been the constant visitor to these women is accepted into society, and if he be *rich* is eagerly *sought* both by mothers having marriageable daughters and by the daughters themselves. But the women with whom they have consorted are *too vile* to be even acknowledged as worthy of Christian burial, to say nothing of common Christian treatment. I have heard women reply when this difficulty was pressed upon them, "We cannot ostracise *men* as we are compelled to *women,* since we are *dependent* on them for *support."* Ah! here's the rub. But do you not see that these *other* sisters are *also* dependent upon men for *their* support, and *mainly* so because you render it next to impossible for them to follow any *legitimate* means of livelihood? And are only those who have been fortunate enough to secure *legal* support entitled to live?

When I hear *that* argument advanced, my heart sinks within me at the degraded condition of my sisters. They submit to a degradation simply because they *see no alternative* except self-support, and they see no means for that. To put on the semblance of holiness they cry out against those who, for like reasons, submit to like degradation; the only difference between the two being in a licensed ceremony, and a slip of printed paper costing twenty-five cents and upward.

The good women of one of the interior cities of New York some two years since organized a movement to put down prostitution. They were, by stratagem, to find out who visited houses of prostitution, and then were to ostracise them. They pushed the matter until they found their own husbands, brothers and sons involved, and then suddenly desisted, and nothing has since been heard of the eradication of prostitution in that city. If the same experiment were to be tried in New York the result would be the same. The supporters of prostitution would be found to be those whom women cannot ostracise. The same disability excuses the presence of women in the very home, and I need not tell you that Mormonism is practiced in *other* places beside Utah. But what is the logic of these things? Why, simply this: A woman, be she wife or mistress, who consorts with a man who consorts with *other* women, is equally, with *them and him*, morally responsible, since the receiver is held to be as culpable as the thief.

The false and hollow relations of the sexes are thus resolved into the mere question of the *dependence* of women upon men for support, and women, whether married or single, are supported *by* men because they *are* women and their opposites in sex. I can see no moral difference between a woman who marries and lives with a man because he can provide for her wants, and the woman who is *not* married, but who is provided for at the same price. There is a *legal* difference, to be sure, upon one side of which is set the seal of respectability, but there is no virtue in law. In the *fact* of law, however, is the evidence of the lack of virtue, since if the law be *required* to enforce virtue, its real presence is wanting; and women need to comprehend this truth.

The sexual relation, must be rescued from this *insidious* form of slavery. Women must rise from their position as *ministers* to the passions of men to be their equals. Their entire system of education must be changed. They must be trained to be *like* men, permanent and independent individualities, and not their mere appendages or adjuncts, with them forming but one member of society. They must be the companions of men from *choice*, *never* from necessity.

It is a libel upon nature and God to say this world is not calculated to make women, equally with men, self-reliant and self-supporting individuals. In present customs, however, this is apparently impossible. There must come a change, and one of the direct steps to it will be found in the newly claimed political equality of women with men. This attained, one degree of subjugation will be removed. Next will come, following equality of right, equality of duty, which includes the duty of self-hood, or independence as an individual. Nature is male and female throughout, and each sex is equally dependent upon nature for sustenance. It is an infamous thing to say a condition of society which requires women to enter into and maintain sexual relations with men is their legitimate method of protecting life. Sexual relations should be the result of entirely different motives than for the purpose of physical support. The *spirit* of the present theory is, that they are entered upon and maintained as a *means* of physical gratification, regardless of the consequences which may result therefrom, and are administered by the dictum of the husband, which is often in direct opposition to the will and wish of the wife. She has *no* control over her own person, having been taught to "submit herself to her husband."

I protest against this form of slavery, I *protest* against the custom which compels women to give the control of their maternal functions over to anybody. It should be *theirs* to determine *when*, and under what circumstances, the greatest of all constructive processes—the formation of an immortal soul—should be begun. It is a *fearful* responsibility with which women are intrusted by nature, and the very *last* thing that they should be compelled to do is to *perform* the office of that responsibility against their will, under improper conditions or by disgusting means.

What can be more terrible than for a delicate, sensitively organized woman to be compelled to endure the presence of a beast in the shape of a man, who knows nothing beyond the blind passion with which he is filled, and to which is often added the delirium of intoxication? You do not need to be informed that there are many persons who, during the acquaintance preceding marriage, preserve a delicacy, tenderness and regard for womanly sensitiveness and modest refinement which are characteristic of true women, thus winning and drawing out their love-nature to the extreme, but who, when the decree has been pronounced which makes them indissolubly theirs, cast all these aside and reveal themselves in their *true* character, as without regard, human or divine, for aught save their own desires. I know I speak the truth, and you too know I speak the truth, when I say that thousands of the most noble, loving-natured women by whom the world was ever blessed, prepared for, and desirous of pouring their whole life into the bond of union, prophesied by marriage, have had all these generous and warm impulses thrust back upon them by the rude monster into which the previous gentleman developed. To these natures thus frosted and stultified in their fresh youth and vigor, life becomes a burden almost too terrible to be borne, and thousands of pallid cheeks, sunken eyes, distorted imaginations and diseased functions testify too directly and truly to leave a shade of doubt as to their real cause. Yet women, in the first instance, and men through them as their mothers, with an ignorant persistence worthy only of the most savage despotism, seem determined that it shall not be investigated; and so upon this voluntary ignorance and willful persistence society builds. It is *high* time, however, that they should be investigated, *high* time that your sisters and daughters should no longer be led to the *altar* like sheep to the shambles, in ignorance of the uncertainties they must inevitably encounter. For it is no slight thing to hazard a life's happiness upon a single act.

I deem it a false and perverse modesty that shuts off discussion, and consequently knowledge, upon *these* subjects. They are *vital*, and I never performed a duty which I felt *more* called upon to perform than I *now* do in denouncing as *barbarous* the ignorance which is allowed to prevail among young women about to enter those relations which, under present customs, as often bring a life-long *misery* as happiness.

Mistakes made in this most important duty of life can never be rectified ; a commentary upon the system which of itself is sufficient in the sight of common sense to forever condemn it. In marriage, however, common sense is *dispensed* with, and a *usage* substituted there-for which barbarism has bequeathed us, and which becomes *more* barbarous as the spiritual natures of women gain the ascendancy over the mere material. The former slaves, before realizing that freedom was their God-appointed right, did not feel the *horrors* of their condition. But when, here and there, some among them began to have an *interior* knowledge that they were held in obedience by an *unrighteous power*, they then began to *rebel* in their souls. So, too, is it with women. So long as they knew nothing beyond a blind and servile obedience and perfect self-abnegation to the will and wish of men, they did not rebel; but the time *has* arrived wherein, here and there, a soul is awakened by some terrible ordeal, or some divine inspiration, to the fact that women as much as men are *personalities, responsible* to themselves for the use which they permit to be made of themselves, and they rebel demanding freedom, freedom to hold their own lives and bodies from the demoralizing influence of sexual relations that are not founded in and maintained by love. And this rebellion will continue, too, until love, unshackled, shall be free to go to bless the object that can call it forth, and until, when called forth, it shall be respected as holy, pure and true. Every day *farther* and wider does it spread, and *bolder* does it speak. None *too soon* will the yoke fall by which the unwilling are made to render a hypocritical obedience to the despotism of public opinion, which, distorted and blinded by a sham sentimentality, is a false standard of morals and virtue, and which is utterly destructive to true morality and to real virtue, which can only be fostered and cultivated by freedom of the affections.

Free Love, then, is the law by which men and women of all grades and kinds are attracted to or repelled from each other, and does not describe the results accomplished by either; these results depend upon the condition and development of the individual subjects. It is the *natural* operation of the *affectional* motives of the sexes, unbiased by *any* enacted law or *standard* of public opinion. It is the opportunity which gives the opposites in sex the conditions in which the law of chemical affinities raised into the domain of the affections can have unrestricted sway, as it has in *all* departments of nature *except* in enforced sexual relations among men and women.

It is an impossibility to compel incompatible elements of *matter* to unite. So also is it impossible to compel incompatible elements of *human nature* to unite. The sphere of chemical science is to bring together such elements as will produce harmonious compounds. The sphere of social science is to accomplish the same thing in humanity. Anything that stands in the way of this accomplishment in either department is an *obstruction* to the natural order of the universe. There would be just as much common sense for the chemist to write a law *commanding* that two incompatible elements should unite, or that two, once united, should so remain, even if a third, having a stronger affinity for one of them than they have for each other, should be introduced, as it is for chemists of society to attempt to do the same by individuals; for both are impossible. If in chemistry two properties are united by which the environment is not profited, it is the same law of affinity which operates as where a compound is made that is of the greatest service to society. This law holds in social chemistry; the results obtained from social compounds will be just such as their respective properties determine.

Thus I might go on almost infinitely to illustrate the difference which *must* be recognized between the operations of a law and the *law itself.* Now the whole difficulty in marriage law is that it endeavors to *compel* unity between elements in which it is impossible; consequently there is an attempt made to subvert not only the general order of the universe, but also the special intentions of nature, which are those of God. The results, then, flowing from operations of the law of Free Love will be *high, pure* and *lasting,* or *low, debauched and promiscuous, just in the degree* that those loving, are high or low in the scale of sexual progress; while each and all are strictly natural, and therefore legitimate in their respective spheres.

Promiscuity in sexuality is simply the *anarchical stage of development* wherein the passions rule supreme. When spirituality comes in and rescues the real man or woman from the domain of the purely material, promiscuity is simply impossible. As promiscuity is the analogue to anarchy, so is spirituality to scientific selection and adjustment. Therefore I am fully persuaded that the very highest sexual unions are those that are monogamic, and that these are perfect in proportion as they are lasting. Now if to this be added the fact that the highest kind of love is that which is utterly freed from and devoid of *selfishness,* and whose *highest* gratification comes from rendering its object the *greatest* amount of happiness, let that happiness depend upon whatever it may, then you have my ideal of the highest order of love and the most perfect degree of order to which humanity can attain. An affection that does not desire to bless its object, instead of appropriating it by a selfish possession to its own uses, is not worthy the name of love. Love is that which exists to *do* good, not merely to *get good,* which is constantly giving instead of desiring.

A Cæsar is admired by humanity, but a Christ is revered. Those persons who have lived and sacrificed themselves most for the good of humanity, without thought of recompense, are held in greatest respect. Christians believe that Christ died to save the world, giving His life as a ransom therefor. That was the greatest gift He could make to show His love for mankind.

The general test of love to-day is entirely different from that which Christ gave. That is now deemed the greatest love which has the strongest and most uncontrollable wish to be made happy, by the appropriation, and if need be the sacrifice, of all the preferences of its object. It says: "Be mine. Whatever may be your wish, yield it up to me." How different would the world be were this sort of selfishness supplanted by the Christ love, which says: Let this cup pass from me. Nevertheless, not my will but thine be done. Were the relations of the sexes thus regulated, misery, crime and vice would be banished, and the pale, wan face of female humanity replaced by one glowing with radiant delight and healthful bloom, and the heart of humanity beat with a heightened vigor and renewed strength, and its intellect cleared of all shadows, sorrows and blights. Contemplate this, and then denounce me for advocating Freedom if you can, and I will bear your curse with a better resignation.

Oh! my brothers and sisters, let me entreat you to have more faith in the self-regulating efficacy of freedom. Do you not see how beautifully it works among us in other respects? In America everybody is free to worship God according to the dictates of his own conscience, or even not to worship anything, notwithstanding you or I may think that very wicked or wrong. The respect for freedom we make paramount over our individual opinions, and the result is peace and harmony, when the people of other countries are still throtling and destroying each other to enforce their individual opinions on others. Free Love is only the appreciation of this beautiful principle of freedom. One step further I entreat you to trust it still, and though you may see a thousand dangers, I see peace and happiness and steady improvement as the result.

To more specifically define Free Love I would say that I prefer to use the word *love* with *lust* as its antithesis, *love* representing the spritual and *lust* the animal; the perfect and harmonious interrelations of the two being the perfected human. This use has its justification in other pairs of words; as good and evil; heat and cold; light and dark; up and down; north and south; which in *principle* are the same, but in *practice* we are obliged to judge of them as *relatively* different. The point from which judgment is made is that which we occupy, or are related to, individually, at any given time. Thus what would be up to one person might be down to another differently situated, along the line which up and down describe. So also is it of good and evil. What is good to one low down the ladder may not only be, but actually is, evil to one further ascended; nevertheless it is the same ladder up which both climb. It is the comprehension of this scientific fact that guarantees the *best* religion. And it is the *non-comprehension* of it that sets us as judges of our brothers and sisters, who are below us in the scale of development, to whom we should reach down the kind and loving hand of assistance, rather than force them to retreat farther away from us by unkindness, denunciation and hate.

In fine, and to resume: We have found that humanity is composed of men and women of all grades of development, from the most hideous human monster up to the highest perfected saint: that all of them, under our theory of government, are entitled to worship God after the dictates of their several consciences; that God is worshiped just as essentially in political and social thought and action as He is in religious thought and action; that no second person or persons have any right to interfere with the action of the individual unless he interfere with others' rights, and then only to protect such rights; that the thoughts and actions of all individuals, whether high and pure, or low and debauched, are equally entitled to the protection of the laws, and, through them, to that of all members of the community. Religious thought and action already receive the equal protection of the laws. Political thought and action are about to secure the equal protection of the laws. What social thought and action demand of the laws and their administrators is the same protection which Religion has, and Politics is about to have.

I know full well how strong is the appeal that can be made in behalf of marriage, an appeal based on the sanctions of usage and inherited respect, and on the sanctions of religion reinforced by the sanctions of law. I know how much can be said, and how forcibly it can be said, on the ground that women, and especially that the children born of the union of the sexes, must be protected, and must, therefore, have the solemn contract of the husband and father to that effect. I know how long and how powerfully the ideality and sentiment of mankind have clustered, as it were in a halo, around this time-honored institution of marriage. And yet I solemnly believe that *all that* belongs to a dispensation of force and contract, and of a low and unworthy sense of mutual ownership, which is passing, and which is destined rapidly to pass, completely away ; not to leave us without love, nor without the happiness and beauty of the most tender relation of human souls; nor without security for woman, and ample protection for children; but to lift us to a higher level in the enjoyment of every blessing. I believe in *love with liberty ;* in *protection without slavery ;* in *the care and culture of offspring by new and better methods, and without the tragedy of self-immolation on the part of parents.* I believe in the family, *spiritually constituted*, expanded, amplified, and scientifically and artistically organized, as a unitary home. I believe in the most wonderful transformation of human society as about to come, as even now at the very door, through general progress, science and the influential intervention of the spirit world. I believe in more than all that the millennium has ever signified to the most religious mind; and I believe that in order to prepare minds to contemplate and desire and enact the new and better life, it is necessary that the old and still prevalent superstitious veneration for the legal marriage tie be relaxed and weakened ; not to pander to immorality, but as introductory to a nobler manhood and a more glorified womanhood; as, indeed, the veritable gateway to a paradise regained.

Do not criticise me, therefore, from a commonplace point of view. Question me, first, of the grounds of my faith. Conceive, if you can, the outlook for that humanity which comes trooping through the long, bright vista of futurity, as seen by the eyes of a devout spiritualist and a transcendental socialist. My whole nature is prophetic. I do not and cannot live merely in the present. Credit, first, the burden of my prophecy ; and from the new standing-ground so projected forth into the future, look back upon our times, and so judge of my doctrine; and if, still, you cannot concede either the premises or the conclusion, you may, perhaps, think more kindly of me personally, as an amiable enthusiast, than if you deemed me deliberately wicked in seeking to disturb the foundations of our existing social order.

I prize dearly the good opinion of my fellow-beings. I would, *so gladly*, have you think well of me, and not ill. It is because I love you all, and love your well-being still more than I love you, that I tell you my vision of the future, and that I would willingly disturb your confidence, so long cherished, in the old dead or dying-out past. Believe me honest, my dear friends, and so forgive and think of me lovingly in turn, even if you are compelled still to regard me as deceived. I repeat, that I love you all; that I love every human creature, and their well being; and that I believe, with the profoundest conviction, that what I have urged in this discourse is conducive to that end.

Thus have I explained to you what Social Freedom or, as some choose to denominate it, Free Love, is, and what its advocates demand. Society says, to grant it is to precipitate itself into anarchy. I oppose to this arbitrary assumption the logic of general freedom, and aver that order and harmony will be secured where anarchy now reigns. The order of nature will soon determine whether society is or I am right. Let that be as it may, I repeat: "The love that I cannot command is not mine; let me not disturb myself about it, nor attempt to filch it from its rightful owner. A heart that I supposed mine has drifted and gone. Shall I go in pursuit? Shall I forcibly capture the truant and transfix it with the barb of my selfish affection, and pin it to the wall of my chamber? Rather let me leave my doors and windows open, intent only on living so nobly that the best cannot fail to be drawn to me by an irresistible attraction."

SOCIOLOGY

(2)

Victoria C. Woodhull's Complete and Detailed Version
of the Beecher-Tilton Affair . . . 1872.

The "article" that "burst like a bomb-shell" and initiated the disclosure appeared in *Woodhull & Claflin's Weekly* (Nov. 2, 1872, pp. 9-13).

VICTORIA C. WOODHULL'S

COMPLETE AND DETAILED VERSION

OF THE

BEECHER-TILTON AFFAIR.

Woe unto you, Scribes and Pharisees, hypocrites! for ye are like unto whited sepulchres, which, indeed, appear beautiful outward, but are within full of dead men's bones, and of all uncleanness.

Even so ye also outwardly appear righteous unto men, but within ye are full of hypocrisy and iniquity.—MATT. xxiii., 27, 28.

FOR SALE BY ALL BOOKSELLERS AND DEALERS IN PERIODICALS, ETC.

Price, Twenty-five Cents.

The Trade Supplied on Favorable Terms by

J. BRADLEY ADAMS,

816 F STREET, OPPOSITE PATENT OFFICE,

WASHINGTON, D. C.

WHY THIS PAMPHLET IS PUBLISHED.

The Pluto-theocracy of Brooklyn is attempting to crush Mrs. Woodhull without giving her the opportunity she seeks to prove the charges preferred by her against Rev. Henry Ward Beecher, the well-known Pastor of Plymouth Church, of that city. The press and the telegraph have been used, from Maine to California, to create the impression that there is no foundation whatever for the statement of Mrs. Woodhull that Mr. Beecher has adulterously violated, for the last past ten years, *habitually and systematically*, that decalogue which he professes to believe, was a direct order issued personally by the Almighty Creator of the Universe to mankind, through Moses, and for expounding and defending which; he, Mr. Beecher, has been receiving from his congregation, for several years, a higher salary than is paid to any other clergyman in the United States. The same agencies have also been used to revile Mrs. Woodhull, and to bring her into public disrepute by stigmatizing her as a slanderer, a spiritualist, a free-lover, a social revolutionist, and a very wicked woman generally ; and all this by people who, if in a witness-box, would have to acknowledge that they know nothing of her except from hearsay.

This organized and costly effort of Mr. Beecher's wealthy friends had the effect, at first, of creating a good deal of public sympathy with that gentleman, and arousing a general feeling of indignation against Mrs. Woodhull. But, as might have been readily foreseen by those who went into the dangerous business of manufacturing public opinion on *ex parte* testimony, a powerful reaction has already commenced. After the first excitement was over, Christian people began to ask each other, in whispers, and cautiously, "Why has not Mr. Beecher instituted legal proceedings against this wicked woman, that she may be convicted of this atrocious libel, and be punished?" And soon after, the question was on the tongue of every man who has the true interests of Christianity at heart, as he met an acquaintance whom he believed also to be a Christian, "If Mr. Beecher is too tender-hearted to have this vile woman tried, convicted and imprisoned, why does he not get Mrs. Paulina Wright Davis and Mrs. Elizabeth Cady Stanton, two ladies of good family, high culture and the first social standing, whose characters are irreproachable and whose veracity would not be questioned, to publicly deny, over their own signatures, the allegations of Mrs. Woodhull that they told her the first information they received of Mr. Beecher practicing habitually the free-love which he denounced from the pulpit was from Mr. and Mrs. Tilton themselves?"

After a while, zealous Christians grew impatient, and, ceasing to whisper, asked each other boldly, "Why does not Mr. Beecher get Mr. Frank Moulton, a member of the Plymouth Church, to deny, publicly, the truth of Mrs. Woodhull's statement, that, after Mr. Tilton's discovery of his wife's infidelity, and her confession to him of her criminal relations with Mr. Beecher for more than ten years, he, Moulton, at Mr. Tilton's request, and as his friend, called upon Mr. Beecher, and, pistol in hand, compelled him to give up a paper which he, Beecher, had prepared, and had forced or induced Mr. Tilton to sign, declaring that there had been no criminal intimacy between them. "Why," ask these zealous Christians, now grown impatient, "does not Mr. Beecher get Mr. Moulton to deny that he ever performed, substantially, this service for his friend Tilton?"

The above and similar questions are no longer asked in whispers or in corners. Many men and women who have the progress of practical Christianity at heart are indignant at the contemptuous inaction of the far-famed Brooklyn preacher, who thus allows a great scandal on the church to stand unrefuted. And others, their numbers daily increasing, are beginning to avow their belief that there may be something in this charge, after all. "Why," they ask, " is Mr. Tilton himself, the whilom fast and bold friend and enthusiastic biographer of Mrs. Woodhull, entirely silent?" " Does Mr. Beecher think," ask others, " that because a silly charge which had, of course, to be dropped, of issuing an obscene publication, was preferred against Mrs. Woodhull, or because she has been arrested for libel by an obscure libertine, that the grave charges she prefers against one of the most distinguished pillars of the church, she claiming to possess partial documentary evidence, and naming her living witnesses, all of them persons of good standing in the community—does Mr. Beecher think that he can retain the confidence of the Christian public, and his pastorship of a Christian church, to the advantage of the cause he professes to serve, by allowing these charges to remain disproved?"

A very large and increasing proportion of the thinking people of the community, including the most active and zealous Christians, are beginning to say, frankly, that this silence of Mr. Beecher will not answer, that Mr. Tilton's reticence is ominous, and that the fact that not one witness cited by Mrs. Woodhull has contradicted her statements, tells fearfully against Mr. Beecher—that the whole thing looks as if he was afraid to go into court and have this affair thoroughly ventilated.

It is even darkly hinted that Mrs. Woodhull's arrest, ostensibly on another charge, was indirectly instigated by Mr. Beecher's friends, and that they are anxious she shall be convicted of slandering a shameless, avowed libertine, and imprisoned, that they may have an opportunity to purchase her eternal silence on the Beecher matter by effecting her release. Indeed, every mail leaving New York bears increasingly strange rumors to all parts of the country regarding this remarkable case ; and the general idea of an "impending crisis" in the history of the Plymouth Church of Brooklyn strongly prevails.

Under all these circumstances, it is not strange that there is a great demand for the original article by Mrs. Woodhull which has created this intense excitement in religious circles all over the country. People are anxious to read it, and to form their own opinions, instead of continuing to rely on the garbled ex parte statements regarding it which are being scattered broadcast over the land by Mr. Beecher's friends and admirers. Hence the publication of this pamphlet, which is a verbatim copy of Mrs. Woodhull's statement.

THE BEECHER-TILTON SCANDAL CASE.

I propose, as a commencement of a series of aggressive moral warfare on the social question, to begin in this article with ventilating one of the most stupendous scandals which has ever occurred in any community. I refer to that which has been whispered broad-cast for the last two or three years through the cities of New York and Brooklyn, touching the character and conduct of the Rev. HENRY WARD BEECHER in his relations with the family of THEODORE TILTON. I intend that this article shall burst like a bomb-shell into the ranks of the moralistic social camp.

I am engaged in officering, and in some sense conducting, a social revolution on the marriage question. I have strong convictions to the effect that this institution, as a *bond* or *promise* to love one another to the end of life, and forego all other loves or passional gratifications, has outlived its day of usefulness ; that the most intelligent and really virtuous of our citizens, especially in the large cities of Christendom, have outgrown it ; are constantly and systematically unfaithful to it ; despise and revolt against it, as a slavery, in their hearts ; and only submit to the semblance of fidelity to it from the dread of a sham public opinion, based on the ideas of the past, and which no longer really represent the convictions of any body. The doctrines of scientific socialism have profoundly penetrated and permeated public opinion. No thought has so rapidly and completely carried the conviction of the thinking portions of the community as stirpiculture. The absurdity is too palpable, when it is pointed out, that we give a hundred times more attention to the laws of breeding as applied to horses and cattle and pigs, and even to our barn-yard fowls, than we do to the same laws as applied to human beings. It is equally obvious, on a little reflection, that stirpiculture, or the scientific propagation and cultivation of the human animal, demands free love, or freedom of the varied union of the sexes under the dictates of the highest and best knowledge on the subject, as an essential and precedent condition. These considerations are too palpable to be ignored, and they look to the complete and early supercedure of the old and traditional institution of marriage, by the substitution of some better system for the maintenance of women as mothers, and of children as progeny. All intelligent people know these facts and look for the coming of some wiser and better system of social life. The supercedure of marriage in the near future, by some kind of socialistic arrangement, is as much a foregone conclusion with all the best thinkers of to-day as was the approaching dissolution of slavery no more than five or ten years before its actual abolition in the late war.

But, in the meantime, men and women tremble on the brink of the revolution and hesitate to avow their convictions, while yet partly aware of their rights, and urged by the legitimate impulses of nature, they act upon the new doctrines while they profess obedience to the old. In this manner an organized hypocrisy has become the tone of our modern society. Poltroonery, cowardice and deception rule the hour. The continuance, for generations, of such utter falsity, touching one of the most sacred interests of humanity, will almost eradicate the sense of honesty from the human soul. Every consideration of sound expediency demands that these days be shortened ; that somebody lead the van in announcement of the higher order of life.

Impelled by such views, I entered the combat with old errors, as I believe them to be, and brought forward, in addition to the wise and powerful words which others have uttered on the subject, the arguments which my own inspiration and reflections suggested. No sooner had I done so than the howl of persecution sounded in my ears. Instead of replying to my arguments, I was assaulted with shameful abuse. I was young and inexperienced in the business of reform, and astounded to find what, as I have since learned from the veterans in the cause, is the usual fact, that the most persistent and slanderous and foul-mouthed accusations came from precisely those who, as I often happened to know, stood nearest to me in their convictions, and whose lives, privately, were a protest against the very repression which I denounce. It was a paradox which I could not understand, that I was denounced as utterly bad for affirming the rights of others, to do as they did; denounced by the very persons whom my doctrines could alone justify, and who claimed, at the same time to be conscientious and good men. My position led, nevertheless, to continuous confidences relating to people's own opinions and lives and the opinions and lives of others.

My mind became charged with a whole literature of astonishing disclosures. The lives of almost the whole army of spiritualistic and social reformers, of all the schools were laid open before me. But the matter did not stop there. I found that, to a great extent, the social revolution was as far advanced among leading lights of the business and wealthy circles, and of the various professions, not excluding the clergy and the churches, as among technical reformers.

It was, nevertheless, from these very quarters that I was most severely assailed. It was vexatious and trying, I confess, for one of my temper, to stand under the galling fire of personalities from parties who should have been my warmest advocates, or who should, else, have reformed their lives in accordance with a morality which they wished the public to understand they professed. I was sorely and repeatedly tempted to retort, in personalities, to these attacks. But simply as personality, or or personal defense, or spiteful retort, I have almost wholly abstained during these years of sharp conflict from making any use of the rich resources at my command for that kind of attack.

But, in the meantime, the question came to press itself upon my consideration: Had I any right, having assumed the championship of social freedom, to forego the use of half the weapons which the facts no less than the philosophy of the subject placed at my command for conducting the war—through any mere tenderness to those who were virtual traitors to the truth which they knew and were surreptitiously acting upon? Had not the sacred cause of human rights and human well-being a paramount claim over my own conduct? Was I not, in withholding the facts and conniving at a putrid mass of seething falsehood and hypocrisy, in some sense a partaker in these crimes; and was I not, in fact, shrinking from the responsibility of making the exposure more through regard for my own sensitiveness and dislike to be hurt than from any true sympathy with those who would be called upon to suffer?

These questions once before my mind would never be disposed of until they were fairly settled upon their own merits, and apart, so far as I could separate them, from my own feelings or the feelings of those who were more directly involved. I have come slowly, deliberately, and I may add reluctantly, to my conclusions. I went back to and studied the history of other reforms. I found that GARRISON not only denounced slavery in the abstract, but that he attacked it in the concrete. It was not only "the sum of all villainies," but it was the particular villainy of this and that and the other great and influential man, North and South, in the community. Reputations had to suffer. He bravely and persistently called things by their right names. He pointed out and depicted the individual instances of cruelty. He dragged to the light and scathed and stigmatized the individual offenders. He made them a hissing and a by-word, so far as in him lay. He shocked the public sensibilities by actual and vivid pictures of slaveholding atrocities, and sent spies into the enemies' camp to search out the instances. The world cried shame! and said it was scandalous, and stopped their ears and blinded their eyes, that their own sensibilities might not be hurt by these horrid revelations. They cast the blanket of their charities and sympathies around the real offenders for their misfortune in being brought to the light, and denounced the informer as a malignant and cruel wretch for not covering up scenes too dreadful to be thought upon; as if it were not a thousand times more dreadful that they should be enacted. But the brave old cyclops ignored alike their criticisms, their protests, and their real and their mock sensibilities, and hammered away at his anvil, forging thunderbolts of the gods; and nobody now says he was wrong. A new public opinion had to be created, and he knew that people had to be shocked, and that individual personal feelings had to be hurt. As Bismarck is reported to have said : "If an omelet has to be made some eggs have to be broken." Every revolution has its terrible cost, if not in blood and treasure, then still in the less tangible but alike real sentimental injury of thousands of sufferers. The preliminary and paramount question is : Ought the revolution to be made, cost what it may? Is the cost to humanity greater of permitting the standing evil to exist? and if so, then let the cost be incurred, fall where it must. If justice to humanity demand the given expenditure, then accepting the particular enterprise of reform, we accept all its necessary consequences, and enter upon our work, fraught, it may be, with repugnance to ourselves as it is necessarily with repugnance to others.

I have said that I came slowly, deliberately and reluctantly to the adoption of this method of warfare. I was also hindered and delayed by the fact that if I entered upon it at all I saw no way of avoiding making the first onslaught in the most distinguished quarters. It would be cowardice in me to unearth the peccadillos of little men, and to leave untouched the derelictions and offences of the magnates of social and intellectual power and position. How slowly I have moved in this matter, and how reluctantly it may be inferred, will appear from these little points of history.

More than two years ago these two cities—New York and Brooklyn—were rife with rumors of an awful scandal in Plymouth Church. These rumors were whispered and covertly alluded to in almost every circle. But the very enormity of the facts, as the world views such matters, hushed agitation and prevented exposure. The press, warned by the laws of libel, and by a tacit and in the main honorable *consensus* to ignore all such rumors until they enter the courts or become otherwise matters of irrepressible notoriety, abstained from any direct notice of the subject, and the rumors themselves were finally stifled or forgotten. A few persons only knew something directly of the facts, but among them, situated as I was, I happened to be one. Already the question pressed on me whether I ought not to use the event to forward the cause of social freedom, but I only saw clear in the matter to the limited extent of throwing out some feelers to the public on the subject. It was often a matter of long and anxious consultation between me and my cabinet of confidential advisers.

In June, 1876, WOODHULL & CLAFLIN'S WEEKLY published an article in reply to HENRY C. BOWEN'S attack on myself in the columns of *The Independent*, the editorship of which had just been vacated by THEODORE TILTON. In this article the following paragraph occurred : "At this very moment awful and herculean efforts are being made in a neighboring city to suppress the most terrific scandal which has ever astonished and convulsed any community. Clergy, congregation and community will be alike hurled into more than all the consternation which the great explosion in Paris carried to that unfortunate city, if this effort at suppression fail."

Subsequently I published a letter in both World and Times in which was the following sentence : " I know a clergyman of eminence in Brooklyn who lives in concubinage with the wife of another clergyman of equal eminence."

It was generally and well understood among the people of the press especially. that both of these references were to this case of Mr. BEECHER'S, and it came to be generally suspected that I was better informed regarding the facts of the case than others, and was reserving publicity of my knowledge to a more convenient season. This suspicion was heightened nearly into conviction when it transpired that THEODORE TILTON was an earnest and apparently conscientious advocate of many of my radical theories, as appeared in his far-famed biography of me, and in numerous other publications in The Golden Age and elsewhere. Mr. TILTON'S warmest friends were shocked at his course, and when he added to his remarkable proceedings his brilliant advocacy of my Fourteenth Amendment theory, in his letters to HORACE GREELEY, CHAS. SUMNER and MATT. CARPENTER, they considered him irremediably committed to the most radical of all radicals. Assurance was made doubly sure when he presided at Steinway Hall, when I, for the first time, fully and boldly advanced my free-love doctrines. It was noted, however, that this man who stood before the world so fully committed to the broadest principles of liberty, made it convenient to be conspicuously absent from the convention of the Woman Suffragists at Washington last January. All sorts of rumors were thereupon rife. Some said he had " gone back" on his advocacy of free love ; some said a rupture had taken place between him and the leaders of the suffrage movement, and many were the theories brought forward to explain the facts. But the real cause did not transpire until Mr. TILTON was found at Cincinnati urging as a candidate the very man whom he had recently so severely castigated with his most caustic pen. It was then wisely surmised that political ambition, and the editorial chair of The Tribune, and his life-long personal devotion to Mr. Greeley, were the inducements which had sufficed to turn his head and heart away, temporarily at least, from our movement.

About this time rumors floated out that Mrs. WOODHULL, disgusted at the recent conduct of Mr. TILTON and the advice given him by certain of his friends, was animadverting in not very measured terms upon their conduct. An article specifying matters involving several of these persons, obtained considerable circulation, and with other circumstances, such as the definite statement of facts, with names and places, indicatad that the time was at hand, nigh even unto the door, when the things that had remained hidden should be brought to light, and the whole affair be made public.

Sometime in August last there appeared in the Evening Telegram a paragraph which hinted broadly at the nature of the impending *expose*, About this time, a gentleman from abroad, to whom I had related some of the facts in my possession, repeated them to a member of Mr. BEECHER'S church, who denounced the whole story as an infamous libel ; but some days later he acknowledged both to his friend and me that he had inquired into the matter, and learned that it was a " damning fact." This gentleman occupies a responsible position, and his word is good for all that he utters. Such was the facility with which confirmations were obtained when sought for. When, therefore, those who were conversant with the case, saw in the Boston Herald and other papers that I had made a public statement regarding the whole matter, they were not in the least surprised. It shows that the press had concluded that it was time to recognise the sensation which, whether they would or not, was destined soon to shake the social structure from its foundation.

A reporter was then specially detailed to interview me in order, as he said, that the matter might be published in certain of the New York papers. Why that interview has been suppressed is not possible to affirm with certainty, but it is easy to guess. An impecunious reporter can be bought off with a few hundred dollars. And there are those who would readily pay thousands to shut the columns of the press against this exposure. Fortunately I have a nearly verbatim copy of the report, as the interviewer prepared it, and in this shape I shall now present it to the public.

But before proceeding to the main matter, let me relate, more in detail, the facts which finally determined me to enter upon this adventurous and responsible method of agitation.

In September, 1871, I was elected at the annual convention at Troy, President of the National Association of Spiritualists. I had never consociated with the Spiritualists, although for many years both a Spiritualist and a medium myself, with rare and wonderful experiences of my own from my childhood up. I went to this convention merely as a spectator, with no previous concert or machinery of any kind, and was myself as absolutely taken by surprise by my nomination and election as could have been any one present. It was said editorially in our paper, September 30, 1871, and said truly: " Her surprise at her reception, and her nomination to the Presidency of the Society was equaled only by the gratitude which she felt, and will ever feel, at the unexpected and tumultuous kindness with which she was then and their honored beyond her desert."

In WOODHULL & CLAFLIN'S WEEKLY, of Nov. 11, 1871, I addressed a President's message to the American Association of Spiritualists. In that document I made use of these words : " A new and mightier power than all the rings and caucuses, than all the venal legislatures and congresses, has already entered the arena. Not only are all the reform parties coalescent in the reform plane, but they have *already* coalesced in spirit, under the new lead, and ' a nation will be born in a day.' They have already taken possession of the public conviction. Somewhat unconsciously, but really, all the people look to the coming'of a new era ; but all of them are not so well aware as we are that the spirit world has always exerted a great and diversified influence over this, while it is not till quite recently that the spiritual development of this world has made it possible for the other to maintain real and continuous relations with it.

" Your enthusiastic acceptance of me, and your election of me as your President, was, in a sense, hardly your act. It was an event prepared for you, and to which you were impelled by the superior powers to which both you and I are subject. It was only one step in a series of rapid and astounding events, which will, in a marvellously short time, change the entire face of the social world."

This and similar to this was the complete avowal which I then made of my faith, in the spiritual ordering of human events, and especially of a grand series of events, now in actual and rapid progress, and tending to culminate in the complete dissolution of the old social order, and in the institution of a new and celestial order of humanity in the world. And let me now take occasion to affirm, that all the, otherwise viewed, terrible events which I am about to recite as having occurred in Plymouth Church, are merely parts of the same drama which have been cautiously and laboriously prepared to astound men into the consciousness of the possibilities of a better life ; and that I believe that all the parties to this *embroglio* have been, throughout, the unconscious agents of the higher powers. It is this belief, more than anything else, which finally reconciles me to enact my part in the matter, which is that of the mere *nuncia* to the world of the facts which have happened, and so of the new step in the dissolution of the Old and in the inauguration of the New.

At a large and enthusiastic National Convention of the reformers of all schools, held in Apollo Hall, New York, the 11th and 12th of May, 1872,

I was put in nomination as the candidate of the Equal Rights Party for the Presidency of the United States. Despite the brilliant promise of appearances at the inception of this movement, a counter current of fatality seemed from that time to attend both it and me. The press, suddenly divided between the other two great parties, refused all notice of the new reformatory movement; a series of pecuniary disasters stripped us, for the time being, of the means of continuing our own weekly publication, and forced us into a desperate struggle for mere existence. I had not even the means of communicating my condition to my own circle of friends. At the same time my health failed from mere exhaustion. The inauguration of the new party, and my nomination, seemed to fall dead upon the country; and, to cap the climax, a new batch of slanders and injurious inuendoes permeated the community in respect to my condition and character.

Circumstances being in this state, the year rolled round, and the next annual convention of the National Association of Spiritualists occurred in September, 1872, at Boston. I went there—dragged by the sense of duty—tired, sick and discouraged, as to my own future, to surrender my charge as President of the Association, feeling as if I were distrusted and unpopular, and with no consolation but the consciousness of having striven to do right, and my abiding faith in the wisdom and help of the spirit world.

Arrived at the great assemblage, I felt around me everywhere, not indeed a positive hostility, not even a fixed spirit of unfriendliness, but one of painful uncertainty and doubt. I listened to the speeches of others and tried to gather the sentiment of the great meeting. I rose finally to my feet to render an account of my stewardship, to surrender the charge, and retire. Standing there before that audience, I was seized by one of those overwhelming gusts of inspiration which sometimes come upon me, from I know not where; taken out of myself; hurried away from the immediate question of discussion, and made, by some power stronger than I, to pour out into the ears of that assembly, and, as I was told subsequently, in a rhapsody of indignant eloquence, with circumstantial detail, the whole history of the BEECHER and TILTON scandal in Plymouth Church, and to announce in prophetic terms something of the bearing of those events upon the future of Spiritualism. I know perhaps less than any of those present, all that I did actually say. They tell me that I used some naughty words upon that occasion. All that, I know is, that if I swore, *I did not swear profanely.* Some said, with the tears streaming from their eyes, *that I swore divinely.* That I could not have shocked or horrified the audience was shown by the fact that in the immense hall, packed to the ceiling, and as absolutely to my own surprise as at my first election of Troy, I was re-elected President of the Association. Still impressed by my own previous convictions, that my labors in that connection were ended, I promptly declined the office. The convention, however, refused to accept my declinature.

The public press of Boston professed holy horror at the freedom of my speech, and restricted their reports to the narrowest limits, carefully suppressing what I had said of the conduct of the great clergyman. The report went forward, however, through various channels, in a muffled and mutilated form, the general conclusion being, probably, with the uninformed, simply that Mrs. Woodhull had publicly slandered Mr. Beecher.

Added, therefore, to all other considerations, I am now placed in the situation that I must either endure unjustly the imputation of being a slanderer, or I must resume my previously formed purpose, and relate in formal terms, for the whole public, the simple facts of the case as they have come to my knowledge, and so justify, in cool deliberation, the words I uttered, almost unintentionally, and by a sudden impulse, at Boston.

I accept the situation, and enter advisedly upon the task I have undertaken, knowing the responsibilities of the act and its possible consequences. I am impelled by no hostility whatever to Mr. BEECHER, nor by any personal pique toward him or any other person. I recognize in the facts a fixed determination in the Spirit world to bring this subject to the light of day for high and important uses to the world. They demand of me my co-operation, and they shall have it, no matter what the consequences may be to me personally.

The following is the re-statement from notes, aided by my recollection, of the interviewing upon this subject by the press reporter already alluded to :

REPORTER.—" Mrs. Woodhull, I have called to ask if you are prepared and willing to furnish a full statement of the BEECHER-TILTON scandal for publication in the city papers ?"

MRS. WOODHULL.—" I do not know that I ought to object to repeating whatever I know in relation to it. You understand, of course, that I take a different view of such matters from those usually avowed by other people. Still I have good reason to think that far more people entertain views corresponding to mine than dare to assert them or openly live up to them."

REPORTER.—" How, Mrs. WOODHULL, would you state in the most condensed way your opinions on this subject, as they differ from those avowed and ostensibly lived by the public at large ?"

MRS. WOODHULL.—" I believe that the marriage institution, like slavery and monarchy, and many other things which have been good or necessary in their day, is now *effete*, and in a general sense injurious, instead of being beneficial to the community, although of course it must continue to linger until better institutions can be formed. I mean by marriage, in this connection, any *forced* or *obligatory tie* between the sexes, *any legal intervention* or *constraint* to prevent people from adjusting their love relations precisely as they do their religious affairs in this country, in complete personal freedom ; changing and improving them from time to time, and according to circumstances."

REPORTER.—" I confess, then, I cannot understand why you of all persons should have any fault to find with Mr. BEECHER, even assuming everything to be true of him which I have hitherto heard only vaguely hinted at."

MRS. WOODHULL.—" *I* have no fault to find with him in any such sense as you mean, nor in any such sense as that in which the world will condemn him. I have no doubt that he has done the very best which he could do under all the circumstances—with his demanding physical nature, and with the terrible restrictions upon clergymen's lives, imposed by that ignorant public opinion about physiological laws, which they, nevertheless, more, perhaps, than any other class, do their best to perpetuate. The fault I find with Mr. BEECHER is of a wholly different character, as I have told him repeatedly and frankly, and as he knows very well. It is, indeed, the exact opposite to that for which the world will condemn him. I condemn him because I know, and have had every opportunity to know, that he entertains, on conviction, substantially the same views which I entertain on the social question ; that, under the influence of these convictions, he has lived for many years, perhaps for his whole adult life, in a manner which the religious and moralistic public ostensibly, and to some extent really, condemn ; that he has permitted himself, nevertheless, to be overawed by public opinion, to profess to believe otherwise than as he does believe, to help, persistently, to maintain, for these many years that very social slavery under which he was chaffing, and against which he was secretly revolting both in thought and practice ; and that he has, in a word, consented, and still consents to be a hypocrite. The fault with which I, therefore, charge him, is not infidelity to the old ideas, but unfaithfulness to the new. He is in heart, in conviction and in life, an ultra socialist reformer ; while in seeming and pretension he is the upholder of the old social slavery, and, therefore, does what he can to crush out and oppose me and those who act and believe with me in forwarding the great social revolution. I know. myself, so little of the sentiment of fear, I have so little respect for an ignorant and prejudiced public opinion, I am so accustomed to say the thing that I think and do the thing that I believe to be right, that I doubt not I am in danger of having far too little sympathy with the real difficulties of a man situated as Mr. BEECHER has been, and is, when he contemplates the idea of facing social opprobrium. Speaking from my feelings, I am prone to denounce him as a poltroon, a coward and a sneak ; not, as I tell you, for anything that he has done, and for which the world would condemn him, but for failing to do what it seems to me so clear he ought to do ; for failing, in a word, to stand shoulder to shoulder with me and others who are endeavoring to hasten a social regeneration which he believes in."

REPORTER.—" You speak very confidently, Mrs. WOODHULL, of Mr. BEECHER'S opinions and life. Will you now please to resume that subject, and tell me exactly what you know of both.'

MRS. WOODHULL.—" I had vaguely heard rumors of some scandal in regard to Mr. BEECHER, which I put aside as mere rumor and idle gossip of the hour, and gave to them no attention whatever. The first serious intimation I had that there was something more than mere gossip in the matter came to me in the committee room at Washington, where the suffrage women congregated during the winter of 1870, when I was there to urge my views on the Fourteenth Amendment. It was hinted in the room that some of the women, Mrs. ISABELLA BEECHER HOOKER, a sister of Mr. BEECHER, among the number, would snub Mrs. WOODHULL on account of her social opinions and antecedents. Instantly a gentleman, a stranger to me, stepped forward and said : " It would ill become these women, and especially a BEECHER, to talk of antecedents or to cast any smirch upon Mrs. WOODHULL, for I am reliably assured that HENRY WARD BEECHER preaches to at least twenty of his mistresses every Sunday."

" I paid no special attention to the remark at the time, as I was very intensely engaged in the business which had called me there ; but it afterward forcibly recurred to me with the thought also that it was strange that such a remark, made in such a presence, had seemed to have a subduing effect instead of arousing indignation. The women who were there could not have treated me better than they did. Whether this strange remark had any influence in overcoming their objections to me I do not know : but it is certain they were not set against me by it ; and, all of them, Mrs. HOOKER included, subsequently professed the warmest friendship for me."

REPORTER.—" After this, I presume you sought for the solution of the gentleman's remark."

Mrs. WOODHULL.—" No, I did not. It was brought up subsequently, in an intimate conversation between her and me, by Mrs. PAULINE WRIGHT DAVIS. without any seeking on my part, and to my very great surprise. Mrs. DAVIS had been, it seems, a frequent visitor at Mr. TILTON's house in Brooklyn—they having long been associated in the Woman's Rights movement—and she stood upon certain terms of intimacy in the family. Almost at the same time to which I have referred, when I was in Washington, she called, as she told me, at Mr. TILTON's. Mrs. TILTON met her at the door and burst into tears, exclaiming : ' Oh, Mrs. DAVIS, have you come to see me ? For six months I have been shut up from the world, and I thought no one ever would come again to visit me." In the interview that followed, Mrs. TILTON spoke freely of a long series of intimate, and so-called criminal relations, on her part, with the Rev. HENRY WARD BEECHER ; of the discovery of the facts by Mr. TILTON ; of the abuse she had suffered from him in consequence, and of her heart-broken condition. She seemed to allude to the whole thing as to something already generally known, or known in a considerable circle, and impossible to be concealed ; and attributed the long absence of Mrs. DAVIS from the house to her knowledge of the facts. She was, as she stated at the time, recovering from the effects of a miscarriage of a child of six months. The miscarriage was induced by the ill-treatment of Mr. TILTON in his rage at the discovery of her criminal intimacy with Mr. BEECHER, and, as he believed, the great probability that she was *enciente* by Mr. BEECHER instead of himself. Mrs. TILTON confessed to Mrs. DAVIS the intimacy with Mr. BEECHER, and that it had been of years' standing. She also said that she had loved Mr. BEECHER before she married Mr. TILTON, and that now the burden of her sorrow was greatly augmented by the knowledge that Mr. BEECHER was untrue to her. She had not only to endure the rupture with her husband, but also the certainty that, notwithstanding his repeated assurance of his faithfulness to her, he had recently had illicit intercourse, under most extraordinary circumstances, with another person. Said Mrs. DAVIS: ' I came away from that house, my soul bowed down with grief at the heart-broken condition of that poor woman, and I felt that I ought not to leave Brooklyn until I had stripped the mask from that infamous, hypocritical scoundrel, BEECHER.' In May, after returning home, Mrs. DAVIS wrote me a letter, from which I will read a paragraph to show that we conversed on this subject."

" ' EXTRACT FROM A LETTER.

" ' DEAR VICTORIA : I thought of you half of last night, dreamed of you and prayed for you.
" ' I believe you are raised up of God to do a wonderful work, and I believe that you will unmask the hypocrisy of a class that none others dare touch. God help you and save you. The more I think of that *mass of Beecher corruption* the more I desire its opening.
" ' Ever yours, lovingly,
" ' PAULINA WRIGHT DAVIS.
" ' PROVIDENCE, R. I., May, 1871."

REPORTER.—" Djd you inform Mrs. DAVIS of your intention to expose this matter, as she intimates in the letter ?"
MRS. WOODHULL.—" I said in effect to her, that the matter would become public, and that I felt that I should be instrumental in making it so. But I was not decided about the course I should pursue. I next heard the whole story from Mrs. ELIZABETH CADY STANTON."
REPORTER.—" Indeed ! Is Mrs. STANTON also mixed up in this affair ? Does she know the facts ? How could the matter have been kept so long quiet when so many people are cognizant of it ?"
MRS. WOODHULL.—" The existence of the skeleton in the closet may be very widely known, and many people may have the key to the terrible secret, but still hesitate to open the door for the great outside world to gaze in upon it. This grand woman did indeed know the same facts, and from Mr. TILTON himself. I shall never forget the occasion of her first rehearsal of it to me at my residence, 15 East Thirty-eighth street, in a visit made to me during the Apollo Hall Convention in May, 1871. It seems that Mr. TILTON, in agony at the discovery of what he deemed his wife's perfidy and his pastor's treachery, retreated to Mrs. STANTON's residence at Tenafly, where he detailed to her the entire story. Said Mrs. STANTON, ' I never saw such a manifestation of mental agony. He

raved and tore his hair, and seemed upon the very verge of insanity.'
'Oh!' said he, 'that that damned lecherous scoundrel should have de-
filed my bed for ten years, and at the same time have professed to be my
best friend! Had he come like a man to me and confessed his guilt, I
could perhaps have endured it, but to have him creep like a snake into
my house leaving his pollution behind him, and I so blind as not to see,
and esteeming him all the while as a saint—oh! it is too much. And
when I think how for years she, upon whom I had bestowed all my
heart's love, could have lied and deceived me so, I lose all faith in humanity. I do not believe there is any honor, any truth left in anybody
in the world.' Mrs. STANTON continued and repeated to me the sad story,
which it is unnecessary to recite, as I prefer giving it as Mr. TILTON himself told it me, subsequently, with his own lips."

REPORTER.—" Is it possible that Mr. TILTON confided this story to you?
It seems too monstrous to be believed!"

MRS. WOODHULL.—" He certainly did, and what is more, I am persuaded
that in his inmost mind he will not be otherwise than glad when the
skeleton in his closet is revealed to the world, if thereby the abuses
which lurk like vipers under the cloak of social conservatism may be
exposed and the causes removed. Mr. TILTON looks deeper into the soul
of things than most men, and is braver than most."

REPORTER.—" How did your acquaintance with Mr. TILTON begin?"

MRS. WOODHULL.—Upon the information received from Mrs. DAVIS and
Mrs. STANTON I based what I said in the WEEKLY, and in the letters in the
Times and World, referring to the matter. I was nearly determined,
though still not quite so, that what I, equally with those who gave me
the information, believed, but for wholly other reasons, to be a most important social circumstance, should be exposed, my reasons being, as I
have explained to you, not those of the world ; and I took that method to
cause inquiry and create agitation regarding it. The day that the letter
appeared in the World Mr. TILTON came to my office, No. 44 Broad street,
and, showing me the letter, asked : ' Whom do you mean by that?' ' Mr.
TILTON,' said I. ' I mean you and Mr. BEECHER.' I then told him what I
knew, what I thought of it, and that I felt that I had a mission to bring
it to the knowledge of the world, and that I had nearly determined to
do so."

" I said to him much else on the subject; and he said : ' Mrs. WOODHULL,
you are the first person I have ever met who has dared to, or else who
could, tell me the truth.' He acknowledged that the facts, as I had heard
them, were true, but declared that I did not yet know the extent of the
depravity of that man—meaning Mr. BEECHER. ' But,' said he, ' do not
take any steps now. I have carried my heart as a stone in my breast for
months, for the sake of ELIZABETH, my wife, who is broken-hearted as I
am. I have had courage to endure rather than to add more to her weight
of sorrow. For her sake I have allowed that rascal to go unscathed. I
have curbed my feelings when every impulse urged me to throttle and
strangle him. Let me take you over to ELIZABETH, and you will find her
in no condition to be dragged before the public ; and I know you will
have compassion on her.' And I went and saw her, and I agreed with
him on the propriety of delay."

REPORTER.—" Was it during this interview that Mr. TILTON explained
to you all that you know of the matter?"

MRS. WOODHULL.—" Oh, no. His revelations were made subsequently
at sundry times, and during months of friendly interconrse, as occasion
brought the subject up. I will, however, condense his statements to me,
and state the facts as he related them, as consecutively as possible. I
kept notes of the conversation as they occurred from time to time, but

the matter is so much impressed on my mind that I have no hesitation in relating them from memory."

REPORTER.—" Do you not fear that by taking the responsibility of this *expose* you may involve yourself in trouble? Even if all you relate should be true, may not those involved deny it *in toto*, even the fact of their having made the statements?"

MRS. WOODHULL.—"I do not fear anything of the sort. I know this thing must come out, and the statement of the plain ungarnished truth will outweigh all the perjuries that can be invented, if it come to that pass. I have been charged with attempts at blackmailing, but I tell you, sir, there is not money enough in these two cities to purchase my silence in this matter. I believe it is my duty and my mission to carry the torch to light up and destroy the heap of rottenness, which, in the name of religion, marital sanctity, and social purity, now passes as the social system. I know there are other churches just as false, other pastors just as recreant to their professed ideas of morality—by their immorality you know I mean their hypocrisy. I am glad that just this one case comes to me to be exposed. This is a great congregation. He is a most eminent man. When a beacon is fired on the mountain, the little hills are lighted up. This exposition will send inquisition through all the churches and what is termed conservative society."

REPORTER.—" You speak like some wierd prophetess, madam."

MRS. WOODHULL.—"I am a prophetess—I am an evangel—I am a Saviour, if you would but see it; but I, too, come not to bring peace, but a sword."

Mrs. Woodhull then resumed, saying: "Mr. TILTON first began to have suspicions of Mr. BEECHER on his own return from a long lecturing tour through the West. He questioned his little daughter, privately, in his study, regarding what had transpired in his absence. 'The tale of iniquitous horror that was revealed to me was,' he said, ' enough to turn the heart of a stranger to stone, to say nothing of a husband and father.' It was not the fact of the intimacy alone, but in addition to that, the terrible orgies—so he said—of which his house had been made the scene, and the boldness with which matters had been carried on in the presence of his children. ' These things drove me mad,' said he, 'and I went to ELIZABETH and confronted her with the child and the damning tale she had told me. My wife did not deny the charge nor attempt any palliation. She was then *enceinte*, and I felt sure that the child would not be my child. I stripped the wedding ring from her finger. I tore the picture of Mr. BEECHER from my wall and stamped it in pieces. Indeed I do not know what I did not do. I only look back to it as a time too horrible to retain any exact remembrance of. She miscarried the child and it was buried. For two weeks, night and day, I might have been found walking to and from that grave, in a state bordering on distraction. I could not realize the fact that I was what I was. I stamped the ring with which we had plighted our troth deep into the soil that covered the fruit of my wife's infidelity. I had friends, many and firm and good, but I could not go to them with this grief, and I suppose I should have remained silent through life, had not an occasion arisen which demanded that I should seek counsel. Mr. BEECHER learned that I had discovered the fact, and what had transpired between ELIZABETH and myself, and when I was absent, he called at my house and compelled or induced his victim to sign a statement he had prepared, declaring, that so far as he, Mr. BEECHER, was concerned, there was no truth in my charges, and that there had never been any criminal intimacy between them. Upon learning this, as I did, I felt, of course, again outraged, and could endure secrecy no longer. I had one friend who was like a brother, Mr. FRANK MOULTON. I went to him and stated the case fully. We were both members of Plymouth Church. My friend took a pistol, went to Mr. BEECHER and demanded the letter of Mrs. TILTON, under penalty of instant death."

Mrs. Woodhull here remarked that Mr. MOULTON had himself, also, since described to her this interview, with all the piteous and abject beseeching of Mr. BEECHER not to be exposed to the public.

"Mr. MOULTON obtained the letter," said Mrs. W., "and told me that he had it in his safe, where he should keep it until required for further use. After this, Mr. TILTON's house was no house for him, and he seldom slept or eat there, but frequented the house of his friend MOULTON, who sympathized deeply with him. Mrs. TILTON was also absent days at a time, and. as Mr. TILTON informed me, seemed bent on destroying her life. I went, as I have said, to see her, and found her, indeed, a wretched wreck of a woman, whose troubles were greater than she could bear. She made no secret of the facts before me. Mr. BEECHER's selfish, cowardly cruelty, in endeavoring to shield himself and create public opinion against TILTON, added poignancy to her anxieties. She seemed indifferent as to what should become of herself, but labored under fear that murder might be done on her account."

"This was the condition of affairs at the time that Mr. TILTON came to me. I attempted to show him the true solution of the imbroglio, and the folly that it was for a man like him, a representative man of the ideas of the future, to stand whining over inevitable events connected with this transition age and the social revolution of which we are in the midst. I told him that the fault and the wrong were neither in Mr. BEECHER. nor in Mrs. TILTON, nor in himself; but that it was in the false social institutions under which we still live, while the more advanced men and women of the world have outgrown them in spirit ; and that. practical-everybody is living a false life, by professing a conformity which they do not feel and do not live, and which they cannot feel and live any more than the grown boy can re-enter the clothes of his early childhood. I recalled to his attention splendid passages of his own rhetoric, in which he had unconsciously justified all the freedom that he was now condemning, when it came home to his own door, and was endeavoring, in the spirit of a tyrant. to repress.

"I ridiculed the *maudlin sentiment* and *mock heroics* and '*dreadful suzz*' he was exhibiting over an event the most natural in the world, and the most intrinsically innocent ; having in it not a bit more of real criminality than the awful wickedness of 'negro-stealing' formerly charged, in perfect good faith, by the slaveholders, on every one who helped the escape of a slave. I assumed at once, and got a sufficient admission, as I always do in such cases, that he was not exactly a vestal virgin himself ; that his real life was something very different from the 'awful virtue' he was preaching, especially for women, as if women could 'sin' in this matter without men, and men without women, and which, he *pretended*, even to himself, to believe in the face and eyes of his own life, and the lives of nearly all the greatest and best men and women that he knew : that the dreadful 'suzz' was merely a *bogus sentimentality*, pumped in his imagination, because our sickly religious literature, and Sunday-school morality, and pulpit pharaseeism had humbugged him all his life into the belief that *he ought to feel and act* in this harlequin and absurd way on such an occasion—that, in a word, neither Mr. BEECHER nor Mrs. TILTON had done any wrong. but that it was he who was playing the part of a fool and a tyrant ; that it was he and the factitious or manufactured public opinion back of him, that was wrong ; that this babyish whining and stage-acting were the real absurdity and disgrace—the unmanly part of the whole transaction, and that we only needed another Cervantes to satirize such stuff as it deserves, to squelch it instantly and forever. I tried to show him that a true manliness would protect and love to protect / would glory in protecting the absolute freedom of the woman who was loved, whether called wife, mistress, or by any other name, and that the true sense of honor in the future will be, *not to know even* what relations our lovers have with any and all other persons than ourselves—as true courtesy never seeks to spy over or to pry into other people's private affairs.

"I believe I succeeded in pointing out to him that his own life was essentially no better than Mr. BEECHER'S, and that he stood in no position to throw the first stone at Mrs. TILTON or her reverend paramour. I showed him again and again that the wrong point, and the radically wrong thing, if not indeed, quite the only wrong thing in the matter, was the barbarous idea of ownership in human beings, which was essentially the same in the two institutions of slavery and marriage. Mrs. TILTON had in turn grown increasedly unhappy when she found that Mr. BEECHER had turned some part of his exuberant affections upon some other object. There was, in her, therefore, the same sentiment of the real slaveholder. Let it be once understood that whosoever is true to himself or herself is thereby, and necessarily, true to all others, and the whole social question will be solved. The barter and sale of wives stands on the same moral footing as the barter and sale of slaves. The god-implanted human affections cannot, and will not, be any longer subordinated to these external, legal restrictions and conventional engagements. Every human being belongs to himself or herself by a higher title than any which, by surrenders or arrangements or promises, he or she can confer upon any other human being. Self-ownership is inalienable. These truths are the latest and greatest discoveries in true science.

"Perhaps Mr. BEECHER knows and feels all this, and if so, in that knowledge consists his sole and his real justification ; only the world around him has not yet grown to it ; institutions are not yet adapted to it ; and he is not brave enough to bear his open testimony to the truth he knows.

"All this I said to Mr. TILTON ; and I urged upon him to make this providential circumstance in his life the occasion upon which he should, himself, come forward to the front and stand with the true champions of social freedom."

REPORTER.—"Then Mr. TILTON became, as it were, your pupil, and you instructed him in your theories."

Mrs. WOODHULL.—"Yes, I suppose that is a correct statement ; and the verification of my views, springing up before my eyes on this occasion, out of the very midst of religion and moral prejudices, was, I assure you, an interesting study for me, and a profound corroboration of the righteousness of what you call 'my theories.' Mr. TILTON'S conduct toward Mr. BEECHER and toward his wife began from that time to be so magnanimous and grand—by which I mean simply just and right—so unlike that which most other men's would have been, that it stamped him, in my mind, as one of the noblest souls that lived, and one capable of playing a great *role* in the social revolution which is now so rapidly progressing.

"I never could, however, induce him to stand wholly, and unreservedly, and on principle, upon the free-love platform ; and I always, therefore, feared that he might for a time vacillate or go backward. But he opened his house to Mr. BEECHER, saying to him, in the presence of Mrs. TILTON : 'You love each other. Mr. BEECHER, this is a distressed woman ; if it be in your power to alleviate her condition and make her life less a burden than it now is, be yours the part to do it. You have nothing to fear from me.' From that time Mr. BEECHER was, so to speak, the slave of Mr. TILTON and Mr. MOULTON. He consulted them in every matter of any importance. It was at this time that Mr. TILTON introduced Mr. BEECHER to me, and I met him frequently both at Mr. TILTON'S and at Mr. MOULTON'S. We discussed the social problem freely in all its varied bearings, and I found that Mr. BEECHER agreed with nearly all my views upon the question."

REPORTER.—"Do you mean to say that Mr. BEECHER disapproves of the present marriage system?"

MRS. WOODHULL.—"I mean to say just this—that Mr. BEECHER told me that marriage is the grave of love, and that he never married a couple that he did not feel condemned."

REPORTER.—"What excuse did Mr. BEECHER give for not avowing these sentiments publicly?"

MRS. WOODHULL.—"Oh, the moral coward's inevitable excuse—that of inexpediency. He said he was twenty years ahead of his church; that he preached the truth just as fast as he thought his people could bear it. I said to him, 'Then, Mr. BEECHER, you are defrauding your people. You confess that you do not preach the truth as you know it, while they pay for and persuade themselves you are giving them your best thought.' He replied: 'I know that our whole social system is corrupt. I know that marriage, as it exists to-day, is the course of society. We shall never have a better state until children are begotten and bred on the scientific plan. Stirpiculture is what we need.' 'Then,' said I, 'Mr. BEECHER, why do you not go into your pulpit and preach that science?' He replied: 'If I were to do so I should preach to empty seats. It would be the ruin of my church.' 'Then,' said I, 'you are as big a fraud as any time-serving preacher, and I now believe you are all frauds. I gave you credit for ignorant honesty, but I find you are all alike—all trying to hide, or afraid to speak the truth. A sorry pass has this Christian country come to, paying 40,000 ministers to lie to it from Sunday to Sunday, to hide from them the truth that has been given them to promulgate.'"

REPORTER.—"It seems you took a good deal of pains to draw Mr. BEECHER out."

MRS. WOODHULL.—"I did. I thought him a man who would dare a good deal for the truth, and that, having lived the life he had, and entertaining the private convictions he did, I could perhaps persuade him that it was his true policy to come out and openly avow his principles, and be a thorough consistent radical, and thus justify his life in some measure, if not wholly, to the public."

REPORTER.—"Was Mr. BEECHER aware that you knew his relations to Mrs. TILTON?"

MRS. WOODHULL.—"Of course he was. It was because that I knew of them that he first consented to meet me. He could never receive me until he knew that I was aware of the real character he wore under the mask of his reputation. Is it not remarkable how a little knowledge of this sort brings down the most top-lofty from the stilts on which they lift themselves above the common level?"

REPORTER.—"Do you still regard Mr. BEECHER as a moral coward?"

MRS. WOODHULL.—"I have found him destitute of moral courage enough to meet this tremendous demand upon him. In minor things, I know that he has manifested courage. He could not be induced to take the bold step I demanded of him, simply for the sake of truth and righteousness. I did not entirely despair of him until about a year ago. I was then contemplating my Steinway Hall speech on Social Freedom, and prepared it in the hope of being able to persuade Mr. BEECHER to preside for me, and thus make a way for himself into a consistent life on the radical platform. I made my speech as soft as I conscientiously could. I toned it down in order that it might not frighten him. When it was in type, I went to his study and gave him a copy, and asked him to read it carefully and give me his candid opinion concerning it. Meantime, I had told Mr. TILTON and Mr. MOULTON that I was going to ask Mr. BEECHER to preside, and they agreed to press the matter with him. I explained to them that the only safety he had was in coming out as soon as possible an advocate of social freedom, and thus palliate, if he could not completely justify, his practices, by founding them at least on principle. I told them that this introduction of me would bridge the way. Both the gentlemen agreed with me in the view, and I was for a time almost sure that my desire would be accomplished. A few days before the lecture, I sent a note to Mr. BEECHER asking him to preside for me. This alarmed him. He went with it to Messrs. TILTON and MOULTON asking advice. They gave it in the affirmative, telling him they considered it eminently fitting that he should pursue the course indicated by me as his only safety ; but it was not urged in such a way as to indicate that they had known the request was to have been made. Matters remained undecided until the day of the lecture, when I went over again to press Mr. BEECHER to a decision. I had then a long private interview with him, urging all the arguments I could to induce him to consent. He said he agreed perfectly with what I was to say, but that he could not stand on the platform at Steinway Hall and introduce me. He said, 'I should sink through the floor. I am a moral coward on this subject, and I know it, and I am not fit to stand by you, who go there to speak what you know to be the truth ; I should stand there a living lie.' He got upon the sofa on his knees beside me, and taking my face between his hands, while the tears streamed down his cheeks, begged me to let him off. Becoming thoroughly disgusted with what seemed to me pusillanimity, I left the room under the control of a feeling of contempt for the man, and reported to my friends what he had said. They then took me again with them and endeavored to persuade him. Mr. TILTON said to him : ' Mr. BEECHER, some day you have got to fall ; go and introduce this woman and win the radicals of the country, and it will break your fall.' ' Do you think,' said BEECHER, ' that this thing will come out to the world?' Mr. TILTON replied : 'Nothing is more certain in earth or heaven, Mr. BEECHER ; and this may be your last chance to save yourself from complete ruin.'

" Mr. BEECHER replied : 'I can never endure such a terror. Oh! if it must come, let me know of it twenty-four hours in advance, that I may take my own life. I cannot, cannot face this thing !'

" Thoroughly out of all patience, I turned on my heel and said : ' Mr. BEECHER, if I am compelled to go upon that platform alone, I shall begin by telling the audience why I am alone, and why you are not with me,' and I again left the room. I afterward learned that Mr. BEECHER, frightened at what I had said, promised, before parting with Mr. TILTON, that he would preside if he could bring his courage up to the terrible ordeal.

" It was four minutes of the time for me go forward to the platform at Steinway Hall when Mr. TILTON and Mr. MOULTON came into the anteroom asking for Mr. BEECHER. When I told them he had not come, they expressed astonishment. I told them I should faithfully keep my word, let the consequences be what they might. At that moment word was sent me that there was an organized attempt to break up the meeting, and that threats were being made against my life if I dared to speak what it was understood I intended to speak. Mr. TILTON then insisted on going on the platform with me and presiding, to which I finally agreed, and that I should not at that time mention Mr. BEECHER. I shall never forget the brave words he uttered in introducing me. They had a magic influence on the audience, and drew the sting of those who intended to harm me. However much Mr. TILTON may have since regretted his course regarding me, and whatever he may say about it, I shall always admire the moral courage that enabled him to stand with me on that platform, and face that, in part, defiant audience. It is hard to bear the criticisms of vulgar minds, who can see in social freedom nothing but licentiousness and debauchery, and the inevitable misrepresentation of the entire press, which is as perfectly subsidized against reason and common sense, when social subjects are discussed, as is the religious press when any other science is discussed which is supposed to militate against the Bible as the direct word of God to man. The editors are equally bigots, or else as dishonest as the clergy. The nightmare of public opinion, which they are still professionally engaged in making, enslaves and condemns them both."

Mrs. WOODHULL concluded by saying that since her Steinway Hall speech she had surrendered all hope of easing the fall of Mr. BEECHER, that she had not attempted to see him, and had not in fact seen him. She only added one other fact, which was, that Mr. BEECHER endeavored to induce Mr. TILTON to withdraw from his membership in Plymouth Church, to leave him, Mr. BEECHER, free from the embarrassment of his presence there ; and that Mr. TILTON had indignantly rejected the proposition, determined to hold the position with a view to such contingencies as might subsequently occur.

So much for the interviewing which was to have been published some months ago ; but when it failed or was suppressed, I was still so far undecided that I took no steps in the matter, and had no definite plan for the future in respect to it, until the events, as I have recited them, which occurred at Boston. Since then I have not doubted that I must make up my mind definitely to act aggressively in this matter, and to use the facts in my knowledge to compel a more widespread discussion of the social question. I take the step deliberately, as an agitator and social revolutionist, which is my profession. I commit no breach of confidence, as no confidences have been made to me, except as I have compelled them, with a full knowledge that I was endeavoring to induce or to force the parties to come to the front along with me in the announcement and advocacy of the principles of social revolution. Messrs. BEECHER and TILTON, and other half-way reformers, are to me like the border States in the great rebellion. They are liable to fall, with the great weight of their influence, on either side in the contest, and I hold it to be legitimate generalship to compel them to declare on the side of truth and progress

My position is justly analagous with that of warfare. The public, Mr. BEECHER included, would gladly crush me if they could—will do so if they can—to prevent me from forcing on them considerations of the utmost importance. My mission is, on the other hand, to utter the unpopular truth, and make it efficient by whatsoever legitimate means ; and means are legitimate as a war measure which would be highly reprehensible in a state of peace. I believe, as the law of peace, in the right of privacy, in the sanctity of individual relations. It is nobody's business but their own, in the absolute view, what Mr. BEECHER and Mrs. TILTON have done, or may choose at any time to do, as between themselves. And the world needs, too, to be taught just that lesson. I am the champion of that very right of privacy and of individual sovereignty. But that is only one side of the case. I need, and the world needs, Mr. BEECHER's powerful championship of this very right. The world is on the very crisis of its final fight for liberty. The victory may fall on the wrong side, and his own liberty and mine, and the world s, be again crushed out, or repressed for another century, for the want of fidelity in him to the new truth. It is not, therefore, Mr. BEECHER as the individual that I pursue, but Mr. BEECHER as the representative man ; Mr. BEECHER as a power in the world ; and Mr. BEECHER as my auxiliary in a great war for freedom, or Mr. BEECHER as a violent enemy and a powerful hindrance to all that I am bent on accomplishing.

To Mr. BEECHER, as the individual citizen, I tender, therefore, my humble apology, meaning and deeply feeling what I say. for this or any interference on my part with his private conduct. I hold that Mr. TILTON himself, that Mrs. BEECHER herself, have no more right to inquire. or to know, or to spy over with a view to knowing. what has transpired between Mr. BEECHER and Mrs. TILTON than they have to know what I ate for breakfast or where I shall spend my next evening ; and that Mr. BEECHER's congregation and the public at large have just as little right to know or to inquire. I hold that the so-called morality of society is a complicated mass of sheer impertinence, and a scandal on the civilization of this advanced century; that the system of social espionage under which we live is damnable, and that the very first axiom of a true morality is for the people *to mind their own business,* and learn to respect, religiously, the social freedom and the sacred social privacy of all others ; but it was the paradox of Christ, that as the Prince of Peace. he still brought on earth, not *peace,* but *a sword.* It is the paradox of life that, in order to have peace, we must first have war ; and it is the paradox of my position that, believing in the right of privacy and in the perfect right of Mr. BEECHER, socially, morally, and divinely, to have sought the embraces of Mrs. TILTON, or of any other woman or women whom he loved and who loved him, and being a promulgator and a public champion of those very rights, I still invade the most secret and sacred affairs of his life, and drag them to the light, and expose him to the opprobrium and villification of the public. I do again, and with deep sincerity. ask his forgiveness. But the case is exceptional, and what I do I do for a great purpose. The social world is in the very agony of its new birth, or, to resume the warlike simile, the leaders of progress are in the very act of storming the last act of bigotry and error. Somebody must be hurled forward into the gap. I have the power, I think, to compel Mr. Beecher to go forward and to do the duty for humanity from which he shrinks ; and I should, myself, be false to the truth if I were to shrink from compelling him. Whether he sinks or swims in the fiery trial, the agitation by which truth is evolved will have been promoted. And I believe that he will not only survive, but that when forced to the encounter he will rise to the full height of the great enterprise, and will astound and convince the world of the new gospel of freedom, by the depth of his experiences and the force of his argument.

The world, it seems, will never learn not to crucify its Christs, and not to compel the retractation of its Galileos. Mr. BEECHER has lacked the courage to be a martyr, but, like Galileo, while retracting. or concealing and evading, he has known in his heart *that the world still moves ;* and I venture to prophesy, as I have indeed full faith. that he and the other parties to this social drama will yet live to be overwhelmed with gratitude to me for having compelled them to this publicity. The age is pregnant with great events, and this may be the very one which shall be, as it were, the crack of doom to our old and worn out, and false and hypocritical social institutions. When the few first waves of public indignation shall have broken over him, when the nine days' wonder and the astonished clamor of Mrs. Grundy shall have done their worst, and when the pious ejaculations of the sanctimonious shall have been expended, and he finds that he still lives, and that there are brave souls who stand by him, he will, I believe, rise in his power and utter the whole truth. I believe I see clearly and prophetically for him in the future a work a hundred times greater than all he has accomplished in the past. I believe, as I have said, a wise Providence. or. as I term it, and believe it to be, the conscious and well calculated interference of the spirit world, has forecast and prepared those very events as a part of the drama of this great social revolution. Of all the centres of influence on the great broad planet, the destiny that shapes our ends, bent on breaking up an old civilization and ushering in a new one, could have found no such spot for its vantage ground as Plymouth Church, no such man for the hero of the plot as its reverend pastor, and, it may be, no such heroine as the gentle cultured, and, perhaps, hereafter to be sainted wife of Plymouth Church's most distinguished layman. Indeed I think that Mrs. TILTON has had, at least at times, a clearer intuition guiding her, a better sense of right, and more courage than her reverend lover ; for, on one occasion, Mr. TILTON told me that he took home to her one of my threatening notices, and told her that that meant her and Mr. BEECHER, and that the exposure must and would come ; and he added that she calmly replied : "I am prepared for it. If the new social gospel must have its martyrs, and if I must be one of them, I am prepared for it."

" In conclusion, let us again consider, for a moment, the right and the wrong of this whole transaction. Let us see whether the wrong is not on the side where the public puts the right, and the right on the side where the public puts the wrong. The immense physical potency of Mr. BEECHER, and the indomitable urgency of his great nature for the intimacy and embraces of the noble and cultured women about him, instead of being a bad thing as the world thinks, or thinks that it thinks, is one of the noblest and grandest of the endowments of this truly great and representative man. The amative impulse is the physiological basis of character. It is this which emanates zest and magnetic power to his whole audience through the organism of the great preacher. Plymouth Church has lived and fed, and the healthy vigor of public opinion for the last quarter of a century has been augmented and strengthened from the physical amativeness of HENRY WARD BEECHER. The scientific world know the physiological facts of this nature, but they have waited for a weak woman to have the moral courage to tell the world such truths.— Passional starvation, enforced on such a nature, so richly endowed, by the ignorance and prejudice of the past, is a horrid cruelty. The bigoted public, to which the great preacher ministered, while literally eating and drinking of his flesh and blood, condemned him, in their ignorance, to live without food. Every great man of Mr. BEECHER'S type has had, in the past, and will ever have, the need for, and the right to, the loving manifestations of many women, and when the public graduates out of the ignorance and prejudice of its childhood, it will recognize this necessity and its own past injustice. Mr. BEECHER'S grand and amative nature is not, then, the bad element in the whole matter, but intrinsically a good thing, and one of God's best gifts to the world.

So again, the tender, loving, womanly concessiveness of Mrs. TILTON, her susceptibility to the charm of the great preacher's magnetism, her love of loving and being loved, none of these were the bad thing which the world thinks them, or thinks that it thinks them, or professes to think that it thinks them to be. On the contrary they are all of them the best thing—the best and most beautiful of things, the loveliest and most divine of things which belong to the patrimony of mankind.

So again, it was not the coming together of these two loving natures in the most intimate embrace, nor was it that nature blessed that embrace with the natural fruits of love which was the bad element in this whole transaction. They, on the contrary, were good elements, beautiful and divine elements, and among God's best things to man.

The evil and the whole evil in this whole matter, then, lies elsewhere. It lies in a false and artificial or manufactured opinion, in respect to this very question of what is good or what is evil in such matters. It lies in the belief that society has the right to prohibit, to prescribe and regulate, or in any manner to interfere with the private love manifestations of its members, any more than it has to prescribe their food and their drink. It lies in the belief consequent upon this, that lovers own their lovers, husbands their wives and wives their husbands, and that they have the right to complain of, to spy over, and to interfere, even to the extent of murder, with every other or outside manifestation of love. It lies in the *compulsory hypocrisy and systematic falsehood* which is thus enforced and inwrought into the very structure of society, and in the consequent and wide-spread injury to the whole community.

Mr. BEECHER knows all this, and if by my act he is compelled to tell the world that he knows it, and to force men to the conviction that it is true, he may well thank God that I live, and that circumstances have concurred to emancipate him, despite of himself, from his terrible thraldom, and to emancipate, through him, in the future, millions of others

Still, in conclusion, let me add, that in my view, and in the view of others who think with me, and of all, as I believe, who think rightly on the subject, Mr. BEECHER is to-day, and after all that I have felt called upon to reveal of his life, as good, as pure, and as noble a man as he ever was in the past, or as the world has held him to be, and that Mrs. TILTON is still the pure, charming, cultured woman. It is, then, the public opinion that is wrong, and not the individuals, who must, nevertheless, for a time suffer its persecution.

Mrs. ISABELLA HOOKER BEECHER has, from the time that I met her in Washington, stood my fast friend, and given me manifold proofs of her esteem, knowing, as she did, both my radical opinions and my free life. I have been told—not by her, but upon what I believe to be perfectly good authority—that she has for months, perhaps for years past, known the life of her brother, and urged on him to announce publicly his radical convictions, and assured him that if he would do so, she, at least, would stand by him. I know, too, by intimate intercourse, the opinions, and to a great extent the lives, of nearly all the leading reformatory men and women in the land ; and I know that Mr. BEECHER, passing through this crucial ordeal, retrieving himself and standing upon the most radical platform, need not stand alone for an hour, but that an army of glorious and emancipated spirits will gather spontaneously and instantaneously around him, and that the new social republic will have been forever established.　　　　　　　　　　VICTORIA C. WOODHULL.

I publish the following letter. not to attempt to justify the exposure given above, but to show that I am not alone in the belief that benefit will accrue to the world from it. It may have been Mr. PARKER who moved me to the utterances made at Boston. I have no doubt it was he, since I have been so informed both by himself and his friends. I desire it to be distinctly understood, however, that I do not wish to shoulder any of the responsibility on the spirit world for what I have done, although I know I shall have its support in whatever way I may need it in carrying forward this system of social warfare. The public will, ere long, learn that if it attempt to stop the social revolution which is impending, it has more than one weak woman to contend against.　　　　　　　　　　V. C. W.

---

14 RINGGOLD ST., PROVIDENCE, R. I., }
September 16, 1872. }

MY DEAR VICTORIA :

My husband and myself called on Friday evening, accompanied by Mrs. Colonel Pope, of Harrison street, on Mrs. J. H. Conant,, and found her at home ; Dr. Pyke was with her. He, the Doctor, entered into conversation with me concerning your attack upon Beecher, as he termed it, which I defended, whereupon Theodore Parker controlled Mrs. Conant, and spoke in substance as follows :

"When Henry Ward Beecher, knowing spiritualism to be true, stood in his own pulpit and denounced it as ' one of the most dangerous humbugs of the day,' the spirit world felt that it had pleaded and borne with him long enough, and that they would unmask and show him to the world a hypocrite as he is. This it has done, and it mattered little whether Mrs. Conant, Victoria Woodhull, or Laura Cuppy Smith was the instrument used. The spirit world has not yet completed its work. Other canting hypocrites remain to be proclaimed to the public in their true colors, and the Scripture shall be verified, ' There is nothing secret that shall not be made known, nothing hidden that shall not be revealed.' If I could have divested my medium of the *influence of persons in the form* I should have proclaimed this through her lips on the platform of John A. Andrews' hall on Wednesday afternoon."

I think I have given you Theodore Parker's words verbatim.

The same evening I was conversing with E. B. Beckwith, a prominent lawyer of Boston, who remarked that there seemed to him to be a retribution following the Beechers, and that you could use in your own behalf the same argument in vindication of your exposure of Beecher that Mrs. Stowe and her family had used in her defence with regard to the Byron affair, with this addition, that you had not accused the living, who could defend themselves, of half so base a crime as she laid to the charge of the poet and a sister woman, the dead who could not reply. I thought the suggestion too good to be lost, shall use it myself freely, and send it to you.

LAURA CUPPY SMITH.

SOCIOLOGY

(3)

The Naked Truth; or, the Situation Reviewed! . . . 1873.

Delivered in Cooper Institute, New York, January 9, 1873. Reproduced from *Woodhull & Claflin's Weekly* (Jan. 25, 1873, pp. 3-7, 14-15). Preceded on page two by an address of the same title prepared for delivery on the same platform by Tennie C. Claflin, but not delivered. The original columns are here reduced, divided and realigned; original type column width 5-5/8 inches.

VICTORIA C. WOODHULL'S ADDRESS.

My Friends and Fellow-Citizens :—I come into your presence from a cell in the American Bastile, to which I was consigned by the cowardly servility of the age. I am still held under heavy bonds to return to that cell, or to meet my trial in a United States Court, upon a scandalous charge trumped up by the ignorant or the corrupt officers of the law, conspiring with others to deprive me, under the falsest and shallowest pretences, of my inherited previleges as an American citizen. In my person, the freedom of the press is assailed, and stricken down, and such has been the adverse concurrence of circumstances that the press itself has tacitly consented, almost with unanimity, to this sacrilegious invasion of one of the most sacred of civil rights. Public opinion too has been abused into concurring for a moment with this outrage.

But I have no intention of entering upon a specific defense of myself to-night. I was not unaware of what would be done when the method of social agitation, which furnished the grounds for the tyrannous exercise of power, was begun, and I am not disappointed. I was informed of the old United States statute, regarding the transmission of obscene literature through the mails, and also of the law as amended last June to specially meet this case. To suppress our paper was the only method of precedure by which the old *regime* could meet our argumentation; but its representatives, though wise in their own conceit, have unwittingly played directly into my hands, and for the benefit and ultimate triumph of the very thing they sought to crush.

In this, which to me, is the higher and truer sense, instead of being my enemies and persecutors, as they are in spirit and purpose, they are my active, most efficient and most effective allies ; and I wish it to be distinctly understood at the very outset, that whatever I may feel called upon to say in arguing the subject upon the plane, and for the more complete understanding of the people, I here and now claim that Mr. Comstock, the characteristic agent of the Young Men's Christian Association, acting under the inspiration of Messrs. Bowen, Claflin & Co., members of Plymouth Church ; that District Attorney Noah Davis, and his assistant, General Davies, and Mr. Commissioner Osborne, backed up by those who are determined, as was stated in the *Tribune*, "to run her to the earth if it took every hour of his life and every dollar of his fortune," and the United States Grand Jury ; that Mr. Challis, with his hundred thousand dollars, and Mr. Justice Fowler ; in a word, that all and every one of them who have had any active or passive hand in what, in the common acceptance, is personal and vindictive persecution, though personally enemies to me, are, indeed, my most esteemed friends, without whom and their recent active and well-calculated interference, no such vantage as the present revolution has attained could possibly have been gained.

Therefore, without further argument, I hold that I am justified in claiming them all as my faithful though unwilling allies in the social revolution in which I am engaged ; and to whatever length their ire, their hate, their vindictiveness, their bitter foolishness, their stupidity or ignorance may push them on in their line of action, they inevitably proceed just so much the further to secure the rapid and complete success of the latest, greatest and grandest revolution of the centuries, to the inauguration and completion which I am thoroughly and entirely devoted and consecrated.

But from this morally philosophic standpoint of observation, which is the one from which I wish it to be understood that I wage my warfare and upon which I can have no enemies, I shall descend to the more common plan of general controversy to discuss the matter with you, and from this position I am compelled, in the first place, to arraign the courts : secondly, as the moulder of public opinion, the press ; thirdly, a bigoted, ignorant, and persecuting public opinion. Moreover I am also compelled, and here you must pardon the frankness of my speech, to arraign you who are my friends and who are my fellow-citizens, for moral cowardice and traitorousness to the spirit of American institutions.

But in all this I "shall criticise them with as little personality as I can give to action, all of which has been so personal. I shall withhold, too, as far as I can, every expression of resentment ; and no one who knows all I knew of this matter, would fail to credit me with singular and great moderation. For behind what I shall relate, there are other histories every incident of which I have rescued from the obscurity to which they were confided and as I think of them, it is with difficulty that I restrain my just indignation," but I shall confine myself to a calm and dispassionate discussion of what is already before the public, leaving other things to rise to the surface when circumstances which do not care to control, shall permit or compel them. Saul of Tarsus, when he stood by and held the garments of them who stoned the martyr Stephen, took on his soul the guilt of the blood of "the first martyr," and you, in so far as you have consented, even tacitly and inertly, to the unheard-of persecution which has been directed against my sister and me in the name of the law, have been implicated in that great wrong, and perhaps before I am done, you will perceive your unconscious guilt to have been far greater than you have heretofore supposed. But I repent of the intention of arraigning you, even before entering upon its execution..

You may rightly plead, in mitigation to the fact, that the newspapers have systematically abstained hitherto from presenting our side of the case ; that the officers of the law, pretend ing to act on behalf of the people and in the interests of public virtue, have interfered with the high hand, have seized our types, have broken up our business, have purloined our private papers, have suppressed our paper in transitu in the mails, have thrown us into jail, and have so cut us off from the means of communicating with the public that our voice could not be heard ; that the truth of the matter, as we see it and know it to be, has never come to your knowledge ; and that you have been obliged, therefore, in a great measure, to form your opinions in ignorance of the facts.

My sister and myself are now indicted in the United States Court on the preposterous charge of sending obscene literature through the United States mail—a charge which the officers of the Government will never dare to bring to a trial, as they cannot afford themselves to be brought into complete ridicule. If anything which I can say in this address, or which I can say or write at any time, can provoke or sting them into the folly and madness of exposing the weakness and the damnable outrage of this unhallowed proceeding against peaceable and law-abiding citizens, by bringing the case to trial, I shall consider that success the most fortunate event of my life. But I now predict before you, and make my formal record of that prediction for future reference and use, that I shall fail, utterly fail in the attempt. The District Attorney, and everybody concerned in this nefarious matter have either already accomplished all they aimed at, by covering my sister and me with the odium of being prisoners and accused of a scandalous offense, or they have had enough of the whole matter, seeing that it was a blunder from the start, and wish themselves fairly rid of it.

I repeat my prediction, and make it as marked and distinct as possible : the United States Government will never proceed to trial, in the case now on their court docket in the Southern District of New York, against Victoria C. Woodhull and Tennie C. Claflin, for violating the statute of Congress against transmitting obscene literature through the mails. They will never dare to do it. On the other hand, I predict that the Government will not enter a *nolle prosequi*, and make thereby the only honorable reparation, to some slight extent, which it would be in their power to make, for the outrage they have committed on our individual rights. And, my friends, you must not forget that, when an individual is wronged, by the superaction of law officers, the whole people is thereby outraged. I predict, however, that the course they will pursue will be to hold the case over our heads, as a threat, to delay and postpone it from time to time, to pretend that they intend to bring us to trial, and yet never to do so in fact ; in the hope that fortune will favor them in getting them out of the scrape, through our death or poverty, or virtual surrender to the force of a long-continued persecution.

But they reckon without their host. The cards of fate are shuffled for a different deal. I give notice here and now, I hope the occasion is a sufficiently public one, that the publication office of WOODHULL & CLAFLIN'S WEEKLY is at 48 Broad street, New York city, and that from that office there will soon be issued and sold to all applicants a revised edition of the suppressed number of WOODHULL & CLAFLIN'S WEEKLY, containing the "Beecher-Tilton Scandal," and that within a few weeks there will probably have been sent a million copies of it to every part of the world, so that the whole public shall be my jury and decide whether there is anything obscene in that earnest and all-important statement.

The United States officials can afford anything else better than to become utterly ridiculous in the eyes of the legal profession and of the public generally; and they know already that there is not a respectable lawyer or citizen, who has read our journal and knows its character, who supposes for a moment that the United States have any case against us. They can even better afford to be known as persecutors of individuals, having the rights only of public prosecutors, rather than to continue to hold to the charge of obscenity. The pretension is too flimsy to bear a moment's inspection.

The issue of our paper in question, that of Nov. 2, 1872, is, undoubtedly, one of the boldest we have ever issued in the war we are conducting in behalf of progress, free thought and untrammelled lives; breaking the way for future generations; but throughout all its fifty closely printed columns, there is only one passage, and that of only three lines, to be found in the article now known as the Challis article, which the most fastidious literary critic, who was honest, could by any possibility construe into obscenity; and that is not half so bad as a hundred isolated passages which might be selected from the bible, and which pious fathers and mothers and moral teachers, and perhaps they who belong to the Young Men's Christian Association, read in the family before prayers, to youth of both sexes, morning and evening, all over the land.

But neither the zealot Comstock, nor the District Attorney, nor the Grand Jury had, as yet, got their eye on this dreadful three-line paragraph when they had my sister and me arrested and, with unseemly haste, indicted for obscenity. Their procedure was based entirely on the "Beecher-Tilton Scandal," and it was an after-thought altogether when the Assistant District Attorney said in court that he "meant the whole paper"—an after-thought for which I am greatly obliged to him, as it puts him in my power in ways of which he is, as yet, totally unconscious.

Their action was, as they then avowed, entirely for the purpose of "protecting the reputation of revered citizens," as if it were any part of their business to protect the reputation of anybody by instituting an arbitrary censorship of the press in this free country, or except in an action for libel which had not been instituted nor even thought of; as if Americans were living under the paternal wing of self-constituted legal protectors, self-constituted tyrants, otherwise speaking; and finally, as if the charge of obscenity was in any way related to that of the attack on, or the defense of, "revered citizens."

The law was open to Mr. Beecher and others for any wrong done them, and they did not move in the matter, for reasons which were alike satisfactory to them, and to us, at the time, and which are now rapidly becoming satisfactory to the whole public. What right, then, had the District Attorney, and through his agency and solicitation, the Grand Jury—the United States, in other words—through their representatives to interfere, and still, without charging any libel, to trump up another factitious and scandalous, flimsy and ridiculous, irrelevant and preposterous charge, to get, by indirection, at the result they wished to achieve—that, in a word, of simply stopping our mouths at any cost, to protect the reputations of "revered citizens," and entirely irrespective of the question whether we were telling the truth or not, or of the other question, whether our motives were good or bad? As in the case of the slave-holders and Garrison, it was not a question of the truth, nor of the motive, but of the absolute necessity for their keeping us hush on the subject.

Now, it so happens that in another case, that of Challis against Col. Blood, entirely apart from that of the United States against my sister and me, the whole Challis article came before the public and was published in full, or, as the lawyers say, *verbatim, literatim et punctatim*, in the New York *Herald*, and various other newspapers; has been, in a word, pretty extensively circulated over the country in other newspaper columns than our own, and Mr. Comstock has not informed upon, and Mr. District Attorney Noah Davis has not presented, and the Grand Jury have not indicted the publishers of the *Herald* and the other papers.

Is it that men are so generally accustomed to say and print obscenity that these paragons of purity and protectors of pious and revered citizens don't mind that? Is it that the masculine sex has the monopoly of obscenity as they have of tobacco and bad whisky? Is it that obscenity is any less obscenity when it appears in the *Tribune* or the *Times* or the *Herald*? Or is it that those publishers are known to be rich and powerful, while we were supposed, from our recent misfortunes, to be poor, and possibly friendless? Or is it, after all, that the whole world knows that these respectable and well to-do publishers and editors don't mean anything by it, except merely to make money in the ordinary course of business, while it feels instinctively that we are in earnest, and mean to do what we can to put an end to the vicious conditions of society, obscenity among the rest of them? Is it, then, the old story that the craft is in danger, that practices and habits and modes of life exist, and are held to be respectable, and must be protected, which are so obscene in their character, that we cannot even mention them without seeming to be, ourselves, guilty of obscenity? Is it the old cry of "stop thief," merely to turn away attention? Is it the old fear that the temple of the great goddess Diana should be despised, and her magnificence should be destroyed, whom all Asia and the world worshipeth? Finish out the reading of the nineteenth chapter of the Acts of the Apostles, when you go home to your houses, and inwardly reflect on it and digest the old story, and you will understand the whole subject better than by the reading of all the newspapers.

It is not the question of Henry Ward Beecher, nor of Theodore Tilton, nor of Theodore Tilton's Wife, nor of Victoria C. Woodhull, nor of John H. Noyes, nor of Stephen Pearl Andrews, nor of Brigham Young, nor of all these combined, nor of a thousand more like them; but it is the question of a new gospel, of the new "word of God," adapted to this age and generation, as the truth of that olden day was to that. Put for the Jesus then preached, the Logos that "became flesh and dwelt among us, and we beheld his glory * * * full of grace and truth," first chapter of John; put in the place of this narrower and more infantile conception, ALL TRUTH WHATSOEVER, *scientific, socialistic, universal,* and read for Paul and Silas, and Barnabas and Timotheus, and Erastus, and the other faithful missionaries of that day, the Mary Woolstencrofts, the Fanny Wrights, the Owens, the St. Simons, the Fourriers, the Comtes, the Garrisons, the Warrens, the Andrews, the Noyes, the Woodhulls—in a word, the expounders and the agitators for liberty, and a new order of social affairs, in this epoch all over the world—and the old book may be read again; and every word will be true still, and true in a higher sense, or at any rate in a farther on development. The teachers and reformers of this, the social era, are but the prototypes, under other names, of the teachers and reformers of all other and past eras. But *new* truths will always persist in being *new.* The world is always *taken again by surprise,* and *on its weak side,* by every new gospel, by every new dispensation of truth, and betrayed again into the unseemly conduct of receiving and treating its annunciators as enemies of the public welfare and as criminals to be persecuted or punished? I might, perhaps, complete the parallel by substituting Henry Ward Beecher in the place of Nicodemus, and somebody, I will not even guess who, in the place of Judas Iscariot. Whoever he may be his name will pass into history; perhaps in some subsequent edition of one of the gospels or of the Acts of the Apostles, which may be part of the standard religious literature of the next eighteen centuries.

But I am diverted from my direct purpose which was to point out to you the inconsistencies of our honorable representatives of the law, and to show you why they will not dare to arrest me again, for defying them, and doing again precisely what I did, just as innocently and rightfully, before.

I have told you that the New York *Herald* has boldly and unhesitatingly reprinted the most objectionable matter which was contained in the number of our paper which was suppressed by violent and illegal seizures, and for which we were arrested. Not only this, but, in our very next issue, we deliberately reprinted the language of that terrible three-line sentence, the same as contained in the *Herald*, repeating it several times; and we have not been complained of for doing so.

But that is not all. George Francis Train, like a true knight-errant as he is, flew to our side as a champion, when we were in prison, and, treating the matter with his peculiar idiosyncrasy, he published and had circulated broadcast through the city and sent through the mails, several numbers of a newspaper sheet which he styled *The Train Ligue*. In it, he repeated and paraded and rang the changes in every possible way, upon every one of the possible objectionable passages in our whole paper, being purposely, if we were obscene in a direct, simple statement of facts, ten times more audaciously obscene in reproducing us, flaunting his utterances in the very faces of those distinguished legal authorities who had arrested us, " stumping them," as the boys say, with every insulting circumstance of provocation to arrest him on the same charge.

But the heroes of the United States law had become wary in conducting the warfare. They saw that they had already, so to speak, " put their foot in it;" or, permit me still to be homely in my expressions, and "not to put too fine a point upon it," they " smelt a rat," after the District Attorney found that revered citizens could not be brought into court. *They couldn't afford to become utterly ridiculous*, and there was something in the atmosphere, that warned them that they were becoming, *just a little ridiculous*, *just a little odious*, and *just a little contemptible* already ; *contemptible* for their ignorance of the law and of the literature they assumed to judge of ; *contemptible* for their ignorance of the American principle of the freedom, of the citizen and the press ; *contemptible* for their unconscionable usurpation of authority, and contemptible, above all, for their ungallant and ungentlemanly discrimination against women, in their exercise of their judicial functions when there were so many men who could be charged as we were charged.

You now see why the District Attorney will not have me arrested again for repeating my offense against "revered citizens"—offense, forsooth!—for exercising my simple and unquestionable rights as an editor and an advocate of social reform. He can't arrest all the James Gordon Bennetts, all the George Francis Trains and all the Victoria C. Woodhulls; and he can't, in the face and eyes of this exposure, arrest Tennie and me and throw us again into Ludlow-street Jail, for publishing precisely the same things which they publish, and which Train published, purposely exaggerated, to show that they dare not trouble him. He cannot arrest us unless he is ready to arrest us all, or along with us, all the other editors in the city.

The District Attorney can't afford to arrest everybody who says a naughty word, not even to carry out his assumed new office of protector of the reputation of "revered citizens." Pushed one step too far, his procedure in that direction incurs ridicule. "Come shortly off," not impartially carried out; not applied even to those who flaunt their offenses and try to get arrested, in order to bring out the absurdity, it will at a certain point provoke universal indignation. The United States District Attorney cannot afford either to have a ridiculous cognomen annexed to his name. That would swamp him in this community. "A hasty plate of soup" tacked to the reputation of even a great man, and in good-natured jocosity, haunted and annoyed him to his grave. The District Attorney is not even a great man, and *his* nickname may have real meaning in it. I warn him not to defy the stab of a steel pen! Inventive genius sometimes displays itself in other ways than in devising new offenses against the law or new offices as public protectors of the reputation of revered citizens.

Another reason why the Government cannot, very well, proceed to trial, is this: Since our arrest, Attorney-General Williams, of President Grant's Cabinet, has, at the instance and by request of Postmaster-General Creswell, rendered an opinion having a direct bearing upon this case, as follows:

"Post-office officials have no right to open or detain letters or other matter transmitted through the Post-office, though they may know they contain obscene matter. And Postmasters have no more authority to open letters, other than those addressed to themselves, than have other citizens of the United States."

Coupled with this, we have the denial of the officials of the New York Post-office, as to their complicity in the outrage committed upon the mails. Mr. Knapp, the special agent of the Post-office Department, said he read the paper of November 2 from beginning to end, and he would not take any responsibility, such as the District Attorney desired him to take, to hold the entire mail on account of alleged obscenity. Therefore, under the opinion of the Attorney-General, and the disclaimer of Mr. Knapp, the District Attorney stands in the position of having, with the cognizance of somebody, robbed the mail of the package of papers upon which the charge was based. Do you not see, then, that Mr. District Attorney Davis or Mr. Assistant District Attorney Davies cannot afford to move further in this matter?

The fellow Comstock is, I think, too conceitedly egotistic to realize the position into which his action has placed him. He is also, I think, just enough fool and knave combined, to believe he can himself "put up a job" and then make others responsible for it. He it was instead of ourselves who procured the placing in the Post-office of the package complained of, by buying the papers and having them addressed and sent to the Post-office on his own account, by a person having neither right or authority to act for my sister and me.

The watchword that led Mr. Greeley to an untimely grave was "Anything to beat Grant;" but the watchword of this set of worthies who, by arresting us, hoped to squelch the WEEKLY, is anything to save "revered citizens" who have unwritten private histories. Obdurate as they must have been, ever to have attempted such a proceeding; impervious to common sense and impossible of wise judgment as they were, to seek to evade the very issue they had themselves evoked, by an indictment grown, like a mushroom, in a single night. I do not think that even they are so utterly foolhardy, in respect to their future reputation, as to push what has already been fully passed upon and adversely to them decided by all thoughtful people.

I tell you, Mr. District Attorney, very frankly, I have your head "in chancery," and I intend to punch it. I believe this is a correct use of the language of the ring, although I am not, literally, a pugilist; and I may make a mistake in the thing said, but not in the thing meant. That you may rest assured of, unless you mend your manners, and then I may have larger game to fly at and may forget my little appointment with you. In the meantime please don't have me arrested,—forgetting my sex—for this unfortunate allusion, to the prize ring, *on a charge of being a prize-fighter*; for I perceive, now I have said it, that this verbal expression holds precisely the same relation to an offense against the laws prohibiting pugilistic encounters, by professional bruisers, as what we published in our paper, holds to an offense against the laws prohibiting obscene literature.

Pickwick, as a prosecuting official, enhances the dangers of literature generally. By some mental obfuscation of such a public functionary, there is no telling how soon some woman may be arrested for adultery, for kissing her own boy baby. I commend the subject to the consideration of the Young Men's Christian Association. The blue laws of Connecticut had the advantage of being printed, after a sort; but these new rip raps of journalism are not laid down on any chart. They must be sought for in the experiences of women thrust into Ludlow-street Jail, through the professional ignorance, stupidity, and lack of common intelligence, or what not, of men who happen to fill the public offices.

I would not be misunderstood, and you might not understand me if I were not to explain that Mr. Train is arrested ; but you must remember that it did not come through the efforts of the gentleman of whom I have been speaking, although the case was, I believe, urgently presented for his action. The two cases present this paradox : while the United States authorities acted upon our case only after the State authorities had refused to take cognizance of it, the State authorities acted upon the case of Mr. Train only after the United States authorities had refused to take cognizance of it. Therefore, though Mr. Train is under arrest, upon a charge of obscenity, what I have said of the District Attorney, with whom I have an account to settle, is, nevertheless, strictly true.

Again : This affair with Mr. Train is, to me, utterly incomprehensible. I can very well understand why the youthful zeal of the Christian Young Men should stand horrified at the doctrines of the WEEKLY, especially when they are accompanied by personal illustrations of the mysteries of godliness ; but that their reverential piety should pretend to be shocked because Mr. Train, in his zeal to expound the Bible to the understanding of those who are not as familiar with it as they should be, considering that they account themselves as good Christians, is, as I said, simply incomprehensible. Can it be possible that he is a better Biblical scholar than are the representatives of the Young Men's Christian Association, that he should have found a phase of religion in their Holy Book of which they knew nothing ? It seems that this must be so, since there is no other explanation for their conduct in arresting him for quoting the Bible on them, except that they are themselves actually ashamed to have the attention of the world called to the true character of the Book which they claim to be the infallible word of their God.

I speak with no feeling of disrespect for this venerable Book, or of Him whom they claim as its Author ; but what must we think of a God who speaks language to his people that, when used by others than by those of their own household, even His Elect feel called upon to prosecute the intruder upon what is all their own, for obscenity ? If Mr. Train is guilty of obscenity for printing extracts from the Bible, is not the American Bible Society equally guilty for printing the same in the Bible as a whole ? Nor can they dodge the issue they themselves have evoked, by saying that the charge is not based upon the Bible quotations, since those quotations form, by far, the most objectionable part of the *Train Ligue;* and I am free to confess that, if any language can be called obscene, the extracts in question must be so considered ; and it is clear that Mr. Train so considered them, since his nice sense of honor would not permit him to plead "not guilty" to the charge of obscenity.

But I do not quite understand how the beyond-discretion zealousness of the Christian Young Men is going to extricate them from the ridiculous position into which they have been led. Of course it was ridiculous for them to have arrested my sister and me for obscenity for the language contained in the WEEKLY of November 2d, and not to arrest Mr. Train for the infinitely more obscene language contained in the *Train Ligue*. I pitied them for the scrape into which their hate of me had betrayed them. Having put their foot into it, in our case, they did not know exactly how to escape ridicule and permit Mr. Train to pass unnoticed, he having purposely flaunted them; and, as it usually occurs when people are in a predicament, in attempting to get out of it, they have the more perceptibly floundered in it. Perhaps but a few of the community realized, in fact, how deeply they "got into it," in our case; but now the whole community cannot fail to know the full extent to which the Only Elect will go — the utter folly they will commit, the altogether frantic efforts they will put forth to save the only escape known to them from the hell of which they stand in mortal fear.

But excuse me, that I have not as yet told you anything of what this is all about. The events that I alluded to have formed so intense a portion of my life for the last few weeks, that I forget that the truth of the matter has never even been stated to you. The press, for reasons which I will state presently, has been just as nearly silent, as it has been possible to be. Only the fact that we had been arrested and thrown into jail, because we had been doing something, or saying something, awfully naughty, which even must not be mentioned—and that we, who until recently, have rather been petted and favored by the public, had suddenly become awfully bad people, was suffered to go out to the world. Meantime we have bided our time and waited for the storm to blow over, to see whether it was really we or somebody else who had been hurt.

I speak of myself as conducting a warfare on the present impacted mass of love and hate, of confidence and jealousy, of prudery and flippancy, of deceit and hypocrisy, marital infidelity, sexual debauchery, seduction, abortion and consequent general moral degradation, all mingled in frightful confusion, and labeled the social system. When I think of this as being the foundation of morality, as it is called, I wonder if to the label it ought not to be added, "to be well shaken before taken." Unfortunately, however, it *is* a warfare, because the world will insist on making war on me and my ideas. For myself, I love *everybody; every human being*, and have no desire in my soul to fight or contest with anybody; I would far rather be engaged in teaching what I know, and in learning of others who are wiser than I am, what they know. Least of all, have I any piques to gratify, or any personal hostilities to wage with any one.

In the prosecution of a mission to which I feel myself called, for the annunciation of ideas, and, for so much of warfare and attack, as the natural reaction against those ideas has provoked, or may provoke or demand, I resolved to lay open to the world, something of the convictions and of the lives of leading individuals in the community, which would go to strengthen my position, if they were known, and which, while concealed and believed to be wholly opposite, went to weaken it, and to render my task and the task of others who openly stand with me, infinitely harder.

In accordance with this determination, and for reasons which are more elaborately set forth in the article itself, we published in our issue of November 2d, the Beecher-Tilton Scandal. In that article I stated what I happened very well to know to be true, by means therein fully stated, that Henry Ward Beecher is, on conviction, a free-lover, as I am, and as many of the noblest and wisest of the representative men and women of the land, and of the world, really are, whether they have or have not the moral courage—by which I mean fidelity to their convictions—to avow it ; and, to make good my assertions in respect to his theory—derived, probably, as many as fifteen or twenty years ago, from the writings and counsels of Fourrier, Warren, Andrews and other great socialistic thinkers—I stated, with detail and circumstances, facts which were also in my knowledge, derived in a great part from Mr. Beecher himself, in a way which dispensed me from any obligation of confidence, to the effect that he had not hesitated to live his own life of social freedom in his own way, and I added, that these facts were well known to a considerable circle of Mr. Beecher's church and congregation, and that I had been taken into this circle socially and intimately, because they learned that I had become possessed of these facts (in the first instance through Paulina Wright Davis and Elizabeth Cady Stanton, and subsequently through Mr. Tilton himself, and others), and because they feared that I would publish them, and because by communicating them unreservedly, they hoped to divert me from my purpose to use them in behalf of the interests of social emancipation, and the great principle of human freedom.

In finally making this publication, I was actuated by no other motive. To make this fact, if possible, comprehensible to you and the public, I will again state for the hundredth time what I mean, and what the great thinkers who have come to conviction on this subject, which they have been trying for half a century to intimate or communicate to the world, mean, by social freedom or free love ; an idea which it seems so very difficult for the majority of mankind to understand, or rather which they seem determined not to understand.

Free love means nothing more and nothing less, in kind, than free worship, freedom of the press, freedom of conscience, free trade, free thought, freedom of locomotion (without a passport system), free schools, free government, and the hundred other precious, special systems of social freedom, which the great heroes of thought have fought for, and partially secured for the world, during this last period of the world's growth and expansion. It is all one and the same thing, it is just freedom and nothing else. It is simply impossible that any great thinker like Mr. Beecher, if the subject is once fairly brought before his mind, can see the matter in any other light; and, if he is on the side of freedom at all, if he believes in the American principle, in the Declaration of Independence, in anything distinctly American, that he should come to any other conclusion, than that the compulsory regulation of our love affairs by statute law, is a remnant, as slavery was, of an old and opposite order of things, is simply ridiculous.

Mr. Beecher believes in free worship, that is to say, in the freedom of every individual to worship God as he sees fit, or not to worship him at all; he believes also in freedom of conscience, and also, doubtless, that every act of his life should be made a matter of conscience; how then can he or could he be anything else than a free lover? How can I regulate my life by my conscience, in the most secret and sacred things, if it has already been regulated for me by the hurried and ignorant legislation of a set of crude and corrupt legislators at Albany? It is the question whether our virtue, if we have any, shall be something vital and self regulating, or whether it shall be something dead, formal and legal, merely.

But what, in the next place, is freedom? Folks talk and think—I fear, my dear hearers, that you yourselves still think—that freedom means merely the license to do something bad. Is there, then, no need of freedom equally to do good things and right things? How easily you understand all this subject if we take it into any other sphere than just this one of love. We Americans believe in the freedom of worship, which is eminently an American doctrine. It is already secured, for at least this country. Does it follow that all Americans rush at once into devil worship? Do they as a matter of fact, erect altars and churches to the devil? Is it true, even, of the majority, that they do so? You know it is not; and yet anybody is perfectly free here—anywhere from the broad Atlantic to the broader Pacific—to erect altars and churches to the devil; and if they did so, you and I, Mr. Beecher, and the most conservative and orthodox divines, all over the land, would stand staunchly up together, as one man, in defense of their perfect (civic) right to do so; for if anybody can say, arbitrarily, that anybody else, shall not worship the devil, that same somebody may next say, in the same arbitrary way, that nobody shall worship God.

If anybody have the right to prohibit the erection of a Chinese joss temple on our shores, he must have equally the right to prohibit baptism by immersion or by sprinkling, or the elevation of the host, or the saying of mass.

As the condition of our freedom, therefore, we as Americans, *insist on the freedom of others, on the right of others*, to do even that, and just that, which we, as individuals, *believe to be wrong.* Nay, more, I hope that the doctrine reaches far deeper; that it is not *because it is the condition of our own freedom,* that we assent to all this, but that it is that THAT *itself is our religion;* not merely or chiefly that, in certain times, it favors and secures us, which is still a selfish and insecure basis for freedom, but that we *penetrate to the divine essence of the idea,* and see and know that this ultra, radical idea of freedom *is the profoundest of moral truths and of sound solutions;* and hence that we are devotees for its maintenance and defense, because it is intrinsically true, and whether it works well or ill for our individual predictions at the time.

I know that this is a fearful and tremendous doctrine. I know that it is the most searching and testing of all doctrines, of the fidelity and honesty of our own love of truth. I doubt if one in a million of this great American people, who have nevertheless, founded their institutions on the idea, have yet penetrated to the full significance of the idea. I doubt whether you, any of you, fully realize the profundity of the moral convictions, on which this Government was founded. And yet in this matter of worship, we have substantially realized the ideal. A hundred churches lift their spires to heaven, side by side, in the same city, dedicated to as many different orders of worship and creed, and all the congregations, peacefully and with mutual respect, pursue, from Sabbath to Sabbath, their various attractions and convictions; and all this, simply because we have wisely concluded (after thousands of years or bloodshed and strife over the subject) to say "hands off;" and to remit the whole subject to the conscience, to the judgment, to the good taste (or the bad taste), in a word, to the individuality of the individual—which is freedom.

Now let us return to the matter of love. The real thinkers believe, that this same principle will work the same harmonious and beautiful results, in this sphere also, and will completely and divinely regulate in the end, and, coupled with all other good influences, all our social disharmonies. They believe that our social disharmonies, those, I mean, of the family, are prolonged and aggravated, by the futile attempts of legislation to regulate them, just as the religious strifes of the past were fomented by a similar outside interference; and that, left entirely to themselves, they will regulate themselves.

It is not now the question whether this is true or not. I am simply saying that those who have thought most about it believe it is true. I believe it, and Mr. Beecher believes it; and thousands of the most thoughtful and refined people, who do not dare to approve it, except cautiously to each other, believe it; and it is your prejudices, and the prejudices of the people at large, which compel them to hypocrisy in concealing opinions, which they cannot, nevertheless, be wholly hindered from acting upon. And it is not, as the country people believe, because the cities are more vicious, but simply because they are more enlightened about the real significance of freedom, that these doctrines prevail more extensively in the great cities.

But now see, again, how you, and the people at large, misunderstand us on this subject. I have said sometimes and often, that I live my own free life in accordance with my doctrine ; and I said in my Steinway Hall speech, something to the effect, that I have the right to change my love every day or every night if I choose to do so ; and the public press, and the public itself, cry out in chorus, Mrs. Woodhull confesses that she lives an utterly abandoned life ; she lives and sleeps with two or three or five hundred or some other egregious number of men.

Now all this is very absurd, and the public will come, at some early day, to be very much ashamed of it. Let us return to the matter of worship ; and suppose I had been engaged in fighting the battle for that freedom ; and suppose I had said, I go to church or not, as I please, and I have a right to go to a different church, and worship God in a different way, every Sunday of my life, and suppose on the strength of this, the public said, Mrs. Woodhull confesses that she has no religious convictions whatever, and that she is an out-and-out infidel, or that one church is no better than another, and all are equally bad, etc. Why, the merest tyro in reasoning would see how utterly inconsequential were these conclusions, and would set down their holders as the stupidest of asses.

Now, probably there are not ten in this audience—in many an audience that I address there is not one—who know or have any right to assume to know, from anything I ever said, or from anything they know of my life, whether I live the life of a nun, or whether I live as the exclusive wife of one man, or whether I am what the cry indicates. Mrs. Hooker and several other of my anxious female friends, who have had the opportunity to know most about my life, have on various occasions, taken the pains to assure the public that I am one of the most exclusive and monogamic of matrons. For my own part I have been perfectly willing that the world should think just the other way, if that same public choose to humbug itself into whatsoever preposterous idea—both to accustom the world to accept the idea of freedom for others, who might want a broader social sphere than I do, and also to give the world just this lesson—that it is none of its business (except for very special occasions) what my private life is, as it is none of my business (except for very special occasions) what the private life of anybody else is.

Do you not now begin to understand, that whosoever believes in the better policy, for society, of leaving the love affairs of the community to regulate themselves, instead of trusting to legislation to regulate them, is a free lover ; and that being a free lover no more determines that one is low or promiscuous in one's habits, than believing that people shall have the right to choose their own food, determines that the person who believes so, has the personal habit of living on rotten meat or bad eggs.

But, I think I hear you say : " Well, possibly we might agree with you, that the mere abstract doctrine of free love is all right, at least for some millennial order of society in the future ; and we might accept Mr. Beecher and forgive him, if he has really been forced by his convictions to this conclusion. But you go immensely beyond this, and tell the world that Mr. Beecher not only believes it as a doctrine, but that he lives it promiscuously or, at least, outside of his own marriage relation ; and, then, that he has been secret and hypocritical in doing so.

Well, as to the first of these points, if we have really agreed that freedom is the true doctrine, then that means that it is none of your business, and none of mine how he lives or with whom ; any more than it is what he eats or when he sleeps ; except (exceptionally), for the moment, as an example, for teaching you and me this very lesson, new and strange in our several ideas, it is true, that it is none of our business. Undoubtedly, I have a general interest that you and all others should eat healthy and good food, but you have a far more special and direct interest in the matter, and it would be sheer impertinence for me to interfere, even if you should insist on eating very bad food.

Our old habits, under the marriage *regime*, now happily coming to an end, have made us all intolerably impertinent; until our social order is an impacted conspiracy of mutual spies and informers, so dense, so tyrannous, so awful, that if it were political, no civilized community world or could endure it; and such that the socially enfranchised communities of the future will look back upon it, with the same horror with which we regard the atrocious despotisms of Comodius or Caligula. Mrs. Grundy has a despotism, a million times more overwhelming and degrading, over the entire populations of England and New England, and generally, of all other countries, than ever any Nero or Tarquin had over Rome. Like slavery, hers is a despotism, which reaches every homestead, and is all pervading, and utterly terrific, to all but the stoutest hearted heroes and heroines ; and religion, which seldom establishes anything, but only consecrates what is, has consecrated this severe despotism. Better, a thousand times say, with nonchalance, like Cain, " Am I my brother's keeper?" than to belong to this hellish conspiracy to keep our brothers and sisters, so hugged by the iron arms of false morality and custom, that the life and spontaniety is all pressed out of them. Anybody, with half an ear, who knew the meaning of logic, who has listened to Mr. Beecher's stirring sermons on individuality, interspersed along through the last twenty years, would have heard in them the whisperings of social emancipation.

If, therefore, Mr. Beecher, in being true to the new doctrine of freedom, has been infidel and false to the old, that is none of our business, except to rejoice, if it come incidently to our knowledge; and if he has on any grounds been unwise, he is the one to learn the fact, and to improve in the use of freedom, by availing himself of the privileges which it alone confers, to improve. And if we had any business to know, yet, how could we know? Solomon says, "The heart of man knoweth its own bitterness." Are any of us competent to tell what domestic sufferings have been endured by the man and the woman in the two involved households; or by the men and the women in any households; and what consolations must come, or the heart must break! I know nothing of promiscuity by Mr. Beecher. I suppose variety is not necessarily promiscuity, any more upon the social keyboard, than it is upon the keyboard of the piano; and every soul must find for itself, the harmony of its own chords.

As to the second point: that I have charged Mr. Beecher, and that the facts charge him with hypocrisy and concealment. I have, it is true, complained of him, in behalf of truth and freedom, that he has hid, in some measure, his light under a bushel; but that, I think, is far more your fault and the fault of his congregation, the fault of the world; in fine, of the social despotism I have talked of, then it is his fault individually. It is part of what his brother, Rev. Edward Beecher, once so appropriately named "The Organic Sin." It will be time for us to insist, therefore, that he repent when we remove from him the repressive force of our own past bigotries and prejudices. It is our constant assumption that our great teachers, in the pulpit and elsewhere, have truths of which we are ignorant. How much do we know of how terribly we are all the time tempting them, compelling them even, to resort to hypocrisy and concealment by our unreadinesss to hear the truth.

But let me ask this question: Would Mr. Beecher's congregation have tolerated him in preaching the doctrine, or doing the acts? If not, and if the doctrine and the acts are both right for him to accept and act, then they do not stand in any place to reproach him. "Let them first cast the beam out of their own eye," and so of the great repressive public. Mr. Beecher, would, I assure you, feel himself the most emancipated dominie that ever stood in a pulpit, if his congregation and the public were simply prepared to permit him to preach to them this very sermon; for the preaching of which, because he is not emancipated, I am called upon to fill his place. Every member of his church and congregation will read this lay sermon, when it is printed and circulated among them, and they may take every word of it for what he would most gladly say to them, if their prejudicies did not forbid him to tell them the whole truth.

But on the whole I have no quarrel whatever, with either the preacher or his congregation. The deportment of both, under the exposure which I felt called upon to make, of the doctrine and the life of the pastor, has been magnificent and unprecedented, whether we regard it as a manifestation of convictions, or merely as a splendid instance of pure strategy. The statement which I made dealt too much in detail, involved too large a number of distinguished individuals; great writers and speakers, competent to answer for themselves, touched upon circumstances too well known, by too large a number of persons, showed too intimate an acquaintance with both the public and private aspects of the subject, and was, in every respect, too convincing of its truth upon the bare face of it, to be met successfully, in any other way, than by that perfect silence and masterly inactivity which have characterized the church, congregation, pastor and all the individuals without a single exception.

The public has stood aghast, with anxious expectation, for some denial from some quarter, of the truth of these allegations; but days passed into weeks and weeks rolled into months, and not a word of denial, nor even of explanation had been volunteered from any source; until the conviction has now gradually settled down upon the public mind, that there is no answer or explanation which can possibly be made. The whole case has been suffered to go by default. The admission has virtually been made; or, in any event, has been assumed by the people to have been made, that what I stated, and all that I stated was a simple narrative of the truth, which both pastor and congregation, have been compelled, in this tacit way, to admit.

The scene which these people have enacted, during these weeks and months, has been one of the most lofty and magnanimous which any people on earth, ever manifested toward a great leader of opinion. The language and the deportment of Plymouth Church and congregation, toward the pastor of Plymouth Church, was and is, not that of disbelief in the statements made—the probability, the almost certainty, of which many of them in private admit; but it has been the sublime faith of true devotees to their great leader, that to whatever point his convictions may have led him—whatsoever the course of life he may have conscienciously adopted, that they, too, believed in it to the extent of justifying and standing by him, through all the vicissitudes of fate, which may result, from his own fidelity to his own convictions.

They have said to him almost unanimously: Whether these allegations be true or not, we do not feel bound even to inquire; whether they be true or not, we believe in *you*, Henry Ward Beecher; we accept you as our teacher, and you as our instructor, in any new and higher truth; and if there be any truth, which you have felt bound to withhold from us, and yet, which you have not felt required to forego in your own life, we wait in confidence—we abide in faith, until the circumstances, and the growth in public opinion, shall enable us to come to a better understanding of that which you have already learned.

The scene has been, from the first, sublime. Mr. Beecher has gone forth, preaching, praying and pouring forth his great soul of inspiration, as if nothing had happened. His elders and deacons have gathered around him as a solid phalanx, saying: "Make no explanation—not even to us; we ask none; we will see that the church and congregation accept and maintain the same tacit league of acquiescence." And they have done so; and church, and congregation, and the public—to a large extent—have quietly subsided into the acceptance of his position, whatsoever it may be.

By this magnanimous system of tactics, which could not have been carried out at any former period of the world's history—which could not have been carried out, probably, in any other church and congregation in the world—which marks grandly and sublimely the exalted influence which the great preacher has rightly acquired, during all these years, over the minds of his people—what otherwise would have been a disastrous fall, has been broken, opinion has been modified, adverse judgment of the conduct itself, mollified, and the way prepared for the ulterior acceptance, by the whole world, of that which, but a few weeks before, it would have been deemed impossible to have projected, in any form, into the public thought, in such a way, as to secure acceptance.

The cause, in so far as it implied any charge deemed immoral by old standards, or unwise has been suffered to go, as I have said, by default; but, not only that—not only has a defeat been warded off, but a positive triumph for new ideas, has been secured ·by this masterly inactivity. Not only has it been found safe for an orthodox preacher, and for a great leader of opinion, to commit every breach of the old and *effete* code of morals, and to stand upon the tacit admission of the fact, *mildly* but *firmly*—surrounded by his cohorts of elders, deacons and people—defying all criticism; but, more than this, that same conduct and that same sublime justification of that conduct on the part of his congregation and people—or what amounts to the same thing, their utter refusal even to investigate, what they half believe to be true, or what they admit may have been true, and holding Mr. Beecher in any event all right, or sufficiently right to command their allegiance—have almost lifted humanity up to a new plane—have prepared for its new departure in morals—have reversed the currents of opinion of the ages past, and have opened the way for the fullest and freest discussion of every social problem.

From this time forward, the question is no longer, what has been thought and taught to be right in social affairs, no longer merely, what has descended to us by tradition, and what has been consecrated to us by religion; but it is the new and higher question, of what is virtually true in the social relations, which is presented for our consideration; of what is natural and right ; of what would lead to the highest and best results in the social architecture of the future; of what is our duty in respect to that future ; of what, in other words, are the the signs of the times; what is the nature and tendency of the age we live in, and who are the men and the women who can lead the world to higher and better condictions? What of the night, how far are we along toward the breaking of the perfect day ? What is the significance of modern socialism, of Christian socialism, and what of all the socialisms, and prophecies of the hour in respect to the future?

These and ten thousand others pressing and urgent questions which ignorance, prejudice and the impacted and obstinate reluctance of the community, to investigate radically new subjects, have hitherto hindered and kept back, are now fairly launched upon the tide of public investigation, and can no longer be charged upon a few erratic individuals, as a restless disposition to disturb the public peace. These great questions which are now pressing forward in the place 'of the old anti-slavery agitation, or the temperance reform, and of the woman's rights movement specifically, and of the hundred and one subjects and questions of reform, which have occupied the public attention during the last three or four decades, have been more fostered and favored, with reference to their early triumphant solution, by the conduct of Mr. Beecher and his congregation in this matter, than by any preceding event. I felt assured that in some way, which I was incompetent fully to foresee, the step which I took to force Mr. Beecher and his people, more openly into the current of reform, would have this desired result ; but I see clearly now, that in no possible, other way, could so much have been achieved, in behalf of this result, as by this course of tacit admission and quiet default, into which their good instincts have directed them. If I ever had any, I have, therefore, no longer, any quarrel, as it now stands, with anybody about this matter.

I have said, that no one of the numerous parties mentioned by me in connection with this subject, has uttered one word of denial or explanation. There was an evidently unauthorized paragraph floating through the newspapers, to the purport that Elizabeth Cady Stanton had denied the truth of what I have stated; but the item bore no authentication of her signature and was evidently untrue. She has not denied and will not deny what I have said in the matter. A correspondent of the Hartford *Times* forwarding a communication from Philadelphia, adverting to the subject, says:

"But Mrs. E. Cady Stanton's course needs explanation. The papers have stated that Mrs. Stanton, being at Lewistown, Me., on reading Mrs. Woodhull's story, denounced it as far as it related to herself. Perhaps she did deny something. But Mrs. S. is a public woman, and knows how to write; why have we not a card from her, explaining the matter in full? I will tell you, Mr. Editor: simply because Mrs. Stanton dare not imperil her own reputation for veracity; for she has herself charged Mr. Beecher, to parties residing in this city and known to me, the writer, and elsewhere, with very much the same offenses of which Mrs. Woodhull speaks."

Mrs. Stanton knows all these facts too well, has mentioned them too extensively, has too much respect for her own veracity, and knows me too well in the earnestness and veracity of my serious averments, and in the boldness and energy with which I prosecute my undertakings, wantonly to deny any statement which she has made to me, and to others along with me, in relation to this important affair. She is also too deeply interested in the general progress of social emancipation to wish even, in any manner, to injure the effect which this particular campaign, in the great social warfare, is now so happily producing. None of the persons involved will hereafter, any more than they have hitherto, deny the statement I have made of the facts. The same writer in the Hartford *Times*, just quoted from, has the following with regard to Mr. Moulton:

"And now a word regarding Mr. Frank Moulton. Of the integrity, culture and fine social position of this gentleman we are fully assured;

and we are also authentically informed that *his* 'painful silence' means a great deal; for whether Mr. Moulton, at the point of a pistol, extorted from Mr. Beecher such a paper as Mrs. Woodhull defines or not, it is certain that he forced Mr. Beecher to deliver up a paper of some kind. Mr. Moulton is a gentleman, who does not go to vulgar extremes; and the fact that he felt obliged to compel Mr. Beecher to deliver up that paper, *as he did*, is sufficient evidence that the paper was an important one, and Mr. Moulton considered that Mr. Beecher had forfeited esteem as a gentleman, if not as a Christian. If Mr. Beecher, relying upon his former reputation, scornfully refuses to notice Mrs. W.'s main charges, perhaps he could be induced to explain the cause of Mr. Moulton's ungracious visits to him. One thing is sure, namely, that if Mr. M. ever breaks his 'painful silence' (for he will not lie), it will be found that an important paper was wrested by him from Mr. Beecher; and that this paper relates to the act which Mr. Beecher, for reasons of his own, does not yet see fit to make public."

The moment the silence should be broken, that defense or denial should be attempted, that discussion should be instituted, a hundred witnesses would spring up on every side, confirming, in generals and in particulars, all that I have said; and among these witnesses not a few would be from among the members of Plymouth Church I therefore repeat, that no sublimer spectacle has been witnessed, in any age, than the perfect reticence and complete personifiation of the policy of inaction, on the part of all the parties concerned. We may therefore dismiss them from our large list of obstacles in the way of social progress, and may enroll them at once, and for all future time, as at least the tacit friends and co-operators with the army of social emancipation.

But I promised to tell you why the press has been silent. It was partly because they were astonished by the magnitude and revolutionary nature of the facts stated; because they were therefore taken, as it were, unawares and unprepared with any well-defined opinions on the subject: and because the subject was too pregnant with importance to be dealt with in the ordinary flippant way. It was, partly, because of a highly honorable sentiment of friendship and veneration for Mr. Beecher which pervades in fact, the whole country, and which is similar in kind to the feeling which has controlled so powerfully his church and congregation; and from a general unreadiness to do or say anything, which would embarrass him in selecting his own system of tactics and his own method of defense, in the serious delemma into which he had been thrown. It was in part sympathy with the new ideas, with which fully one-half of the members of the press in this city, are more or less imbued, and the hope that if left alone, the matter would, in some way, turn out favorably for the cause of a reform, in which they were to some extent interested, while still unprepared to incur the odium of its defense; and it was in part the fear of that despotism of opinion, under which we all live, and which has, hitherto, almost preemptorily forbidden the free discussion of the social problem.

But no one of these causes, nor all of them combined, could have long prevented the open protest of the press against the abuse of the power of the law and the assault on the rights of free speech and free publication, which were involved in our arrest, if we had remained incarcerated, or could prevent it now, if we should be again arrested.

The New York *Herald* generously opened its columns (paying only its peppercorn of allegiance to Mrs. Grundy in its editorial columns) for me in my defense while I was in jail. The Brooklyn *Eagle* published a succession of caustic editorials, arraigning the officers of the law for their usurpation, and urging Mr. Beecher and his congregation to take the only legitimate measures for defending against, or denying my statement, if they were to be defended against or denied, at all. The Catholic newspapers of the country, republished extensively from us, and showed but an ill-concealed exultation, that Protestant clergymen were not exempt from the liability to the same charges which Protestants, in their so-claimed superior purity, have delighted to make against Catholic clergymen. In a word, the sympathies of the Catholics of these two cities, and perhaps of the country at large, are strongly with us in this contest; and I wish to acknowledge my great obligations to leading Catholics who have busied themselves in aiding me, in the securing of bail, and in other important matters, during my incarceration.

The Protestant pulpit had also begun to growl forth its disapprobation of Mr. Beecher's position. In a sermon preached in the West Church, Boston, on November 4, 1872, by Rev. C. A. Bartol, reported in the *Liberal Christian* of Saturday, December 7, this distinguished clergyman says:

"Having such a good opinion of ourselves makes us think lightly of our guilt. We eat and wipe our mouth; but we cannot outface witnesses of our error; and it is a mistake to leave specific indictments unexamined, as if simple standing could put them down. Not were we high as Colossus! The grim accusations of the woman in jail in New York will serve the commonwealth if they lead to a probing of those deepest wounds inflicted on it by secret iniquity; while the multiplication of crimes of violence arising out of jarring affectional relations ought, if anything can, short of the last fire and last war, to alarm custodians of order and Christians in their pews."

And again:

"For, the only safety is truth. A lie is no more safe than good. Things cannot be hushed up, nor crimes concealed more than flames. If anybody charges me with a sin, I shall not rely on my reputation; I shall demand investigation, and you for my investigators straightway. What corruption is that crow of suspicion after? He is not flying through the air for nothing! The church dares not explore the evil? Then let its members bear the stain!"

Socialism, the belief that just as great changes are impending, and must be effected for the ultimate good of mankind, in the relation of the sexes—in the more widespread influence of love—in the elevation of love out of its lower forms of mere passional excitement, of its purification, without repression or destruction of any part, however, of the sentiment; the belief that the construction of our homes must be radically changed, to accommodate these new ideas; that industry must be organized around the great composite home or hive of people; that women must be cared for and sustained, not in domestic bondage, but in complete freedom, and all that stands connected and related with these beliefs—in a word, Socialism is no longer confined to the few agitators and radical thinkers—is no longer to be traced home to French infidelity or free-thinking, but is widely diffused, even in the most religious circles, and where the sentiments of piety most profoundly prevail.

John H. Noyes and the Oneida Community, with their system of complex marriage or practical Free Love, were the outbirth, not of French Socialism, but of New England Revivalism, and of the more vital interpretation of the spirit and letter of the New Testament. Prof. Upham, who has recently died, and who stood for fifty years at the head of New England theology, a vital pietist of the Madame Guion school, was for many years a full convert, through his study of the Scripture, to the belief that, unlimited freedom in the relations of the sexes would, in the Millennial order, supersede our present marital restrictions. These doctrines were taught by him, in a subdued and partial sense, to the hundreds of young men who have gone forth from Bowdoin College to preach, and to pursue the various professions, during the past generation.

During the last twenty years Prof. Upham has steadily visited, from year to year, and communed with Noyes and Andrews and all the other leaders of the most advanced social doctrines. He has encouraged and upheld them by his great words, filled with religious unction and sound philosophy. He has believed that men and women were to be lifted to higher and still higher excellencies, through the deepest and most varied experiences of the heart, and that the doctrine of Love divine, as promulgated by Christ, meant nothing less, and nothing else, than the ultimate introduction upon the earth of a complete social emancipation.

I have heard Mr. Andrews say that he has been closeted, at his own house, with no less than five or six of the leading Doctors of Divinity of the country, during a single year, in the closest and most confidential consultation in respect to these great subjects; and I might occupy the remaining portion of my hour in detailing to you the simple evidences of what I can now only reaffirm as the fact: and which is, that the whole public sentiment of this great Republic is permeated and honey-combed with the belief in, and expectation of, an early and complete overturn of the existing social order, and the introduction of a higher type of morality and social truth.

Now then, in what manner can those who would stave off the discussion, those who dread the light, either with regard to existing evils or future remedies, proceed, other than by charging obscenity or indecency, upon those who persist in the discussion? Anything and everything short of these real offenses against the law, is permitted and authorized, and justified by our Republican institutions; by our doctrine of the freedom of the press, and by our habits of thought as a people. The obscurantists and old fogies, the resisting and unready conservatives have, therefore, no other grounds of defense, no other possible means of repression; no other hopes of success, in keeping under and down, the uprising tendency to ventilate this whole subject, except by charging upon the champions of reform, these disgusting offences. Necessarily the subjects dealt with, are of a delicate nature; necessarily the public mind has to be accustomed to the treating of, and to the reading about, and to the consideration of things, which have hitherto been tabood or held to be improper for public discussion.

The science of physiology is liable to the same imputation, and has been struggling for the last twenty years for admission, in the most limited way, into our public schools, although vastly the most important of the sciences for the young, simply on the ground, that it is next to impossible to treat it, without some infringment upon established preju- dices. Socialism inevitably incurs a similar liability; it is impossible to present or discuss the evils or the remedies, in which all socialism deals, without, at times, saying things, in very plain speech, about matters which are ordinarily hushed up or barely referred to by allusion.

But the world grows in its strength and capacity for facing the consideration of every subject. At one time the whole com- munity was shocked and agitated, in respect to the exhibition of nude figures in statuary and painting, here in America, as against the puritanical notions of a previous generation : but all that has gone past, and the beautiful works of art, which base themselves upon the culture and admiration of the human fig- ure, are now familiar visitants in every family.

The admission of women to the ranks of the medical profes- sion, has been hooted at and hindered on the same grounds. A prurient and fastidious morality would, in a thousand ways, keep back the progress of the world ; but the world's progress moves in too powerful a current to be repressed. Mystery and mock modesty are giving way, rapidly, before universal enlight- enment, and this little puny effort, of the inferior law officers, of the United States Government at New York, to repress the freedom, and hinder the discussion, of great and vital questions ; to institute a censorship over thought and morals and free speech, is too ridiculous and is too much an anachronism, too much out of harmony, both with our institutions and the spirit of the age in which we live, to be more than a mere ripple upon the surface. The time has gone past for such measures to inter- vene, successfully, in the intellectual discussion of the age. The tocsin of a new order of thinking and acting, was inaugu- rated, for this country and the world, when Jefferson affirmed, in a single terse epigram, that error need never be feared so long as the truth is left free to combat it.

But let us consider for a moment, what it is which constitutes obscenity or indecency or indelicacy. Where is the line to be drawn between what it is proper to discuss, or speak of, or put in type, and what ought to be, or may rightly be suppressed by the law? And in reply, I would say, that nothing said with an earnest purpose and for a good end, is or can be obscene. If any other standard than this be erected the very first book to be condemned and burned for obscenity is the Bible itself. The next books will be the law books. Not a book on medical juris prudence can be permitted to be printed or sent through the mails. The next will be the medical books. I have in my library an anatomical atlas and other works of the kind which must be instantly repressed.

I am having, at this time, an exhaustive collection made of all the passages in the Bible which may be considered, by this mode of interpretation, obscenity ; and I am having, through my counsel, a similar collection made, of the prints, discussions and expositions to be found in the legal and medical books.

am having a similar research made throughout the literature of the world; although, in this respect, I have been nearly saved from the necessity of labor, by a remarkable work which has already performed this service.

Near the end of the war, Mr. Secretary Harlan, of the Department of the Interior at Washington, moved by spasm of piety, removed the distinguished poet and philanthropist, Walt Whitman, from an office which he held in his department, on the ground of the obscenity of some of his poems. Having no appreciation of the legitimate license of genius to deal with the most delicate subjects, and, reading the sublimest passages of inspiration, with the bleared ignorance of uncultured stupidity, he thought it belonged to him, as the Young Men's Christian Association, through its pious agent, think it belongs to them to oversee the morals of the community, and he removed Whitman from office. Unaware of the fact that Rabelais, Montaigne, Hudibras, Sterne, Burns, Byron and Shakspeare himself, and fully a thousand other great poets and philosophers, fill the libraries of the most refined people in all countries, and that their works abound in pictures and allusions which, in the mouths of vulgar people, would be vulgar and obscene, the pious Secretary made his ridiculous raid upon the most representative and characteristic of American poets.

Immediately, however, a storm of indignation arose. The Secretary of another department conferred on Whitman a higher office, and Whitman's literary friend, William O'Connor, wrote in defense, a pamphlet, called "The Good Gray Poet," which is the most exhaustive display of the freedom which has been accorded to genius, in this direction, which is to be found anywhere in literature. The work itself is a credit to the literary craft. [Here followed copious quotations from the Book referred to.]

My counsel have taken this whole subject in hand; and, in case the Government of the United States ever dare, which I have assured you they will not, to press the case against me and my sister for trial, the court house, the public press and the country will be flooded with such oceans of reading matter of an unusual character from all these sources, from the Bible down to the last novelette, that those who have moved in this business will, it is hoped, be fully satiated with the results.

Such are some of the great words of the great poets found in defense of the free scope and untrammeled career of genius in literature. I recur, now, for one moment, in conclusion, to the more direct and far more weighty purpose of this discourse. I stand here to make my defense of the spirit of this age; of that drift toward social freedom, which is now bursting all bounds, and insisting upon the complete enfranchisement of the human affections.

The head and the hand are already free. Free-thinking and free-acting within the just limits which inhibit encroachment, are now grandly tolerated in the world, except in that one department of human affairs, which includes the sentiment of love. In that local centre of our lives we are still slaves. The land mourns with the bitterness of its bondage. The reverend clergymen who have labored earnestly and honestly to fasten still on the community their traditional ideas of morality, never permitting themselves even to ask if there is anything wrong in their methods; or if there is, perchance, some better way, have felt the reaction of the vital forces within their own persons and within the community and the age in which they live, as severely as any other class. The old fear of hell-fire has lost its repressive terrors, even over their consciences and lives. Somebody, it is said, has gathered the names of no less than seven hundred preachers of all sects and denominations, who have been driven from their pulpits within the last four years, and in this country alone ; their congregations and the public scandalized, and themselves and their families disgraced and socially ruined by their sexual offences against the effete and false systems of their own moral teachings.

All the other classes of society suffer no less terribly. There is a skeleton in every house. There is hardly a family of ten persons in the land which does not contain in its numbers, some one or more poor, wretched, heart-broken or tortured victim of our ill-advised laws and perverted notions of purity and prosperity ; and sometimes every adult person in the entire household is such a victim of repression or compression, or else of starvation, or else, still, of gorging and satiety of their sexual nature.

Every third person of the audience I am now addressing is a conscious, and to some extent a rebellious slave under this tyrannical social system, begotten of other ideas than those that now prevail, and which was, perhaps, well enough adapted to other times, but which now has become a galling tyranny over their domestic lives, and *they* know that what I say is true. Most of the remainder of my audience, and they are simply representatives of the country at large, if not so consciously, are still unconsciously dragging out a miserable social existence of domestic wretchedness, a common lot of the homes of the people, derived from the same bad brood of pernicious causes.

Repulsions, discontent and mutual torment, haunt the household everywhere. Brothels and social hells crowd the streets and avenues; passional starvation, enforced by law and a factitious public opinion on the one hand, and sickly and weary wives, and even husbands, on the other hand, overwrought, disgusted, and literally murdered, in their utter incompetency to meet the legitimate demands of healthy natures, coupled with them; ten thousand forms of domestic damnation cropping and bursting out in ten thousand ways, through all the avenues of life; and everybody crying, "Peace! peace! when there is no peace;" and the few who dare to speak of these evils and to call for a remedy, hounded to the death by the same old persecuting spirit, which, from the earliest ages, has met and martyred every new and struggling reformatory idea.

But there is, nevertheless, a brighter side to the picture. The dawn of the better day is already shining over the hill-tops of the gorgeous orient. Sexual freedom, the last to be claimed for man, in the long struggle for universal emancipation—the least understood and the most feared of all the freedoms, but destined to be the most beneficent of any—will burst upon the world, through a short and sharp encounter with the forces of evil. We who are assembled in this very hall to-night, will, many of us, meet in a few months or years, to celebrate the glorious incoming of the age of a rounded-out and completed Human Freedom. The passions, instead of being regarded as we have been taught to regard them, as merely satanic or malign forces to be repressed or enslaved, will be recognized for what they are; as the *voice of God* in the soul; as the promptings of our best nature; as the holy premonitions of a divine harmony in society, so soon as they shall be understood and adjusted under the beneficent influences of freedom.

Rising up out of our false notions of propriety and purity; coming to know that everything is proper which enhances happiness and injures no one; and that everything, *whatsoever*, is pure that is healthful and natural, we shall greet each other on that joyous occasion with smiles of a benign joy, while looking back with a touch of sadness through the past hours of the long night of social bondage; and shall prepare, from that day, for the perfect and pure blessedness of the coming millennium of the absolute liberty of the Human Heart.

SOCIOLOGY

(4)

To Women Who Have an Interest in Humanity
Present and Future . . . 1874.

Reproduced from *Woodhull & Claflin's Weekly* (October 31, 1874, p. 9). The original columns are here reduced, divided and realigned; original type column width four inches.

WOMEN WHO HAVE AN INTEREST IN HUMANITY, PRES-
ENT AND FUTURE—PERSONAL GREETING:

ring these three years in which I have been before the
c urging the necessity of sexual reform, though often
I to do so, I have steadily declined to address women
; I have always said that there is nothing in the most
ugh discussion of any subject that ought not to be
ed to, quietly and earnestly, by both men and women.
oth sexes are parties to the unnatural and damaging
ons that have cursed the world by a race of physically
nerate children, so should they both be students to
re the way out of these terrific conditions. But wore so frightened at the idea of hearing these matters
d about before the men who have demoralized them so
, and I have had to guard my speech so carefully, lest
who had the courage to come out to hear me should
ared away, that I have finally concluded to give way to
con-iderations and include in my lectures one
ess to women alone in each place I may
In doing this I shall not really depart from
rinciples by which I have, until now, refused to speak
e sex alone; since the final reason that has induced me
the sex alone; since the final reason that has induced me
ly. I have made some new discoveries in regard to
in's sexual powers and maternal functions, which are
ently proper for her to inquire into as a sex, as they
to her specifically—to her endowments, over and
which men have no more than an indirect interest,
o paramount right. Woman, as I have frequently
and written, is rightfully Queen in the domain of sex;
ving so, she is the natural sovereign of all that sex im-
and she has no right to relinquish her sovereignty by
r sale to anybody; indeed, it is her special duty to ever
ain and guard it inviolate and sacred, permitting no
ion upon its rights and no intrusion into its sanctities.
e learned what woman has forfeited by an opposite
e; and how, through this course, she has really been
Eve" through whom the first transgression came, by
the whole race has been cursed. She has parted
her birthright for less than a mess of potage, and has
arily gone into, and remains in, a slavery with which
was never other slavery to compare. For what slavery
re, or was there ever, to be compared in its degrada-
o that of surrendering to others the control of those
ons through whose operations immortal souls are cre
This divine work has been entrusted by Nature and
d to woman; but she has been false to her God and
to Nature—a traitor to a trust confided to her than
there is none equal in magnitude, importance and
ness in the world.

But in spite of all this trust, in spite of the confidence reposed in her by her Creator; in spite of the crown of her
womanhood she has ingloriously, ignominiously and traitor-
ously permitted herself to become the mere servant, the slave,
instead of remaining the Queen that she ought to have been,
and has consented to the servility of bartering her crown
for money and for food; when to have retained her rightful
place upon the throne, and to have enforced her rights proud
ly, would have been to have had absolute sway over both continually. What by virtue of her functions she has been entitled to of right, she has consented to supplicate for by the
sacrifice of her womanhood.

Now all this must be reversed. Woman has got to resume
her natural position, and man must gracefully yield up his
control and rule over her sexual and maternal functions; or
else she must rebel and accept the consequences. Woman
must be free; must be sovereign again and command the obedience of man, and to become a servant where he has been
lord so long.

But woman has been in slavery for such a length of time
that she is in utter ignorance, not only of her powers and
functions, but also of what has resulted from her apostasy.
Therefore she must be enlightened; she requires to be informed—to be awakened to a sense of her crime and her
responsibility. It is my mission, as far as possible, to do
this work, and, in order to reach the hearts of my sex, I am going to speak to them separately, so that I may unhesitatingly
pour out my soul's deepest convictions and show them how,
through sorrows, trials and sufferings, these truths have
been brought home to me. I shall speak what I have learned
through saddest experience; but having come up through
that experience with fresh rays of light warming my heart,
I should, in turn, be recreant to my mission if I were to
neglect to do what I can for the emancipation of my sex as
a whole.

In brief, then, I propose to show woman how she best may
redeem herself, and next the race; show her the secret
by which she shall be emancipated from her slavery of thousands of years, which shall install her sovereign in the domain of sex, and which will save her in the future from undesired pregnancy and unwilling child-bearing ; through the
realization of which alone can the curse of the race be removed; and, that I may do this as widely—to as large a
number—as possible, I shall speak to them alone, whenever
and wherever the opportunity shall permit. The little experience I have already had in this new departure has convinced me that I am right in having taken it, and I trust
that those of my sex who have any comprehension of the
import of what I have to say to women, will rally them
together, and, so far as may be, prepare them to make a new
Declaration of Independence and a new departure—this time
in that department of society which is basic and vital.

VICTORIA C. WOODHULL.

SOCIOLOGY

(5)

Tried As By Fire . . . 1874.

TRIED AS BY FIRE;

OR,

THE TRUE AND THE FALSE,

SOCIALLY.

AN ORATION DELIVERED BY

VICTORIA C. WOODHULL,

IN ALL

The Principal Cities and Towns of the Country during an engagement of

ONE HUNDRED AND FIFTY CONSECUTIVE NIGHTS,

TO AUDIENCES TOGETHER NUMBERING.

A QUARTER OF A MILLION OF PEOPLE.

——•——

New York:
WOODHULL & CLAFLIN.
1874.

PROSPECTUS.

WOODHULL & CLAFLIN'S WEEKLY.

[The only Paper in the World conducted, absolutely, upon the Principles of a Free Press.]

It advocates a new goverumeut in which the people will be their own legislators, and the officials the executors of their will.

It advocates, as parts of the new government—

1. A new political system in which all persons of adult age will participate.

2. A new land system in which every individual will be entitled to the free use of a proper proportion of the land.

3. A new industrial system, in which each individual will remain possessed of all his or her productions.

4. A new commercial system in which "cost," instead of "demand and supply," will determine the price of everything and abolish the system of profit-making.

5. A new financial system, in which the government will be the source, custodian and transmitter of   money, and in which usury will have no place.

6. A new sexual system, in which mutual consent, entirely free from money or any inducement other than love, shall be the governing law, individuals being left to make their own regulations; and in which society, when the individual shall fail, shall be responsible for the proper rearing of children.

7. A new educational system, in which all children born shall have the same advantages of physical, industrial, mental and moral culture, and thus be equally prepared at maturi:y to enter upon active, responsible and useful lives.

All of which will constitute the various parts of a new social order, in which all the human rights of the individual will be associated to form the harmonious organization of the peoples into the grand human family, of which every person in the world will be a member.

Criticism and objections specially invited.

The WEEKLY is issued every Saturday.

Subscription price, $3 per year; $1.50 six months; or 10c. single copy, to be had of any Newsdealer in the world, who can order it from the following General Agents:

The American News Co., New York City;

The New York News Co., New York City;

The National News Co., New York City;

The New England News Co., Boston, Mass.

The Central News Co., Philadelphia, Pa.;

The Western News Co., Chicago, Ill.

Sample copies, mailed on application, free.

VICTORIA C. WOODHULL AND TENNIE C. CLAFLIN, Editors and Proprietors.

COL. J. H. BLOOD, Managing Editor.

All communications should be addressed

WOODHULL & CLAFLIN'S WEEKLY,

Box 3,791, New York City.

TRIED AS BY FIRE;

Or, The True and The False, Socially.

For what purpose has this audience assembled; and what
does it expect of me? Consider this question well now, since I
propose to perform my duty regardless alike of approval or dis-.
approval. In this duty you may listen to speech, such as, perhaps, you never heard from a public platform before.

You have been invited to hear the social problem discussed;
to see it placed in the crucible of analysis to be tried by the hot.
flames of truth, the fire meanwhile fed by stern facts, and stirred
to intensest heat, until the dross shall rise to the surface and
gradually disappear in fumes which may be unpleasant to the
senses, but leaving behind the purified residuum gathered, indicating clearly what is true and what false in the tested subject
—the sexual relations.

This is my task, not to be explained as it progresses in
terms of glittering generalities, or of poetic fancy, or in gingerly
words that may leave any in doubt as to what is intended, but
plainly, honestly and earnestly, so that no one can misunderstand; but which will clearly set forth the conditions requisite
to the health of these relations and the ignorance and abuse producing their diseases, and show what all knew, well enough, but
few dare acknowledge to themselves, even: that there is much
that is rotten in Denmark.

You are here as my guests, knowing in advance upon what
subject I should speak; and I shall expect from you, individually and collectively, that courteous treatment which would be
my due under any other circumstances than these, in which I
might be your hostess, and you my guests. I shall not utter a
word, phrase or sentence, except such as I conscientiously believe to be true, and that ought, for the good of the race, to be
uttered. Nor shall I, in the course of my speech, plain, bold,
even bald as it may be, use any expressions that, by the remotest
construction, trench upon the boundaries of the vulgar. I shall,
however, call things by their plain, Saxon names, holding that
there is no part of the beautiful, human mechanism for which
the pure in heart and thought ought be able to blush while
it is under consideration.

I have asked this question and given this explanation for
the purpose. at the outset, of permitting any here, who may not

desire to listen to such plain speech as I have indicated, to **retire** now, so that others may not be disturbed, later in the evening, by their removal.

We now understand each other. It is not expected, it is not desired, that I withhold any fact I may have to offer, or advice I may have to give, regarding a subject which, more than any other, ought to command the attention of all enlightened people; but which, from falsely conceived ideas and a wrongly educated public opinion, is, more than any other, anathematized by almost the whole world.

People may pretend to blush, and the editors may write of me as indecent and vulgar, and say I have no shame to speak as I shall, what they will not dare to print. But, after all, ought not they and you and I rather to blush with real shame that such things as I shall mention, exist to be spoken about? I say, shame upon the newspapers, upon the preachers, teachers and doctors, that it is necessary for me to tell you what they ought long ago to have freely discussed, and have thus relieved me of this unpleasant task! I say, shame upon them all! and if the papers must perforce reproduce this word, let them be honest enough to properly apply it to the existing facts that of themselves are obscene and vulgar, and not to the speaker, who deals with them, not because it is either her nature or pleasure, but because she desires, like Boards of Health dealing with nuisances, to abate them.

Therefore if any vulgar or indecent thoughts arise in the mind of any person when these things are discussed, they do not attach to the speaker, but belong wholly to the individual; hence whatever may be thought now, or said hereafter, by any of you, or written about them at any time, is, by no possible, far-fetched construction, an insult or imputation offered me. On the contrary it is a degradation to their subjects or authors, indicating the moral standpoint from which they, and not I, view the subject; and an insult to their mothers, to be explained by bad rearing and worse moral teaching. So do not think that, when I pick up the paper and read the nasty things that are said of me, I feel insulted or hurt; but rather believe that I pity those who write them, and feel that they have need of a loving mother or a darling sister, to snatch them from a degradation in which they can see only vulgarity or vileness, where there is really, nothing except purity and holiness.

If any of these mothers or sisters have such sons or brothers, let me beg of them to never let their yearning affections cease their efforts, nor their entreaties and tears to flow, until they are rescued—until they are restored to manhood.

No man who respects his mother or loves his sister, can speak disparagingly of any woman; however low she may seem to have sunk, she is still a woman. I want every man to remember this. Every woman is, or, at some time, has been a sister or daughter; and if she be now "out upon the cold world," do not forget that some son or brother helped, perhaps forced her there. Nor can it be amiss for men to ask: "Am I pure enough to make my judgments just?"

Let these thoughts check the rising frown and the cruel words you would bestow upon any unfortunate woman, in whatever condition, and call forth your love and sympathy instead, in some practical way for her rescue or assistance.

[Thus preliminarily introduced, I pass to the consideration of the true and the false in the relation of the sexes:]

The sexual relations of humanity are fundamental to its continuous existence, and are, therefore, the most important into which men and women enter. It is vital that they should be entered into properly, that they should be understood clearly, and, still more so, that they should be lived rightly. Nevertheless, the world has virtually declared that this shall not be. It denies all knowledge of them to the young, and permits the youth and the maiden to walk blindfolded into their exploration, ignorant even of their own functions, only taking special care that the journey, once begun, may never be retraced or stopped. It has left the travelers, as it were, in the mid-ocean of what may be their eternal happiness, if the course pursued be right; or their certain destruction if the chosen way be wrong, without chart or compass, subjected to winds which drive them, they know not where, and to currents and counter-currents, for which no haven of safety is provided; and, alas! they too often go down to untimely graves, victims to a willful ignorance. Such are the results of modern social regulations.

I am conducting a campaign against marriage, with the view of revolutionizing the present theory and practice. I have strong convictions that, as a bond or promise to love another until death, it is a fraud upon human happiness; and that it has outlived its day of usefulness. These convictions make me earnest, and I enter the fight, meaning to do the institution all possible harm in the shortest space of time ; meaning to use whatever weapons may fall in my way with which to stab it to the heart, so that its decaying carcase may be buried, and clear the way for a higher and a better institution.

I speak only what I know, when I say that the most intelligent and really virtuous people of all classes have outgrown this institution ; that they are constantly and systematically unfaithful to it; despise and revolt against it as a slavery; and only submit to a semblance of fidelity to it, from the dread of a falsely educated public opinion and a sham morality, which are based on the ideas of the past, but which no longer really represent the convictions of anybody.

Nor is this hypocritical allegiance the only or the greatest or gravest consideration that is capturing the opinions of the really intelligent. It is rapidly entering into the public thought, that there should be, at least, as much attention given to breeding and rearing children, as is given to horses, cattle, pigs, fowls and fruit. A little reflection shows that the scientific propagation of children is a thing of paramount importance; as much above and beyond that of personal property as children are above dogs and cats. And this conviction, practically considered, also shows that the union of the sexes, for propagation, should be consummated under the highest and best knowledge, and in such manner and by such methods as will produce the best results. These considerations are so palpable that they cannot be ignored; and they look to the early supercedure of the institution of marriage by some better system for the maintenance of women as mothers, and children as progeny. This is as much a foregone conclusion with all the best thinkers of to-day as was the approaching dissolution of slavery, no more than ten years before its final fall.

But in the meantime men and women tremble on the verge of the revolution, and hesitate to avow their convictions; but aware of their rights, and urged by the impulses of their natures, they act upon the new theories while professing allegiance to the old. In this way an organized hypocrisy has become a main feature of modern society, and poltroonery, cowardice and deception rule supreme in its domain. The continuation of such falsity for a generation, touching one of the most sacred interests of humanity, will eradicate the source of honesty from the human soul. Every consideration of expediency, therefore, demands that some one lead the van in a relentless warfare against marriage, so that its days may be made short.

This is my mission. I entered the contest, bringing forward, in addition to the wise and powerful words of others, such arguments as my own inspirations and reflections suggested. No sooner had I done this, however, than the howl of persecution sounded in my ears. Instead of replying to my arguments, I was assaulted with shameful abuse; and I was astonished to find that the most persistent and slanderous and foul-mouthed accusations came from precisely those whom I happened often to know should have been, from their practices, the last to raise their voices against any one, and whom, if I had felt so disposed, I could have easily silenced. But simply as personality or personal defense, or spiteful retort, I have almost wholly abstained during these years of sharp conflict from making use of the rich resources at my command for this kind of attack and defense, and, passing the vile abuse which has beset me, have steadfastly pressed on in the warfare.

In a single instance only have I departed from this course. Circumstances conspired to put me in possession of certain facts regarding the most prominent divine in the land, and from him I learned that he too was not only false to the old dispensation, but unfaithful to the new—a double hypocrisy, over which I hesitated many months, doubting if I should use it. It was not that I desired or had any right to personally attack this individual ; but something had to be done to break down the partition walls of prejudice that prevented public consideration of the sexual problem, and fully to launch it upon the tide of popular discussion. This revolution, like every other that ever preceded it, and as every other that ever will follow it, must have its terrific cost, if not in blood and treasure, then still in the less tangible but equally real sentimental injury of thousands of sufferers. It was necessary that somebody should be hurt. I cast the thunderbolt into the very centre of the socio-religio-moralistic camp of the enemy and struck their chieftain, and the world trembled at the blow. In twenty years not anybody will say that I was wrong, any more than anybody now says that the old leaders of the anti-slavery revolution were wrong in attacking slavery in the concrete.

My purpose was accomplished. Whereas, before, none had dared to broach the sexual question, it is now on everybody's lips ; and where it would have been impossible for a man, even, to address a public, promiscuous audience anywhere without being mobbed, a woman may now travel the country over, and from its best rostrums, speak the last truth about sexuality, and receive respectful attention, even enthusiastic encouragement. The world has come to its senses—has been roused to the real import and meaning of this terrible question, and to realize that only through its full and candid examination may we hope to save the future from utter demoralization.

But why do I war upon marriage ? I reply frankly : First, because it stands directly in the way of any improvement in the race, insisting upon conditions under which improvement is impossible ; and second, because it is, as I verily believe, the most terrible curse from which humanity now suffers, entailing more misery, sickness and premature death than all other causes combined. It is at once the bane of happiness to the present, and the demon of prophetic miseries to the future—miseries now concealed beneath its deceptive exterior, gilded over by priestcraft and law, to be inwrought in the constitutions of coming generations to mildew and poison their lives.

Of what in reality does this thing consist, which, while hanging like a pall over the world, is pretendedly the basis of its civilization ? The union of the opposites in sex is an instinct inherent in the constitutions of mankind ; but legal marriage is an invention of man, and so far as it performs anything, it defeats and perverts this natural instinct. Marriage is a license for sexual commerce to be carried on without regard to the consent or dissent of this instinct. Everything else that men and women may desire to do, except to have sexual commerce, may be and is done without marriage.

Marriage, then, is a license merely—a permission to do something that it is inferred or understood ought not to be done without it. In other words, marriage is an assumption by the community that it can regulate the sexual instincts of individuals better than they can themselves; and they have been so well regulated that there is scarcely such a thing known as a natural sexual instinct in the race ; indeed, the regulations have been so at war with nature that this instinct has become a morbid disease, running rampant or riotous in one sex, and feeding its insatiable maw upon the vitality of the other, finally resulting in disgust or impotency in both.

Isn't this a pretty commentary on regulation? Talk of Social Evil bills! The marriage law is the most damnable Social Evil bill—the most consummate outrage on woman—that was ever conceived. Those who are called prostitutes, whom these bills assume to regulate, are free women, sexually, when compared to the slavery of the poor wife. They are at liberty, at least to refuse ; but she knows no such escape. "Wives, submit yourselves to your husbands," is the spirit and the universal practice of marriage.

Of all the horrid brutalities of this age, I know of none so horrid as those that are sanctioned and defended by marriage. Night after night there are thousands of rapes committed, under cover of this accursed license ; and millions—yes, I say it boldly, knowing whereof I speak—millions of poor, heart-broken, suffering wives are compelled to minister to the lechery of insatiable husbands, when every instinct of body and sentiment of soul revolts in loathing and disgust. All married persons know this is truth, although they may feign to shut their eyes and ears to the horrid thing, and pretend to believe it is not. The world has got to be startled from this pretense into realizing that there is nothing else now existing among pretendedly enlightened nations, except marriage, that invests men with the right to debauch women, sexually, against their wills. Yet marriage is held to be synonomous with morality ! I say, eternal damnation sink such morality !

When I think of the indignities which women suffer in marriage, I cannot conceive how they are restrained from open rebellion. Compelled to submit their bodies to disgusting pollution ! Oh, Shame ! where hast thou fled, that the fair face of womanhood is not suffused with thy protesting blushes, stinging her, at least into self-respect, if not into freedom itself ! Am I too severe ? No, I am only just !

Prate of the abolition of slavery ! There was never servitude in the world like this one of marriage. It not only holds the body to whatever polluting use—abstracting its vitality, prostituting its most sacred functions, and leaving them degraded, debauched and diseased—but utterly damning the soul for all aspiration, and sinking it in moral and spiritual torpor. Marriage not slavery ! Who shall dare affirm it? let woman practically assert her sexual freedom and see to what it will lead ! It is useless to mince terms. We want the truth ; and that which I have about this abomination I will continue to give, until it is abolished.

It is useless to cry, "Peace! Peace! when there is no peace." It is worse than useless to cry, Freedom! Freedom! when there is nothing but slavery. Let those who will, however, in spite of the truth, go home and attempt to maintain it there, and they will wake up to find themselves sold, delivered and bound, legally, to serve their masters sexually, but, refusing to do which, there will be a penalty, if not the lash. Now, husbands! now, wives! isn't this true? You know it is. And isn't it shameful that it is true?

Is this too sweeping? What was it that condemned slavery? Was it that all slaves were cruelly treated? Not the most ultra-Abolitionist ever pretended it! They admitted that the majority were contented, comfortable and happy. Can the same be said, truly, of the slaves to marriage, now?

But it was claimed and proven, as I claim and shall prove of marriage, that the instances of extreme cruelty were sufficiently numerous to condemn the system, and to demand its abolition. Proportionally, the instances of extreme cruelty in marriage are double what they were in slavery, and cover a much broader field, involving all the known methods by which the body can be tortured and the heart crushed. I could narrate personal cases of various kinds, for a week, and not exhaust my stock; but I cannot pause to do so. Judged by the logic of the past, this institution stands condemned, and will be soon relegated to the limbo of the past.

But there is another picture of this holy institution, scarcely less to be deprecated than are its actual cruelties; and little, if any, less degrading to womanhood: All men and women now living together, who ought to continue to so live, would so continue were marriage laws repealed. Is this true or false? This depends upon the truth or falsity of the following further propositions: Marriage may be consummated by men and women who love mutually; or, marriage may be consummated by men and women who have no love. If it be said that the former is false and the latter true, it is denied that love has anything to do with marriage—an affirmation, virtually, that they who hate may marry rightly; but if, on the contrary, the former is true and the latter false, it is agreed, constructively, that all I ever said or ever can say is true,

Now which is it? Has love, or ought it to have anything to do with marriage? Who will dare say that love should not be a precedent to marriage? But when this is affirmed, the legitimate corollary is not seen: That, since marriage should not begin without love, it should cease when love is gone. To accept the former, is to declare the latter. And no logician, however subtle, can escape it. Nor can you escape it; nor could I, although I labored for years to do so.

But if there are any who are in doubt as to what is right and true, I offer a test that will decide it. Let the married who live together, who would separate were the law repealed, rise!

Not any here of that stripe ; or, if there are, they are ashamed to make a public confession of it. I should be so, too, were I sailing the voyage of life in such a ship. Ask any audience, or any individual, this question, and the result would be the same. What is the inference? Clearly that, if people really do live together who do not love, they are ashamed of it, and, consequently, of the law that holds them ; and that they want the world to think that they love each other, and choose to live together on that account, regardless of the law.

Who is there in the community who would like to have it understood that there is no love at home? Isn't it the fact, on the contrary, that those whose homes are loveless, and who fight and wrangle and fuss continually take special pains to conceal these things from the world? Everybody knows it is. What more sweeping condemnation could there be than this, both of the law which compels it and the practice itself? None! It is the hot-bed of hypocrisy, deceit and lust, and is doing more to demoralize the world than all other practices combined.

I am justified, therefore, in concluding that all people who are not practical free lovers, living together for love, are theoretically so, and are ashamed to confess that their practices do not accord with their theories ; or, in other words, are ashamed that their practice is enforced lust instead of free love. These are the alternatives, and the only ones, and I don't intend that the people shall escape them. Every one of you—every one of the people generally—either practices Free Love or enforced lust, and the world shall understand when people denounce me as a Free Lover they announce themselves as enforced lusters ; and I'll placard their backs and they shall walk up and down the world with this mark of depravity, as they have intended that I should do for having the moral courage, which they lack, to make my theories and practices agree.

There is but one objection, then, to the abolition of this last and greatest of all the slaveries, that, from the popular standpoint, has any validity whatever. This one is the *dernier resort* to which every opposing orator flies when driven from other positions: What will become of the children? Ah! that is the rub, is it? And it is asked with an air of *nonchalance* and self-complacency that seems to say, "Now I have you on the hip." This is the question that everybody asks ; but it is not seen that it is answered when the other position is abandoned. The assumption is this: if there were no marriage "the family" would cease to exist, and children would be left on the world. But this preposterous proposition is refuted by the denial and proof that "the family" exists by virtue of law. If the law were abrogated, and men and women should generally live on as now, which they say they would by denying that they live together on account of the law, what would be the difficulty about the children? And yet this bugbear has been pumped up into the imaginations of the people until it is regarded almost universally as an antidote to all allegations against marriage.

But aside from all this there are direct proofs, equally fatal to the children antidote. Are there men and women here who, in the face of this audience, or anywhere else, who, in the face of any other audience, would dare stand up and confess that they would abandon their children if the law of marriage were repealed? I have never been able to find such a person. If there are such here I want to see them. Barnum would pay a big price for such animals. I shall never be able to accept the doctrine of total depravity as applicable to any person until I meet such a specimen. The Darwinian order of descent acknowledges no such connecting link.

Oh, no! Of course WE could never neglect our children under any circumstances, but we fear that our neighbors might, therefore it wouldn't be quite expedient to give them an opportunity. If I were to go to your neighbors they would say the same of you. So the world goes on—one-half of it submitting to a semblance of law which they really despise, pretending that it is necessary on their neighbors' account—the old pharisaical godliness, "I am holier than thou," and I thank God that "I am not as other men are."

If people are really honest, however, in this opinion of their neighbors they should settle the matter. Let them go to their neighbors and say, "Now, my friends, here is a law upon the statute books that is an expensive one to administer, which, so far as I am concerned, might as well be repealed; but I fear if it be done that you would abandon your children and perhaps do a great many other bad things that I, with my superior honor and manhood, could not stoop to do." My opinion is that neigbors would help them out of doors much more rapidly than they entered, especially if there should be heavy boots ready for service, with this advice gratis, if in the rapidity of the movement it shouldn't be forgotten: "You had better go home and take care of your own family, and you won't have so much time to worry yourself about mine."

It is this stuff that is the matter with the world. Everybody, individually, is ready for freedom, but regards everybody else, collectively, as being in danger. Everybody is afraid that everybody else's wife and daughters would go to the bad if social freedom were to obtain, and their children to the dogs if the leash of the law were to be let loose. And these are what are offered as arguments against the introduction of freedom into the social relations.

It is an imputation that neither you, nor I, nor anybody else would submit to for a moment were we to consider its insolence. It is an insult alike to the manhood of man and the womanhood of woman, and an outrage upon good sense and common decency.

But I would not leave the children question under the

impression that I think their present conditions are by any means what they ought to be. Indeed I believe that they could not well be worse, and that an equally radical revolution is required in the methods of rearing and educating the young as there in begetting them. But right begetting stands first in importance, hence the marriage question is the first one to be revolutionized.

Without going into details, such methods for rearing and educating children should obtain as will give to them the right to live to adult age, each having had equal advantages in all directions with every other child ; that shall assure each the capacity and acquirements for good citizenship; and equal pecuniary end wments, so that all may begin adult life equal. Freedom without equality is a fraud ; and both these, without justice, a snare. There is but one question to ask : How can children be born, reared and instructed to make them the best men and women, physically, mentally and morally. If the answer demand the abrogation of so-called parental rights and authority they must go. The best interests of children, at whatever cost, is the proper motto. It's useless to waste time upon the present generation. Let it go ; but its ignorance and stupid blundering should not be transmitted to the next.

Nor should one-half of all the children born continue to die before reaching the age of five years, sacrificed, as they now are, to the inexcusable ignorance of mothers—murdered, it ought rather to be said, by the popular barbarity which condones ignorance of sexual matters. This fact is a commentary upon our social relations that transforms them into horrid tragedies and stamps the mark of Cain upon every mother. When a ship founders at sea, with the loss of a few hundred lives, the whole world is shocked at the horror ; but it sleeps quietly over the still greater horror of double that number of children—babes, almost—falling victims, daily, to these fell destroyers, the so-called safeguards of society, maintained by the canting hypocrisy of its fifty thousand ministerial frauds who know better, and the sham morality and mock-modesty of their willing dupes.

Some time ago, when lecturing in Massachusetts, a lady said : "Do you see that woman at the window opposite, weeping? She buried her daughter to-day—her only child, fourteen years old."

Without thought, I asked, "What was the matter with her ?"

She replied, "Can't you imagine—a girl, and fourteen years of age? Last summer I carried one of your papers there, in which there was an article entitled, "Sexual Vice in Children." After I had left, she took the tongs and threw it out of the window. To-day she has buried her only child, because she did not read and follow the advice contained in that article. Six days ago her little daughter arrived at puberty. Ignorant of its meaning and frightened at what she could not understand, she, unknown to her mother, washed out her clothes, and put them on. To-day she is in her grave. Now, Mrs. Woodhull, what is your verdict against that mother?"

I replied, "It is the same that ought to be rendered against every mother in the land who can so criminally neglect the education of her daughters upon so vital a matter as this, whether, as in this instance, it is fatal or not: Murderer!"

Infancy and childhood ought to be the most healthy periods of life; but they are ten times more fatal than any other. Of this sickening fact there can be but one verdict: Cut off at the age of from one day to five years, by maternal ignorance. This is still more evident when we remember that, from the very moment children begin to take care of themselves, the death rate diminishes. Think of these things, and then let it be said, if it can, that the social question ought not to be discussed publicly! Why, there is nothing else worthy to be discussed, so long as this remains unsolved! It should be the topic of conversation at the breakfast table, at dinner, at supper—everywhere—until the whole matter is well understood by everybody.

Will the press dare, hereafter, to condemn me for pressing it upon the attention of parents—for showing them the fearful ignorance and its frightful results? No! not directly; but instead of reporting what I say, so that the public may learn, they will daub me with the feculence of their own thoughts, and say I am vulgar and indecent, and ought to be avoided by everybody; and the too-confiding people will repeat the villainous lies in good faith.

A step beyond marriage as a means to gain sexual relations reaches the relations themselves, their uses and abuses. Here a query arises: Which is the end to be gained? Is it marriage merely, regardless of the character of the relations which it legalizes; or is it proper, natural, healthful, useful relations, such as will bless the parties themselves and the children who result? In other words, is it happiness, and peace, and comfort, and health, and all the good which can follow; or is it the legal union regardless of results?

Let us see. There will scarcely be found in this late day any intelligent person who will maintain that marriage ought ever to be consummated by persons between whom there is no love. The argument is, that men and women who love each other may consummate that love after being legally married but not otherwise; and if either party refuse to consummate the marriage, it becomes void. This establishes the theory that the principal feature of marriage is legal. But this controverts the common consent that love is a necessary precedent. Almost the whole word is in a "mull" over the confusion of ideas caused by the attempt to make these contradictions harmonize—desiring to live out their interior convictions, but fearing to do so lest they incur the legal or social penalty; desiring that their natural instincts and sentiments should be their guides, but fearing to let them lest they be accounted followers of the baser passions.

The law, then, and the real convictions of the people are at variance; but since the latter are inherent in the constitution of man, while the former is a contrivance of his intellect, invented for specific purposes, it must be concluded that the latter ought to take precedence in determining· the conduct of life. And when it is remembered that the law binds together only those people who otherwise would separate, this conclusion becomes inevitable.

After careful observation I have deliberately concluded that there are two classes only who have anything more than an imaginary interest in maintaining the marriage system : The hypocritical priests who get their fees for forging the chains and the blackguard lawyers who get bigger ones for breaking the fetters. The former have an average of ten dollars a job, and some of them a hundred jobs a year ; while the latter, not quite up to the former in number, to keep even with them, raise their average price per job to two hundred and fifty dollars. A thousand dollars a year for the priests ! How should people know whether they ought to marry or not without asking their consent ? Of course marriage is divine ! A thousand dollars a year for the lawyers ! How could people be supposed to know whether they ought to separate or not until the lawyer has got his fee ? Of course virtue must have a legal standard. How could morality and modesty be preserved unless the priest got his ten dollars ; or how could husbands and wives be prevented from killing each other unless the lawyer got his two hundred and fifty ? Will the priest ever cease his cant about the former, or the lawyer change the law about the latter so long as the people are fools enough to pay them fees ? They who suppose they may, don't yet understand how much divinity there is in this marriage business.

The real question at issue then is one entirely apart from law, relating wholly to the conditions that make up the unity, whether they are such as judged by the results, warrant the unity that is sought. What are proper and what improper sexual relations is the problem to be solved, and it is that one which of all others is most fraught with the interests, the happiness and the real well-being of humanity. Upon these relations, as I shall show, depend not only the health, happiness and prosperity of the present generation, but the very existence of future generations.

That existence is involved in these relations. If they be pure and good and withal natural, which they must be to be pure and good, then the existence which they make possible will be of the same character ; but if they be impure, bad, and withal unnatural, which if they are they must be impure and bad, then the existence which they make possible will be of like character. A pure fountain sends forth pure waters, but the stream flowing from an impure source will assuredly be unclean. To make the fountains of life—the sexual relations—pure, is the work of the reformer, so that the streams they send forth may flow through coming ages uncontaminated by any inherited contagion.

There are a few propositions necessary to be laid down that will become self-evident as the subject develops: 1. A man or woman who has perfect physical health, has natural and healthful sexual relations. 2. A man or woman, married or single, old or young, professional prostitute or *roue*, or a professed nun or celibate, who has bad general health—and suffers from any chronic disease—has unnatural and unhealthy sensual conditions. 3. A man and woman, living together, who have perfect physical health, have natural and healthful sexual relations, and will have healthy offspring. Such a union is God-ordained, if it do not have the approval of the law or the sanction of the priest; and no man can put it asunder. 4. If either or both of the parties to a union have generally poor physical health—suffer from any chronic disease—such parties have unnatural and unhealthful sexual relations, and their progeny will be puling, weakly, miserable, damned. Such a union is God-condemned if it have the approval of all the laws, and the blessing of all the priests in the world ; and as corollary to all these, this : All diseases not to be attributed to so-called accidental causes are the result of improper, or the want of proper, sexual, conditions ; and this applies to all ages and to both sexes.

It may now be asked : What are proper sexual conditions? I reply : Sexual commerce that is based upon reciprocal love and mutual desire, and that ultimates in equal and mutual benefit, is proper and healthful ; while improper sexual commerce is that which is not based upon reciprocal love and mutual desire, and that cannot, therefore, ultimate in equal or mutual benefit. Children begotten by the former commerce will never be bad children physically, mentally or morally ; but such as are begotten by the latter commerce will inevitably be bad children, either physically, mentally or morally, or, which is more likely to be the case, partially bad throughout.

I desire to be fully understood upon this part of the subject. I have been generally denounced by the press as an advocate of promiscuousness in the sexual relations. I want you to fully comprehend the measure of truth there is in this charge. Hence I repeat that there is but one class of cases where commerce of the sexes is in strict accordance with nature, and that, in this class, there are always present, First, love of each by each of the parties ; second, a desire for the commerce on the part of each, arising from the previous love ; and third, mutual and reciprocal benefit.

Of improper sexual commerce there are several classes : First, that class where it is claimed by legal right, as in marriage ; second, where the female, to please the male, accords it without any desire on her own part; third, where, for money, for a home, for any present, as a payment for any claim, whether pecuniary or of gratitude, or for any motive whatever other than love, the female yields it to the male; fourth, where there is mutual love and desire, but where, for any reason, there is such want of adaptation as to make mutual consummation impossible.

This is the promiscuousness that I advocate now, and that I have, from the first, advocated.

Will the representatives of the press, who have covered me with their abuse until I am regarded with horror all over the land as a person whose presence is contamination and whose touch contagion, correct their foul lies by stating these propositions, and, so far as they can at this late day, do me justice? We shall see!

"But," said a prominent woman of this country, with whom I was recently discussing these maxims in sexuality, "how are you going to prevent all this intercourse of the sexes, which you condemn?"

"Ah!" said I, "that's the question. I have no right nor has anybody else any right to prevent it in any such sense as you infer."

This is a matter that must be remanded back from law, back from public inteference, to individuals, who alone have the sovereignty over it. No person or set of persons, however learned and wise, have any right, power or capacity, to determine legally for another when commerce is proper or when it shall occur. It is not a matter of law to be administered by the public, but a question of education to be gained by individuals—a scientific problem to expound and elucidate which, should be one of the chief duties of all teachers and reformers. Every person in the world, before arriving at the age in which the sexual instinct is developed, should be taught all there is known about its uses and abuses, so that he or she shall not ignorantly drift upon the shoals whereon so many lives are wrecked.

I advocate complete freedom for sexuality the same as for religion. The charge of promiscuousness is laid in this fact, and some intelligent minds have thought it was a sound charge, until its inconsistency and utter absurdity have been pointed out to them. This is the proposition: I advocate sexual freedom for all people—freedom for the monogamist to practice monogamy, for the varietist to be a varietist still, for the promiscuous to remain promiscuous. Am I, therefore, an advocate of promiscuousness, variety or monogamy? Not necessarily either. I might do all this and be myself a celibate and an advocate of celibacy. To advocate freedom in sexual things and also the right of individuals to choose each for himself to which class to belong, is by no means synonymous with the advocacy of the class which he chooses. Advocating the right to do a thing and advocating the doing of that thing are two entirely separate and different matters.

Is not this too clear to be misunderstood? I will make it still clearer, lest some may not see it. As I said, I not only advocate sexual freedom, but also religious freedom. I claim that every individual has the right to be a Pagan, Christian, Jew, Mohammedan, Quaker, Oneida Perfectionist, Calvinist, Baptist, Methodist, Trinitarian, Unitarian, Universalist, or whatever else he has a mind or the will to be. Every person advocates the same right—the same freedom—and I am sure if an attempt were made to subvert this right in this country, every hand would be raised against it. I am, however, neither one nor any of these, but a Spiritualist, and I bend all my religious energies to the advocacy of Spiritualism.

Nobody would think of calling me a Romanist because I say that everybody has the right to be a Catholic; but, transfer the question from religion to sexuality, and because I advocate the same theory for this that I do for religion, I am denounced as an advocate of promiscuousness. Did any of you ever hear that I ever said that the monogamist has no right to practice monogamy? Was I ever known to assert that all people should be promiscuous, or varietists? No! What am I, then? I cannot be all of them. Why then class me as promiscuous? I will tell you why: Simply to brand me with supposed infamy, and to frighten the people so that they shall not come to an understanding of these things. That's the reason, and the press knows it.

There is an honest difference of opinion among its advocates in regard to what will be the result of sexual freedom, but none in regard to freedom itself. Some thinkers of wide experience in social matters have concluded that ultimately there will be no constant sexual relation; that change will be the order of society. Others, equally honest and conscientious, believe that a select variety will be the order; while others, still, hold just as firmly that the perfected union of one man and one woman is the highest order. I do not remember ever to have made a speech on this subject in which I did not affirm my belief in the latter order. Not because I desired to soften the feeling against me by so doing, but because I conscientiously believe that in such conditions will be found the highest attainable happiness; and I urge education, discussion and enlightenment upon the subject, believing that they will tend to carry the people toward this condition. Therefore, while I advocate the right of the promiscuously inclined to be promiscuous if they will, I ought to be classed as a monogamist. But if freedom be right in the abstract it does not matter whether monogamy or promiscuousness be the ultimate, since let it be which it may it will be right.

I cannot illustrate the ridiculous ideas of promiscuousness

better than by relating an incident that once happened to me while traveling from Washington to New York. I was approached by an intelligent woman, who, learning who I was, desired to hear my opinions for herself. In the conversation that ensued she remarked, "Oh, Mrs. Woodhull, is it true that you are a promiscuous woman?"

I replied, quietly, "Well, I do not know what you would call promiscuousness. Let me ask you a question, and then I may be able to determine."

Looking her in the face I saw the figure 4 appear upon her forehead. I said, "Madame, I believe you have known at least four different men sexually. Is that true?"

"Oh, yes! I am now living with my fourth husband."

Turning away from her with affected disdain I replied, "Madame, you are altogether too promiscuous for me."

Society permits a woman to have a dozen men, legally, in as many years, and she is all right. She's sound on the Goose Question. But if a woman live with her sexual mate without the payment of the fee, she is all wrong; she is a prostitute. And this is called purity, called morality! I say damn such morals. Such purity stinks. Logically, there is room for no other conclusion than this: That let the highest order of sexuality be what it may, the monogamists have no more right to enforce monogamy by law, as the rule of society, than the promiscuous have to enforce promiscuousness as the order to be observed. Society does, however, attempt to enforce monogamy, but it makes a bad failure.

The Oneida Communists, on the contrary, do not permit monogamic attachments. If they are found springing up, the parties are compelled to separate. If we are to judge which is the better rule by the results, nobody who has ever visited Oneida will hesitate a moment in the decision. Judged by its fruits—by its prosperity, its honesty, its morality, its health—Oneida is the best order of society now on the earth. Its enforced promiscuousness is preferable even to our enforced monogamy, and for very good reasons, which will become evident further on.

Suffice it, here, that promiscuous sexuality among people who have no love attachments, is not so debased a condition as is that which prevails so widely in marriage, where passion in the male, vents itself at the expense of disgust in the female. I know these are bitter pills for those to swallow who think that purity consists in fidelity to marriage. But whether bitter or sweet, they are true; and though I may be cursed now, if they purge the people of their false and absurd notions about sexual purity, I shall some day have their thanks for administering them. I offer you the remedy of Free Love as an antidote for enforced lust, and the world will have to take it before the disease can be cured.

So much for promiscuousness. But what of prostitution,

what of love and what of lust? Terrible words are these in the vocabulary of modern society, but still more so in that of social reform! The question with it is, not as to what is the popular meaning of these terms, but what is their natural, their scientific significance as tested by exact analysis or the stern logic of experience?

Prostitution is popularly applied to certain kinds of sexual commerce? but it has a much wider application, extending to every faculty, function and capacity of the body and mind. It means a perverted, unnatural or excessive use of a capacity. A person who overworks his body or brain is a prostitute. The unhealthy use of anything is its prostitution. They prostitute their stomachs who over-eat or over-drink. Therefore, prostitution, sexually, means a great deal more than intercourse obtained in houses of ill-fame for money. In a scientific sense, it means all sexual commerce that has not a proper basis in love and desire. There may be prostitution in marriage, and proper commerce in the bawdy house. It depends upon the specific conditions attending the act itself, and not where or how it is obtained.

In the exact sense, the woman who sells her body promiscuously is no more a prostitute than she is who sells herself in marriage without love. She is only a different kind of a prostitute. Nor are either of them any more prostitutes than are the countless wives who nightly yield their unwilling bodies to lecherous husbands, whose aim is sexual gratification without regard to the effect upon their victims. The difference is this: In the latter cases the men have legal permission to use the women whether they desire or object, while in the former the woman consults her own wishes—it is a slip of paper costing twenty-five cents and upward, good during life, that a man carries about with him to save the expense of purchasing, from time to time, elsewhere.

. It's a sharp trick played by men upon women, by which they acquire the legal right to debauch them without cost, and to make it unnecessary for them to visit professional prostitutes, whose sexual services can only be obtained for money. Now, isn't this true? Men know it is. Those who haven't a wife know very well that they procure for money what they would otherwise have by law. And what is more disgraceful still, is that thousands of men marry because they cannot afford the cost of satisfying their sexual demands with prostitutes. You and I and everybody else know that what I say is true, and yet the sanctity of marriage—the holy sacrament—is talked of as if it had existence! Bosh! It's an insult to common honesty to trade in such stuff and call it holy. Holy! To me it is nastiness; or if there is any worse name, call it that.

I know hundreds of wives who confess privately that they would not live another day with their husbands if they had any other method of support; and yet pass the poor prostitute as though her touch were leprous. As between the two, the legal prostitute is the more depraved at heart. It is axiomatic, that only those women are really pure whose sympathies go out to the unfortunate whom society has driven to the street and brothel by its unjust anathema; who can visit them without contamination; whose virtue is so assured that it is above suspicion. If there is any sister in this place so low that no other woman will visit her, tell me; there will my feet wend their way. If there is any child so wretched that none will care for it, there will my mother's heart wander.

Why should Christian women shun the outcasts of society? The Master whom they profess, habitually made them His companions. What excuse can they offer for a departure from His example? None! But it adds to their long lists of crimes the sin of hypocrisy. Let them beware lest the harlots get into the Kingdom before them.

What a commentary upon the divinity of marriage are the watering places during the summer seasons! The mercenary "mammas" trot out their daughters on exhibition, as though they were so many stud of horses, to be hawked to the highest bidder. It's the man who can pay the most money who is sought; it makes no difference how he got it, nor what are his antecedents. It doesn't matter if he is just from the hands of the physician, cured of a loathsome disease; if he have the cash he is the man. To him who bids highest, in the parlance of the auctioneer, the article is knocked down.

Everybody knows that this is the ruling spirit, not at watering places only, but in so-called best society everywhere. Marriages of love become rarer year after year, while those of convenience are proportionately on the increase. How much better is this than the actual exposure and sale, of Oriental practice? Yet we boast of superior intelligence, purity and morals! and we prate of the holy marriage covenant! Verily, we "make clean the outside of the platter, but within are dead men's bones and all uncleanliness."

I respect and honor the needy woman who, to procure food for herself and child, sells her body to some stranger for the necessary money; but for that legal virtue which sells itself for a lifetime for a home, with an abhorrence of the purchaser, and which at the same time says to the former, "I am holier than thou," I have only the supremest contempt. If there is anything that is vulgar it is a modern fashionable marriage. The long retinue, the church, the priest—all to do what? To give the bride, sexually, to the bridegroom. It is a public notice that these people, who have been everything else to each other, are now united sexually. Why, modesty itself should forbid such a parade!

But would you break up that which is called prostitution? The women can do it if they will. The virtuous women of an eastern city recently made an effort. They called secret meetings, and resolved to visit "the houses" and learn who it was that supported them, and then afterward to ostracize them. The visiting began. The New York papers were filled with the matter; day after day column after column was devoted to this crusade. After a week it suddenly stopped. The press was mystified. What was the matter? Had the women succeeded? Nothing could be learned. Finally one of the keenest of the metropolitan Bohemians determined to solve the matter. He visited this inland city; but not a word from the recently zealous women. They said they had abandoned the project; but would give no reason. At last he visited the keepers of the houses, and from them he got the key to the sudden closing of the campaign. "The women," they said, "pressed their investigations until they pressed themselves into the faces of the best men of the city, some of them their husbands and brothers; and considering that they could not ostracize this class of persons they went home and delivered 'Caudle Lectures' instead."

Now I will tell you wherein they failed, and why they were not honest. When they found their best men—their husbands and brothers—were supporting these women—consorting with them of course—they should have taken them home and seated them at their tables beside their companion, and said: "If you are good enough for our husbands to consort with, you are good enough to sit at our tables with them, and to occupy their homes with us, and to visit where we visit, and generally to be our companions."

If the women, in every city where there are professional prostitutes, would organize, and agree to bring the women home to the men who visit them, prostitution, so called, would be abolished at once. It is the women who stand in the way. They, knowing that their husbands visit these women, continue to live on, doing their best to damn the women, but saying nothing about the men. They probably forget that the wife who consorts with the man whom she knows consorts with prostitutes, is just as bad as they are.

But where is prostitution in its greatest luxury? At Washington. There are to be found the most elegant mansions, most sumptuously furnished. Why all this magnificence? Why, indeed! Because in Washington there are assembled the best, the most brilliant men in the nation—the men to whom the people have committed the national interests and who conduct the national affairs. Of course there should be all the elegance that wealth can furnish for the accommodation of such men. And there is; of course there : And they know how to appreciate it, I can assure you.

Everybody knows what the "third house" in Washington is. It consists of the lobbyists who are there to obtain legislation—to push this little scheme, or that small appropriation. Large sums of money are expended by this lobby. When a particular scheme is to come up, its friends distribute ten, fifteen and even twenty thousand dollars among the mistresses of these houses. Why? To secure their influence with Representatives and Senators. You needn't take my word for this; anybody who will inquire can learn the truth. Of course none of these gentlemen ever visit these houses to get under this purchased influence. Oh no! It is exerted upon them by these women magnetically, from afar off, of course it is.

I say it boldly, that it is the best men of the country who support the houses of prostitution. It isn't your young men, but the husbands and fathers of the country, who occupy positions of honor and trust. It is not the hard-working, industrial masses at all, but those who have money and time to expend for such purposes, who are really the old hoary-headed villains of the country. The young haven't money enough to support themselves. So when you condemn the poor women, whom you have helped to drive to such a life, remember to visit your wrath upon the best men of the country as well.

And when legislators discuss Social Evil bills let the women demand equality for their outraged sisters. These bills are professedly to prevent the spread of venereal diseases, and they provide for the medical examination and registration of women to effect it. Now if they really wish to stop these diseases and make the business safe, why not register and examine every man who visits these houses before he is admitted. A house of prostitution, free from disease cannot be contaminated, except through the visits of diseased men. Examine the men, then, and deny admission to the diseased, and there will be an end of the business. How many Social Evil bills would be passed under such conditions? Echo answers, "How many?"

But we are told that prostitution is a "necessary evil," and long articles are published tending to establish this proposition. Necessary for what? So that men may satiate their sexual demands. This is the plain English of it! Mothers, what does this say to you? This, and it is a blotch of infamy upon womanhood that can never be effaced except by woman herself rising in the dignity and divinity of her maternal nature and making a falsity of the damning fact: that you must yearly contribute a certain percentage of your daughters to fill the infernal maw of prostitution; give them up to be sunk in infamy, to be abhorred of their sisters and despised of their brothers; in a word, to walk the prostitutes' road to hell.

Necessary evil! Necessary indeed! Isn't it rather your shame, and my shame, and the dishonor of womanhood and the disgrace of manhood that should make the stones weep to contemplate—a million of innocent, virgin girls of from twelve to sixteen years of age—your daughters, mine, perhaps sacrificed to this "necessary evil" every fifteen years! Think of it, mothers, and let the blush of shame never fade from your cheeks until this infamy is blotted from existence; or until you have made the victims of this "necessary evil" as respectable as its promoters and supporters.

Statistics inform us that there are two hundred and fifty thousand professional prostitutes in the country, nearly one-tenth of whom are in New York City; and that these are visited and supported by not less than two and a half millions of men —one-third of the voting population of the country. Think of it! A quarter of a million professional female prostitutes and two and a half millions of professional male prostitutes, or ten men to one woman. And yet Congress is wonderfully concerned about Utah. Consistency is a jewel which Congressmen don't seem to carry about with them. They must be jealous of the Mormons. If the proportions were reversed so that there would be ten women to one man on their side of the question, they would probably let Brigham alone, and think it rather a nice thing to be a Mormon ; but Brigham has got the better of them; 'twas very wicked of him to go and do such a thing ; very, very wicked that he should, in a small way, presume to imitate both the meekest and the wisest of the Biblical fathers.

But love and lust are terms equally misapplied even by the most brilliant minds. Love is an universal principle. It is the life of the universe. It is that power called attraction which holds all things together. It is that force which unites the two elements from which water is formed and the two natures of which a sexual unit is composed. It uplifts the mountains and depresses the valleys ; causes the water to flow and the clouds to float; the lily to blossom and the violet to bloom ; the dew to fall and the storm to descend ; it is the living and motive power of the world ; it is God.

The Christian tells the same story, but he speaks in a language which he does not understand—God is Love. If this be so, then Love is God ; then all the love there is, is God ; but this love they tell us is free. I have been endeavoring to convince them of the truth of their own most cherished, though heretofore meaningless proverb, so that they may appreciate its beauty and bask in its glory, and for my pains I am dubbed "the Devil." I have tried to show that all love must be as they say that God is—Free ; that love cannot be confined to the limits of a man-made law any more than God can be shut up in a creed. Attempt to put the limits of a written law about love, saying, thus far and no farther, and love is destroyed. It is no longer love, because it is limited, and love, being God, cannot be limited.

When a limit is placed upon anything that by nature is free, its action becomes perverted. All the various attractions in the world are but so many methods by which love manifests itself. The attraction which draws the opposites in sex together is sexual love. The perverted action of sexual love, when limited by law or otherwise, is lust. All sexual manifestations that are not free are the perverted action of love—are lust. So, logically, the methods enforced by man to ensure purity convert love into lust. Legal sexuality is enforced lust. All the D. D.'s and LL. D.'s in the world, though they have all the mental gifts and the tongues of angels, cannot controvert the proposition.

This brings us to a still more serious part of my subject. Remember I am to withhold nothing—no fact, no advice. We are now face to face with the most startling and the most common fact connected with the miseries of marriage. But I know of no author, no speaker who has dared to call attention to, or to suggest a remedy for it, or even to hint at it as needing a remedy, or to recognize its existence in any manner.

It will be remembered that early in the evening I showed that marriage when analyzed, is a license to cohabit sexually. Now I am going to show that the enforcement of this method eventually defeats the original object. I state it without fear of contradiction by fact or of refutation by argument that it is the common experience among the married who have lived together strictly according to the marriage covenant, for from five to ten years, that they are sexually estranged. There may be, I know there are, exceptions to this rule, but they are the exceptions and not the rule. It is a lamentable fact that all over this country there is a prolonged wail going up on account of this condition. Sexual estrangement in from five to ten years! Think of it, men and women whom Nature has blessed with such possibilities for happiness as are conferred on no other order of creation—your God-ordained capacity blasted, prostituted to death, by enforced sexual relations where there is neither attraction or sexual adaptation; and by ignorance of sexual science!

Some may assert, as many do, that failure in sexual strength is intellectual and spiritual gain. Don't harbor the unnatural lie. Sexuality is the physiological basis of character and must be preserved as its balance and perfection. To kill out the sexual instinct by any unnatural practice or repression, is to emasculate character; is to take away that which makes what remains impotent for good—fruitless, not less intellectually and spiritually than sexually.

It is to do even more than this. From the moment that the sexual instinct is dead in any person, male or female, from that moment such person begins actually to die. It is the fountain from which life proceeds. Dry up the fountain and the stream will disappear. It is only a question of time, and of how much is obtained from other fountains, when the stream will discharge its last waters into the great ocean of life.

Others again seem to glory over the fact that they never had any sexual desire, and to think that this desire is vulgar. What! Vulgar! The instinct that creates immortal souls vulgar! Who dare stand up amid Nature, all prolific and beautiful, whose pulses are ever bounding with the creative desire, and utter such sacrilege! Vulgar, indeed! Vulgar, rather, must be the mind that can conceive such blasphemy. No sexual passion, say you? Say, rather, a sexual idiot, and confess that your life is a failure, your body an abortion, and no longer bind your shame upon your brow or herald it as purity. Call such stuff purity. Bah! Be honest, rather, and say it is depravity.

It is not the possession of strong sexual powers that is to be deprecated. They are that necessary part of human character which is never lacking in those who leave their names standing high in the historic roll. The intellect, largely developed, without a strong animal basis is never prolific of good in any direction. Evenly balanced natures, in which there are equal development and activity of all departments are those which move the world palpably forward for good; but if superiority of any kind is desirable at all, let it be in the animal, since with this right, the others may be cultivated to its standard. If this be wanting, however, all possible cultivation, intellectually, will only carry the individual further away from balance, and make the character still more "out of tune" with nature. These are physiological facts inherent in the constitution of mankind, and they cannot be ignored with impunity. No reliable theory of progressive civilization can ever be established that does not make them its chief corner stone, because they are the foundation upon which civilization rests.

It is the misuse, the abuse, the prostitution of the sexual instinct that is to be deprecated. Like all other capacities, it needs to be educated, cultivated, exercised rightly, and to do this is to live in accordance with nature and as commanded by the higher law, that law which every one finds deep-seated in his soul, and whose voice is the truest guide. When the world shall rise from its degradation into the sphere of this law, when the sexual act shall be the religion of the world, as it is now my religion, then, and then only, may we reasonably hope that its redemption is nigh.

What other religion so near alike to God—the all-loving, all-creating Father; or so much in harmony with Nature—the ever-receptive and ever-evolving Mother. Let your religious faith be what it may if it do not include the sexual act it is impotent. Make that act the most divine of all your worship. Let it be unto you without spot or blemish. Let it rise unto God a continual incense of piety and holiness, and be henceforth resurrected from the debauch in which the ages have sunk it. This is my religion—the fundamental principles for the generation of the race. Let it be yours and all mankind's, and with no other, the salvation long sought, long prayed for, long prophesied and long sung will soon be found. Discard it, put its life and health-giving blessings aside, and all the other religions ever conceived or dreamed, or that may be conceived of dreamed, combined, will be impotent to usher in the glad time.

Oh! that my lips were smitten with the inspiration of an archangel, that I might reach your hearts and show you the better life; that I might pierce your understandings and force in upon them the mighty import of these truths. Oh! that I could so appeal to my brothers everywhere, that forever after they would regard women as of angelic order, to be approached only as they would approach the enthroned Goddess of Purity, upon whose presence none would dare presume, and whose favors it is theirs to merit and receive, rather than to command and appropriate. Look not upon her for selfish purposes, but rather to bless her, let that blessing depend upon what it may, even if to bless is not to possess. Other love than this is selfishness, and a profanation of the Holy Word. That is love which will bless the object, even if to do so is to yield it. Remember that it is a pretension and a fraud to think of ownership in, or control over, the person of a woman. This is her inheritance, never to be bartered, never to be sold, never to be given away, even; but only to be exchanged, blessing for blessing, when an all-absorbing, all-embracing, all-desiring love points out the way.

And my sisters. Oh! what shall I say to them; how awaken them to realize the awful responsibilities conferred through their maternal functions. How shall I arouse, how startle them into a comprehension of the divinity of maternity; how sting them, if nothing else will do it, into self-respect? How shall I show them the destruction they have sown broadcast over the earth; how exhibit the black damnation, the sin, misery, shame, crime, disgrace, that come home to them as mothers; how stab their hearts with the awful monstrosities with which they have desecrated the earth; how bring to their hearts, to wring them in bitter anguish, the wild ravings of the maniac, the senseless drivel of the chattering idiot, the horrid delirium of the drunkard, the desolate moans of the "outcasts," the heart-sobs of criminals, the dreaded spectacle of the murderer, face to face with death? Ah! how adequately shall I bring these things—all these—home to the mothers of humanity; how make them feel the horrid misery that they have wrought by the outrage and desecration of their divine maternal functions?

Oh! mothers, that I could make you feel these things as I know them. I do not appeal to you as a novice, ignorant of what I speak, merely to excite your sympathies, but as one having learned through long years of bitter experience. Go where I have been; visit the prisons, insane asylums and the glittering hells that I have visited; see the maniac mother at the cell door of her son, to be hanged in the morning, as I have seen her—cursing God, cursing man, cursing until nothing but curses filled the air, and until their fury flecked her face with foam, that her crime should be visited upon her poor, poor boy. Follow her home, and when the agony of the gallows has come and gone, ask her the meaning of all this, and she will tell you, as she has told me: "That boy was forced upon me; I did not want him; I was worn out by child-bearing; and I tried, in every way I knew, to kill him in my womb. I thought of nothing else until it was too late to think of that. I failed. He was born; and I have made him a murderer. He committed the deed, and has suffered an ignominious death; but I am the real criminal.

"But I did not do this willfully. I had never been taught any better—never been told the fearful effect of such acts and deeds upon the unborn child. I followed the common practices of my friends. I did not know I was stamping my child with the brand of Cain. But all this did not save him. He was hanged for my crime."

But look upon another scene. Go home with me and see desolation and devastation in another form. The cold, iron bolt has entered my heart and left my life a blank, in ashes upon my lips. Wherever I go I carry a living corpse in my breast, the vacant stare of whose living counterpart meets me at the door of my home. My boy, now nineteen years of age, who should have been my pride and my joy, has never been blessed by the dawning of reasoning. I was married at fourteen, ignorant of every thing that related to my maternal functions. For this ignorance, and because I knew no better than to surrender my maternal functions to a drunken man, I am cursed with this living death. Do you think my mother's heart does not yearn for the love of my boy? Do you think I do not realize the awful condition to which I have consigned him? Do you think I would not willingly give my life to make him what he has a right to be? Do you think his face is not ever before me pressing me on to declare these terrible social laws to the world? Do you think with this sorrow seated on my soul I can ever sit quietly down and permit women to go on ignorantly repeating my crime? Do you think I can ever cease to hurl the bitterest imprecations against the accursed thing that has made my life one long misery? Do you think I can ever hesitate to warn the young maidens against my fate, or to advise them never to surrender the control of their maternal functions to any man! Ah! if you do, you do not know the agony that rests here. Not to do less than I am doing were madness; it were worse than crime; it were the essence of ten thousand crimes concentrated in one soul to sink it in eternal infamy.

Nor is this all that urges me onward. A few months ago I laid a beautiful sister away in Greenwood. Above her is written, "Cut off by marriage at thirty-one years." She had always opposed my social theories, though I knew her life was being sacrificed to a legal marriage. When on her death-bed she called me to her and said, "My darling sister, I am going to die. Oh! if I could have had the moral courage to have stood by you and to have broken loose from my thralldom I should not have been here. I knew you were right; but I could not endure the obloquy that the ungrateful world was heaping upon you. Knowing that I am to die I wanted to see you alone and ask your forgiveness for the anguish I have caused you by joining with the world to crush you out. It is meet that I should be sacrificed. I deserve it. It is just. But I shall soon be freed from the galling chains I dared not break myself, and will then be near you to make you bold and strong, and in so far as I can, repair the injury I have done."

My brothers and sisters, I never walk upon a platform without feeling the presence of that darling sister; and I now see her beautiful face flitting above me, hear her sweet voice encouraging me, and feel her magnetic power inspiring me to do my duty. "Cut off by marriage at thirty-one" rings in my ears, and I repeat it to the world as the mournful refrain of millions of wives, who, like her, were its victims; who, like her, after suffering untold miseries for years, went down to untimely graves murdered by the men to whom marriage sold them sexually.

When I review the conditions under which humanity is born I am surprised, not so much that it is so bad, but that it is so good. I do not wonder that there are all classes of criminals, that there are all sorts of diseases, that there are all grades of intellect; I do not wonder that debauchery and drunkenness meet us at every hand, and that lust in adults and sexual vice in children are sapping the life of the people; nor that in summing them all up and calculating their effects that the conclusion is reached that unless there soon come a change the American people will be blotted out. And then tell me that I shall not discuss the sexual question! I should like to see the power or law that can prevent me.

You remember that little game was tried in New York, and failed. When I published the biography of the American Pope, the United States authorities, urged on by the minions of the Church—the Y. M. C. Assassination Association—swooped down upon me and carried me off to jail, not for libel on the Pope, but for obscenity. I remained there quietly enough for some weeks, trusting that the outrage upon the freedom of the press and free speech would rouse the people to my defense against such an unwarrantable act. But Beecher was bigger than a free press—of more consequence than free speech. His danger cowed the whole country into silence; and the people sneaked after the trail of the popular preacher, in abject submission. "It was well worth the while of the United States to protect the reputation of a revered citizen," said District-Attorney Noah Davis; and the whole country complacently repeated it.

What was a little woman, in jail, compared with Mr. Beecher! What if a free press and free speech were imprisoned with her—were struck down in her person! What were they to the American people when Mr. Beecher was in danger; and through him the whole rascally set of fifty thousand preachers; and through them, again, the Christian Church everywhere! If she were to rot in jail, what was that beside the necessity of "hushing things up;" of strangling the scandal before it should spread into other churches all over the country and show them all rotten? Simply nothing.

It was the United States that held me illegally imprisoned. It was the people everywhere, you among the rest. But you did not raise a single voice at the outrage. You left me powerless in the cell of the State while the Church carried the key. But if you were dead to the infamy, I was not. I saw it was useless to wait for the people to protest, so I gave battle alone. I went into the combat single-handed against both Church and State led on by all their minions, and with the aid of honest Judge Blatchford, I whipped the whole cowardly crowd. I will speak what I will; and I will publish the truth about any professional hypocrite when I think I can render the world a service by so doing. I have just come from a second fight with them. In the first it was free press and free speech, that triumphed. In the second it was Free Love, and the victory in both instances was complete. I don't think they will try it over again; but if they do, I'll fight them again, armed with truth and with justice, and have no fears for the result.

But to return from this digression, let us inquire the real end to be gained by reform. The pretense of every reform ever advanced has been to better the condition of the people. But first and last—one and all—they have dealt with existing conditions—with effects—endeavoring to mitigate and cure evils, instead of preventing them. No sooner is one evil cured than the causes that produced it send forth another that requires to be cured; and thus reform, traveling in circles, has made but little real advance, except in the direction of intellectual development, in which a different practice has prevailed. People are better, intellectually, than they were; but not so physically or morally.

There can be a better race only by having better children. If they are bad, good men and women are impossible. There can be better children only through better conditions of generation; a better understanding by women of the processes of gestation, and better methods of rearing and education. These propositions are self-evident, and point directly to the sexual relations as the place to begin the work of improving the race. All effects in other directions, however promising, will prove futile for permanent good. The necessity for regeneration must be replaced by proper generation. If all women in the country were to join the temperance crusaders they might, for the time, decrease drunkenness; but the moment they should cease their efforts it would return. Now let these women go home and breed no more drunkards, and the remedy will be effectual. And so of all other vices and crimes.

Not long ago, when passing through Janesville, Wisconsin, a young man who had heard me lecture about the pre-natal effect of the mother's conduct upon the child, came and asked me to look at his breast. I did so. It was covered with bottles. When his mother was carrying him she was in the habit of going into her uncle's liquor store and tasting his liquor. The result was she "marked" him with bottles. Of course this young man is a confirmed drunkard. He might be importuned into signing the pledge a hundred times, but he would always break it at the first opportunity. And what is true of him is also true of nearly every other drunkard. They are made so by their mothers, or else they inherit it from their fathers. The temperance crusade, then, must begin in the home, in the marriage bed, in begetting children, and in proper surroundings and influences for the mother during gestation. Nothing else will ever cure the world of drunkenness, or any other vice.

The power of the mother over the unborn child, for evil, is too well attested by too many facts to need further elucidation. But it teaches a lesson of mighty import which ought to receive universal consideration. If her powers for ill are so marked, what must they be for good, when exercised under an enlightened understanding! Nothing is more certain than that mothers can make their children just what they want them to be, limited only by the inherited tendencies of the father.

There are, then, but two questions in this whole matter of reforming the world ; but they are vital and inseparable. The first is, to discover and develop the science of proper generation, so that all the inherited tendencies may be good; and the second is, that the germ life, once properly begun, may not be subjected to any deleterious influences, either during the period of gestation or development on to adult age.

This is the meaning of social reform. It means better children, and it doesn't care how they are to be obtained—only to obtain them. Any methods that will secure them are good, are true, are pure, are virtuous methods. The question to be asked of the mothers of the future will not be, "Who is the father?" but, "How good is the child?" If it be not good it will be a disgrace to the mother, no matter if the father is her legal husband.

I say it, and I want the world to know that I say it, that a woman who bears a dozen or less scraggy, scrawny, puny, half-made-up children, by a legal father, is a disgrace to her sex and a curse to the community ; while she who bears as many perfect specimens of humanity, no matter if it be by as many different fathers, is an honor to womanhood and a blessing to the world. And I defy both the priests and the law to prove this false.

Every sensible man and woman will have to admit it. It is a self-evident proposition.

In August, 1873, at the Silver Lake camp meeting, I said, before fifteen thousand persons, that no one knows who his father is. Think of it for a moment, and you will see how impossible it is that he should know. Can any person make oath that he knows who it was who, in unity with his mother, was his father? He may swear that he has been told so, but that does not amount to knowledge. I made this statement, not specially to declare this fact, but to enforce the argument that it doesn't make any difference who may be the father of any child, if he is only a good child and an honor to his mother. I have repeated this statement a hundred times since, and never a hiss. Hasn't the sexual question grappled with the thoughts of the people? This is an evidence not to be misunderstood.

But among all the radical things I have never quite equaled one recently published in *The Popular Science Monthly*, in an article written by Mr. Herbert Spencer, the acknowledged philosopher of the age. Quoting from an eminent English surgeon, he says: "It is a lamentable truth that the troubles which respectable, hard-working married women undergo are more trying to the health and detrimental to the looks than any of the irregularities of the harlot's career." What a commentary is this on the marriage institution! Much the larger part of the married women of the world in a worse condition, as to health and looks, than are the harlots! Take that home with you, and think of it, and see if you can come to any other conclusion than that an institution that produces such results in women, needs to be replaced by something better. Now don't forget that these are not my words, and say that I advocate prostitution; but remember that they are the words of the highest authority in philosophy and science now living, published in the most popular monthly in the country, and give them weight accordingly.

There are many popular fallacies about prostitution. Statistics inform us that the average life of prostitutes is about four years; but this does not show the real causes of such fatality. It leaves it to be inferred that it is in the fact of prostitution merely. It does not say that it is caused by dissolute living, and drinking, and by the diseases which usually accompany promiscuous intercourse.

The real truth about this is that those prostitutes who never drink, and who never permit themselves to become diseased are among the healthiest of women, and hold their beauty and vigor to an advanced age. Is this a startling assertion? Anybody who will take the trouble can easily confirm it. I do not make it without the most unmistakable proof, which is open to all inquirers, as it was to me, to obtain. It was necessary for me to know by personal investigation, and it shows me as it will everybody else that what Herbert Spencer writes in *The Pop-*

ular Science Monthly is true : that the promiscuous life of the harlot is less detrimental to health and beauty than is the common life of the married slave. The reason is simple and clear. Promiscuous intercourse, when sexual conditions are imperfect, when the act is not based on mutual love and desire, is better than so-called monogamic intercourse under the same conditions, made more intolerable by a deep-seated disgust. But by no means is this an argument against monogamy. It is an argument against legal monogamy when the monogamy of nature is wanting; and, as such, is the most convincing that can be offered in favor of monogamy founded upon love. Free relations of any kind are better than any can be that are enforced These are the logical deductions from the facts. I did not create the facts, so if you have fault to find, find it with them and not me. I merely offer them to you for consideration, so that you may think of and discuss this subject understandingly.

I have already said that the salvation of the world can come only through better children. This fact has been widely recognized by all so-called Christian denominations. Each is very anxious to get hold of the children. The Romanist says : "Give me the children for twenty-five years and I will make the world Catholic." True enough. They have taken a step in the right direction, but only a step. They say : give me the children, good or bad. The reformer, who shall really save the world, must go another step and see that there are none but good children born. Then the root of the matter will be reached.

But how to accomplish this is now the vital question. Many may think that I am too severe on my sex—on the mothers ; but I wish I could be ten times more so, because, and I say it in sorrow, this is a work for the mothers, to the fearful importance of which I fear they cannot be roused. They have a terrible responsibility resting upon them and a fearful preliminary task to perform. They have got first to conquer their sexual liberty, so that their maternal functions shall be under their own control at all times ; and next to guard them from contamination, so that their children may be pure.

I do not complain of women as willfully sending the race onward to destruction, I only wish to show them that they are doing it, and to urge them by every argument that my woman's nature can suggest, or my mother's heart conceive, to stop the desolation. What can I say ? How shall I plead with them to reach their hearts and rouse them into consciousness upon this terrible theme ? Shall I remind them again of the death of one half of their children ? Shall I show them the still-born babes, strangled at birth because they are not wanted ? Shall I tell them that the birth-rate among the more intelligent classes has decreased one-half in twenty years by abortions ; and that, unless these things cease, the race will ultimately be blotted out ?

Or shall I turn to the other side of the picture and show them the awful fact that nine women in ten are so diseased, sexually, as to make them unfit to become mothers, brought to this condition by their efforts to prevent pregnancy, or to procure abortions, or by continually submitting to undesired intercourse until the sexual instinct is dead; and that if these conditions go on for twenty years it will be impossible for women even to become pregnant?

Or, again, shall I ask them to look on the faces of their children and see the history of sexual vice indelibly written—their boys and their girls, the former in the first stages of self-abuse, or, having too late discovered their danger, in the last stages of spermatorrhea; and the latter, pale, yellow and dejected from irregularities, or, having too late discovered their cause, prostrated by leucorrhœa and prolapsus uteri?

And having done this, shall I ask them if they wonder that these things are so, when they remember that they were constantly debauched by the insatiable lust of their husbands during the whole period in which they were bearing these children beneath their hearts? What else can be expected than premature and precocious development of the sexual passions in children when, during their gestation, the influence of this passion is continually forced upon them; or what else than that this passion should be vented in vicious ways which carry their victims down to certain destruction?

Or what other pictures can I bring to lay at the feet of mothers to show them the horrors they are working for humanity by this willing sexual slavery in which they slumber as if nothing were the matter? Oh! let me plead with mothers in the name of future generations to rescue your divinely ordered maternity from the horrid debauch in which it is plunged. Let me implore you for your own soul's future happiness to emancipate yourselves, at whatever cost, from the awful crime of sexual slavery, so that you may dedicate your lives to the good of future generations rather than to expend them in ministering to the lustful demands of legal masters. Let me urge upon you, for your own sakes, the strict observance of the laws of your sexual natures, and to never permit their divine instincts to be trifled with or debauched by any man, whether he be husband or lover. Let me beg of you, for humanity's sake, to rescue yourselves from this thralldom of license, snatch yourselves from the rude grasp of lust, and elevate yourselves from the quagmire of disgust into which license and lust have cast you, so that womanhood may once more become Queen of purity, nobility and virtue.

Instead of supporting churches and sending missionaries to the heathen; of praying and singing to convert the liquor-sellers; of building and supporting hospitals for foundlings and for women about to become illegal mothers; of erecting penitentiaries, insane asylums, alms-houses and gallows, let the women come together in solemn conclave and register an eternal vow that they will never bear any more children to fill these places. Let them swear by the God of humanity that they will never again become pregnant of an undesired child. Let them enter a solemn oath that they will never again surrender their sexual or maternal functions to be outraged by undesired commerce. Let the women come together and do these things in earnest and the world will be saved from that time.

I repeat that I do not complain of women as willful perpetrators of all these crimes; but I charge it home upon the intelligent men, upon the teachers, preachers, and doctors especially, that they willfully keep the rest of the world in ignorance of the truths about sexual debauchery. But still more specially do I hurl this indictment against the editors. They know these truths, but they know also if women generally come to a knowledge of them that the sexual domination of man will cease. Hence by blackguarding me they hope to frighten the women away, so that I may not reach their ears. But, thank heaven, they cannot entirely shut them out. Some there are who, having suffered, and knowing there is something wrong somewhere, have the moral courage to come for the facts, and they go away and repeat them to others, until there is a general inquiry among women all over the country to offset this attempt at suppression on the part of men. Some papers also dare sometimes to hint at the facts; sometimes publishing what I say, but taking care to condemn me editorially, so as to make the editorial censure wash the reportorial facts.

The scientific journals and monthlies are filled with articles leading directly to the solution of this question where ten years ago there was not so much as a word to be seen in any publication about sexual subjects, even hinting in the remotest manner that there was anything rotten sexually. If I do nothing else I know that I have awakened investigation on this subject. If all I have said is error; if the truth lie in altogether different directions from those in which I point, out of the discussion now going on the truth will be evolved.

But what is more surprising to me than everything else is that the Chicago *Times*—a paper in which I have been perhaps more vilely abused than in any other—in its issue of April 5th, published, editorially, the following statement: "Could society by some omnipotent fiat determine that, from to-day no sexual intercourse should occur, save in cases where there is a *mens sana in corpore sana* (meaning sound minds in sound bodies) less than half a century hence would witness the closing of hospitals, saloons, penitentiaries and 'houses;' the extinction, almost to a man, of physicians; and the cessation of nearly every movement whose purpose is the lessening of human suffering and vice. Taxes would sink to the minimum; men and women would tread the earth with the springy, buoyant step of perfect health; and the millennium would commence its glorious reign upon this our sin-bestridden and disease-cursed earth." I have never said more than this. If you will not listen to my pleading, accept those of the most influential and widely-circulated journal of the great North-West, and I will rest content to let it speak for me.

Now can you understand for what I have been made the victim of such vile abuse? The truths which I have presented to you are those I have always sought to enforce. I have always contended that, if there is to be any ostracism for prostitution, the men should suffer equally with the women; that the seducer should be held up to the same scorn and contempt that is visited upon the seduced. I have asked for equality—nothing more; and I will accept nothing less for my sex, let them heap whatever contumely they may upon me.

It would appear from their opposition that women do not want the ostracism of male prostitutes, or to be deprived of them as companions; that they do not want the seducer debarred from their society, and he is usually a "lion" among them; that they do not want to own and control their maternal functions and sexual instincts; that they do not want to have the right to say when they shall bear children and when not'; but, on the contrary, that they want to be owned, want to be supported by men, in return for the sexual favors which they can confer. They don't want reform; they want things to remain as they are.

Isn't this a legitimate conclusion? Think of it, women of the nineteenth century! Shall your names go down to posterity in such connection? Let me warn you this is where they are going. In September, 1872, I said, before a convention in Boston: I believed that, in twenty years, the daughters of to-day, then grown, would regard their mothers as having been the real prostitutes of this time. If what I have presented are facts, wouldn't it be a just verdict?

A popular objection against Free Love is, that it breaks up families. My answer to this indictment is, that a family which falls in pieces when Free Love strikes it, is already broken up, and waiting for a loophole out of which to escape; and as the press have coupled my name with this *role*, the discontented think it a good thing to shift whatever opprobrium there may be connected with their cases, upon Woodhull. Thus I become the pack-horse for thousands who have no more conception of Free Love than a donkey has of mathematics.

But I'll tell you what I do. If a husband or a wife get discontented and uneasy, and chafe in their bonds, I advise such to seek out the ulcers, come to a mutual understanding, talk out the hidden and corroding cause, sum up the difficulties and grievances and see if they are of such character and magnitude as to preclude all hope for peace and happiness, and not under any circumstances call in the services of a blackguard lawyer.

I ask men and women to be honest with each other. If any

find their attachments growing cold—their love waning—say so, and not continue the pretense while the real love is lavished elsewhere. I ask men and women to be thoughtful of each other's needs and desires. If a wife find her husband spending his evenings away from home, let her be sure there is something wrong; and when he goes again, put on hat and shawl and accompany him. If it is to the club, the bar-room, the billiard table, the theatre, the opera or the house of ill-fame, tell him that any place which he frequents is good enough for you to visit. Face him in his discontent, and say: "What is the matter, my darling? What is it in which I fail that you must spend your evenings away from me? Has your love for me gone, or what is the matter? Tell me? It is useless to continue an unhappy life when there is so easy a remedy. If you do not love me any longer, take me into your confidence; let me be your friend and adviser."

If there is any basis of hope left, this course will develop it; and there are hundreds of families who owe their present unity and happiness to having followed it. It is an error into which people naturally fall who think that my supporters are among the dissatisfied families. It is precisely the reverse of this. It is the families which cannot be separated or broken up which believe in the efficacy of freedom as a regulative element. My most bitter opponents among my own sex, are the professional prostitutes who know I am going to break up their business, and the ignorant wives who read little and think less, and who are in constant fear of losing their "Paw," over whom they have none except a legal control; and among the opposite sex, those who are habitually unfaithful to marriage, and the ministers who know their nice arrangements will be spoiled, and the lawyers, whose divorce business will be ruined by freedom. Ask any of these, when found denouncing Mrs. Woodhull, if they ever heard her speak, or ever read her paper or speeches, the reply will be, "No! and I don't want to."

But I would remind these exceedingly virtuous people that the Catholic says, that every one who was not married by the Catholic method is living in prostitution. So please remember when they cast their epithets about so freely, that there is a greater authority than they are, which denounces them in equally opprobrious terms. This class say that those living together who are not married as they are, are prostitutes; the Catholic Church looks at them, and, because they are not married as it marries, calls them by the same name.

For my part I look beyond the ceremony and the law, and observe the facts; and if I find people living together in hate and disgust, whether married after the Protestant fashion or the Catholic style, I say they are prostituting their sexual functions, and in sight of the God of Nature are prostitutes.

Let us consider briefly the doctrine of stirpiculture, hinted at in the *Times* quotation. Nobody, more than I, feels the need of scientific propagation; but there is something in men and women of which science can neither take cognizance or control. Men and women are more than animals; and this additional quantity must be recognized in any successful theory about this matter. Stirpiculture, popularly understood, means that the best men and women, physically, produce the best children. This theory may be, and doubtless is, true as applied to animals; but observation does not bear out its truth among men and women. Many physically perfect men and women bear bad children. With them, the theory as stated needs to be supplemented as follows: Provided love exists between them.

Women cannot bear their best children except by the men they love best and for whom they have the keenest desire. If these are for the best men, physically, so much the better. There are instances where the husband or the wife, and some, where both, from inherited causes, have bad health, who rear families of robust children; but in these cases there is a sexual unity which exalts the creative act far above the possibility of inherited contagion; while others whose children should apparently rank high, physically and mentally, are remarkably deficient in both regards. Nothing is more common than mediocre children in families representing the intellect and morality of the age; nor the brightest gems where none would think of finding them.

These facts are too common to be ignored; and they lead unerringly to the conclusion that this science, as applied to animals, cannot be practiced by men and women. It would find an insuperable argument in the repugnance which exists instinctively in women against consorting with men for whom they have no love. Women would revolt against such a theory, and the disgust that would accompany its practice would have a deleterious influence upon the intended result far outweighing any benefit that might be anticipated from mere physical perfection. This alone is a fatal objection, and makes it necessary that other considerations should enter any successful theory for the scientific breeding of humanity.

But of what use is it to talk of stirpiculture while marriage exists? The very first necessity is freedom for woman, sexually. What can a woman do with a theory so long as she belongs, legally, to any man? It is preposterous to think of it. Argue stirpiculture to a woman who is compelled to submit herself, sexually, to a legal master whenever he demands it, even to the extent of brutality! It is simply nonsense. Talk of scientific propagation to a woman bound to a man whose system is loaded with venereal, scrofula or other loathsome disease! It is absurd. Present any theory of sexual intercourse for the observance of women, so long as they have no control over their maternal functions! It is insanity. When men do not and will not respect either the wishes or desires of their wives, or the remittant bodily conditions peculiar to women, nor their physical health, however bad it may be—of what use is it to offer women a theory to regulate reproduction! Better spend breath asking the sun to stand still or the moon to visit the earth, than commit the absurdity of offering stirpiculture to married women.

When any of the old-fashioned religious denominations have revivals, they extend a general invitation to sinners to come forward and relate their experiences and be converted; to tell how bad they were before they were better. If this is a good thing to do religiously, why would it not be equally good socially? I'll take the first six married women anywhere, and if they are forced to tell the whole truth about their sexual experience, there would be no further argument necessary to prove that it's idle to talk of stirpiculture so long as women do not own and control their sexual organs; therefore, the first thing for women to do, is to declare themselves free; to assert their individual sovereignty sexually. Until they have the moral courage to do this, and therefore to rescue themselves from prostitution, stirpiculture will do for those to play with who dare not touch the main question.

I have been shown, instinctively, as you would call it, clairvoyantly as I would say, the solution of this whole matter; but have not yet been able to reason it out so as to demonstrate it logically. But when impregnation takes place under perfect conditions of love and desire and their mutual consummation, the same process occurs regarding physical impurities as related to the new germ life, that takes place when water is changed to ice. For instance, ice formed from salt water is not salt ice. Salt is a foreign substance to water, and in its natural changes is cast off. So impurities of the human system are foreign substances which, in perfected sexual conditions, form no part of the transmitted qualities. These conditions are to be found only where there is that perfect sexual exaltation which blends two beings in one—"two souls with but a single thought, two hearts that beat as one," that thought and beat being to reproduce their counterpart. Into such an act, no impurity can enter. It is God's sublimest creative impulse; and he who can think of it except in reverence, awe and gratitude, is unfit to enter its sacred chambers. Who can think of its wonders and beauties; its bliss and its holiness, and not worship Him who hath given such possibilities to man!

If this be so, and I feel I know it is, the doctrine of heredity and transmission will have to be remodeled, or rather abandoned, and the solution sought by them obtained in the science of sexuality—which is the science of life. I am the more inclined to this theory from the fact that some men, while sexually poisonous to some women, are a life-giving element to others. The private histories of the divorced and remarried, offer many facts of this kind, and they must form a part of any basis upon which a sexual science can be built.

I should be glad to follow stirpiculture further, but I must leave it by making these propositions, which to me are self-evident:

First—The highest order of humanity results from sexual relations in which love and desire are the only elements present.

Second—The lowest order of humanity results from sexual relations where there is disgust instead of delight, and endurance instead of reciprocity.

Third—The intermediate orders of humanity result from various modifications of these two extremes.

What then is to be inferred from all this, is the purity at which I aim, and to which sexual freedom, as I believe and teach it, will lead. Can any who have heard me, conceive that what I have said tends toward greater sexual debauchery and degradation than now exists? If there are any such they have misconceived the natural tendency of freedom. To pretend to believe that the giving of freedom to woman will plunge her deeper in vice, is to insult all womanhood; it is to pronounce upon woman the verdict that she is by nature inclined to sexual change, and this every woman knows is a lie. I hurl the infamous insinuation back in the teeth of whoever dare make it, as a libel upon my sex, based upon the practices of men and not upon the natural instincts of women.

I make the claim boldly, that from the very moment woman is emancipated from the necessity of yielding the control of her sexual organs to man to insure a home, food and clothing, the doom of sexual demoralization will be sealed. From that moment there will be no sexual intercourse except such as is desired by women. It will be a complete revolution in sexual matters, in which men will have to take a back seat and be content to be servants where they have been masters so long. The present system is at variance with everything in nature. Everywhere, except among men and women, the female has supreme authority in the domain of sex, and the male never pretends to oppose it, nor to appeal from its decisions. Compare men and women with the animals and see how far below them they have fallen in this regard. Yet among animals the principle of freedom is thoroughly exemplified. Why are they not degraded, debauched and diseased? Simply because the female is the dominant power in sex. What would be the result among animals were the barbarous rule of marriage enforced; were the female to be compelled to submit herself without reserve to the lecherous instincts of the male? It would be the same that has obtained among women—disease everywhere, until there is scarcely a sexually healthy woman past the age of puberty to be found. This is the purity, this the morality, this the divinity of marriage. Oh, God! is there no power that can restore woman to the level of the brutes? Is their nothing that can rescue her from this shameless condition, from this pollution, this nastiness?

To woman, by nature, belongs the right of sexual determination. When the instinct is aroused in her, then and then only should commerce follow. When woman rises from sexual slavery into freedom, into the ownership and control of her sexual organs, and man is obliged to respect this freedom, then will this instinct become pure and holy; then will woman be raised from the iniquity and morbidness in which she now wallows for existence, and the intensity and glory of her creative functions be increased a hundred-fold; then may men and women, like the beasts or the birds, if they will, herd together, and the instinct in woman, by the law of natural attraction and adaptation, rouse in man its answering counterpart, and its counterpart only.

This is the purity at which I aim; this is the holiness to which I would have woman and, through her functions, the sexual relations elevated; this is the glory with which I would have woman crowned; this is what it means to be virtuous; this what it means to be pure. Again I ask, is there a man or woman who hears me who will ever dare hereafter to associate this doctrine with the debased and the low, and call it an attempt to descend further into lust and license?

Oh, woman! would that the beautiful, the shining, the redeemed of heaven could come to you in their white-robed purity and sing in your ears the blessed song of the angels who "neither marry nor are given in marriage," and who live in their own natural element of freedom. Oh! that they could come to you as they have to me, and show how, through you, as represented by Eve—through your sexual slavery to men—has sin, and misery and crime been introduced into the world; and how through the assertion and maintenance of your sexual freedom and purity only, can "the seed of the woman bruise the serpent's head," and humanity be restored to its original sexual purity, the Scripture fulfilled and the millennium ushered in.

Instead of opposing this doctrine, the Churches should see that through its propagation only can their sacred prophecies be realized. Instead of denouncing me the ministers ought to be my most earnest advocates, not merely because through the theory of Free Love only can their lives be justified, but because by its practice alone can salvation come to the world. They have been working at the wrong end of salvation; they have been trying to save souls while their bodies were damned. Now let them save bodies, and the souls will take care of themselves. I should be glad to believe that these clerical persons are honest, but I cannot. They know the sad lives of thousands of women, suffering and yearning for comfort and sympathy; these women go to their pastors for relief, and I have the very best of reasons for believing, indeed, I know that in numerous instances, they not only get that for which they yearn, but also that further comfort and sympathy to which the others naturally lead, and which the ministers know they can so safely administer. This is another reason to be added to the matter of fees, which I have already mentioned, why this class do not wish the marriage relations disturbed. The ministers, lawyers and doctors have a monopoly of this field, and they intend to keep it.

The world will have a genuine surprise some day when it shall awaken to the truth, as I know it, about the churches; to a knowledge of the kind of currency in which lawyers often receive their divorce fees. As this, however, is none of my business, I shall let the world take its own time about it. But I sometimes think it would be only a just reward for their stupidity were husbands to be shown why it is that their wives are so earnest in religious matters. Everybody knows that the churches would totter and tumble if it were not for the women. Men have mostly grown out of churches, and attend them because their families wish it, so that the "pew rent" may be paid. There are many churches besides Plymouth in which half the women are in love with their pastors; and in these cases I think it safe to say, as it is in that of Plymouth, it is usually reciprocated.

But as to the difficulty of freedom for woman : There is but one, and that is pecuniary independence. I know that opposers refer to the condition of women in Greece and Rome, when there were few restrictions sexually, and use it as an argument against freedom now. But it doesn't apply, and I will show you why. In those times it mattered not whether there were marriage laws or not. In either case woman was dependent upon her sex for support ; if married, then upon her husband ; if not married, then upon her lover.

So the mere abolition of marriage does not necessarily mean sexual freedom for woman. I do not hesitate to admit that marriage has played its necessary part in the evolution of society ; nor that among a people where women have a very limited position in the industrial organization, that it provides them a support. I will go so far even as to say that, so long as women prefer to depend upon the sale of their sexual favors rather than upon their industrial capacities for support, that marriage may be deemed a sort of protection. But I also hold that, to a woman who prefers rather to rely upon her own talent for support, marriage is intolerable.

This is the same argument that was used by the slaveholders. "Slaves," they said, "were better off as slaves than they could be, free They need to be taken care of ; and until they are capable of self-support it is best that slavery continue." The slaves themselves generally coincided with this idea. Only a few of the more intelligent saw that the argument was a deceit.

So now do most women coincide with the same argument as applied to marriage. Only a few who have solved the question for themselves, see that it is fallacious. In spite of the argument the anti-slavery revolution came, and violently cast the slaves upon their own resources. Who is there who now dare say their condition is not improved? So will it be with women. They will hesitate to take the responsibility of freedom. They will say: "I prefer to rely upon my sex a little longer." But the revolution will come eventually, and thrust them upon their own resources; and in ten years nobody will be found to doubt that their condition has been improved.

But the old argument as applied to women is fallacious in still another way, as I will show. Suppose that all the women in the land, on a given day, should rise and throw off the yoke of marriage, and declare and hold themselves free, how long would it be before the men would accede to any terms? Do you think it would be a month—three weeks—two weeks? I haven't the slightest idea that they would hold out a single week. Women are entirely unaware of their power. Like an elephant led by a string, they are subordinated by a writing, drawn up by just those who are most interested in holding them in slavery. I am sometimes almost out of patience at the servility with which women fawn upon their masters, when they might lead them by the nose wherever they please.

It is sometimes asked: "If what you say is true, and that marriage is a curse, why did not the deprecated results obtain years ago?" I will show you why. It will be remembered that it used to be said by the slaveholders, that the moment a slave got the freedom crotchet into his head he was no longer of any account. A negro was a good slave so long as the idea of freedom was not born in his soul. Whenever this birth occurred he began to feel the galling of his chains.

It is the same with women. So long as they entertain the idea that their natural destiny is to be owned and cared for by some man, whom they are to repay by the surrender of their person, they are good, legal wives; but from the moment the notion that they have an individual right to themselves—to the control of their bodies and maternal functions—has birth in their souls, they become bad wives. They rebel in their souls, if not in words and deeds; and the legal claims of their husbands become a constant source of annoyance, and the enforcement of their legal rights an unbearable thing.

It is this repugnance, this sexual rebellion, that is causing the degradation and widespread disease among women, sexually; and this reacts upon man, and degrades him. The mind, in rebellion at the enslaved condition, has such an effect upon the sexual act that it becomes impossible for its subject to respond or reciprocate; and the organs suffer the natural penalty.

In speaking of this almost anomalous condition in woman, Dr. John M. Scudder, Professor of the Diseases of Women in the Cincinnati Medical College, says: "If the act is complete, so that both body and mind are satisfied, no disease arises, though there be frequent repetitions; but if the act be incomplete, the organs being irritated merely, and the mind not satisfied, then disease will surely follow. 'There is no doubt that the proper gratification of the function is conducive to health and longevity; or that its abuse leads to disease and shortens life. Therefore," he adds, "the wife should not lose control of her person in marriage. ·It is hers· to rule supreme in this regard. This is a law of life, and is violated in no species except in man."

What better confirmation could there be of all that I have been trying to enforce upon you, than these words from this large-hearted man and widely-experienced physician? Every wife should obtain the book from which I quote these words, and study it carefully. It is entitled, "The Reproductive Organs," and has just been published by Wilstach, Baldwin & Co., of Cincinnati, Ohio.

I said at the outset that I am endeavoring to effect a revolution in marriage, or rather to replace the institution by a better method of providing for women as mothers and children as progeny. Everybody admits that our social system is far from perfect. Society, like everything else in the universe, evolves by natural laws. Marriage is not the perfect condition. It will be replaced by another and more perfect, which will be a legitimate outcome of the old. As republicanism in politics is a legitimate child of constitutional monarchy, so in socialism shall personal freedom be the offspring of legal limitation; and when it shall come, not anybody will doubt its parentage or question its legitimacy. .

Sexual freedom, then, means the abolition of prostitution both in and out of marriage; means the emancipation of woman from sexual slavery and her coming into ownership and control of her own body; means the end of her pecuniary dependence upon man, so that she may never even seemingly, have to procure whatever she may desire or need by sexual favors; means the abrogation of forced pregnancy, of ante-natal murder, of undesired children; means the birth of love-children only, endowed by every inherited virtue that the highest exaltation can confer at conception, by every influence for good to be obtained during gestation, and by the wisest guidance and instruction on to manhood, industrially, intellectually and sexually.

It means no more sickness, no more poverty, no more crime: it means peace, plenty and security, health, purity and virtue; it·means the replacement of money-getting as the aim of life by the desire to do good; the closing of hospitals and asylums, and the transformation of prisons, jails and penitentiaries into workshops and scientific schools; and of lawyers, doctors and ministers into industrial artizans; it means equality, fraternity and justice raised from the existence which they now have in name only, into practical life; it means individual happiness, national prosperity and universal good.

Ultimately, it means more than this even. It means the establishment of co-operative homes, in which thousands who now suffer in every sense shall enjoy all the comforts and luxuries of life, in the place of the isolated households which have no care for the misery and destitution of their neighbors. It means for our cities, the conversion of innumerable huts into immense hotels, as residences ; and the combination of all industrial enterprises upon the same plan; and for the country, the co-operative conduct of agriculture by the maximum of improvements for labor-saving, and the consequent reduction of muscular toil to the minimum. And it means the inter-co-operation of all these in a grand industrial organization to take the places of the present governments of the world, whose social basis shall be all people united in the great human family as brothers and sisters.

So after all I am a very promiscuous Free Lover. I want the love of you all, promiscuously. It makes no difference who or what you are, old or young, black or white, Pagan, Jew, or Christian, I want to love you all and be loved by you all ; and I mean to have your love. If you will not give it to me now, these young, for whom I plead, will in after years bless Victoria Woodhull for daring to speak for their salvation. It requires a strong and a pure woman to go before the world and attack its most cherished institution. No one who has not passed through the fiery furnace of affliction, and been purged of selfishness by the stern hand of adversity, and become emancipated from public opinion, could stand the load of opprobium that I have been forced to carry. I sometimes grow weary under its weight and sigh for rest, but my duty to my sex, spurs me on. Therefore I want your sympathy, your sustaining love, to go with me and bless me ; and when I leave you for other fields of labor and stand upon other rostrums, fearing I may not be able to do my duty, I want to feel the yearnings of your hearts following me with prayers that my efforts may be blessed. I want the blessings of these fathers, the affections of these sons, the benedictions of these mothers and the prayers of these daughters to follow me everywhere, to give me strength to endure the labor, courage to speak the truth and a continued faith that the right will triumph.

And may the guardian angels who are hovering over you carry the benign light of freedom home to your souls to bless each sorrowing heart, to relieve each suffering body, and to comfort each distressed spirit as it hath need, is the blessing which I leave with you.

SOCIOLOGY

(6)

Stirpiculture . . . 1888

STIRPICULTURE;

OR,

THE SCIENTIFIC PROPAGATION OF THE HUMAN RACE.

BY

VICTORIA CLAFLIN WOODHULL MARTIN,

17, *Hyde Park Gate, S.W.*

FEBRUARY, 1888.

London, England.

ETERNAL JUSTICE.

By Charles Mackay.

———◆———

I.

The man is thought a knave, or fool
 Or bigot, plotting crime,
Who, for the advancement of his kind,
 Is wiser than his time.
For him the hemlock shall distil ;
 For him the axe be bared ;
For him the gibbet shall be built ;
 For him the stake prepared.
Him shall the scorn and wrath of men
 Pursue with deadly aim ;
And malice, envy, spite, and lies
 Shall desecrate his name.
But Truth shall conquer at the last,
 For round and round we run ;
And ever the Right comes uppermost,
 And ever is Justice done.

II.

Pace through thy cell, old Socrates,
 Cheerily to and fro ;
Trust to the impulse of thy soul,
 And let the poison flow.
They may shatter to earth the lamp of clay
 That holds a light divine,
But they cannot quench the fire of thought
 By any such deadly wine.
They cannot blot thy spoken words
 From the memory of man,
By all the poison ever was brewed
 Since time its course began.
To-day abhorred, to-morrow adored,
 So round and round we run ;
And ever the Truth comes uppermost,
 And ever is Justice done.

III.

Plod, Friar Bacon, in thy cave ;
    Be wiser than thy peers ;
Augment the range of human power,
    And trust to coming years.
They may call thee wizard, and monk accursed,
    And load thee with dispraise ;
Thou wert born five hundred years too soon
    For the comfort of thy days ;
But not too soon for humankind.
    Time hath reward in store ;
And the demons of our sires become
    The saints that we adore.
The blind can see, the slave is lord,
    So round and round we run ;
And ever the wrong is proved to be wrong,
    And ever is Justice done !

IV.

Keep, Galileo, to thy thought,
    And nerve thy soul to bear ;
They may gloat o'er the senseless words they wring
    From the pangs of thy despair ;
They may veil their eyes, but they cannot hide
    The sun's meridian glow ;
The heel of a priest may tread thee down,
    And a tyrant work thee woe ;
But never a truth has been destroyed ;
    They may curse it and call it crime ;
Pervert and betray, or slander and slay
    Its teachers for a time ;
But the sunshine aye shall light the sky,
    As round and round we run ;
And the Truth shall ever come uppermost,
    And Justice shall be done.

V.

And live there now such men as these—
    With thoughts like the great of old !
Many have died in their misery,
    And left their thought untold ;
And many live, and are ranked as mad,
    And placed in the cold world's ban,
For sending their bright far-seeing souls
    Three centuries in the van.
They toil in penury and grief,
    Unknown, if not maligned ;
Forlorn, forlorn, bearing the scorn
    Of the meanest of mankind !
But yet the world goes round and round,
    And the genial seasons run ;
And ever the Truth comes uppermost,
    And ever is Justice done !

STIRPICULTURE;

OR,

THE SCIENTIFIC PROPAGATION OF THE HUMAN RACE.

————◆————

THE goal to be attained, is the motive which impels people to action. Scarcely any action is performed without an end in view. Therefore mankind has acquired the habit of seeking for the ulterior motive which actuated this or that deed. All civilized nations have a code of laws. The motive which induced the framing of these laws was the necessity of having fixed rules which would regulate the aggregations of families into societies and states; the goal to be attained was the commonweal of the people.

Sociology may be compared to the construction of a building : the myriads of poor are the foundation; the rest of the structure corresponds to the different grades of society. The last could not exist without the first named. It is the struggling masses who are the foundation ; and if the foundation be rotten or insecure, the rest of the structure must eventually crumble. We must not consider the durability of the structure from the upper portion, that is, the upper classes, to whom the existing social condition is well enough ; but we must look to the foundation of the structure, or, in other words, the millions of wretched humanity who are daily increasing and whose condition is becoming inevitably more miserable. The architect of this building corresponds to the Government; and, before he commences to build, he must be quite sure that the foundations are all right, so as to give strength and support to the whole. To be a great architect is to be highly endowed. The ancient Greeks realized the great importance of this eminent ability, whether it was as the architect of a building, a government, or, above all, as the architect of a human being. The Greeks have reflected upon modern nations all that is highest in classical art. Their then existing popular government brought to perfection philosophy and literature, and was a masterpiece of administrative construction ; and history tells us of instances wherein their perception of the beautiful was so keen of what the human body might attain, that they brought the finest statuary and works of art before the pregnant mother to impress her that she might create a perfect model of human architecture.

We shall always find people devoting their lives to perfecting beautiful orchids or some other rare plant; astronomers are searching the sidereal universe to find some new star ; amateur breeders in the highest circles of society are devoting their time and their money to perfect their horses and cattle; farmers employ different food for the different effects they wish to have in their sheep,—fine wool, or excessive fat, &c.; all the influences of temperature, air, food, and external surroundings, are brought to bear to perfect the animal and vegetable organisms: but to waste a moment's reflection over the solution of perfecting so miserable a creature as man, what he may become, to what standard he may attain—impossible, the discussion is vulgar. The consequence is that people are not shocked to read and discuss the terrible crimes which may be committed by so low and vulgar a creature as man, or the horrible descriptions of want and misery accumulating on every side among the poor; but they are shocked at anyone's daring to talk of the causes that made this crime and misery possible.

Even the discussion of these social evils can scarcely mitigate the degraded condition of the people whom it is most necessary to reach. Among the poor, to all that appeals to the worst side of man's nature is given full scope. In the terrible fight for existence, they are obliged to work hard all day, and sometimes far into the night, having no time to pause, to consider the terrible evil that they are daily making greater by this crime of reproducing in their offspring their own debilitated condition both of body and of mind. They are perpetuating the hereditary curse from which they are daily praying that death may release them; but from which they are too weak, morally and physically, to abstain from cursing their children with. And these children have not only the hereditary instincts of crime to contend against, but are made familiar from their infancy with vice of every description. And when we read in the daily papers, that crime among children is becoming more prevalent, who is responsible ? When our cities are counting their outcasts and paupers by the tens of thousands, to whom are we to look for relief; when those in authority, who represent the people, remain apathetic, or say, when appealed to, that they are powerless to offer a remedy ?

In the pulpit, and in every department of life, leaders and teachers are shutting their eyes to this growing evil ; but still they say that there has been no suffering like the present; and they make charitable appeals for countless starving, ignorant people, regardless of the causes that make these charities possible. And yet they insist that the people are not prepared for the discussion of the scientific propagation of the race. *The time never was nor ever will be ready for the cowards who fear to be included among the agitators of an unpopular subject.*

It is man who requires to be perfected ; and in order to do this we must first understand the laws operating upon his social and physical condition. First, that condition of sociology which made certain human laws compulsory, and which created the necessity for the erection of public buildings to enforce them.

Moses studied for thirty years at the court of Pharaoh, and was initiated by the priests into those laws governing human society which preceded them.

With this knowledge, he constructed laws and institutions which have been more or less modified and adapted by each succeeding government according to the degree of civilization that each nation has attained. The Ten Commandments have become an integral part of the codified laws. The Government does not leave these commandments as optional moral laws, but makes them obligatory. For example, the law says:—

Thou shalt not kill.

Thou shalt not commit adultery.

Thou shalt not steal.

Thou shalt not bear false witness against thy neighbour—that is, thou shalt not perjure thyself. If you break these laws you must suffer the penalty. The Government has the authority to enforce obedience, and therefore immense capabilities of forming the character of its subjects. By the very fact of punishing these offences, it creates a repugnance in the minds of people; and in successive generations, it is not so much the law which is the restraint, as the association that has been engendered with these crimes. It has created a horror in the human *mind* of murder, of adultery, of theft, of perjury. Why cannot it go further and add something towards perfecting the human *body*? Let the Government incorporate as part of its laws the following commandments :—

Thou shalt not marry when malformed or diseased.

Thou shalt not produce His image in ignorance.

Thou shalt not defile His Temple.

Let it make it a crime against the nation, as it is

against God's Divine laws, to break these commandments, to thrust the results of their ignorance on the body social to be supported at the expense of the nation. Then in successive generations these crimes, too, may be regarded with horror and repugnance. It is no longer a question of expediency, but one of absolute necessity, which the Government will be obliged to deal with.

What is the commonweal of the public? It is to inaugurate such laws as will react with beneficial effects on its subjects. And as population increases and intellectual growth advances these laws should not remain stationary, so as to retard progress, but should be revised to keep pace with the times. The laws which were made to legislate for our forefathers, should not be allowed to become our legislators. Inertia is not progress. It is owing to the ever advancing nations that civilization has reached its present altitude. The most conservative throughout nature are ever the slowest in development.

We build institutions in order to incarcerate the insane, the idiots, the epileptics, the drunkards, the criminals, &c. If the lower organism of animals were subject to such infirmities and propensities, we should soon exterminate them; and yet we have not thought it needful to take measures to eradicate them from the highest organism, man. All such propensities have been contracted or acquired by the parental organism, or during the life of the individual itself, and have become hereditary in the offspring, reproducing itself

so exactly as to develop itself at the same age in the
offspring as when acquired by the parent.

What will the future enlightened ages think of the
women who are calmly looking on, oblivious of the fact
that their husbands are at work erecting the very
edifices in which they, in their ignorance as human
architects, may see their offspring incarcerated; or if
not their own children, some other mother's child?
And in after years, in visiting these buildings, they
will see the result of their ignorance in the brutish
faces of the inmates with the legible stamp of hereditary sensuality and vice. Every building erected to
meet the exigencies of this ignorance will be a reproach
to all womanhood. Do people realize, that nowhere
on the face of the earth is there a building erected to
teach people how to perfect the human body? The
sooner mankind awaken to the all-important truth,
that you cannot force people into moral conduct, into
a better social condition—that you must educate them
—the sooner we shall have emptied the buildings
erected to contain those monstrosities.

The phase of civilization which envelops in mystery
the origin of life conceals within itself the greatest
incentive to the very crimes that intelligence would
dissipate. Well did Sokrates define virtue as knowledge, and vice as ignorance. This truth should be
brought home to every woman, and she should be
made to feel that she is criminally responsible for all
the misery from which the human race is suffering
through her ignorance of the vital subject of proper

generation. The vulgar prejudices of a narrow-minded people have, in woman, cloaked with ignorance the fundamental principles of life in which our mothers should be most educated—an ignorance which is powerless to inspire in their husbands and sons that chivalry and respect due to every other mother's daughter. The mothers are incapable of teaching their children what they themselves have not been taught, leave their sons and daughters in ignorance of those dangers which await them at the very threshold of the struggle for existence, leave them to take their chance in this unsympathetic, pitiless world, leaving them to weep tears of blood over the dying embers of a misspent life !

Mankind has forgotten the lesson taught by the Hindus five thousand years ago—that to degrade or to oppress woman involves the physical and moral degradation of man; that the assumption of superiority and tyranny of the master, which for ages man has assumed over woman, has almost extinguished that Divine spark in her which alone has the power to regenerate humanity.

We cannot over-estimate the influence for good or evil that the mother has over her child. Who can train with such loving tenderness the shooting tendrils of the young inquiring mind ? Who can with such unerring judgment instruct the child in those dangers which surround the developing manhood and woman-hood ? Who is so capable of awakening the soul to a higher life ? And when this is realized, and superstition and ignorance give way to a reign of intelligence, and the full comprehension that there is nothing so vulgar as ignorance, then medical statistics will not have to tell us that one half of our sons on reaching manhood are unfit to become fathers, and that one half of our daughters on reaching maturity are unfit to become mothers. For it is this class of the unfit, who, on becoming parents, engender in their children the hereditary consequences of their thoughtless marriages, thereby sealing the doom of unborn generations. The marriages of such individuals produce epileptics, idiots, neurotics, insane inebriates; and by far the larger number become criminals. Nearly all the crime committed is the result of the inherited weak blood, or a malformation, or disease of the brain. It is familiar to everyone that when the brain is injured a corresponding loss of intellectual activity supervenes, causing in some cases a total lapse of memory, or hallucinations which occasion the most extraordinary actions on the part of its victim. If we know the cause producing this effect, we regard them as irresponsible beings and try to alleviate their sufferings; but where the cause producing this effect is unknown to us, where these hallucinations and extraordinary actions are the result of an hereditary diseased formation of the brain, or injurious conditions of life reacting on the brain, we regard them as hardened criminals and hold them as responsible citizens. It only proves to us how little the psychical as well as the physical part of man is understood. We should

not treat these unfortunates as criminals, as responsible
beings ; we should treat them as having a diseased
mental condition. For it is the co-operation of the
different parts of the body which insure the organization of the whole ; injure one part, and the whole
suffers ; debauch the stomach, and the whole is
debauched ; disease the mind, and the whole is
diseased ; outrage nature, and monstrosities are the
result. By the magnitude of these social evils we are
overwhelmed, but of their origin we have been
neglectful.

When we are able to make the study of man take
precedence over all others ; when we are able to reduce
the psychical part of man to a science ; when we are
able from these conclusions to perfect his moral and
physical condition ; when we are able to judge our own
actions with the same justice as we judge another's ;
when we are no longer the slaves of habit ; when
we realize that within us is a little community which
requires to be properly governed, so that anarchy will
not take possession, thereby causing destruction to the
whole ; when we realize that passion is the barbarous
state of man, and reason is the civilized state, then we
shall no longer look into the vacant faces of people and
see no response to the question of decaying nations.
Why has this crime of ignorance been allowed during
these thousands of years of civilization ?

We have only to visit the poorer quarters of our
towns and see the slaves of drunkenness and disease, to
realize upon how slight a basis is built the security of

our modern civilization. What a lesson might be taught in administrative government. For no matter to what perfection we may attain in mechanics, art, or sciences, man is the concentric pivot around which all revolve, and without which everything is an illusion. That immeasurable space, with its innumerable stars and glowing suns, piercing the mists enveloping worlds, and all the elements waging the fierce battle of life, are only realities in as far as man's intellectual power is capable of understanding them as such. The faults existing, and inharmonious notes producing discord, originate in man. The more the brain of man develops, the more the unity of inanimate and animate nature will be understood, so that ultimately the gulf dividing the two will be spanned, and a violation against one of nature's laws will be impossible.

" Know ye not that ye are the temple of God ? "

" If any man defile the temple of God, him shall God destroy ; for the temple of God is holy, which *temple* ye are."—1 *Corinthians iii.* 16 *and* 17.

———

THE votaries of truth are ever tortured and crucified by the bigoted and ignorant. The philosophers of ancient history realized greater truths than they dared proclaim to an ignorant populace. Preachers, all over the civilized world to-day, are in advance of their congregations; but they teach their philosophy, as of old, according to the calibre of the people, and not the truth that they realized. The spirit may be willing, but the flesh is weak. In the past, divines have been able to wield an immense power through the ignorance of those to whom they preached. To-day people are thinking for themselves, and the more they comprehend, the more the Church loses its power; and it will continue to do so, unless it have something better to offer than hitherto.

The time has come for the strong food of which St. Paul speaks :—" I have fed you with milk, and not with meat : for hitherto ye were not able to bear it, neither yet now are ye able." (1 Corinthians iii. 2.) " For everyone that useth milk is unskilful in the word of righteousness : for he is a *babe*. But strong *meat* belongeth to them that are of full age, even those who by reason of use have their senses exercised to discern both *good* and *evil*." (Hebrews v. 13-14.) Now, St. Paul meant that intellectually we are as yet infants, too weak to grapple with the truth that must come to us before we shall be able to solve the mysterious problem of life. Has habit paralyzed the impulse of nobler thought ? Is tradition too great a giant to cope with ? Must we crush the hunger in our hearts that is craving for the truth, and die like so many beasts of burden ? More and more intense becomes the craving desire to unravel life's tangled web. Whence comes the Divine spark that electrifies the clod into animation ; and, having spent its force, whither goes the vital element ? From the lowest form of animal life we are beginning to recognize the highest type of intellectual growth. Religion is to us the belief in the unseen ; and science is the knowable, which, after all, is only the manifestation of the unseen.

We trust no more to those illuminations of the soul which have inspired each new discovery and elucidated many mysteries of science. Yet the spiritual must have had a part in all the great truths that have burst upon the world, though little understood are the ethical laws which govern mankind. That matter can never be annihilated, is the first principle we learn in science. It may be resolvable into compounds, or even into elements ; but that it ceases to be a substance is impossible. Once having lived, we can never know death. Death is a misapplied term : " Both animals and plants have their origin in a particle of nucleated protoplasm which not only dies and is resolvable into mineral and lifeless constituents, but is always dying ; and, strange as the paradox may seem, could not live unless it died " (Professor Huxley). " That which thou sowest is not quickened, unless it die." (1 Corinthians xv. 36.)

The laws of evolution are, no doubt, the solution of many problems of science ; but the exponents of evolution have not been able to produce life, nor to solve this enigma. Five or ten thousand years have not materially changed man. The philosophy taught by Christna and Buddha, thousands of years ago, was grander in its conception than anything we have at the present time. Do we excel the ancient Greeks in art to-day ? And again, our laws are simply a repetition of the old Hindu laws dating back more than three thousand years before the Christian era. And in all these years of evolution we have not been able to better them. Five thousand years ought to improve mankind ; but the people are in the same depraved condition now as then. If any change has been made it has been for the worse, which proves to us that there is something radically wrong in the social economy.

Faint glimmerings of the truth were perceived by a few redeemers even in the first epochs of history ; but

it has had to filter through cycle after cycle until
woman could be educated to realize her true position
as a creator—the architect of the human race. And
that Divine martyr, Jesus, foresaw that ages upon ages
must roll away ere the human heart could comprehend
the true significance of the curse which was marring
the masterpiece of God in the Eden of his body.

The tradition that our first parents sinned has been
generally accepted : whether, according to the Vedas,
it was the Adema and Heva (meaning in Sanscrit the
first man and the first woman) on the island of Ceylon,
or the Adam and Eve of the Christian Bible. A
tradition of which the world makes a fable, but, rightly
understood, conveys the greatest lesson ever taught.
In the Hindu version, the man was the tempter, and it
was at the prayer of the woman that God pardoned
man. The Christian rendition makes the woman the
tempter. It matters little which it was, but that they
both sinned is evident; and, according to the record,
for the sin that they committed, all their decendants were
to be cursed until mankind should learn to sin no more.

First we must comprehend what the primordial
curse really was from which we are suffering to-day,
and endeavour, if possible, to remove that curse. We
will take the Christian version of the Bible (Genesis
iii. 5, 16): "God doth know that in the day ye eat
thereof, then your eyes shall be opened, and ye shall
be as gods, knowing *good* and *evil*." . . . . "Unto
the woman he said, I will greatly multiply thy sorrow
and thy conception ; in sorrow thou shalt bring forth

children; and thy desire shall be to thy husband, and
he shall rule over thee." This was the curse that fell
upon the human race when universal man and universal woman were driven out of Eden. No miscon-
ception as to the true meaning of this curse can arise :
woman, in whom burneth the lamp of God, was to be
degraded into an unholy vessel! Each generation has
suffered from this curse, and none more than the
present. So general is it to-day, that there is not a
place on the globe which does not degrade woman—
universal degradation! O God! to what depths has
thine Eve fallen !

In studying the lives of all Redeemers, from the time
of the birth of Christna of Hindustan, born of the
virgin Devanaguy, to the birth of Jesus of Nazareth,
born of the Virgin Mary, we learn that, although each
Saviour was accredited with Divine conception, they
were born of mortal mothers. The mothers, through
the long anxious months of gestative growth, moulded
and stamped the characters of these Divine martyrs.
No matter how mythical the conception, it was an awful
realistic fact to the woman who gave each child birth.
It was she who went into the very valley and shadow
of death to usher in this new life. It was she alone
who was the architect of the yet unborn being. And
through her awakening to the awful responsibility that
she has occupied as a creator, down to the present day,
will come the redemption of mankind, for her power is
just as potent for good or evil on the future unborn
generations as it was in the beginning of time.

The illuminated soul of Jesus understood this truth, and all His teachings were for the comprehension of this reality. "Destroy this temple, and in three days I will raise it up." . . . "But He spake of the Temple of His body." (John ii. 19, 21.)

Even at His Crucifixion the ignorant mob for whom He suffered the martyrdom of death, mocked Him, "Ah! Thou that destroyest the Temple and buildest it in three days! save Thyself."

Christ realized that the redemption of the race must come through the appreciation of the body; and this truth His *Apostles* preached, whereas preachers of to-day, after two thousand years, are still talking of the soul, not having the moral courage to grapple with this truth. And the ignorant cry out, "Rather let us die in our corruption than discuss the procreative principle of life." Hence nature has one fearful blotch to mar her sublimity—a deformed, diseased image of God, rotting away with its own debauchery; scarcely one of His handiwork comprehending the marvellous truth, "Know ye not that ye are the Temple of God, and that the Spirit of God dwelleth in you?" (1 Corinthians iii. 16.)

Jesus, in His Divine person, gave the world the living example of the triumph of the spiritual over the animal. Jesus tried to deliver man from the curse which was put upon Him in the Eden of his body. His teaching was the dawning of a new era. But to this truth the people, whirled in the maëlstrom of their own passions, paid little heed.

Sacerdotalism has so twisted and misrepresented every great thought, that mankind know not what is truth and what is error, and superhuman efforts are needed to lift humanity from the bogs of ignorance. Rather give us the stoic philosophy of Epictetus or of Marcus Antoninus than that religion which panders to ignorance. It is the very weakness and cowardice of the few who lead that is spreading desolation throughout the land. We see people cursed to-day with hereditary diseases, hereditary brutish passions, and with hereditary criminal instincts. What can we expect from the man born with alcoholized brain cells but a drunkard ? Can we expect anything else than brutish ungovernable passions from men and women, when we consider that the mother-architect during the period of gestation was subject to unbridled passion and brutal treatment until all her capabilities for moulding the character of her yet unborn child for good were destroyed ? Can we have anything but murderous instincts from the unwelcome child whom the mother did everything to kill before giving it life, and who engraved upon the child's plastic brain the desire to murder ? And when the gallows demands its victim, which one should be hanged ? The cruel irony of fate makes mankind the slaves of congenital instincts and congenital deformities. What availeth it to talk to man of his soul, when body and mind are torn by an hereditary disease until reason totters ? The law of compensation is inexorable. For religion, men and women have had the courage to be torn to pieces. For

religion they have had the courage to be burnt at the
stake. For religion, healthy men and women have
doomed themselves to perpetual celibacy. The
religion of the future, which will be founded on the
great truth that the human body is the Temple of God,
will awaken mankind to the awful responsibility of
creating His image when unfit to do so.

This Temple has been so defaced and brutalized that
one can no longer apply to it the word human. Can
it be possible that the masterpiece of God is drugged
in opium hells scattered over the so-called civilized
earth? Are those God's creatures that fill the hot-
beds of infamy which swarm in all large towns? Are
those God's creatures that people the houses for
lepers? Are all those malformed, misshapen beings His
image? And are all those brutish faces that crowd the
prisoners' dock a part of Him? Happily, men and
women are no longer satisfied with food for the body
alone; their souls hunger for the knowledge that will
give them the mastery over themselves.

The ignorance which surrounds the awful procreative problem makes mankind abject slaves. How long
ere the piercing rays of science shall dissipate the mists
of prejudice and superstition, leaving us to see, and
inciting us to aspire after, that altitude of perfection which, when attained, will make us indeed a race
of gods?

24

SOME THOUGHTS ABOUT AMERICA.

----·----

"While they promise them liberty, they themselves are
the servants of corruption."—2 *Peter ii.* 19.

THIS is pre-eminently an age of progress. A
restless dissatisfaction with the old order of
things pervades every heart. The needs of the people
grow daily greater, and they will not submit to being
ignored. If there be a cesspool in a street, the neigh-
bours do not hastily cover it up so that it may be hidden
from the public view. No ; they have the very bottom
dredged that their loved ones may not sicken and
die from the malaria. But the social and political
cesspools may go on gathering in the germs of deadly
miasma, while each human soul vies with the other
to ignore the fatal effects, until the nation is ready
to faint under its own corruption. I say social and

political cesspools, because one is the outcome of the other.

The government of a nation indicates more than anything else the character of its people. The laws that are needed and enforced determine the degree of civilization which that nation has attained, and the extent to which the people are capable of governing themselves. The laws demonstrate whether the people are the slaves of their own passions, or whether they feel the true dignity of manhood, and are conscious that they have control over a kingdom that they within themselves can make or mar. We have nowhere on the face of the globe a government which aims at perfecting its people. Upon the slightest provocation nations and individuals alike are ready to resort to brute force which was the government of the lowest type of civilization, and from which we to-day are not educated enough to free ourselves.

The best land if left uncultivated grows the rankest weeds, so the country with the greatest possibilities, if governed unwisely, may commit the most fatal errors.

More than a hundred years have come and gone since that momentous day when our Declaration of Independence was signed. What a promise of future achievement! No shackles of autocratic despotism to weigh down the American people! They were free—free to mould their own future greatness.

Let us see how this promise has been fulfilled. The

century has seen many Presidents in office; men who
have had glorious opportunities to show the world
that our Government was the highest type of human
advancement—that they were self-made men, an
example of indomitable courage and perseverance,
and that through these qualities they had attained
the highest office America had to bestow; that they
were worthy of the nation's confidence, and would
work for that nation's greatness to the best of their
ability—to realize, in fact, an ideal republican government. Have we in any one respect attained this? Has
any European country any confidence in our officials?
Have we ourselves any reliance on the integrity of
our representatives? Is it the best man to whom is
intrusted the highest office? Is he put in office by
the voice of the people, or by the political wire-pullers
who have their own self-aggrandisement in view?
We call ours a republican government. Does that
mean that it is framed for and by the people, or for
and by the select few? We see in every department
diplomacy and trickery indifferent to the cry of the
great mass of starving individuals. We shall have
to give an answer to their demands before many years
elapse. But unless this problem be met and grappled
with soon, America will have one of the most terrible
revolutions that has ever shaken the world. A political,
social, and moral earthquake is concentrating its force
beneath the very foundations of our so-called free
country.

The laws of the United States are constructed to

deal with effects only, and do not take into consideration the causes.

Good care is taken that each State shall have its prisons, lunatic, idiotic, inebriate, foundling, and other asylums ; but not one building is erected nor one law enforced that would teach the people how not to contribute to these over-crowded receptacles of human misery. And yet the American Government can boast of the surplus in the United States treasury with which it is at a loss what to do.

Never a consideration or thought for the thousands of human beasts of burden who live from hand to mouth, to whom justice, nature, and God are dead letters.

But they are regaled by the Press with a description of what the President has had for breakfast, luncheon, or dinner, how many calls he has had, how many times he has shaken hands, &c. To what great uses is put the highest office that America can confer for the organizing of peace, prosperity, and good will to all!

Let us review the situation. Paupers, tramps, and professional beggars are largely on the increase. Statistics show that the same name will constantly recur among the diseased and criminal classes, and that pauperism is hereditary. Say that one criminal may be the ancestor of a thousand criminals, and one pauper the ancestor of a thousand paupers. Are these not questions that are seriously connected from an economical and social point of view with our Government ? Have any of our Presidents tried to meet this question, or in any way tried to alleviate the anxiety of the people?

The social question has reached an acute stage. We may arrest the disease for a short time, but all the more terrible will be the malady when grappled with. We see thousands and thousands of parasites born every year who have no means of subsistence, who are destined to fasten upon their fellow-creatures, draining the vitality and strength of the nation, and precipitating its downfall.

It is not so much to political power that a country owes its greatness, but to that social fabric upon which all laws are based. All of our politicians are ready to deal with the effects, but not one of them is brave enough to penetrate the substratum of society and deal with the cause. A weak and vacillating leader does more to destroy a nation's greatness than does a really bad man. Our Government should be the example to the world, but above its doors of State are written in letters of blood, " *Mene, Mene, Tekel, Upharsin.*" The people want the leader capable of grappling with this hydra-headed social monster and one who understands the terrible urgency of this question. For they will no longer tolerate in power the men who assert that the masses are too ignorant to comprehend the true cause of these social upheavals. The Government should make it possible for the masses to be educated on these vital subjects, that they may no longer in ignorance thrust upon the body social the myriads of paupers, and those who, to eke out a miserable existence, are forced through incompetency for labour to accept the smallest pittance. They thereby exhaust the demand for the skilled artisan, they lower the standard of labour,but above all they curse humanity by doubling their kind every few years, until all our large towns are over-populated. Education and the proper understanding of the procreative principle of life are the only checks to over-population. And this was the curse, not the blessing, which was put upon woman when she was driven out of Eden : " *Unto the woman he said, I will greatly multiply thy sorrow and thy conception; in sorrow thou shalt bring forth children ; and thy desire shall be to thy husband, and he shall rule over thee.*" (Gen. iii. 17.)

Yes, read your Bible again, not with the understanding dwarfed and blinded by the bigotry and darkness of centuries, but with the true comprehension that we to-day are suffering from the very curse that was put upon Eve in the Eden of her body. Go anywhere among the most miserable of any community, and you will find there the largest number of improvident marriages. Mere girls and boys, married and not married, become parents before complete maturity. And herein lies the germ of the world's discontent ; and the disease is not in the crust which covers the ulcer, but in the core of the ulcer itself. Until that is probed with a daring and skilful hand, socialism and poverty will go on increasing, for the people who will not, or do not know how to, work, are the superfluous, or, in other words, ought never to have been born. For as Jesus turned and said to the women who were following Him, "*Weep not for me, but weep for yourselves, and for your children. For, behold, the days are coming, in which they shall say, Blessed are the barren, and the wombs that never bare, and the paps that never gave suck.*" (St. Luke xxiii. 28-29.) To those in power the little bacillus of socialism has no awful import; it is only when the consequences begin to fret them that they will turn their attention to the germ.

We have agricultural fairs all over the civilized world; each one is competing with the other to breed the finest horses and cattle, and prizes are awarded for so doing. In the animal kingdom in a few years we shall have none but domestic animals, and those in a higher state of perfection. All wandering herds will have been exterminated. But in the human kingdom, vagabondage is on the increase; and even the children of these vagabonds, when taken to reformatories or put into schools, sooner or later find their way back to swell the ranks of that rapidly increasing pauper class, who are lower than animals, having no instinct of domesticity. If the animal kingdom were subject to the debauchery, the foul air, the unwholesome food, the filthy abodes, the prevalent diseases that the human race has to contend with, in five years it would be extinct.

A man could not put on again the clothes of his childhood, he has outgrown them. The laws which clothed our constitution over a hundred years ago, when the American nation was in its infancy, are too small and too narrow in their limits for the intellectual demands of her people at the present day. The people have grown beyond them. To-day is as pregnant with revolution for independence, and as laden with as mighty import as was that memorable day in Philadelphia, when Tom Paine rose to the situation and said : " What this country wants is independence, and I mean revolution;" what the people want now is independence of thought and action and a revolution of old systems and ideas.

The Constitution of America, tattered and torn, has been hallowed by the blood of her noblest sons fighting for freedom. And that same spirit of freedom is only slumbering in the breasts of her sons and daughters to-day. And when she realizes that she is the leading nation of the world, she will rise to the occasion, and shake off the shackles of the Old World's diseased and worn-out social systems which are gradually creeping in and destroying her young life.

Victoria Woodhull Martin.

February, 1888.

SOCIOLOGY

(7)

The Rapid Multiplication of the Unfit . . . 1891.

THE RAPID MULTIPLICATION

OF

THE UNFIT.

BY

VICTORIA C. WOODHULL MARTIN.

17, HYDE PARK GATE, LONDON ;

AND

142, WEST 70TH STREET, NEW YORK CITY, U.S.A.

1891.

THE RAPID MULTIPLICATION

OF

THE UNFIT.

ONE of the most fruitful sources of error is the supposition or the taking for granted that others will
see and comprehend human nature as we see and
comprehend it. An individual judges a social
problem from his or her understanding. He or she
has longings, desires, emotions, and sensations, and
he or she imagines that others have the same
sensations, that they will respond to the same stimuli
in exactly the same manner and with the same degree
of intensity in a given circumstance, in a definite
social order.

There are often greater differences between individuals of the same race than between individuals
of different races. Some are more richly endowed
with more highly evolved nervous systems. If we
wish to understand the basis of a superior faculty, we
study how the nervous system of the individual has

1 *

become specialized. In the same way if we wish to understand the inferiority of individuals we study in what way their nervous systems are defective. It is this differentiation of the nervous system which separates man from man more effectually than geographical isolation in our modern civilization. The period of reaction to tactual, to auditory, to visual sensations, depends upon the physiological condition of the central nervous system.

Animals possess eyes, the structure is apparently the same, but what a difference in function. Human beings possess hands which are apparently alike in structure, but what a vast difference in delicacy of touch, in muscular sensibility between them. Some have taste highly developed, as, for instance, wine tasters or tea tasters. With many very often the sense of taste is defective. Cutaneous sensibility, with some is developed to an abnormal degree. Persons with keen bodily perception are often affected by changes in the weather, or shiver at the approach of particular individuals, or feel approaching danger. Many animals have this faculty developed to a higher degree than human beings. Again, we have thick-skinned individuals with very slight cutaneous sensibility. This has passed into the popular expres sion that a person is thick-skinned, you can't hurt or affect him; or it is often said that he or she is callous, hardened, unfeeling, insensible to anything you may say or do.

We do certain things, because in the doing we derive satisfaction and pleasure, we avoid doing certain things because they give us pain. If we study the physiology of pleasure and pain, we find that the person with highly developed bodily perception and the thick-skinned individual are two widely different animals; and this difference arises from the fact that the same stimulus applied to the two individuals will vary in intensity and therefore will produce a different effect. In Michael Foster's " Text Book on Physiology," he says, that " a slight stimulus, such as " gentle contact of the skin with some body, will pro- " duce one kind of movement; and a strong stimulus, " such as a sharp prick applied to the same spot of skin, " will call forth quite a different movement. When a " decapitated snake or newt is suspended and the skin " of the tail lightly touched with the finger, the tail " bends towards the finger; when the skin is pricked " or burnt, the tail is turned away from the offending " object. And so in many other instances.

" It must be remembered of course that a difference " in the intensity of the stimulus entails a difference in " the characters of the afferent impulses; gentle contact " gives rise to what we call a sensation of touch, while " a sharp prick gives rise to pain, consciousness being

" differently affected in the two cases because the
" afferent impulses are different." The difference in the
intensity of the same stimulus applied to the sensitive
person, to the thick-skinned person, and the diseased
person would affect their consciousness differently.
The stimulus, which would be so intense to the
sensitive person as to produce pain, would to the
thick-skinned person only produce a sensation of
touch. The coarse brutal word which would give
rise to pain in the sensitive individual would give a
sensation of satisfaction to the person with slight
sensibility.

If pleasure and pain actuate our movements or
determine the character of our movements, we have
ample proof that influences which give pleasure to one
class of individual may give pain to another. More
light is thrown on this subject in another paragraph
in Michael Foster's " Text Book on Physiology":
" The clinical histories of diseases of the spinal cord in
" man bring to light in a fairly clear manner a fact of
" some importance, namely, that the several impulses
" which form the basis of the several kinds of sensa-
" tions, of touch, heat, cold, and pain, and of the
" muscular sense, are transmitted along the cord in
" different ways and presumably by different struc-
" tures. For disease may impair one of these sensa-
" tions and leave the others intact.

"Thus cases of spinal disease are recorded, in "which on one side of the body or in one limb ordinary "tactile sensations seemed to be little impaired, and "yet sensations of pain were absent; when a needle was "thrust into the skin no pain was felt, though the "patient was aware that the needle had been pressed "upon the skin at a particular spot; and conversely "in other cases pain has been felt upon the insertion "of a needle, though mere contact with or pressure on "the skin could not be appreciated. Again, cases are "recorded in which the skin was sensitive to touch or "pain, but not to variations of temperature; it is "further stated that cases have been met with in "which cold could be appreciated but not heat, and "vice versâ."

Many persons cannot be affected with kind words and mild treatment, but must be dealt with harshly or firmly. The psychical appreciation of the slighter stimulus is blocked, it is analogous to the one in whom touch could not be appreciated but on the insertion of the needle pain could be felt.

Certain poisons in the blood augment the excitability of the central nervous system, others deaden the sensibility. The fatigue products in the blood have a depressing influence on the central nervous system; imbecility, stupidity, dullness, imply lessened excitability of the nervous system. To arouse dull

or stupid people it requires a stronger stimulus than
it requires for normal individuals, just as it requires
a stronger stimulus to arouse a tired animal into
action than a fresh one.

In the same way that we build insane asylums to
house our insane because they have lost their mental
balance, so we build pauper institutions for those
who have lost their physical balance. The vaga-
bond, the pauper, is as much born and made one
as the man of insane temperament under stress
demonstrates his neurotic heredity and the criminal
his pathological condition. The terrible effects on
posterity of depleting our workers and then allowing
them in ignorance to breed is the burning question for
humanity. The physical condition of the population
of a manufacturing town is proverbial.

It is said that in a new country where the land
has not yet been appropriated, there is no such thing
as the unemployed or the pauper. When colonists
first settle upon a piece of land there is plenty of
outdoor exercise, manly pursuits, work which does
not cause physical deterioration. But after a time as
population increases and sedentary occupations take
the place of active pursuits, crowded enclosed work-
rooms supplant work in the open air, the energy of
the workers is gradually sapped by artificial life in
cities, and they become the progenitors of a class

physically enfeebled, spiritless, incapable of sustained effort. Work is carried on by means of the contractions of muscular fibres. Michael Foster says, in his " Text Book on Physiology," that " inter-" ference with the normal blood stream is followed " by a gradual diminution in the responses to stimuli " and the muscle loses all its irritability and becomes " rigid . . . . with regard to the quality of the " blood thus essential to the maintenance or res-" toration of irritability, our knowledge is definite " to one factor only, viz. the oxygen. If blood " deprived of its oxygen be sent through a muscle " removed from the body, irritability so far from " being maintained seems to have its disappearance " hastened. In fact, if venous blood continues to be " driven through a muscle, the irritability of the " muscle is lost even more rapidly than in the entire " absence of blood. It would seem that venous blood " is more injurious than none at all. If exhaustion be " not carried too far the muscle may however be " revived by a proper supply of oxygenated blood." The pallid faces and stunted growth of some of our town-bred workers tell their own tales. If exhaustion be carried too far in the living organism fatigue ensues, and in fatigue the muscles are slow to respond to stimuli. Individuals who are tired move and think more slowly and are less energetic. It can

2

be imagined how terrible are the physical results that ensue to those whose normal condition is one of fatigue.

Power of endurance in individuals is not equal; so that we could not say that eight hours' work or that less or more is beneficial to all alike. One may work eight hours continuously and not be exhausted, whereas another may be totally exhausted in six. Physicians warn us that if we do not allow sufficient rest to a tired organ to recuperate, waste products accumulate producing poisons which are a fruitful source of disease. The most active agent in generating the unfit is fatigue poison. If a large percentage of histories of family degeneration can be traced in the offspring of parents who have passed the prime of life, how much larger must the percentage of family degeneration be that is due to physical exhaustion from overwork or the lack of sufficient light and fresh air.

After great physical exhaustion the stomach is tired, it is often unable to digest heavy and coarse food, nature calls for something light, liquid of some kind, broth, tea, alcohol, and the like. And to this cause may be assigned the reason why the consumption of tea, alcohol, and opiates of different kinds is so largely on the increase. Animals who are over-tired or sick turn away from food. Anæmia is brought on by insufficient nutriment. Persons suffering from anæmia become apathetic, listless; the brain if no longer supplied with sufficient nutriment becomes torpid, the vital activity is lowered. Such persons have no energy to make an effort, they have no power of taking the initiative.

It is said that one in every five of the population of London does die or is destined to die in a hospital, the workhouse, or pauper lunatic asylum. *Pari passu* with this statistical statement the cry is growing louder for more public institutions to house the incapable, and it is urged that all stigma should be removed from them.

In visiting one of these institutions a short time since, in one of the wards I saw a little child moving about with the aid of a chair, its body being too big and heavy for its legs ; in another ward a nurse, who was carrying a baby covered with scrofulous sores, asked me if I would adopt it. The baby had no one to claim it and they were only waiting to find someone who would take charge of it. There were cases of hip disease, some had been successfully operated upon. There was one with spina bifida. The doctor took great pride in showing me a child on whom he had just operated for hare-lip ; my attention was drawn to the success he had had in delivering a mother of an idiotic baby. What is the destiny of these children ? They require able-bodied

2 *

nurses from their birth, and able-bodied physicians to spend their valuable time over them. They are scarcely ever able to shift for themselves, they are a care all their lives, and at last swell the ranks of the one in five who die in the hospital, the workhouse, or pauper lunatic asylum.

The relationship between the abnormal palate and the brain is being recognized by all physicians who have made any study of the subject. They are consequently enabled to predict that in all probability the child with cleft palate will either be semi-idiotic, a criminal, or a lunatic, especially if subjected to the stress of poverty or adverse conditions, in any case will add to the burden already heavy laid on the community by the incapable. And the chances are they will be among the five who will die in the workhouse, hospital, or pauper lunatic asylum.

The following extract I copied from a paper :—

"A woman named Abigail Cochrane, who has just died at "Kilmalcolm at 84 years of age, was a pauper from the cradle "to the grave. She was born in Greenock in 1807, and was "imbecile from her earliest youth. It is estimated that she cost "the public purse between £2000 and £3000."

As in the case of Abigail Cochrane, each one of our human failures adds a considerable item to the burden, already large, put upon the healthy useful citizens. And if our present industrial workers are overtaxed, overburdened, and under the strain their health is undermined, what benefit will their progeny be to future generations ? How are superior qualities to be transmitted to the offspring, if for generations the economic pressure has been so great as to deteriorate the physical constitution of their progenitors ?

Physiology teaches us that conscious life is the result of the nature of the afferent or sensory impulses which reach the central nervous system, the physiological condition of the central grey matter, and the efferent impulses the central nervous system gives rise to which result in different movements. We know blue from red because they differentially stimulate the retina. Consciousness is differently affected because the afferent impulses are different. We recognize two different sounds because they differentially stimulate the auditory nerves. Consciousness is differently affected because the afferent impulses are different. We know already that the *character* of the afferent impulses varies with the intensity of the stimulus, and if the central nervous system is thrown into activity by the summation of afferent impulses reaching it, those who from over-exertion or disease have their sensibility or excitability lessened, their nervous systems are fed in less degree. Such persons would require stronger stimuli than normal healthy individuals to produce a given effect, for their central nervous systems either do not react at all to a given stimulus or else very feebly, with the results that they are dull or stupid. In one an afferent impulse may be so intense as to invoke a nerve storm, with another it may be too weak to have an effect.

Many are so deficient in sensibility that although afferent impulses may be started by the most beautiful pictures, sculpture, divine strains of music, noble and humane examples, in fact the most sublime combinations of nature and art, they will awaken no response, they will arouse no efferent processes of noble thoughts and actions. This accounts for the fact that certain persons only take pleasure in vulgar low resorts and the companionship of coarse people. They seek their affinities. The saying is, that a man is known by the company he keeps ; in other words, his nervous system is similarly developed.

If we study the nervous system of the pauper class, we find that instead of their nervous energy being economically expended, there is lavish, uneven and wasteful expenditure which is of no great benefit to the individual nor to society. They are organically deficient; they inherit defective, ill-regulated nervous systems, or their nervous systems become badly adjusted through irregular habits, bad training, or diseases. They are incapable of sustained effort. They prefer jobs to regular work, spasmodic efforts to work for a few hours or days, and these efforts are followed by a reaction of utter inability to make further exertion. They can assign no reason why any sustained effort is wearisome to the last degree. These characteristics are symptomatic of retrogression, or they are the reappearance of a more primitive type.

There are savages who will work hard to collect material things, and then will debauch and idle away weeks and months until the pangs of hunger compel them to make another effort to work. In this we have the simplest condition of economic pressure. It is said that the special characteristic of the savage is that he has no thought for the morrow. He eats until he can eat no more, then goes hungry until he finds more food. These very characteristics we see exhibited among our own savages. I saw a poor man, who said he was hungry and had been given some bread and cheese, eat until his hunger was appeased and then throw the bread and cheese which remained into the street; he could not or did not realize that in a few hours he would be hungry again. I have frequently seen bread thrown away by such and lying in the street. To them bread had been given once, it would be given again, or they would go hungry until the pangs of hunger compelled them to make a further effort to procure more. It is a waste of words to say that these individuals are paupers because they have not been careful, thrifty, and temperate. We might lecture for hours to them on the advantages of industry, we might urge our plea with the fervour of a divine oracle, the afferent impulses we give rise to arouse no response in those torpid brains. For our plea to have an effect they must be given new nervous systems and healthy rich blood, in other words, they must not be bred. It is characteristic of those organically defective that it is the voluntary part of their nature which is most affected. They have not the *will* to make any exertion, they fall into the conditions which circumstances place them. With the offspring of parents suffering from fatigue or other poison, compulsory education may be enforced, but our efforts will not be repaid by healthy useful individuals unless they spring from a healthy source.

Political economists have said that the conscientious, the right-minded, will not marry until they are in a position to do so, and herein is the *crux* of the social problem. The more highly developed human beings yield less and less readily to the dictates of sexual passion alone. They judge and consider consequences.

They profit by the experiences of others and therefore avoid doing that which will bring sorrow to those whom they love. High motives deter the fit from marrying until they are in a position to do so. Among the better classes marriage is being deferred more and more, the standard of living is becoming higher among them, and more time is given to education, whereas the unfit who are not deterred by any qualms of conscience or apprehension of consequences go on multiplying. And as the more highly developed are not perpetuated, or if perpetuated it is in fewer numbers, the thoughtless, improvident, degenerate, and diseased, multiply upon us.

An educated man made the remark a short time ago, " The cause of so much misery among the poor "to-day is over-population, it is their reckless indul-"gence in large families. I am too poor to marry, I "can't afford to have a family, I wish I could, and yet "I am called upon to pay taxes to educate and help "to support others' paupers." Here is a man who was accustomed to a certain standard of living, and who therefore did not care to have offspring who would not have the same advantages as he had had, or to have a family who might become a burden on others. An example of the conscientious not marrying until he could afford it, a result which is most disastrous in its effects on the quality of the human race.

A man may possess a noble character and have a magnificent physique, but if he do not perpetuate these qualities they do not survive. A man may be diseased, stupid or reckless, but withal he marries and raises a large family: his qualities are perpetuated, but it is not the survival of the fittest. Many men break their health down by overwork, and the terrible strain is seen in the physical condition of their children. Many men have not over exerted themselves, and have had no scruples about living on the charity of their relations or friends, and hence their children do not suffer from the depleted physical condition of their fathers; but are these children the survival of fittest? Moral checks which would appeal to the superior intellectual mind, do not influence the unfit. In the majority of cases they have not a nervous system sufficiently developed to appreciate these motives.

A great many seem to think that interference with marriages of the unfit will only give greater opportunities to races, lower in the scale of development who are multiplying so fast, to overcome and conquer the more advanced races. We have an example of this in the rapid multiplication of the negroes in America, who at some not far distant day will outnumber and overrun the whites if the rapid increase be not checked. Eventually, if America is owned and governed by negroes, would it be the survival of the fittest? The outlook is as ominous in Europe.

Mr. Raines states in his census of the population of India, that the returns show an increase of thirty millions in the population in ten years, the total being 285,000,000. Add to this number 400,000,000, or probably more in China, and it looks as if these vast hordes may yet overrun and wipe out Western civilization. With this spectre looming up in the distance it is considered a dangerous policy to advocate any theory which would tend to limit the population of Western nations. The argument holds good if we wish simply to limit the numbers of the population of the fit, but has no application with regard to the marriages of the unfit. An American child brought up in China, if it had a defective nervous system, will demonstrate it in China ; and a Chinese child brought up in Europe, if born of diseased parents, will demonstrate its hereditary condition here. We find often that physical causes, not numbers, determine whether races shall be conquerors or conquered. Stamina often gives the victory to a race. Generalship indicates superior development of the general.

But in any attempt to raise the standard of humanity, to aid evolution, we must take into consideration that it is not the survival of the fittest, but the survival of the unfit by means of their rapid multiplication in societies as presently organized.

Any cause which determines the mating of individuals has a direct influence on the quality of the human race. All artificial social inducements for the mating of unsuitable individuals are instruments for the multiplication of the unfit. To prove how detrimental our present social life is to the human race, we have only to ask how many of the marriages which take place would be consummated if there were no social inducements, no fear of public opinion, no regard for the law, if there were no other inducement but the fact that he is male and she female, and that they are physiologically mated. How many who to-day are not mated would under such a state come together and propagate, and how many who to-day propagate from other inducements than love would no longer not do so? One great cause of the rapid multiplication of the unfit over the fit, is our false social system which places so many obstacles to prevent the coming together of our best men and women.

How many opportunities has a girl to find her physiological mate in her little set—even if she were free to choose? Sexual selection has very little scope in our conventional system. Take the many instances of women who marry for a home, very often the only choice between that and starvation, and ask if there could be a greater perversion of the sexual instinct. I have heard it said, "What a good marriage Mr. —— "has made, he married a girl with fifty thousand "pounds, more or less; *she* is ugly and unattractive, "but what a windfall for him." A suitable marriage is often considered the one which will relieve the man from his debts or the marriage which will raise him or her up in the social or financial world. Money bags are highly valued in the marriage mart, and the, at present, artificial sign indicating that you, the vulgar, might not know the value of this piece of human flesh, so we tabulate him Lord or Prince.

Thousands of examples might here be given of the marriages *de convenance* of old men and young girls, and of young men and aged women which are so frequent nowadays. When these marriages are fruitful they too often produce idiots, murderers, or otherwise unfit. There are many social barriers which prevent the respectable poor from making physiologically suitable marriages. A respectable working woman said, "I work with a great many "men, but after business hours I do not dare go "about with any of them, for immediately all kinds of "reports would be circulated which would ruin my "reputation." The reckless or unfit not being deterred by any false restrictions go on multiplying.

Under our present industrial system there is a strong tendency against the survival of the fittest. If we take the life histories of two men, one honest the other dishonest, we shall find that nearly everything is in favour of the clever dishonest man in a plutocracy. Stanley Jevons gives us an example of how reckless speculation can be carried on at the expense of a credulous confiding public. "It now "becomes possible to create a fictitious supply of a "commodity, that is, to make people believe that a "supply exists which does not exist. The possessor "of a promissory note or warrant regards the docu- "ment as equivalent to the commodity named thereon. "It is only necessary then to print off, fill up, and "sign an additional number of such notes in order to "have a corresponding supply of commodity to sell. "It is true that the issue of promises involves their "fulfilment at a future day; but the future is "unknown, and the issuer may believe that before the "fulfilment is likely to be demanded the price of "the commodity will have fallen. Thus, if pig-iron "warrants could be issued in unlimited quantities "(irrespective of the stocks actually in the stores at "Glasgow), an unscrupulous band of speculators "might perhaps make large profits by selling great "quantities of iron for future delivery. *After* "*suddenly and excessively depressing the price of* "*pig-iron they might succeed in gradually buying up* "*enough at lower prices to meet* the warrants when "presented. This kind of 'bear' operations has "certainly been successful in other markets."

"About ten years ago it became the practice to "rig the market as regards the shares of particular "joint-stock banking companies. A party would be "formed, perhaps *owning none of the shares of the* "*elected company,* and they would proceed to sell con- "siderable quantities of the shares, hoping so to "*damage* the *reputation* of the company and *lower* the "*value of the stock* as to be able to buy up enough "before delivery would be required. This noxious "kind of speculation was checked by an Act of "Parliament (30 Victoria, c. 29, 1867), which now "requires the seller of bank shares to specify the "numbers of the registered proprietors of the shares "which he is selling for future delivery." In another paragraph of the same work, a further example of modern business transactions is given. The italics are my own in all three paragraphs. "Great "injustice arises in some cases from this defective "state of the gold currency. I have heard of "one case in which an *inexperienced* person, after "receiving several hundred pounds in gold from "a bullion dealer in the City of London, took "them straight to the Bank of England for deposit. "Most of the sovereigns were there found to be

"light, and a prodigious charge was made upon the
"unfortunate depositor. The dealer in bullion had
"evidently paid him the residuum of a mass of
"coins, from which he had picked the heavy ones.
"In a still worst case, lately reported to me, a man
"presented a post-office order at St. Martin's-le-
"Grand, and carried the sovereigns received to the
"stamp-office at Somerset House, where the coins
"were weighed, and some of them found to be
"deficient. Here a man was, so to say, defrauded
"between two Government offices."

Examples may be given to illustrate how the
inexperienced are at the mercy of clever speculators. A man wishes to possess certain railroad
shares, so that he can control a certain railroad ;
he offers to buy these shares, but the possessors,
knowing they have good value for their money,
refuse to sell ; then the clever speculator goes to
work to bring pressure to bear to force them to sell
their shares, by creating a panic, or by spreading
rumours to damage their credit; by this means, if
they have many promissory notes or bills to meet,
or money tied up, they may be obliged to realize on
their shares, and the great financier has accomplished
a *coup d'état*. An instance of the modern code of
business ethics came under my notice a few weeks
ago. A millionaire tried to negotiate a bill of
exchange with a friend ; fortunately, the friend had

been made aware that the rate of exchange had
fallen, otherwise this clever financier would have
made perhaps a handsome profit out of his friend.
Many examples might be given how the dishonest
man, by trickery, bribery, furthers a scheme and
amasses a fortune. And with this fortune he can
pay the cleverest lawyers to defend him, if necessary,
with his ill-gotten gains. The honest man in the
time of distress pays his debts honourably, aids his
friends, and takes advantage of no one, and, the consequence is, becomes poor. They both have children,
the dishonest wealthy man can have the best professors, send his children to the best schools, his
children will have better food and clothing, in time
of sickness have the best medical attendance; they
will have frequent changes from town to country,
opportunities to travel and see the world; and having
a favourable environment and not being subjected
to the stress of poverty or conditions which would
develop the latent bad they will acquire polish,
become cultured, and with these superior advantages
our *jeunesse dorée* will have their pick in the marriage
market, where very often our fairest and tenderest
flowers are knocked down to the highest bidder.
And it is said, Would you take the reward of merit
away? The honest man's sons, whose father has
become impoverished, perhaps while they were still

young, may even have to do manual labour, they
will be subjected to the stress of poverty, they will
not have the best professors that *money* can procure
in this world, where superior opportunities should be
the reward of merit ; they may have no opportunities
to acquire polish and refinement, they may not become
cultured in the terrible struggle with poverty.

Take an example of two men who are in the same
line of business and are competing against each other.
They are both individualists, and we are told that by
their competing, prices are kept down and that we
get a superior article for our money, and so forth.
One of these men has capital to the amount of two
hundred thousand pounds outside of his business,
and the other has capital to the amount of one
hundred thousand pounds. The one who has two
hundred thousand pounds says, I can afford to undersell or underbid or carry on my business at a loss of
one hundred thousand pounds ; by that time I have
ruined him, I have attracted all his customers from
his establishment to mine, and when I have the
monopoly I can gradually raise my prices till they
give me a fair profit and my business is doubled.

This course is being pursued in nearly every line
of business, the margin of profit is being run so close
that old-established firms are obliged to sell out or
continue business at a loss. I know of many instances

where men have said, I can't take your order at a certain price for it will leave me no profit, I have to pay my workpeople, my rent, and support my family, and I can't do that unless I make a fair profit. Or, again, it is said, I can't do the job for such a price, but in many cases the man will be forced to become a sweater and will turn round and say to the workpeople, If you will work at so much an hour, I will take the job, I will make no profit out of it, if you don't feel disposed to work for so little, the order will be given to a competing firm who will perhaps do the job at a loss to attract a customer. I wished to investigate this subject for myself, and I have taken special pains to compare prices. For example, I went to shops which only sold certain articles, and then to universal providers or general providers. I found in one instance at a small shop the price was just double what I could buy the same article for at the large shop which sold nearly everything. I said to the proprietor, I can buy this at M——'s for fourpence. He took his book out to show me that he paid his manufacturer more than that wholesale. He said to me, they must have bought in a job lot or are selling them at a *loss* to attract customers to buy other things on which they make their profit.

In other instances, with other articles I had to

pay four shillings to the special dealer which allowed a *fair* profit, for what I could buy for three shillings within a penny or two more or less at the general providers. I found that the cheaper price was *cost* price to the manufacturers. Of course, the big houses are attracting the customers away from the small retailers and eventually they must go to the wall. As long as the small retailer was making a profit at *fair* prices, he was an employer, but with ruin staring him in the face he is obliged to give up his business and goes as an *employée*.

A hypothetical case will illustrate the effects of the modern tendency of concentrating several small industries into one large establishment : five small shops sell trimmings and buttons, the sixth, a big shop, sells these articles cheaper, or perhaps at first sells them at cost price to attract the customers, so that the people who require these articles go to the big shop. Therefore the five small shops are obliged to close, and the five former employers go to the big shop and become *employées* in the trimming department. This is said to be a departure in the direction of progress, because labour requires time—so time enters as an important factor in determining cost, and the time is saved in buying many articles at one shop, instead of being obliged to go about to many shops to find the required articles. The men, however, who have gone over to the big shop do not receive a share in the profits, but the sixth gets the former profits of the other five. The children of the five, the majority, fall several grades lower in the social scale, because with their altered fortunes they are obliged to leave school earlier, and the time they were giving to mental and physical culture must now be given up to work for bare subsistence. Whereas the children of the sixth, the minority, rises several grades higher.

I asked a saleswoman in one of these shops if the women received pretty fair wages. She answered, " We are the poorest paid workwomen in the City, " the firm makes such small profits they can't afford to " pay more." I asked her if they had any difficulty in getting workwomen. " No," she answered, " they " are never obliged to advertise, there are hundreds on " the list ready to take the place of one who falls out." I need scarcely say that many of the applicants were from the other ruined firms.

Before we can be quite sure that centralization of wealth and industries is in the direction of progress, the bodily degeneration caused in the production must be taken into account as part of the cost against the value of the utility. If labour must be regulated by supply and demand, the quantity of inferior people will create a demand for a quantity of inferior goods. Our requirements demand certain economic goods ; in proportion as our taste becomes more highly educated the more difficult it will be to satisfy it. It is urged that the poor have so many useful things that formerly they were not able to possess, because they can be turned out by the quantity, and very cheap. The utility of certain articles of apparel is of more importance than the beauty. We get the hundred indifferently-made coats to-day where we used to get the one well-made before. And my opinion is, that we had better go back to sheep skins, because the utilities are used up or worn out, and have left no product, whereas the beautiful thing left the product in a developed æsthetic sense. Æsthetic taste enters very considerably into the value of an object. A picture may have no value to the vulgar, uneducated eye, but to the connoisseur who discerns its worth it has great value. The being able to appraise the value of an object, pre-supposes a faculty in the appraiser which the majority of ordinary people do not possess. So, then, if we wish a demand for this superior article, we must educate and develop this faculty in the individual.

If the great artist has no one to appreciate his genius it goes begging, if the superior workman gets no one to buy his work he falls back into the ranks of the many who supply the demand for the uneducated, undeveloped taste.

Among other causes which conduce to the rapid multiplication of the unfit, it has been suggested that the reason why the poor are so prolific is that they are underfed, that abundance of rich food lessens fertility. From experiments on flowering and fruit plants, it has been proved that by checking the *nutritive* conditions of the plant the reproductive power is increased; the roots of fruit trees are cut in order that they may yield abundant fruit. Darwin has already mentioned this subject in his work on animals and plants under domestication. He refers to some authors who have attempted to show that fertility increases and decreases in an inverse ratio to the amount of food. Darwin goes on to say, " This strange doc-" trine has apparently arisen from individual animals " when supplied with an inordinate quantity of food, " and from plants of many kinds when grown on " excessively rich soil, as on a dunghill, becoming " sterile." In another chapter Darwin again refers to this subject in a paragraph, beginning, *sterility from the excessive development of the organs of Growth or Vegetation.* " To make European vegetables under " the hot climate of India yield seed, it is necessary to " check their growth; and when one-third grown, " these are taken up and their stems and *tap-roots* are "cut or mutilated. So it is with hybrids; for instance, "Professor Lecoq had three plants of Mirabilis which, "though they grew luxuriantly and flowered, were "quite sterile ; *but after beating one with a stick until* "*a few branches alone were left, these at once yielded* "*good seed.*" There is other evidence bearing on this subject, especially the experiments of M. Maupas and others with infusoria, which have shown that when food became scarce the conjugal appetite increased, and when food was plentiful there was no conjugal inclination. There are certain worms which produce parthenogenetically when food is plentiful, and sexually when food is scarce, showing the intimate relation between nutrition and reproduction.

Opposed to this theory is the statement that population increases with the increase of food, that is, the number of animals increase rapidly where food is plentiful, and in times of dearth or scarcity the number decreases. The increase is ascribed to the increase in the number of marriages in prosperous periods. But among the very poor, where the increase is most rapid, I do not think this increase of population is due entirely to the *legal* marriage. It is very difficult to reconcile the naturalist's and the political economist's theories; the naturalist's that reproduction is augmented by the scarcity of food, the political economist's theory that population increases or diminishes inversely with the price of corn. Other checks may be at work which tend to obscure the value of the first theory ; it may be that the food supply, falling below the minimum necessary to sustain life in a healthy condition, causes diseases or otherwise incapacitates human beings in the struggle against adverse conditions in an industrial crisis.

To sum up some of the principal causes in the rapid multiplication of the unfit, we may class them under two heads, namely, Physiological and Psychological.

Among the probable Psychological causes are:—

(1.) The more intelligent the individuals the more they think of consequences and the less likely are they to be influenced by sexual passion alone. Later marriages among the upper classes with the result of having fewer children, and if too long deferred the marriages are infertile. The improvident therefore would marry first and would rear the largest number of offspring. The sense of responsibility developes with age, but the very poor marry at very early ages.

(2.) Among the unfit easier modes of becoming acquainted, less prudery, more freedom in the intercourse of the sexes.

(3.) The mystery and secresy which envelopes these natural functions, too often create a morbid desire which often leads to masturbation and other practices.

(4.) Marriages among the upper classes for money and position, or the marriages of those who have not sufficient opportunities under our present social decrees to seek and find a more suitable partner.

(5.) The sexual passion excited by the intermingling of the sexes in overcrowded tenements; whole families often sleeping in one room. A lady who has a home for girls to help them through their first confinement, and to save first offenders, if possible, said: "It is appalling the number of " girls who come here who have been seduced by " their own brothers."

Among the probable Physiological causes are:—

(1.) Marriages of the immature, those who have passed the prime of life, or the physically exhausted, which produce offspring lacking in vigour and mental power, and only too often absolute idiocy is the result.

(2.) Inbreeding, especially if the parents are very similar, which intensifies morbid tendencies, the offspring from these marriages suffer from impaired mental power and lack of vigour; although close inbreeding gives a tendency towards idiocy, it also inclines towards insanity. It is said that insanity is one of the scourges of Newfoundland where intermarriage obtains. This also may be the result of the parents having been subjected to the same conditions of life.

(3.) Too great a difference between parents, for instance, cross-marriage, which give a tendency to reversion, as Darwin has so clearly demonstrated. Disease affecting the reproductive system also favours a tendency to reversion. It is said that cross-breeding is analogous to disease by producing an abnormal condition of ovum and sperm. From these marriages are supplied our criminals and the monstrosities. As Darwin says, " A similar tendency to " the recovery of long-lost characters holds good even " with the instincts of crossed animals. There are " some breeds of fowls which are called ' everlasting " layers,' because they have lost the instinct of incuba- " tion ; and so rare is it for them to incubate that I " have seen notices published in works on poultry, " when hens of such breeds have taken to sit. Yet the " aboriginal species was of course a good incubator; " and with birds in a state of nature hardly any instinct " is so strong as this. Now, so many cases have been " recorded of the crossed offspring from two races, " neither of which are incubators, becoming first-rate " sitters, that the reappearance of this instinct must be " attributed to reversion from crossing." The reappearance of long-lost characters also occurs when disease affects the ovaries and testes. In disease of the ovaries, characters which have been latent in the female may become actual or effective. It seems incredible with our modern ideas of ethics that instincts or characters which it may have taken thousands of years of civilization to modify or suppress, should reappear as the result of influences which have affected the reproductive organs of the parents in a single generation. It especially strikes us with horror when we realize how common diseases of these organs are to-day.

(4.) Artificial preventive checks, which are more within the reach of the well-to-do classes than the very poor. Especially as these would affect the reproductive organs unfavourably and by this means gives a tendency to reversion.

(5.) The extreme susceptibility of the reproductive organs to changed or unnatural conditions, whether these be psychical or physical. The perversion of the sexual instinct often destroys all natural feeling, instance ancient and modern infanticide, fœticide, overlaying, suffocating infants, slow starvation, the frequent falls which are only too often premeditated, and many other instances of perverted natural feelings. The accounts of the perverted sexual instinct among certain tribes and even among modern nations may be due to unnatural conditions affecting the reproductive system; and to this fact also may be attributed prehistoric cannibalism, anthropophagy. Darwin remarks under the heading sterility from changed conditions, showing the extreme susceptibility of the reproductive organs to these changes: " When conception takes place under confinement, " the young are often born dead, or die soon, or are " ill-formed. This frequently occurs in the Zoo-" logical Gardens, and, according to Rengger, with " native animals confined in Paraguay. The mother's " milk often fails. We may also attribute to the dis-" turbance of the sexual functions the frequent " occurrence of that monstrous instinct which leads " the mother to devour her own offspring."

(7.) Disease, unless it directly affects the reproductive organs, seems to have no direct influence in lessening fertility. Diseased animals if left to nature would in all probability die off. Medical science, however, keeps them alive in order that they may propagate their kind.

(8.) The evident correlation between the brain and generative organs, the more the brain is exercised or when the female is given abundant rich food; in fact, the more the vegetative organs are developed in the female, especially where this is excessive, sterility is often the result. We have analagous cases in rich seedless fruit and double flowers.

The extreme delicacy of the females of the upper

classes from their artificial life is also a cause of lessened fertility. Also the sowing of the wild oats of the young men of the upper classes, is too often the cause of the sterility of the females whom they marry.

To disease in the parents may be attributed the largest share in generating the unfit. I read some time ago an article on Hydrocephalus, written by a doctor, who states that hydrocephalus occurs in about one in three thousand confinements, and that if syphilis, which is *such a common disease,* were the cause of hydrocephalus, why hydrocephalus would be more common still. To look up the family history of a patient is now a common practice. I had a girl in my employ whose conduct was very strange; I found on enquiry that her father and brother were in an insane asylum, and it will only be a short time when she will have to be placed under restraint.

The best minds of to-day have accepted the fact that if superior people are desired, they must be bred; and if imbeciles, criminals, paupers, and otherwise unfit are undesirable citizens they must not be bred.

The first principle of the breeder's art is to weed out the inferior animals to avoid conditions which give a tendency to reversion and then to bring together superior animals under the most favourable conditions. We can produce numerous modifications of structure by careful selection of different animals, and there is no reason why, if society were differently organized, that we should not be able to modify and improve the human species to the same extent. In order to do this we must make a religion of the procreative principle. Our girls and boys must be taught how sacred is the life-giving principle. The most wonderful of all the forces at work throughout nature.

Our young men and women should realize the purpose for which they are uniting in the holiest bond of physical life. And by this means we would have inaugurated the upper million and the lower ten. Any social conditions which tend to transpose these terms are subversive of the true interests of humanity.

VICTORIA C. WOODHULL MARTIN.

Part II

POLITICAL THEORY

Introduction by Madeleine B. Stern

Sporting a blue naval costume and an Alpine hat, and armed with the Constitution of the United States, Victoria Woodhull went to Washington in December 1870. The MEMORIAL which had been framed with the help of her friends and advisers, the radical thinkers Stephen Pearl Andrews and James Harvey Blood, was to be presented to Congress. It was indeed an epoch-making document. Against the background of an unsuccessful twenty-year feminist struggle to achieve the franchise, the WOODHULL MEMORIAL was at once novel, simple and powerful. Instead of demanding a new Amendment for the granting of woman suffrage, it brazenly postulated that no new Amendment was required to enfranchise women. As citizens they already possessed that right, a right guaranteed by the Fourteenth and Fifteenth Amendments which had been adopted to insure citizens of the franchise regardless of race or color.

The MEMORIAL, followed by Victoria's ADDRESS TO THE HOUSE JUDICIARY COMMITTEE in January 1871, thus raised the vexed problem of woman suffrage into a question of constitutional law and in so doing deeply impressed the suffragettes, among them Susan B. Anthony and Isabella Beecher Hooker. For a time, until they were distressed by rumors of her unsavory reputation, the feminists saw in La Woodhull the Paladin "best fitted to rescue" their cause "from dusty oblivion."

The Woodhull argument, entrenched in the philosophy of Stephen Pearl Andrews and especially his interpretation of the Constitution, made clear that "with the right to vote sex has nothing to do." A few distinguished law-makers concurred, notably Congressman Albert Gallatin Riddle, who held that by a just construction of the Fourteenth and Fifteenth Amendments women were entitled to vote. Benjamin Franklin Butler, Radical Republican, Member of Congress, and champion of woman's rights, agreed with this interpretation which he elaborated upon as co-author of the Judiciary Committee's Minority Report on the MEMORIAL.

The Majority Report, however, penned by John Armor Bingham, Congressman from Ohio, recommended that the WOODHULL MEMORIAL be laid on the table and that the petitioner's prayer be not granted.

Despite her failure, the petitioner pursued her purpose. At the N
vember elections Victoria Woodhull led a group of thirty-two women
the polls, delivered a peroration on the science of government for t
benefit of the inspectors, and made a courageous albeit unsuccessf
attempt to cast her ballot.

In her LECTURE ON CONSTITUTIONAL EQUALITY Victoria e
broidered upon her arguments. Quoting Franklin and Madison, Ch
Justice Taney and the distinguished orator in the cause of emancipatic
Senator Charles Sumner, she announced that if the Negro had been giv
the franchise, women were equally entitled to it, for "if you speak o
race you include both sexes." Without the franchise, women were tax
to maintain a government in whose administration they were denied
voice. Congress, she advised, should forthwith pass a Declaratory A
setting forth the right of all citizens to vote; otherwise, Victo
Woodhull threatened secession.

She reiterated her theme in CARPENTER AND CARTTER R
VIEWED. Both Matthew Hale Carpenter, Senator from Wisconsin, a
David Kellogg Cartter, Chief Justice of the Supreme Court of the D
trict of Columbia, disagreed with her interpretation of the Fourteen
and Fifteenth Amendments. In her speech before the National Suffra
Association in Washington on January 10, 1872, Victoria Woodh
gave both these anti-feminists a dressing-down based upon a close lc
ical analysis of race and sex, states' rights and court decisions. S
touched upon the Dred Scott Case when Chief Justice Taney, befc
deciding in 1857 that Congress had no power to exclude slavery frc
the territories, dilated upon the term, citizen. She referred to the T
ritory of Wyoming whose Legislature had been the first to grant su
frage to women in 1869. She cited a succession of points of law, dou
less marshaled by her editor-friend, the erstwhile attorney, Steph
Pearl Andrews. And after all the references and citations had been ma
she concluded that, while one million Negroes could now exercise t
right of franchise, fifteen million women could not. Yet, she affirme
"I submit that I have established, first: that by the mere fact of bei
citizens women are possessed of the elective franchise; and second, th
the elective franchise is one of the privileges of the Fourteenth Amer
ment which the States shall not abridge; that the States cannot regula
the suffrage out of existence, as they attempt to do, and have done,
the case of women; and finally, that whether it was, or was not, the
tent of the framers of the Fourteenth Amendment to give women t
elective franchise, *they have done so*, past all hope of retreat."

A generation after that summing-up, during the Panic Year of 189
the State of Colorado granted women the right to vote for its Preside

al Electors. It was an act that had little or no influence upon the ection in which McKinley triumphantly carried both the West and the Mid-West after a bitter campaign against Bryan. But it did prompt Victoria Woodhull, who by then had become Victoria Woodhull Martin f London, to review the circumstances of her MEMORIAL and AD-DRESS TO THE HOUSE JUDICIARY COMMITTEE and to comment pon feminist reaction to her efforts which, she believed, had given "an mmediate impetus to the movement." In her article, WOMAN SUF-'RAGE IN THE UNITED STATES, she asserted: "It was at this time 1870-1871) that the movement reached its flood in America. It has ow come forward with a rush again, and if taken at the flood, will ssuredly lead to victory. The victory will be achieved on the constitu-ional plea which I advanced at Washington twenty-five years ago."

On both counts Victoria Woodhull was wrong. A new Amendment would be required to enfranchise women and another generation would ass before this was accomplished.

Months before her MEMORIAL had been presented to Congress, Victoria Woodhull determined to test the issue involved by running for olitical office. On April 2, 1870, she flung her hat into the ring with a MANIFESTO which appeared in the *New York Herald* announcing her andidacy for the Presidency of the United States, the first such pro-osal in American political history.

The thought was swiftly transmuted into action. A Victoria League was organized to support her candidacy. In May 1872 at an Apollo Hall onvention, Victoria Woodhull was officially nominated and a grand ally at Cooper Institute ratified the nomination of the Equal Rights arty. *Woodhull & Claflin's Weekly* was used as a campaign sheet; to the une of "John Brown's Body" her constituents chanted, "Victoria's narching on."

Her NEW PARTY PLATFORM—the platform of the Equal Rights arty—was a mélange of the revolutionary theories of Stephen Pearl Andrews and James Harvey Blood, and the French socialist reformers, Fourier and Jean Godin, founder of a Palace of Industry for workers in Guise, France. It aimed at the reconstruction of the most important unctions of government, the advancement of labor, the freedom of wo-man. It opposed monopoly and the death penalty. It championed the ight-hour day, free land, and a one-term Presidency terminated by a .fe pension and a seat in the Senate. It promised civil service reform and .ational education, a foreign policy reflecting the expanding influence f the United States, a system of social security and a program that would respect the rights of humanity rather than the rights of property. ignificantly, it envisioned a Grand International Tribunal for the arbitration of differences.

Internationalism was a concept especially congenial to Stephen Pear
Andrews. He thought in international—sometimes even interplanetary—
terms, and his influence upon Victoria Woodhull's political thinking
during the 1870's was profound. One of the most important works bear
ing the Woodhull byline is A PAGE OF AMERICAN HISTORY. CON
STITUTION OF THE UNITED STATES OF THE WORLD. This pre
cursor of a League of Nations enunciates the doctrine of interdepend
ence, allows for the development of the arts and sciences, guarantees the
elective franchise to all adult citizens, and views the producer as entitle
to the total proceeds of his labor. It looks to a socialist welfare state fo
"the abolition of Pauperism . . . upon the principle that if people canno
obtain employment government should supply it to them; if they wil
not labor, government should compel them sufficiently to support them
selves; if they cannot labor, government should maintain them."

Unfortunately, by the time Grant was re-elected in November 1872
the Equal Rights Party had no electoral ticket and its erstwhile cand
date was in Ludlow Street Jail, charged with transmitting obscene li
erature through the mails.

Now, a century later, the Utopian doctrines outlined in Victori
Woodhull's platform and in the writings that bear her name are investe
with a special relevancy. Many of the concepts defined therein have b
come part of the national legal fabric. The writings and speeches i
which they were adumbrated one hundred years ago thus form a di
tinguished and important part of the radical political literature of th
country.

POLITICAL THEORY

(1)

Congressional Reports . . . on the Woodhull Memorial . . . 1871.

CONGRESSIONAL REPORTS

ON

WOMAN SUFFRAGE.

The Majority and Minority Reports

OF THE

JUDICIARY COMMITTEE

OF THE

HOUSE OF REPRESENTATIVES

ON THE

WOODHULL MEMORIAL.

NEW YORK:

WOODHULL, CLAFLIN & CO, No. 44 BROAD STREET.

1871.

CONSTITUTIONAL EQUALITY.

To the Hon. the Judiciary Committees of the Senate and the House of Representatives of the Congress of the United States:

The undersigned, Victoria C. Woodhull, having most respectfully memorialized Congress for the passage of such laws as in its wisdom shall seem necessary and proper to carry into effect the rights vested by the Constitution of the United States in the citizens to vote, without regard to sex, begs leave to submit to your honorable body the following in favor of her prayer in said Memorial which has been referred to your Committee:

The public law of the world is founded upon the conceded fact that sovereignty cannot be forfeited or renounced. The sovereign power of this country is perpetual in the politically-organized people of the United States, and can neither be relinquished nor abandoned by any portion of them. The people in this Republic who confer sovereignty are its citizens: in a monarchy the people are the subjects of sovereignty. All citizens of a republic by rightful act or implication confer sovereign power. All people of a monarchy are subjects who exist under its supreme shield and enjoy its immunities.

The subject of a monarch takes municipal immunities from the sovereign as a gracious favor; but the woman citizen of this country has the inalienable "sovereign" right of self-government in *her own proper person*. Those who look upon woman's status by the dim light of the common law, which unfolded itself under the feudal and military institutions that establish right upon physical power, cannot find any analogy in the status of the woman citizen of this country, *where the broad sunshine of our Constitution has enfranchised all.*

As sovereignty cannot be forfeited, relinquished or abandoned, those from whom it flows—the citizens—are equal in conferring the power, and should be equal in the enjoyment of its benefits and in the exercise of its rights and privileges.

One portion of citizens have no power to deprive another portion of rights and privileges such as are possessed and exercised by themselves. The male citizen has no more right to deprive the female citizen of the free, public, political expression of opinion than the female citizen has to deprive the male citizen thereof.

The sovereign will of the people is expressed in our written Constitution, which is the supreme law of the land. The Constitution makes no distinction of sex. The Constitution defines a woman born or naturalized in the United States, and subject to the jurisdiction thereof, to be a citizen. It recognizes the right of citizens to vote. It declares that the right of citizens of the United States to vote shall not be denied or abridged by the United States or by any State on account of "race, color or previous condition of servitude."

Women, white and black, belong to races; although to different races. A race of people comprises all the people, male and female. The right to vote cannot be denied on account of race. All people included in the term race have the right to vote, unless otherwise prohibited.

Women of all races are white, black or some intermediate color. Color comprises all people, of all races and both sexes. The right to vote cannot be denied on account of color. All people included in the term color have the right to vote unless otherwise prohibited.

With the right to vote sex has nothing to do. Race and color include all people of both sexes. All people of both sexes have the right to vote, unless prohibited by special limiting terms less comprehensive than race or color. No such limiting terms exist in the Constitution.

Women, white and black, have from time immemorial groaned under what is properly termed in the Constitution "previous condition of servitude."

Women are the equals of men before the law, and are equal in all their rights as citizens.

Women are debarred from voting in some parts of the United States, although they are allowed to exercise that right elsewhere.

Women were formerly permitted to vote in places where they are now debarred therefrom.

The Naturalization Laws of the United States expressly provide for the naturalization of women.

But the right to vote has only lately been distinctly declared by the Constitution to be inalienable, under three distinct conditions—in all of which woman is distinctly embraced.

The citizen who is taxed should also have a voice in the subject

matter of taxation. " No taxation without representation" is a right
which was fundamentally established at the very birth of our country's
independence ; and by what ethics does any free government impose
taxes on women without giving them a voice upon the subject or a
participation in the public declaration as to how and by whom these
taxes shall be applied for common public use ?

Women are free to own and to control property, separate and
apart from males, and they are held responsible in their own proper
persons, in every particular, as well as men, in and out of court.

Women have the same inalienable right to life, liberty and the
pursuit of happiness that men have. Why have they not this right
politically, as well as men ?

Women constitute a majority of the people of this country—they
hold vast portions of the nation's wealth and pay a proportionate share
of the taxes. They are intrusted with the most holy duties and the
most vital responsibilities of society ; they bear, rear and educate men ;
they train and mould their characters; they inspire the noblest impulses in men ; they often hold the accumulated fortunes of a man's
life for the safety of the family and as guardians of the infants, and
yet they are debarred from uttering any opinion, by public vote, as to
the management by public servants of these interests ; they are the
secret counsellors, the best advisers, the most devoted aids in the most
trying periods of men's lives, and yet men shrink from trusting them
in the common questions of ordinary politics. Men trust women in
the market, in the shop, on the highway and the railroad, and in all
other public places and assemblies, but when they propose to carry a
slip of paper with a name upon it to the polls, they fear them. Nevertheless, as citizens women have the right to vote; they are part and
parcel of that great element in which the sovereign power of the land
had birth : and it is by usurpation only that men debar them from
their right to vote. The American nation, in its march onward and
upward, cannot publicly choke the intellectual and political activity
of half its citizens by narrow statutes. The will of the entire people
is the true basis of republican government, and a free expression of
that will by the public vote of all citizens, without distinctions of
race, color, occupation or sex, is the only means by which that will can
be ascertained. As the world has advanced in civilization and culture ; as mind has risen in its dominion over matter ; as the principle
of justice and moral right has gained sway, and merely physically organized power has yielded thereto ; as the might of right has sup-

planted the right of might, so have the rights of women become more
fully recognized, and that recognition is the result of the development
of the minds of men, which through the ages she has polished, and
thereby heightened the lustre of civilization.

It was reserved for our great country to recognize by constitutional
enactment that political equality of all citizens which religion, affection
and common sense should have long since accorded; it was reserved
for America to sweep away the mist of prejudice and ignorance, and
that chivalric condescension of a darker age, for in the language of
Holy Writ, "The night is far spent, the day is at hand, let us therefore
cast off the work of darkness, and let us put on the armor of light.
Let us walk honestly as in the day."

It may be argued against the proposition that tnere still remains
upon the statute books of some States the word "male" to an exclusion, but as the Constitution in its paramount character can only be
read by the light of the established principle, *ita lex Scripta est;* and as
the subject of sex is not mentioned and the Constitution is not limited
either in terms or by necessary implication in the general rights of citizens to vote, this right cannot be limited on account of anything in the
spirit of inferior or previous enactments upon a subject which is
not mentioned in the supreme law. A different construction would
destroy a vested right in a portion of the citizens, and this no legislature
has a right to do without compensation, and nothing can compensate a
citizen for the loss of his or her suffrage—its value is equal to the value
of life. Neither can it be presumed that women are to be kept from the
polls as a mere police regulation: it is to be hoped, at least, that police
regulations in their case need not be very active. The effect of the
amendments to the Constitution must be to annul the power over this
subject in the States whether past, present or future, which is contrary
to the amendments. The amendments would even arrest the action of
the Supreme Court in cases pending before it prior to their adoption,
and operate as an absolute prohibition to the exercise of any other jurisdiction than merely to dismiss the suit.

3 Dall., 382 ; 6 Wheaton, 405 ; 9 Id., 868 ; 3d Circ., Pa., 1832.

And if the restrictions contained in the Constitution as to color,
race or servitude, were designed to limit the State governments in reference to their own citizens, and were intended to operate also as restrictions on the Federal power, and to prevent interference with the rights
of the State and its citizens, how then can the State restrict citizens of
the United States in the exercise of rights not mentioned in any restric-

tive clause in reference to actions on the part of those citizens having reference solely to the necessary functions of the General Government, such as the election of representatives and senators to Congress, whose election the Constitution expressly gives Congress the power to regulate?

S. C., 1847 : Fox vs. Ohio, 5 Howard, 410.

Your memorialist complains of the existence of State Laws, and prays Congress, by appropriate legislation, to declare them, as they are, annulled, and to give vitality to the Constitution under its power to make and alter the regulations of the States contravening the same.

It may be urged in opposition that the Courts have power, and should declare upon this subject.

The Supreme Court has the power, and it would be its duty so to declare the law ; but the Court will not do so unless a determination of such point as shall arise make it necessary to the determination of a controversy, and hence a case must be presented in which there can be no rational doubt. All this would subject the aggrieved parties to much dilatory. expensive and needless litigation, which your memorialist prays your Honorable Body to dispense with by appropriate legislation, as there can be no purpose in special arguments " ad inconvenienti," enlarging or contracting the import of the language of theConstitution.

Therefore, Believing firmly in the right of citizens to freely approach those in whose hands their destiny is placed, under the Providence of God, your memorialist has frankly, but humbly, appealed to you, and prays that the wisdom of Congress may be moved to action in this matter for the benefit and the increased happiness of our beloved country.

Most respectfully submitted,

VICTORIA C. WOODHULL.

Dated NEW YORK, January 2, 1871.

THE MEMORIAL OF VICTORIA C. WOODHULL.

To the Honorable the Senate and House of Representatives of the United States in Congress assembled, respectfully showeth:

That she was born in the State of Ohio, and is above the age of twenty-one years; that she has resided in the State of New York during the past three years; that she is still a resident thereof, and that she is a citizen of the United States, as declared by the XIV. Article of Amendments to the Constitution of the United States.

That since the adoption of the XV. Article of Amendments to the Constitution, neither the State of New York nor any other State, nor any Territory, has passed any law to abridge the right of any citizen of the United States to vote, as established by said article, neither on account of sex or otherwise:

That, nevertheless, the right to vote is denied to women citizens of the United States, by the operation of Election Laws in the several States and Territories, which laws were enacted prior to the adoption of the said XV. Article, and which are inconsistent with the Constitution as amended, and therefore, are void and of no effect; but which, being still enforced by the said States and Territories, render the Constitution inoperative as regards the right of women citizens to vote:

And whereas, Article VI., Section 2, declares "That this Constitution, and the laws of the United States which shall be made in pursuance thereof, and all treaties made, or which shall be made under the authority of the United States, shall be the supreme law of the land; and all judges in every State shall be bound thereby, anything in the Constitution and laws of any State to the contrary notwithstanding:"

And whereas, no distinction between citizens is made in the Constitution of the United States on account of sex; but the XV. article of Amendments to it provides that "No State shall make or enforce any law which shall abridge the privileges and immunities of citizens of the United States, nor deny to any person within its jurisdiction the equal protection of the laws."

And whereas, Congress has power to make laws which shall be necessary and proper for carrying into execution all powers vested by the Constitution in the Government of the United States, and to make or alter all regulations in relation to holding elections for senators or representatives, and especially to enforce, by appropriate legislation, the provisions of the said XIV. Article:

And whereas, the continuance of the enforcement of said local election laws, denying and abridging the right of citizens to vote on account of sex, is a grievance to your memorialist and to various other persons, citizens of the United States, being women—

Therefore, your memorialist would most respectfully petition your Honorable Bodies to make such laws as in the wisdom of Congress shall be necessary and proper for carrying into execution the right vested by the Constitution in the Citizens of the United States to vote, without regard to sex.

And your memorialist will ever pray.   VICTORIA C. WOODHULL.

Dated NEW YORK CITY, December 19, 1870.

41st Congress, 3d Session.	HOUSE OF REPRESENTATIVES.	Report No. 22.

VICTORIA C. WOODHULL.

JANUARY 30, 1871.—Recommitted to the Committee on the Judiciary and ordered to be printed.

Mr. BINGHAM, from the Committee on the Judiciary, made the following

REPORT.

The Committee on the Judiciary, to whom was referred the Memorial of Victoria C. Woodhull, having considered the same, make the following report:

The Memorialist asks the enactment of a law by Congress which shall secure to citizens of the United States in the several States the right to vote " without regard to sex." Since the adoption of the fourteenth amendment of the Constitution, there is no longer any reason to doubt that all persons, born or naturalized in the United States, and subject to the jurisdiction thereof, are citizens of the United States and of the State wherein they reside, for that is the express declaration of the amendment.

The clause of the fourteenth amendment, " No State shall make or enforce any law which shall abridge the privileges or immuni es of citizens of the United States," does not, in the opinion of the committee, refer to privileges and immunities of citizens of the United States other than those privileges and immunities embraced in the original text of the Constitution, Article 1V., Section 2. The fourteenth amendment, it is believed, did not add to the privileges or immunities before mentioned, but was deemed necessary for their enforcement, as an express limitation upon the powers of the States. It has been judicially determined that the first eight articles of amendment of the Constitution were not limitations on the power of the States, and it was apprehended that the same might be held of the provision of the second section, fourth article.

To remedy this defect of the Constitution, the express limitations upon the States contained in the first section of the fourteenth amendment, together with the grant of power to Congress to enforce them by legislation, were incorporated in the Constitution. The words " citizens of the United States," and " citizens of the States," as employed in the fourteenth amendment, did not change or modify the relations of citizens of the State and Nation as they existed under the original Constitution.

Attorney General Bates gave the opinion that the Constitution uses the word " citizen," only to express the political quality of the individual in his relation to the Nation ; to declare that he is a member of the body politic, and bound to it by the reciprocal obligation of allegiance on the one side and protection on the other. The phrase " a citizen of the United States," without addition or qualification, means neither more nor less than a member of the Nation. (Opinion of Attorney General Bates on citizenship.)

The Supreme Court of the United States has ruled that, according to the express words and clear meaning of the second section, fourth article of the Constitution, no privileges are secured by it except those which belong to citizenship. (Connor et al. vs. Elliott et al., 18 Howard, 593.,

In Corfield vs. Coryell, 4 Washington Circuit Court Reports, 380, the court say :

The inquiry is, what are the privileges and immunities of citizens in the several States ? We feel no hesitation in confining these expressions to those privileges and immunities which are in their nature fundamental; which belong of right to the citizens of all free governments; and which have at all times been enjoyed by the citizens of the several States which compose this Union, from the time of their becoming free, independent and sovereign. What these fundamental principles are would, perhaps, be more tedious than difficult to enumerate. They may, however, be all comprehended under the following general heads: Protection by the Government; the enjoyment of life and liberty, with the right to acquire and possess property of every kind, and to pursue and obtain happiness and safety, subject, nevertheless, to such restraints as the Government may justly prescribe for the general good of the whole; the right of a citizen of one State to pass through or to reside in any other State, for the purpose of trade, agriculture, professional pursuits, or otherwise; to claim the benefit of the writ of *habeas corpus*; to institute and maintain actions of any kind in the courts of the State; to take, hold, and dispose of property, either real or personal; and an exemption from higher taxes or impositions than are paid by the other citizens of the State, may be mentioned as some of the particular privileges and immunities of citizens which are clearly embraced by the general description of privileges deemed to be fundamental; to which may be added the elective franchise, as regulated and established by the laws or Constitution of the State in which it is to be exercised.   *   *   * But we cannot accede to the proposition which was insisted on by the counsel, that under this provision of the Constitution, sec. 2., art. 4, the citizens of the several States are permitted to participate in all the rights which belong exclusively to the citizens of any other particular State.

The learned Justice Story declared that the intention of the clause—"the citizens of each State shall be entitled to all the privileges and immunities of citizens in the several States"—was to confer on the citizens of each State a general citizenship, and communicated all the privileges and immunities which a citizen of the same State would be entitled to under the same circumstances. (Story on the Constitution, vol. 2, p. 605.)

In the case of the Bank of the United States *vs.* Primrose, in the Supreme Court of the United States, Mr. Webster said:

That this article in the Constitution (art. 4., sec. 2) does not confer on the citizens of each State political rights in every other State, is admitted. A citizen of Pennsylvania cannot go into Virginia and vote at any election in that State, though when he has acquired a residence in Virginia, and is otherwise qualified and is required by the constitution (of Virginia), he becomes, without formal adoption as a citizen of Virginia, a citizen of that State politically. (Webster's Works, vol. 6, p. 112.)

It must be obvious that Mr. Webster was of opinion that the privileges and immunities of citizens, guaranteed to them in the several States, did not include the privilege of the elective franchise otherwise than as secured by the State Constitution. For, after making the statement above quoted, that a citizen of Pennsylvania cannot go into Virginia and vote, Mr. Webster adds, "but for the purposes of trade, commerce, buying and selling, it is evidently not in the power of any State to impose any hindrance or embrassment, &c., upon citizens of other States, or to place them, going there, upon a different footing from her own citizens." (Ib.)

The proposition is clear that no citizen of the United States can rightfully vote in any State of this Union who has not the qualifications required by the Constitution of the State in which the right is claimed to be exercised, except as to such conditions in the constitutions of such States as deny the right to vote to citizens resident therein "on account of race, color, or previous condition of servitude."

The adoption of the fifteenth amendment to the Constitution imposing these three limitations upon the power of the several States, was by necessary implication, a declaration that the States had the power to regulate by a uniform rule the conditions upon which the elective franchise should be exercised by citizens of the United States resident therein. The limitations specified in the fifteenth amendment exclude the conclusion that a State of this Union, having a government republican in form, may not prescribe conditions upon which alone citizens may vote other than those prohibited. It can hardly be said that a State law which excludes from voting women citizens, minor citizens, and non-resident citizens of the United States, on account of sex, minority or domicil, is a denial of the right to vote on account of race, color, or previous condition of servitude.

It may be further added that the second section of the fourteenth amendment, by the provision that "when the right to vote at any election for the choice of electors of President and Vice-President of the United States, Representatives in Congress, or executive and judicial officers of the State, or the members of the legislature thereof, is denied to any of the male inhabitants of such State, being twenty-one years of age, a citizen of the United Sates, or in any way abridged, except for participation in rebellion or other crime, the basis of representation therein shall be reduced in the proportion which the number of such male citizens shall bear to the whole number of male citizens twenty-one years of age in such State," implies that the several States may restrict the elective franchise as to other than male citizens. In disposing of this question effect must be given, if possible, to every provision of the Constitution. Article 1, section 2, of the Constitution provides:

That the House of Representatives shall be composed of members chosen every second year by the people of the several States, and the electors in each State shall have the qualifications requisite for electors of the most numerous branch of the State legislature.

This provision has always been construed to vest in the several States the exclusive right to prescribe the qualifications of electors for the most numerous branch of the State legislature, and therefore for members of Congress. And this interpretation is supported by section 4, article 1, of the Constitution, which provides—

That the time, places, and manner of holding elections for Senators and Representatives shall be prescribed in each State by the legislature thereof; but the Congress may at any time by law make or alter such regulations except as to the place of choosing Senators.

Now it is submitted, if it had been intended that Congress should prescribe the qualifications of electors, that the grant would have read: The Congress may at any time by law make or alter such regulations, and also prescribe the qualifications of electors, &c. The power, on the contrary, is limited exclusively to the time, place and manner, and does not extend to the qualification of the electors. This power to prescribe the qualification of electors in the several States has always been exercised, and is, to-day, by the several States of the Union; and we apprehend, until the Constitution shall be changed, will continue to be so exercised, subject only to the express limitations imposed by the Constitution upon the several States, before noticed. We are of opinion, therefore, that it is not competent for the Congress of the United States to establish by law the right to vote without regard to sex in the several States of this Union, without the consent of the people of such States, and against their constitutions and laws; and that such legislation would be, in our judgment, a violation of the Constitution of the United States, and of the rights reserved to the States respectively by the Constitution. Is it is undoubtedly the right of the people of the several States so to reform their constitutions and laws as to secure the equal exercise of the right of suffrage, at all elections held therein under the Constitution of the United States, to all citizens, without regard to sex; and as public opinion creates constitutions and governments in the several States, it is not to be doubted that whenever, in any State, the people are of opinion that such a reform is advisable, it will be made.

If, however, as is claimed in the memorial referred to, the right to vote "is vested by the Constitution in the citizens of the United States without regard to sex," that right can be established in the courts without further legislation.

The suggestion is made that Congress, by a mere declaratory act, shall say that the construction claimed in the memorial is the true construction of the Constitution, or in other words, that by the Constitution of the United States the right to vote is vested in citizens of the United States "without regard to sex," anything in the constitution and laws of any State to the contrary notwithstanding. In the opinion of the committee, such declaratory act is not authorized by the Constitution nor within the legislative power of Congress. We therefore recommend the adoption of the following resolution:

Resolved, That the prayer of the petitioner be not granted, that the memorial be laid on the table, and that the Committee on the Judiciary be discharged from the further consideration of the subject.

| 41st Congress, 3d Session. | HOUSE OF REPRESENTATIVES. | Report No. V., Part 2. |

VICTORIA C. WOODHULL.

FEBRUARY 1, 1871.—Ordered to be Printed.

Mr. LOUGHRIDGE, from the Committee on the Judiciary, submitted the following as the

VIEWS OF THE MINORITY.

In the matter of the Memorial of Victoria C. Woodhull, referred by the House to the Committee on the Judiciary, the undersigned, members of the Committee, being unable to agree to the report of the committee, present the following as their views upon the subject of the Memorial:

The memorialist sets forth that she is a native born citizen of the United States, and a resident thereof; that she is of adult age, and has resided in the State of New York for three years past; that by the Constitution of the United States she is guaranteed the right of suffrage; but that she is, by the laws of the State of New York, denied the exercise of that right; and that by the laws of different States and Territories the privilege of voting is denied to all the female citizens of the United States; and petitions for relief by the enactment of some law to enforce the provisions of the Constitution, by which such right is guaranteed.

The question presented is one of exceeding interest and importance, involving as it does the constitutional rights not only of the memorialist but of more than one half of the citizens of the United States—a question of constitutional law in which the civil and natural rights of the citizen are involved. Questions of property or of expediency have nothing to do with it. The question is not "Would it be expedient to extend the right of suffrage to women," but, "Have women citizens that right by the Constitution as it is."

A question of this kind should be met fairly and investigated in that generous and liberal spirit characteristic of the age, and decided upon principles of justice, of right, and of law.

It is claimed by many that to concede to woman the right of suffrage would be an innovation upon the laws of nature, and upon the theory and practice of the world for ages in the past, and especially an innovation upon the common law of England, which was originally the law of this country, and which is the foundation of our legal fabric.

If we were to admit the truth of this, it is yet no argument against the proposition, if the right claimed exists, and is established by the Constitution of the United States. The question is to be decided by the Constitution and the fundamental principles of our Government, and not by the usage and dogmas of the past.

It is a gratifying fact that the world is advancing in political science, and gradually adopting more liberal and rational theories of government,

The establishment of this Government upon the principles of the declaration of Independence was in itself a great innovation upon the theories and practice of the world, and opened a new chapter in the history of the human race, and its progress toward perfect civil and political liberty.

But it is not admitted that the universal usage of the past has been in opposition to the exercise of political power by women. The highest positions of civil power have from time to time been filled by women in all ages of the world, and the question of the right of woman to a voice in government is not a new one by any means, but has been agitated, and the right acknowledged and exercised, in governments far less free and liberal than ours.

In the Roman Republic, during its long and glorious career, women occupied a higher position, as to political rights and privileges, than in any other contemporaneous government. In England unmarried women have, by the laws of that country, always been competent to vote and to hold civil offices, if qualified in other respects; at least such is the weight of authority. In "Callis upon Sewers," an old English work, will be found a discussion of the question as to the right of women to hold office in England.

The learned and distinguished author uses the following language:

And for temporal governments I have observed women to have from time to time been admitted to the highest places; for in ancient Roman histories I find Eudocia and Theodora admitted at several times into the sole government of the empire; and here in England our late famous Queen Elizabeth, whose government was most renowned; and Semiramis governed Syria; and the Queen of the South, which came to visit Solomon, for anything that appears to the contrary, was a sole queen; and to fall a degree lower, we have precedents that King Richard the First and King Henry the Fifth appointed by commissions their mothers to be regents of this realm in their absence in France.

But yet I will descend a step lower; and doth not our law, temporal and spiritual, admit of women to be executrixes and administratrixes? And thereby they have the rule or ordering of great estates, and many times they are guardianesses in chivalry, and have hereby also the government of many great heirs in the kingdom and of their own estates.

So by these cases it appeareth that the common law of this kingdom submitted many things to their government; yet the statute of justices of the peace is like to Jethro's counsel to Moses, for there they speak of men to be justices, and thereby seemeth to exclude women; but our statute of sewers is, "Commission of sewers shall be granted by the King to such person and persons as the lords should appoint." So the word persons stands indifferently for either sex. I am of the opinion, for the authorities, reasons and causes aforesaid, that this honorable countess being put into the commission of the sewers, the same is warrantable by the law; and the ordinances and decrees made by her and the other commissions of sewers are not to be impeached for that cause of her sex.

As it is said by a recent writer:

Even a present in England the idea of women holding official station is not so strange as in the United States. The Countess of Pembroke had the office of sheriff of Westmoreland and exercised it in person. At the assizes she sat with the judges on the bench. In a reported case it is stated by counsel and assented to by the court that a woman is capable of serving in almost all the offices of the kingdom.

As to the right of women to vote by the common law of England, the authorities are clear. In the English Law Magazine for 1868-'69, vol. 26, page 120, will be found reported the case of the application of JANE ALLEN, who claimed to be entered upon the list of voters of the Parish of St. Giles, under the reform act of 1867, which act provides as follows: Every man shall, in and after the year 1868, be entitled to be registered as a voter, and when registered to vote for a member or members to serve in Parliament, who is qualified as follows: 1st. Is of full age and not subject to any legal incapacity, &c., &c.

It was decided by the court that the claimant had the right to be registered and to vote; that by the English law, the term man, as used in that statute, included woman. In that case the common law of England upon that question was fully and ably reviewed, and we may be excused for quoting at some length:

And as to what has been said of there being no such adjudged cases, I must say that it is perfectly clear that not perhaps in either of three cases reported by Mr. Sharn, but in those of Catharine vs. Surry, Coates vs. Lyle, and Holt vs. Lyle, three cases of somewhat greater antiquity, the right of women freeholders was allowed by the courts. These three cases were decided by the judges in the reign of James I (A. D. 1612). Although no printed report of them exists, I find that in the case of Olive vs. Ingraham, they were repeatedly cited by the lord chief justice of the Kings Bench in the course of four great arguments in that case, the case being reargued three times (7 Mod., 264), and the greatest respect was manifested by the whole court for those precedents. Their importance is all the greater when we consider what the matter was upon which King James' judges sitting in Westminster Hall had to decide. It was not simply the case of a mere occupier, inhabitant, or scot or lot voter. Therefore the question did not turn upon the purport of a special custom, or a charter, or a local act of Parliament, or even of the common right in this or that borough. But it was that very matter and question which has been mooted in the dictum of Lord Coke, the freeholder's franchise in the shire, and upon that the decision in each case expressly was, that a feme sole shall vote if she hath a freehold, and that if she be not a feme sole, but a feme covert having freehold, then her husband during her coverture shall vote in her right. These, then, are so many express decisions which at once displace Lord Coke's unsupported assertion and declare the law so as to constrain my judgment. It is sometimes said, when reference is made to precedents of this kind, that they have never been approved by the bar. But that cannot be said of these. Hakewell, the contemporary of Lord Coke and one of the greatest of all parliamentary lawyers then living—for even Selden and Granvil were not greater than Hakewell—left behind him the manuscript to which I have referred, with his comments on those cases.

Sir William Lee, chief justice, in his judgment in the case of Olive vs. Ingraham, expressly says that he had persued them, and that they contained the expression of Hakewell's entire approval of the principles upon which they were decided, and of the results deduced; and we have the statement of Lord Chief Justice Lee, who had carefully examined those cases, that in the case of Holt vs. Lyle, it was determined that a feme sole freeholder may claim a vote for Parliament men; but if married, her husband must vote for her.

In the case of Olive vs. Ingraham, Justice Probyn, says:

The case of Holt vs. Lyle, lately mentioned by our Lord Chief Justice, is a very strong case; "They who pay ought to choose whom they shall pay." And the Lord Chief Justice seemed to have assented to that general proposition, as authority for the correlative proposition, that "women, when *sole*, had a right to vote." At all events, there is here the strongest possible evidence that in the reign of James I, the *feme sole*, being a freeholder of a country, or what is the same thing, of a county, of a city, or town, or borough, where, of custom, freeholders had the right to vote, not only had, but exercised the parliamentary franchise. If married, she could not vote in respect merely of her freehold, not because of the incapacities of coverture, but for this simple reason, that, by the act of marriage, which is an act of law, the title of the *feme sole* freeholder becomes vested for life in the husband. The qualification to vote was not personal, but real; consequently, her right to vote became suspended as soon and for as long as she was married. I am bound to consider that the question as to what weight is due to the dictum of my Lord Coke is entirely disposed of by those cases from the reign of James I and George II, and that the authority of the latter is unimpeached by any later authority, as the cases of Rex. *vs.* Stubles, and Regina *vs.* Aberavon, abundantly show.

In Austey's Notes on the New Reform Act of 1867, the authorities and precedents upon the right of women to vote in England are examined and summed up, and the author concludes:

It is submitted that the weight of authority is very greatly in favor of the female right of suffrage. Indeed, the authority against it is contained in the short and hasty dictum of Lord Coke, refered to above. It was set down by him in his last and least authoritive institute, and it is certain that he has been followed neither by the great lawyers of his time nor by the judicature. The principles of the law in relation to the suffrage of females will be found in Coates *vs.* Lyle, Holt *vs* Ingraham, and The King *vs.* Stubles, cases decided under the strict rules for the construction of statutes.

It cannot be questioned that from time whereof the memory of man runneth not to the contrary, unmarried women have been by the laws of England competent voters, subject to the freehold qualification which applied alike to men and women. Married women could not vote because they were not freeholders; by the common law their property upon marriage became vested in the husband.

So that it appears that the admission of woman to participation in the affairs of government would not be so much of an innovation upon the theories and usage of the past as is by some supposed.

In England the theory was that in property representation, all property should be represented. Here the theory is that of personal representation, which of course, if carried out fully, includes the representation of all property. In England, as we have seen, the owner of the property, whether male or female was entitled to representation, no distinction being made on account of sex. If the doctrine contended for by the majority of the committee be correct, then this Government is less liberal upon this question than the government of England has been for hundreds of years, for there is in this country a large class of citizens of adult age, and owners in their own right of large amounts of property, and who pay a large proportion of the taxes to support the Government, who are denied any representation whatever, either for themselves or their property—unmarried women, of whom it cannot be said that their interests are represented by their husbands. In their case, neither the English nor the American theory of representation is carried out, and this utter denial of representation is justified upon the ground alone that this class of citizens are women.

Surely we cannot be so much less liberal than our English ancestors! Surely the Constitution of this Republic does not sanction an injustice so indefensible as that!

By the fourteenth amendment of the Constitution of the United States, what constitutes citizenship of the United States, is for the first time declared, and who are included by the term citizen. Upon this question, before that time, there had been much discussion judicial, political and general, and no distinct and definite definition of qualification had been settled.

The people of the United States determined this question by the fourteenth amendment to the Constitution, which declares that—

All persons born or naturalized in the United States and subject to the jurisdiction thereof are citizens of the United States, and of the State wherein they reside. No State shall make or enforce any law which shall abridge the privileges or immunities of citizens of the United States; nor shall any State deprive any person of life, liberty, or property, without due process of law; nor deny to any person within its jurisdiction the equal protection of the law.

This amendment, after declaring who are citizens of the United States, and thus fixing but one grade of citizenship, which insures to all citizens alike all the privileges, immunities and rights which accrue to that condition, goes on in the same section and prohibits these privileges and immunities from abridgment by the States.

Whatever these "privileges and immunities" are, they attach to the female citizen equally with the male. It is implied by this amendment that they are inherent, that they belong to citizenship as such, for they are not therein specified or enumerated.

The majority of the committee hold that the privileges guaranteed by the fourteenth amendment do not refer to any other than the privileges embraced in section 2, of article 4, of the original text.

The committee certainly did not duly consider this unjustified statement.

Section 2, of article 4, provides for the privileges of "citizens of the *States*," while the first section of the fourteenth amendment protects the privileges of "*citizens of the United States.*" The terms citizens of the *States* and citizens of the *United States* are by no means convertible.

A circuit court of the United States seems to hold a different view of this question from that stated by the committee.

In the case of The Live Stock Association *vs.* Crescent City (1st Abbott, 396), Justice Bradley, of the Supreme Court of the United States, delivering the opinion, uses the following language in relation to the 1st clause of the 14th amendment:

The new prohibition that "no State shall make or enforce any law which shall abridge the privileges or immunities of citizens of the United States" is not identical with the clause in the Constitution which declared that "the citizens of each State shall be entitled to all the privileges and immunities of citizens in the several States." It embraces much more.

It is possible that those who framed the article were not themselves aware of the far-reaching character of its terms, yet if the amendment does in fact bear a broader meaning, and does extend its protecting shield over those who were never thought of when it was conceived and put in form, and does reach social evils which were never before prohibited by constitutional enactment, it is to be presumed that the American people, in giving it their *imprimatur*, understood what they were doing and meant to decree what in fact they have decreed.

The "privileges and immunities" secured by the original Constitution were only such as each State gave to its own citizens, * * * * but the fourteenth amendment prohibits any State from abridging the privileges or immunities of citizens of the United States, whether its own citizens or any others. It not merely requires equality of privileges, but it demands that the privileges and immunities of all citizens shall be absolutely unabridged and unimpaired.

In the same opinion, after enumerating some of the "privileges" of the citizens, such as were pertinent to the case on trial, but declining to enumerate all, the court further says:

These privileges cannot be invaded without sapping the very foundation of republican government. A republican government is not merely a government of the people, but it is a free government. * * * * It was very ably contended on the part of the defendants that the fourteenth amendment was intended only to secure to all citizens equal capacities before the law. That was at first our view of it. But it does not so read. The language is, "No State shall abridge the privileges or immunities of citizens of the United States." What are the privileges and immunities of the citizens of the United States? Are they capacities merely? Are they not also rights?

The court in this seems to intimate very strongly that the amendment was intended to secure the natural rights of citizens, as well as their equal capacities before the law.

In a case in the supreme court of Georgia, in 1869, the question was before the court whether a negro was competent to hold office in the State of Georgia. The case was ably argued on both sides, Mr. Akerman, the present Attorney-General of the United States, being of counsel for the petitioner. Although the point was made and argued fully, that the right to vote and hold office were both included in the privileges and immunities of citizens, and were thus guaranteed by the fourteenth amendment, yet that point was not directly passed upon by the court, the court holding that under the laws and constitution of Georgia the negro citizen had the right claimed. In delivering the opinion, Chief Justice Brown said:

It is necessary to the decision of this case to inquire what are the "privileges and immunities" of a citizen, which are guaranteed by the fourteenth amendment, to the Constitution of the United States. Whatever they may be, they are protected against all abridgement by legislation * * Whether the "privileges and immunities" of the citizen embrace political rights, including the right to hold office, I need not now inquire. If they do, that right is guaranteed alike by the Constitution of the United States and of Georgia, and is beyond the control of the legislature.

In the opinion of Justice McKay, among other propositions, he lays down the following.

2d. The rights of the people of this State, white and black, are not granted to them by the constitution thereof; the object and effect of that instrument is not to *give*, but to restrain, deny, regulate and guarantee rights, and all persons recognized by that constitution as citizens of the State have *equal, legal and political rights*, except as *otherwise expressly declared*.

3d. It is the settled and uniform sense of the word "citizen," when used in reference to the citizens of the separate States of the United States, and to their rights as such citizens, that it describes a person entitled to every right, *legal and political*, enjoyed by any person in that State, unless there be some express exceptions made by positive law covering the particular persons, whose rights are in question.

In the course of the argument of this case, Mr. Akerman used the following language upon the point, as to whether citizenship carried with it the right to hold office:

"It may be profitable to inquire how the term (citizen) has been understood in Georgia. * * * It will be seen that men whom Georgians have been accustomed to revere believed that citizenship in Georgia carried with it the right to hold office in the absence of positive restrictions."

The majority of the committee having started out with the erroneous hypothesis that the term "privileges of citizens of the United States," as used in the fourteenth amendment, means no more than the term "privileges of citizens," as used in section 2 of article 4, discuss the question thus:

"The right of suffrage was not included in the privileges of citizens as used in section 2, article 4, therefore that right is not included in the privileges of citizens of the United States, as used in the fourteenth amendment."

Their premise being erroneous their whole argument fails. But if they were correct in their premise, we yet claim that their second position is not sustained by the authorities, and is shown to be fallacious by a consideration of the principles of free government.

We claim that from the very nature of our government, the right of suffrage is a fundamental right of citizenship, not only included in the term "privileges of citizens of the United States," as used in the fourteenth amendment, but also included in the term as used in section 2 of article 4, and in this we claim we are sustained both by the authorities and by reason.

In *Abbott vs. Bayley*, (6 Pick., 92,) the supreme court of Massachusetts says:

"The privileges and immunities" secured to the people of each State, in every other State, can be applied only to the case of a removal from one State into another. By such removal they become citizens of the adopted State without naturalization and have a right to sue and be sued as citizens; and yet this privilege is qualified and not absolute, for they cannot enjoy the right of suffrage or eligibility to office without such *term of residence* as shall be prescribed by the constitution and laws of the State into which they shall remove.

This case fully recognizes the right of suffrage as one of the "privileges of the citizen," subject to the right of the State to *regulate* as to the *term of residence*—the same principle was laid down in Corfield *vs.* Correll.

In the case of *Corfield vs. Correll* in the Supreme Court of the United States, Justice Washington, in delivering the opinion of the court, used the following language.

"The privilege and immunities conceded by the Constitution of the United States to citizens in the several States," are to be confined to those which are in their nature fundamental, and belong of right to the citizens of all free governments. Such are the rights of protection of life and liberty, and to acquire and enjoy property, and to pay no higher impositions than other citizens, and to pass through or reside in the State at pleasure, and to enjoy the elective franchise as regulated and established by the laws or constitution of the State in which it is to be exercised

And this is cited approvingly by Chancellor Kent. (2 Kent, sec. 72.)

This case is cited by the majority of the committee, as sustaining their view of the law, but we are unable so to understand it. It is for them an exceedingly unfortunate citation.

In that case the court enumerated some of the "privileges of ci izens," such as are "*in their nature fundamental and belong of right to the citizens of all free governments,*" (mark the language), and among those rights, place the "right of the elective franchise" in the same category with those great rights of life, *liberty* and *property.* And yet the committee cite this case to show that this right is *not* a fundamental right of the citizen!

But it is added by the court that the right of the elective franchise, "is to be enjoyed as regulated and established by the State in which it is to be exercised."

These words are supposed to qualify the right, or rather take it out of the l.st of fundamental rights, where the court had just placed it. The court is made to say by this attempt in the same sentence, "the elective franchise *is* a fundamental right of the citizen, and it is *not* a fundamental right." It is a "fundamental right," provided the State sees fit to grant the right. It is a "fundamental right of the citizen," but it does not exist, unless the laws of the State give it. A singular species of "fundamental rights!" Is there not a clear distinction between the regulation of a right and its destruction? The State may regulate the right, but it may not destroy it.

What is the meaning of "regulate" and "establish?" Webster says:—Regulate—to put in good order. Establish—to make stable or firm.

This decision then is, that "the elective franchise is a fundamental right of the citizen of all free governments, to be enjoyed by the citizen, under such laws as the State may enact to regulate the right and make it stable or firm." Chancellor Kent in the section referred to, in giving the *substance* of this opinion, leaves out the word establish, regarding the word regulate as sufficiently giving the meaning of the court.

This case is, in our opinion, a very strong one against the theory of the majority of the committee.

The committee cite the language of Mr. Webster, as counsel in United States *vs.* Primrose.

We indorse every word in that extract. We do not claim that a citizen of Pennsylvania can go into Virginia and vote in Virginia, being a citizen of Pennsylvania. No person has ever contended for such an absurdity. We claim that when the citizen of the United States becomes a citizen of Virginia, that the State of Virginia has neither right nor power to abridge the privileges of such citizen by denying him entirely the right of suffrage, and thus all political rights. The authorities cited by the majority of the committee do not seem to meet the case—certainly do not sustain their theory.

The case of Cooper *vs.* The Mayor of Savannah, (4 Geo., 72) involved the question whether a free negro was a citizen of the United States? The court, in the opinion says:

Free persons of color have never been recognized as citizens of Georgia; they are not entitled to bear arms, vote for members of the legislature, or hold any c vil office; they have no poli ical rights, but have personal rights, one of which is personal liverty.

That they could not vote, hold office, &c., was held evidence that they were not regarded as citizens.

In the Supreme Court of the United States, in the case of Scott vs. Sanford, (19 Howard, p. 476,) Mr. Justice Daniel, in delivering his opinion, used the following language as to the rights and qualities of citizenship:

For who it may be asked is a citizen? What do the character and status of citizens import? Without fear of contradiction, it does not import the condition of being private property, the subject of individual power and ownership. Upon a principle of etymology alone, the term citizen, as derived from *civitas*, conveys the idea of connection or identification with the State or government, and a participation in its functions. But beyond this there is not, it is believed, to be found, in the theories of writers on government, or in any actual experiment heretofore tried, an exposition of the term citizen which has not been understood as conferring the actual possession and enjoyment, or the perfect right of acquisition and enjoyment, of an entire equality of privileges, civil and political.

And in the same case Chief Justice Taney said: "The words 'people of the United States' and 'citizens' are synonymous terms, and mean the same thing; they both describe the political body, who, according to our republican institutions, form the sovereignty, and who hold the power, and conduct the Government through their representatives. They are what we familiarly call the sovereign people, and every citizen is one of this people, and a constituent member of this sovereignty." (19 Howard, 404.)

In an important case in the Supreme Court of the United States, Chief Justice Jay, in delivering the opinion of the court, said: "At the Revolution the sovereignty devolved on the people, and they are truly the sovereigns of the country, but they are sovereigns without subjects, (unless the African slaves may be so called,) and have none to govern but themselves. The citizens of America are equal as fellow-citizens, and joint tenants of the sovereignty." (Chishol vs. Georgia, 2 Dallas, 470.)

In Conner vs. Elliott, (18 Howard,) Justice Curtis, in declining to give an enumeration of all the "privileges" of the citizen, said "According to the express words and clear meaning of the clause, no privileges are secured except those that belong to citizenship."

The Supreme Court said, in Corfield vs. Coryell, that the elective franchise is such privilege ; therefore, according to Justice Curtis, it belongs to citizenship. In a case in the Supreme Court of Kentucky, (1 Littell's Ky. Reports, p. 333,) the court say :

No one can, therefore, in the correct sense of the term be a citizen of a State who is not entitled upon the terms prescribed by the institutions of the State to all the rights and privileges conferred by these institutions upon the highest class of society.

Mr. Wirt, when Attorney General of the United States, in an official opinion to be found on p. 508, 1st volume Opinions of Attorney Generals, came to the conclusion that the negroes were not citizens of the United States, for the reason that they had very few of the "privileges" of citizens, and among the "privileges of citizens" of which they were deprived, that they could not vote at any election.

Webster defines a citizen to be a person, native or naturalized, who has the privilege of voting for public officers, and who is qualified to fill offices in the gift of the people.

Worcester defines the word thus : "An inhabitant of a republic who enjoys the rights of a citizen or freeman, and who has a right to vote for public officers as a citizen of of the United States."

Bouvier, in his Law Dictionary, defines the term citizen thus : "One who, under the Constitution and laws of the United States, has a right to vote for Representatives in Congress and other public officers, and who is qualified to fill offices in the gift of the people."

Aristotle defines a "citizen" to be one who is a *partner in the legislative and judicial* power, and who shares in the honors of the state." (Aristotle de Repub., lib. 3, cap. 5, D.)

The essential properties of Athenian citizenship consisted in the share possessed by every citizen in the legislature, in the election of magistrates and in the courts of justice. (See Smith's Dictionary of Greek Antiquities, p. 289.)

The possession of the *jus suffragii*, at least, if not also of the *jus honorum*, is the principle which governs at this day in defining citizenship in the countries deriving their jurisprudence from the civil law. (Wheaton's International Law, p. 892.)

The Dutch publicist, Thorbecke, says:

What constitutes the distinctive character of our epoch is the development of the right of citizenship. In its most extended, as well as its most restricted sense, it includes a great many properties.

The right of citizenship is the right of voting in the government of the local, provincial or national community of which one is a member. In this last sense the right of citizenship signifies a participation in the right of voting, in the general government, as member of the State.

(Rev. & Fr. Etr., tom. v, p. 383.)

In a recent work of some research, written in opposition to female suffrage, the author takes the ground that women are not citizens, and urges that as a reason why they can properly be denied the elective franchise, his theory being that if full citizens they would be entitled to the ballot. He uses the following language:

It is a question about which there may be some diversity of opinion what constitutes citizenship or who are citizens. In a loose and improper sense the word citizen is sometimes used to denote any inhabitant of the country, but this is not a correct use of the word. Those, and no others, are properly citizens who were parties to the original compact by which the government was formed, or their successors who are qualified to take part in the affairs of government by their votes in the election of public officers.

Women and children are represented by their domestic directors or heads in whose wills theirs is supposed to be included. They, as well as others not entitled to vote, are not properly citizens, but are members of the State, fully entitled to the protection of its laws. A citizen, then, is a person entitled to vote in the elections. He is one of those in whom the sovereign power of the State resides. (Jones on Suffrage, p. 48.)

But all such fallacious theories as this are swept away by the fourteenth amendment, which abolishes the theory of different grades of citizenship, or different grades of rights and privileges, and declares all persons born in the country or naturalized in it to be citizens, in the broadest and fullest sense of the term, leaving no room for cavil, and guaranteeing to all citizens the rights and privileges of citizens of the republic.

We think we are justified in saying that the weight of authority sustains us in the view we take of this question. But considering the nature of it, it is a question depending much for its solution upon a consideration of the government under which citizenship is claimed. Citizenship in Turkey or Russia is essentially different in its rights and privileges from citizenship in the United States. In the former, citizenship means no more than the right to the protection of his absolute rights, and the "citizen" is a subject; nothing more. Here, in the language of Chief Justice Jay, there are no subjects. All, native-born and naturalized, are citizens of the highest class; here *all citizens are sovereigns*, each citizen bearing a portion of the supreme sovereignty, and therefore it must necessarily be that the right to a voice in the Government is the right and privilege of a citizen as such, and that which is undefined in the Constitution is undefined because it is self-evident.

Could a State disfranchise and deprive of the right to a vote all citizens who have red hair; or all citizens under six feet in height? All will consent that the States could not make such arbitrary distinctions the ground for denial of political privileges; that it would be a violation of the first article of the fourteenth amendment; that it would be abridging the privileges of citizens. And yet the denial of the elective franchise to citizens on account of sex is equally as arbitrary as the distinction on account of stature, or color of hair, or any other physical distinction.

These privileges of the citizen exist independent of the Constitution. They are not derived from the Constitution or the laws, but are the means of asserting and protecting rights that existed before any civil governments were formed—the right of life, liberty and property. Says Paine, in his Dissertation upon the Principles of Government:

The right of voting for representatives is the primary right, by which other rights are protected. To take away this right is to reduce man to a state of slavery, for slavery consists in being subject to the will of another; and he that has not a vote in the election of representatives is, in this case. The proposal, therefore, to disfranchise any class of men is as criminal as the proposal to take away property.

In a state of nature, before governments were formed, each person possessed the natural right to defend his liberty, his life and his property from the aggressions of his fellow men. When he enters into the free government he does not surrender that right, but agrees to exercise it, not by brute force, but by the ballot, by his individual voice in making the laws that dispose of, control and regulate those rights.

The right to a voice in the government is but the natural right of protection of one's life, liberty and property, by personal strength and brute force, so modified as to be exercised in the form of a vote, through the machinery of a free government.

The right of self-protection, it will not be denied, exists in all equally in a state of nature, and the substitute for it exists equally in all the citizens after a free government is formed, for the free government is by all and for all.

The people "ordained and established" the Constitution. Such is the language of the preamble. "We, the people." Can it be said that the people acquire their privileges from the instrument that they themselves establish? Does the creature extend rights, privileges, and immunities to the creator? No; the people retain all the rights which they have not surrendered; and if the people have not given to the Government the power to deprive them of their elective franchise, they possess it by virtue of citizenship.

The true theory of this Government, and of all free governments, was laid down by our fathers in the Declaration of Independence, and declared to be "self-evident." "All men are endowed by their Creator with certain inalienable rights; among these are life, liberty, and the pursuit of happiness. That to secure these rights governments are instituted among men, deriving all their just powers from the consent of the governed."

Here is the great truth, the vital principle, upon which our Government is founded, and which demonstrates that the right of a voice in the conduct of the government, and the selection of the rulers, is a right and privilege of all citizens.

Another of the self-evident truths laid down in that instrument is:

That whenever any form of government becomes destructive of these ends, it is the right of the people to alter or abolish it, and to institute a new government, laying its foundations on such principles, and organizing its powers in such form, as to them shall seem most likely to effect their safety and happiness.

How can the people carry out this right without the exercise of the ballot; and is not the ballot then a fundamental right and a privilege of the citizen, not given to him by the Constitution, but inherent, as a necessity, from the very nature of government?

Benjamin Franklin wrote:

That every man of the commonalty, except infants, insane persons and criminals, is, of common right, and by the laws of God, a freeman, and entitled to the free enjoyment of liberty. That liberty or freedom consists in having an actual share in the appointment of those who frame the laws, and who are to be the guardians of every man; life, property, and peace, for the all of one man is as dear to him as the all of another, and the poor man has an equal right but more need to have representatives in the legislature than the rich one. That they who have no voice nor vote in the electing of representatives do not enjoy liberty, but are absolutely enslaved to those who have votes and to their representatives; for to be enslaved is to have governors whom other men have set over us, and be subject to laws made by the representatives of others, without having had representatives of our own to give consent in our behalf.—Franklin's Works, vol. 2, p. 372.

James Madison said:

Under every view of the subject it seems indispensable that the mass of the citizens should not be without a voice in making the laws which they are to obey, and in choosing the magistrates who are to administer them.—Madison Papers, vol. 3, p. 14.

Taxation without representation is abhorrent to every principle of natural or civil liberty. It was this injustice that drove our fathers into revolution against the mother country.

The very act of taxing exercised over those who are not represented appears to me to be depriving them of one of their most essential rights as freemen, and if continued, seems to be, in effect, an entire disfranchisement of every civil right. For what one civil right is worth a rush after a man's property is subject to be taken from him at pleasure without his consent? If a man is not his own assessor, in person or by deputy, his liberty is gone, or he is entirely at the mercy of others.—Otis's Rights of the Colonies, p. 58.

Nor are these principles original with the people of this country. Long before they were ever uttered on this continent they were declared by Englishmen. Said Lord Summers, a truly great lawyer of England:

Amongst all the rights and privileges appertaining unto us, that of having a share in the legislation, and being governed by such laws as we ourselves shall cause, is the most fundamental and essential, as well as the most advantageous and beneficial.

Said the learned and profound Hooker:

By the natural law whereunto Almighty God hath made all subject, the lawful power of making laws to command whole politic societies of men, belongeth so properly unto the same entire societies, that for any prince or potentate of what kind soever upon earth to exercise the same of himself, (or themselves,) and not either by express commission immediately received from God, or else by authority derived at the first from their consent upon whose persons they impose laws, it is no better than mere tyranny! Agreeable to the same just privileges of natural equity, is that maxim for the English constitution, that "Law to bind all must be assented to by all;" and there can be no legal appearance of assent without some degree of representation.

The great champion of liberty, Granville Sharpe, declared that—

All British subjects, whether in Great Britain, Ireland, or the colonies, are equally free by the laws of nature; they certainly are equally entitled to the same natural rights that are essential for their own preservation, because this privilege of "having a share in the legislation" is not merely a British right, peculiar to this island, but it is also a natural right, which cannot without the most flagrant and stimulating injustice be withdrawn from any part of the British empire by any worldly authority whatsoever.

No tax can be levied without manifest robbery and injustice where this legal and constitutional representation is wanting, because the English law abhors the idea of taking the least property from freemen without their free consent.

It is iniquitous (iniquum est, says the maxim) that freemen should not have the free disposal of their own effects. and whatever is iniquitous can never be made lawful by any authority on earth, not even by the united authority of king, lords, and commons, for that would be contrary to the eternal laws of God, which are supreme.

In an essay upon the "first principles of government," by Priestly, an English writer of great ability, written over a century since, is the following definition of political liberty:

Political liberty I would say, consists in power, which the members of the state reserve to themselves, of arriving at the public offices, or at least of having votes in the nomination of those who fill them.

In countries where every member of the society enjoys an equal power of arriving at the supreme offices, and consequently of directing the strength and sentiments of the whole community, there is a state of the most perfect political liberty.

On the other hand, in countries where a man is excluded from these offices, or from the power of voting for proper persons to fill them, *that man*, whatever be the form of the government, has no share in the government and therefore has no political liberty at all. And since every man retains and can never be deprived of his natural right of relieving himself from all oppression, that is, from everything that has been imposed upon him without his own consent, this must be the only true and proper foundation of all the governments subsisting in the world, and that to which the people who compose them have an inalienable right to bring them back.

It was from these great champions of liberty in England that our forefathers received their inspiration and the principles which they adopted, incorporated into the Declaration of Independence, and made the foundation and framework of our Government. And yet it is claimed that we have a Government which tramples upon these elementary principles of political liberty, in denying to one-half its adult citizens all political liberty, and subjecting them to the tyranny of taxation without representation. It cannot be.

When we desire to construe the Constitution, or to ascertain the powers of the Government and the rights of the citizens, it is legitimate and necessary to recur to those principles and make them the guide in such investigation.

It is an oft-repeated maxim set forth in the bills of rights of many of the State constitutions that "the frequent recurrence to fundamental principles is necessary for the preservation of liberty and good government."

Recurring to those principles, so plain, so natural, so like political axioms, it would seem that to say that one-half the citizens of this republican Government, simply and only on account of their sex, can legally be denied the right to a voice in the Government, the laws of which they are held to obey, and which takes from them their property by taxation, is so flagrantly in opposition to the principles of free government, and the theory of political liberty, that no man could seriously advocate it.

But it is said in opposition to the "citizen's right" of suffrage that at the time of the establishment of the Constitution, women were in all the States denied the right of voting, and that no one claimed at the time that the Constitution of the United States would change their status ; that if such a change was intended it would have been explicitly declared in the Constitution or at least carried into practice by those who framed the Constitution, and, therefore, such a construction of it is against what must have been the intention of the framers.

This is a very unsafe rule of construction. As has been said, the Constitution necessarily deals in general principles; these principles are to be carried out to their legitimate conclusion and result by legislation, and we are to judge of the intention of those who established the Constitution by what they say, guided by what they declare on the face of the instrument to be their object.

It is said by Judge Story, in Story on Constitution, "Contemporary construction is properly resorted to to illustrate and confirm the text. * * *It can never abrogate the text; it can never fritter away its obvious sense; it can never narrow down its true limitations.*"

It is a well-settled rule that in the construction of the Construction, the objects for which it was established, being expressed in the instrument, should have great influence ; and when words and phrases are used which are capable of different constructions, that construction should be given which is the most consonant with the declared objects of the instrument.

We go to the preamble to ascertain the objects and purpose of the instrument. Webster defines preamble thus: "The introductory part of a statute, which states the reason and intent of the law."

In the preamble, then, more certainly than in any other way, aside from the language of the instrument, we find the intent.

Judge Story says:

The importance of examining the preamble for the purpose of expounding the language of a statute has been long felt and universally conceded in all juridical discussion. It is an admitted maxim * * that the preamble is a key to open the mind of the matters as to the mischiefs to be remedied and the objects to be accomplished by the statute. * * It is properly resorted to where doubts or ambiguities arise upon the words of the enacting part, for if they are clear and unambiguous, there seems little room for interpretation, except in cases leading to an obvious absurdity or to a direct overthrow of the intention expressed in the preamble. (Story on the Constitution, sec. 457.)

Try this question by a consideration of the objects for which the Constitution was established, as set forth in the preamble, "to establish justice." Does it establish justice to deprive of all representation or voice in the Government one-half of its adult citizens and compel them to pay taxes to and support a Government in which they have no representation ? Is "taxation without representation" justice established?

"To insure domestic tranquillity." Does it insure domestic tranquillity to give all the political power to one class of citizens, and deprive another class of any participation in the government? No. The sure means of tranquillity is to give "equal political rights to all," that all may stand "equal before the law."

"To provide for the common defense." We have seen that the only defense the citizen has against oppression and wrong is by his voice and vote in the selection of the rulers and law makers. Does it, then, "provide for the common defense," to deny to one half the adult citizens of the republic that voice and vote?

"To secure the *blessings of liberty* to ourselves and our posterity." As has been already said, *there can be no political liberty* to any *citizen deprived of a voice in the government.* This is self-evident; it needs no demonstration. Does it, then, "secure the blessings of liberty to ourselves and our posterity," to deprive one half the citizens of adult age of this right and privilege?

Tried by the expressed objects for which the Constitution was established, as declared by the people themselves, this denial to the women citizens of the country of the right and privilege of voting is directly in contravention of these objects, and must, therefore, be contrary to the spirit and letter of the entire instrument.

And according to rule of construction referred to, no "contemporaneous construction, however universal it may be, can be allowed to set aside the expressed objects of the makers, as declared in the instrument." The construction which we claim for the 1st section of the fourteenth amendment is in perfect accord with those expressed objects; and even if there were anything in the original text of the Constitution at variance with the true construction of that section, the amendment must control. Yet we believe that there is nothing in the original text at variance with what we claim to be the true construction of the amendment.

It is claimed by the majority of the committee that the adoption of the fifteenth amendment was by necessary implication a declaration that the States had the power to deny the right of suffrage to citizens for any other reasons than those of race, color, or previous condition of servitude.

We deny that the fundamental rights of the American citizen can be taken away by "implication."

There is no such law for the construction of the Constitution of our country. The law is the reverse—that the fundamental rights of citizens are not to be taken away by implication, and a constitutional provision for the protection of one class can certainly not be used to destroy or impair the same rights in another class.

It is too violent a construction of an amendment, which prohibits States from, or the United States from, abridging the right of a citizen to vote, by reason of race, color, or previous condition of servitude, to say that by implication it conceded to the States the power to deny that right for any other reason. On that theory the States could confine the right of suffrage to a small minority, and make the State government aristocratic, overthrowing their republican form.

The fifteenth article of amendment to the Constitution clearly recognizes the right to vote, as one of the rights of a citizen of the United States. This is the language:

"The right of citizens of the United States to vote shall not be denied or abridged by the United States, or by any State, on account of race, color, or previous condition of servitude."

Here is stated, first, the existence of a *right.* Second, its nature. Whose right is it? The right of citizens of the United States. What is the right? The right to vote. And this right of citizens of the United States, States are forbidden to abridge. Can there be a more direct recognition of a right? Can that be *abridged* which does not *exist?* The denial of the power to abridge the right, recognizes the existence of the right. Is it said that this right exists by virtue of State citizenship, and State laws and Constitutions? Mark the language: "The right of citizens of the *United States* to vote;" not citizens of *States.* The right is recognized as existing independent of State citizenship.

But it may be said, if the States had no power to abridge the right of suffrage, why the necessity of prohibiting them?

There may not have been a necessity; it may have been done through caution, and because the peculiar condition of the colored citizens at that time rendered it necessary to place their rights beyond doubt or cavil.

It is laid down as a rule of construction by Judge Story that the natural import of a single clause is not to be narrowed so as to exclude implied powers resulting from its character simply because there is another clause which enumerates certain powers which might otherwise be deemed implied powers within its scope, for in such cases we are not to assume that the affirmative specification excludes all other implications. (2d Story on Constitution, sec. 449.)

There are numerous instances in the Constitution where a general power is given to Congress, and afterward a particular power given, which was included in the former; yet the general power is not to be narrowed, because the particular power is given. On this same principle the fact that by the fifteenth amendment the States are specifically forbidden to deny the right of suffrage on account of race, color, or previous condition of servitude, does not narrow the general provision in the fourteenth amendment which guarantees the privileges of all the citizens against abridgment by the States on any account.

The rule of interpretation relied upon by the committee in their construction of the fifteenth amendment is, "that the expression of one thing is the exclusion of another," or the specification of particulars is the exclusion of generals.

Of these maxims Judge Story says:

They are susceptible of being applied, and often are ingeniously applied, to the subversion of the text and the objects of the instrument. The truth is, in order to ascertain how far an affirmative or negative provision excludes or implies others, we must look to the nature of the provision, the subject-matter, the objects, and the scope of the instrument; these and these only can properly determine the rule of construction. (2 Story, 448.)

It is claimed by the committee that the second section of the fourteenth amendment implies that the several States may restrict the right of suffrage as to other than male citizens. We may say of this as we have said of the theory of the committee upon the effect of the fifteenth amendment. It is a proposal to take away from the citizens guarantees of fundamental rights, by implication, which have been previously given in absolute terms.

The first section includes all citizens in its guarantees, and includes all the "privileges and immunities" of citizenship and guards them against abridgment, and under no recognized or reasonable rule of construction can it be claimed that by implication from the provisions of the second section the States may not only abridge but entirely destroy one of the highest privileges of the citizen to one half the citizens of the country. What we have said in relation to the committee's construction of the effect of the fifteenth amendment applies equally to this.

The object of the first section of this amendment was to secure all the rights, privileges, and immunities of all the citizens against invasion by the States. The object of the second section was to fix a rule or system of apportionment for Representatives and taxation; and the provision referred to, in relation to the exclusion of males from the right of suffrage, might be regarded as in the nature of a penalty in case of denial of that right to that class. While it, to a certain extent, protected that class of citizens, it left the others where the previous provisions of the constitution placed them. To protect the colored man more fully than was done by that penalty was the object of the fifteenth amendment.

In no event can it be said to be more than the recognition of an existing fact, that only the male citizens were, by the State laws, allowed to vote, and that existing order of things was recognized in the rule of representation, just as the institution of slavery was recognized in the original Constitution, in the article fixing the basis of representation, by the provision that only three-fifths of all the slaves ("other persons") should be counted. There slavery was recognized as an existing fact, and yet the Constitution never sanctioned slavery, but, on the contrary, had it been carried out according to its true construction, slavery could not have existed under it; so that the recognition of facts in the Constitution must not be held to be a sanction of what is so recognized.

The majority of the committee say that this section implies that the States may deny suffrage to others than male citizens. If it implies anything it implies that the States may deny the franchise to all the citizens. It does not provide that they shall not deny the right to male citizens, but only provides that if they do so deny they shall not have representation for them.

So, according to that argument, by the second section of the fourteenth amendment the power of the States is conceded to entirely take away the right of suffrage, even from that privileged class, the male citizens. And thus this rule of "implication" goes too far, and fritters away all the guarantees of the Constitution of the right of suffrage, the highest of the privileges of the citizen; and herein is demonstrated the reason and safety of the rule that fundamental rights are not to be taken away by implication, but only by express provision.

When the advocates of a privileged class of citizens under the Constitution are driven to implication to sustain the the theory of taxation without representation, and American citizenship without political liberty, the cause must be weak indeed.

It is claimed by the majority that by section 2, article 1, the Constitution recognizes the power in States to declare who shall and who shall not exercise the elective franchise. That section reads as follows:

The House of Representatives shall be composed of members chosen every second year by the people of the several States, and the electors in each state shall have the qualifications requisite for electors of the most numerous branch of the State legislature.

The first clause of this section declares *who* shall choose the Representatives—mark the language—"Representatives *shall be chosen by the people* of the States," not by the male people, not by certain classes of the people, but by the people; so that the construction sought to be given this section, by which it would recognize the power of the State to disfranchise one-half the citizens, as in direct contravention of the first clause of the section, and of its whole spirit, as well as of the objects of the instrument. The States clearly have no power to nullify the express provisions that the election shall be by the people, by any laws limiting the election to a moiety of the people.

It is true the section recognizes the power in the State to regulate the qualifications of the electors; but as we have already said, the power to regulate is a very different thing from the power to destroy.

The two clauses must be taken together, and both considered in connection with the declared purpose and objects of the constitution.

The Constitution is necessarily confined to the statement of general principles. There are regulations necessary to be made as to the qualifications of voters, as to their proper age, their domicile, the length of residence necessary to entitle the citizen to vote in a given State or place. These particulars could not be provided in the Constitution but are necessarily left to the States, and this section is thus construed as to be in harmony with itself, and with the expressed objects of the framers of the Constitution and the principles of free government.

When the majority of the committee can demonstrate that "the people of the States," and one-half the people of the States, are equivalent terms, or that when the Constitution provides that the Representatives shall be elected by the people, its requirements are met by an election in which less than one-half the adult people are allowed to vote, then it will be admitted that this section, to some extent sustains them.

The committee say, that if it had been intended that Congress shou d prescribe the qualifications of electors, the grant would have given Congress that power specifically. We do not claim that Congress has that power; on the contrary, admit that the States have it; but the section of the Constitution *does* prescribe who the electors shall be. That is what we claim—nothing more. They shall be "the people;" their qualifications may be regulated by the States; but to the claim of the majority of the committee that they may be "qualified" out of existence, we cannot assent.

We are told that the acquiescence by the people, since the adoption of the Constitution, in the denial of political rights to women citizens, and the general understanding that such denial was in conformity with the Constitution, should be taken to settle the construction of that instrument.

Any force this argument may have it can only apply to the original text, and not to the fourteenth amendment, which is of but recent date.

But, as a general principle, this theory is fallacious. It would stop all political progress; it would put an end to all original thought, and put the people under that tyranny with which the friends of liberty have always had to contend—the tyranny of precedent.

From the beginning, our Government has been right in theory, but wrong in practice. The Constitution, had it been carried out in its true spirit, and its principles enforced, would have stricken the chains from every slave in the republic long since. Yet, for all this, it was but a few years since declared, by the highest judicial tribunal of the republic, that, according to the "general understanding," the black man in this country had no rights the white man was bound to respect. General understanding and acquiescence is a very unsafe rule by which to try questions of constitutional law, and precedents are not infallible guides toward liberty and the rights of man.

Without any law to authorize it, slavery existed in England, and was sustained and perpetuated by popular opinion, universal custom, and the acquiescence of all departments of the government as well as by the subjects of its oppression. A few fearless champions of liberty struggled against the universal sentiment, and contended that, by the laws of England slavery could not exist in the kingdom; and though for years unable to obtain a hearing in any British court, the Sommersett case was finally tried in the Court of King's Bench in 1771, Lord Mansfield presiding, wherein that great and good man, after a long and patient hearing, declared that no law of England allowed or approved of slavery, and discharged the negro. And it was then judicially declared that no slave could breathe upon the soil of England, although slavery had up to that time existed for centuries, under the then existing laws. The laws were right, but the practice and public opinion were wrong.

It is said by the majority of the committee that "if the right of female citizens to suffrage is vested by the Constitution, that right can be established in the courts."

We respectfully submit that, with regard to the competency and qualification of electors for members of this House, the courts have no jurisdiction.

This House is the sole judge of the election return and qualification of its own members. (article 1, section 5, of Constitution;) and it is for the House alone to decide upon a contest, who are, and who are not, competent and qualified to vote. The judicial department cannot thus invade the prerogatives of the political department.

And it is therefore perfectly proper, in our opinion, for the House to pass a declaratory resolution, which would be an index to the action of the House, should the question be brought before it by a contest for a seat.

We, therefore, recommend to the House the adoption of the following resolution:

Resolved, by the House of Representatives, That the right of suffrage is one of the inalienable rights of citizens of the United States, subject to regulation by the States, through equal and just laws.

That this right is included in the "privileges of citizens of the United States," which are guaranteed by section 1 of article 14 of amendments to the Constitution of the United States; and that women citizens, who are otherwise qualified by the laws of the State where they reside, are competent voters for Representatives in Congress.

WM. LOUGHRIDGE.
BENJ. F. BUTLER.

H. Rep. 22, pt. 2——3

EQUAL SUFFRAGE.

IMMENSE MEETING LAST NIGHT AT LINCOLN HALL—THE RIGHT OF WOMEN TO VOTE
DISCUSSED—MRS. VICTORIA WOODHULL AND MRS. ISABELLA BEECHER HOOKER
ARGUE FROM A CONSTITUTIONAL STANDPOINT—GENERAL BUTLER'S REMARKS.

A vast concourse of intelligent men and women sat in Lincoln Hall last evening, and listened with rapt attention to the masterly argument delivered by Mrs. Woodhull upon the legal aspects of female suffrage. Long before the commencement of the lecture the ushers were busy in procuring chairs for those who could not find other seats, and with all that, men and women stood by scores all around the sides of the room.

At 8 o'clock Mrs. Paulina Davis advanced to the footlights and stated the object of the lecture in a few clear, earnest words, and then introduced Mrs. Woodhull.

This was her first attempt at public speaking. During the remarks of Mrs. Davis she had sat with perfect external composure, but those who knew her face saw at a glance that nothing but a tremendous effort of will enabled her to maintain that demeanor. When she commenced to speak her voice was clear, distinct, and without the least tremor. She said, in opening, that while she had invited the people to listen to an argument, she must acknowledge that their speaker made no pretension to oratory. The lecture was based upon the same points which have more than once been stated in these columns, and need not, therefore, be restated. They were brought out more fully and sustained by more extended citations of precedent; they had also the force of a woman speaking with the unconscious power and earnestness of irrevocable conviction of a just and soon to be triumphant cause. Mrs. Woodhull discussed fully the principles of government, and the circumstances out of which it sprung from the tyranny of George III., and applied them to the question in discussion. Then the days of reconstruction were passed in review; laws, declarations and speeches were quoted; some of them from men who oppose female suffrage, and contrasted with the position assumed by the majority of the Judiciary Committee. It was said that the Constitution did not give women the right of suffrage; nor more does it give it to the men. Where, then, do they get it? They inherit it from their God.

When Mrs. Woodhull commenced speaking her face was perfectly colorless, and she was obliged to stop an instant between each sentence to gain strength to utter the next. It was a grand exhibition of will. But as she progressed and became warmed in her argument, much of the fire and freedom of her ordinary conversation returned, her face flushed and she was herself. The lecture was a triumph, and she demonstrated the fact that, with a little experience, Mrs. Woodhull will be as strong upon the rostrum as she is with the pen.

After the conclusion of this argument, Isabella Beecher Hooker, a sister of Henry Ward Beecher, spoke upon the moral view of the question. And if there were anything wanting to prove that a legal right should not be abridged, Mrs. Hooker most emphatically presented it.

Gen. Butler was loudly called for after Mrs. Hooker retired, and in answer thereto gave, in his peculiarly terse and vivid manner, his reasons for joining in the minority report of the Judiciary Committee on the Woodhull Memorial, of which the following is a synopsis:

He said a lady had petitioned Congress for the protection of her rights. The petition required a change of laws, and therefore had been referred to the Judiciary Committee, of which he was a member. He had examined the question coolly and deliberately, as a lawyer, and had not asked whether it was best to grant the franchise or not. He must learn first if women were citizens. None but citizens of the United States could register a ship at our ports, none others could pre-empt land or receive passports; but that he found that from time immemorial in this country women had registered ships, pre-empted land, and secured passports without question. Mrs. Woodhull's first point was therefore sustained. She was a citizen. The right of a citizen to vote for his rulers was a right outside of all constitutions and laws; it was an inherent right of every citizen, as he understood the principles of the government. The second point of the petition was therefore established; and the third, that she was denied the right to vote in New York, was conceded. He had, therefore, signed the minority report. The majority of the Committee held that the right to vote could only be obtained through State laws, and in that they lost the distinction between voting for a State and a United States officer. He held that all the States' rights which interfered with Congress in enforcing the rights of citizens of the United States were buried forever in the red sea of blood that had flowed south of the Potomac. If the committee was right, how could Congress pass the bill enforcing the right of citizens to vote in the several States yesterday? But they ask us why minors can't vote if women can. If all citizens may vote, how can we exclude the minor citizen, the pauper, the idiot, the criminal, being citizens. There was a difference here. All minors were excluded, so all were equal. All idiots were excluded, so there was no distinction. This objection was the slimmest he ever heard. Qualifying and guarding the right was quite different from abridging it. The right to vote anywhere might be guarded for the protection of the ballot-box, but could not be abridged.

Mrs. Woodhull's position on this question is indorsed by many members of Congress, among whom are the following: Hon. B. F. BUTLER, Mass.; Hon. G. W. WOODWARD, Penn.; Hon. J. H. ELA, N. H.; Hon. N. P. BANKS, Mass.; Hon. WM. LOUGHRIDGE, Iowa; Hon. WM. LAWRENCE, Ohio; Hon. S. C. POMEROY, Kas.; Hon. G. W. JULIAN, Ind.; Hon. JOHN LYNCH, Maine.

POLITICAL THEORY

(2)

A Lecture on Constitutional Equality . . . 1871.

A variant printing, somewhat abridged (24 pp.) and slightly altered in text appeared with an identical title-page.

A LECTURE

ON

CONSTITUTIONAL EQUALITY

DELIVERED AT

LINCOLN HALL, WASHINGTON, D. C.,

THURSDAY, FEBRUARY 16, 1871,

BY

VICTORIA C. WOODHULL.

NEW YORK:

JOURNEYMEN PRINTERS' CO-OPERATIVE ASSOCIATION,

No. 30 BEEKMAN STREET.

1871.

LECTURE

It was an honest zeal which first influenced me to appear before the public as a champion of a cause which receives alike the jeers of the common multitude and the railery of the select few. It is an honest zeal in the same, that inspires me with confidence to continue before it as its advocate, when but too conscious that I am of that portion of the people who are denied the privileges of freedom; who are not permitted the rights of citizens; and who are without voice, in the pursuit of justice, as one of that sovereignty to whom this government owes its existence, and to whom it will be held accountable, as it holds all accountable who set themselves against Human Rights.

I have no doubt it seems strange to many of you that a woman should appear before the people in this public manner for political pur poses, and it is due both to you and myself that I should give my reasons for so doing.

On the 19th of December, 1870, I memorialized Congress, setting forth what I believed to be the truth and right regarding Equal Suf-frage for all citizens. This memorial was referred to the Judiciary Committees of Congress. On the 12th of January I appeared before the House Judiciary Committee and submitted to them the Constitutional and Legal points upon which I predicated such equality. January 20th Mr. Bingham, on behalf of the majority of said Committee, submitted his report to the House in which, while he admitted all my basic propositions, Congress was recommended to take no action. February 1st Messrs. Loughridge and Butler of said Committee submitted a report in their own behalf, which fully sustained the positions. I assumed and recommended that Congress *should* pass a Declaratory Act, forever settling the mooted question of suffrage.

Thus it is seen that equally able men differ upon a simple point of Constitutional Law, and it is fair to presume that Congress will also differ *when* these Reports come up for action. That a proposition involving such momentous results as this, should receive a one-third vote upon first coming before Congress has raised it to an importance, which spreads alarm on all sides among the opposition. So long as it was not made to appear that women were denied Constitutional rights, no opposition was aroused; but now that new light is shed, by which it is seen that such is the case, all the Conservative weapons of bitterness, hatred and malice are marshalled in the hope to extinguish it, before it can enlighten the masses of the people, who are always true to freedom and justice.

Public opinion is against Equality, but it is simply from prejudice, which requires but to be informed to pass away. No greater prejudice exists against equality than there did against the proposition that the world was a globe. This passed away under the influence of better information, so also will present prejudice pass, when better informed upon the question of equality.

I trust you will pardon me the expression when I say that I do not comprehend how there can exist an honest and perfect appreciation of the fundamental propositions upon which the superstructure of our government is based, and, at the same time, an honest hostility to the legitimate deductions of them, therefore I appear before you to expound as best I may the law involved by these propositions and to point out the inconsistencies of those who evince hostility to such deductions.

I come before you, to declare that my sex are entitled to the inalienable right to life, liberty and the pursuit of happiness. The first two I cannot be deprived of except for cause and by due process of law; but upon the last, a right is usurped to place restrictions so general as to include the whole of my sex, and for which no reasons of public good can be assigned. I ask the right to pursue happiness by having a voice in that government to which I am accountable. I have not forfeited that right, still I am denied. Was assumed arbitrary authority ever more arbitrarily exercised? In practice, then, our laws are false to the principles which we profess. I have the right to life, to liberty, unless I forfeit it by an infringement upon others' rights, in which case the State becomes the arbiter and deprives me of them for the public good. I also have the right to pursue happiness, unless I forfeit it in the same way, and am denied it accordingly. It cannot be said, with any justice, that my pursuit of happiness in voting for any man for office, would be an infringement of one of his rights as a citizen or as an individual. I hold, then, that in denying me this right without my having forfeited it, that departure is made from the principles of the Constitution, and also from the true principles of government, for I am denied a right born with me, and which is inalienable. Nor can it be objected that women had no part in organizing this government. They were not denied. To-day we seek a voice in government and *are* denied. There are *thousands* of male citizens in the country who seldom or never vote. They are not denied : they pursue happiness by not voting. Could it be assumed, because this body of citizens do not choose to exercise the right to vote, that they could be *permanently* denied the exercise thereof? *If* not, *neither* should it be assumed to deny women, who wish to vote, the right to do so.

And were it true that a majority of women do not wish to vote, it would be *no* reason why those who do, should be denied. If a right exist, and only *one in a million* desires to exercise it, *no* government should deny its enjoyment to that one. If the thousands of men who do not choose to vote should send their petitions to Congress, asking them to prevent others who do vote from so doing, would they listen to them? I went before Congress, to ask for myself and others of my sex, who wish to pursue our happiness by participating in government, protection in such pursuit, and I was told that Congress has not the necessary power.

If there are women who do not desire to have a voice in the laws to which they are accountable, and which they must contribute to support, let them speak for themselves ; but they should not assume to speak for me, or for those whom I represent.

So much for the fundamental propositions upon which government is organized. Women did not join in the act of constructing the Constitution. So far as I know, none expressed a desire so to do, and consequently were not denied. But *what* is government, and *what* a Republican form of government? Government is national existence organized. Government of some form exists everywhere, but none would assume to say that the government of *China* is similar to that of *England*, or that of *Germany* to that of the *United States.* When government is fashioned *for* the people it is not a republican form, but when fashioned *by* the people it is a republican government. *Our* form of government is supposed to emanate from the people, and whatever control it possesses *over* the people is supposed to be exercised by and with their consent; and even more than this, *by their direct will and wish.* If, at any time, there are powers exercised by a government which emanates from, and is dependent upon, the will of the people, which the majority of the people do not desire to be continued, they have it in their power, and it is their duty, to compel their suspension. If, at any time, the majority of the people from whom has emanated, and who support a republican form of government, desire that it should assume *new* functions, exercise more extended control or provide for *new* circumstances, *not* existent at its primary organization, they have the power and it is their duty to *compel* their government to take such action as is necessary to secure the form that shall be acceptable.

The people are virtually the government, and *it* is simply the concentration and expression of their will and wisdom through which they assume form as a body politic or as a nation. The government is an embodiment of the people, and as *they* change so also must it change. In this significant fact lie all the true beauty and wisdom of our form of polity. It can be changed without actual revolution, and consequently possesses the inherent qualities of permanency. It is capable of adaptation to all contingences and circumstances, and provides how changes shall be made. It nowhere positively declares that its citizens, or the people, if you please, shall *not* have the right to vote under its provisions: and, *mark you* it nowhere provides that any portion of the people *shall* vote.

Before government was organized there were no citizens, but there were *people*, and these people had the *human right* to organize a government under which they could become citizens. In the absence of organized government, individual government alone exists, every individual having the human right to control himself and herself.

Now, if a people—an aggregate of individuals—not having a government, undertake to construct one, wherein but *one-half* should engage, the *other* half taking no part therein, and its functions should be exercised over the *whole*, it is *plain* that so far as the non-engaged part would be concerned, it would be an *usurped* authority that dispossessed them of the inherent right which all people have in organized government. But so long as the unconsulted part quietly acquiesce in such a government, there could be none to question its right to control. At the moment, however, when the unconsulted portion should demur from such government, they would begin to assert the right to self-government, possessed equally by all. The fact that such right had not been made known by expression, could in no wise invalidate it. It would remain an inherent possession, and whenever expressed it could be maintained and enjoyed.

The condition of the people of this country to-day is this:

I and others of my sex find ourselves controlled by a form of government in the inauguration of which we had no voice, and in whose administration we are denied the right to participate, though we are a large part of the people of this country. Was George III.'s rule, which he endeavored to exercise over our fathers, less clearly an assumed rule than is this to which we are subjected? He exercised it over them without their consent and against their wish and will, and naturally they rebelled. Do men of the United States assume and exercise any less arbitrary rule over us than *that* was? No, not one whit the less. To be sure his cabinet were *few*, while they are *many;* but the principle is the same; in both cases the inherent elemental right to self-government is equally over-ridden by the assumption of power. But the authority King George's Parliament exercised was even more consistent than *this* is which they assume and exercise: his government made no pretension to emanation from the people.

When our fathers launched "Taxation without representation is tyranny" against King George, were they consistent? Certainly. Were they justified? Yes; for out of it came our national independence. The Revolutionary war, which gave our country independence, grew from this tyranny. Was that war justifiable? Most assuredly it was. We find that the same declarations of tyranny were raised by Congress in the lengthy discussions upon enfranchising the negro. Such senti- ments as the following were often repeated, and with great effect: "A considerable part of the people of the United States embraced under the preamble to the Constitution, 'We, the people,' are left without repre sentation in the government; but, nevertheless, held within the grasp of taxation of all kinds, direct and indirect, tariff and excise, State and national. This is tyranny, or else our fathers were wrong when they protested against a kindred injustice. This principle is funda- mental. It cannot be violated without again dishonoring the fathers," whose rights were so ably and eloquently asserted and defended by James Otis, who, in his "Right of the Colonies," says: "The very act of taxing exercised over those who are not represented, appears to me to be depriving them of one of their most essential rights as free- men, and if continued, seems to be, in effect, an entire disfranchisement of every civil right. For what one civil right is worth a rush after a man's property is subject to be taken from him at pleasure without his consent? If a man is not his own assessor, in person or by deputy, his liberty is gone, or he is entirely at the mercy of others." Could *stronger words* than these be found or used in favor of universal suf frage? They applied with sufficient force *then* to rouse a few men, whose souls were fired with its injustice, to resist a powerful oppressor. It was one of the most forcible arguments by which the cause of the negro was advocated. *Is it* any less forcible in its application to women? Is the tyranny now exercised over women under, as some say, the authority of the government—but we say, without any au- thority—any less tyrannous than that over our fathers? or than that of the negro, for whom many plead so earnestly? Or is *nothing* tyranny for women? If a civil right is "not worth a rush" to a *man* when he is taxed and not represented, how much is it worth to a woman? If a "*man's* liberty is gone," and he is "at the mercy of others" when thus taxed, what becomes of *woman's* under the same tyranny? If "every man of sound mind should vote," by what principle can every *woman* of sound mind be deprived of voting? Or are all women of *unsound* mind? Not exactly; they are found to be very proper persons as the assigns of men in many instances.

In the records of the early days of the Republic, there are found *numerous* authorities bearing directly upon this point, such as, "That by the law of nature no man has a right to impose laws more than to levy taxes upon another; that the free man pays no taxes, as the freeman submits to no law but such as emanate from the body in which he is represented." If the freeman pays no taxes without representation, how is it that the free woman is compelled to do so? Not long since I was notified by a United States officer that if I did not pay a certain tax the government had imposed upon me, my property would be levied upon and sold for that purpose. Is *this* tyranny, or can men find some *other* word to take the place of that used by our fathers so freely, and by Congress, not so long ago as to be forgotten, with such powerful effect? Has oppression become less odious, that in these days twenty of the forty millions of people who compose the sovereign people of this country must *quietly* submit to what has been, in all ages of representative government, denounced as *tyranny?*

But let us hear more of the principles which actuated our fathers: "All men having sufficient evidence of permanent common interest with, and attachment to, the community, have the right of suffrage, and cannot be taxed or deprived of their property for public uses without their own consent or that of their representatives so elected, nor bound by any law to which they have not in like manner assented for the public good."—*Virginia Bill of Rights, Jan.* 12, 1776.

So it appears that our fathers declared that *no one* should be bound by *any* law in the making of which he had no voice. *How* would this principle operate to-day should I refuse to pay the taxes levied against me without my consent and in direct opposition to my wishes? Would I be justified in declaring that I would not pay? I might be *justified*, but I do not think I should escape the tyranny.

Franklin said, "That every man of the community, except infants, insane people and criminals, is of common right, and by the laws of

God, a freeman, and entitled to the free enjoyment of liberty. *That freedom or liberty consists in having an actual share in the appointment of those who frame* the laws, and who are to be the guardians of every man, for the all of one man is as dear to him as the all of another man; and the poor man has an equal right, but more need, to have representatives than the rich one." "That they who have no voice nor vote in the election of representatives do not enjoy liberty, but are *absolutely enslaved;* for to be enslaved is to have governors whom others have set over us."

If freedom consists in having an *actual share* in appointing those who frame the laws, are not the women of this country in absolute *bondage*, and can government, in the face of the XV. Amendment, assume to deny them the right to vote, being in this "condition of servitude?" According to Franklin we are absolutely enslaved, for there *are* " governors set over us by other men," and we are " subject to the laws " they make. Is *not* Franklin good authority in matters of freedom? Again, rehearsing the arguments that have emanated from Congress and applying them to the present case, we learn that "It is idle to show that, in certain instances, the fathers failed to apply the sublime principles which they declared. Their failure can be *no* apology for those on whom the duty is now cast." Shall it be an apology *now?* Shall the omission of others to do justice keep the government from measuring it to those who now cry out for it? I went before Congress like Richelieu to his king asking for justice. Will they deny it as he did until the exigencies of the case compel them?

I *am* subject to tyranny! I am taxed in every conceivable way. For publishing a paper I must pay—for engaging in the banking and brokerage business I must pay—of what it is my fortune to acquire each year I must turn over a certain per cent.—I must pay high prices for tea, coffee and sugar : to *all* these must I submit, that *men's* government may be maintained, a government in the administration of which I am denied a voice, and from its edicts there is no appeal. I must submit to a heavy advance upon the first cost of *nearly everything I wear* in order that industries in which I have no interest may exist at my expense. I am compelled to pay extravagant rates of fare wherever

I travel, because the franchises, extended to gigantic corporations, enable them to *sap* the vitality of the country, to make their *managers
money kings*, by means of which they boast of being able to control not
only legislators but even a State judiciary.

To be compelled to submit to *these* extortions that *such* ends may
be gained, upon *any* pretext or under *any* circumstances, is bad enough ;
but to be compelled to submit to them, and also denied the right to
cast my vote *against* them, is a tyranny *more* odious than that which,
being rebelled against, gave this country independence.

But usurpations do not stop here. The Constitution, as it stood
on the day of its original adoption, under the interpretation of
that day, guided by the principle of *self*-government, admits *perfect* equality among the people. There are *no* limitations contained in it by which any part of the people from whom it emanated
could be placed *unequally* with any other part. Permit me to quote
from a speech delivered by Mr. Sumner, in the Senate of the United
States, March 7, 1866, upon the following proposition :

Representatives shall be appointed among the several States which
may be included in this Union, according to their respective number of
persons included in each State, excluding Indians not taxed : Provided, That whenever the elective franchise shall be denied or abridged
by any State on account of race or color, all persons therein of such race
or color shall be excluded from the basis of representation. " Adopt
this," said Mr. Sumner, "and you will stimulate anew the war of race
upon race. Slavery itself was a war of race upon race, and this is only
a new form of this terrible war. Adopt it, and you will put millions of
fellow-citizens under the ban of excommunication. You will declare
that they have no political rights which 'white men' are bound to respect. Adopt it, and you will cover the country with dishonor. Adopt
it, and you will fix the stigma upon the very name of Republic." In
express terms there is an *admission of the idea* of inequality of rights
founded on race and color. That this unrepublican idea should be
allowed to find a place in the text of the Constitution, will excite es-
pecial wonder, when it is considered how conscientiously our fathers
excluded from that text the kindred idea of property in man. Mr.

Madison "thought it wrong to admit in the Constitution the idea of property in man." "But," says Mr. Sumner, "is it less wrong to admit in the Constitution, the idea of inequality of rights founded on race and color?" Is it not, *I* ask, a *graver* wrong to insist that *one-half the people of all races* and colors have not equal right, because they are *women;* and *this* too when there are *no* provisions contained in the Constitution which can by *any* possibility be construed to give the other half disfranchising power? Fathers, husbands, brothers, sons, does not your blood tingle with shame in your veins at this ignoble distinction? How can you look in your sisters' faces and declare they shall not enjoy the citizen's rights, granted to the lowest orders and classes in the human race?

Therefore it is, that instead of growing in republican liberty, we are departing from it. From an unassuming, acquiescent part of society, woman has gradually passed to an individualized human being, and as she has advanced, one after another evident right of the common people has been accorded to her. She has now become so *much* individualized as to demand the full and unrestrained exercise of *all* the rights which can be predicated of a people constructing a government based on individual sovereignty. She asks it, and shall Congress deny her?

The formal abolition of slavery created several millions of male negro citizens, who, a portion of the acknowledged citizens assumed to say, were *not* entitled to equal rights with themselves. To get over this difficulty, Congress in its wisdom saw fit to propose a XIV. Amendment to the Constitution, which passed into a law by ratification by the States. Sec. I. of the Amendment declares: "All persons, born or naturalized in the United States, and subject to the jurisdiction thereof, are citizens of the United States and of the State wherein they reside. No State shall make or enforce any law which shall abridge the privileges and immunities of citizens of the United States. Nor shall any State deprive any person of life, liberty and property without due process of law, nor deny any person within its jurisdiction the equal protection of the law."

But there is an objection raised to our broad interpretation of this Amendment, and that is obtained from the wording of the second section thereof: "But whenever the right to vote," etc., " is denied to any of the male inhabitants of such State, being twenty-one years of age, and citizens of the United States," etc., etc., " the basis of representation then shall be reduced in the proportion which the number of such male citizens shall bear to the whole number of male citizens twenty-one years of age." *Consisteney* is said to be a bright jewel when possessed, but I doubt its possession by those who have the boldness to advance *this* as an argument in opposition to this point. We surely have a right to use the logic of objectors in interpreting their own propositions, and we therefore reply, *ita lex scripta est.* If the Constitution mean *nothing* but what is expressed, how can it be presumed to infer anything from the use of the word *male* in this second section, except what it expresses ? The *right* of women to vote, or the *denial* of that right to them, *is not* involved by this section under the furthest fetched application.

I am perfectly well aware of the attempt which was made in the Congress of 1866 to add a special, but indirectly restrictory clause, to the Constitution, providing that the basis of representation should be the then recognized legal voters. It was perceived that the arguments advanced for political equality for the negro were equally potent for women. The inconsistency of women forming a part of the basis of representation, and being denied participation in it, was *too* apparent to escape sagacious minds. The attempt, however, did not succeed. Its promoters *did not dare* openly to avow their intentions, but it is known that they *felt* the time would come when women would claim equal political rights, which could not consistently be denied them, unless, when it should be *necessary so to do*, that proper restrictory legislation should be contained in the Constitution.

The only point which I can see the report of the majority of the Judiciary Committee attempts to make against my demand, I propose to meet by quoting authority, which I am positive no one will think of questioning.

Chief Justice Taney in Howard, Rep., 404, thus defines the words people and citizen. The words *"people of the United States"* and *citizens* are *synonymous* terms and mean the *same thing*. They *both* describe the *political* body, *who*, according to our republican institutions, *form* the *sovereignty* and who *hold* the power and *conduct* the government through their representatives. They are what we *familiarly* call the *sovereign* people, and *every* citizen is *one* of this people and a *constituent* member of this sovereignty.

Ibid, p. 476 : "There is not, it is believed, to be found in the theories of writers on government, or in any actual experiment heretofore tried, *any* exposition of the term *citizen*, which has not been considered as conferring the *actual possession* and *enjoyment* of the *perfect right* of acquisition and enjoyment of an *entire* equality of privileges, *civil* and *political.*" Such authority as this, couched in such strong words, leaves no doubt about the Constitutional meaning of these terms.

I do not think it possible that the Congress or the people of the United States, when they shall give this matter due consideration, will refuse to accept *such* authority upon the rights of citizens, the decisions of the report referred to, to the contrary notwithstanding. The XIV. Amendment has compelled said Committee to admit *just enough too much* to make their *entire* position untenable. Being citizens, women are of the "sovereign people," and entitled to the enjoyment of an "*entire equality of privileges, civil and political.*"

After the adoption of the XIV. Amendment it was found that still more legislation was required to secure the exercise of the right to vote to all who by it were declared to be citizens, and the following comprehensive amendment was passed by Congress and ratified by the States : "The right of citizens of the United States to vote shall not be denied or abridged by the United States or by any State on account of race, color or previous condition of servitude." Nothing could be more explicit than this language, and nothing more comprehensive. "But," says the objector, ever on the alert, "it may be denied on account of sex." It must be remembered "that is law which is written," and that all *inferences* drawn must be in accord with the *general intent* of the instrument involved by the inference. *If* the right to vote cannot be denied on account of race, *how* can it be denied on account of a constituent part of race, unless the power of denial is specially *expressed* The larger *always* includes the smaller, which, if reserved, the reservation must be expressed. No *inference* can be allowed to determine that *any* part of the citizens covered by the term *race*, can be denied the right to vote, unless the denial is expressed. It seems to me that no logic can be plainer than this. Had this amendment recited that the right to vote should not be denied on account of race, except to *females*, it would have left the right of denial to the States, but *even then*, under the XIV. Amendment, the denial would have to be made, with women participating therein, and although there are those who assert that the majority of women do not desire to vote, I think none of you can imagine that, *possessing* the right, they would remain at home and premit it to be taken away.

This Amendment is *just as much* a part of the Constitution as though it had been one of its original provisions. The effect of the Constitution, as it *now* stands, upon the *present* citizens must be the same that it would have been upon the citizens at the time of its original adoption, had it contained *all* its present provisions. Previous to its adoption there were no citizens of the United States. Immediately it was adopted persons became citizens, but had not voted as citizens of the United States under it. Under *these* circumstances, with *these* provisions *in* the Constitution, which declare that Representatives shall be elected *by the people;* that *all people* are *citizens*, and that the right to vote shall not be denied on account of race, color or previous condition of servitude, I ask Congress, and I ask them upon their solemn oaths, to give vitality to the provisions of the Constitution, and to guarantee a republican form of government to every State, *who* among the people, persons, citizens, who resided in the States, could have been denied the right to vote for Representatives? We must regard this Amendment as though there had been no negroes requiring enfranchisement. We must divorce our minds from the negro and look at the Constitution *as it is.* We must not be biased by surrounding circumstances. It must apply to these conditions and interpret them. It is the basis of equality constructed *by all* and *for all*, and from which all partake of *equal* rights, privileges and immunities.

Because this Amendment was framed to apply to the African race and to *black* people and to those who had been slaves, it must not be concluded that it has no *broader* application. Whoever it may include, under logical construction, to them the right to vote shall not be denied. Take the African race and the black color and the previous slaves out of the way, and what application would this Amendment *then* have? This is the way to test these things, the way to arrive at what they mean. *Who* will pretend to say this Amendment would mean nothing were there no negroes, and there had been no Southern slaves? Who will pretend to say that the Amendment would mean nothing in the coming election, provided that there never before had been an election under the Constitution? If you provide a Constitutional amendment, having *one* race specially in view, it must not be forgotten that there are *other* races besides. Thirty-seven States constitute the United States. If you speak of the United States you speak of all the States, for they are all included. If you speak of a *part* of the United States, you must designate *what* part, in order that it may be known what you mean. A race is composed of two sexes. If you speak of a race you include both sexes. If you speak of a *part* of a race, you must designate *which* part in order to make yourselves intelligible.

The same line of reasoning applies to the word color, although some assume to say that color in this Amendment means black, as white is no color. But how should any know what specific color is referred to in this Amendment? One might say it was intended to mean a copper color; another a mulatto color, and still another that of a Spaniard or an Italian. How can any one determine absolutely that the word race or color in this Amendment referred to the African race and to black color? Hence you must see the complete absurdity of interpreting this to mean *any* special race or color, or *any* number of races and colors less than the whole number.

I have learned that high judicial authority has been invoked upon this question of law, and that this authority has declared that neither the XIV. nor XV. Amendment gave anybody the right to vote. I think I give the exact words. I have not claimed that the XV. Amendment gave *any one* the right to vote. There is no language in either the XIV. or XV. Amendment which confers rights not possessed: but I will state what these Amendments *do* say, and if it is not equal to the declaration of the right of all to vote I confess that my perceptions are at fault for I cannot perceive the difference. They declare positively—not negatively—that "All persons born or naturalized in the United States are citizens of the United States," and mark you, of the State wherein they reside. I am a person, one of the sovereign people, a citizen of the United States and of the State of New York. Does the State of New York enforce any law which abridges my privileges or immunities as a citizen? Is it nothing to be denied the right to vote? What privileges and immunities have I differing from those of the subjects of the most *absolute* monarch? They are subject to such laws as he sees fit to impose. Am I subject to any laws other than are imposed upon me? It does not appear possible to me that men are conscious of the tyranny they exercise over women. It may be mildly exercised, but it is, nevertheless, absolute tyranny. I can have what they will give. Could the veriest slave have less? Therefore, government permits the State of New York, in the face of the XIV. Amendment, to enforce laws which abridge my privileges and immunities, as well as those of every other woman who resides therein, who is responsible, taxed and who contributes to the maintenance of an organized government.

"But," says the authority, "neither does the XV. Amendment give anybody the right to vote." What does it do? or was it an utter abortion of Congressional wisdom? "The right to vote shall not be denied on account of race, color or previous condition of servitude." The right to vote, then, is possessed. It may be, as some say, a negative admission of the existence of the right; nevertheless, it is an admission, and one under which I claim to be a voter.

I now come to the previous condition of servitude, and there is much *more* in this than is at first apparent. We had become so accustomed to regard African slavery as servitude that we forgot there were other conditions of servitude besides. Slavery or a condition of servitude is, plainly speaking, subjection to the will of others. The negroes were subject to the will of their masters, were in a condition of servitude and had no power or authority as citizens over themselves.

I make the plain and broad assertion, that the women of this country are as *much* subject to men as the slaves were to their masters. The extent of the subjection may be less and its severity milder, but it is a complete subjection nevertheless. What can women do that men deny them? What could not the slave have done if not denied?

It is not the women who are happily situated, whose husbands hold positions of honor and trust, who are blessed by the bestowal of wealth, comforts and 'ease that I plead for. These do not feel their condition of servitude any more than the happy, well-treated slave felt her condition. Had slavery been of this kind it is at least questionable if it would not still have been in existence; but it was not all of this kind. Its barbarities, horrors and inhumanities roused the blood of some who were free, and by their efforts the male portion of a race were elevated by Congress to the exercise of the rights of citizenship. Thus would I have Congress regard woman, and shape their action, *not* from the condition of those who are so well cared for as not to wish a change to enlarge their sphere of action, but for the *toiling female millions*, who have human rights which should be respected.

It may be affirmed that the exercise of suffrage will not ameliorate their conditions. I affirm that it will, and for authority will refer to the improved condition of our fathers and also to the improved condition of the negroes since they acquired the rights of citizenship; since they were enfranchised : *and how enfranchised?* The XV. Amendment does not grant them the right to vote. Neither does it to me ; *but it forbids* that a right already possessed shall be denied. If the male negroes, as citizens, possessed the right to vote, shall it be assumed that women citizens do not possess the same right?

It is said the Amendment does not give any one the right to vote. Suppose we admit that for a moment. I think men will desire to disown it. If the XIV. and XV. Amendments give none the right to vote, let me ask them where they obtain their right to vote? Do they get it from the Constitution? Nowhere does it say "the right to vote," except in this XV. Amendment. Do they vote by right, or is this another usurpation which they exercise? Where do they get their right to vote? I will tell them where they get their right to vote. They inherit it from their God, and every one of the sovereign people inherits it from the same infinite source, Who knows no such ignoble limitation as that of sex. The right to vote is *higher* than State laws, *higher* than countries' constitutions. It can neither be given nor taken by laws or by constitutions. These are but means for its exercise, and when our laws and constitutions shall have been reduced to *this* standard we shall have a republican form of government, and not till then

One more point and I shall dismiss this Amendment. It has been insisted, again and again, that the denial may be made on account of sex, and that it was not intended by those who framed this Amendment to make such a broad application and such a sweeping enfranchisement as my interpretation embraces. This is not the first time, even in legislation, that people, having a single point in view which they were determined to gain, have overreached themselves; happily, however, this time it was in the cause of liberty, humanity and equal rights.

All law may not be the deductions of logic, but where law does not apply fact and logic must. Here, however, law and fact do apply, while the deductions are very clear.

This Amendment declares that the right to vote shall not be denied on account of race. The class of opposers who still wish to deny women the right to vote, declare this means the *African* race. Let us see how this would read. The right to vote shall not be denied on account of the African race. To WHOM shall it not be denied on account of the African race? *This* certainly does not inform us, for it simply declares that it shall not be denied on account of the *African* race. Therefore, if this Amendment were even modified by saying the African race, it would still fail to leave any room for denial. But it does *not say African* race, and cannot, therefore, be interpreted to *mean* the African race, when there are so many other races represented in this country. Who would pretend that though the right to vote could not be denied to the African race, it *might be* denied to the Teuton, the Celt or the Scandinavian? Under any other interpretation of this Amendment than the broad one I make, the right to vote *may* be denied to *any* race or *all* other races except the African.

Does Congress desire that an interpretation shall stand upon the

Constitution, that, should the time come when the Anglo-Saxons would not be predominant, would permit other races to unite and deny the right to vote to the Anglo-Saxon race? *See* the dilemma in which this matter is placed by persisting in denying women the right to vote?

There is but one construction the language of this Amendment is susceptible of, and this becomes apparent if the section is properly rendered. It simply means that the right to vote shall not be denied on account of race to ANYBODY. By the interpolation of this word the sense of this Amendment is complete and unmistakable. From the simple negative it changes it to an all-powerful command, by which the sovereign people declare that the right to vote shall not be denied by the United States nor by any State to any person of any race.

We are now prepared to dispose of the sex argument. If the right to vote shall not be denied to any person of any race, how shall it be denied to the female part of all races? Even if it could be denied on account of sex, I ask, what warrant men have to presume that it is the *female* sex to whom such denial can be made instead of the *male* sex? Men, you are wrong, and you stand convicted before the world of denying me, a woman, the right to vote, not by any right of law, but simply because you have usurped the power so to do, just as all other tyrants in all ages have, to rule their subjects. The extent of the tyranny in either case being limited only by the power to enforce it.

And this brings us to the "qualification" argument; which before entering upon I must premise by saying, I consider it the most *stupid* of them all. If there is little of sound logic in the other objections, in this there is none at all. It is the purest attempt at *quackery* that was ever palmed off upon a nation.

The only reason that can be offered for which women can be denied the right to vote is that they do not "possess the requisite qualifications for electors of the most numerous branch of the State Legislature." Article I, section 2 of the Federal Constitution.

Again: "The times, places and manner of holding elections for Senators and Representatives shall be prescribed in each State by the Legislature thereof; but the Congress may at any time by law makers, alter such regulations." Federal Constitution; article 1, section 6, paragraph 1.

Upon *these* two words, "qualifications" and "regulations," must be based the whole authority for denying to women the right to vote. It has been said that the right to vote exists, but has been denied. A person being denied the right to vote is disfranchised. Are the terms qualification, regulation and disfranchisement synonymous? Qualifications are what citizens can acquire, and after having acquired can use them or not. Disfranchisement cannot be overcome. Anything that is made a qualification, which cannot be attained, which is an impossibility, is not a qualification, either within the meaning of the Constitution or of dictionaries. Sex cannot be made a disqualification. To be denied the right to vote on account of sex is the pure essence of disfranchisement; for how can a person, a citizen, being a woman, obtain the qualification of being a man? I regret that I am compelled to impugn your good sense by the argument, but I have had "sex" sounded in my ears until I can scarcely *think* of it with patience or *speak* of it with courtesy. Sex is a quality obtained by nature, and with what degree of regard for common honesty shall men continue to call this a *disqualification* which women must overcome? Was ever a more intolerable thing? It is like saying to the starving, "You may eat; here is a stone." The kingdom of human rights cannot be invaded to furnish qualifications for voters; these qualifications must be of a character equally attainable by all citizens. No more can be required of woman than of man. If men become qualified by residence, property, education, character, age, etc., so, too must women be able to qualify by the same means.

I do not care what qualifications the States require for electors. What I ask is, that they shall apply equally to all citizens of the United States, whether they are men or women. For men to say to women, "You shall not vote because you are women" is *intolerable;* is *unbearable,* and it will not do for Congress to quietly allow this disfranchisement to continue. Congress *has* the power to make and alter the regulations of a State, and I respectfully ask Congress to make and alter the regulations of the State of New York, so that I shall not be disfranchised under the misnomer of the qualification of sex.

Nor is authority wanting upon this point, and that, too, from our fathers who framed the State Constitutions, of which we hear so much, and who thought so differently from what is now predicated of them.

Mr. Madison, as a member of the Virginia Convention said: "*Some* States might regulate the elections on the principle of *equality*, and *others* might regulate them otherwise. Should the people of any State, by any means, be deprived of the right of suffrage IT WAS DEEMED PROPER THAT IT SHOULD BE REMEDIED BY THE GENERAL GOVERNMENT." One half of *all* citizens of the United States are disfranchised because they are not men, a something to which they can never attain. Nature has made a distinction which it is impossible to get over. How do the arguments which were used in Congress not many months ago, pale before the awful magnitude of this National dishonor? They were then entreated to not continue the disfranchisement of a *few* millions of negroes, but they *unblushingly* continue the disfranchisement of *many* millions of women.

If there are good and consistent reasons why some should not be electors let them be applied without regard to sex or any other general condition. Let men as well as women be subject to them. If they include me I will not complain; I will but ask that every man shall be prevented for the same reasons I am, and for none other. If men were unreasonably prevented from suffrage I would as earnestly plead their cause. No person felt more for the emancipated negro race than myself; but with their enfranchisement I could not forget that the whole female sex was laboring under the same disabilities from which they were raised. Negroes could not qualify to become voters, Congress assisted them and they are voters; hence I went to Congress to plead for women. The negro found many advocates—men whose souls were large enough to take in all God's family. But with this great effort they closed. Woman must be her own advocate. Few of the male sex—few of those who battled so manfully for the negro—now come forward and lift their voices against this *thrice* greater, this *terrible* wrong.

Slavery will ever be regarded by all our descendants as a foul blotch upon the escutcheon of this country's honor, which ages alone can wash away. Congress know this, but they do not yet know how much *more* foul will this greater wrong be regarded by future ages. It should be the task of the next Congress to remove this damning thing. That Congress which recognized negroes as citizens is already reverenced for its mighty work. So, too, will that Congress which shall recognize women as citizens of equal rights with the negro be regarded with reverence in proportion to the magnitude of the result of its labors.

I assume then—

1st. That the rights, privileges and immunities of all citizens are equal.

2d. That no citizens as a class can be denied the right to vote, except they first forfeit it as a class.

3d. That the qualifications which a State may require of electors must be such as can be acquired by all persons by the same means.

4th. That the State may make regulations but cannot enforce prohibitions.

5th. That anything that may be required which is impossible of one-half of the people or any considerable class, possessing all the other qualifications required for electors, is not a qualification, but disfranchisement.

6th. That a State which disfranchises any part of its citizens on account of any natural quality is not possessed of a Republican form of government.

7th. That if a State has not a Republican form of government it is the solemn duty of Congress, under its Constitutional obligations, to guarantee it to its citizens resident therein.

Thus have I endeavored, as briefly as possible, to place before you my reasons for claiming the right to vote for myself and others of my sex who desire it. Neither upon general principles nor by special provision of the Constitution can I perceive that men have any right to deny it to us. So long as we did not *claim* it, it was not denied, but I do now claim that I am, *equally* with men, possessed of the right to vote, and if *no others* of my sex claim it, I will stand alone and reiterate my claim, and if the right is possessed, men have *no power* other than an usurped one to deny me.

The first official duty of every Congressman is to take a solemn oath to support and give vitality to the Constitution of the United States, not as they would, or might wish it to be, but as it is. That Constitution declares that women are citizens, and that citizens shall not be denied the right to vote. In the face of these facts, how can they, with that oath recorded, deliberately set at naught these plain declarations ?

I went before Congress to demand a right, and memorialized them, setting forth my grievances, and frankly and fully to the extent of my ability I endeavored to make my claim clear. This is a vital matter, fraught with more momentous events than have ever yet dawned upon the world. Through it civilization will make a giant stride from barbarism toward perfection—a stride which will land the human race near the haven where every person living will become a law unto himself, where there shall be no need of Constitutions, Houses of Congress and Executives, such as are necessary now.

Regarding it as I do, it becomes to me the most sacred duty of my life to attain to my rights under the Constitution.

I think I have examined this subject quite thoroughly; to me it appears very plain, but to others it may not. I have no doubt about the common rights of citizens under the original text of the Constitution. There is *no room* for doubt since the addition of the XIV. and XV. Amendments. Whatever doubt there may yet be in the minds of opponents, I now propose to show you that whether equality is Constitutional or not, Congress has *already* given its verdict in favor of my position, whether *intentionally* or *unwittingly* I *know* nor *care* not; it is *sufficient* that it is given, and *that*, too, in the form of *positive* law.

Permit me to return for a moment to Mr. Bingham, who has played so prominent a part, who has wrought so much better than he knew. In his report adverse to my memorial, which asked for an Act to place the right of all citizens to vote above question, he says in the outset:

"Since the adoption of the XIV. Amendment of the Constitution there is no longer any reason to doubt that *all persons* born or naturalized in the United States, and subject to the jurisdiction thereof, *are* citizens of the United States and of the State wherein they reside." And in closing : " We are of opinion, therefore, that it is not competent for Congress to establish by law the right to vote, without regard to sex, in the several States of this Union, without the *consent* of the *people* of such States, and against their constitutions and laws ; and that such legislation would be, in our judgment, a violation of the Constitution of the United States and of the rights reserved to the States. We therefore recommend that the prayer of the petitioner be not granted."

This report was made to the House of Representatives, January 30, 1871. It is almost impossible to conceive that the author of this report was the same person who drew the XIV. Amendment, and AN ACT to enforce the rights of citizens of the United States to vote in the several States of the Union, and for other purposes, approved May 31, 1870. If Mr. Bingham can harmonize these three instruments and maintain himself before the people of the United States as the great legal authority of the Congress of the United States, he will accomplish something no other person living would be able to *do*. But let us refer to this act of less than a year ago, which I have taken the precaution to produce, section 2 of which is as follows :

And be it further enacted, That if, by or under the authority of the constitution or laws of any State, or the laws of any Territory, any act is or shall be required to be done as a prerequisite or qualification for voting, and by such constitution or laws persons or officers are or shall be charged with the performance of duties in furnishing to citizens an opportunity to perform such prerequisite, or to become qualified to vote, it shall be the duty of every such person or officer to give to all citizens of the United States the same and equal opportunity to perform such prerequisite, and to become qualified to vote without distinction of race, color or previous condition of servitude ; and if any such person or officer shall refuse or knowingly omit to give full effect to this section, he shall, for every such offence, forfeit and pay the sum of five hundred dollars to the person aggrieved thereby, to be recovered by an action on the case, with full costs and such allowance for counsel fees as the court shall deem just, and shall also, for every such offence, be deemed guilty of a misdemeanor, and shall, on conviction thereof, be fined not less than five hundred dollars, or be imprisoned not less than one month and not more than one year, or both, at the discretion of the court.

SEC. 3. *And be it further enacted,* That whenever, by or under the authority of the constitution or laws of any State, or the laws of any Territory, any act is or shall be required to [be] done by any citizen as a prerequisite to qualify or entitle him to vote, the offer of any such citizen to perform the act required to be done as aforesaid shall, if it fail to be carried into execution by reason of the wrongful act or omission aforesaid of the person or officer charged with the duty of receiving or permitting such performance or offer to perform or acting thereon, be deemed and held as a performance in law of such act; and the person so offering and failing as aforesaid, and being otherwise qualified, shall be entitled to vote in the same manner and to the same extent as if he had in fact performed such act; and any judge, inspector or other officer of election whose duty it is or shall be to receive, count, certify, register, report or give effect to the vote of such citizen upon the presentation by him of his affidavit stating such offer and the time and place thereof, and the name of the officer or person whose duty it was to act thereon, and that he was wrongfully prevented by such person or officer from performing such act, shall for every such offence forfeit and pay the sum of five hundred dollars to the person aggrieved thereby, to be recovered by an action on the case, with full costs and such allowance for counsel fees as the court shall deem just, and shall also for every such offence be guilty of a misdemeanor, and shall, on conviction thereof, be fined not less than five hundred dollars, or be imprisoned not less than one month and not more than one year, or both, at the discretion of the court.

SEC. 16. *And be it further enacted*, That all persons within the jurisdiction of the United States shall have the same right in every State and Territory in the United States to make and enforce contracts, to sue, be parties, give evidence, and to the full and equal benefit of all laws and proceedings for the security of person and property as is enjoyed by white citizens, and shall be subject to like punishment, pains, penalties, taxes, licenses and exactions of every kind, and none other, any law, statute, ordinance, regulation or custom to the contrary notwithstanding. No tax or charge shall be imposed or enforced by any State upon any person immigrating thereto from a foreign country which is not equally imposed and enforced upon every person immigrating to such State from any other foreign country; and any law of any State in conflict with this provision is hereby declared null and void

Thus we find Mr. Bingham, in the XIV. Amendment, declaring that *all persons are citizens ;* in an Act approved May 31, 1870, making it a penal offence for any officer of election in any State to refuse to permit *all citizens* the *same* and *equal* opportunities to perform the prerequisites to become qualified to vote ; less than a year afterward informing us that women are *not citizens*, and on January 30, 1871—less than two months thereafter—very decidedly expressing a contrary opinion, and adding that Congress has no power to enforce their rights as citizens in the States, which is a complete stultification of the Act of last May. At present Mr. Bingham does not think women are entitled to vote. What he may think to-morrow or next month it would be quite impossible to predict. Whether we are to account for his inconsistencies by presuming that he has not attained to the knowledge that the States, through their respective legislatures, by the act of adopting and ratifying the XIV. and XV. Amendments, did remove all obstructions to the right of women citizens to vote or by some other disability of mind it is impossible to determine.

What did Congress ask the States to do? To ratify the Amendments. They did ratify them, and thereby enfranchised women as citizens. Mr. Bingham does not yet seem to comprehend what the States were asked to do, nor that they did what was requested of them.

It is clear from the report of the majority of the Judiciary Committee, that they take the view that there is "something" in the Constitutions or Laws of the States which is contrary to the language, spirit, intent and purpose of these Amendments, and that this inconsistent something must be removed by the States. I contend that by the adoption of these Amendments, the States did legislate upon the subject, and remove all inconsistencies and all obstructions to the right to vote; leaving them as parts and parcels of the "Supreme Law," before which *all existing legislation contrary* to and *inconsistent* therewith *did* fall, and was rendered null and void.

The Constitution can be amended as follows: "Congress, whenever two-thirds of both Houses shall deem it necessary, shall propose Amendments to the Constitution, which shall be valid to all intents and purposes as part of this Constitution, when ratified by the legislatures of three-fourths of the several States," Article V. Again it says: "This Constitution and the laws of the United States which shall be made under authority of the United States, shall be the supreme law of the land," Article VI.

These amendments *were* thus proposed by two-thirds of both Houses—*were* thus *ratified* by the Legislatures of three-fourths of the several States, and were thus formally legislated upon by all the several State Legislatures and *adopted* by them in the due and solemn manner in which they pass all laws. From the moment the official declaration was made that they *were* so adopted by State legislation, they became a part of the "supreme law of the land," which they *never* could have become without such legislation.

Are not these amendments in question, as a part of the supreme law, the *very creatures* of the State Legislatures, and as *such* do they not supercede all legislative acts in *all the* States not in harmony therewith? Nor can the States *recede* from these acts without similar formal legislation in which three-fourths of all the States must concur. *And what do they establish?* *The status of every native born or naturalized person in the country as a citizen of the United States and of the State, and the right to vote as vested in every such person.* And to go further: The State of New York has declared—Article I. of the Constitution of New York—and every other State holds that: "No *member of this State shall be disfranchised* or deprived of *any* of the rights or privileges secured to *any* citizen thereof—unless by the law of the land or the judgment of his peers." As the State cannot pass any law which deprives *any* citizen of his or her citizenship and the declared right to vote, it follows that the Legislatures *have* acted directly upon this question by the adoption of these amendments, and *forever* precluded themselves from receding, except by a similar proceeding, viz.: by another amendment to the Constitution which would annul and repeal the XIV. and XV. Amendments.

These amendments are therefore not only the law of the *United States*, but the Constitutional law of New York and *every other* State in the Union.

Therefore, I would have Congress, in the pursuit of its duty, to enforce the Constitution by appropriate legislation, *pass* a Declaratory Act plainly setting forth the right of *all* citizens to vote, and thus render unnecessary the thousands of suits for damages which will otherwise arise. What legislation could be *more* appropriate than defining the rights of *one-half* the citizens of the country, when they are in question? This matter has passed *beyond* the States. They have delegated this power to *Congress* by these Amendments. Could the legislatures of the States think of legislating upon the question of *who* are citizens? *How* can they then upon the *rights* of these *same* citizens, which are no less clearly a part of the Constitution than the fact of citizenship.

There are some conscientious persons, I am informed, who object to petitioning Congress to pass a Declaratory Act, for the reason that since they possess the right it is beneath their dignity to petition for what they already have. But do they stop to consider how long they may be obliged to wait for the exercise of suffrage? Do they think men will voluntarily grant it? If they do they will be mistaken. But they say, "The courts will give it to us." Will they do so without the asking? If so, it will be a great departure from their usual practice.

It seems to me that petitioning Congress to enforce the provisions of these Amendments is eminently proper, and that any who object thereto either do not understand the powers and duties of Congress or do not wish so easy a solution of the franchise question, which solution cannot be expected from the courts, as a decision therein may be deferred for years.

A Washington correspondent of the Tribune of May 2d, speaking of this matter, says:

"There is no probability that the women of this District will vote by the next Presidential election, if they depend on a decision of the Courts in their favor for the privilege. The action is brought in the Circuit Court of the District, which will adjourn before reaching the case. It cannot, then, be decided until the October term; but, no matter what the decision may be, the case will be appealed to the United States Supreme Court, which, judging from the present condition of its docket, will not be able to render an opinion in less than two or three years."

The matter of time is an important element in this issue. I am aware that women do not yet fully appreciate the terrible power of the ballot, and that they have made no calculations what they will do should the right to vote be accorded them the next session of Congress. I hold that when women are fully decided in their minds that they are entitled by law to the elective franchise, it is their solemn duty to determine how they shall use this new power.

The enfranchisement of ten millions of women, is a revolution such as the world has never seen, and effects will follow it commensurate with its magnitude and importance. Whatever the women of the country shall determine to do that will be done. It seems to me that nothing could be more wise and judicious than for them even now to begin to consider what they will do.

I have had ample occasion to learn the true worth of present political parties, and I unhesitatingly pronounce it as my firm conviction if they rule this country twenty years to come as badly as they have for twenty years past, that our liberties will be lost, or that the parties will be washed out by such rivers of blood as the late war never produced. I do not speak this unadvisedly. I know there are men in Congress—great men—who know that unless change for the better come this will.

What do the Republican leaders care for the interests of the people if they do not contribute to their strength. They have prostituted and are prostituting the whole power of the government to their own selfish purposes. They have wrung the very last possible dollar from the industries of the country and are now hoarding it in the vaults of the Treasury. One hundred and thirty millions of dollars in actual cash is a great power, a dangerous power it might be made by unscrupulous men, and I do not think but that there are those near the head of the government who are ambitious and unscrupulous enough to take advantage of any favorable opportunity in which to make use of this power.

True the republican party did a mighty work to which all future ages will look back with reverence. True that they opened the door, unwittingly though it was done, to our enfranchisement. True that they have made the name of slavery odious, and added new lustre to that of freedom.

But having delivered us from one damnation shall they be permitted to sell us to another, compared to which the first is but a cipher? They have told us that the Southern slave oligarchy had virtual control of the government for many years, and that the terrible war which we waged was the only means by which this power could be humbled.

But do they tell us of a still more formidable oligarchy which is now fastening upon the vitals of the country? Do they tell us that they have given four hundred millions of acres of the public domain, millions of dollars and tens of millions of credit to build up this new tyrant? Do they tell us that this tyrant is even now sufficiently powerful to buy up the whole legislation of the country, to secure the confirmation of any nomination which it desires made, and to bribe officials everywhere to the non-performance of their duty? Do they tell us matters have been so arranged that all the revenue they can extract from the people is turned over to this power, by which process the vitality of the country is being gradually absorbed? No, not a bit of it. This they will leave us to learn through bitter experience as we were left to learn what were the fruits of forty years plotting by the slave oligarchy. This new oligarchy has plotted less than ten years and it has already attained the most threatening and alarming proportions.

Shall we turn to the Democratic party with the hope that they may prove the necessary salvation from the wrath to come. To do this would indeed be to show the dire extremity to which we are driven. I hold that the Democratic party is directly responsible for the late war. The Democratic party South would not have rebelled had not the Democratic party North promised them their support. Can we expect anything better from them than from the Republican party? They are not now making themselves so antagonistic to the true interests of the country as are the Republicans, simply because they have not got the power so to do. But where they have the power, their leaders do not hesitate to make the most use of it to their own aggrandisement.

Therefore, it is my conviction, arrived at after the most serious and careful consideration, that it will be equally suicidal for the Woman Suffragists to attach themselves to either of these parties. They must not—cannot afford to—be a mere negative element in the political strife which is sure to ensue in the next Presidential election. They must assume a positive attitude upon a basis compatible with the principles of freedom, equality and justice which their enfranchisement would so gloriously demonstrate as the true principles of a republican form of government. I do not assume to speak for any one. I know I speak in direct opposition to the wishes of many by whom I am surrounded. Nevertheless, I should fail to do my duty, did I conceal what I feel to be the true interests of my sex, and through them, those of humanity; for the interests of humanity will never be understood or appreciated until women are permitted to demonstrate what they are, and how they shall be subserved. I have thus as briefly as possible given what I concieve to be the position which the Woman's Rights Party occupies at this time, their prospective power, importance and duties, and the dangers by which this country is threatened, from which they may save it.

If Congress refuse to listen to and grant what women ask, there is but one course left them to pursue. Women have no government. Men have organized a government, and they maintain it to the utter exclusion of women. Women are as much members of the nation as men are, and they have the same human right to govern themselves which men have. Men have none but an usurped right to the arbitrary control of women. Shall free, intelligent, reasoning, thinking women longer submit to being robbed of their common rights. Men fashioned a government based on their own *enunciation* of principles: that taxation without representation is tyranny; and that all just government exists by the consent of the governed. Proceeding upon *these* axioms, they formed a Constitution declaring all persons to be citizens, that one of the rights of a citizen is the right to vote, and that no power within the nation shall either make or enforce laws interfering with the citizen's rights. And yet men deny women the first and greatest of all the rights of citizenship, the right to vote.

Under such glaring inconsistencies, such unwarrantable tyranny, such unscrupulous despotism. what is there left women to do but to become the mothers of the future government.

We will have our rights. We say no longer by your leave. We have besought, argued and convinced, but we have failed; *and we will not fail.*

We will try you *just once more.* If the very next Congress refuse women all the legitimate results of citizenship; if they indeed merely so much as fail oy a proper declaratory act to withdraw every obstacle to the most ample exercise of the franchise, then we give here and now, deliberate notification of what we will do next.

There is one alternative left, and we have resolved on that. This convention is for the purpose of this declaration. As surely as one year passes, from this day, and this right is not fully, frankly and unequivocally considered, we shall proceed to call another convention expressly to frame a new constitution and to erect a new goverment, complete in all its parts, and to take measures to maintain it as effectually as men do theirs.

If for people to govern themselves is so unimportant a matter as men now assert it to be, they could not justify themselves in interfering. If, on the contrary, it is the important thing we conceive it to be, they can but applaud us for exercising our right.

We mean treason ; we mean secession, and on a thousand times grander scale than was that of the South. We are plotting revolution ; we will overslough this bogus republic and plant a government of righteousness in its stead, which shall not only profess to derive its power from the consent of the governed, but shall do so in reality.

We rebel against, denounce and defy this arbitrary, usurping and tyrannical government which has been framed and imposed on us without our consent, and even without so much as entertaining the idea that it was or could be of the slightest consequence what we should think of it, or how our interests should be affected by it, or even that we existed at all, except in the simple case in which we might be found guilty of some offense against its behests, when it has not failed to visit on us its sanctions with as much rigor as if we owed rightful allegiance to it ; which we do not, and which, in the future, we will not even pretend to do.

This new government, if we are compelled to form it, shall be in principles largely like that government which the better inspirations of of our fathers compelled them to indite in terms in the Constitution, but from which they and their sons have so scandalously departed in their legal constructions and actual practice. It shall be applicable, not to women alone, but to all persons who shall trausfer their allegance to it, and shall be in every practicable way a higher and more scientific development of the governmental idea.

We have learned the imperfections of men's government, by lessons of bitter injustice, and hope to build so well that men will desert from the less to the more perfect. And when, by our receiving justice, or by our own actions, the old and false shall be replaced by the new and true ; when for tyranny and exclusiveness shall be inaugurated equality and fraternity, and the way prepared for the rapid development of social reconstruction throughout.

Because I have taken this bold and positive position; because I have advocated radical political action; because I have announced a new party and myself as a candidate for the next Presidency, I am charged with being influenced by an unwarrantable ambition. Though this is scarcely the place for the introduction of a privileged question, I will, however, take this occasion to, once and for all time, state I have no personal ambition whatever. All that I have done, I did because I believed the interests of humanity would be advanced thereby.

Had I been ambitious to become the next president I should have proceeded very differently to accomplish it. I did announce myself as a candidate, and this simple fact has done a great work in compelling people to ask: and why not? This service I have rendered women at the expense of any ambition I might have had, which is apparent if the matter be but candidly considered.

In conclusion, permit me again to recur to the importance of following up the advantages we have already gained, by rapid and decisive blows for complete victory. Let us do this through the courts wherever possible, and by direct appeals to Congress during the next session. And I again declare it as my candid belief that if women will do one-half their duty until Congress meets, that they will be compelled to pass such laws as are necessary to enforce the provisions of the XIV. and XV. Articles of Amendments to the Constitution, one of which is equal political right for all citizens.

But should they fail, then for the alternative.

POLITICAL THEORY

(3)

Carpenter and Cartter Reviewed . . . 1872.

Reprinted in *Woodhull & Claflin's Weekly* (May 24, 1873, pp. 4-7, 10).

CARPENTER AND CARTTER

REVIEWED:

A SPEECH

BEFORE THE

National Suffrage Association,

AT

LINCOLN HALL, WASHINGTON, D. C., JAN. 10, 1872.

BY

VICTORIA C. WOODHULL.

NEW YORK:
WOODHULL, CLAFLIN & CO., PUBLISHERS,
44 Broad Street.

1872.

PROSPECTUS.

WOODHULL & CLAFLIN'S WEEKLY.

[The only Paper in the World conducted, absolutely, upon the Principles of a Free Press.]

It advocates a new government in which the people will be their own legislators, and the officials the executors of their will.

It advocates, as parts of the new government—

1. A new political system in which all persons of adult age will participate.

2. A new land system in which every individual will be entitled to the free use of a proper proportion of the land.

3. A new industrial system, in which each individual will remain possessed of all his or her productions.

4. A new commercial system in which "cost," instead of "demand and supply," will determine the price of everything and abolish the system of profit-making.

5. A new financial system, in which the government will be the source, custodian and transmitter of   money, and in which usury will have no place.

6. A new sexual system, in which mutual consent, entirely free from money or any inducement other than love, shall be the governing law, individuals being left to make their own regulations; and in which society, when the individual shall fail, shall be responsible for the proper rearing of children.

7. A new educational system, in which all children born shall have the same advantages of physical, industrial, mental and moral culture, and thus be equally prepared at matur' y to enter upon active, responsible and useful lives.

All of which will constitute the various parts of a new social order, in which all the human rights of the individual will be associated to form the harmonious organization of the peoples into the grand human family, of which every person in the world will be a member.

Criticism and objections specially invited.

The WEEKLY is issued every Saturday.

Subscription price, $3 per year; $1.50 six months; or 10c. single copy, to be had of any Newsdealer in the world, who can order it from the following General Agents:

The American News Co., New York City;

The New York News Co., New York City;

The National News Co., New York City;

The New England News Co., Boston, Mass.

The Central News Co., Philadelphia, Pa.;

The Western News Co., Chicago, Ill.

Sample copies, mailed on application, free.

VICTORIA C. WOODHULL AND TENNIE C. CLAFLIN, Editors and Proprietors.

COL. J. H. BLOOD, Managing Editor.

All communications should be addressed

WOODHULL & CLAFLIN'S WEEKLY,

Box 3,791, New York City.

A REVIEW

NEW DOCTRINE OF STATE RIGHTS.

"We hold these truths to be self-evident; that all men are created equal; that they are endowed by their Creator with certain inalienable rights; that among these are life, liberty, and the pursuit of happiness; that to secure these rights, governments are instituted among men, deriving their just powers from the consent of the governed."

Such, my friends, are the propositions which resulted from that famous Philadelphia Conference, in which Washington, Franklin, Rush and Adams, when hesitating and undecided, called on Tom Paine to solve their difficulty. Rising from his seat when he had attentively listened to their doubts and queries, and, towering high above them, Mr. Paine answered them : "We want independence, and I mean revolution."

And our wants to-day are what their wants were at that time. We want independence ; and if we can't get it without it, we mean revolution. Do you doubt that we are in slavery ? Franklin himself said to be enslaved is to have governors appointed over us by other men. Women have governors appointed over them by other men, and, according to Franklin, are absolutely enslaved. Freedom has been the watchword which has echoed through the centuries, and to-day it rises higher, and touches the souls of mankind with a profounder meaning than ever before. With each succeeding year it has gathered in volume, and expanded its boundaries, until every human soul leaps with a new pulsation when touched by its magnetic power.

Something more than a year ago I went before Congress with a simple petition, setting forth that I was a citizen of the United States and of the State of New York, under the provisions of the Fourteenth Amendment to the Constitution of the United States, and that the State of New York unlawfully deprived me of one of the dearest rights of a citizen, in direct contravention of that Amendment, and asking for the necessary legislation to prevent the continuation of such tyranny.

I adopted that course because I believed myself aggrieved as set forth, and because I believed I had just as good a right to participate in government as most men had, and because I was not willing to await the willingness of men to graciously say, "We will now consent that you shall vote." I did not ask any other woman whether she believed as I believed, or if she felt as I felt. I acted of my own accord, scarcely realizing that my demand would grow into the great National Question it since has.

But why did I go to Congress with my demand? I will tell you. I had carefully watched the legislation of Congress following the war, which was fought and won upon the very idea upon which all that legislation was founded—and that was the sovereignty of the United States over that of the States. It was held by all Republicans, up to the time of my demand upon Congress, that that was the result of the war and the effect of the Amendments.

I saw that all the qualifications for electors, of which use had been made by the States, were wiped out by the Amendments and the Force Act; I saw that the provisions of race, color, and previous condition of servitude, removed all restrictions upon the right of negroes to vote, although, as in the State of New York, they were not prevented from voting because they were negroes, but because they did not have the property qualification; I saw all these restrictions and obstacles melt away before the potent concentration of power, by which the sovereign people of the whole country forbid the sovereign people of any people to discriminate against citizens who owed their first allegiance to the United States.

I saw that I was first a citizen of the United States, and, by virtue of so being, also a citizen of the State of New York, and that the State had no right to even require me to conform to any of its regulations in order to be entitled to be recognized as a citizen.

But the State of New York did assume to interfere with my rights as a citizen of the United States, by depriving me of the right to participate in the government of the United States. Therefore, as a citizen of the United States, I appealed to the Government of the United States for redress. Was I right or was I wrong? But how was I met? By the flat contradiction of my whole demand. It was denied that I was a citizen. I was simply a woman—not even a person, since to be a person was to be a citizen.

That was a year ago. How does the question stand to-day? Then, the Republican Party claimed to have demolished—aye, destroyed—the doctrine of States' rights. Now they are compelled either to acknowledge that my demand was a legal and just one, or themselves become the champions of those very doctrines to purge the country from which they murdered hundreds of thousands of their brothers. Thus, what required rivers of blood and years of severest struggle to gain, my simple demand has caused them to abandon. Verily, there must be a mighty power behind that demand, to cause the Republican Party to even hesitate to grant it. While not to grant it is to enter up a verdict of condemnation against themselves, which time even will never be able to efface.

I hold, then, that I was right in going to Congress to demand redress; and I further hold that everything that has since occurred, connected with this question as relating to women, proves that I was right—proves that we have no hope whatever for redress by any other means. In a State where men specially desire to invite the immigration of women, they were denied an amendment to the state constitution by a vote of six to one. If that is to be taken as a sample of what men will do where they should be specially favorable to women on account of their scarcity, what may we expect in States where women predominate? Do you, my friends, see any hope that way? I confess I do not.

Turn you to Wyoming, and what do we see there as a result of the theory that citizens may be enfranchised and disfranchised at will simply because they don't choose to vote as it is desired that they should vote? Is that the kind of Republicanism under which you want to live? Do you want your State to grant you suffrage one day, and take it away the next? Have men ever undertaken to play that game with their own sex? Not a bit of it. And, were it ever attempted, I think I can name a hundred Congressmen who would launch their oratorical thunder, till the whole country should ring with its echoes. And it would be right. It would be ignoble in them not to do so. But in our case—why, it is quite a different matter. They don't deem it quite expedient. They don't know exactly what use we shall make of the ballot if they permit us to get it. We are only women, you know— between whom and men, it is said, there is an impassable political gulf fixed. But let me simply say to those expedient Congressmen, who think more of their positions and prospects than they do of justice. that they cannot afford to maintain that position.

But let us enter into a close analysis of the situation, and the law which applies. We, as women citizens, are either entitled to vote under the law, or we are not. Let us take it up, and see for ourselves just how the matter stands. We do not need to ask anything. I think we are capable of reading and getting at the real sense of it for ourselves. And if we read, and find that we are entitled to the ballot, under the very laws men have made, we are surely justified in demanding the benefit of such laws.

One of the following positions must be correct. Either the States have the right to deny the right to vote to all citizens, or they have no right to deny it to any citizen. Now, we claim that they have no right to deny any citizen the right to vote. But if we admit that they have no right to deny any citizen the right to vote, we thus claim that that is not a Republican form of government which makes such denial. And if the government which makes such denial is not a Republican government, is that form of government which will admit of such denial a Republican form? I say most emphatically no! But what say the Republican Party?

During last Summer, Mr. Tilton addressed an exhaustive argument to Senator Sumner upon this question, ending by asking him to become the champion of this movement in Congress, as he was the champion of the Slavery movement. Though several months have elapsed, Mr. Sumner has made no reply. Whether he thinks it unworthy his attention, or whether, like many Republicans, he thinks it inexpedient to broach this question upon the eve of a Presidential election,— since they are not capable of seeing how it will affect that election,— or whether he is indifferent to it, we are not able to determine. But I must confess to not a little astonishment that a Senator who played so honorable a part in the destruction of African Slavery, and advocating human rights, and whose speeches only need to be amended by substituting the word "sex" for "negro," to furnish us all the argument we require, should, for any reason whatever, hesitate to become a champion against this greater slavery. I may be in error in supposing he will not. I trust I may be.

But as yet he has made no reply, though another honorable Senator has. And I think we are justified in assuming, and I do assume, that the address of Mr. Tilton to Mr. Sumner was not considered as simply a personal address, but as addressed, through Mr. Sumner, to the Republican Party, and that since Mr. Sumner could not consistently take adverse grounds, and since the party could not permit itself to be committed to Woman Suffrage by an indorsement of it, that Mr. Carpenter was selected as the person to break the force of Mr. Tilton's onset, and to bridge the question over another Presidential election, when, as I have been informed by several prominent men, they will be willing that we get our rights. And to such things, my friends, has our Republic descended. Justice, when placed in the scales with party expediency, is found wanting, and goes by the board. What business have these men to deny us our rights because a Presidential election is impending? Had they a particle of the sense of honor and true patriotism; had they a single feeling of love for their country, as above their love for self and position, they would the more gladly welcome us just at this time. Hence I say, and I declare it boldly, that these men whom other men send to Congress to legislate for themselves and against us, are traitors to their country, and unfit to occupy seats in so honorable a place as the Capitol of this country, representative of freedom to the world, if they for a single moment deny us justice. We ask no favor. We want no alms. We beg for no charity. We demand what is ours of right. And woe betide them if they shut their ears to our demands, since—

> " Ever the right comes uppermost,
> And ever is justice done ;"

But, as I have said, the question is now narrowed down to a very small point—a single point—but around it are grouped several important questions which, it appears to me, must have been either totally ignored, or, at best, but casually observed by those who established it, as the position from which to resist the attack of Woman Suffrage, under the Constitution as it is. It has seemed to me ever since I thought upon this subject that we had a queer sort of a Republican form of government whose Constitution had to be amended in order to meet each new contingency. It appeared to me that " We the people " included all the people. But our wise governors seated in the Capitol inform us quite to the contrary. They tell us that we the people are only those persons whom from time to time their graciousness permits the privilege of interest in government.

That is to say, though our Constitution is based upon individual equality, exact justice and perpetual freedom, yet those whom men choose to legislate have the right to decide who are to be the recipients of these blessings which the Constitution was ordained to guard, protect and defend. Some of you may be able to comprehend such a position, and see its benign results ; but, for my part, I freely confess I am too obtuse. I can understand the simple propositions of the theory of our government ; but, for the life of me, I lose sight of the theory altogether if I attempt to grasp the application which is made of it in practice— since the paradox is too obscure for me to discover its truth. And this Republican Paradox, enunciated by Senator Carpenter, became to me still more enveloped in clouds and fogs after it passed the searching ordeal of Justice Cartter's logic. The Paradox, as stated by Mr. Carpenter (as far as can be discovered from his language), is this : We have a Republican form of government because we are compelled by the Constitution to have it, and it consists of the right of States to deny the right to vote to any citizen, except male negroes, which, after passing through the judicial furnace of Justice Cartter's brain, becomes still further attenuated—since, he says, that to admit the theory that the right to self-government is an inherent right is to destroy our civilization—hence the right don't exist.

Now, before going further, I submit to you whether Justice Cartter's logic, added to Senator Carpenter's wisdom, should not compel us, out of respect to ourselves, if not from deference to them, to adjourn and go home, convinced that we form no part of "We the people," nor of the persons whom this Amendment made citizens; or, if we are citizens, that we must wait with due patience for our gracious masters to extend us the ballot, since they instruct us that we have no rights that men are bound to respect, unless we can shoulder our muskets and fight for them. What say you? Let me tell you, my friends, for my part, instead of going home to wait for the tardy justice hinted at, I will shoulder the musket and fight for freedom, and no longer submit to this degrading vassalage. I say, "Give me freedom or give me death !" and it is time for women to declare their emancipation in terms that shall make the country ring from end to end, rouse each sleepy soul, and cause those who hold sway over them to tremble in their usurped seats.

Since we have not concluded to go home, let us examine the questions that are grouped about the new Republican doctrine of States Rights, as remodeled and announced by the modern Lycurgus, and made law by the later Daniel. And first let us examine as to what a Republican form of government is. Mr. Carpenter says: "It is a strong point in favor of your position, that under the old Constitution it is made the duty of the United States to guarantee a Republican form of government to every State." But he sweeps that point away by the assertion that, since when women did not desire to vote, the States were held to have a Republican form of government; that, though women do now desire the right to vote, and are denied, the States, nevertheless, are Republican. Is that strictly logical? I say, emphatically, NO ! It is neither logic nor common sense, as I will shortly show.

A hundred years ago women made no demand for the exercise of the elective franchise. They simply did not want it. They were not denied it, however; and they freely exercised such other citizen's rights as that of pre-empting lands, obtaining passports, and clearing vessels. Nobody thought of denying them these rights. But it is quite different now since women do demand the elective franchise, thousands strong, and are denied. The argument hurled at us, that the majority of women do not want the ballot, instead of being against our position, is directly and forcibly in its favor—since a government might be held to be Republican which had non-voting citizens from choice, which could not be so held having non-voting citizens from compulsion.

Would Mr. Carpenter assume that to be a Republican form of government which deprived every man of the ballot? We hardly think he would go to that extreme. How, then, can he assume the same of one that denies the ballot to every woman? And do you not see, to admit if all women wanted the ballot that they should have it, is to admit, if any one desires it, it is clearly her right to have it, since rights are individual, not collective? If it is the right of all women, then it follows necessarily that it is the right of each one constituting the all. Is not that a clear statement?

But Mr. Carpenter facetiously says: "The Constitution, deriving its powers from the will of the people, must be construed as it was understood by the people." Admit all that, and it cuts its own throat; since, if the people a hundred years ago construed indefinite language to mean one thing, the people of to-day may very properly give the same language a very different construction. Or are we always to accept the theories of past ages? The Constitution exists to-day under the authority and by the will of the people who exist to-day; and it is for *them* to determine for themselves what a Republican form of government is to-day, not what it may have been held to be a hundred years ago.

But how are we to know whether the States ever had a Republican form of government? Mr. Carpenter says: "The Courts would undoubtedly have held that the States under the old Constitution were Republican;" but, unfortunately, that question was never raised, and of course it was never decided. It seems to me, however, that Mr. Madison did not so understand the matter, since he said: "Some States might regulate the elections on the principle of equality, and others might regulate them otherwise. Should the people of any State by any means be deprived of suffrage, it was deemed proper that it should be remedied by the General Government."

Now, what did Mr. Madison mean by the principle of equality in elections? Mr. Carpenter will hardly contend that he meant admitting one half the citizens to suffrage and excluding the other half, since that would be *inequality*. If Mr. Madison were now here, and should make that assertion, he would at once be set down by our opponents as a shrieker for Woman Suffrage.

If a Republican form of government mean the equality to which Mr. Madison referred, then neither the United States nor any of the States ever had it; and they have not got it now. Mr. Carpenter saw the force of this, and said, " Well, it is a strong point."

A Republican form of government means a government guaranteeing equality of rights among its citizens exercising the right of self-government, in opposition to a monarchical form, in which citizens submit to be ruled by a monarch, as women submit to be ruled in this country by men. There is no mistaking the meaning of these terms. There is no chance left for equivocation, reservation, or interpretation. Ours is either a monarchical or a Republican government, and there is no half-way house at which to stop. Leaving a monarchy, we must go to the other extreme to find a Republic. To do otherwise is to set up a false pretense—is to practice a cheat either upon rights or upon credulity. And I do not mean that men shall think any longer it is upon my credulity that they are practicing. I am for exposing this monstrous fraud, and for compelling the enforcement of that provision of the Constitution which demands a Republican form of government in every State of the Union.

But now let us see about the muddle into which Senator Carpenter, in his zeal to establish his new-fledged doctrines, would precipitate the Fourteenth Amendment. The language of its first section is: " All persons born or naturalized in the United States are citizens of the United States and of the State wherein they reside. No State shall make or enforce any law that shall abridge the privileges and immunities of citizens of the United States, nor deny to any person the equal protection of the laws."

Of this language Mr. Carpenter says : " *Had the Fourteenth Amendment stopped with the first section, I think the right of all citizens, black and white, male and female, to vote and hold office, would have been secured.*" He *thinks* only !

But is such the actual fact ? Had there been no second section, would the right to vote have been secured alike to men and women ? That is the question, and it is the only one. The language is positive. It does not leave any room for doubt, or place for construction to step in and quibble over words. The States shall not (that is the language) make or enforce any law that shall abridge the privileges and immunities of citizens of the United States. Now, everybody who knows anything about the definition given to the term citizen knows it describes a person entitled to participate in government, and that was distinctively and expressly settled as the law of the United States in one of the most important cases that ever came before the Supreme Court of the United States—the Dred Scott case. In delivering the opinion of the Court, Mr. Justice Daniels said : "Who, it may be asked, is a citizen ? What do the character and status of citizens import? Upon a principle of etymology alone the term citizen, as derived from *civitas*, conveys the idea of connection or identification with the State or government, and a participation in its functions. But beyond this there is not, it is believed, to be found in the theories of writers on government, or in any actual experiment heretofore tried, an exposition of the term citizen which has not been understood as conferring the actual possession and enjoyment or the perfect right of acquisition and enjoyment, of an entire equality of privileges, civil and political."

Now, what are political privileges ? Are voting, being elected and appointed to office, political privileges ? If they are not, then there are no political privileges. Take them away from politics and there would be nothing remaining. Then the right to vote is a political privilege which every citizen has the perfect right to possess or acquire and enjoy ; and since every woman born or naturalized in the United States is a citizen, every such woman, by the supreme tribunal of the nation, has the right to vote; and that decision of that tribunal stands the supreme law, unreversed by any later decision.

It inevitably and unavoidably follows, then, that the first section of the Fourteenth Amendment *does* give to "black and white, male and female," the right to vote; and no proposition can be more clearl⁻ and forcibly established.

Now, then, let us see about that second section, upon which Senator Carpenter makes so magnificent a retreat, saying, "Although *all* citizens have been made voters by the first section, the second section clearly recognizes the right of the States to exclude a *portion* of the same from voting." If a portion only, why not the whole—but if only a portion, what portion? "Oh! but—but—but it doesn't tell us who may be excluded. That, you know, we left for the States to decide." And who, pray, are the States? Do they consist of men only, and is it for them, having usurped the power to do so, to say that all women are the portion who may be excluded? Is that the magnificent result obtained by all the wisdom expended since the war in legislation, to which Congress has been almost exclusively devoted? It seems to me that such an abortion is better described by that little game, "first you see it, and then you don't," than anything else that ever emanated from Congressional brains. For the sake of ushering negroes into the mysteries of citizenship, Congress set themselves to work and made everybody citizens; but, being frightened at the grandeur and extent of the result, straightway they turned about and gave the States the right to exclude a *portion* of the newly-made voters from voting, and magnanimously left it to the States to say that that portion should be women. Such patriots; such lovers of their country; such devoted adherents to the right of the States, to do whatever they please with citizens of the United States so that they let men alone, is truly astonishing. And Mr. Carpenter, the Raphael of the nineteenth century, presents them to us in such life-like colors and in such grandeur, that we fain must bow down and worship at their shrine.

But let us analyze these beautiful pictures of the Gods of Wisdom and Justice, to see if indeed they are the only true Gods. We have been so often deceived that we must be pardoned for having become just a little bit skeptical. This Amendment declares that when the right to vote shall be denied by a State to a portion of the male citizens of the United States, the basis of such States' representation shall be reduced, &c.; and this, Mr. Carpenter says, is clearly an acknowledgment of the right of the States to deny the right to vote to women. General Butler a year ago said of a certain argument, that it was "the slimmest he ever heard." That may be the slimmest he had ever heard, but Mr. Carpenter had not then advanced this one, of which we are speaking. I think General Butler will be obliged to revise his assertion in favor of Mr. Carpenter's last effort. When the States shall deny the right to vote to a single man, then they shall have the right because of such denial to deny the same right to all women. Wonderful wisdom; wonderful indeed !

But again: this provision is in the form of a penalty; it provides if any State shall do a certain thing to certain citizens of the United States, that it shall suffer a certain penalty. Now that is all that can be made of the language. And it may be well to remember that that only is law which is written; *ita lex scripta est* is the rule everywhere. It is the only safeguard to law, since if we are at liberty to infer anything we please, then we might as well have no law at all.

But Senator Carpenter tells us, that because the sovereign people have declared, if the States shall assume to commit a certain crime against citizens, they shall suffer a certain penalty, that that gives them the right to commit all other crime against all other citizens with perfect impunity. Undoubtedly Senator Carpenter and Justice Cartter will give to the world a new system of logic; but I hope I shall not be called upon to formulate its rules.

Let us try by the same rule a similar kind of a case outside of voting, and see how it would work. The people say that if a person commit the crime of murder he should be hanged; therefore, any person has the right to commit all other crimes and suffer no penalty at all.

But there is still another face to this remarkable thing, which we are called upon to admire. If men are denied the right to vote, then the representation must be reduced. But all women may be excluded from voting and still be retained in the basis of representation. This pretense, however, is too shallow to dwell upon. Any school-girl of twelve years who could not detect it ought to be accounted a dullard. But these logicians must stick to this line of argument, since it is their last line of defense. Give this up and women suffrage is inevitable. I don't expect them to give it up until driven from it by brute force.

But we will bid adieu to this part of the subject by calling attention to the fact everywhere recognized in law, that anything granted by positive law cannot be taken away by imputation.

Justice Story, in speaking of Constitutional law, said: "Contemporaneous construction is properly resorted to, to illustrate and confirm the text; it can never abrogate the text; it can never fritter away its obvious sense; it can never narrow down its true limitations. There seems little room for interpretation, except in cases leading to an obvious absurdity, or to a direct overthrow of the intention expressed in the preamble."

Now the text to the Fourteenth Amendment is clear and positive making, as Senator Carpenter, even, is compelled to admit, all persons voters. Then, if the common rule is applied, how can the inference drawn by Senator Carpenter, from the indefinite and negative language of the second section, be held to "abrogate that text;" and "fritter away its obvious meaning;" and "narrow down its true limitations," and finally to directly overthrow not only the intent but the positively expressed meaning of the text. In other words, how can what is granted to women in express terms by the first section be taken away from them by the inference it is found convenient to draw from the second section?

"But," says Senator Carpenter, "the Fifteenth Amendment is equally damaging to the right of female suffrage, since if by the Fourteenth Amendment the elective franchise had been secured to every citizen, the Fifteenth Amendment would have been unnecessary." Now mark the consistency of the three points of his argument which we have reached: First, he informs us that the first section of the Fourteenth Amendment secured the right to vote to all citizens, black and white, male and female; second, that all persons having been enfranchised, the second section of the same Amendment confers the power upon the States to disfranchise any citizens, for any reason whatever; and that since the States continued to disfranchise male negroes, the Fifteenth Amendment was necessary to take that power away from the States. Now, if it was the intention of Congress from the first to arrive at this end, why did they proceed by such a roundabout way? Why did they not at once specifically state that all this legislation was for the purpose of securing the votes of male negroes, since that, according to Senator Carpenter, is the final result. The States may deny the right to vote to any citizens except to male negroes. Suffrage in all other cases stands just as it did before the Amendments, the fact of all persons having been made citizens counting for nothing.

All men save negroes voted then. All men, including negroes, vote now. So that the result of all the work and talk about human rights has ended in securing the exercise of the elective franchise to say, a million negroes; and all this was conducted with specific care that the same right should not be secured to 15,000,000 women. In other words, the men of the United States have declared by these Amendments that all men may vote if they choose, but that no woman shall vote under any circumstances whatever. I submit to you if, according to their own showing, this is not what has been accomplished.

But we object to this conclusion, and propose to show that men have proceeded upon an opposite theory quite too long to permit them to shift its application, now that women demand what belongs to them. The Courts have held that all limitations of rights must be made in express terms; we must demand that the same rule shall operate in our case, especially since it has been held to apply in cases arising under this Amendment.

Justice McKay laid down the following proposition: "The rights of the people of a State, white and black, are not granted them by the Constitution thereof; the object and effect of that instrument is not to give but to, restrain duly regulate and guarantee rights; and all persons recognized by the Constitution as citizens of the State have *equal legal and political rights*, except as *otherwise expressly declared.*"

Again: "It is the settled and uniform sense of the word citizen, when used in reference to the citizens of the separate States of the United States, and to have rights as such citizens, that it describes a person entitled to every right, legal and political, enjoyed by any person in that State, unless there be some express exceptions made by positive law covering the particular persons whose rights are in question."

Let me ask, is there any language in these Amendments by which women are excluded from suffrage "by positive law covering the particular persons" whose rights are involved. On the contrary, there is no direct reference made to women whatever, and no particular persons excluded. Therefore, by still another argument we are compelled to conclude that since women in common with all other persons are made citizens, and consequently voters, all women are voters, with the exception of those who have been excluded by express constitutional provisions.

Again: Senator Carpenter tells us that before the adoption of the Fifteenth Amendment any citizen could be. excluded for any reason whatever, but since that adoption any citizen may be excluded for any reason other than race, color, or previous condition of servitude.

.Now I claim, if language have any definite meaning, and if there are any rules of logic by which such meaning is to be arrived at, and if the construction of general law as announced by the Courts has any weight, that the Fifteenth Amendment forbids the denial or abridgment of the right to vote to any citizen whatever. The language is plain and explicit:

"The right of citizens of the United States to vote shall not be denied or abridged by the United States or by any State on account or race, color, or previous condition of servitude."

Now, the question is not what that language was framed to cover, nor what it has been construed to mean; but what does it say, and what would it be considered as meaning if it were to be interpreted by people having no interest in the matter as citizens of the United States, and no knowledge of the circumstances under which it became the law of the land?

It asserts, first, that the right to vote is a citizen's right; and, secondly, that that right shall not be denied or abridged by any government on account of race, color, or previous condition. Now, what do these terms cover? We know that the African race were denied the right to vote, and that by this Amendment the male portion were raised to the exercise of that right. But we also know if the Celtic race had also been denied the same right that they would have been affected in the same way. Hence it must be held to mean that not only are the States prohibited from denying the right to vote to the African race, but also to all other races—that is, that no person of any race shall be denied the right to vote because he belongs to that specific race.

If none can be denied the right to vote on account of race, can any be denied that right on account of anything that goes to make up race?

That is, since the African race cannot be denied the right to vote, can any part of that race be denied? We say, emphatically, NO! The larger always includes the parts of which it is composed, and if the whole is granted a privilege, or the exercise of a right, no part of the whole can be excluded, unless the exclusion of that specific part is expressly provided for, as I have shown it must be by the decisions, quoted, which have never been reversed. If we say the citizens of the United States may vote, it could not be held that the citizens of any of the States could be prevented, unless such States were excluded in definite terms. If the United States could not deny the right to vote to citizens of the United States, they surely could not to the citizens or the State of New York, unless there was a specific provision granting the right to exclude New York. And what applies to citizens in general must apply to all classes of citizens, no part of whom can legally be excluded, except such exclusion is made in express terms, so as to specially declare who are excluded.

But let us look at this provision from another standpoint, that we may judge of it upon some other issue than of voting. Suppose that negroes, instead of having been denied the right to vote, had been denied the right to register vessels or to pre-empt land, which, equally with his right to vote, are citizens' rights; and that the Fifteenth Amendment had read: "The right of citizens of the United States to register vessels and to pre-empt lands shall not be denied by the United States, or by any State, on account of race, color etc.," would that have been construed to leave the privilege of denying those rights to citizens on account of sex? Why are not those rights denied on account of sex? That they are not, under the interpretation of the language or the Amendment, is clear and unmistakable; since what would apply in one class of cases must also apply in all classes of cases. Nobody would think of denying a negro woman the right to register a ship, or to pre-empt land, or to obtain a passport. She is a citizen, and entitled to these citizen's rights; but the moment another citizen's right is involved—that one by which men hold their usurped power—then they are denied the exercise of that right, and are quietly informed that that right may be denied to citizens being women.

The right to vote shall not be denied on account of race. Now, if it may be denied to anybody covered and included by that term, then everybody included by the term race may be excluded for various other reasons, which would render the provision utterly nugatory. To assume such a position would be to make all legislation negative and void. And arguing upon the plea of intent, of which opponents make such constant though thoughtless use, it was the intent of the framers of the Fifteenth Amendment to prevent negroes from being denied the right to vote for any reason whatever.

Now, what does the term race include in comparison with sex? A race is composed of two sexes. Thus sex is a component part of race. But who ever heard that a sex was composed of two or more races? Therefore, if the right to vote cannot be denied on account of race, it cannot be denied on account of sex, which is a constituent part of race, unless it is specially provided, in express terms, that exclusion may be made on account of sex, and stating which sex may be excluded.

Our State constitutions provide that male citizens are electors. Why may we not just as reasonably assume that some male citizens may be excluded for other reasons than simply because they are males? Men say that the women are excluded for other reasons than because they belong to a race. We say that men may also be excluded by the same rule for other reason than because they are males. Is not that statement clear? The several races include all people, and the right to vote cannot be denied on account of race. But a part of the race are denied because they are women. Now, by the other proposition, all men are included in the phrase, " all male citizens," and they cannot be denied the right to vote, but a part of all male citizens, even the negro part, may be excluded for any other reason it may be convenient to invent. That would not be excluding them because they are males, but because they had a certain colored hair, or because they were not a certain number of feet in height, or for any other reason of which use might be made to compel arbitrary distinctions. This would be the same rule which men now apply to the term race. Women are not excluded because they belong to the African, or any other race, but because they are women, who are a part of race; as different colored haired men are a part of the sum total of men; and as different sized men are a part of the sum total of men. But while exclusions are made on account of sex, they are not made upon the other accounts simply because men don't choose to make them; which resolves the whole question into its real position : that men exclude women from voting because they have got the power to do so, and that is the sum and substance and all there is of it since it completes the argument, and the conclusion is impossible of escape.

Do you not see it is as I asserted in the beginning, that this doctrine of Mr. Carpenter's, to which he has committed the Republican party, and which they have made no effort to reverse, is the most complete possible statement of the old and exploded doctrines of States Rights, in a new form, to meet a specific contingency ? It seems to me that it was an unfortunate oversight in the Southern States that they did not take this view of the question ; since, when they were forbidden to deny negroes the right to vote because they belonged to the African race, they might have invented any other reason and have excluded them in spite of Congress. If this doctrine prevail, I do not see why the States may not go on and find reasons to exclude every negro in them from the ballot. Senator Carpenter says they have the right. I am quite certain some of the people of some of the States would like to have it done. Then I say do it and have the sincerity of these self-constituted advocates of freedom and equality put to the test, as to whether their affections run to the negro rather than to women.

We are all aware of the desperate strait in which the Democratic party find themselves. They are seeking in every direction for an escape from the toils the Republicans have woven about them; they supposed themselves "foundered" on the rock of a Centralized Government, from which there was no chance of escape except to accept the situation and make a "New Departure." Even the astute and learned, and legal and excessively constitutional New York *World* lately acknowledged that it was not only the intent, but the effect of the Amendments to vest the control of citizenship in the General Government, and to put it entirely beyond the control of the States. Now, I do not state this of my own knowledge, but I have been privately informed, that Senator Carpenter is ambitious to be the next President, and since he saw that in the Republican party there was no chance for him, he put forth this new doctrine reviving the theory of States Rights as a bid for the Democratic nomination. As I said, I cannot state that this is so, but this I can say: He ought to have it, since he has had the temerity to assert in a new form a doctrine which the most earnest old line Democrats had abandoned not only as impracticable but obsolete.

The further we pursue this argument the clearer it becomes that women are excluded from a right common to all citizens by the despot's right of might, which in all ages has been the argument of tyrants. Each succeeding proposition which we examine results in demonstrating this by a new method. Each analysis proves the logic of the right of men to be the flimsiest assumption, the merest pretense.

But, for all that, we will go through the list. Senator Carpenter says the States have the right to exclude women. This would have been a little more satisfactory had he explained what the States are. Suppose we admit his proposition. There must be some definite method of procedure by which to accomplish it. How must they do it? First, it must be determined what the States are to which this power is intrusted. Next, have the States excluded any citizens from suffrage? Lastly, was that exclusion made in proper form?

States are not certain territorial areas, having definite limits abstracted from their inhabitants. But they are the people and their effects living in such defined limits. It is impossible to conceive of a State without people. A State is a people under the jurisdiction of a certain organized government. I think no person can object to that rendition. Now, the State of New York consists of all the people who are included within specified limits, and over whom its Constitution and Laws hold jurisdiction. Now, have those people ever denied to the women of New York the right to vote? There has never been any such procedure, or any attempt at such procedure. The Courts say that all persons who are citizens are entitled to every right, civil and political, enjoyed by any person in the State, unless excluded by express terms covering the persons excluded. I have examined the Constitution and Laws of New York, and I find no express terms excluding women from equal political rights. There is no such provision existent. By what authority, then, are women denied the right to vote? I answer, by the authority of the right of might.

In the State of Nebraska this question came before the people, but the men absolutely prevented a part of the people from expressing their opinion. And yet they say that the people of Nebraska rejected Woman Suffrage. Was there ever such insults heaped upon a class of citizens as this? Will Senator Carpenter assume that the people of Nebraska have denied women the right to vote? If he cannot, neither can he escape the inevitable conclusion that they are wrongfully and illegally deprived of a right exercised by other citizens of Nebraska, and consequently he must admit that it is the duty of the General Government to interpose its power to prevent the continuation of the wrong.

More recently, in Wyoming, an attempt was even made to take from women the right to vote, exercised by them for two years, and, as Governor Campbell testifies, in a manner worthy of the best citizens. Now, what is the lesson to be learned from this attempt at despotic power in Wyoming? That to allow the right of the States to deny suffrage to any of its citizens is a dangerous precedent, and that it will be a fatal error for women to rely upon this tenure for their rights, since every Governor may not be like Governor Campbell, and some Legislatures may not have even six men out of twenty who will admit that women have any rights that men are bound to respect. Governor Campbell wisely remarks, "If this Legislature deprive women of the right to vote, the next may deprive men."

There is but one position for women to assume, and that they should advocate first, last, and all the time. They must take the Amendments, as they have the legal and established right to take them, to mean just what they say, utterly regardless of whatever might or might not have been the intent of their framers. They have completely reversed the order of government. Formerly citizens were originally citizens of the State. Now they are first citizens of the United States, and by virtue of being so are citizens of the States wherein they reside.

The first duty of every citizen is allegiance to the United States sovereignty; secondly, when it does not interfere with his first allegiance,

allegiance to tne sovereignty of the State. And if the State interfere with any of her privileges as a citizen of the greater sovereignty, then she must appea. for relief to that greater sovereignty. State sovereignty then is merged in the sovereignty of the United States. And the people of this larger sovereignty have decreed that neither that sovereignty nor that of any State shall interfere in any way whatever with the rights of citizens of the United States. This is as we read the Constitution, and all the authority there is supports this reading. Those who read it differently invite all the dangers of a return to despotism. It must be all the people governing themselves; or it *may* be one of them governing all the rest; since to begin discrimination is to open the way to discriminate against all, and to permit a government to deny one class of citizens a right that is exercised by another class, is to admit its right to deny all kinds of rights to all classes of citizens; and there is no escaping that conclusion, unless it be by the remarkable logic of Justice Cartter, which we will presently admire.

There are several other points in Senator Carpenter's "New Departure," which, with these examined, are equally felicitous. But I have not time to notice them here. I wait however to hear him advocate them from his seat in the Senate, and to see his brethren of the Republican party say, Amen!

But we hear opposition from another quarter and must take some time to look after it. Since this constitutional question has been raised this matter has found its way into the Courts, notwithstanding the oft-repeated wail from Boston that the raising of this question by those "ungodly people" has done irreparable harm to the cause. It has ruined the prospects for women, since it has sunk the question from a mere matter of glittering generalities into the depths of Constitutional law. Now, I am willing to accept suffrage, even if we have to drag it through such low and filthy slums as this to get it. I want it, and want it right away. I am even willing to get it by a "Short Cut," across lots, and through a gate left open by those who loved the negroes so well that they forgot there were any women. Even by a "trick" am I willing to get back our rights. When we deal with thieves who have stolen our birthrights, it is not only our right, but our solemn duty to take advantage of all their oversights to make safely off with their booty. I am for stealing every possible march upon them, and for confronting them in the places to which they have fled for safety and security. They have built up a something which we have shown to be a mere pretense, but which they now desire the Courts to confirm, and to thus fortify their position against us forever.

This *entree* into the Courts caused a considerable. flutter among politicians and political journals. Farmer Horace in the *Tribune* recently said that we might as well keep away from the Courts, since if we went there with our troublesome petitions we would be requested to go home and mind our own business. But we did go to the Courts, and the Courts having forgotten the injunctions of the Philosopher, listened.

Justice Howes of Wyoming even rendered a decision in which he declared that all women citizens in the United States acquired the right to vote by the Fourteenth Amendment. And Justice Underwood of Virginia announced, semi-officially, the same doctrine. This frightened the press, and straightway they roused to the fact that there really was such a question before the people. Even the *Nation* in its critical clumsiness felt called upon to enter its protest; and so it went the round, until Justice Cartter, of the Supreme Cour of the District of Columbia, solved the whole question to the complete satisfaction of both parties. He is so remarkably clear in his elucidation of the subject that I am satisfied; and our opponents assert that they are also satisfied. This decision is almost as remarkable in its possibilities as the Amendments themselves appear to be, which it pretends to interpret.

Since that portion of this decision which satisfies me is the latter part, I will begin with that. He says, in giving expression to my own judgment of this clause (the first clause of the Fourteenth Amendment), it does advance them (women) to free citizenship, and clothes them with the right to become voters. Now, I hold that is the law. Women are full-fledged citizens, with the right to become voters in the same manner that men become voters, by qualifying under the existing regulations. But we found the Constitution of the States standing in the way of our becoming voters. Hence, I asked Congress to compel the removal of the obstructions by passing an act forbidding the States to make distinctions of sex a bar to voting Such action will also meet the legal objection raised by Justice Cartter, since he says: "It is a constitutional provision that does not execute itself It is the creation of a constitutional condition that requires the supervention of legislative power to give it effect The capacity to become a voter created by this Amendment lies dormant until made effective by legislative action." Now, while I deny the possibility of such a thing as dormant rights existing in one class of citizens which is active in another class, being equal in other respects, and which require legislation to make them legal, still legislation is the readiest way to compel the removal of the distinctions, and hence we seek it.

But Justice Cartter strikes a blow at the very existence of our theory of government, when he argues that the right to vote is not a natural right, existing regardless of constitutions and laws: He says: "The legal vindication of the natural right of citizens to vote would involve the destruction of civil government, hence the right does not exist." Civil government does exist, even with all the accumulation of male depravity. Justice Cartter in substance tells us if women participate they would destroy it, hence women do not have the right to participate. Complimentary, truly ; isn't it?

Men are bad enough; but women—oh, no, that will never do—they would ruin us. Since some men make bad use of the ballot, therefore women have no right to it. Since some people abuse their stomachs, through their appetites, therefore the right to eat and drink does not exist. Since some people steal, therefore the right to possess anything does not exist. Since some people commit suicide, therefore the right to life does not exist. A wise man! A wondrous wise man! I stand abashed before the awful majesty of such wisdom !

But this is not all the discoveries in constitutional law made by this latter-day Columbus. It has been his fortune to find out that women have been rescued from one unpleasant condition by this Amendment. "It has done so much as to distinguish them from aliens," says this Solomon. "To be an alien," says Webster, "is not to belong to the same country or government;" "belonging to one who is not a citizen;" " estranged;" "foreign;" "not allied;" "adverse to; ' one not entitled to the privileges of a citizen." Now we are informed that we are rescued from these conditions; that we now " belong to the same country and government;" that we are " citizens;" that we are not " estranged," or "foreign;" that we are "allied," and not " adverse to;"and that we are " entitled to the privileges of a citizen." All this may be consistency, and very precious jewels at that, but I am free to confess that my obtuseness will not permit me to appreciate the application of it, made by Justice Cartter.

But, back of all this statement of Justice Cartter, he proposes a principle which is fatal to all his elaboration. By his own argument he proves that our government never had, and has not now got, a legal existence, since civil government can have no legitimate existence anywhere unless it have a lawful beginning somewhere. How can a legal legislative body be organized if there is no one qualified to vote until that right is conferred by legislation? How were the first legislators elected, and who elected them? and if they were elected by the people, who had no right to vote, how shall we go about to establish the validity of our laws? I assume that, if the right to vote or the right to self-government do not exist in the people, independent of constitutions and laws, that there never can be a lawful constitution in existence, since all constitutions and all laws must then emanate from an arbitrary assumption of power on the part of somebody.

It is scarcely necessary to pursue this absurd fallacy, since the matter has been so thoroughly passed upon by a higher authority than Justice Cartter, who must have been oblivious of Chief-Justice Taney's decision in the Dred Scott Case. Justice Cartter assumes that the government confers the right to vote. Hear him rebuked by Taney, who said : " The words 'people of the United States' and 'citizens ' are synonymous terms, and mean the same thing. They both describe the political body, who, according to our republican institutions, form the sovereignty, and who hold the power and conduct the government through their representatives. They are what we familiarly call the sovereign people, and every citizen is one of this people, and a constituent member of this sovereignty."

Can anything be clearer than this exposition, or more pointed as to our claim? Every woman is a member of the sovereignty, who hold the power and conduct the government through their representatives. Against the pandering to despotism of this late decision I oppose the broad republican sentiment of the former one; nor do I fear the judgment of the American people when they shall come to see this matter properly—Senator Carpenter and all whom he represents, and Justice Cartter and his confederates, to the contrary notwithstanding.

But I must call your attention to another fact that this decision brings into the argument, because when it is stripped of subterfuges and inconsistency, it has a few substantial points left. He says that women are made full citizens by a constitutional provision which does not execute itself. He scarcely need have told us that, though I thank him for having done so. If anybody ever saw a constitutional provision executing itself, he has witnessed something that if he can reproduce and take it to Barnum's Menagerie, I am sure he can realize a fortune from it. We go to a deal of trouble and expense, and pay seventy thousand men four years' salary, who do scarcely anything else than work for the election of a President, to execute the constitutional provisions; from all of which we should have been exempt had the Constitution been self-executing. And, moreover, one of these constitutional provisions is specially framed in this view, since it is made one of the positive duties of the President " to take care that the laws be faithfully executed," the provisions of the Constitution itself being the supreme law. Now I ask, in all candor and seriousness, if the President has taken care that this part of the supreme law relating to women was faithfully executed? If Congress want to impeach him they had better take some clear case of neglect of duty, and here, according to Justice Cartter, is a very plain one.

But let us take another view of this question of dormant right raised by Justice Cartter. He says legislation must supervene before it can become a right to be exercised. Is that the view Congress took of the Amendment in its application to negroes? If the negroes acquired any benefits by this Amendment, women also acquired the same benefits. If it made negroes citizens and voters, so also did it make women citizens and voters. Is there any escape from that logic? How did negroes become voters? Did the State make them so? No. This Amendment is all the legislation there has been upon the subject. And if it only made them citizens having the dormant right to become voters, how is it they are voters? As Judge Underwood has naively remarked: If by a constitutional enactment a word of five letters was stricken out of the State Constitutions and Laws, why cannot a word of four letters be also stricken out? Justice Cartter seems to have ignored history in this matter. Or does he hold that the "Force Act" was the legislation that raised negro suffrage from its dormant stage? If so, should not Congress also, and for the same reason, make the same sort of legislation, or rather, enforce the same Act, for the benefit of women?

That Act has never been understood, and I here desire to call the attention of Senator Carpenter to it, since it stabs his whole plea to the heart, and sweeps away the dust with which he endeavored to blind the eyes of thoughtless people. Section 2 of this Act reads as follows:

And be it further enacted, that if, by or under the authority of the Constitution or Laws of any State, or the Laws of any Territory, any Act is or shall be required to be done as a pre-requisite or qualification for voting, and by such Constitution or Laws, persons or officers are or shall be charged with the performance of duties in furnishing to citizens an opportunity to perform such pre-requisite, or to become qualified to vote, it shall be the duty of every such person or officer to give to all citizens of the United States the same and equal opportunity to perform such pre-requisite and to become qualified to vote.

We know this Act was framed for the negro, but we must again demand the attention of our lords and masters. They must not object to being held to laws they have themselves made, and we beg them to remember that having made it the duty of officers of election to give all citizens the same and equal opportunity to become qualified and to vote, that if they intended to make any exception, they should have done so in the Act in specific terms covering the particular citizens intended to be excluded from its benefits. In the name of justice and common sense as well as in that of law, I ask you, my friends, if that is not a reasonable demand. And if they failed to make the requisite exception to exclude women, shall we not claim under the Act? And I will *now* state that Judge Woodward, of Pennsylvania, while I was at Washington last winter, brought this Act to me and said, "There is no question about women being able to vote under it." Many other eminent men have said the same thing to me. But such plain language as is used scarcely needs authoritative exposition to make its meaning clear.

And this brings us face to face with the last argument, to which everybody alike resorts when driven from all other possible positions. Invariably they come at last back to the baby objection, which is considered as a sort of general antidote to Woman Suffrage. "Well," they say, "if all you say is just as you assume it to be, why, babies have got the same right to vote that women have." That is exactly what we claim, only we claim a little more—that men have got no right to vote that the women and babies do not possess. All we ask is that men, women and babies shall exercise the right equally and under the same regulations, as James Madison said they ought, otherwise it was the duty of the government to remedy it.

It is a strange fact that people can never see that this baby objection applies equally and as forcibly to man suffrage as it does to woman suffrage. If it is an objection in the last-mentioned, it is equally so in the first instance. Though this objection is, as General Butler has termed it, "the slimmest he ever heard," I will take the time to sweep it out of our path.

Infants consist of male and female persons. But men would have it inferred that there are no male infants, since they ask, "Are women born in the United States?" and reply, "so are babies." Male and female babies are both born in the United States, and consequently both are citizens, and both possess the right to vote; but the regulations prevent its being exercised until they have resided twenty-one years in the United States. On arriving at that age they have the requisite qualification of age, and both arrive at that qualification by the same process—by living twenty-one years. But just at that point the discrimination between the male and the female, as against the latter, begins. The male is permitted to begin the exercise of the right to vote, while the female is quietly informed that no age to which she can attain will ever qualify her to vote. This is an unequal exercise of power against which I rebel. It is neither a regulation nor the establishment of the citizen's right to vote, but a flat and unqualified denial of it.

Again, criminals, paupers and lunatics are citizens, but, by the common law, by which all legal construction of law is governed, are held to be incompetent to exercise the suffrage. Still there is no inequality here. All criminals, all paupers, all lunatics, be they men or women, are alike excluded. To make men's logic sound they should say that these classes of citizens, being women, should, while those being men should not, be excluded from suffrage. This would make their reasoning consistent. Now, will men say that adult women are to be placed in the same category with these classes of citizens and excluded from the suffrage for the same reasons that they and infants are excluded? But if they are not excluded for the same reason that these classes of citizens are, pray tell us what the reason is for which they are excluded. I have never heard one given.

On arriving at the age of twenty-one, men become entitled to the exercise of the suffrage. Why women should not also become entitled by the same reason, men may be sufficiently wise to determine. I hope they may. I am sure none will be more ready to give them credit than I. But if they cannot give a good, lawful and constitutional reason why women twenty-one years of age cannot vote, then I shall hold their assumptions as valueless.

Now, what did Mr. Madison mean by "the principle of equality?" Evidently he meant equality among citizens in regard to the right of suffrage. Suppose Mr. Madison were now living and should make that declaration, would he not be justly set down as an advocate of the right of women citizens to vote under the provisions of the Constitution; and further, that he would deem it proper that the general government should remedy any inequality in such States as should regulate elections upon the principles of inequality? The Constitution itself now declares that women are citizens, and that the right to vote is a citizen's right. The States deny the right to vote to women citizens. Is not that an inequality, according to Mr. Madison, to be remedied by the general government.

But we suppose Senator Carpenter would at this stage of the argument again remind us of that "fatal" second section of the Fourteenth Amendment. None of our opponents now attempt to say that women are not citizens. That is admitted by them all. Now if to be 'a citizen is to have the right of suffrage, or, if the elective franchise is included among the privileges of citizens, then women have the right to vote. I will prove both propositions, and thus doubly establish our claim by two other methods.

A citizen possesses all his rights of citizenship from birth, else he can never possess them legally as I have shown ; but some of these rights, like the right to bear arms, he does not exercise till the military age; others, like the right to vote, and to possess inherited property, till the legal age; and others, still, like the holding of the higher offices of state, till a yet wiser age ; and till different ages for different offices. No one will pretend to say that there is a single citizen possessing the qualifications, who has not got the right to become President, though he or she cannot do so until thirty-five years of age.

I make the broad assertion that a citizen (whether man or woman) by virtue of simple citizenship (and with nothing else as his or her credentials) possesses constitutionally the right of suffrage. What is a citizen ?

Noah Webster says that "a citizen is a person, native or naturalized, who has the privilege of voting for public officers, and who is qualified to fill offices in the gift of the people."

Worcester says that "a citizen is an inhabitant of a republic who enjoys the rights of a citizen, or freeman, and who has a right to vote for public officers, as a citizen of the United States."

Bouvier's Law Dictionary, which gives the legal meaning of the word, says that "a citizen is one who, under the Constitution and laws of the United States, has a right to vote for Representatives to Congress and other public officers, and who is qualified to fill offices in the gift of the people."

Thorbecke saying that " the right of citizenship is the right of voting in the government of the local, provincial, or national community of which one is a member."

Turning to the courts, I quote the Supreme Court of Kentucky, which declares that "no one can be in the correct sense of the term a citizen of a State who is not entitled, upon the terms prescribed by the institutions of the State, to all the rights and privileges conferred by these institutions upon the highest classes of society."

And, finally, the Supreme Court of the United States, in, perhaps, the most important case that was ever decided—the Dred Scott case— Justice Daniels said, as I have already quoted, that to be a citizen is to have the actual possession and enjoyment, or the perfect right of acquisition and enjoyment, of an entire equality of privileges, civil and political."

Mark the force of the words of Justice Daniels: "*The actual possession and enjoyment, or the perfect right of acquisition and enjoyment, of an entire equality of privileges, civil and political.*"

How lame and how impotent beside such authority as this is the decision of Justice Cartter, that though the amendments had conferred upon women the right to vote, it was a *dormant* right not to be enjoyed *until men should graciously see fit to make it active.*

But let us see more of this business.

In the opinion of Justice McKay, among other propositions, he lays down the following: and here we must again repeat

3d. It is the settled and uniform sense of the word "citizen," when used in reference to the citizens of the separate States of the United States, and to their rights as such citizens, that it describes a person entitled to every right, *legal and political,* enjoyed by any person in that State, unless there be some express exceptions made by positive law covering the particular persons whose rights are in question.

Now, you all know that the phrase "all male citizens" in our State constitutions is what men make use of to prevent women from voting. I ask, in all seriousness, is that an *express exclusion made by positive law* covering the *particular persons* whose rights are in question? It does not even refer to women, and therefore there is no law that covers the particular women whom the men seek to exclude from the exercise of a citizen's right. But even if this were not so—if there *were* express laws in the States, of what force would they be as against the Constitution of the United States, which declares itself to be the *supreme law* of the land, the constitution and laws of any State to the contrary notwithstanding? Now, if the Constitution of the United States give women the right to vote, how can the States take it away or deny its exercise? Some of these wise governors of ours may tell us, but I confess I cannot see how it can be lawfully done.

But, let us look still a little further, since the further we look the clearer our case becomes:

The Supreme Court of Massachusetts says:

"The privileges and immunities" secured to the people of each State, in every other State, can be applied only to the case of a removal from one State into another. By such removal they become citizens of the adopted State without naturalization, and have a right to sue and be sued as citizens; and yet this privilege is qualified and not absolute, for they cannot enjoy the right of suffrage or eligibility to office without such *term of residence* as shall be prescribed by the constitution and laws of the State into which they shall remove.

This case fully recognizes the right of suffrage as one of the "privileges of the citizen," subject to the right of the State to *regulate* as to the *term of residence*—the same principle was laid down in Corfield *vs.* Correll. Justice Washington, in delivering the opinion, used the following language:

"The privileges and immunities conceded by the Constitution of the United States to citizens in the several States," are to be confined to those which are in their nature fundamental, and belong of right to the citizens of all free governments. Such are the rights of protection of life and liberty, and to acquire and enjoy property, and to pay no higher impositions than other citizens, and to pass through or reside in the State at pleasure, and to enjoy the elective franchise as regulated and established by the laws or constitution of the State in which it is to be exercised.

The elective franchise, then, is *one* of the privileges referred to in the Fourteenth Amendment which shall not be abridged. It only remains to be asked, what it is to regulate and establish the elective franchise to complete our case, since the Court says "as regulated and established by the States."

I have never heard any objection made to the regulations established for the protection of the ballot. Nobody objects that a person is forced to reside a year in a State to which he may remove before he can vote. This changing however does not impair the right. But we make this objection. We object that when a man and a woman remove from one State to another, that the woman is not permitted to vote after a years residence. We want these things to fall equally upon all classes of citizens : and they must be made to do so, we no longer say they ought.

To regulate, Webster says, is " to put in order," not to put out of existence. To establish is " to make stable and firm," not to nullify and destroy. Now, that is all we ask. We demand that our elective franchise shall be so " put in order " that we may have the enjoyment of a perfect equality of political privilege with men, and that it shall be made " stable and firm." We want nothing but what the law gives us, and that, too, in terms *so plain* that " the wayfaring man, though a fool, can understand."

But men say there was " no intent " to enfranchise women. There ought not to have been any need of intent, and I do not know how they can say there was any, but since they do, I presume both men and women will be compelled to leave that matter as the Supreme Court of the United States has decided it. Justice Bradley, in delivering the opinion of the Court in the case of The Live Stock Association vs. The Crescent City, said :

" It is possible that those who framed the article were not themselves aware of the far-reaching character of its terms, yet if the amendment *does* in fact bear a broader meaning and *does* extend its protecting shield over those who were never thought of when it was conceived and put in form, and *does* reach social evils which were never before prohibited by constitutional enactment, *it is to be presumed* that the American people, in giving it their *imprimatur understood* what they were doing and *meant* to decree what in fact they *have* decreed."

Again I say, if words have any definite meaning. or Court decisions any weight, I submit that I have established, first : that by the mere fact of being citizens women are possessed of the elective franchise ; and second, that the elective franchise is one of the privileges of the Fourteenth Amendment which the States shall not abridge ; that the States cannot regulate the suffrage out of existence, as they attempt to do, and have done, in the case of women ; and finally, that whether it was, or was not, the intent of the framers of the Fourteenth Amendment to give women the elective franchise, *they have done so*, past all hope of retreat, except by getting woman's consent to another Amendment to the Constitution repealing the Fourteenth.

But let us look at this matter in the light of a common business transaction, and see it in a still more ridiculous position. There are joint-stock companies in which women are stockholders. What would even men say if the male stockholders of such companies should get secretly together and pass a resolution reciting that all male stockholders may vote? Do you think the female stockholders would submit to such a usurpation of powers? But women submit to a still more despotic and tyrannical usurpation. Our government is a joint stock company, in which *every* citizen has an interest, and yet men, without even so much as consulting women, have denied them all right to participate in the administration of that interest. Is that despotism, or can a better term be found by which to designate it?

Thus have I carefully gone through the arguments, *pro* and *con*, and as I think, both legally and logically, fully established the fact that women have, not only just as clear a natural right to participate in government as men have, but also that they have a constitutional and legal right conferred by the Supreme Court, and therefore that they are illegally, unconstitutionally, and tyrannically excluded. But the majority of men oppose us, and as men only have power, they may under the present form of government, continue to exclude us. Suppose there are fourteen millions of adult citizens who would vote—seven millions of men and seven millions women. At least two millions of the men are in favor of Woman Suffrage. Add them to the seven millions women, and our majority would be nine millions to five millions. Shall that majority remain bound hand and foot by such a minority? But men say that women won't vote? That is too late in the day. Wyoming has nailed that lie fast.

Now shall we quietly submit to have five millions men domineer over and insult seven millions women and two millions men. If men think so I am sure they will be mistaken. There is one thing left to be done. If, under our present Constitution, we cannot obtain our rights, we will project one under which we shall be able to get them, and that too without depriving anybody else of theirs. These nine millions citizens are entitled to a Constitution to represent them, and they have got the power to inaugurate it. I do not propose they shall wait ' sixty years" for justice. I want it here and now; and I intend, at least, to propose a way to get it; and not only to get this justice, but also a way by which justice shall be secured to all classes ; and especially to those millions who toil all their lives only to see the results of their labor poured through channels constructed by our wise legislators into the coffers of the already rich—a justice which shall set this tide in the opposite direction, until equality shall be restored, and until no man or woman shall be able to exist from the sweat and toil of another. We have spoken of revolution before, and what I shall now propose means revolution—means a complete transformation of the present condition of things—means the voice of the people heard as the government of this country, in the place of Congress and Legislatures, who have usurped our rights, and who presume to deal them out to us by the teaspoonful, and even this only when they see fit, or think it expedient.

POLITICAL THEORY

(4)

Woman Suffrage in the United States . . . 1896.

Reproduced from *The Humanitarian* (July 1896, pp. 1-8); published in London and edited by Victoria Woodhull.

THE
HUMANITARIAN.

VOL. IX. [ENTERED AT STATIONERS' HALL.]   JULY, 1896.   [NEW SERIES.]   NO. I.

WOMAN SUFFRAGE IN THE UNITED STATES.

BY THE EDITOR.

THE cause which is bringing woman suffrage in America to the front with a rush is the forthcoming Presidential election, and more particularly the fact that the women of the State of Colorado will be permitted by Colorado to vote for the Presidential electors of that State. Thus, for the first time in the history of the United States, women will have a direct voice in the election of the President. If the Presidential election be a close one, and there is every possibility of its becoming so, the votes of the women of Colorado may suffice to turn the balance of power, and then, the President would owe his election to women.* This then is the situation; one unparalleled in the history of America, and in a wider sense in the history of humanity.

If it be conceded that the women of the State of Colorado should vote for the President at the Presidential election of 1896, on what grounds of reason or justice shall the women of the other States of the Union be debarred from voting too? To permit the women of Colorado to vote at the Presidential Election and to exclude the women of the remaining States will be an illogical and invidious position which cannot be maintained. The cause of woman suffrage in America is virtually won. And it has been won on the ground which I have all along urged was the only one which could lead to victory, namely, on the plea that the Federal Constitution of the United States, as it stands, permits the suffrage of women. The plea put forward by the women of Colorado to-day is no new plea. It is the same which I put before the Judicial Committee of Congress at Washington in 1870—now more than a-quarter of a century ago.

In 1870 not only was it unpopular, but it was dormant. The Women's Suffrage Convention had been in existence for twenty years, it had held many meetings and presented many petitions, but

---

* See "North American Review," May, 1896, p. 632, where my original argument of 1871 is re-stated in a letter, signed W. S. Harwood.

it had achieved nothing except from the educational point of view. Countless resolutions had been passed.

The object of the Women's Suffrage Convention had been to obtain the franchise by amending the Constitution. The whole gist of my contention from the first was, and is, that no amendment is necessary since the suffrage was already granted to both sexes by the written Constitution. We were not pleading for a privilege, but demanding a right. This is the identical position of the women of Colorado to-day.

In the autumn of 1870, acting on my own initiative, I prepared a Memorial setting forth the Constitutional view and went to Washington to get it presented to Congress. It was not an easy task. However, all difficulties were overcome by the 22nd December, when the Memorial was duly presented to Congress; in the Senate by Senator Harris, in the House of Representatives by the Hon. W. P. Julian, an early friend of the woman's cause. In this Memorial I set forth clearly my claim to vote as a citizen of the United States, not basing the demand upon any legal opinion or suffragist's essay, but on the written words of the Constitution itself, and especially upon Section 1 of Article XIV, which runs as follows :—

"*All persons born or naturalized in the United States, and subject to the jurisdiction thereof, are citizens of the United States and of the State wherein they reside. No State shall make or enforce any law which shall abridge the privileges or immunities of citizens of the United States ; nor shall any State deprive any person of life, liberty or property, without due process of law ; nor deny to any person within its jurisdiction the equal protection of the laws.*"

This article, it will be seen, expressly defines who are citizens of the United States, and makes no restriction as to sex, for the word "persons" cannot by any legal or verbal sophistry be twisted to exclude women.

I also supported my case on the 15th Amendment of the Constitution, which decrees that :

"*The right of citizens of the United States to vote shall not be denied or abridged by the United States or by any State on account of race, color, or previous condition of servitude.*"

The Memorial was a brief one, but it opened up an entirely new point of constitutional law, and one which had not struck anyone before. It impressed both Houses of Congress so much that it was carefully considered, referred to the Judiciary Committee, and ordered to be printed in the official *Globe.* The sensation which followed upon its publication outside Congress was immense, and I at once followed up the advantage by demanding a personal hearing before the Judiciary Committee, when the Memorial should come up for consideration. Such a demand had never before been made by a woman, but it was granted, and the hearing was fixed for the 11th January, 1871. Upon this being known, the Woman's Suffrage Convention, then sitting at Washington, resolved to support me. To quote from the Secretary's report : " Hearing this important step taken by Victoria Woodhull, a stranger to the Convention, a conference was held between the parties, resulting in a friendly agreement that with the consent of the Chairman of the Committee, Mrs. Isabella Beecher Hooker, on the part of the Convention, should at the same time, through a constitutional lawyer, the Hon. H. G. Riddle, ex-Member of Congress, defend the Memorialists (30,000 women) whose names were already before Congress, asking also to exercise the right of ballot."*

I shall never forget the 11th January, 1871 ; it will always remain as one of the most memorable days of my life. And it was also a memorable day in the history of the woman's movement in America, for it was the first time that a woman's voice was heard in the Judiciary Chamber. The Chamber was thronged when I rose to address the Committee, and around the table were seated some of the most eminent jurists of America, and by me were all the best known among the woman suffragists of the day. My argument took some time to deliver, for it was lengthy and I had fortified it by frequent reference to the great Constitutional authorities. It was in the main an amplification of the plea put forward in the Memorial, and supported by every consideration which I could think of as likely to advance the cause and influence the judges. But the dominant note running through the whole was that women demanded the vote as a right under the existing Constitution ; in short the very ground on which the women of Colorado are now claiming the vote. The argument which I advanced then is the one which has led to their victory to-day.

The Committee heard me with careful attention, and at the end announced that they would take time to consider their decision. Three weeks later, on January 30th, 1871, Mr. Bingham submitted

---

* Letter of Mrs. Griffing, Secretary of the Committee of the Woman's Suffrage Convention. Appendix to the history of the Decade Meeting of Oct. 20, 1870.

the Majority Report to the House of Representatives. It admitted all the basic proposition, of my Memorial, yet recommended that the petition should not be granted. On the following day, Judge Loughbridge and General B. F. Butler, two of the acutest legal intellects of America, presented the Minority Report. They reviewed and upheld all my contentions and fortified them by copious quotations from constitutional lawyers. They recommended that Congress should pass a Declaratory Act for ever settling the disputed question of woman suffrage.

This Minority Report and the agitation which had preceded it gave an immediate impetus to the movement. A Special Committee of the Woman's Convention at Washington was formed, consisting of Mrs. Isabella Beecher Hooker, Mrs. J. S. Griffing, Mrs. M. B. Bowen, Susan B. Anthony, Paulina Wright Davis, and Ruth Carr Denison (prominent women suffragists of the day), and a special effort was made to advance the cause.

I entered upon my Presidential Campaign, by announcing myself as a candidate for the Presidential Election of 1872. This I did chiefly for the purpose of bringing home to the mind of the community woman's right to fill any office in America, from the Presidency down. The storm of ridicule and abuse which followed this move may be imagined, nevertheless I addressed meetings in almost every town and city of the Union in pursuit of my candidature, and was nominated for the Presidency at an immense gathering at Apollo Hall, New York. Also to drive home another object lesson, my sister and I presented ourselves at the ballot to record our votes. They were refused amid a scene of great excitement.

It was at this time (1870-1871) that the movement reached its flood in America. It has now come forward with a rush again, and if taken at the flood, will assuredly lead to victory. The victory will be achieved on the constitutional plea which I advanced at Washington twenty-five years ago.

In a characteristic letter to the London *Times* recently, Professor Goldwin Smith from his Canadian coign of vantage, reviewed the position of woman suffrage in America (of course unfavourably), and came to the conclusion that the movement was retrogressing. I do not propose to answer the points raised by Professor Goldwin Smith— some minor inaccuracies in his letter were ably dealt with by Mrs. Fawcett. I prefer to take a wider view. The woman's movement generally has gained ground, but the suffrage phase of it has not kept pace with the general advance. I am aware that certain points have

VICTORIA VICTA!—VICTORIA WOODHULL AND TENNIE C. CLAFLIN AT THE POLLS IN THE CITY OF NEW YORK, ON ELECTION DAY, NOV. 7TH.—THEY PRESENT THEIR BALLOTS, BUT ARE DENIED THE EXERCISE OF THE ELECTIVE FRANCHISE.

been gained here and there, but with the exception of Colorado, the progress of the cause generally is very far short of what we confidently hoped and anticipated it would be twenty-five years ago. The reasons of this are not far to seek. I stated them in a recent letter to the London *Times* in answer to Professor Goldwin Smith, and I again assert them here. The first reason is to be found in the internal dissensions, divisions and jealousies which have been the bane of the suffrage movement from the beginning. Those who would govern others must first learn to govern themselves. Soon after I raised the constitutional question in 1870–71, the woman suffragists drifted away from it and back again to the old and discredited methods and worn-out cries. Yet it is on the constitutional plea alone that they can win—the fact that the Federal Constitution as it stands admits women to every political right—and the ultimate triumph of the movement in America will be secured in this way alone.

In England while other aspects of the woman's movement have gained ground, this has moved slowly. Little has been achieved beyond a "monster petition," despite the platitudes of vote-catching Ministers, the bill was relinquished in the last Parliament amid ribald laughter, and this Session it has been dropped with a silence which is almost more contemptuous. Clearly then the question is not in the forefront of practical politics, and a great deal remains to be accomplished before it can arrive there.

Suffrage is only one phase of the larger question of woman's emancipation. More important is the question of her social and economic position. Her financial independence underlies all the rest.

Victoria Woodhull Martin.

NOTE.—The illustrations inserted in the foregoing article are reproduced from plates which appeared in the contemporary press.—EDITOR.

POLITICAL THEORY
(5)
"The Woodhull Manifesto" . . . 1870.

Originally appeared in the *New York Herald* (April 2, 1870, p. 8). Here reproduced from Victoria C. Woodhull, *The Argument for Woman's Electoral Rights. ... A Review of My Work at Washington, D.C., in 1870-1871* (London 1887).

I now turn to the record of my own work. Having clearly satisfied my own mind that the existing Constitutions of my country conferred this franchise on all citizens, independently of the accident of sex, and that all rights attaching to the possession of the franchise followed necessarily on with its exercise, I determined to bring matters to an issue by claiming my rights in their highest form of expression, and declared myself a candidate for the Presidency in the following terms :—

[Reprinted from the *New York Herald* of April 2nd, 1870.]

The disorganized condition of parties in the United States at the present time affords a favourable opportunity for a review of the political situation and for comment on the issues which are likely to come up for settlement in the Presidental election in 1872. As I happen to be the most prominent representative of the only unrepresented class in the republic, and perhaps the most practical exponent of the principles of equality, I request the favour of being permitted to address the public through the medium of the *Herald*. While others of my sex devoted themselves to a crusade against the laws that shackle the women of the country, I asserted my individual independence ; while others prayed for the good time coming, I worked for it; while others argued the equality of woman with man, I proved it by successfully engaging in business ; while others sought to show that there was no valid reason why women should be treated, socially and politically, as being inferior to man, I boldly entered the arena of politics and business and exercised the rights I already possessed. I therefore claim the right to speak for the unenfranchised women of the country, and believing as I do that the prejudices which still exist in the popular mind against women in public life will soon disappear, I now announce myself as candidate for the Presidency.

I am well aware that in assuming this position I shall evoke more ridicule than enthusiasm at the outset. But this is an epoch of sudden changes and startling surprises. What may appear absurd to-day will assume a serious aspect to-morrow. I am content to wait until my claim for recognition as a candidate shall receive the calm consideration of the press and the public. The blacks were cattle in 1860; a negro now sits in Jeff Davis' seat in the United States Senate. The sentiment of the country was, even in 1863, against negro suffrage; now the negro's right to vote is acknowledged by the Constitution of the United States. Let those, therefore, who ridiculed the negro's claim to exercise the right to "life, liberty and the pursuit of happiness," and who lived to see him vote and hold high public office, ridicule the aspirations of the women of the country for complete political equality as much as they please. They cannot roll back the rising tide of reform. The world moves.

That great Governmental changes were to follow the enfranchisement of the negro I have long foreseen. While the curse of slavery covered the land progress was enchained, but when it was swept away in the torrent of war, the voice of justice was heard, and it became evident that the last weak barrier against complete political and social equality must soon give way. All that has been said and written hitherto in support of equality for woman has had its proper effect on the public mind, just as the anti-slavery speeches before secession were effective; but a candidate and a policy are required to prove it. Lincoln's election showed the strength of the feeling against the peculiar institution; my candidature for the Presidency will, I confidently expect, develop the fact that the principles of equal rights for all have taken deep root. The advocates of political equality for women have, besides a respectable known strength, a great undercurrent of unexpressed power, which is only awaiting a fit opportunity to show itself. By the general and decided test I propose, we shall be able to understand the woman question aright, or at least have done much towards presenting the issue involved in proper shape. I claim to possess the strength and courage to be the subject of that test, and look forward confidently to a trumphant issue of the canvass.

The present position of political parties is anomalous. They are not inspired by any great principles of policy or economy; there is no live issue up for discussion.

A great national question is wanted, to prevent a descent into pure sectionalism. That question exists in the issue, whether woman shall remain sunk below the right granted to the negro, or be elevated to all the political rights enjoyed by man. The simple issue whether woman should not have this complete political equality with the negro is the only one to be tried, and none more important is likely to arise before the Presidential election. But besides the question of equality others of great magnitude are necessarily included. The platform that is to succeed in the coming election must enunciate the *general* principles of enlightened justice and economy.

A complete reform in our system of prison discipline, having specially in view the welfare of the families of criminals, whose labour should not be lost to them; the rearrangement of the system and control of internal improvements; the adoption of some better means for caring for the helpless and indigent; the establishment of strictly neutral and reciprocal relations with all foreign Powers who will unite to better the condition of the productive class, and the adoption of such principles as shall recognize this class as the true wealth of the country, and give it a just position beside capital, thus introducing a practical plan for universal government upon the most enlightened basis, for the actual, not the imaginary benefit of mankind.

These important changes can only be expected to follow a complete departure from the beaten tracks of political parties and their machinery; and this, I believe my canvass of 1872 will effect.

With the view of spreading to the people ideas which hitherto have not been placed before them, and which they may, by reflection, carefully amplify for their own benefit, I have written several papers on governmental questions of importance and will submit them in due order. For the present the foregoing must suffice. I anticipate criticism; but however unfavourable the comment this letter may evoke I trust that my sincerity will not be called in question. I have deliberately and of my own accord placed myself before the people as a candidate for the Presidency of the United States, and having the means, courage, energy and strength necessary for the race, intend to contest it to the close.

VICTORIA C. WOODHULL.

POLITICAL THEORY

(6)

A New Political Party and A New Party Platform . . . 1871.

A New Political Party

AND

A New Party Platform.

At the Suffrage Convention held in Apollo Hall, May 11th and 12th, 1871, by request of Mrs. LUCRETIA MOTT, the following Platform of Principles of a Just Government was read by VICTORIA C. WOODHULL, and is embodied in this history that it may have a wide circulation and be deeply considered in all its bearings on the future of this country.

SUFFRAGE is a common right of citizenship. Women have the right of suffrage. *Logically* it cannot be escaped. Syllogistically it is self-evident, thus :—

First—All persons—men and women—are citizens.

Second—Citizens have the right to vote.

Third—Women have the right to vote.

Though the right to vote be now denied, it must eventually be accorded. Women can be neither Democrats nor Republicans. They must be something more than Democratic or Republican. They must be humanitarian. They must become a positive element in governmental affairs. They have thought little; they must be brought to think more. To suggest food for thought, a new party and a new platform is proposed for the consideration of women and men: the party, the Cosmopolitical—the platform a series of reforms, to wit:

A reform in representation, by which all Legislative Bodies and the Presidential Electoral College shall be so elected that minorities as well as majorities shall have direct representation.

A complete reform in Executive and Departmental conduct, by which the President and the Secretaries of the United States, and the Governors and State Officers, shall be forced to recognize that they are the servants of the people, appointed to attend to the business of the people, and not for the purpose of perpetuating their official positions, or of securing the plunder of public trusts for the enrichment of their political adherents and supporters.

A reform in the tenure of office, by which the Presidency shall be limited to one term, with a retiring life pension, and a permanent seat in the Federal Senate, where his Presidential experience may become serviceable to the nation, and on the dignity and life emolument of Presidential Senator he shall be placed above all other political position, and be excluded from all professional pursuits.

A radical reform in our Civil Service, by which the Government, in its executive capacity, shall at all times secure faithful and efficient officers, and the people trustworthy servants, whose appointment shall be entirely removed from, and be made independent of, the influence and control of the legislative branch of the Government, and who shall be removed for "cause" only, and who shall be held strictly to frequent public accounting to superiors for all their official transactions, which shall for ever dispose of the corrupt practices induced by the allurements of the motto of present political parties, that " to the victor belong the spoils," which is a remnant of arbitrarily assumed authority, unworthy of a government emanating from the whole people.

A complete reform in our system of Internal improvements, which connect and bind together the several States in commercial unity, to the end that they shall be conducted so as to administer to the best interests of the whole people, for whose benefit they were first permitted, and are now protected; by which the General Government, in the use of its postal powers and in the exercise of its duties in regulating commerce between the States, shall secure the transportation of passengers, merchandize and the mails, from one extremity of the country to the opposite, and throughout its whole area, at the actual cost of maintaining such improvements, plus legitimate interest upon their original cost of construction, thus converting them into public benefits, instead of their remaining, as now, hereditary taxes upon the industries of the country.

A complete reform in commercial and navigation laws, by which American built or purchased ships and American seamen shall be practically protected by the admission of all that is required for construction of the first, or the use and maintenance of either, free in bond or on board.

A reform in the relations of the employer and employed, by which shall be secured the practice of the great natural law, of one-third of time to labour, one-third to recreation, and one-third to rest, that by this, intellectual improvement and physical development may go on to that perfection which the Almighty Creator designed.

A reform in the principles of protection and revenue, by which the largest home and foreign demand shall be created and sustained for products of American industry of every kind; by which this industry shall be freed from the ruinous effects consequent upon frequent changes in these systems; by which shall be secured that constant employment to working-men and working-women throughout the country which will maintain them upon an equality in all kinds and classes of industry; by which a continuous prosperity—which, if not so marked by rapid accumulation, shall possess the merit of permanency—will be secured to all, which in due time will reduce the cost of all products to a minimum value; by which the labouring poor shall be relieved of the onerous tax, now indirectly imposed upon them by Government; by which the burden of governmental support shall be placed where it properly belongs, and by which an unlimited national wealth will gradually accumulate, the ratio of taxation upon which will become so insignificant in amount as to be no burden to the people.

A reform by which the power of legislative bodies to levy taxes shall be limited to the actual necessities of the legitimate functions of Government in its protection of the rights of persons, property and nationality; and by which they shall be deprived of the power to exempt any property from taxation ; or to make any distinctions directly or indirectly among citizens in taxation for the support of Government; or to give or loan the public property or credit to individuals or corporations to promote any enterprise whatever.

A reform in the system of criminal jurisprudence, by which the death penalty shall no longer be inflicted; and by which, during that term, a portion of the prison employment shall be for, and the product thereof be faithfully paid over to, the support of the criminal's family ; and by which our so-called prisons shall be virtually transformed into vast reformatory workshops, from which the unfortunate may emerge to be useful members of society, instead of the alienated citizens they now are.

The institution of such supervisatory control and surveillance over the now low orders of society as shall compel them to industry, and provide for the helpless, and thus banish those institutions of pauperism and

10 *

beggary which are fastening upon the vitals of society, and are so prolific of crime and suffering in certain communities.

The organization of a general system of national education which shall positively secure to every child of the country such an education in the arts, sciences and general knowledge as will render them profitable and useful members of society, and the entire proceeds of the public domain should be religiously devoted to this end.

Such change in our general foreign policy as shall plainly indicate that we realize and appreciate the important position which has been assigned us as a nation by the common order of civilization; which shall indicate our supreme faith in that form of government which emanates from, and is supported by the whole people, and that such government must eventually be uniform throughout the world; which shall also have in view the establishment of a Grand International Tribunal, to which all disputes of peoples and nations shall be referred for final arbitration and settlement, without appeal to arms; said Tribunal maintaining only such an International army and navy as would be necessary to enforce its decrees, and thus secure the return of the fifteen millions of men who now compose the standing armies of the world, to industrial and productive pursuits.

A reform by which the functions of Government shall be limited to the enactment of general laws; and be absolutely prohibited from enacting any special law upon any pretext whatever; by which all laws shall be repealed which are made use of by Government to interfere with the rights of adult individuals to pursue happiness as they may choose; or with the legitimate consequences of such pursuit; or with contracts between individuals, of whatever kind, or their consequences, which will place the intercourse of persons with each other upon their individual honour, with no appeal, and the intercourse of the general people upon the principles of common honesty; which will be a nearer approach to self-government and a wider departure from arbitrary control than has ever been exemplified. And finally, that all legislative action shall be approved by the people before becoming law.

Thus in the best sense do I claim to be the friend and exponent of the most complete equality to which humanity can attain; of the broadest individual freedom compatible with the public good, and that supreme justice which shall know no distinction among citizens upon any ground whatever, in the administration and the execution of the laws; and also, to be a faithful worker in the cause of human advancement; and especially to be the co-labourer with those who strive to better the condition of the poor and friendless; to secure to the great mass of working people the just reward of their toil. I claim from these, and from all others in the social scale, that support in the bold political course I have taken which shall give me the strength and the position to carry out these needed reforms, which shall secure to them, in return, the blessings which the Creator designed the human race should enjoy.

If I obtain this support, woman's strength and woman's will, with God's support, if He vouchsafe it, shall open to them, and to this country, a new career of greatness in the race of nations, which can only be secured by that fearless course of truth from which the nations of the earth, under despotic male governments, have so far departed.

VICTORIA C. WOODHULL.

NEW YORK,
January 10*th*, 1871.

POLITICAL THEORY

(7)

The Correspondence Between the Victoria League and
Victoria C. Woodhull . . . 1871.

THE CORRESPONDENCE

THE VICTORIA LEAGUE

AND

VICTORIA C. WOODHULL.

THE FIRST CANDIDATE FOR THE NEXT PRESIDENCY.

THE LETTER OF NOMINATION.

NEW YORK, July 4, 1871.

MRS. VICTORIA C. WOODHULL:

Madam—A number of your fellow-citizens, both men and women, have formed themselves into a working committee, borrowing its title from your name, and calling itself THE VICTORIA LEAGUE.

Our object is to form a new national political organization, composed of the progressive elements in the existing Republican and Democratic parties, together with the women of the Republic, who have been hitherto disfranchised, but to whom the Fourteenth and Fifteenth Amendments of the Constitution, properly interpreted, guarantee, equally with men, the right of suffrage.

This new political organization will be called THE EQUAL RIGHTS Party, and its platform will consist solely and only of a declaration of the equal civil and political rights of all American citizens, without distinction of sex. We shall ask Congress at its next session to pass an act, founded on this interpretation of the Constitution, protecting women in the immediate exercise of the elective franchise in all parts of the United States, subject only to the same restrictions and regulations which are imposed by local laws on other classes of citizens.

We shall urge all women who possess the political qualifications of other citizens, in the respective States in which they reside, to assume and exercise the right of suffrage without further hesitation or delay.

We ask you to become the standard-bearer of this idea before the people, and for this purpose nominate you as our candidate for President of the United States, to be voted for in 1872 by the combined suffrages of both sexes. If our plans merit your approval, and our nomination meet your acceptance, we trust that you will take occasion, in your reply to this letter, to express your views in full concerning the political rights of women under the Fourteenth and Fifteenth Amendments.

Offering to you, Madam, the assurance of our great esteem, and harboring in our minds the cheerful prescience of victory which your name inspires, we remain,

Cordially yours,

THE VICTORIA LEAGUE.

THE LETTER OF ACCEPTANCE.

NEW YORK, July 20, 1871.

Fellow Citizens of the Victoria League :

I beg you not to regard my delay in replying to your flattering invitation to become the candidate of the Equal Rights party for the Presidency as evincing indifference on my part. The delay has, in fact, been occasioned by just the opposite cause ; the state of mingled emotion, anxiety and reflection into which the serious proposition from a responsible source that I should accept such a nomination has thrown me. It is true that I have, now nearly a year ago, *announced myself* as a candidate for the high office in question, but that was rather for the mere purpose of lifting a banner, of provoking agitation and for giving emphasis to an opinion, and a rallying point for the great unorganized party of progress.

But the case is now different. Things have progressed to an astonishing degree during this year past. I may have been qualified to raise an excitement, to inaugurate a definite movement, to seize an outpost, and even, perhaps, to project a programme. But does it follow that I am the proper person to become the permanent " standard bearer," as you phrase it, of a great political party, and actually to guide the State.

Little as the public think it, a woman who is now nominated may be elected next year. Less change of opinion than has occurred already, in the same direction, will place her in the White House. The American people are generous and noble, and when their hearts are touched they are susceptible of a grand enthusiasm. They are also—the *men* of the nation I mean now—capable of a gallantry toward my sex, which would rival the devotion of the age of chivalry. They are also essentially just ; and when the thought shall really come home to them, with the cogency of conviction, that they have, through thoughtlessness, been all along acting unjustly to their mothers and wives and daughters, by depriving them of political rights, it may happen that there will come up a great swelling-tide of reactionary sentiment which will make a sudden revolution.

I feel that I *know* that just the right woman to touch the right chord of the public sympathy and confidence—if the right woman could be found—would arouse such a tempest of popularity as the country has never seen, and as a consequence should ride triumphantly on the tide of a joyous popular tumult to the supreme political position.

Just at this moment, also, the two great political parties of the past are positively without any issue. General Washington's popularity extinguished for the moment all partizan opposition, and made of the whole nation one grand fraternizing party. The advent of the first woman to the Presidential chair may be the occasion of the next great national fraternization—of the jubilee of the whole people; and this grand event may be, and, to say more, to my prophetic vision, is, at this very moment, actually impending.

It is possible, therefore, that if I am your candidate, I may be elected. And the question recurs, am I the woman, among all the noble women of the land, who can either touch the true chord of sympathy in the national heart to secure the first result, or to manifest that high grade of feminine wisdom which should characterize the first Woman President of the United States ?

It is this momentous question which gives me pause; and, after even this long delay, I find it no easy matter calmly to assume the responsibilities to which you invite me.

But there has been another cause of delay. You ask me to state the argument in full for the political rights of women, under the Fourteenth and Fifteenth Amendments, and I have tried to comply with your request. I have returned repeatedly to the task. But, gentlemen and ladies, *I have lost all inspiration for that work.* "Let the dead bury their dead." *I made my argument on that subject, last winter, before the Judiciary Committee of the House of Representatives, ——aided by these noble auxiliaries, Mrs. Paulina Wright Davis and Mrs. Harriet Beecher Hooker. I had the good fortune, also, to call out from that committee that unanswerable minority report signed by Benjamin F. Butler and Judge William Loughridge—an instrument which constitutes a Gibraltar of woman's political rights against which all opposition is vain, and which has already grown to be the settled constitutional law in both the judicial and the popular opinion on that whole subject.

A very distinguished lawyer of this city said the other day, and the same fact is repeated almost daily, that no man of high legal position would now dare to risk his reputation by denying the conclusiveness of that argument and report.

The only shadow of an adverse argument which survives is based on the assumption that the amendments did not explicitly contemplate the case of women. The framers and adopters of these provisions did not intend, it is said, to confer rights on us, but only on the negro. That perhaps may be true; but it is equally true that they just as little intended to *exclude* or *except* women. The probable truth is that these law-makers did not at the time so much as think of the existence of women—so completely has woman been unconsciously ignored, until the last winter, at Washington, by these male politicians, as being in any way entitled to political rights.

How, then, does the matter stand ? Why, just in this way. That, the legislators having had no intention whatsoever, for or against, in respect to this application of the law, the intention of the legislators, apart from the words used, cannot be appealed to on either side; and we are driven to fall back on the naked interpretation of the words themselves, and to gather all that we have any right to presume of *intention*, from the strict legal interpretation of the language employed.

If we have got the concession of our rights from the mere fact that those who were in the exercise of power had so little respect for or so little thought even of our rights that *they forgot to take steps to defraud us out of them,* shall we be called upon to carry courtesy so far as to decline to take advantage of their forgetfulness? Some may think we ought to do that way; but we propose to do otherwise, and to avail ourselves of all which the indifference or the unconscious contempt of men in power may carelessly have thro' in our way. If they have left down the bars, we shall qu' ly walk in; especially as it is only coming home to our o' pasture.

I propose to *rendezvous*, again, at Washington the com' winter. No Representative or Senator will be more punct' than I. But I do not go there *to argue* the question of ' rights. The argument is concluded. I shall go, accom nied by a corps of the representative women of the land *insist* on the *practical recognition* of rights which are alrea by the public verdict, *theoretically established* and conced We shall demand that that be made existent *de facto* wh already exists *de jure*. We shall claim the passage o Declaratory Act, merely the signing of the judgment on basis of the verdict already rendered in our favor; and to the political trickster or pettifogger who shall dare to hin our rights by any motion in arrest of judgment or ot' wise for delay.

I expect to succeed. I do not expect that the women ' leave Washington this very winter until after such Decl tory Act shall form part of the statutes of the country. is simply scandalous that a nation whose very existence out of the axiom, *no taxation without representation,* and fought for that principle to the death, should persist f single year, after the subject is fairly broached, to im' on us taxation and to refuse us representation; or that a y' ple whose fundamental political idea is opposition to class-legislation should disfranchise, by the act of a mino the very largest *class* of its citizens.

The early coming of female participation in the busines' legislation is inevitable; and from now on, destruction await the politician who does not heed the rising tide. The tion of every public man on this question is noted, and Nemesis of political destiny will overtake every recrean the true principles of a real republic, which involves the eq' ity of woman. Republicanism *shall have* its fair trial, whi never has had hitherto. If female suffrage is an exp' ment, so was republicanism itself; and this is the next periment to be tried in the order of governmental evolu' And as it absolutely has to be tried, those who would prob the crisis of its inauguration are mere obstructionists, enemies of the public peace. In many a revolution the disturbers are, when the matter is looked at deeply, th' who oppose it. If a thing is in accordance with the spir' the age, it cannot be successfully resisted ; and who does know that the spirit of this age is unbounded emancipat'

It is the merest waste of time, therefore, to fight longer over this dead issue. Let both the old effete dying-out political parties be wise at once. Let them ' cept the situation," and inaugurate from now the still gr' "new departure." Slavery has been abolished. The w' waits for this other and more hidden, but no less real, ' ery of restrictions on woman to be, likewise, hustled o' existence and relegated to the limbo of the dead past.

My countrymen, do not regard this concession as a de' But noble, gallant and loving men do not shrink from d even at the hands of a woman. They sometimes say they *love to be conquered.* How noble the vanquishm which will be only the surrender to your sisters and love rights which have been unjustly—but thoughtlessly, on part as much as on yours—withheld.

Moreover, do not fear the nature of woman! L' be your glory and your choice to make her free to the r' most—to expand into her most glorious possible womanh Do not think that you must prescribe the law of her b' Perhaps even now you are *needing something* in your culture, something for the development of your own hi

*Instead of making the argument in question a part of this reply as requested by you. I enclose it herewith as a separate document.

hood, which can only be derived from the environment truly enfranchised womanhood, such as the world has ·r yet seen. Among the Quakers or Friends women, gh not wholly free, have, for more than a century stood, any respects, side by side with and as the equal helpers of ; and no such disaster has resulted to the characters of er men or women as is feared from the admission of wo- into politics ; but quite the reverse.

y brothers! we are not, and cannot be, your enemies. among you, on the contrary, that we look to find our rs and dearest friends—our protectors and our chosen perators in the responsible business of life. We have no rests which are not intimately linked with your inter- and with the interests of your children. We want noth- which is not right, and as right for you and for them is us.

e know, too, that this strife between women and men, this ial alienation of the two hemispheres of humanity in this is working most deleterious results, and especially upon characters of the next immediate generation. Children e no fathers and no mothers while men and women dis- t and repel each other, even in that mild sense which struggle implies. And yet the struggle cannot end, ause it *ought not* to end—and because we cannot consent , it *should* end—until our perfectly equal rights and free- , socially and politically, are completely established. Whosoever obstructs or hinders the earliest possible con- ion of what we ask is therefore, either ignorantly or ntionally, perverse.

far from wishing to degrade you, my brothers, we ld be so glad that we would rejoice with exceeding great if we could find you manly and god-like enough to com- d our worship. The greatest misfortune of women is there are so few great and truly noble men; and it is greatest misfortune of men, and perhaps, as yet, a greater fortune on their part—for women have been hitherto nped and degraded—that there are so few great and truly le women. I am saddened when I think of the weary te of commonplace and inferior natures.

e need, my brothers and sisters, all our conjoint exer- s to found and rear the grand edifice of future society. ry day used in simply removing restrictions and obstruc- s, and still worse, in maintaining them, is a day lost n the nobler occupation. This bondage of woman is the withe that binds us to the dead past. Sever it, and we into the freedom of a new future.

erhaps I should also mention in this connection the oppres- weight which capital, in its greedy ignorance, still lays n labor. The freedom of woman and the freedom of laborer are conjointly the cause of humanity. Industry, nce and the home must all be rightly adjusted, as tran- nal to the higher order. Democrats and Republicans st make haste to take up these great new issues, or the on of the women and the workingmen and the Interna- alists will render their further existence, as parties, un- essary. The National Labor Union, just now con- ing at St. Louis, has, for the first time, invited women n equal terms to that convention. It is, of course, no- d that neither Republicans nor Democrats have, with e exceptions in Massachusetts, invited us yet into their itical assemblages.

t may be thought that my demands are too urgent, and expectations too immediate and too large. But that been thought before now; and yet the realization has ceded the hope.

t the last meeting of Congress my Memorial set forth t since the adoption of the Fifteenth Article of the Amend- nts to the Constitution, no State or Territory either has abridged, or has the right to abridge, the right of the citizens to vote; and that the *status* of women as citizens is com- pletely established. At that time it was only a small but bold wing of either party that dared to express sympa- thy with this new announcement. At this day, however, only eight or nine months later, the real leaders of both the Republican and Democratic parties stand squarely upon this platform of doctrine, and are lending their influence to mold the action of their parties in that direction. The names of SUMNER, WADE, MORTON, TRUMBULL, WILSON, CARPENTER, SPRAGUE, NYE, POMEROY, STEARNS, HARRIS, ARNELL, MAYNARD, BANKS, JULIAN, BURDETT, LYNCH, WOODWARD, ELA, MORRILL, VALLANDIGHAM, KERR, CHASE, and BLACK, with a host of others that might be mentioned, fill the list of great politicians—and there are none greater— who have given in their allegiance to woman's suffrage.

Indeed, I stand almost appalled at the success of what has been already attempted. And it is not alone the states- men. The public press also is already virtually converted. It is everywhere admitted that it is only a question of time. Why not then shorten the time to the utmost? The work of a single day in Congress may end the agitation and quietly begin the new *regime*. The change will be far less than has occurred within the twelvemonth. Revolutions are often completed at the time from which chronology dates their commencement; and this revolution has, in fact, definitively ended. Nobody sneers now at woman's suffrage. Everybody has already " in thought accepted the new situa- tion;" and the real revolution is always that which takes place *in the thoughts* of the people. All else is merely the re- cording of the verdict and the incidentals of the execution.

I cannot speak of pride, for that is not the feeling; but I cannot repress a sense of solemn joy and lofty exultation— something like that, perhaps, of Miriam upon the shore of the Red Sea, celebrating the rescue of her people under the guidance of the marvelous cloud by day and pillar of fire by night—when I reflect on what the spirits in heaven, aided by devoted spirits in the flesh, are so rapidly and so marvelous- ly accomplishing for the complete enfranchisement of my sex, and, through them, of all humanity.

If, fellow-citizens, with these views, with this faith and this hope, under God, and with such powers as I have, dedi- cated to their service, you still think that I am the fitting woman to represent this movement—to be, as you say, its "standard bearer"—I cannot and will not decline such nom- ination as you may see fit to make of me to the public.

Perhaps I ought not to pass unnoticed your courteous and graceful allusion to what you deem the favoring omen of my name. It is true that a Victoria rules the great rival nation opposite to us on the other shore of the Atlantic, and it might grace the amity just sealed between the two nations, and be a new security of peace, if a twin sisterhood of Vic- torias were to preside over the two nations. It is true, also, that in its mere etymology the name signifies *Victory!* and the victory for the right is what we are bent on securing. It is again true, also, that to some minds there is a consonant harmony between the idea and the word, so that its eu- phonious utterance seems to their imaginations to be itself a genius of success. However this may be, I have some- times thought, myself, that there is, perhaps, something prov- idential and prophetic in the fact that my parents were prompted to confer on me a name which forbids the very thought of failure ; and, as the great Napoleon believed the star of his destiny, you will at least excuse me, and charge it to the credulity of the woman, if I believe also in fatality of triumph as somehow inhering in my name.

With profound esteem, your obedient servant,
VICTORIA C. WOODHULL.

POLITICAL THEORY

(8)

Correspondence of the Equal Rights Party . . . 1872.

Reproduced from *Woodhull & Claflin's Weekly* (June 15, 1872, pp. 8-9). Columns here reduced, divided and realigned. Original type column width four inches.

LETTER OF NOTIFICATION.

NEW YORK, June 3, 1872.

CTORIA C. WOODHULL.—Dear Madam: The National Convention of the Equal Rights Party who recently assembled in Apollo Hall in this city, has instructed the undersigned officers of the Convention to inform you that you have been nominated by acclamation as its candidate for the Presidency of the United States. The Platform and Resolutions unanimously adopted by the Convention we also submit to your consideration, and request your acceptance of the same as well as of the nomination.

J. D. REYMERT, *President.*

ANNA M. MIDDLEBROOK.
JOHN T. ELLIOT.
ISAAC FRAZIER,
LAVINA C. DUNDORE.
JOHN M. SPEAR.

Vice Presidents.

HARRIET B. BURTON
GEORGE R. ALLEN.

Secretaries.

RUTH W. S. BRIGGS, *Treasurer.*

LETTER OF ACCEPTANCE.

NEW YORK, June 5, 1872.

J. D. Reymert, President of the Nominating Convention of Equal Rights Party, and Associates:

GENTLEMEN AND LADIES: Your communication received this morning conveying the formal statement to me of the simple fact that the Equal Rights Party, recently represented in convention in this city, has nominated me as the chief standard-bearer of the party in the coming conflict, recalls the vivid sensations of gratitude, renewed responsibility and profound humility with which I was overwhelmed on that memorable evening when the spontaneous acclaim of a great, enthusiastic and admirable assembly of male and female citizens, gave me the same information without waiting for the formalities of announcement. You speak almost as if this simple fact were one of the ordinary events of politics. But to my apprehension it is far more than that. It is not even a common-place historical event. The joint assemblage of all the reformers, of all schools, for the first time in the history of the great transition which human society is undergoing, blended and fused in the same spirit, coming to agree to stand upon the same form of ideas and measures, and nominating by an outburst of inspiration a woman known to be representative of most advanced and unmitigated radicalism, and because she was so known; and a negro, one of the boldest of the champions and defenders of human rights, a representative and a representative woman of the two oppressed and oppressed classes, for the two highest offices in the gift of a great people—such an occurrence rises in my mind into the sublimity and pregnant significance of the grander class of the events of history. It is an event which marks in various senses a climacteric; and more than that, even; the reversal of the current of human affairs, from the drift towards selfish ambition and class interests, towards magnanimity and justice; the disposition to impose wrong, to a generous readiness to make reparation; from the low, semi-barbarous greed for the use of an authority, to the gallant and truly civilized manner of well-bred gentlemen and ladies, to cede the place of her to those whom brute force might otherwise repress. It is the first redemption in politics of the pledge given in the prophecy, that "the first shall be last, and the last first." In a word, it is the appropriate inauguration of the EQUAL RIGHTS PARTY; which, in its larger aspect, contemplates not American politics merely, or alone; but the establishment of justice throughout the world. It is also the subordination of party among reformers themselves, to the unity of a common ...

This last aspect of the subject cannot be too much insisted on. The reformers in the world are the strongest party in the world; the mightiest political power in the world the moment they unite. The conservative world knows that fact better, even, than the reformers themselves; knows the meaning of such a union, and trembles in the prospect or the presence of its actual occurrence.

The reformers have been kept asunder by various causes; and divided and weakened, they have been conquered. Their intensity in the perception of particular and different evils, and of their remedies, has tended to divide them. But they are coming now to perceive that the greatest of all evils, relatively to their conflict with the common enemy the organized injustice of society, is the diversity in their own views, carried to the extent of defeating their common action. The higher truth is unity in the midst of their diversity, the unity of a combined phalanx for action; with the freedom of absolute toleration. The organization of the Equal Rights party is the expression of the fact that the cohorts of reform have at length arrived at this solid center of united activity.

Another cause for the division of the ranks of reformers has been the different degrees of radicalism, by which they have been severally characterized. Those a little behind have feared to trust those a little in advance; until at length it is clearly seen that they are all travelling along the same road, and destined to reach the same goal—the absolute dissolution of the old order of social managements, and the erection of a totally new order, on the two bases of freedom and justice.

This point once gained, everything is gained. Reformers, instead of falling asunder like a rope of sand, at every strain will be consolidated, by their co-operation, into a mighty strength, from the moment that they can no longer be frightened by any other degree of radicalism beyond where they severally stand. *They have evidently reached that point when they nominate me.* It has been the purpose of my life to administer to them *that test.* I have uttered as radical thoughts in behalf of social and individual freedom (short of encroachment), as I could find the power to frame into words; and you have called me to the front, not, I presume, in spite of the fact, but *in virtue of the fact,* as that I have been so plain-spoken. At all events, I stand by all that I have uttered. If by retracting one word I have written or spoken in behalf of human emancipation *from all the slaveries,* except merely to remove misapprehensions, I could be proclaimed, to-morrow, Empress of the World, I would not retract. What I have said stands; and, by your nomination, I understand you to mean that you stand with it; not in the details, nor necessarily, in the form of utterance, but in the general spirit of ultra devotion to human rights.

Nor is it to be understood, that in accepting your generous and enthusiastic nomination of me, a woman, I resign one iota of my right to be equally free-spoken in the future. The Presidential chair could be no bribe for my silence, and I am glad that you do not so intend it. It has been the curse of this country and of the political arena, and is in some sense the vice of republican institutions, that the promise and the attainment of office are alike a padlock upon the lips of honest expression; but, I pledge you my honor, that I will make one exception, if there be no other, to that rule. By accepting my course in the past, and by conceding me your confidence for the future, you aid me in my determination to utter still grander truths hereafter. My work for the reorganization of society will never cease until social, industrial, political and educational liberty and equality, be achieved for all.

No one understands better than I do that all those great results cannot be attained through merely political means. Disruptive agitation is only a way for the achievement of freedom; and freedom itself, when achieved, is no more than opportunity. What we must come to in the end is the scientific organization of society, under the leadership of, and in devoted allegiance to, the best thought in the world, consecrated to the highest uses. Politics, in the ordinary or vulgar sense of the term will, in preponderance, give way to social science. Knowledge will take the place of merely blind experiment, and, in a great measure, of inspirational guidance itself. The actual establishment of the Social and Industrial Palace, at Guise, as detailed in the April number of *Harper's Monthly Magazine,* and as one of the solutions of the labor and capital question, is a greater event than the outcome of any war that ever was fought.

Still wars have been, and, perhaps, still are a necessity, and so of the violent affirmation of rights, until rights are conceded and peace inaugurated upon a right basis. The uses of political movements, and more especially this one of them, are to wipe away hindrances. It is chiefly in breaking down the old and ushering in the new, that I know that I have a special function to perform; and in doing this humanitarian work, my inspirations and my spiritual previsions reveal to me views which I look upon with dread. I do not hold my life dear, except for its value to this cause, but an ordinary courage might shrink from what I foresee will oppose itself to this movement. I know not that I understand, myself, the full meaning of scenes which open to my inner vision. Is it possible that the wealthy and well to do in our midst, who have fattened from the country's industries will be blinded to the signs of the times, and refuse justice to those "who have reaped down their fields, until, as with the slaveholders of the South, calamity overtakes them? Is it possible they can believe that the working men and the women are not in earnest in their demands, and that nothing but a bloody commune will convince them?

I did intend to make some comment on the utterly trivial and foolish character of the platforms of the other political parties, in the face of the tremendous issues which are really rising on this nation; but I will restrain myself to a single point. Horace Greeley, in his letter of acceptance of the nomination made of him at Cincinnati, prates of "solemn constitutional obligations to maintain the equal rights of all citizens," meaning thereby the equal rights of all *male* citizens, ignoring completely and contemptuously the rights of more than a full half of the citizens of the United States; with, in a word, the same superciliousness with which the slaveholders spoke, a few years since, of the rights of the people, never meaning or including the rights of the slave. Mr. Greeley does this not by oversight or thoughtlessness, which would be sufficiently insulting; but with deliberate insult; for no one knows better than he, or is more awake to the fact, that the women of the country are earnestly and persistently insisting that they shall go for something in the civil constitution of the State. He repeats, that there should "henceforth be no privileged class, and no disfranchised caste within the limits of our union"; referring to the disfranchised *slave-holders*, but never in the least to the *women.* So, again, his "impartial suffrage," and his being "President not only of a party, but of the whole people," if elected, means President of his own "caste" and "class," and the self-appointed ruler of all others.

It may be expected that I shall make some reference to our own platform, some exposition of my own views of its principles. But this is scarcely necessary, since it is well known that everything which is legitimately a deduction from the principles of freedom, equality and justice, finds a hearty response in my heart a cordial reception in my mind. However, the pride I feel for that grand enunciation of human rights, will not permit me to pass it by in utter silence. The scope of its application, the comprehensiveness of its theories, the supreme devotion to principle of its construction, are of themselves sufficiently soul-inspiring to demand the undivided sympathy of the best humanitarians; out when to these considerations are added the causes which at this time demand such a construction of such principles, and the results to be attained when they shall have found form in law, glorious visions of the future rise in resplendent grandeur in my soul, lifting it from the temporary and transitional things of the present into a comprehension of humanity redeemed from all its arbitrary conditions relieved of all its heavy yokes of bondage, and ushered into millennial perfections prophesied and promised by all prophets since the world began.

The Equal Rights Party in constructing this platform has not attempted to evade even a single issue that presents itself, nor to envelop in mist and doubt the methods by which it proposes to meet it. By the use of the plainest words, in the terses language and with the most startling directness, has it announced both its purposes and its methods. It did not seek to find a way to avoid the prejudices of gaunt, fossilized conserv-

atism, nor yet the cowardice of respectable, time-serving radic ism; but, in the vulgar sense of the terms, ignoring all pol and all expediency, it struck directly at the heart of the syst that has borne the bitter fruits upon which so large a prop tion of the people feed, proposing its utter overthrow.

In all this I most heartily concur. I do not believe in ho winking the people in order that they may be decie into giving their support to any movement. I believe cause which commands our zeal and devotion to be in it sufficiently potent to guarantee for itself a successful issue know there are those who condemn our methods; but I that the people are greater than any individuals, that they *do* understand the issues now rising into form demanding solution; in fact that even now they are anxio awaiting the more forcible and direct presentation, of issues so that there may be a more tangible, and the same time a more substantial point around wh to rally. All this is provided for and presented in this form. The principles of the various reformatory movem are there gathered and formulated into a single structure, ing to their respective advocates a more forcible enunciatio their several propositions than they have ever before obtai

I said the platform strikes directly at the heart of system under which we live. By this I mean very much than the present governmental structure. I mean the farther reaching theory of the uses of government. Heret governments have been maintained almost wholly o the idea that they are for the protection of prop hitherto legislation has altogether overlooked hum ty, and proceeded as if there were no such thing as hu rights, which were entitled to respect. It is now prop to reverse completely this order of things and to make hu rights the pivotal center around which legislation shall clus the rights of property ever remaining of second importance, or as the means only to greater and better e Under our present system people are, perhaps it may be, alm unconsciously compelled to make property the chief end and aim of life; are compelled to live, as if with death, all existe ceases. The reversal of all this will the reversal of the ca which compel it, and the people instead of living the the of individual selfishness, will come up to the realization of fact that each one is but a part of one perfect whole, which cludes all; and that the interests and well being of every i vidual member of the whole are best promoted when the in ests and well being of the whole are made the govern motives.

Thus to set forth completely its purposes and methods Equal Rights party declares its intention to construct, from principles it enunciates, a new organic law, which will ad the full possession and the free exercise of every human ri for all individuals. Trampling the theories vitalized present constitutions, National and State, under its fe boldly pushes on, announcing that all criminal and civil shall be National in application, and uniform in execut thus proposing to administer a death-blow to the system which vast hordes of the officials of so-called justice live grow fat upon the dissensions among the people, and thus storing to the people their long-lost right to self-govern of which they have, in their blind devotion to the mere ward semblance of freedom, permitted themselves to be prived.

Not only has it claimed the sacred right of self-gov ment, but also the almost equally important measure, tha people themselves shall be their own law-makers; and that Congress and Legislatures shall be restricted to their le mate duties as working committees, whose acts must be proved by, before becoming binding upon, the people. single plank in this platform will, when carried out in pra do more to abolish corrupt legislation than all the ever proposed by legislative bodies. All well informed sons, know that the people have nothing to do with pr legislation; know that it is capital wealth—in one form another, that controls not only the law-making, but the executing power, as well. The people no longer re

gs, lobbies and cliques to attend to their business, and in
opting the *referendum* as one of the demanded reforms they
pose to wipe them out of existence.

gain, the people are becoming sick of legalized monopolies.
y know of no reason why the government should grant
rtered privileges to any man or any set of men which per-
him or them to absorb all surplus earnings, while they
on year after year eating the hard crusts of industrial de-
dence, their legalized masters rolling in luxuries they have
earned. Into this condition it is proposed to introduce
tle of the leaven of equality and equity, so that every man,
and every woman also, shall be con firmed and protected
he possession of all the results of their labors.

ut in abolishing monopolies they do not intend also to
ian the systems that have grown up under them.
se they propose to wrest from the hands of the powerful
orations which now possess them, and to whom all the
fits accrue, and take them into their own hands and reap
their advantages. The one thousand millions of dollars
cess of costs of maintenance which our present system of
rnal improvements makes it possible for railroad corpora-
s to wring yearly from the industries of the country, the
le propose to retain in their own hands; and also to as-
e their management, so that it shall be impossible to com-
he public to pay seven dollars per ton for the transporta-
of coal less than two hundred miles, to satisfy the insatia-
maw of the Dividends Takers.

ither do they propose longer to quietly submit to the loss
eir interest in the public domain. This is a heritage in-
ably vouchsafed to them by the fact of its being natural
ritance. No person can ever acquire title—a just title—an
lute ownership—to any of the wealth which, upon coming
existence, they found awaiting them. Not only do they in-
that there shall be no more land-grabbing, but they far-
intend that the hundreds of millions of acres of land that
already been "grabbed" shall be reclaimed and here-
held for free occupancy by actual settlers.

e Equal Rights party further proposes that the innumera-
eeches called money-lenders, now fastened upon the vitals
e productive classes, shall be choked off and com-
d to give up their profession, and from filching their sup-
from the people, to turn to supporting themselves by prove industry. The people are sick of paying to capitalists
ally thirty millions of dollars for the exclusive privilege
h they possess of furnishing a circulating medium, when
public can furnish its own circulating medium at the
cost of the paper and printing.

e Equal Rights party also proposes that so long as govern-
is maintained wholly upon the theory that it is for the
ection of property instead of individual human rights, that
erty shall pay the expenses of its maintenance, and upon
proposition that the more wealth an individual possesses
arger should be his proportion of the expense incurred
ts protection; and also during the transition from the
e, to an equitable, system of industry, that the laborer
be legally protected against the exactions made upon his
ical strength, and that the National and State eight hour
shall be enforced, if not by the Government, then, rising
eir sovereign capacity, by the people themselves; and also
the laborer shall be guaranteed a just compensation for his
and still further that every person who desires to do so,
have the opportunity to labor without being under the
ssity of begging for employment, and, failing to obtain it,
eing his family grow gaunt and weak from the pinching
ts of unsatisfied hunger.

it is a duty of Government to secure to individuals the
ts which the Declaration pronounces to be inalienable, the
duty is not performed, when hundreds, thousands, aye,
ons of human beings, men, women and children, wander
the streets of our cities and the highways of our country, hungry, ragged and cold, vainly seeking in this land of plenty,
where physical want should be unknown, for the honorable
means of support; and if, perchance, to save themselves from
actual starvation, they take a portion of what, perhaps, they
themselves produced, then they are hurried to the station
houses their own hands have builded. Instead of the continuation of such impeachments of our civilization, the Government must become the paternal guardian of these classes of
its citizens, guaranteeing them the employment they require.

The Equal Rights Party declares against the present system
of criminal jurisprudence, denies the right of government
to assume a jurisdiction which belongs to the immutable
government of the Universe, and proposes to transform the
instruments of punishment into methods of reformation.

It also agrees with the propositions of Horace Greeley as to
universal amnesty and impartial suffrage, but differs entirely
from him in his applications of them. Universal amnesty, it
holds, should include not only those who once rebelled against
the Government, but also all of that sex which, though never
rebellious *de facto*, is equally under the ban, and that impartial suffrage should be something more than a cheat, used for
the purpose of beguiling the people; in fact, that it should be
considered as applying to all citizens, which he denies.
The Equal Rights Party also proposes that the people shall
resume the appointing power, and reduce all Executive officials, including even the President, to be their servants instead of investing them with a power that virtually transforms them into masters.

It also maintains that every son and daughter of the nation
is entitled to equal opportunities for acquiring an education,
which shall be, not only intellectual, but also industrial. In
so doing it strikes a fatal blow at the most insiduous of all
existing despotisms, and the most demoralizing of all monopolies, viz.: that of educational superiority; and it furthermore
demands that the Government shall supervize, and be held responsible for the methods by which such National education
shall be conducted.

The Equal Rights party also recognizes the destiny of nations, and affirms its purpose to be, to work in consonance therewith. It accepts the prophecy of all ages, that the time shall
come when, instead of a multitude of constantly opposing nations, the whole world shall be united under a single paternal
government, whose citizens shall become a common brotherhood owning a common origin and inheriting a common destiny.

I return, in conclusion, to what I have said of the transitional nature of the impending political revolution. When this conflict shall be concluded, either with or without actual bloodshed; when the spirit of conceding justice shall have been
secured, either by convincement or force; the call will be made
on all sides for constructive science and wisdom. Sociology
is the rising science of the day. The writings and living
thoughts of the great students of social phenomena of all
ages, in the strictly scientific point of view, will become the
common property of the whole people. In the mean time let
us do well the preliminary work. Let there be, first, a *whole
people*; let there be freedom; let there be the universal desire
for the reign of justice; then there will be a fitting preparation
for the final grand organization of all human affairs.

Finally, I gratefully accept the nomination made of me, and
pledge myself to every honorable means to secure, at the earli
est possible day, the triumph of the principles enunciated in
the platform, which being those of justice, and for the welfare
of humanity, I know they must shortly succeed.

Your obedient servant,   VICTORIA C. WOODHULL.

POLITICAL THEORY
(9)

"Speech at the Ratification Meeting of the
Equal Rights Party" . . . 1872.

SPEECH OF VICTORIA C. WOODHULL.

t is an unusual—I may, perhaps, say, an unprecedented—
ng for a person bearing a nomination for the highest office
the gift of the people, to appear before them as an advo-
e of the cause represented by such nomination. But the
vement which the Equal Rights party has inaugurated is it-
f also unprecedented ; and this fact is sufficient apology, if,
deed, apology be needed at all, for my appearance before
u to-night. Besides, as you well know, I am not much
en to the habit of conforming to conventionalities. In fact,
here be one thing that I hold more lightly in esteem than
r other, it is the doing, or the refraining from doing, any-
ng, simply because it is in accordance with an established cus-
n so to do. The greater question with me is, is it right, and if
answer be in the affirmative, or the negative, it is the final ar-
ator. The grand effort which is about to be put forth in
interest of humanity, demands the best and most self-sac-
cing devotion of every living soul which can feel and ap-
ciate its great need ; and to promote such a cause I am will-
g to depart widely, if it need be, from the well-beaten track of
my predecessors and contemporaries, and stand boldly be-
e you, advocating the cause which is equally dear to all our
rts, and urging upon you all to lose no opportunity to help
he glorious work.

ut what is this work? What is humanity suffering, from
ch it needs to be redeemed ?

do not know that it can be more succinctly, and at the
e time, so comprehensively set forth, as it has been done in
platform constructed by the People's Convention in Apollo
, on the 10th of May. It is true, however, that this plat-
n relates more specifically to methods than to the reasons
them, or to the results to be gained by them. Therefore,
ought perhaps, to inquire into the diseases by which we are
cted; and also into the conditions to which our methods
forward. The theory of our government justifies the
tio that every human being is in the eyes of the theory,
l in life. Admitting this, there is no escaping the fact,
the uses of government should be to foster, protect and
mote the possession of equality. How does the condition
society reply to this standard for government? Is there
thing that even approaches to equality in any of the va-
s phases of life? I unhesitatingly answer, no! Look
re we may, to whatever class of people or condition, and
face of equality, we find the greatest, gravest, aye, the most
ble distinctions, existing in every thing with which law has
ht to do. Everything is made to turn upon the rights of
erty, and nothing upon the rights of humanity.

he monarch was once the point around which all legislation
olved. In this country, this has been so far changed, that,
the man king, is substituted the king, capital; while we all
ember that, not many years ago, cotton, through slavery,
king. But we also remember that this king was de-
oned, and the throne itself washed away by a torrent of
aan blood. But behind the place where its gaunt form
d, stands another, now revealed by its destruction, with still
e subtle grasp upon the vital life of this country, and that
g is wealth. To its demands the entire industry of the
atry is compelled to pay tribute; to its decrees, every in-
trial knee is compelled to bow; at its beck and nod, every
y hand stays its task and trembles lest its task shall be
pleted. This king, though so newly installed, already
aks itself so firmly seated upon the throne, that it even
s to the length of ignoring all law, which the politicians
cted, by which to catch the votes of the laborers.

he Legislature of the State of New York, on the 20th day of
y, 1870, passed the following law:

"Section 1. On and after the passage of this act, eight hours
shall constitute a legal day's work, for all classes of mechanics, workingmen and laborers, excepting those engaged in
farm and domestic labor; but overwork, for an extra compensation, by agreement between employer and employe, is hereby
permitted."

Now this stands to-day the law in this State. But are its
decrees respected by king wealth? But this, even, is not all
the law held in contempt. The Congress of the United States
passed a law similar in its provisions to this one of this State.
Nothing, however, is sufficiently authoritative to command
itself to this despot that is attempting to ride rough shod over
every right of the workingman, which interferes with the immense revenues it is accustomed to toll from them.

But this superiority to law is even surpassed in insolence by
the bravado with which it is assumed that you, and not it, are
the law breakers and defiers. When workingmen come together and jointly agree to demand that the law shall be respected, in their behalf, this presuming tyrant prates to you
in the most approved style of hypocritical cant, of your obligations as peaceable, law-abiding citizens.

When I consider what the working people of this country
have endured, I am lost in wonder and astonishment at their
patience and forbearance; not that they have simply remained
thus patient and forbearing, but that they have not long since
risen in their sovereign might, to do and redress their own
wrong in the most summary and thorough manner. But has
their forbearance earned them any consideration ? No! but on
the contrary it has encouraged the despot to attempt still greater demands, to make still more extensive exactions year
after year. If he wants more rent, larger profits, greater discounts, more mortgages, more costly residences, more sumptuous equipages, more servants to answer its call, in a word,
more of every thing that by your labor you can furnish them,
for you do furnish and pay for them all in the end; and this
fact should be borne more vividly in mind when this despot is
to be approached by you.

You should know that instead of this power being your
master, it should be your servant. Since all it is it owes to
you. Let this fact permeate every thought of your souls, and
never again permit yourselves to approach this king with
doffed hats or upon bended knee. I would have every workman or workwoman feel that he or she is equal in all respects
to any wealthy person who lives upon the alms of industry;
upon which every one who does not labor does live. Such, are
in no wise a whit better than your meanest paupers.

But to return to the demands of labor. In this city there
have been perhaps, as many as fifty thousand men upon strike,
to compel the enforcement of the law which I have quoted.
Some trades have succeeded, others have not as yet; while others still are being caught by compromises. Now, I say, if it is
right to compromise, it is wrong to strike. They who having
struck in consent with the general movement, compromise
without the consent of the movement are traitors, just as much
traitors as if they had sold themselves to the enemy upon the
eve of a great battle. It is the right of those who do not wish
to strike, to remain quietly at their work, and no man has any
right forcibly to interfere with them; but a deserter is not entitled to any consideration.

But this King offers compromises to be accepted in lieu of
full justice. When the law says a pound of flesh and not a
drop of blood, it wants to take a portion of blood; when the
law says eight hours, it proffers you nine hours. Do you
know, that in admitting the nine hours, where it has until
now exacted ten, it admits the justice of all that is claimed.
If it be not right for the King to exact ten hours, when the bond
provides but eight, how can it be just to attempt to reply to
this, but I trust their logic may fall upon already convinced ears.

I know all the hardships it may be necessary for some to endure. I know how cruel it is to see those dependent upon the weekly wages for the comforts of life, deprived of them. But we should remember that unless we have the courage to endure even to death, we are not worthy to count ourselves the sons and daughters of the men and women, who barefooted trod the wintry roads of Valley Forge, blood marking their way. It would have been easy for those heroes of the revolution to have sold themselves for British gold and thereby obtained relief; as it is easy now for you to sell yourselves for the gold of this King. But had they sold out, or deserted to their foe, you, of to-day, would not have had, even the blessings you now enjoy. Even so it is with you. If you do not now show the same determined devotion to freedom and justice, you will not be able to bequeath to your children that for which they will look back to you as now we look back to our fathers. Stand firm, then, in your demands. Yield not a single inch; and even it require you to walk the streets of this opulent city without shoes, remember that you but imitate your noble, your valiant fathers; and that as they by their steadfastness won their cause, so also will you, by similar steadfastness win your cause.

I would not be understood as advocating violence to gain your ends. I would have every conceivable method tried, and proven a failure before resorting to the final one. I would have every laborer in the country demand that eight hours should constitute a day's work, and stick to the demand, until this proud king is willing to do them justice. But if, after doing everything, you still fail to compel it to respect the law, why then, take the execution of it into your own hands : and such being your right may also become even your duty.

But for a moment, laying aside this part of the subbject, permit me to tell you that for all the wrongs that working people suffer, they are themselves *chiefly* at fault. You should not lay all the blame upon the shoulders of this king. It is all your own work. You have created this king, placed it upon the throne, and more even than that, it is you who maintain the throne. Every year at every election you vote that this king shall continue to rule over you : shall continue to enslave you out of all you earn. It was, as it were, but yesterday, when you shouted " Long live this king !"—and to-morrow you will again resume the old cry ; to-morrow you will march to the polls and cast your votes as this king commands, and the next day again cry out against his despotism.

In this city there are one hundred and twenty-five thousand workingmen's votes; but is there a workingman sent to Albany ? or to Washington ? No; you have sent the satellites of this king up and down there; who, after getting there, turn upon and laugh at your foolishness. You may not like these things; they may not be palatable, but nevertheless they are true, and if they are bitter pills, it would do you good to swallow them and permit them to cleanse your system of this capacity for truckling to this king.

To-day you cry " down with this king !" I advise you upon the next election day to not only utter the same cry, but to also by your votes re-echo it until it resoundings shall shake the throne upon which it sits. But I desire to call your attention to a fact of which perhaps you have not seriously thought. Who, let me ask you, have produced all the wealth which this country possesses ? Have they who hold and call it theirs? You know better than that. You know that all our Vanderbilts, Stewarts and Astors have never earned as much as the weakest man among you. Have they, then, an equitable title to what they possess ?

I will admit, if it please them, that it is possible they may have a legal title, though there may be good reasons to question even that; but an equitable title, never ! The wealth that these persons hold, in equity, belongs to those who produced Who has done this ? Why, the people have done it, and it longs to the people, and to them, in good time, it must be rendered. All these people know all this, and the wiser them are forestalling pub ic judgment by expending la sums in investments made in the interests of the so-cal lower classes. They also are aware that the time is near hand when their accumulations will be tax d out of th hands. If a person owning ten thousand dollars in proper which he produced, is taxed one per cent., Mr. Stewart, who has his half a hundred millions, must be taxed, sa twenty-five per cent.—under such a system how long wo his wealth last ? But it is not the Stewarts alone, nor chie who rob the indurtries. They may take their thousand dollars annually, but there is another class which takes millions. I mean the bondholders. For the twenty-five h dred million dollars that the people are said to owe this cla it is demanded, that there shall in interest and principal, returned nearly five thousand millions. Now how do we pose to escape this extortion ? In this way: The people this debt in interest-bearing bonds; these they propose pay at once in National currency, and thus stop yearly drain upon the producing classes of one hundred fifty million dollars. Will this do one any injustice? The money lenders will have received the face of their lo while the people will have transformed an interest bea debt into a non interest bearing debt; a redeemable indeb ness into a permanent circulating medium, which the faith credit of the people will always make current. Thus, at stroke, will the gold and interest despots be forever dethron

These are but portions of the work that the people must form, before there will be any such thing as industrial equ possible; but they are important portions. Now the ques arises, what will the people do to help this their redemp along, toward consummation ? We all know that all polit movements require a money support. This one, looking Equal Rights for the people cannot expect, especially in early stage, any aid from wealth. This will not come un shall be a necessity for wealth to enlist in the cause to save self; that time will come; but until it does come, the mo ment must look to those, in the direct interest whom it is inaugurated. Is the end to be ga worthy of this support? For years those you who are now called upon have given up your all, in demand made by the means of the systems that this movem will overturn. When *this* is accomplished, the millions paid into the pockets of Wealth, will remain in the pocke industrial people ; and instead of there being the *very rich* and the *very poor many*, all will be rich enough to have al comforts that wealth and enjoyment demand. I say, the attain to such a condition should enlist the aid of every l er in this country ; and I further add that if the indu classes come to the support of this movement in the mann deserves to be supported, the entire revolution can be pe bly accomplished by the next election ; and I know they come to its support. I know that the true policy of thes demption has been felt in many a heart, and spreading these, all the noble hearts in the country, which have borne down by toil, will catch up the glad inspiration, bearing it along its path as it proceeds, shall grow broade wider, until it shall have swept over the whole land ; and its course shall have been ended, not so much as a single trary inequality, not a single injustice, shall be left in p to prey upon the laboring masses.

A Page of American History. Constitution of the United States of the World . . . 1870.

Originally published in 1870, and reprinted substantially the same as *A New Constitution for the United States of the World Proposed by Victoria C. Woodhull* (1872).

A Page of American History.

CONSTITUTION

OF THE

UNITED STATES OF THE WORLD.

AN ADDRESS

BY

VICTORIA C. WOODHULL.

DELIVERED IN LINCOLN HALL, WASHINGTON, U.S.A., IN 1870.

*The First Suggestion of its kind made in America,
and commented on widely by the Press.*

DECLARATION OF PURPOSE.

We, the people of the United States—a National Union— and of the several States as its component parts, proceeding upon the Natural Right inherent in humanity, and in order to secure a perfect and enduring Union ; to establish equality as a birth-right ; to administer common justice ; to secure peace, tranquillity and prosperity ; to provide for the common defense ; to promote the general welfare ; to secure the blessings of freedom, and protection for the exercise of individual capacities to ourselves and our posterity ; and to erect a government which shall be the center around which the nations may aggregate, until ours shall become a Universal Republic, do ordain and establish this Constitution of the United States of the World ; which shall be the Supreme Law wherever it shall have, or acquire, jurisdiction.

DECLARATION OF INTERDEPENDENCE.

All persons are born free and equal, in a political sense (in every sense except heredity), and are entitled to the right to life, which is inalienable ; and to liberty and the pursuit of happiness ; and these shall be absolutely unabridged, except when limited in the individual for the security of the community against crime or other human diseases.

DECLARATION OF THE RIGHTS OF PERSONS.

All persons are entitled to the full and unrestrained use of all their natural and acquired powers and capacities ; but such use by the individual, or by aggregations of individuals, shall never extend to infringement upon, or abridgment of, the same use in other persons.

DECLARATION OF THE RIGHTS OF THE COMMUNITY.

The community has the right, under this Constitution, to organize and maintain government, by which every individual shall be protected in the exercise of personal rights, and prevented from interfering with those of others. But by organizing government the people shall surrender no rights.

DECLARATION OF THE SPHERE OF GOVERNMENT.

It shall be the sphere of the government to perform the duties required of it by the people under the guidance of this Constitution ; and the government shall be vested with the power to perform them, and be limited to such performance.

ARTICLE I.

The Government shall consist of :
The Legislative Department ;
The Executive Department ; and
The Judicial Department.

ARTICLE II.

SEC. 1.—The Legislative Department shall consist of :
A Senate, and
A House of Representatives ;

Which shall be known as the Congress of the United States ; and all legislative power is vested in the Congress.

SEC. 2.—1. The Senate shall consist of two Senators from each State, to be chosen by the Legislature thereof, and each Senator shall have one vote.

2. The United States shall be divided into five Congressional Districts, as follows :

3. The First Congressional District shall consist of the following States, to wit : Maine, West Virginia, Kentucky, North Carolina, Indiana, Iowa, Nevada and Texas ; and its proportion of all new States that may be admitted into the Union.

4. The Second Congressional District shall consist of the following States, to wit : Virginia, Pennsylvania, Rhode Island, Missouri, California, Vermont, Kansas and Nebraska ; and its proportion of all new States that may be admitted into the Union.

5. The Third Congressional District shall consist of the following States, to wit : Maryland, Massachusetts, Ohio, Florida, Oregon, Minnesota and Delaware ; and its proportion of all new States that may be admitted into the Union.

6. The Fourth Congressional District shall consist of the following States, to wit : Louisiana, Michigan, Connecticut, Georgia, Illinois, Tennessee and New Jersey ; and its proportion of all new States that may be admitted into the Union.

7. The Fifth Congressional District shall consist of the following States, to wit : New York, Wisconsin, New Hampshire, Arkansas, South Carolina, Mississippi and Alabama ; and its proportion of all new States that may be admitted into the Union.

SEC. 3.—1. At the Sessions of the Legislatures in all the States next preceding the expiration of the terms of Senators first expiring, the Legislatures of the respective States shall elect Senators for a term of years necessary to complete five years from the time of the adoption of this Constitution ; and at the Sessions of the Legislatures next preceding the expiration of the remaining Senators, the Legislatures shall elect Senators for a term, to complete ten years from the time of the adoption of this Constitution.

2. At the Sessions of the Legislatures next preceding the expiration of the terms of the Senators elected as aforesaid, the Legislatures in the First District shall elect Senators for the full and regular term of ten years ; in the Second District, for the term of nine years ; in the Third District, for the term of eight years ; in the Fourth District, for the term of seven years ; and in the Fifth District, for the term of six years ; and thereafter, in each of the districts for the full and regular term of ten years.

SEC. 4.—1. When vacancies shall occur in the Senate, by death, resignation or otherwise, the Legislatures shall elect Senators to fill the unexpired terms.

2. Any person thirty years of age who shall have been a citizen of the United States nine years, and of the State one year, may be elected Senator from such State.

SEC. 5.—1. The House of Representatives shall consist of Representatives chosen by the people, as hereinafter provided.

2. The terms of all Representatives who shall compose the House of Representatives at the time of the adoption of this Constitution, shall expire on the fourth day of March next succeeding the first election after the said adoption.

3. At the first election after the adoption of this Constitution, the First Congressional District, together with the Territories of Washington and Arizona, shall elect Representatives for the term of one year ; the Second District, together with the Territories of Wyoming and Colorado, for the term of two years ; the Third District, together with the Territories of Montana and the District of Columbia, for the term of three years ; the Fourth District, together with the Territories of Utah and New Mexico, for the term of four years ; and in the Fifth District, together with the Territories of Idaho and Dakota, for the term of five years ; and thereafter, in all the Districts and their Territories, upon the expiration of the terms provided above, all elections for Representatives shall be for the full term of five years.

SEC. 6.—1. Representatives shall be apportioned among the States according to their respective population, not exceeding one Representative for every hundred thousand adult citizens ; but each State and Territory shall have at least one Representative.

2. When vacancies shall occur in the House of Representatives, the Executives in the State from which they occur shall issue writs of election to fill them ; but there shall be no election at any other time than upon the general annual election day hereinafter provided.

3. Any person twenty-five years of age who shall have been a citizen of the United States seven years, and of the State one year, may be elected Representative to the Congress from such State.

ARTICLE III.

SEC. 1.—1. The Congress shall assemble twice every year, the first term beginning on the first Monday in January, and the second on the first Monday in September ; and these two shall constitute one Congress ; and the first Congress which shall convene after the adoption of this Constitution shall be known as the First Congress of the United States of the World.

2. A person bearing the credentials required by the Congress, setting forth that such person was duly elected to be a Congressman, which shall be *prima facie* evidence that the person was duly elected, is entitled to a seat in Congress.

3. A majority of each House shall constitute a quorum, but a smaller number may adjourn from day to day, and be authorised to compel the attendance of absent members, under such rules as may be prescribed by the Congress.

4. Each House may prescribe and enforce the rules of its proceedings, except that without the unanimous consent of the House the " ayes and nays " shall not be demanded, except upon the final passage of bills and resolutions.

5. Each House shall keep a journal of its proceedings, an abstract of which, together with all bills and resolutions introduced, and all bills and resolutions passed, having been duly approved by the President, shall be regularly published in the Congressional Journal, which shall be provided by law.

6. Neither House shall, without the consent of the other adjourn for more than one week ; and final adjournments of both Houses shall be provided for at least twenty days before taking place.

SEC. 2.—1. Congressmen shall receive stated salaries, without mileage, as compensation for their services, to be ascertained by law, which law may be revised every tenth year ; and such salary shall be paid by the States which they severally represent, upon the certificate of the Clerk of the House to which they belong, that they are entitled to the same.

2. Congressmen shall be exempt from arrest in all cases, except for treason, felony, and breach of the peace.

3. Congressmen shall not perform the functions of or hold any other civil offices whatever during the term for which they shall be elected.

SEC. 3.—1. All bills shall originate in the House of Representatives.

2. Every bill which shall have passed the House of Representatives shall be sent to the Senate for its approval ; but if, instead of approval, the Senate shall propose amendments, the bill with the proposed amendments shall be returned to the House for its concurrence. If the House do not concur, then a Committee of Conference, to consist of an equal number from each House, shall be appointed, upon whose action the House shall finally act, and again send the bill to the Senate for final concurrence or rejection ; and if it be rejected, the provisions which shall secure its rejection shall not be considered again during that Congress ; but if the Senate concur, then the bill shall be sent to the President of the United States. If he approve, he shall sign the same ; but if he disapprove it, he shall return it to the House of Representives, with his reasons therefor, which shall be entered upon the Journal, and they shall proceed to reconsider it. If, after such reconsideration, the House shall still adhere to its previous action, by a vote of a majority, the bill shall be considered as finally enacted by the Congress.

3. At the ending of each Congress all the bills that shall have received the approval of the President, or which shall have been finally enacted by Congress, together with such as

shall remain in the hands of the President after the final adjournment of Congress, shall be turned over to the Register of United States Laws, and be by him referred, through the Governors of the several States and Territories, to the people for their approval, to be by them voted upon at the next general election, before becoming law ; and if any bill fail to receive a majority of the votes of all the citizens voting upon it, then it shall be considered as rejected by the people ; and it shall not become a law.

4. After the final adjournment of Congress at the end of any session, the House of Representatives shall remain in semi-session one week, for the purpose of reconsidering any Bill which the President may desire to return with his objections. If the President, however, shall inform the House that he will return no Bill, then the House may disperse ; and all Bills not thus returned to the House by the President within the first five days of the semi-session shall be held to be approved by him and ready to be referred to the people.

5. All Bills which shall become laws by the approval of the people, shall be printed by the Register of United States Laws, and furnished to the States, and to the various Departments of the Government, and also preserved as shall be provided by law.

ARTICLE IV.

Sec. 1.—The Congress of the United States shall, as soon as practicable, and in the order prescribed, enact laws and prescribe rules and regulations, to provide for the government of the people, in accordance with the tenor and provisions of this Constitution, and as set forth in the Principles of its Declarations.

Sec. 2.—The Congress shall prescribe a form for a Constitution which shall be common to, and adopted by, each State now constituting one of the United States ; as well as adopted by every State that may hereafter be admitted into the Union.

Sec. 3.—1. The Congress shall provide uniform laws to raise a revenue to maintain the Government of the United State as organised under this Constitution. But no means shall be resorted to, which shall fall unequally, either upon citizens or upon States, except as hereinafter provided.

2. To maintain the equality of all citizens before the laws.

3. To secure the equal right to the exercise of all common rights.

4. To establish a general system of Criminal Jurisprudence.

5. To establish a general system of Common Law.

6. To regulate the naturalization of foreigners ; commerce between the States, and with other nations ; Marriage : Divorce ; and Education ; each according to the principles of the Declarations.

7. To fix the standards of weight and measures.

8. To establish Post Offices, Post Roads, Post Railroads, Post Telegraphs ; and a Postal Money Order System to meet all the demands of exchange ; and affix such Postal Rates for the same as shall be deemed necessary to maintain them ; or to provide for their maintenarce for the public benefit.

9. To provide for the maintenance of an Army of, not to exceed ten maximum Regiments, in time of peace ; and a Navy ; and to regulate and govern the same.

10. To provide at once for the admission, free of duty, of every article of commerce not produced in the United States ; and to provide for the free admission of all commodities classed as the necessities of life, when the general system of Revenue shall have been inaugurated.

11. To provide a regular reduction in the existing Tariff, which shall entirely abolish the system in its application to all foreign importations from countries opening their Ports to the commerce of the United States free.

SEC. 2.—The Congress shall have power :

1. To provide for organising the Militia of States, and in time of war, for calling it into the service of the United States.

2. To provide for the promotion of the Arts and Sciences ; and for that purpose may secure for limited times, not to exceed twenty years, to Authors and Inventors, the exclusive

right to their respective writings, discoveries and inventions ; or at their discretion to purchase the same for the general benefit of the people.

3. To establish a National Money System, and to provide for loaning the money to the people, either as a means of Revenue, or at the cost of maintaining the system ; and to regulate and affix the value of the same by providing for its conversion into United States Bonds, drawing a rate of interest not to exceed the established rate in the increase of the general wealth of the country ; or, when less than that rate, the rate of the taxation laid on loans of money made to the people ; the Bonds also to be convertible into money at the option of the holder ; and to order the payment of any part of the public debt at any time at par in the National Money.

4. To inaugurate a system of surveillance over, and care for, the destitute classes, looking to their utilization as members of society, and to the abolition of Pauperism and Beggary, upon the principle that if people cannot obtain employment government should supply it to them ; if they will not labor, government should compel them sufficiently to support themselves ; if they cannot labor, government should maintain them.

5. To inaugurate and provide for the maintenance of a system of Industrial Education, which may be made general for all children, based upon the proposition that they belong to society as a whole, in a still more general and important sense, than to the individuals of it who are their parents ; and especially that it is the duty of the Government to become the guardian and protector of all children whose interests are not maintained and protected by their parents ; and provide for and adopt all children relinquished to society by their parents.

6. To inaugurate a new system of Prison Discipline, based upon the proposition that to be restrained of liberty is not as punishment for crime, since all rewards and punishments are administered by the immutable laws of the universe ; but that it is a necessary precaution for the safety of the community ; and which shall secure to every person restrained, or to the family, if dependent, the entire net proceeds of all labor performed.

7. To inaugurate a system of justice and equality as to property rights, based upon the proposition that the producer is entitled to the total proceeds of labor, which shall prevent the accumulation of wealth in the hands of non-producers ; and to provide for the gradual return to the People of all monopolies of land by individuals, based upon the principle that the soil is, or should be, as common property as the air is, or the water, by requiring that upon the decease of persons seized of personal property to a greater amount than a sum to be ascertained by law, or of landed estate, such property and estate shall revert to the Government, for the benefit of the People ; and when such system shall be inaugurated, then to forbid all sales and transfers of land, as well as gifts and nominal sales of other property, and to establish rules and regulations for its use, of all such property and estate, by the people for the public benefit, all of which looks to the practical recognition of the greatest of all human facts, the unity of the human race, having common interests and purposes, and to the perfect practice of the theory of equality, upon which this Constitution is founded.

8. To increase the rate of taxation on accumulations of wealth in excess of one hundred thousand dollars in the following manner, to wit : If the tax on one hundred thousand dollars be one-half of one per cent., on over one hundred thousand dollars it shall be one per cent. ; on over two hundred thousand dollars it shall be two per cent. ; on over three hundred thousand dollars it shall be three per cent. ; on over four hundred thousand dollars it shall be four per cent. ; on over five hundred thousand dollars it shall be five per cent. ; on over seven hundred and fifty thousand dollars it shall be ten per cent. ; on over one million dollars it shall be fifteen per cent. ; on over one million five hundred thousand dollars it shall be twenty per cent. ; on over two million dollars it shall be twenty-five per cent. ; and in the same proportions upon any other basic rate than upon one-half of one per cent. upon $100,000.

9. To inaugurate and provide for a system of National Railways, based upon the proposition that whatever involves the direct interests of the public should be in the hands and under the control of the people, for the public welfare, and to that end may purchase existing railways, at a price to be ascertained by law, but not greater than the same could be constructed for, or construct new roads, as the circumstances shall seem to require ; and the system shall be operated

either at the cost of maintenance or for the public benefit from the public funds.

10. To inaugurate a system of Public Markets for all the products of the world, having in view the abolition of the system of middle-men or hucksters, and which shall secure to producers the entire amount paid by consumers, less only the cost of transportation and distribution.

11. To abolish the Tariff, and provide for the control of the importation of foreign goods, in such quantities only as the demands of the country shall require ; and to determine the price at which such imports shall be sold to the people by general law, except as is herein otherwise provided for free admission.

12. To inaugurate a system that shall give employees, equally with employers, a direct interest in the results of their co-operation for production ; which shall, after the payment to the employer of the same rate of interest for the money invested by him as is paid for the use of the National Money ; and the payment of salaries to the employees and the employers, and all other legitimate expenses, divide the net profits in an equitable manner among them.

13. To provide for the return to the people of all mineral, coal, oil and salt lands, and for their operation for the public benefit.

14. And to propose to the several Nations of the world a plan for an International Tribunal to which all disputes of Nations shall be referred for arbitration and settlement ; which plan shall also include provisions for an International Army and Navy to enforce the edicts of the Tribunal and to maintain the peace of the world.

ARTICLE V.

SEC. 1.—1. No taxes shall be levied by any legislative body in the United States, except for the legitimate purposes of government in protecting the rights of persons and nationality. Neither shall any legislative body have power to exempt any property whatever from taxation ; or to discriminate in favour of any property as to rate, except as is herein otherwise provided ; and there shall be no methods of taxation that shall, in any manner, protect certain classes of the people at the expense of certain other classes, except as herein otherwise provided in Article IV., Section II., Par. 8 and 11. And no special taxes of any kind shall be levied, upon any pretext or for any purpose whatever.

2. All taxes, whether for National, State, County or Municipal purposes, shall be laid and collected by one Revenue System, with the exceptions to which reference is made in the preceding paragraph.

Sec. 2.—No legislative body in the United States shall have power to give or loan the public property or credit to individuals, or to corporations, to promote any enterprise, or for any purpose whatever.

Sec. 3.—No money shall be drawn from any Treasury of the people, in the United States, unless in consequence of appropriations made by law ; and a regular detailed account of receipts and expenditures, giving each separate item in the accounts, of all public moneys, shall be published ; those arising in the accounts of the United States and the several States, weekly ; and those upon the accounts of other subdivisions, weekly or monthly ; and the accounts of the United States and of the States shall be published in a periodical issued for the purpose, at the expense of the public, in a manner to be determined by law.

ARTICLE VI.

All legislation by all legislative bodies shall be in the form of General Laws ; and no special legislation for any purpose shall be considered by any legislative body in the United States ; and all laws enacted to cover special cases shall be absolutely null and void, and shall be held and maintained to be so by the General Government, as the special representative and conservator of the rights of the people ; provided, however, that the Government of the United States, the States, or of any sub-divisions of a State may provide for any special internal improvement when instructed so to do by a vote of the citizens of their respective jurisdictions.

ARTICLE VII.

Sec. 1.—1. The Executive power of the United States shall be vested in a President and a Ministerial Cabinet.

2. Any person thirty-five years of age, who shall have been a citizen of the United States fifteen years, shall be eligible to the office of President or to the Ministerial Cabinet.

3. The President and the Ministerial Cabinet shall hold their offices during the term of ten years, and together with the Vice-President, chosen for the same term, shall be elected as follows :

The tickets of the several Presidential and Ministerial Cabinet Electoral Parties, in each State, shall consist of one person from each Congressional Representative District ; and the number of Electors to which each ticket shall be entitled shall be in the same proportion to the whole number of electors to which the State is entitled, as the total vote cast for each ticket shall bear to the whole number of votes cast for all the tickets ; to be taken from the districts standing at the heads of the several tickets : but disregarding all fractional remainders.

4. The sum of the unrepresented fractional balances of votes in the several States shall be determined by the Electoral College ; and the Electors to which each ticket shall be found to be entitled shall be chosen by the Electors of the several tickets chosen by the States, already in the Electoral College ; and such Electors shall be entitled to vote, the same as though regularly elected by the people.

5. During the month of December following the Presidential Election, the President shall issue a proclamation convening the Electoral College in the Hall of the House of Representatives of the United States, on a stated day in the following month. where they shall organise by electing from their number a Presiding Officer, a Secretary and Tellers : and they shall then proceed to elect by ballot :

1st. A President.

2d. A Vice-President.

3d. A Secretary of the Department of International Relations.

4th. A Secretary of the Department of Home Relations.

5th. A Secretary of the Department of Finance.

6th. A Secretary of the Department of Revenue.

7th. A Secretary of the Department of Expenditures.

8th. A Secretary of the Department of Internal Improvements.

9th. A Secretary of the Department of Postal and Telegraphic Service.

10th. A Secretary of the Department of War.

11th. A Secretary of the Department of the Navy.

12th. A Secretary of the Department of Commerce.

13th. A Secretary of the Department of Criminal Jurisprudence and of Common Law

14th. A Secretary of the Department of Education.

15th. A Secretary of the Department of Reformatory and Criminal Labor.

16th. A Secretary of the Department of National Insurance.

17th. A Secretary of the Department of Statistics.

18th. An Attorney-General of the United States.

19th. The Judges of the Supreme Court of the United States, when there shall be vacancies.

6. The election shall be conducted in the following manner, to wit :

If no candidate shall receive a majority of the votes of all the Electors constituting the College within the first ten ballots, then the candidate receiving the smallest number of votes shall be dropped from the list of candidates, after each ballot, until an election shall be had ; and the candidates thus elected for the respective offices shall be declared duly elected to fill them for the next term of ten years.

7. In case of death or unavoidable absence of Electors entitled to be present and vote in the Electoral College, the Electors present, on the ticket to which they belong, shall provide substitutes to act in the stead of the absentees, and they shall have the power to perform the functions as though regularly elected.

8. No person shall be eligible to the offices of President, Vice-President, or to the Ministerial Cabinet, for a second term ; nor shall any person once occupying either of these offices be eligible to any of them for the succeeding term.

9. The President, on retiring from the office, shall succeed to a seat in the Senate of the United States, as Presidential Senator, with the same powers and entitled to the same pay as other Senators, but to be paid by the United States ; and shall be excluded from all professional pursuits.

10. In case of a vacancy occurring in the office of President, the Vice-President shall succeed to the office for the unexpired term.

11. In case of a vacancy occurring in the Ministerial Cabinet, it shall be filled by an election on joint ballot by the Congress of the United States.

12. The duties pertaining to each department of the Ministerial Cabinet shall be defined and prescribed by the Congress, according to their respective and appropriate spheres, indicated by their names.

SEC. 2.—1. The President shall be Commander-in-Chief of the Army and Navy of the United States, and of the Militia when in the service of the United States ; and may require the opinion, in writing, of the Secretary of any Executive Department upon any subject relating to the Department.

2. The President shall have power, by and with the consent of the Senate, to make treaties with other nations, provided two-thirds of the Senate concur ; and shall nominate, and by and with the consent of the Senate shall appoint, all foreign officers, and all other officers of the United States not herein otherwise provided, and which shall be established by law.

3. The President shall on each assembling of Congress, and at such other times as may be deemed necessary, give to the Congress information of the state of the country, or its foreign relations, and recommend to their consideration such measures as shall be deemed expedient or necessary.

4. The President may, on extraordinary occasions, convene both Houses of Congress.

5. The President shall receive ambassadors from other nations, as well as all public ministers.

6. The President shall see that all the laws are faithfully executed, and shall exercise a general supervision over the entire Executive of the United States, and commission all officers of the United States.

7. The Vice-President shall preside over the Senate of the United States, and vote when the Senate is tied.

ARTICLE VIII.

SEC. 1.—Full faith and credit shall be given in each State to the public acts, records, and judicial proceedings of every other State ; and Congress shall by general law prescribe the manner in which such acts, records, and proceedings shall be proved, and the effect thereof.

SEC. 2.—A person charged with crime who shall be found in another State, shall, on demand of the Executive authority of the State having jurisdiction of the crime, be delivered up to be removed to such State.

ARTICLE IX.

SEC. 1.—1. No incorporated company existing in the United States, or under the authority of any law of the United States, shall, upon any pretext, issue stock certificates to represent a greater sum than the actual amount of money paid in ; nor shall any incorporated company make any stock or scrip dividends, nor money dividends to exceed four per cent., for any current year, upon its entire stock ; nor shall any such company be permitted to, in any manner whatever, evade the letter or the spirit of these provisions ; but whenever the earnings shall produce a sum in excess of the operating expenses, and four per cent. upon the capital stock, then the rate of charges shall be changed so as to reduce the earnings to the standard of four per cent. Any net earnings in excess of four per cent. for any current year, shall be paid over to the General Government.

2. Any company or corporation which shall evade or attempt to evade any of the provisions of this Article, shall upon proof of the same forfeit their charter to the people ; and the Government, for and in the name of the people, shall

assume the conduct of the affairs of such company, either paying to the stockholders the original amount of their investment, or the net earnings up to four per cent. per annum.

3. The provisions of Article IV., Section 8, for taxation, shall apply to the individuals comprising stock companies ; but the taxes shall be collected from the companies.

4. The Congress shall have power to enforce and carry out the provisions of this Article by appropriate legislation.

ARTICLE X.

SEC. 1.—1. New States may be admitted into the Union whenever the people living within the limits of the proposed jurisdiction shall, by vote of the majority, decide to organize as a State under the General State Constitution ; provided, however, that such proposed State shall contain a sufficient population to entitle it to at least one Representative in Congress.

2. The Congress shall have power to make all needed rules and regulations for all the Territorial and other public property, provided, however, that they shall have no power to in any manner dispose by sale of any property whatever, except as provided by law for property other than land.

3. The Congress shall grant to any adult citizen of the United States, applying for the same, any desired and unoccupied part of the public land, excepting mineral, coal, oil and salt lands, not to exceed one hundred and sixty acres, so long as such citizens shall pay regularly to the Government the yearly tax required, and to be ascertained by law for such occupancy ; but such tax shall not exceed the general rate for other property elsewhere in the Union.

4. Whenever the inhabitants of any Territory not already included in the Union shall have signified, by a vote of the majority, their desire to be admitted, they shall be admitted, after organizing as a State, under the General State Constitution, and when not having sufficient population to be admitted as a State, then as a Territory under the General Law established by Congress for the government of Territories.

5. All Territories shall be entitled to one Representative to Congress, who shall be entitled to vote upon all questions which do not specially refer to the Government of the States, or to the States as such.

ARTICLE XI.

SEC. 1.—1. The Judicial Power of the United States shall be vested in one Supreme Court of the United States, to consist of five Judges—one from each Congressional Division of the Union ; and of a Supreme Court of the several States, to consist of three Judges ; and of District Courts in the several States, one for each Congressional District ; and of such other Inferior Courts as may be ordained and established by the Legislature of the States, by authority of the State Constitutions.

2. The Judicial Power shall extend to all cases in law and equity arising under this Constitution, and the laws which shall be made by its authority ; and to all treaties made, or which shall be made, under their authority ; to all cases affecting Ambassadors, other public Ministers, or Consuls ; to all cases of admiralty and maritime jurisdiction ; to controversies to which the United States shall be a party ; to controversies between two or more States ; between a State and citizens of another State ; between the citizens of different States ; between the citizens of the same State claiming under grants of different States ; and between a State or the citizens thereof and foreign States, citizens, or subjects.

3. The District Courts of the several States shall have original jurisdiction over all cases occurring within the limits of their respective districts, with such exceptions, and under such regulations, as the Congress may make.

4. Appeals may be made from the District Courts of the States to the Supreme Courts of the States, and from the Supreme Courts of the States to the Supreme Court of the United States, in all cases where the Supreme Courts of the States are not a unit, under such rules and regulations as shall be prescribed by Congress.

5. The Congress may provide Courts for the several Territories.

ARTICLE XII.

The United States shall guarantee equality of rights, privileges and duties to all the States as States; to all the citizens of the several States as individuals, and shall see to it that no State shall enforce any law which shall trespass upon individual rights as declared to be such by this Constitution.

ARTICLE XIII.

Sec. 1.—1. All persons born, or who shall have been, or shall hereafter be, naturalized in the United States, and subject to the jurisdiction thereof, are citizens of the United States, and of the State wherein they reside.

2. The citizens of the United States shall consist of two classes, to wit: Adult citizens and Minor citizens.

3. Adult citizens shall consist of all citizens who shall have attained to the age of eighteen years and upward.

4. Minor citizens shall consist of all citizens who shall not have attained the age of eighteen years.

5. All adult citizens except Idiots and the Insane shall exercise the Elective Franchise at their pleasure, for all purposes, subject to the following regulation only :—

For all United States officers, without reservations;

For all State officers and Representatives to Congress, after a residence in the State for three months;

For all other officers, after a residence within the limits of their jurisdiction for one month;

When not restrained of their liberty, being charged with, or after conviction of and restraint for, some crime. In all other cases the elective franchise shall be absolutely un-abridged.

5. All citizens, while serving in the Army or Navy of the United States, or as officers of the United States, shall be entitled to vote for United States officers only, except as may

be provided by Congress for officers within their respective organizations.

ARTICLE XIV.

SEC. 1.—1. All elections in all the States shall be held simultaneously on the first Monday in November of each year, beginning at six o'clock in the morning and closing at six o'clock in the evening.

2. All judicial officers, all legislative officers, except United States Senators, and all executive officers provided by or under the authority of this Constitution to officiate as heads of departments, divisions, and sub-divisions, shall be elected by the votes of the people among whom they are to have jurisdiction; and all other officers in such jurisdiction shall be appointed by them, and hold their offices during good behavior; and shall be removed for cause only and in such manner as shall be ascertained by law.

3. Representatives to Congress, Representatives and Senators to the several State Legislatures, by Congressional districts, and all lesser legislative bodies, and all Judges of all Courts, shall be elected in the same manner by which it is provided that the Electoral College shall be elected, except that the districts having the largest fractional remainder of votes shall be taken to complete the quota of officers, and that the officers elected shall be those who shall have received the largest vote instead of in the order of numbered districts or divisions on each ticket.

4. All executive officers not otherwise provided, whether of the United States or the States, may be elected by a majority or plurality vote, or by minority representation, as may be provided by law.

5. No officer elected by the people shall ever be required to take an oath of office or to give bond for the performance of the duties of the office; the fact of election being *prima facie* evidence that the people accept the officer as capable and honest.

6. No officer elected by the people shall be removed from office during the term for which the election was had, except by a vote of the people in the same manner as in the election of the officer.

ARTICLE XV.

SEC. I.—I. The Congress shall have power to pass no law that shall in any manner deny, abridge, or interfere with the most complete exercise of every power, capacity, and talent possessed by the individual ; but shall guarantee every individual peaceful pursuit therein, as against all other individuals.

2. That shall in any manner deny, abridge, or interfere with the right of two or more individuals to contract together in whatever manner, but shall guarantee protection to all contracting parties as against all interference.

SEC. I. All contracts between individuals shall stand upon their own merits and upon the integrity and capacity of the parties involved, without appeal by them to any power for redress ; provided, however, that when contracting parties, at the time of making a contract, shall declare in the contract that they, not having mutual confidence in their ability and integrity to faithfully perform the same, desire the guarantee of other parties, or that Government shall enforce them, then the Government may have the power to take cognizance of an appeal to it, through proper forms, to be prescribed by law, but not otherwise.

2. Laws may be made to compel the enforcement of pecuniary contracts on the part of incorporated companies organized under the authority of law ; since their integrity and capacity may depend upon the perfectness of the laws by which they exist, which are the people's provisions, and not upon the honor and integrity of the individuals composing the company ; and to require the record or publication of such contracts as may affect and indirectly involve the community.

3. No oath or affirmation shall be required by law of any person upon any pretext, or for any purpose whatever. But in any processes of law where evidence is required or given, if it be established that such evidence is false testimony, the person giving it may be held accountable in a manner to be ascertained by law.

ARTICLE XVI.

SEC. 1.—1. It is expressly understood that the Government thus organized has no power conferred upon it except that which is necessary to carry out the instructions of the people, as expressed through the laws framed by their representatives, and approved by themselves, according to the provisions of this Constitution.

2. The people may, by direct vote at any time, instruct their chosen representatives in regard to any issue before them, and all legislative bodies are to be held to be the representatives of the people, and not of their own ideas as opposed to the will of the people.

ARTICLE XVII.

The United States shall compel every State to maintain within its limits a Republican form of government upon all matters in all its legislation and administration ; and such a form is pronounced to be one in which the rights of all adult citizens to participate is absolutely unabridged except by forfeiture ; and in which the equal interests of all minor citizens are secured.

ARTICLE XVIII.

This Constitution may be amended in the same manner in which all laws are required to be passed, by the Congress of the United States and the approval of the people ; provided, however, that all such amendments shall be approved by a vote of three-fifths of the entire vote cast.

ARTICLE XIX.

SEC. 1.—1. The House of Representatives shall have the power, whenever in the judgment of three-fifths of its members it shall be proper to do so, to submit to the people an Amendment to this Constitution abolishing all Senatorial bodies, which shall become the law when approved by the requisite vote of the people.

2. The people may, at any time, without the initiative on the part of the Congress, amend, or abolish parts of this Constitution by a vote of three-fifths of the adult citizens, and the people shall have the right to vote upon any proposition of this kind at any General Election ; and all such votes shall have the same force and effect as though made upon subjects submitted to them by the Congress.

3. This Constitution shall be held to be adopted by the people whenever three-fifths of the whole number of adult citizens of the United States, according to the last census, shall have given it their approval ; and they may then constitutionally proceed to organize the government as herein provided ; but all other and previous legislation under the old Constitution shall continue in full force and effect, until the necessary legislation supplementary to, and in place of it, shall have been provided.

4. Nothing in this Constitution or in the legislation authorized under it shall be held as invalidating contracts existing at the time of its adoption, except in cases herein otherwise expressly provided.

Part III

ECONOMICS

Introduction by Madeleine B. Stern

The American Labor Reform League, a heterogeneous group of anarchists, socialists and radical reformers of various persuasions—all bent upon giving labor its due—was launched at Cooper Institute in May 1871. One of the highlights of the occasion was a speech by Victoria Woodhull (A LECTURE ON THE GREAT SOCIAL PROBLEM OF LABOR & CAPITAL).

This avant-garde feminist had already allied herself with the International Workingmen's Association organized by Karl Marx in 1864, and on December 30, 1871, her *Weekly* would make history by publishing, for the first time in this country, an English translation of the *Communist Manifesto*. At this point in her life, therefore, the oppression of the masses—the subjugation of the "Lower Millions" to the "Upper Ten"—was a popular theme both in the Woodhull drawing room and at the Woodhull lecture stand.

By May 1871, when she addressed the American Labor Reform League, the distance between the extremes of wealth and poverty in America seemed indeed unbridgeable. Corruption in government often abetted the exploitation of the masses. The background was set for the long struggle between labor and capital.

There were three principal roots of the evil flower of oppression: Land, Railways, Money. "Land-Grabbers" had seized the soil until, it was said, approximately one-fortieth of the population owned most of the country's real estate; government land grants to private corporations increased this disproportion. With government's acquiescence, the railways now crossing and criss-crossing the country in a nexus of iron and steel also speculated in land. Their fraudulent practices included excessive freight charges, poor service and exorbitant profits. One of the notorious offenders was the Credit Mobilier of America, a company used by leaders of the Union Pacific Line until it was discredited in 1872.

Land-Grabbing and excessive railway profits culminated in corporate monopolies that developed with unprecedented speed during the '70's. Probably the most flagrant type of monopoly was the Money monopoly. Here, too, government played a pejorative role, for both the National Banking Acts and the protective tariff, originally adopted as emergency

Civil War measures, were continued during the 1870's, favoring select industries and private bankers who manipulated the stock market at will.

In such a climate the merchant princes—later to be styled the robber barons—flourished. Among those "slaveholders" of the North were John Jacob Astor, capitalist owner of inherited land, and William Henry Vanderbilt, manipulator of stocks; A. T. Stewart, merchant founder of a great New York emporium, and Thomas Scott, railway magnate. To Victoria Woodhull and her associates their brand of rugged individualism endangered the sovereign individuality of the laborer.

To counteract it, therefore, she became the mouthpiece of the radical reformers, proposing a series of solutions for the three major evils of the time. For Land-Grabbing she would substitute Free Land or Land Reform, advocated by such agrarians as George Henry Evans and Joshua Ingalls. As Victoria Woodhull phrased it, "the soil upon which we stand is as *common* property as the air is by which we are surrounded." The land belonged to the people. Upon the death of its present owners—the Land Oligarchy—it should revert to the people. As for the railroads, they should be nationalized. The Grange, a farm organization which had attacked railway monopoly, had set the stage for concerted action. Eventually the people should take possession of the entire railroad system of the country. To destroy the Money monopoly, the protective tariff should be replaced by free trade and a system of progressive taxation should be introduced; the public debt should be repudiated and stocks, along with high interest rates, should be abolished.

The philosophy underlying such solutions was clear: labor was the source of all capital. Under the present nefarious system all the results of labor accrued to the privileged few; under the Woodhull system—an amalgam of the theories of the nineteenth-century radical pamphleteers Ezra Heywood and Josiah Warren, Lysander Spooner and William B. Greene—co-operative industry would give labor an interest in the products of their labor; "equitable commerce"—a system by which the price of a piece of merchandise was determined only by its cost plus the time spent in selling it—would eliminate profit; the country's wealth would be vested in its rightful owners, the laborers who had produced it.

To this quasi-communistic-socialistic blueprint Victoria Woodhull added a sociological program that would provide for penal reform and compulsory industrial education, and obviate unemployment by the governmental guarantee of continuous labor at equitable wages.

An IMPENDING REVOLUTION, Victoria Woodhull insisted, could be forestalled only by the REFORMATION elaborated in her blueprint. And indeed, with the activity of the Commune, the insurrectionary government that took possession of Paris in 1871, with the failure of Jay

Cooke & Company and of other great American financial houses, and with the Panic of 1873, the question of REFORMATION OR REVOLUTION, WHICH? was brought closer to the country's doorstep.

Victoria Woodhull's master plan included still another tenet: the economic independence of the laboring woman. This was a subject in which most feminists were, in one way or another, involved—an involvement reflected by the relations maintained for a time between the New England Labor Reform League and the National Woman Suffrage Association, as well as by Elizabeth Cady Stanton's vice-presidency of the American Labor Reform League in 1872.

Victoria Woodhull's involvement in woman's economic independence in particular and in the science of economics in general was more pronounced than that of most feminists. As the first woman stockbroker in this country she was aware, not only through consultations with her advisers, but through firsthand experience, of the machinations of Wall Street and the perplexities and PRINCIPLES OF FINANCE. She was, apparently, familiar with the economic problems of the time, from the deterioration of greenbacks after the Civil War to the panics that were becoming "periodic cataclysms," from the pendulum swing between inflation and deflation to the complexities of credit and overproduction. Thanks to her close association with James Harvey Blood and Stephen Pearl Andrews, she was also doubtless cognizant of the remedies prescribed in such reform tracts as Lysander Spooner's *New System of Paper Currency* and William B. Greene's *Mutual Banking*. To counteract the concentration of wealth in the coffers of the privileged few and to increase the purchasing power of the majority, the petticoat financier offered a simple panacea: since gold was merely an arbitrary and fluctuating standard of value, it should be replaced by what was variously styled a People's Money, a National Currency, HUMANITARIAN MONEY—a medium at once measurable, fixed, and based upon equitable exchange.

Despite this suggestion, the equitable division of wealth remained "the unsolved riddle" a generation after the Woodhull lecture on THE PRINCIPLES OF FINANCE. In 1890, forced into extensive purchases of silver, the American government was thought by many to have endangered the gold standard. The agitation of the Populist Party, recruited largely from farmers of the South and West, and the Panic of 1893 following Cleveland's election, accentuated the FINANCIAL CRISIS IN AMERICA. The conflict between gold, the "hard money" of Wall Street, and free silver, the "poor man's money," became a major issue in the McKinley-Bryan campaign of 1896. Victoria Woodhull, then in her fifties, was, if possible, more engrossed than ever in matters of finance since she had married a financier, John Biddulph Martin of Martin's Bank, London.

To some extent, during her later moneyed years, she sustained the views of her less prosperous days. She still preached that the masses be given "a more equitable and increased purchasing power," that the most be produced at the least cost, that the standard of living of the poor be raised, that the monetary system be reconstructed. To those ends she studied, under her husband's guidance, the writings of the distinguished English economists William Stanley Jevons and Henry D. Macleod and the French economist Frédéric Bastiat. She reviewed the famous law on the relative value of coins formulated by Sir Thomas Gresham who indicated that intrinsically valuable currency would be hoarded while currency of less intrinsic value would remain in circulation and become devaluated. Doubtless she consulted often on monetary matters with her banker husband as she had once consulted with his predecessor, James Harvey Blood.

In some respects Mrs. John Biddulph Martin was far more "Establishment" in her views on economics than Victoria C. Woodhull had been. Mellowed with years and with prosperity, she was frequently able to find a measure of truth in the traditional, conservative opinions she had formerly scoffed. Occasionally she looked down a pseudo-aristo-cratic nose at the economic perplexities created by such a problem as immigration. On one count, however, she was far ahead of her time, foreshadowing a Keynsian view of the deleterious effects of parsimony and thrift: "Society is so interdependent to-day," she wrote in 1892, "and the interaction of relative forces so great, and what is real economy so little understood, that retrenching or economising during a period of hard times not only lowers the general standard of living, but may have other disastrous effects."

To raise that general standard, she looked to the future (WHAT OF THE FUTURE?). In 1896, on the eve of the Boer War, she envisioned a time when science, which "knows no nationality," would transform the face of the world, when eugenics would uplift mankind; when a humanitarian politico-economic system would amalgamate the universe into one "harmonious whole." To bring that day nearer, Victoria Woodhull covered reams of paper, filled countless columns of print, and delivered innumerable lectures. Such portions of her work as are here reprinted epitomize the reform program of a nineteenth-century agitator for woman's rights who notably enlarged the sphere of feminist thought by delving into matters of state and matters of finance. Revolutionary, provocative, often prophetic, the theories she enunciated still claim attention.

ECONOMICS

(1)

A Lecture on The Great Social Problem of Labor & Capital . . . 1871.

A LECTURE

ON

THE GREAT SOCIAL PROBLEM

OF

LABOR & CAPITAL,

DELIVERED AT

COOPER INSTITUTE, NEW YORK CITY,

On Monday, May 8, 1871,

BEFORE THE

REFORM LABOR LEAGUE,

BY

VICTORIA C. WOODHULL.

NEW YORK:
JOURNEYMEN PRINTERS' CO-OPERATIVE ASSOCIATION,
No. 30 BEEKMAN STREET.

1871.

THE GREAT SOCIAL PROBLEM;

LABOR AND CAPITAL.

Three great questions, each based in human equality, the immediate future must solve, namely, Political Rights, Social Order and Moral
Responsibility. The first unattained, the second is impossible, and the
third preposterous. The first attained, the second will be organized,
and the third naturally follow. Every human being is entitled to certain inalienable rights, of which no constitution or law can dispossess
him, but every human being is also subject to certain duties flowing
from the possession of such rights, which he should no more evade than
he should be deprived of their possession.

Therefore it is that we find humanity a body of interdependent
persons, every individual of whom sustains certain dependent relations
to the aggregate, and is entitled to certain protection from the aggregate,
against infringement by others. The interest and rights of each individual are therefore merged in a community of interests and rights, and
the legitimate functions of government are to maintain and protect, so
that by no possibility may the community of interest be made subservient to individual interest, or to the special interest of any number of
individuals less than the whole.

From this position, which principal and reason sustain, it follows
that my first postulate is true; that social order cannot exist unless political right is equally possessed by all among whom it is sought to be
maintained; for if a government is organized to maintain it, in which
but a portion of the community participate—or worse still, in which a
portion are denied participation—there is a departure from the principle
of equality of right among the members of the community, which must
ever prove fatal to humanity.

So long as inequalities exist among the members of a community, first made possible and afterward maintained by *law, so* long will there be inharmonies in the community. This is a self-evident proposition. And so long as there are inharmonies in the community, there can be *no* equality of Moral responsibility, because the inharmony arising from unequal distribution and exercise of rights, to which all are equally entitled, places those who are *below* equality at the mercy of those who have usurped this quantity, and who are thus *above* equality. In such condition, equal responsibility is not justice, and hence our second postulate is maintained.

As there are three great questions pressing for settlement, so, too, do these questions find their legitimate basis in three great principles, which should guide every action of individuals and communities, and by which all results should be tried, and these are: Freedom, Equality and Justice. With the first, the second should be maintained by the ruling of the third, which would be perfect government, since the purposes for which government is organized would be secured to every individual.

Is our government based in these principles, and is it administered according to this formula? If not, why not? What is lacking which is right and what is superabundant which is wrong? Dismissing whatever relates to the first and third of the great questions named, the second, the social problem, will be considered. The sub-question of labor and capital, or the causes of the very unequal distributions of material possessions which obtain under government as now administered, is but a part of the greater one of social order.

Under a government which expresses the will of those over whom its functions are exercised, there can be no question to settle as between such government and the people. But there *is* a question between this people and their government, and it must be settled, and the settlement falls upon the present age to perform.

I fear that the principles involved in this controversy are little understood by the masses who join in it. I fear that portions of the people array themselves against other portions, without comprehending what is the difficulty which they represent, and from which they profess to suffer and desire relief. I fear, while those who do suffer are looking among the leaves and branches of the wrong for its cause, the roots are taking deeper and firmer hold of the vitals of society, and its trunk increasing to still more formidable proportions, and that before they who suffer become conscious of it supreme control will have been obtained over them.

But, says the poor laborer: "What right has my neighbor to all his wealth to produce which he never lifted his hand, while I who did assist in its production, am year after year compelled to continue producing, only to see him obtain all the benefit." As between you, my friend, and him, as individuals, he may have all right to his accumulations; but as between you and him as equal members of the community, and the *community*, he can have none; because the right and interests of the individual cannot properly exist in antagonism to those of the community, of whom you and he are equally constituent parts. Special rights and interests cannot legitimately exist in, and be maintained at the expense of, the general welfare. The general welfare of a people consists in having the greatest possible amount of happiness, and general happiness is not possible where there is such cause of complaint as the one mentioned. So long as the general good of the whole is possible, the greatest good of the greatest number is the object to be obtained through government. Whatever the professions of government are, its practices secure the supposed good of the very select few at the direct expense of the common masses.

Hence, I predicate that so long as the attempt is made to remedy the ills of which society has just cause of complaint, by temporary policies, expedient make-shifts and trimming among effects, instead of leaving all these to take care of themselves, and going to the "Root of the matter," just so long success will not crown the efforts.

But how shall we get at the "Root of the matter?" There is but one way, and that is to go back to the beginning and build better, by putting no bricks in the walls of the edifice to be erected except such as have been trimmed, squared and tested by the principles upon which all government should be constructed.

The people who maintain the present government in this country are not aborigines. As a people they have no primordial right to the soil upon which they live, any more than they have to the air they breathe, which is fully as important to life as is the soil. How comes this distinction to be made by humans between the elements upon which human life depends? How is it, that, in an aggregate population of forty millions of individuals, that less than a fortieth part have usurped the right to all the soil which belongs by natural right to the whole? This is an inequality of most alarming proportions. Every fortieth person has usurped the natural rights of the other thirty-nine, and what is worse than all, they are protected in it by the government.

If a person have in his possession a stolen article, it matters not through how many hands it may have passed, it is nevertheless stolen property and may be reclaimed by the owner upon proof. Now let us try the professed ownership of the soil by this rule, never minding the practice by which it was obtained, which by the way reminds me of that which prevailed in the armies during the late war : a person would steal a horse and "swap" him, and thus obtain one of his own. Suppose a person were to go into the public domain—there is a great deal of unappreciated meaning in that word—and fence off three hundred and twenty acres of soil and call it his own, and should afterward sell the same to another person who should take possession thereof, and that not long thereafter Uncle Sam should pass that way and observe what had occurred, and the question of title should arise, could the party in possession *hold* as against Uncle Sam? Not a bit of it. Let me ask what *better* title *any* person has to any soil he may *profess* to own than this one would have. I do not care through how many generations it may have descended, traced far enough back, the title will be found to have been a *squatter's*, and that *that* squatter took possession of some of the public domain, which belonged to all the people as represented and organized in government.

.The conditions of ownership of soil are founded on no *better* principles than that would be had the whole present population of this country been suddenly transplanted to its soil from some other country, and had "grabbed" their present possessions. In principles of human rights, I say, there would be *no distinction* between this process and that by which they do possess it. Whatever *legal* rights there may be they can never destroy *human* right.

The first government this country knew after its discovery held the public domain in trust for the people ; as they increased, the number for whom the government held the public domain also increased. It was neither the people nor government who owned the soil. It was landed upon, seized and retained. Such a procedure should be called stealing. Its people or government never had a just title to a foot of soil in this or any other country, and cannot convey such a title.

The soil upon which we stand is as *common* property as the air is by which we are surrounded. It is really a wonder that schemers have not before this set afloat some feasible plan for bottling the atmosphere, and dealing it out for considerations to those who should be so unfortunate as not to have " gobbled" some on their own account. For my part I can see no difference in principle between dealing in *air*, *soil* or *water*. They are are all composed of the same elements, and are constantly being converted into each other. Thus then we arrive at the *foundation* for all *material* monopolies. From *this* process of stealing the rights of the people all the other and *lesser* thefts have come, by which the great proportion of people are defrauded of their natural inheritance. *Two* wrongs can never make one right. If a few people have possession of the rights of the many, the many cannot reclaim them, and the few retain them. The few *must* give way to the many.

Every person whom this government represents has a *natural, human* right to the use of his *just* proportion of the public soil, and government should *secure* this right to all, they, individually, paying to the fund for its support a certain amount of the *proceeds* obtained by its use. *This* is the true use which should be made of the public domain.

But what use is government making of it. Hon. George W. Julian, in a speech made in the last session of the 41st Congress, enumerated *twenty-three* bills that passed the Senate granting seventy-five million six thousand three hundred and twenty acres. Beside them there were then pending in the Senate bills granting one hundred and fifteen million, two hundred and eighteen thousand, five hundred acres. Adding these proposed donations to those already made to the various Pacific Roads, and the enormous aggregate of more than four hundred million of acres is found to have been diverted from *public* to *private* use, and are exceeding in extent that of any *ten* of the present number of States.

The enormity of thus defrauding the people of the public domain is beyond comprehension, and can only be appreciated when we are reminded that many of those who have thus betrayed the public interest are now reputed to be possessed of *vast* wealth. We do not pretend to charge that these gentlemen obtained personal benefit from their action upon these various bills. Not by any means. We only desire that the people should know how *easy* it is for their public servants to *acquire riches* while in their service, and to the contemporaneous fact that the proportionate increase of their wealth coincides very *remarkably* with the size of the successful Land-Grabbing Schemes.

If Land-Grabbing continue at the rate it has the past few years, how long will the people have any public domain? That already voted away would have given two million five hundred thousand familes 160 acres each. Does a conception of the magnitude of these plundering operations begin to dawn upon your minds? Two million five hundred thousand families might have been provided with homes and farms and removed from indigence and poverty by allowing them the use of these lands. They would have tilled and made them *productive*; where they will now be idle until the occupation of *contiguous* lands shall increase the market value to seven, ten and even *fifteen* dollars per acre, which these *same families* will be *obliged* to pay for them. If it were simply a scheme to develop that vast territory lying west of the States, so that it should prove a source of revenue to government and thus indirectly to the public, why did not the government *build* these roads and *retain possession* of them for the people instead of building them with the people's *money* and *property*, and then giving them to private individuals?

Hundreds of millions of dollars—*enough to pay the whole national debt*—have been swallowed up and forever lost to the people by the manner these Railroads have been subsidized and built. The development theory has set men wild, and with them *anything* is justifiable which will build a railroad into or through *unoccupied* territory. It is quite time that the people should set about devising means to *stop* this wholesale system of plundering the public, and I seriously mistake if in the next presidential election the voices of the people do not speak *in thunder tones* their disapproval of these practices.

Time does not permit me to dwell longer upon *this* part of the subject. But let me advise every one of you to obtain and carefully read the speech of Mr. Julian, to which I have referred. Also, permit me to mention that Mr. Julian is one of those who retired from Congressional duty on the 4th of March possessed of as little worldly goods as when he entered upon his public career—a fact which speaks more for his honor and integrity than can any word of mine.

Corporate Monopolies are the *legitimate* offspring of Landed Monopolies, and though perhaps not so *immediately* alarming in their audacity or mendacity, are nevertheless a *constant leech* upon *all* the producing interests of the country. Though in nearly every instance these are *theoretically* based in some supposed benefit to flow to the public, their *practice* is universally beyond their legitimate functions, and consequently detrimental. No government has any *legitimate* right to grant special privileges to *any* man, or any *set* of men, by which they may be enabled to acquire a superiority over other men, or by which they may be in position to *compel* others to pay exorbitant charges for the use they may desire to make of like privileges.

Special grants of, and protection to, corporate powers, are only permissable upon the supposition that the *people* will be benefited by them. Take, for instance, our great system of Railroads. Everybody knows of what immense benefit they have been to the country in a general sense. Government foreseeing their *necessity*, and being pressed forward by the great results of the initial roads, thought only of granting all the powers and aid required to build and put them in operation, never stopping to think that the time *might* come when they would oppress the people.

That time *has*, however, come, and one of the great questions of the immediate future will be how to curb and control the rapaciousness of these obese corporations. Few people realize the enormity of the frauds practised by them. They know that the roads are kept in operation and that they are obliged to pay such and such prices to make use of their accommodations. Here their knowledge ceases. They look upon the immense array of figures put forth from time to time, *pretending* to be statements for information, but which are, in *most* cases, statements for *deception*. None but experts can ever arrive at their *real* significance. They perhaps inform us that the Directory have been able to pay a *ten per cent. dividend.* But they do not inform us what the basis of that per cent. is. They do not tell us that their stocks are worth, 50, 75, 100 or 125 per cent. of their par value, because they are able to pay two, four, six, eight or ten per cent. dividends upon such value. They do not inform us that the par value of all their stocks is a *hundred* millions of dollars, while the real value of what it represents is perhaps no more than *ten* millions. Oh no; this information they wish concealed within the gorgeous parlors of the Directory. Permit me to point out how the producing interests of the country are *swindled* out of their hard-earned products by these *patents* upon their industry, by giving some cases in point. In 1891, the capital stock of the Cleveland, Painesville and Ashtabula Railroad was three million dollars; an eight per cent. dividend required that its patrons should pay to that road during a year two hundred and forty thousand dollars in excess of its actual working expenses. In 1867, or in six years, the capital stock was increased to three and a quarter times its original amount, or to nine millions seven hundred and fifty thousand dollars. To pay an eight per cent. dividend upon this increase, required that this Company should extort from its patrons the large sum of five hundred and forty thousand dollars, which, added to the dividend on its *original* capital stock, increased it to twenty-six per cent. So that upon every dollar of actual investment the holders of said stocks in the year 1857, and every year thereafter, received *twenty-six* per cent.

Is it to be wondered that everybody who knows anything about railroad management is *convinced* of the desirability of such stocks?

Again: From New York to Chicago, via the New York Central and Lake Shore Roads, is 982 miles. These roads were built at a cost of about eighty-four and a half millions dollars. The amount of their present stock, upon which there is paid eight per cent. per annum dividends, is one hundred and sixty-four million dollars. To pay the dividends upon their cost requires six millions seven hundred and fifty thousand dollars. To pay the dividend upon their present stock requires twelve millions eight hundred thousand dollars, or in other words, these Companies must *steal from the people* the *enormous* amount of six million dollars annually, that they may be able to pay to the holders of their stocks their regular dividends.

Allowing that there are fifty-five thousand miles of railroads in the country, and calculating them upon the basis of these last mentioned, at what enormous an array of figures do we arrive. The cost of all the railroads would be the sum of four billions seven hundred thousand millions. And supposing all their stocks to have been watered to the extent previously calculated, and that eight per cent. dividends are paid thereon, we find that there must be added to the charges collected from the people to pay operating expenses and legitimate interest upon their original cost, the enormous sum of *three hundred and fifty* millions dollars.

What think you, laboring, wealth-producing people of the United States, of a government which granted franchises to a few individuals by which they may be able not only to extract from your hard earnings some four hundred million dollars interest upon their actual investments, but also *to steal the further* sum of three hundred and fifty million dollars? When all of you realize the enormity of *these swindles* which are practiced upon you by the *sanction* of the government, do you think you will endure it patiently?

I would also call your attention to another interesting bit of fact. All these immense sums come either *directly* or *indirectly* from the laboring classes. Why so? Because the middle-men who transact all the business between the producer and consumer of the respective articles of commerce, must make their profits, whether the railroads swindle the people or not. None of it comes from them. Not at all They are beyond the reach of this rapaciousness. But the weary laborer when he contemplates the results of his year's *hard* work, which he has just shipped to market, *knows* that they will net him just so much less than the market price of them as these *railroads* are pleased to charge him for transportation.

Should government levy a tax of ten cents per bushel upon wheat or corn it would rouse the people to revolt, but these gigantic *Monopolies* may levy ten cents per bushel extra upon both wheat and corn, or five dollars a ton extra on coal, to enable them to pay dividends on fictitious stocks, and never a word is said. What applies to the producer of wheat and corn and coal also applies with *equal* force to all other producers. They realize just so much *less* for their products than they *should*, as they are compelled to pay *more* than they ought for costs of transportation.

Do you realize the magnitude of this matter? The government has placed these Railroad Companies in the position to filch from you an amount *equal to that required* to *maintain* itself, and *which*, if so applied, would relieve you from *all* kinds of taxation.

By Section VIII., Paragraph 1, of the Constitution of the United States, government is granted the power to provide for the *general welfare*. Does the kind of legislation referred to provide for the general welfare? No, a thousand times no. The general welfare is by it *sacrificed*, and a few *railroad* managers made *money-kings*, who are ambitious to obtain the power to control *not only* the condition of the *producing* and *consuming* people, but also to dictate to the government which created them—a more unlimited, unwarrantable, unjustifiable and insolent ambition and contempt for the public than was that of an Alexander or a Napoleon.

Listen to what the Lancaster (Penn.) Intelligencer says of perhaps the most corrupt of all railroad monopolies, the Pennsylvania Central Railroad:

" The Pennsylvania Central have nominally bought up a majority of the members of the legislature, who have bound themselves to vote as they may be directed. The agents of the railroad could be seen at all times in the loby or on the floor of the two houses watching the course of legislation, and forwarding or checking the passage of bills. No men in Harrisburgh are better known and none have a more distinctive and well recognized avocation than these lobby agents of the Pennsylvania Railroad. They have learned by long experience how to ply their foul trade successfully, and are adepts in all the arts of intrigue, and skilled in every species of corruption and bribery."

Not long since, when the question of adjournment was before the legislature, a member rose and said in effect: "*If Thos. Scott has no more business with the legislature, I think we should adjourn.*" Now this Thos. Scott is the Vice-President and the active manager of the affairs of this road Mr. Scott lately became President of the Union Pacific, and thus virtually controls a line of railroad extending from New York to

San Francisco, by which immense power, it is said, he intends also to control the next Presidential Election. It *remains* to be seen whether the working men and women of this country will continue *criminally* blind to their interests and permit such a scheme to be consummated. Whatever party Thos. Scott supports, may be set down as certain to be entirely antagonistic to their interest, no matter by what professions they may seek to obtain support.

What is true of the Pennsylvania Central Railroad Company and its managers, is true to a greater or less degree of *every* railroad company in the country; and not only of every railroad company but of *every other monopoly* which flourishes at the *expense* of the *productive* interests of the country, at whose expense *all monopolies must flourish*, if they flourish at all. The power these corporations possess is full of danger to the freedom of this country. Combined, they could control all legislation, and carry every election. The New York Herald not long since spoke editorially thus : " Now it is possible the American people may not be alarmed at the probable effects a combination of capital and influence of these vast railroad corporations may have upon the future of the country, upon the permanency of its institutions and the perpetuity of its political liberties ; but, in view of *possible* contingencies, we think we are justified in cautioning the people against the possible creation of a railroad oligarchy here who may prove as dangerous to the nation as was the Southern cotton oligarchy in times past."

" This subject is one of considerable interest to the American people, and the election of members to the next Congress should be graduated accordingly."

We know that the Pennsylvania Railroad Company controls the legislature of the State ; that the Central and Erie combined can control that of New York ; the Baltimore and Ohio that of Maryland, that all the Railroad interests of *every* State can control the Legislatures of their respective States, and that the *combined* Railroad Interests of all the States can control Congress.

The National Banking System is another element of power which is *too powerful* to be ignored. Its representatives even now assume to *dictate* to Congress upon measures of finance. 'Tis true this system was inaugurated in an hour of national peril and necessity. It looked well, it worked well, and all was serene with the public, for plenty of money meant *quick* transit, *rapid* sales and facilities in exchange. But the public now begin to understand that the Bankers are *too* happy over their privileges, which permit a double means of obtaining the people's money. They obtain interest from the people on deposits of Government Bonds, and also from the people triple interest on their circulation which they obtain by means of their Bonds. It was a *good day* for the Bankers, and at that time it was the *best thing* the government could do. Every one was happy *then*. The times, however, are changed. Everybody is *not* happy now. The people are not happy over the payment every year of thirty millions of dollars to these banks, in consideration for their having stepped forward to the assistance of the government in its time of need. The people remember that they too stepped forward and offered their lives without consideration. The banks have been well paid, and should retire from their unequal privileges *satisfied* with their gains, and be no longer permitted to remain patented charges upon the industries of the country. The yearly profit of these Banks, which they make from the use of a currency for which the people are in a measure responsible, is sufficient to pay the entire expenses of our National Government. Thus we have two distinct monopolies, each of whose profits are equal to all the expenses of the Federal Government. Please think of that!

The interests of *all* monopolies are mutual. To attack *one* is to put them *all* on the defence. Should the Bank and Railroad Interests of the country *combine*—and there is an effort now being made to that end—what would not they be able to do? This is a matter of the most *serious* import, which tends to a despotism *more* intolerable than that exercised by any of the monarchies of the old world.

The inquiry comes up: How shall this danger be averted or controlled? Experience teaches that there can be *no* legislation limiting their privileges that can not be rendered impotent or be evaded by them. We may not hope for relief from *this* source. There is but one resort left. Since they *will trespass* upon the welfare of the *entire* people to their own aggrandisement, paying no attention and giving no thought to their rights, they must be dispossessed of their power. Primarily they were permitted for the public good. They were constructed and the public welfare was subserved. The public welfare now demands that they shall not become *hereditary* drains upon the vitality of the country.

But, says one, government has no right to take the railroads away from these thieving corporations. The government of the United States has the Constitutional right to do *anything* which the public welfare demands, and the Human Rights of the people *demand* that they shall not be made to pay twenty dollars to be transported from New York to Chicago when the cost is but five, the other fifteen going to promote the interests of a would-be-despotism, which is endeavoring to fasten itself upon the country.

The same results which have followed the inauguration of our Postal System for the transportation of the people's letters would also follow a *like* system extended to the transportation of their merchandise and themselves. If government had the right to take the *former* from private hands, so also has it the power to take the *latter*, and the exigency is a thousand times more formidable and urgent.

Under a *proper* Civil Service the railroads of the United States would be managed with all the *regularity* which pertains to the mails, and, with the official intgerity which, as a rule, characterizes our Postal, Military and Naval Service.

We lay it down as a general proposition that *all* legislation of the *special order* kind, which grants rights or privileges to individuals or corporations, to do what they could not *without* such grant, is a *monopoly* to be *sustained* at the *expense* of the *industrial* or *productive* classes.

All special legislation, I do not care of what *kind* or *grade*, or what *interest* it is to *protect* or *maintain*, is a *direct* blow at the wealth-producing people, for in the *end* the entire benefit which accrues to such interest, comes home to *their* doors and is by *them* paid. Equality which the Constitution pre-supposes among the people, and which it was framed to maintain, is an *impossibility* under *any* such practices, and it is for *this* reason that I have entered my protest *against* everything of the kind which is in our present governmental systems.

I call the system of Protective Tariff a *huge* fallacy, gotten up by the *money* interests to compel *labor* to maintain pursuits which it is assumed could not otherwise exist. The *results* of this system tersely stated are these: It interferes with the natural demand and supply—the natural ebb and flow—of the products of the world, by imposing upon certain of them such tribute that it is impracticable for them to get to the locality of natural demand, so that a special few who inhabit that locality are enabled to produce the same by a greatly increased cost, which the consumer must pay in order to obtain them.

It does not matter how much this plain statement may be *twisted* and *bent* by the alluring sophistries and glittering generalities of the *Protected*, it can never be robbed of its force as a statement, and can *never* be gainsaid. If it be any general benefit for a thousand people to pay one person fifty per cent. more for a desired article than it could be obtained for from a *foreign* producer, simply because it is of *home* production, we should be most happy to hear the demonstration. The argument used is, that the *one* man being protected in the manufacture of *this* article can give employment to a certain number of laborers, who in turn become the consumers of the products of these thousand people. But to make this position tenable it must be proved that laborers *thus* employed, would not be able to apply themselves to *any other* labor than the production of the article in question. This investigation leads to such an intricacy of cause and effect, and of reactionary benefit, that those who attempt to make it, prefer to *accept* the declaration that protection is a good thing to have, *rather* than acknowledge themselves lost in the *fog* and *obscurity* which they are asked to explore to determine the fact of the case.

But, says the Protectionist, pretending to speak in the interests of the laborer, when it is his own which are in jeopardy, would you place the *laboring* classes of this country in competition with the *pauper* labor of Europe. Not by any means. But I will tell you, Mr. Protectionist, what you are doing. You are putting the laboring classes of this country in a *position* which will very soon reduce them to the *condition* which you call pauper labor of other countries, for your practice tends to build up monopolies to which labor becomes every year more and more subservient.

The same results will follow in this country which have obtained in England, which, of all countries of the world, has most thoroughly tested this matter—because the greatest manufacturing country of the world—and her experience is literally conclusive. Let us glance at this beautiful system as practiced there. Its history gives some reliable data more instructive than all the essays of a thousand political econ omists, with all their theories of what might, could, would or should be, if something were to occur which has not and never can. It is no doubt one of the most self-satisfactory things in the world to figure national prosperity, compelling the figures to fit the ends desired, and forgetting to-day the facts of yesterday.

Mons. Guizot speaking in the French Corps Legislatiff, in 1846, said that the free trade policy of England had three results.

1st. It *maintained* and *augmented* the amount of labor.

2d. It *lowered* the prices of the necessaries of life of the laboring classes.

3d. It *diminishes* the terrible oscillations to which those prices were exposed.

In the following year, in consequence of the free-trade *vs.* protec tionist excitement, certain statistics were laid before the English House of Commons, more particularly as to plate-glass, the manufacturers of which had loudly declaimed that free-trade would ruin them, asserting that the continued existence of their business had only been insured by by protection. The statistics were as follows:

In the year 1819 the duty was 98 shillings per cwt., the price per foot was 25 shillings with weekly sales of 3,000 feet. In 1829 the duty was reduced to 60 shillings; the price fell to 12 shillings per foot, with weekly sales of 5,000 feet. In 1849 the duty was removed; the price fell to 5 shillings per foot, with weekly sales of 10,000 feet. In 1836, when the duty was 60 shillings per foot, there 2,500 hands employed and 250,000 pounds sterling invested in the manufacture. In 1849, when there was no duty, there were 12,000 hands employed and 1,000,000 pounds sterling invested in its manufacture.

There was no English plate-glass exported to the United States in 1846, while in 1847 more was so exported than *to all the rest of the world* in 1846.

Comment on the above figures seems altogether superfluous, for the reason that *nothing* that can be said can present a *stronger* case in favor of free trade. We may, however, point out that from 1819 to 1827, under a protective tariff, lowering the duty 30 per cent. reduced the price of the article 52 per cent., and increased its weekly sales 66 per cent. We deduce from this a consumption of 66 per cent. more under the 60s. per cwt. duty than under the 98s. per cwt. duty, and that there were 66 per cent. more laborers engaged in the manufacture under the *lesser* tariff than under the *greater*.

Pursuing still further the official figures, we find that in the year 1847, when *all* the duty was taken off, the amount of labor engaged in the manufacture increased 480 per cent., as compared with the year 1836, when the duty was 60s. per cwt.

It is also notable that the increase in consumption and productiveness followed *exactly* in the wake of the *reduction* in the tariff.

We will now turn to the repeal of the corn laws in England, which was made a test case as to the merits of free trade, the conflict lasting from 1842 to 1846. In 1842 there was a sliding scale of duties in force, that is to say, the duty varied according to the price of corn ; the average of the duty was, however, 16s. per qr. This scale of duties lasted until 1846, when it was lowered to an average of 4s. per qr. ; the average amount of duty collected under the first-named tariff being £372,500 per annum, while in 1849, under a nominal tariff, the duty collected was £615,814 per annum.

The commencement of the free trade agitation found Sir Robert Peel, the Duke of Welliignton and Mr. Gladstone protectionists. In 1846, Sir Robert Peel, speaking in favor of a reduction of the tariff on corn, renounced his protectionist ideas, and became a free trader. In his speech he said he claimed the principle of *yielding* both to the *force of argument* and *conviction*, and of *acting* on the results of *enlarged experience;* and that " he was about to review the duties which applied to many articles the produce and manufacture of other States ; that for the last three years, since the policy of acting on the principle of repealing and reducing certain duties had been acknowledged, there had been *increased* productiveness of revenue, *increased* demand for labor, *increased* commerce, as well as *comfort, contentment* and *peace* in the country, and he was about to proceed on the assumption that the repeal of *prohibitory* and the relaxation of *protective* tariffs is in itself a wise principle."

In 1846, Lord Russell said, "He believed it would have been better for the English farmers if the duty on imported corn had been reduced still lower in 1842."

And the Duke of Wellington voted for the reduction of the duty on corn. In 1815 Mr. Bennett (member of Parliament for Wiltshire) said that "Farmers could not grow wheat under a less protective duty than 96s. a quarter, yet he had since supported a minister who proposed to levy 56s. a quarter."

Mr. Gladstone, who, in 1842, opposed Lord Morpeth's free trade measures, has since become one of the most prominent of free trade champions.

The Earl of Derby, who had been a strenuous opposer of free trade, said, in the House of Commons in 1852, "That after the decision of the country in the recent elections, in favor of free trade, he was prepared to bow to its decisions." And in the same year the Queen in her speech *congratulated* Parliament on the *beneficial* results of *free trade* legislation.

We thus gather that free trade has not only given satisfaction to the *people* wherever it has been practiced, but has absolutely *convinced* its very opponents. In the matter of corn, at the very commencement of the free-trade agitation, the duty was 96s. per quarter; at the close and triumph of free trade it was 1s. a quarter, the results of each reduction only paving the way for a still greater one; had the opponents of free trade been able to show injurious effects from any one reduction of the tariff, the downward movement would have ceased, and probably a reaction have set in.

But the *primary* and *insuperable* objection to the policy of protection is, that under it *equality* to all citizens is impossible. Whatever favorably *appearing* argument may be adduced in its favor, tried by *this* comprehensive principle, it will surely fall to the ground. There is a no more *fatal* idea than that *high* prices are an evidence of prosperity. The very *reverse* is really the case. Real wealth and prosperity do not consist in high prices, but in the *quantities* which are actually possessed. Prices under a protective policy, which, is at all times open to change, must *always* fluctuate with every such change. A person *rich* this year may become *poor* next. Disaster, destruction, ruin and general alarm and want of confidence have always followed changes in the protective policy in this country. Prices which, under protection, are stimulated to *undue* proportions, on the removal or reduction of tariffs, fall as far *below* the actual mean as they were *above* it. High prices at the expense of permanency *are not* the ultimatum to be sought by *any* people of *any* country. The true point to seek is, the employment of industries in *those* directions *where most* can be produced at *least* expense, in the accumulation of the products of which, the country must become more rapidly wealthy than in the production of the *least* at the *greatest* expense.

If by protection this country become *enriched* at the expense of England, there would be a chance for a anrgument for protection : but such is not the case. The total " impositions" made on importations is a *direct* tax upon *one* part of the people for the benefit of the other part, but which results in benefit to nobody. Those whom it is supposed to benefit would be better off were they engaged in some pursuits which would be *self-supporting* and which if they did not bring them so large *present* wages, would have the *greater* advantage of permanency. It is no particular object, and we consider it an *empty honor*, for this country to manufacture articles at a cost of one hundred per cent. over what the same are produced elsewhere for ; the only object gained being, that we may be able to say that they are produced at home, and that we pay double price that they may be thus produced.

The fallacies of protection are well illustrated by supposing that a dozen individuals, possessed of a thousand dollars each, should attempt to get rich by gambling among themselves. The sum total of their funds would be no larger if it were finally in the hands of one of their number. To *add* to their money they must *win* from some *outside* party. Protecting industries works similar results. It compels *one* part of the people to gamble with *another* part and finally results in the accumulation of all the wealth of the country in the hands of the few. It is impossible to add to the wealth of the country by making its farmer pay large prices to its manufacturers. Large products over consumption sent to other countries are the desideratum, our own citizens being the agents for their transportation. If the various interests of a country only produce a sufficient amount to meet the demands among themselves, how can they add to the aggregate wealth?

What would the manufacturers of Massachusetts say, were it attempted to enforce protection to the *farmers* of the state by levying a fifty per cent duty on Western produce, in order that *they* might be able to compete with the Western farmer and thus supply *all* the subsistence there used? Or what would Illinois say, were everything which she requires of Massachusetts, compelled to pay an *equal* duty before it could reach her for consumption. It is true the Constitution prohibits such a thing, but what better *principle* is followed in applying that which is prohibited as between states to the Commercial intercourse between nations? Protection is a short-sighted unprincipled and unreasonable policy and like land-grabbing, tends to the establishment of monopolies.

In the great problem of the assimilation of the world's interests, which is being rapidly solved, it must be learned that the United States is as yet but *part* of the world, and that the *best* interests of *individual* nations are subserved when the *best* interests of *all* nations are consulted. The same rule holds good in this application that is true in regard to the individuals of a country; the best interests of each lie in promoting the best interests of all. Under this rule, carried to its *perfect* working, the industries of the world would localize, where *each* would produce the most of its peculiar products at the *least* average cost, which being given over to commerce, would be transported to such parts of the world as demand them in exchange for products produced by *its* local ized industries in the *greatest* quantities at the least cost. Thus would be introduced a grand system of economy, which would result in fixed and unchangeable channels of commerce, and the employment of the industries of the whole world according to the *natural* law of demand and supply, which *cannot* produce alternate flood and dearth.

If tariffs for the protection of *industries* are not admissible upon the principle of equality, are they any less to be *deprecated* as systems of *revenue?* Here we touch a point upon which the people are very sensitive, and justly so. The levying of duties upon imported goods is an *indirect* way of taxing that portion of the people who *consume* such goods. The amount obtained by this most unequal and indirect manner of taxing the people was, for the last fiscal year, the large sum of one hundred and ninety-four millions four hundred and forty-eight thousand four hundred and twenty-seven dollars, *every dollar* of which was an *additional tax* gathered from the *individuals* who *finally* purchased and consumed such imports. This would not have been important had it fallen *equally* upon the *taxable* property of the country, upon which general taxes are levied; but one hundred millions of this was collected from woolens, cottons, sugar, molasses, coffee and tea, all of which the *poorest* laborers, who should pay no tax, in common with the *richest* landlords are nearly equal consumers. Thus every laboring man was compelled to pay his ten, twenty or fifty dollars to the government, in proportion to the number of his family.

Working men and women of the United States! how like you this manner of filching your hard-earned dollars under the *fraudulent* name of raising a revenue? It is no wonder that your wages will scarcely meet your families' necessities, when you are thus compelled to pay such *sums* upon the most *common staple* articles of general consumption. It is no wonder you continue to be laborers, never being able to become producers upon your own account, when you who *should not*, and under general and just principles of taxation, *would not*, be called upon to pay a *single* dollar as a *direct* tax, are thus burdened.

Nor are the other means to which government resorts for support, entitled to much more consideration. There is *no* equality for the people in *any* of them, and it is quite evident that the system of revenue for the support of government *must* be remodeled so as to *fall* where it *properly* belongs—*upon the taxable property of the country.* This done, and a sound financial system inaugurated, the laboring classes would begin to be leveled up to a medium and the upper classes to be leveled down to the same basis of material prosperity.

A system of taxation for the maintenance of government should be devised by which one set of officials should collect all the monies which are to be gathered, and thereby introduce a *grand system of economy,* which would save at least *three-fourths* of the expense now incurred by the almost innumerable methods which obtain the people's money without their realizing the amounts they pay. All these things the laboring classes must first understand and then rectify. They will *never* attain *anything* approaching equality in the manner through which government is now administered. Never will the laboring classes become *independent* of the *wealthy* classes, until the *freedom, equality* and *justice* which are the birthright of *every* citizen of the United States are possible of attainment under their government.

Having thus passed in review the Land, Protection and Revenue systems of the country, which, with the finance system, complete the *foundation* on which labor and capital build, the relations which these sustain to each other as represented in practice, can be considered.

A stream can never rise higher than its source except by artificial means. If artificial means are used to elevate the stream above its source, when they are removed, changed or decayed, it will fall to its natural level. This principle holds good in all the varied operations of mind as well as matter. The stability of everything which occupies *unnatural* and *inconsistent* positions through *artificial* and *extraneous* means is never assured—is at all times liable to change, and is ever in danger of present, and certain of ultimate dethronement.

Such is the position of *capital* to *labor* in this country. Labor is the *direct* source of *all* capital and has *produced* all capital. But by the means of *unphilosophic, unnatural* and *unequal* laws capital has *usurped* a position *higher* than its source, and not only *occupies* it, but assumes to *dictate* to and control labor. The responsibility for this condition should not be charged upon the representatives of capital; neither does its cause exist *in* capital or in the capitalist. It is further back than they. *It is in the people* who have *constructed* society and government upon *false principles*, which being administered, permit all the *ills* of which they complain.

If the Constitution and laws of a country make possible certain things, which may be seized upon by a few persons to the injury of all the rest, it can scarcely be expected but there will be those willing to take advantage of it. Were this audience shown that by pursuing a certain course, which would not be in conflict with any existing law— no matter how much there should be law to prevent it—that each one of them could in a given time accumulate a *fortune*, I do not think there are many who would forego the opportunity because it would be at the *expense* of others or of the country.

Therefore, when the labor interest cries out against the oppression of capital, it must remember that had their places been reversed the *labor-ers* instead of the capitalists would have been the oppressing power. It is a great thing for people to be able to look at *both* sides of a question—to see how it would be were it "my bull which had gored your ox."

The cause being in the *people* they must *look to themselves* for the remedy, and they must apply it before they may expect to see their rights adjusted. Between the *real* interests of labor and capital there is an *entire harmony*. Their *true* interests lie in each rendering *complete justice* to the other. In the understanding of *this* point lies the *solution* of the present question. *Strife* may continue—*war* even, may come of strife, but for all that the settlement must follow from a proper adjustment of their relations upon principle.

I am sorry that there is class of self-styled reformers who perpetually stir up strife, making interests antagonistic, and thus more widely separating them. These persons prate with considerable volubility of the *terrible condition* into which things have fallen. As a rule they belong to that class who, being upon the outskirts of society, wait, Micawber-like, for something to turn up by which they may ride into position. But do they present *remedies* for the ills they picture so graphically? Do they tell *whence* they come or *whither* they should go? Let me warn the laborers to beware of such persons; they are wolves in sheep's clothing, who would make *use* of the occasion that they may suck their blood.

The true friends of humanity are they who *find the causes* of their ills and teach them their *remedies*. There is no such obscurity about the conditions of society as to make it impossible for its members to comprehend their defects. But the *laboring* classes being *compelled* to *continuous* industry by these defects, do not have the opportunity to search for the hidden causes. They see others fatten from their labor year after year, and without inquiry why these things are so, at once *jump* to the conclusion that they are the subjects of *personal* tyranny which is *determined* forever to keep them in this condition of vassalage. *This* drives the laborers to resistence; they set about forming themselves into combinations to control hours of labor and wages, not yet comprehending that these are but *remedies*, *not* cures. Society has tried *remedies* long enough. They require to be used continually. *Prevention* is what the people demand, and prevention they *must, will* and *shall* have. But the dose for the cure should not be administered in such large proportions as to prove *worse* than the disease. While endeavoring to *prevent* the ills of society, care must be taken that its *life* is not put in jeopardy.

The judicious architect provides the material for the new, before pulling down the old, and thus leaves no unnecessary interval for anarchy to step in and occupy. Before breaking up the *present* construction of society by *revolution*, which would end in anarchy and confusion, from which better condition might possibly spring, the better condition should be prepared and by general consent *substituted* therefor. Surely, there need be no alarm among the laboring classes. This is a republican form of government, in which *all men* at least, are equal in political power. Political power consists in a majority of votes cast. Of what have the male laboring classes to complain? They *outnumber* and can consequently *outvote* the capitalist class, *ten to one*, and *that* too without turning repeaters, though I am sorry to say the repeaters are generally laborers. Though this is lamentably true, it does not follow that all laborers are repeaters, any more than it formerly did that all Democrats were horse thieves, for insinuating which, a prominent Whig was once called to account. Said the Whig, I did *not* say that *all* Democrats were horse-thieves, but I *did* say that all horse-thieves were Democrats, and for authority I refer to the political statistics of prisons.

I ask the Labor Party of the United States of what have you to complain? I will tell you what. You have *yourselves* of whom to complain, and the *complaint* is a most *grievous* one—one which should ever stand in *condemnation* over you until you shall have *repented* in sack-cloth and ashes. You have permitted the government of this country to be *wrenched* from your grasp, and *year after year* you still permit the few who *hold* it to your detriment to continue their encroachments upon your *liberties* and *rights*. You have *made your own beds* and now you complain of others because you have not *better* ones in which to lie. Where are your friends—your leaders—who dare stand forth and tell you the *truth?* 'Tis true they make fine stump-speeches, but nothing comes of them.

The Labor Party need to *learn* some *wholesome* truths which will *teach* them *when* learned, to look for their redemption from an *entirely* different source to that they have been seeking. It will not avail you to attempt to deal with the contingencies of the present, resorting to small expedients to enable you to dodge along, merely escaping complete shipwreck, to be *again* forced, the next day week or year, to the *same*, to escape *like* shoals.

I have told you that the *foundations* upon which society is built are *imperfect*; of what use is it to continually reform the frame work, and the finish, so long as this foundation remains? Society expresses itself through government. Public opinion is capable of many things but it is *powerless* at present, to *redress* grievances, *correct* errors and *right* wrongs which come of law unless it direct that to be done by proper forms of law.

In proper legislation, then, must the preventative of existing ills be sought, and to *this* end should the Labor Party turn *all* its attention and waste *no more time* and *strength* in *vain* denunciations and foundationless recriminations. Proper *legislation* supposes proper *legistators* and these it is your duty to select and elect. Most of your present legislators State and National, have shown themselves *incompetent* to the work *you* require performed. Waste no more time upon them. *Leave* them to seek their level and *turn* you to others who will *not lose sight* of *your interests* and allow them to *sink* in the *allurements* which place and power present. You must not expect those who are not of you to appreciate your needs. Choose from among *yourselves* and you will not go *far astray.* There are most noble exceptions among those reared in luxury, whose hearts feel your conditions as keenly as you do. These will be your best advocates; but *see to it* that *not a vote* is again worse than withheld.

Further, permit me to call your attention to an important fact: that quite four-fifths of your legislators are lawyers. While we must confess to entertaining the highest respect for them as lawyers, we must be permitted to question if all governmental sagacity is confined to them. They are rarely comprehensive, philosophical and progressive, but rather sticklers for the *specialties* and *forms* to which they were trained and to which, in their *practice* they confine themselves. They practice from *policy* to gain certain ends, and resort to all the quibbles possible to defeat their opponents. They do not practice *from principles* to demonstrate their justice. Consequently lawyers are *not* the best material for legislators, and *this* the Labor Party should specially remember. But I should fail in my duty as a professed friend of humanity, did I not endeavor to point out, that all the results which can be obtained through proper legislation are of but *secondary* importance, yea, of *no* importance except as *means* to be used that *greater* and *better* ends may be reached. One basal fact—one which is greater than all others within humanity— which is entirely ignored in all material practices, *must* be placed as the *foundation* of the perfect structure which you propose to erect. *That* fact is the fact of the COMMON BROTHERHOOD OF THE HUMAN RACE. If this recognition is wanting in your propositions, they had better never be made. This is the touch-stone by which all legislation, all administration and all action should be tested and directed, failing in which a fatal error is committed which will poison all action.

The first duty of every living being, in all things in which people meet and mingle, is to accept the fact that *every other* human being is the offspring of the *same* Almighty power, and *equally* entitled to human rights with himself, and that it can make *no* difference in *this* fact if his *skin* be black, if he be a *pagan* or a *Jew, Christian* or *infidel, spiritualist, materialist* or a *nothingarian*, or *even a woman*. In behalf of this latter class, permit me to express a growing hope for the labor party, grounded upon the fact that many of its prominent men acknowledge the equality of civil, political and social rights.

In the first instance, the question of labor and capital is one of material prosperity and equality; secondly, it reacts upon *all other* human interests—intellectual, moral, physical and religious. None of them can flourish among a people burdened by material want. Either extreme of material interest is deleterious to the *best* advancement of *all* other interests. In the *mean* between the two extremes—in calling up those below and leveling down those above—is found the *perfect* harmony of all.

Because material acquirement has *preceded* all other acquirement, the mistake is made of giving it the most *prominent* position among the several interests. This mistake is the bane of society; for it must be apparent to all *considerate* minds that *capital* being the *result* of labor, is nothing more than the *means* to *further* and *greater* ends. The attainment of great *wealth* will not be the principal aim of the people of the future. It will only be considered that by which *higher* purposes may be gained. It was not until quite recently that the fact of a continuous life was any more than *theoretically* accepted by a few people. The large majority of *all* people still accept it as a theory only. Their practices are such as would naturally obtain, were it *certain* that this life is *all there is* of existence, and that the death of the body is the end of man.

Whatever people may *profess* to believe, their *practice* shows that purely material ends are all they really seek—the gratification of physical desires, and obtaining material comforts and pleasures. A conviction—a real faith—is, however, stealing into the consciousness of humanity that what is termed *death* is only a *change* in the conditions of *life*, by which that portion of individuality which constitutes the veritable man or woman is entered upon a *broader* sphere of existence. As this faith, this knowledge, grows in the human soul, so also will there come a change in the purposes and aims of life. That wealth which will be of most use and benefit when the higher life is entered, will be sought and obtained.

Humanity, when *analytically* considered, is still in its *babyhood*. This becomes evident when we observe how *few* there are who seek the *higher* objects of attainment—intellectual, moral and spiritual wealth. These are the *only* kind of capital with which the pursuits of the future can be begun. Why, then, should humanity, in its greed for *material* wealth, lose all *sight* of, and *care* for, these. If our children are trained for the practical after life, so also should humanity adopt the philosophy of education and train for *their* after life. 'Tis true, this most important fact of life is ignored in government, and *here* is the cause of its failure to meet the requirements of humanity. People demand what they do not really comprehend, but still they know their real wants are unsupplied. Here do we also find that *no* government can be a perfect government which ignores any department of human life—which is not only physical, but mental, moral and religious.

In a *true* condition of society there would be *no such thing as individual* wealth. There would be the wealth of the *community* made use of for the *benefit* of the community. The *extreme* of individual wealth and poverty is in *direct* antagonism to a democratic government, which best expressed is: *the greatest good of the greatest number.* What is for the greatest good of the greatest number in the general sense is also for the *best* interests of every individual and of the whole number. No real benefit can flow to *any* individual by an *apparent* gain through *unjust* means.

Under a system of *exact* justice no person can ever possess what he did not himself produce, or which he did not obtain by a just exchange of something which he did produce. All great accumulations of wealth, in the *abstract* sense, were stolen from the producers. Thus *one* person may unjustly obtain what required a *thousand* persons all their lives to produce. What kind of justice is this to flourish as it does in these days when the religion of Jesus is the *external* garb worn by so great a part of humanity?

I tell you that the *first principles of life* have been *utterly* lost sight of, and that we are floundering about in the great ocean of material infidelity. If we would attain to better things we must stop short in our present course and come back to the point of departure, to wit: to the fact that we are a community of brothers and sisters, owning one Father, the Supreme Ruler of all, and build from that greatest of all human facts.

A party which would become successful and remain in power, must *plant* itself in *this* fact and never lose sight of it in its legislation. It must at all times be *firm* in the advocacy of *all* growth and reform which come from the *action* of fundamental principles. All *sectionalism,* all *favoritism,* all *specialism* must be swallowed in the greater interests of the whole. Whatever would detract from the good of the whole, no matter how much supposed *individual* or *local* benefit it promises, *must* be discountenanced.

If such a party is not shortly organized, conditions will develop which will make it a *necessity,* even *without* organization. It will arise as if by *magic* out of the exigencies of the times, and leaders will rise and come to the front as though heaven-directed, and they will be received by the people with acclamation. The trickery and fraud of elections even, may be suddenly dispensed with, and those will direct who have the inherent right to command, which will be recognized and hailed by the people, long sought and at last obtained. The whole sub-strata of society, in its social and political relations, is in ferment. The terrific strifes which *have* been and *are* being waged, lift the weight of *antecedents* and *customs* from the masses, and they begin to *rise*, demanding *such* recognition as has been and still is *denied* them. The Moses who shall divide the waters of the Red Sea that separates them from *their* Canaan will be their divinely appointed leader whom to oppose will be futile.

A *new order* of things is demanded, and a *new order* there will be, in which common honesty may be consistently sought. There are but *two* ways by which this can come. *One* through violent disruption and destruction of present systems, and temporary anarchy as the result; the other through the *scientific* organization and remodeling of society and *harmonized* conditions. The first will surely come if the people are not rapidly and properly instructed in the scientific needs of society. Nearly every result which is sought to be gained, except in government, is first tried by the tests of science. But in *this*, the most important feature of civilization, we blunder along either partially or totally blind-folded by custom or prejudice, which we so quietly and consistently lay aside in all things else.

There are a *variety of special* questions which arise from the *general* ones to which we have called attention remaining untouched, every one of which is of sufficient importance to command the earnest consideration of all people who have any comprehension of the changes which are to come to this people in the immediate future.

It may be objected to what I have said, that it contains more of destruction than of construction. This, perhaps, is true. It was not my purpose to propose forms by which better things can be had, but rather to call your attention to the principles which have been violated, the results of which are our present inequalities. I have said that these principles must be understood and given expression to through legislation that the present ills may turn to future good. Any other course than this lies through temporary anarchy, which I should regret to think a necessary cure.

In conclusion, I will but lay down a general rule, which can always be relied upon to guide the inquirer to correct conclusions, let the question be what it may, upon whatever subject. All questions which can arise are comprehended in the following:

They are questions of freedom; they are questions of equality, or they are questions of justice.

Reduced to these simple propositions, *every* person becomes a *competent* and, as nearly as may be, a *perfect* judge of all conditions to which society in its evolution is subject. They have but to ask is this compatible with freedom; is this consistent with equality, or is this just? If the mind relieve itself from the dominion of authority, custom and prejudice, it will encounter *no* difficulty in arriving at *legitimate* deductions whenever questioned.

Then let every person who would be counted among the consistent, plant himself upon the principle of human equality, and while demanding for himself all human rights, conceding to all others equal human rights. If but a nucleus of such persons is formed at first, their influence will be contagious, and will rapidly spread, until the time come when this people will have become repossessed of the rights of which they have permitted themselves to be unwarrantably robbed. Then may the ultimate of a republican form of government be attained, and its happy citizens labor together in harmony for the common advancement of humanity.

ECONOMICS

(2)

A Speech on the Impending Revolution . . . 1872.

Reprinted in *Woodhull & Claflin's Weekly* (Nov. 1, 1873, pp. 2-7, 12-15).

Freedom ! Equality !! Justice !!!
These three; but the greatest of these is Justice.

A SPEECH

ON THE

Impending Revolution,

DELIVERED IN

Music Hall, Boston, Thursday, Feb. 1, 1872,

AND THE

Academy of Music, New York, Feb. 20, 1872,

BY

VICTORIA C. WOODHULL.

NEW YORK :
WOODHULL, CLAFLIN & CO., PUBLISHERS,
No. 44 Broad Street.

1872.

THE

IMPENDING REVOLUTION.

Standing upon the apex of the nineteenth century, we look backward through the historic era, and in the distant, dim past catch sight of the feeble outreachings of the roots of humanity, which during thousands of years have evolved into the magnificent civilization by which we are surrounded. Mighty nations have risen and fallen; empires have gathered and wasted; races and peoples have evolved and decayed; but the mystic ebb and flow of the Gigantic Spirit concealed within the universe has continued upon its course, ever increasing in strength and in variety of sequence.

It is true that the results which have flown from this progressive course have very materially changed. Early in its history every achievement was considered great or small, as its conquests by military prowess were great or small. But who in this era would think of placing a Sesostris, or a Semiramis, or even an Alexander, or Cæsar, in comparison as conquerors, with the steamship, the locomotive engine, the electric telegraph, and last and greatest, collecting the efforts of all men, and spreading them world-wide—the printing-press. Where kings and emperors once used the sword to hew their way into the centers of barbarism, the people now make use of their subtle powers of intellect to pierce the heart of ignorance. The conquerors of the present, armed with these keen weapons, are so intertwining the material interests of humanity that, where exclusion was once the rule among nations, intercommunication has made it the exception. Every year some new tie has been added to those which already bound the nations together, until even the continents clasp hands across the oceans, and salute each other in fraternal unity, and the islands stand anxiously waiting for their deliverance.

The grand results of all these magnificent changes have accrued to the benefit of nations as such. All the revolutions of the past have resulted in the building of empires and the dethroning of kings. The grandeur of the Roman Empire consisted in its power, centered in and expressed by its rulers. The glory of France under the great Napoleon was the result of his capacity to use the people. We have no histories making nations famous by the greatness of their peoples. Centralization of power at the head of the government has been the source of all national honor. Under this system grades and castes of people have built themselves, the stronger upon the weaker, and the people as individuals have never appeared upon the surface.

Government has gone through various and important evolutions and changes. First we learn of it as residing in the head of the family, there being no other organization. Next, families aggregated into tribes, with an acknowledged head. Again, tribes united into nations, occupying specified limits, and having an absolute ruler. Then began a double process, which is even now unfinished—the consolidation of nations into races, and the redistribution of power to the people. That which was once absolute in the head of the family, the tribe and the nation, is now shared by the head with the most powerful among the people. These two processes will continue until both are complete—until all nations are merged into races, and all races into one government; and until the power is completely and equally returned to all the people, who will no longer be denominated as belonging to this or that country or government, but as citizens of the world—as members of a common humanity.

"God loves from whole to part. But human soul must from individual to the whole."

It is at once one of the most interesting as well as instructive of studies, to trace the march which civilization has described. Beginning in Asia, it traversed westward by and through the rise and decay of the Assyrian, Egyptian, Persian, Grecian and Roman Empires, each one of which built successively upon the ruins of the preceding, and all culminating in the downfall of the last, whose civilization was disseminated to impregnate that portion of the world then unknown. Modern Europe rose, and when at its height of power, civilization still undeviatingly marching westward, crossed the stormy Atlantic, and implanted itself in the virgin soil of America.

Here, however, an entirely new process was begun. Representatives from all nations, races and tongues here do congregate. Not only do the nations of Europe and Africa pour their restless sons and daughters westward, but the nations of Asia, setting at defiance the previous law of empire, send their children against its tide to meet it and to coalesce. To those who can view humanity as one, this is a fact of great significance, since it proves America to be the center to which the nations naturally tend. But this is only a part of its significance. The more prophetic portion is, that here a new race is being developed, into which will be gathered all the distinctive characteristics of all the various races. Each race is the distinct representative of some special and predominant characteristic, being weak in all others. The new race will combine all these different qualities in one grand character, and shall ultimately gather in all people of all races. Observe the merging of the black and white races. The white does not descend to the black, but the black gradually approaches the white. And this is the prophecy of what shall be :

> "For mankind are one in spirit, and an instinct bears along,
> Round the earth's electric circle, the swift flash of right and wrong;
> Whether conscious or unconscious, yet Humanity's vast frame,
> Through its ocean-sundered fibres, feels the gush of joy or shame :
> In the gain or loss of one race, all the rest have equal claim."

As in this country the future race of the world is being developed, so also will the foundation of the future government be developed, which shall become universal. It was no mere child's play or idle fancy of the old prophets, whose prophecies of a Christ who should rule the world, come trooping down the corridors of time, and from all eras converge upon this. Neither were the Jews entirely at fault when they looked for a Messiah who should reign over the world in temporal as well as in spiritual things, since it is beginning to be comprehended that a reign of justice in temporal things can only follow from the baptism of them by spirituality. And it is the approach of these heretofore widely-separated principles which is to produce the impending revolution. And that revolution will be the final and the ultimate contest between justice and authority, in which the latter will be crushed, never again to raise its despotic head among and to divide the members of a common humanity.

St. Paul said: "Faith, Hope and Charity. These three, but the greatest of these is charity." Beautiful as this triplet may appear to be to the casualist, it cannot bear the test of analysis. It will be replaced in the vocabulary of the future by the more perfect one—Knowledge, Wisdom and Justice. These three, but the greatest of these is Justice. Charity, with its long cloak of justice escaped, has long enough covered a multitude of sins. Justice will in the future demand perfect compensation in all things, whether material, mental or spiritual.

Heretofore justice has only been considered as having relation to matters covered by enacted law, and its demands have been considered as satisfied when the law has had its full course. With Freedom and Equality it has been a mere abstract term with but little significance. There has never been such a thing as freedom for the people. It has always been concession by the government. There has never been an equality for the people. It has always been the stronger, in some sense, preying upon the weaker; and the people have never had justice. When there is authority, whether it be of law, of custom, or of individuals, neither of these can exist except in name. Neither do these principles apply to the people in their collective capacity, but when the people's time shall come they will belong to every individual separately. Equality will exist in freedom and be regulated by justice.

But what does freedom mean? "As free as the winds" is a common expression. But if we stop to inquire what that freedom is, we find that air in motion is under the most complete subjection to different temperatures in different localities, and that these differences arise from conditions entirely independent of the air simply as such. That is to say, the air of itself never changes its temperature. Therefore the freedom of the wind is the freedom to obey commands imposed by conditions to which it is by nature related. So also is water always free to seek its own level. But neither the air or the water of one locality obeys the commands which come from the conditions surrounding another locality. That is to say, that while air and water as a whole are subject to general laws, when individualized, each separate body must be subject to its peculiar relations, and to the law of its conditions. Water in one locality may be pure—hydrogen, nitrogen and oxygen ; while in others it may contain various additional elements, as sodium, calcium or ammonium, and yet each is free. Air in one locality may be twenty degrees above, and in another twenty degrees below, zero; and yet each is free in its own sphere.

Now, individual freedom in its true sense means just the same thing for the people that freedom for the air and water means to them. It means freedom to obey the natural condition of the individual, modified only by the various external forces which are brought to bear upon, and which induce action in, the individual. What that action will be, must be determined solely by the individual and the operating causes, and in no two cases can they be precisely alike ; since no two human beings are precisely alike. Now, is it not plain that freedom means that individuals having the right to it, are subject only to the laws of their own being, and to the relations they sustain to the laws of other things by which they are surrounded?

If, then, freedom mean anything, it means that no individual is subject to any rule or law to be arbitrarily imposed by other individuals. But several individuals may agree among themselves to be governed by certain rules, since that is their freedom to do so. And here is the primal foundation and the only authoritative source of government. No individual can be said to be free and be held accountable to a law to which he or she did not consent.

In the light of that analysis, have the people of this country got freedom ? But should it be objected that such freedom would be liable to abuse, we reply that that is impossible. Since the moment one individual abuses his or her freedom, that moment he or she is encroaching upon the freedom of some one else who is equally entitled to the same right. And the law of the association must protect against such encroachment. And, so far as restraint is concerned, this is the province—the sole province—of law, to protect the rights of individual freedom.

But what is equality, which must be maintained in freedom? A good illustration of what equality among the people means, may be drawn from the equality among the children of a family in the case of an equal division of the property of the deceased father. If the property is divided among them according to their respective merits, that would not be equality.

Now, equality for the people means the equality of the family, extended to all families. It means that no personal merit or demerit can interfere between individuals, so that one may, by arbitration or laws, be placed unequally with another. It means that every individual is entitled to all the natural wealth that he or she requires to minister to the various wants of the body, and to an equal share of all accumulated, artificial wealth—which will appear self-evident when we shall have analyzed wealth. It also means that every person is entitled to equal opportunity for intellectual acquirements, recreation and rest, since the first is necessary to make the performance of the individual's share of duty possible; while the second and third are the natural requirements of the body, independent of the individuality of the person, and which was not self-created but inherited.

Under this analysis have we any such thing as equality in this country? And yet it should be the duty of government, since it is a fundamental portion of its theory, to maintain equality among the people; otherwise the word is but a mere catch, without the slightest signification in fact.

What, then, should be the sphere of justice in maintaining equality in freedom? Clearly to maintain equal conditions among free individuals. But this will appear the more evident as we proceed. The impending revolution, then, will be the strife for the mastery between the authority, despotism, inequalities and injustices of the present, and freedom, equality and justice in their broad and perfect sense, based on the proposition that humanity is one, having a common origin, common interests and purposes, and inheriting a common destiny, which is the complete statement of the religion of Jesus Christ, unadulterated by his professed followers.

But does the impending revolution imply a peaceful change or a bloody struggle ?

No person who will take the trouble to carefully observe the conditions of the various departments of society can fail to discern the terrible earthquakes just ready to burst out upon every side, and which are only now restrained by the thick incrustations with which customs, prejudices and authorities have incased humanity. Indeed, the whole surface of humanity is surging like the billows of the stormy ocean, and it only escapes general and destructive rupture because its composition, like the consciences of its constituent members, is so elastic. But, anon, the restrained furies will overcome the temper of their fastenings, and, rending them asunder, will sweep over the people, submerging them or cleansing them of their gathered debris, as they shall have located themselves, with regard to its coming.

All the struggles of humanity in the centuries which have come and gone have been for freedom—for freedom to think and for freedom to act, as against authority and despotic law, without regard to what should come of that thought and action. But we are now entering upon a struggle for something quite different from this. Having obtained freedom from the despotism of rulers and governments, the rule and despotism of individuals began to usurp the places made vacant by them. Where once the king or the emperor reigned, capital, reinforced by the power of public opinion and religious authorities, now sits and forges chains with which to fetter and bind the people. Where, by divine right, men once demanded the results of the labors of their people, the privileged few, by the means of an ingenious system, facetiously called popular laws, now make the same demand, and with equally decisive results. The demand is answered by the return of the entire proceeds of each year's surplus productions into their coffers. And this is no more true of the pauper laborers of Europe and the slave laborers of Asia than it is of the free labor of America. Six hundred millions people constantly toil all their lives long, while about ten millions sit quietly by gathering and luxuriating in their results.

Simple freedom, then, is not enough. It has not accomplished the redemption of the people. It has only relieved them from one form of slavery to leave them at the mercy of another still more insidious in its character, because more plausible; since, if penury and want exist, accompanied by suffering and privation, under the rule of a monarch, he may justly be held responsible. But when it exists under the reign of freedom, there is no responsibility anywhere, unless it may be said to be in the people themselves, which is equivalent to saying responsibility without application.

To illustrate this distinction without a difference, take the island of Cuba, with its half million inhabitants, and suppose it to be ruled by an absolute monarch, who administers his commands through the usual attachés of the court and the noblemen of the island. Virtually owning the people, he commands them to labor, taking from them all their products, and merely feeding, clothing and sheltering them. In this case it would be the non-laborers who, without any circumlocution, directly obtain all the produced wealth, they simply expending their time and talent in its securing, while the lives of the people who produce it would be simply maintained.

Now advance one step toward popular government—to a constitutional monarchy. In this the same results to the producing people will be maintained, while the noblemen will share the wealth among themselves, allotting a certain share to the monarch.

Coming down to a representative government, of which personal liberty is the basis, the despotism of laws enacted in the interest of privileged classes are substituted for the personal despotism of monarchs and nobles. What the absolute monarch possesses himself of by the right of might, the privileged class in the popular government possess themselves of by the right of law, everything legal being held to be just.

Now is not that precisely the case in this country? Do not all the results of labor accrue to the privileged few? and are not the producing classes just as much enslaved to them as the subjects of an absolute monarch are to him?

With this mortification, however. In the last instance, they suffer from conditions over which they have no control ; whilst in the former case the conditions by which they are enslaved are of their own formation. And I say, I would rather be the unwilling subject of an absolute monarch than the willing slave of my own ignorance, of which advantage is taken by those who spend their time in endeavoring to prove to me that I am free and in singing the glories of my condition, to hoodwink my reason and to blind my perception.

And I further say, that that system of government by which it is possible for a class of people to practice upon my credulity, and, under false pretenses, first entice me to acquiesce in laws by which immense corporations and monopolies are established, and then to induce me to submit to their extortions because they exist according to law, pursuing none but lawful means, is an infernal despotism, compared to which the Russian Czar is a thousand times to be preferred.

This may at first seem a sweeping indictment of our form of government, but I say it is just. Suppose we take our railroad system, now amounting to fifty-five thousand miles. At an average cost of eighty thousand dollars per mile for construction and equipment, its total cost would be four billions four hundred millions dollars. To pay the shareholders an eight per cent. dividend for doing nothing, the industries of the country would have to be taxed three hundred and fifty millions dollars over and above the cost of maintenance and operation. Did this enormous drain from the products of the people stop here, the fertility of the country, made use of by the ingenuity of the people, might possibly keep pace with the demand. But it does not stop there. The net earning of the railroads enables their directors to make larger dividends than eight per cent. Do their managers relinquish this increase in favor of the people ? Never a bit of it. But they increase their stock either by selling new shares, or by making stock or scrip dividends, and to neither process has there been found any legal bar or cure.

Now, what may the result of such a system be ? Why, this. If the stock of all these railroads be increased in the same proportion that some of them have already been increased, it may be raised to a thousand billions of dollars, and the people, instead of being compelled to pay three hundred and fifty millions dollars to provide an eight per cent. dividend on their cost, will have to submit to the extortion of eight hundred million dollars annually to satisfy the demands of these legal despots for an eight per cent. dividend upon stock, a large part of which represent absolutely nothing but the people's stolen money.

A person who would double the size of another's note simply because the profits of his business would permit the payment of twelve per cent. interest, so that instead of paying twelve per cent. upon one hundred dollars, which would be an illegal charge, it would be six per cent. upon two hundred dollars, would be deemed and adjudged guilty of forgery. But these railroad magnates sit in their palatial offices and raise their notes at pleasure, and they are considered public benefactors. It is a crime for a single person to steal a dollar, but a corporation may steal a million dollars, and be canonized as saints.

Oh, the stupid blindness of this people! Swindled every day before their very eyes, and yet they don't seem to know that there is anything wrong, simply because no *law* has been violated. In their eyes everything that is lawful is right, and this has become the curse of the nation. But the opposite—that everything which is right is lawful—don't follow as a part of their philosophy.

No matter what a person does if it is not actionable under the law; he is an honest man and a good church member. But Heaven defend us from being truthful, natural beings, unless the law says we may—since that is to be an infamous scoundrel.

A Vanderbilt may sit in his office and manipulate stocks, or make dividends, by which, in a few years, he amasses fifty millions dollars from the industries of the country, and he is one of the remarkable men of the age. But if a poor, half-starved child were to take a loaf of bread from his cupboard, to prevent starvation, she would be sent first to the Tombs, and thence to Blackwell's Island.

An Astor may sit in his sumptuous apartments, and watch the property bequeathed him by his father, rise in value from one to fifty millions, and everybody bows before his immense power, and worships his business capacity. But if a tenant of his, whose employer had discharged him because he did not vote the Republican ticket, and thereby fails to pay his month's rent to Mr. Astor, the law sets him and his family into the street in midwinter; and, whether he dies of cold or starvation, neither Mr. Astor or anybody else stops to ask, since that is nobody's business but the man's. This is a free country, you know, and why should I trouble myself about that person, because he happens to be so unfortunate as not to be able to pay Mr. Astor his rent?

Mr. Stewart, by business tact, and the various practices known to trade, succeeds, in twenty years, in obtaining from customers whom he has entrapped into purchasing from him fifty millions dollars, and with his gains he builds costly public beneficiaries, and straightway the world makes him a philanthropist. But a poor devil who should come along with a bolt of cloth, which he had succeeded in smuggling into the country, and which, consequently, he could sell at a lower price than Mr. Stewart, who paid the tariff, and is thereby authorized by law to add that sum to the piece, would be cast into prison.

Now these individuals represent three of the principal methods that the privileged classes have invented by which to monopolize the accumulated wealth of the country. But let us analyze the processes, and see if it is wholly by their personal efforts that they gain this end.

Nobody pretends that Mr. Stewart ever produced a single dollar of his vast fortune. He accumulated it by dealing in the productions of others, which he first obtained at low rates, and then sold at a sufficient advance over the cost of handling to make in the aggregate a sum amounting to millions.

Now, I want to ask if all this is not arriving at the same result, by another method, at which the slaveholders of the South arrived, by owning negroes? In the case of the latter, the slaveholder reaped all the benefits of the labors of the negroes. In the former case the merchant princes, together with the various other privileged classes, reap the benefit of the labors of all the working-classes of the country. Every year the excess of the produced wealth of the country finds final lodgment in the pockets of these classes, and they grow richer at each succeeding harvest, while the laborers toil their lives away; and when all their strength and vigor have been transformed into wealth, which has been legally transferred to the capitalists, they are heavy with age, and as destitute as when they began their life of servitude. Did ever Southern slave have meaner end than this?

In all seriousness, is there any common justice in such a state of things? Is it right that the millions should toil all their lives long, scarcely having comfortable food and clothes, while the few manage to control all the benefits? People may pretend that it is justice, and good Christians may excuse it upon that ground, but Christ would never have called it by that name. He would even give him that labored but an hour as much as he that had labored all the day, but to him who labored not at all he would take away even that which he hath. And yet we hear loud professions of Christianity ascending from the pulpit throughout the length and breadth of the land. And when I listen, I cannot help exclaiming, " O, ye hypocrites, how can ye hope to escape the damnation of hell? "

Am I asked, How are these things to be amended? I will tell you in the first place, that they must be remedied; and this particular case of dealing in the labor of the people is to be remedied by abolishing huckstering, or the system of middle-men, and substituting therefor a general system of public markets, conducted by the people through their paid agents, as all other public business is performed. In these markets the products of the country should be received, in first hands, direct from the producers, who should realize their entire proceeds. In this manner the immense fortunes realized by middle-men, and the profits made by the half-dozen different hands through which merchandise travels on its way to consumers, would be saved to the producer. A bushel of apples, purchased in the orchard at twenty-five cents, is finally sold to the consumer at a dollar. Now, either the consumer has paid at least a half dollar too much, or the producer has received a half dollar too little, for the apples; since, under a perfect system, the apples would go direct from the orchard to the market, and thence direct to the consumer.

We are forever talking of political economy, but it appears to me that the most vital points—one of which is our system of huckstery— is entirely overlooked.

Suppose Mr. Stewart, instead of having labored all these years for his own selfish interests, had labored in tne interests of the people? Is it not clear that the half-a-hundred million dollars he has accumulated would have remained with the people who have consumed his goods? Place all other kinds of traffic upon the same proposed basis, and do you not see that the system which makes merchant-princes would be abolished? Neither would it require one-half the people to conduct a general system of markets who are now employed speculating in the results of labor.

In short, every person should either be a producer or a paid agent or officer of consumers and producers, and our entire system of shop-keeping reduced to a magnificent system of immense public markets. In this way there could also be a perfect control exercised over the quality of perishable goods, the want of which is now felt so severely in summer in all large cities, and a thousand unthought of remedies would necessarily suggest themselves as the system should develop.

But let us pass to one of the other branches of this same system. We have in our midst thousands of people of immense wealth who have never even done so much to justify its possession as the merchant-princes have done to justify themselves. I refer to our land monopolists, and to Mr. Astor as their representative. Mr. Astor inherited a large landed estate, which has risen in value to be worth millions of dollars, to which advance Mr. Astor never contributed even a day's labor. He has done nothing except to watch the rise and gather in the rents, while the whole laboring country has been constantly engaged in promoting that advance. What would Mr. Astor have been without the City of New York? And what would the City of New York have been without the United States? You see, my friends, it will not do to view this matter superficially. We live in too analytic an age to permit these things to go on in the way they have been going. There is too much poverty, too much suffering, too much hard work, too many hours of labor for individuals, too many sleepless nights, too many starving poor, too many hungry children, too many in helpless old age, to permit these villanous abuses to continue sheltered under the name of respectability and public order.

But again, and upon a still worse swindle of the people. A person having money goes out into the public domain and acquires an immense tract of land. Shortly a railroad is projected and built, which runs through that tract. It offers a fine location for a station. A city springs up, and that which cost in some instances as little as a shilling per acre, is divided into town lots, and these are reluctantly parted with at five hundred dollars each.

Again, I wish to inquire, in the name of Justice, to whom does that advance belong? To the person who nominally holds the land? What has he done to entitle him to receive dollars for what he only paid cents? Is there any equality—is there any justice—in such a condition? He profits by the action of others; in fact at the public expense, since in its last analysis it is the common public who are the basis of all advance in the value of property.

Now, I say, that that common public is entitled to all the benefits accruing from common efforts; and it is an infamous wrong that makes it accrue to the benefit of a special few. And a system of society which permits such arbitrary distributions of wealth is a disgrace to Christian civilization, whose Author and his Disciples had all things in common. Let professing Christians who, for a pretense, make long prayers, think of that, and then denounce Communism, if they can : and denounce me as a Revolutionist for advocating it, if they dare.

But, is it asked, how is this to be remedied? I answer, very easily ! Since those who possess the accumulated wealth of the country have filched it by legal means from those to whom it justly belongs—the people—it must be returned to them, by legal means if possible, but it must be returned to them in any event. When a person worth millions, dies, instead of leaving it to his children, who have no more title to it than anybody else's children have, it must revert to the people, who really produced it. Do you say that is injustice to the children? I say, No ! And if you ask me how the rich man's children are going to live after his death, I answer, by the same means as the poor man's children live. Let it be remembered that we have had simple freedom quite long enough. By setting all our hopes on freedom we have been robbed of our rights. What we want now is more than freedom—we want equality ! And by the Heaven above us, earth's growing children are going to have it! What right have the children of the rich to be born to luxurious idleness, while the children of the poor are born to, all their lives long, further contribute to their ease? Do they not in common belong to God's human family? If I mistake not, Christ told us so. You will not dispute his authority, I am sure. If, instead of preaching Christ and him crucified quite so much, we should practice his teaching a little more, my word for it, we should all be better Christians.

And when by this process all the land shall have been returned to the people, there will be just as much of it, and it will be equally as productive, and just as much room on it as there is now. But instead of a few people owning the whole of it, and farming it out to all the rest at the best possible prices, the people will possess it themselves in their own right, through just laws, paying for its possession to the government such moderate rates of taxes as shall be necessary to maintain the government.

But I may as well conclude what I have to say regarding railroads, which must also revert back to the people, and be conducted by them for the public benefit, as our common highways are now conducted. Vanderbilt, Scott & Co. are demonstrating it better and better every day that all the railroads of the country can be much more economically and advantageously conducted under one management than under a thousand different managements. They imagine that very soon they will have accomplished a complete consolidation of the entire system, and that by the power of that consolidation they will be able to control the government of this country.

But they will not be the first people who have made slight miscalculations as to ultimate results. Thomas Scott might make a splendid Secretary of the Department of Internal Improvements, for which the new Constitution, which this country is going to adopt, makes provision; but he will never realize his ambition to preside over the railroad system of the country in any other manner.

And I will tell you another benefit that will follow the nationalization of our railroads. You have all heard of the dealing in stocks, of the " bulls " and the " bears," and the " longs " and the " shorts," and the "lame ducks" of Wall street. Well, they will all be abolished. There will be no stocks in which to deal. That sort of speculation, by which gigantic swindlers corner a stock and take it in at their own figures, will, to use a vulgar phrase, be "played out." And if you were to see their customers, as I have seen them, rushing about Broad street to catch sight of the last per cent. of their margins as they disappear in the hungry maw of the complacent brokers, you would agree with me that it ought to be "played out."

Under the system which I propose, not only will stock gambling be abolished, but also all other gambling, and the hundreds of thousands of able-bodied people who are now engaged in it, living from the products of others, will be compelled to go to producing themselves.

But, says the objector, take riches away from people and there will be no incentive to accumulate. But, my dear sir, we don't propose to do anything of the kind, nor to destroy any wealth. There will never be any less wealth than now, but a constant increase upon it. We only propose that the people shall hold it in their own right, instead of its being held in trust for them by a self-appointed few. Instead of having a few millionaires, and millions on the verge of starvation, we propose that all shall possess a comfortable competence—that is, shall possess the results of their own labors.

I can't see where there is a chance for a lack of motive to come in. It seems to me that everybody will have a better and a more certain chance, as well as a better incentive to accumulate. Will the certainty of accumulation destroy the desire to accumulate? Nobody but the most stupid would attempt to maintain that. It is not great wealth in a few individuals that proves a country prosperous, but great general wealth evenly distributed among the people. That country must be the most prosperous and happy where the people are most generally comfortably and happily circumstanced. And in this country, instead of a hundredth part of the people living in palaces and riding in coaches, while the balance live in huts and travel on foot, every person may live in a palace and ride in a coach I leave it to you to decide which is the preferable condition and which the more Christian.

And why should the rich object to this? If everybody has enough and to spare, should that be a subject of complaint? What more do people want, except it be for the purpose of tyrannizing over others dependent upon them? But no objections that may be raised will be potent enough to crush out the demand for equality now rising from an oppressed people. This demand the possessors of wealth cannot afford to ignore. It comes from a patiently-enduring people, who have waited already too long for the realization of the beautiful pictures of freedom which have been painted for them to admire ; for the realization of the songs which poets have sung to its praise. Let me warn, nay, let me implore them not to be deaf to this demand, since they do not know so well as I know what temper there is behind it. I have tested it, and I know it is one that will not much longer brook the denial of justice.

But there is another monopoly of which I must speak—I mean the monopoly of money itself. We have seen how great a tyranny that is which arises from monopolizing the land. But that occurring from the monopoly of money, is a still more insidious and dangerous form of despotism, since its ramifications are more extensive and minute. It may be exercised by the person possessing a hundred, or by the person possessing a million dollars. But what is the process? A person inherits a half million dollars for which he never expended a single day's labor. He sits in his office loaning that sum of money say, in sums of one thousand dollars to one thousand different persons, each of whom conducts a little business which yields just enough to support a family and to pay the interest. These people live for forty years in this manner, and die no better off than when they began life. But during that time they have paid all their extra production to the amount of four thousand dollars, each, to the capitalist; and, finally, the business itself is sold out to pay the principal. And thus it turns out that the capitalist obtains everything those thousand persons earned during their whole lives, they leaving nothing to their families. Now, what better is that result than it would have been had these people been slaves? Could their owners have obtained any more from them? I say they would have obtained less; since, had they been slaves in name, as in fact they were, there would have been times during the forty years that they would not have earned interest over cost of their support. Now, look at the capitalist. For one million dollars, and without the straining of a muscle, he receives five million dollars direct, which, reinvested from time to time as it increases, amounts at the end of the forty years to not less than fifteen millions dollars.

But try another example of a somewhat different kind. A person having four grown children, whom he has reared in luxury, and given all the facilities of education, dies, leaving each of them a farm worth twenty-five thousand dollars. These children having never learned the art of farming are incapable of conducting these farms; but they lease them to four different people for a thousand dollars a year each, and live at ease all their lives, therefrom, never so much as lifting their hands to do an hour's labor. Now, who is it that supports those four people? Is it not clear that it is the people who work the farms? And how did it happen that they had the farms to lease? Simply by an incident for which there was no legitimate general cause, else why do not all children have farms and live without work?

Nor can you, my friends, discover anything approaching equality, or ought that looks like justice in that operation. I tell you nay! It is the most insidious despotism, with a single exception, that is possible among a people. It is a despotism which was condemned in all former times, even by barbarians, and which the Jews were only permitted to enforce upon people of other nations. It is the hideous vampire fastened upon the vitals of our people, sucking—sucking—sucking their very life's blood, leaving just enough to keep up their vitality, that they may manufacture more. It is the heartless monster that will have the exact pound of flesh, even if there be loss of blood to obtain it, and there is no just judge near to prevent the taking, or to hold him to account if he take it. It paralyzes our industries; shuts the gates in the way that leads to our inexhaustible treasures within the bosom of mother earth; strips the stars and stripes from the masts of merchantmen; compels our immense cotton lands to luxuriate in weeds; robs our spindles of the power to turn them; and lays an embargo upon every productive enterprise. Whoever makes a movement to compel the earth to yield her wealth, or to transform that wealth into useful form, must first obtain the consent of this despot, and pay his demands for a license.

Thirteen millions of laborers in this country produce annually four thousand millions dollars of wealth, every dollar of which over and above the cost of living is paid over to appease the demands of this insatiate monster—this horrid demon, whose name is Interest.

We are told that we cannot manufacture railroad iron in this country as cheap as it can be manufactured in England. Yes! And why? Is it because we have no ore or no coal; or that, which is not as good as England has? No! We have on the surface what in England is hundreds of feet in the bowels of the earth, and coal the same; and both of better quality. But money can be put at interest in this country so as to double itself every four years, and be amply secured. What reason have capitalists to construct iron works, or to have their care, when twenty-five per cent. per year is returned them, without care or risk? And what is true of iron is also true of every other natural production. Is it any wonder that our manufacturers are obliged to demand that the people pay an additional per cent. upon everything they eat, drink or wear, that they may be protected in their various productive enterprises, when such exactions are laid upon them by this more than absolute monarch? No! It would indeed be a wonder if it were not so.

Now, do you suppose our markets would be flooded with British goods if our producing and manufacturing interests had all the money they require without interest? If there are any borrowers at ten per cent. who hear my voice, let them answer. No; it is the tribute that industry is compelled to pay to capital that forces our government to exact ten, twenty, fifty, aye, even a hundred per cent. for the privilege of bringing merchandise into this country.

But they tell us if we go to free trade that our country would be flooded with foreign products, so there would be absolutely no production of manufactured goods in the country. Now that would be true, if we should attempt free trade and leave the monster Interest with his grip upon our vitals. And here is the short-sightedness of Free-Traders. If we want free trade, we must, in the first place, attack, throttle and kill this demon, after which we may manufacture at prices that will not only absolutely forbid the importation of almost everything that is now imported, but which will also enable us to play the same game with Europe that Europe has played so long upon us. Free money in this country would abolish every European throne within ten years. And yet people cannot be made to see that this country is their support. With free money what need would we have for a protective tariff? Can any Protectionist answer that?

You see, my friends, that it is the people who catch sight of an idea and pursue it to the death, regardless of relative ideas, who make reform so ridiculous. One reform cannot advance alone. All kinds of reform must go on together. Interest and free trade must go hand in hand; interest, if either, a little ahead.

And in this regard I am free to confess that the National Labor Union's demand for a decrease of interest is the most reasonable single reform now being advocated. We want free trade; but we want free money first, so that not a spindle or forge in this country shall stop at the command of those across the ocean.

But how are we going to get free money? Why, in the very easiest way possible. It is the simplest problem of them all. I am not going into this discussion to prove to you that gold is not money, since everybody ought to know that it has no more the properties of money than cotton, corn and pork have the properties of money. Now, money is that thing which, if every dollar in circulation should be destroyed, there would be no loss of wealth. Gold, cotton, corn and wheat are wealth. Destroy these and there is a loss. But when money is destroyed, there is no more loss than when a promissory note is destroyed. A note is an evidence of debt. It is not wealth, but its representative. So also is money not wealth, but its representative. And if we had a thousand million dollars in circulation to day, there would be no more wealth in the country than there now is, and we would have quite as much wealth if there were two thousand millions dollars, since money and wealth are two entirely distinct things.

But they tell us that unless money is made redeemable in gold, it is not of any account, and that, too, in the face of our miserable green-back system, which was so much better even than gold that it saved the nation when, had we stuck to gold, we should have been destroyed. Oh, but it was a depreciated currency, says some one. Yes, it was a depreciated currency, and we should have ample reason to be thankful if when we come to pay our bonds, we have a depreciated currency with which to liquidate them, instead of being obliged, as we shall, to pay a thousand dollars in cotton for what we realized less than five hundred in gold.

It is not the gold only of a country that constitutes its wealth. What should we care if we had not a single ounce of gold, if we had a thousand million bales of cotton, ten thousand millions bushels of corn and wheat, and a billion dollars' worth of manufactured goods to send to other countries? So you see it is not the gold after all that makes a circulation good, but the sum total of all kinds of wealth. Now, that is what we propose to substitute for gold as the basis for a money issue. And instead of permitting corporations to issue it and remain at liberty to dispose of their property and let the people who hold their circulation whistle for its redemption, we propose that government, which can neither sell our property nor abscond with it, shall issue it for the people and lend it to them at cost; or if you will insist on paying interest for money, why, then, pay it to the government and lessen your taxes that much, instead of paying interest to bankers and supporting government besides.

Now, don't you think that would be rather a good sort of a money system? I know that every manufacturer in the country would like it. But I can tell you who will not like it; and whom we may be compelled to fight before they will permit us to have it; and these are the money-lenders and money-changers, such as it is related the Head of the Christian Church—one Jesus Christ, of whom we hear a great deal said, but whose teachings and doctrines are wofully perverted—scourged out of the Temple at a place known as Jerusalem.

I have not been guilty of frequenting the temples of the country much of late, but if I am not misinformed upon the subject, and unless they have changed since I did frequent them, if Christ should pass through this land of a Sunday, scourge in hand, he would find plenty of work to do in the same line in which he labored so faithfully among the Jews.

But the National Labor Union say they won't be so hard upon these money-lenders as we would be. They are willing that they shall be eased down from the vast height to which they have attained. They say they shall have three per cent. interest instead of six, seven, eight and ten, or as much more as they can steal out of the necessities of the case, by the circumstances and discounts. But they shall be limited to three per cent., and in a way that they cannot evade, as they now evade, lawful interest. It is proposed that government shall issue this money, but that it shall be convertible into a three per cent. interest-bearing bond; so that when money shall be so plenty that it will be worth less than three per cent. in business, it can be invested in bonds drawing three per cent.; and the bonds to also be reconvertible into money, so that the moment business shall demand more money than there should be in circulation—which would increase the value of money to more than three per cent.—the bonds would be converted into money again; and when there should be no more bonds to convert, and money still worth more than three per cent., then the Government shall issue more money to restore the equilibrium. In this way money would always be worth just three per cent. No more nor less, and there would always be just enough; or, in other words, money would be measured, as it never has been, and which has been the cause of all our financial troubles. What would you say to a person who should talk to you about measuring your corn in a bushel that had itself never been measured? But you complacently talk of money being a measure of values, and money has never had a measure regulating its own value.

But this consideration is only a stepping-stone to what shall be. Money must be made free from interest. In fact, I do not know but people who have money should pay something to have it securely loaned, the same as you must pay your Safe Deposit Companies for safely keeping bonds, jewels and other valuables. I think people ought to be made to pay for the safe keeping of money upon the same principle. Money under our present system is the only thing which we possess that does not depreciate in value by use. The more money is used, the more it increases ; a proof complete of the fallacy and its despotism.

The Government now pay the banks thirty millions dollars per year for the privilege of loaning them about three hundred millions national currency, which the banks reloan to the people at an average of ten per cent. It seems to me that is almost too good a thing to last long. If the Government can afford to do this thing, why can't they better afford to loan directly to the people for nothing, and save thirty millions dollars annually? Do you think the people would object? Oh, no; but the bankers would. But for all that the cry of "Down with the tyrant" is raised, and it will never cease until interest shall be among the things that were.

I also desire to call attention to the reduction of the Public Debt, and to the means by which this reduction has been accomplished. The Administration hangs almost all of its hopes upon this fact, while if it were thoroughly understood it would prove its condemnation. It has paid three hundred millions of the debt, they say. Who has paid it? we inquire. It fails to answer. We say that that entire payment has be made by the producing classes of the country, while the capitalists have not reduced their cash balances in the least. In other words, the producers have got no more money now than they had before the debt was paid, while the capitalists have had their bonds changed into money. Now, who have paid that three hundred millions dollars? I repeat the laboring people have done it, just as they pay all public debts and all public expenses, besides constantly adding to the wealth of the capitalists themselves. Can such a state of things continue? Again I tell you nay.

This wrong must be remedied by a system of progressive taxation. If persons having a hundred thousand dollars pay one-half per cent. tax, let those having a million pay ten per cent., or two millions twenty-five per cent. Let there be a penalty placed upon monopolizing the common property, and it will soon cease and equality come in its place. Now, the poorest woman who buys the cheapest calico pays a tax to the Government, while the rich appropriate her labor to pay their dues. Truly said Jesus, "The poor ye have with you always."

Another mode of remedying the existing ills in industry and the distribution of wealth, must be in giving employees an actual interest in the products of their labors, so that ultimately co-operation will be the source of all production, its results being justly distributed among all those who assist in the production. First, pay the employer the same rate of interest for his capital that Government shall charge for loans made to the people; next, the general expenses, including salaries to himself and all employees, the remainder to be equitably divided among all who have an interest in it. Do you not see what a revolution in industrial production such a constitutional provision would effect? And do you not suppose if the workingmen and women of this country understood the justice of it, that they would have it? I intend that they shall have the required information. Already there have been half a million tracts upon these subjects sent broadcast over this land, and the present year shall see double as many more, until every laborer, male and female, shall hold in his or her own hands the method of deliverance from this great oppression.

But there is another consideration, which, more forcibly than any other, shows the suicidal policy which we pursue. If the present rates of interest are continued to be paid upon only the present banking capital and bonds of the country, for twenty-five years to come, the interest, with the principal added, will have absorbed the total present wealth, as well as its perspective increase. And such a consummation as this are the European capitalists now preparing for this country. Europe holds not less than three thousand millions of bonded indebtedness of this country, which is being augmented every month by additional railroad bonds, or some syndicate operation. So do you not see that European capital is gradually, but nevertheless inevitably, absorbing not only all of our annually produced wealth, but also acquiring an increased mortgage every year upon our accumulated wealth? There is no escaping these facts. Figures don't lie. Mathematics is an absolute science from whose edicts there is no escape. And mathematics inform us that we are year by year mortgaging ourselves to European capitalists, who will ultimately step in and foreclose their mortgages, and possess themselves of our all, just as we foreclose our smaller mortgages, when there is no hope of a further increase from interest.

Besides the monopoly of land, money and public conveniences, there is another kind of monopoly still, which may appear rather strange and new to be thus classed, but it is neverthless a terrible tyrant. I refer to the monopoly of education. I hold that a just government is in duty bound to see to it that all its children of both sexes have the same and equal opportunities for acquiring education, and that every person of adult age shall have graduated in the highest departments of learning, as well as in the arts, sciences and practical mechanics. Every person should be compelled to acquire a practical knowledge of some productive branch of labor, because the time will come when all people will be obliged to produce at least as much as they consume, or earn what they consume, as the paid agents of producers. What a revolution would that accomplish? If every person in the world was to work at production two hours a day there would be a larger aggregate produced than there is now. Therefore every person must learn the art of production, and thus be equal in resources to any other person, and Government must undertake the compulsory industrial education of all its children.

Thus I could continue analysis upon analysis, until not a stone in the foundations of our social structure would be left unturned, and all would be found unworthy of our civilization—our boasted Christian civilization. I think Christianity has been preached at, long enough. I go for making a practical application of it at the very foundations of society. I believe in recognizing the broad principle of all religion— that we are all children of one great common parent, God, which, since it disproves the propositions of the Church, that at least a large portion of us are the children of the devil, and renders the services of the clergy to save us from that inheritance unnecessary, will abolish our present system of a licensed and paid ministry. Thirty-five thousand ministers are paid twenty-five millions dollars annually for preaching the gospel in cathedrals costing two hundred and fifty millions dollars; and how many of them ever teach any fact other than that Jesus was crucified, just as though that would save us from the sloughs of ignorance in which we are sunk? Which one of them dare tell his congregation the truth, as he, if he be not a blockhead, knows it? I here and now impeach the clergy of the United States as dishonest and hypocritical, since the best of them acknowledge that they do not dare to preach the whole truth, for, if they should, they would have to preach to empty seats—an admission sufficiently damnable to consign them to the contempt of the world and to the hell of which they prate so knowingly, but whose location they have not been able to determine, and to light the torch which shall fire the last one of these palatial mockeries of true religion.

Why, should Christ appear among these godly Christians as he did among the Jews, he would be arrested as a vagrant, or sent to jail for stealing corn; and in Connecticut, perhaps, for Sabbath-breaking, or for telling the maid at the well "*all she had ever done*," which is now called fortune-telling, or for healing the sick by laying on of hands, which they denominate charlatanry. Christ and his Disciples and the multitude which he gathered together had all things in common. But every pulpit and every paper in this Christian country launch the thunders of their denunciations when that damnable doctrine is now advanced. Now, Christ was a Communist of the strictest sort, and so am I, and of the most extreme kind. I believe that God is the Father of all humanity and that we are brothers and sisters; and that it is not merely a theoretical or hypothetical nothing but a stern reality, to be reduced to a practical recognition. And they who cannot accept and practice this doctrine of Christ, and who still profess to be his followers, are simply stealing the livery of Christ in which to serve the devil in their own souls.

I do not care to what length Christians may stretch their faces of a Sunday, nor how much they pay to support their ministers; nor do I care how long prayers they may make, nor what sermons preach, when they denounce the fundamental principles of the teachings of Christ, I will turn upon and, in his language, utter their own condemnation: "Inasmuch as ye have not done it unto the least of these, ye have not done it unto" Christ. And they may make all the fuss, call me all the hard names, they please; but they can't escape the judgment. And I don't intend they shall have a chance to escape it. I am going to strip the masks of hypocrisy from their faces, and let the world see them as they are. They have had preaching without practice long enough. The people want practice now, and when they get it, they can even afford to do without the preaching.

These privileged classes of the people have an enduring hatred for me, and I am glad they have. I am the friend not only of freedom in all things, and in every form, but also for equality and justice as well. These cannot be inaugurated except through revolution. I am denounced as desiring to precipitate revolution. I acknowledge it. I am for revolution, if to get equality and justice it is required. I only want the people to have what it is their right to have—what the religion of humanity, what Christ, were he the arbiter, would give them. If, in getting that, the people find bayonets opposing them, it will not be their fault if they make their way through them by the aid of bayonets. And these persons who possess the monopolies and who guard them by bayonets, need not comfort themselves with the idea that the people won't fight for their rights. Did they not spring to arms from every quarter to fight for the negro? And will you say they will not do the same against this other slavery, compared to which the former is as an gentle shower to a raging tempest?

Don't flatter yourselves, gentlemen despots, that you are going to escape under that assumption. You will have to yield, and it will be best for you to do it gracefully. You are but as one to seven against them. Numbers will win. It will be your own obduracy if they are goaded on to madness. Do not rely upon their ignorance of the true condition. Upon that you have anchored your hopes as long as it is safe. There are too many reform newspapers in circulation. And though the columns of all our great dailies are shut to their truths, still there are channels through which they flow to the people—aye, even to those who delve in the coal mines of Pennsylvania, seldom seeing the joyous sunshine. And this education shall continue until every person who contributes to the maintenance of another in luxurious idleness shall know how such a result is rendered possible.

Hence, I say, it lies in the hands of those who have maintained this despotism over the common people to yield it up to them and recognize their just relations.

And remember what I say to you to-night: If this that is claimed is not granted—if, beside freedom, equality is not made possible by your giving up this power, by which the laborer is robbed of the results of his labor, before our next centennial birthday, July 4th, 1876, you will have precipitated the most terrible war that the earth has yet known.

For three years before the breaking out of the slavery rebellion I saw and heard with my spiritual senses the marching of armies, the rattle of musketry, and the roar of cannon; and I already hear and see the approach of this more terrible contest. I know it is coming. There is but one way in which it can be averted. There was one way by which the slave war could have been avoided—the abolition of slavery. But the slave oligarchy would not listen to our Garrisons, Sumners, Tiltons and Douglases. They tried the arbitration of war, but they lost their slaves at last. Now, will not these later oligarchies —the land, the railroad, the money aristocracies—learn a lesson from their terrible fate? Will they not listen to the abolitionists—to the Garrisons, the Sumners, the Tiltons and the Douglases—of to-day? Will they try the arbitration of war, which will result as did the last, in the loss of that for which they fight? I would that they should learn wisdom by experience. The slaveholders could have obtained compensation for their negroes. They refused it and lost all. Ponder that lesson well, and do not neglect to give it its true application. You can compromise now, and the same general end be arrived at without the baptism of blood. It shall not be my fault if that baptism comes. Nevertheless, equality and justice are on the march, and they cannot be hindered. They must and will attain their journey's end. The people shall be delivered.

I have several times referred to the methods by which these things may be accomplished. They are impossible under our present Constitution. It is too restricted, too narrow, to admit even an idea of a common humanity. True, its text is complete, but its framework does not carry out the original design. Even George Washington, himself, was accused of treachery for countenancing so great a departure as was made; and the late war justified the grounds upon which that accusation was founded. The text of the Constitution held these truths to be self-evident, "That all men (and women) are born equal and entitled to certain inalienable rights, among which are life, liberty, and the pursuit of happiness." The Constitution should have been erected in harmony with those declarations. It was not. There is no such thing as equality provided for. Life and liberty have not been held inalienable under it; the pursuit of happiness has been outrageously interfered with, and the government has been made to exist without the consent of the governed; and exists to-day against the protests of a large number of its subjects.

Is it to be expected that anything so false as that is to its basic propositions can be made enduring? It is against the constitution of nature itself that it should be so. Nature is always true to itself, and will always vindicate itself. If hedged in and obstructed, it will burst through or find its way around. The needle is not truer to the pole than is Nature to the truth. And Nature is always just. Those propositions were deduced from human rights, regardless of any authority or despotism. Had they been elucidated—had their principles guided the construction of the Constitution itself, all would have been well. What our fathers failed to do is left for this generation to perform; and it must not shirk the duty. It must look the condition squarely in the face, and meet the issue as squarely..

What issues must be met and provided for in order that human rights may be respected and protected? I have already referred to the monopolies that must be abolished. But there are also many other things. I will call attention first to minority representation, which lies at the base of a representative government. The State of Massachusetts has eleven representatives in Congress, and they are all Republicans. Justice would infer that there are no Democrats in the State. But such is not the fact. There are a large body of Democrats. They are not represented. That is the fault of the system of arriving at representation. While it is true that majorities must rule, that is not equal to saying that minorities shall have no voice. But the practice in Massachusetts does say just that. I suspect if it were possible for all the real differences, politically, to be represented, that the Congress-men would stand something as follows: The Democrats would have say, four out of the eleven, the Republicans, say, three, while the remainder would be divided between the Labor and Temprence Re-formers and Woman Suffragists. Indeed, I am not certain if the door were to be opened that there would be any straight Republicans left, since all reformers are, under the present system, compelled to con-gregate together in this party, so as not to entirely throw away their votes. The Democrats are always Democrats. Like the hard-shell Baptists, you always know where to find them.

They are always on hand to vote early, and often also, if opportunity permit. Admit minority representation, and the Republican party in Massachusetts would be abolished, except that part who carry the loaves and eat the fishes. They are as certain to be found "right there" as the Democrats are. I think the Woman Suffragists cover about one-half the Republican party. But a large body of them are Spiritualists and Temperance men, while as many more are Labor Re-formers. But those who are more Labor Reformers than anything else, are perhaps two-sevenths; who are more Woman Suffragists than anything else, are perhaps two-sevenths; who are more Spiritualists than anything else, perhaps two-sevenths; and who are more Tem-perance men than anything else, one-seventh; therefore, if the dele-gation were elected by the representation of minorities, it would stand four Democrats, two Spiritualists, two Labor Reformers, two Woman Suffragists, and one Temperance man. But all of these, how-ever, would be again swallowed up whenever a Human Rights party should be evolved, and that will be the party of the near future, in whose all embracing arms the people, long suffering and long waiting, will at last find repose, while the Goddess of Liberty, with her scales of equality, shall find no more of her subjects to whom justice is not measured out. Then will partisan politics have received its death warrant; then will the people become one in heart, one in soul and one in common purpose—the general good of the general whole. The "greatest good of the greatest number will be supplanted by: "the general welfare, is best maintained when individual interests are best protected." The new government, then, must be the result of minority representation, and all legislative bodies, and, where possible, all executive officers, be so elected, while the people shall retain the appointing as well as the veto power. Our lawmakers must be made law proposers, who shall construct law to be submitted to the people for their approval, in the same manner as our public conventions appoint committees to draft resolutions, which are afterward adopted or rejected by the convention itself. This will make every person a legislator, having a direct interest in every law. The people will then no longer elect representatives to make laws by which they must be bound whether they approve or disapprove. The referendum is the desired end. The referendum is what the people require, and it is what the new Constitution must provide. So that in all future time the people themselves will be their own lawmakers—will be the government.

The people must appoint all their officers, heads of departments and bureaus at regular intervals, and all under assistants, during faithful performance of duty. We want no Civil Service Commissions. Every person who shall be eligible to office under the new government will be competent; and when once familiar with the duties, will not be removed to give room for the friend of some politician belonging to the party in power, since it would be the people in power at all times.

Another matter which must have attention is the sweeping away of that *jeu de'esprit*, our courts of justice, by making all kinds of contracts stand upon the honor and capacity of the contracting parties. All individual matters must be settled by the individuals themselves without appeal to the public. Our present system of enforced collection of debts costs every year more than is realized, and besides maintains a vast army of lawyers, constables and court officers in unproductive employ. All this is wrong, entailing almost untold exactions upon the producing community, who in the end are made to pay all these things.

Further, our system of oaths and bonds must be abolished. This swearing people to tell the truth, and binding them to perform their duty, presupposes that they will lie and neglect their duty. People are always placed upon the side of force and compulsion—never upon that of personal rectitude and honor. The results are what might be expected. It plunges us into the very things we would avoid. There is a philosophy, too, in all these things; since in freedom only can purity exist. Anything that is not free is not pure. Anything that is accompanied by compulsion is no proof of individual honesty.

The new government must also take immediate steps for the abolition of pauperism and beggary. It is an infamous reproach upon this country that there are hundreds of thousands of people who subsist themselves upon individual charity. I do not care whether this is from choice or necessity. I say it is a burning shame, requiring immediate curative steps. The indigent and helpless classes are just as much a part of our social body as the protected and the rich are, and they are entitled to its recognition. Society must no longer punish and compel suffering and death for its own wrongs. It must evolve such a social system as shall leave no single member of the common body to suffer. When one member of the body suffers, the whole body sympathizes. So, also, when a member of the social body suffers, does the whole body suffer. And yet we have pretended philanthrophists and Christians who have never grasped that truth.

Our civilization and our Christianity have been made too much a matter of faith in, and devotion to, the unknownable, divorced from all human relations. We must first recognize and practice the brotherhood of man before we can be made to realize the Paternity of God, since "if we love not our brothers whom we have seen, how can we love God whom we have not seen." Our religious teaching has been too much of punishment, and too little of love; too much of faith, too little of works; too much of sectarianism, too little of humanitarianism; too much of hell-fire arbitration, too little of inevitable law; and too much of self-rightousness, and too little of innate goodness.

And here I cannot forbear to depart from the strict line of my subject to say a word regarding a doctrine, from the effects of which even this country is but slowly recovering—that of eternal damnation! I say, that a people who really believe in a God who could burn his own children in a lake of literal fire and brimstone, " where the worm dieth not and the fire is not quenched," and from which there is no present escape nor future hope, for a single unrepented misdeed, and still profess to honor, love and worship a fiend so infernal as that would make Him, cannot be honest and conscientious, since they must mistake fear for love, and confound sycophancy with worship. It was such a belief that kindled the fires by which the early martyrs perished, by which the Quakers of Massachusetts were burned and the witches hanged, and which invented the terrible Inquisition, with its horrid racks and tortures. These are the legitimate results of such a belief; and if the people of to-day really believed what they profess in their creeds, they would do precisely the same things. And they would be justified, since it would be merciful in them to subject a person to a few moments' torture, to induce him or her to escape the eternal tortures of Hell, the horrors of which all the ingenuity men can command could not invent a torture one-hundredth part as inhuman ; and yet they say our Heavenly Father has prepared this for nineteen-twentieths of humanity.

Thank Heaven, however, the day has come when such libels upon the name of God are rapidly merging into the gray twilight, to soon sink in blank, unfathomable oblivion. Thank Heaven, for its own approach earthward, to strike off the chains of superstition from humanity, and for the first faint glimmering of light shed upon us by its angels' faces, proving to us that humanity, whether of earth or heaven, is :

> " One life for those who live and those who die—
> For those whom sight knows and whom memory."

The Jews would not accept Christ since he came not with temporal power. But Christ will come in the power of the spirit, and shall baptise all humanity. Already His messengers begin to herald the "glad tidings of great joy which shall be unto all people." Already the music of the approaching harmonies are heard from the hill-tops of spirituality singing the approaching millennium. Already its divine notes have pierced some of the dark places of earth, making glad the hearts of their oppressed children, shedding light and truth and joy into their souls. The prophecies of all ages converge upon this, and for their fulfillment, Christ, with all his holy angels, will come to judge the world, and to erect upon it that government already inaugurated in Heaven and long promised Earth, for

> " Decrees are sealed in Heaven's own chancery,
> Proclaiming universal liberty.
> Rulers and kings who will not hear the call,
> In one dread home shall thunder-stricken fall.
>
> " So moves the growing world with march sublime,
> Setting new music to the beats of time.
> Old things decay, and new things ceaseless spring,
> And God's own face is seen in everything."

Therefore it is that there shall soon come a time in which the people will ask for universal liberty, universal equality, and universal justice. Heretofore all branches of reform have been separated each from the other—have been diffusive, working in single and straight lines from a principle outward, utterly regardless of all other movements. Reform has never yet been constructive, but destructive to existing things. Nevertheless, all reform originates primarily from a common cause—the effort of humanity to attain to the full exercise of human right, only attainable through the possession of freedom, equality and justice. Any reform which does not embrace these three principles must necessarily be diffusive, instructive or educational. Each different branch is the squaring of a separate stone, all of which must be brought together and adjusted before even the corner-stone of the perfect and permanent structure can be laid. Republicanism even was not integral in its propositions. It looked simply to personal freedom. Neither equality in its high, or justice in its broad, sense was a portion of its creed. Hence republicanism as represented by the party in power has done its work, and those who prefer to stick to it rather than to come out and rally around a platform perfect in humanitarian principles, will thus show themselves to be more republican than humanitarian.

As a nation we are nearing our first centennial birth-day. A hundred years have come and gone since political freedom was evolved from the womb of civilization. Great as its mission was, great as its results have been, shall the car of progress stop there? Is there nothing more for humanity to accomplish? I tell you there are still mightier and more glorious things to come than human tongue hath spoken or heart conceived. Little did our noble sires imagine what a century would do with what they set in motion. From three to forty millions is a grand, I may almost say a terrible, stride. But with thi step we cannot stop. We must open new channels for the expansion of the human soul.

Up to this time we have expanded almost wholly in a material and intellectual sense. There is a grander expansion than either of these. Wealth and knowledge have brought us power, but we lack wisdom. To material prosperity and intellectual acquirements there must be added moral purity, and then we shall get wisdom. Every. body appears to live as though this life were all there is of life, and that to get from it the most physical enjoyment were the grand thing to be attained. Wealth has been made almost the sole aim of living, whereas it should only be regarded as the means to a better end; as the means by which to accumulate an immense capital with which to begin life in the next and higher stage of existence; and he or she lives best on earth who does the most for humanity.

In this view, what are professing Christians—the churches—doing for the general good to-day? What good can come from preaching without practice, since, though people may be able to say, "All of these have I kept from my youth up," Christ, when he shall come, will reply to them: "Go sell all thou hath and give to the poor, and come and follow me." What clergyman in this city dare stand in his pulpit Sunday after Sunday and insist upon such practice? or what one dare to insist that his church should have all things in common? or what one dare to eat with publicans and sinners, or say to the woman, "Neither do I condemn thee." Or which one of the people dare go to her poor, enslaved and suffering sisters and take them to her heart and home? or be the good Samaritan? I tell you, my friends, beware lest those whom you scorn to know be before you with Christ, who knows the heart. It is not what you pretend that shall make you Christian, but what you do, and if you do right, though the world curse you, yet shall you lay up treasures in Heaven thereby. Therefore, I say that the Christianity of to-day is a failure. It is not the following of Christ, nor the practice of his precepts. True religion will not shut itself up in any church away from humanity; it will not stand idly by and see the people suffer from any misery whatever. It is its sphere to cure all ills, whether moral, social or political. There are no distinctions in humanity. Everything to be truly good and grand, whether it be in politics, society or religion, must be truly moral, and to be truly moral is to live the Golden Rule.

Therefore, it is foolish for the Christian to say, "I have nothing to do with politics, as a Christian. It is the bounden duty of every Christian to support that political party which bases itself upon Human Rights; and if there is no such party existing, then to go about to construct one. It is too late in the century for a Justice of the Supreme Court of the United States to be a political thief and trickster as a politician, while he issues a call asking that the people inject God into the Constitution. Such consummate hypocrisy is an outrage upon the intelligence of the nineteenth century; and it will meet its just reward.

If they would take the precepts of Christ and build a new Constitution upon them, nobody would object; but to be asked to recognize a God whom these people have themselves fashioned and set up, who hath not even human sense of justice, is quite a different thing, and one to which this people will not submit. I could point out to you why this attempt is made just at this time, but I rather prefer to point out how this and all other attempts to put fetters upon the people must be avoided, and how to break the fetters by which they are already galled.

Permit me to ask what practical good arises from the people's coming together and merely passing a set of resolutions. You may pass resolutions with whereases and therefores a mile long, and what will be the result unless they are made practical use of. What would you say to a person who should come before you with a resolution setting forth that whereas, thus and thus, are so and so, therefore some new invention ought to be made to meet the conditions. Why you would at once say to him, "Give us the invention; then we shall be able to judge whether your therefore bears any relation to your whereas."

Now precisely in that way should you judge of resolutions for political reform. We have had resolutions long enough. We now need a working model which will secure freedom, equality and justice to the smallest of our brothers and sisters. Anything less than this is no longer worthy to be considered political reform; and that is not only political reform, but it is also the best application possible of the precepts of Jesus Christ, and therefore the best Christianity, the best religion, since to its creed every human being who is not supremely selfish can subscribe.

In conclusion, therefore, let me urge every soul who desires to be truly Christian to no longer separate Christianity from politics, but to make it the base upon which to build the future political structure. Instead of an amendment to the Constitution, which these hypocrites desire, recognizing a God who is simply the Father of themselves, and a Christ of whom they are the self-appointed representatives, give us a new Constitution, recognizing the human rights of the people to govern themselves, of which they cannot be robbed under any pretext whatever, and my word for it, humanity will not be slow to render due homage to their God. Let that Constitution give a place to every branch of reform, while it shall not so much as militate against the rights of a single individual in the whole world—and we are large enough to begin to say the whole world—and to think of and prepare the way for the time when all nations, kindred and tongues shall be united in a universal government, and the Constitution of the United States of the World be the

SUPREME LAW.

Around this as a New Departure let all reformers rally, and, with a grand impulse and a generous enthusiasm, join in a common effort for the great political revolution, after the accomplishment of which the nations shall have cause to learn war no more.

ECONOMICS

(3)

Reformation or Revolution, Which? . . . 1873.

Reformation or Revolution,

WHICH?

OR,

BEHIND THE POLITICAL SCENES.

A SPEECH DELIVERED IN

COOPER INSTITUTE,

OCTOBER 17, 1873,

BY

VICTORIA C. WOODHULL,

TO AN AUDIENCE OF 4,000 PEOPLE,

Filling to its utmost capacity the Hall, to which hundreds found it impossible to gain admission.

New York:

WOODHULL & CLAFLIN.

1873.

Reformation or Revolution, Which?

Or, Behind the Political Scenes.

It may appear presumptuous, perhaps ridiculous, for a woman to talk to an audience composed largely of men, about politics and government. Men have had the management of these questions so long, it ought at least to be presumed that what they do not know is not worth talking about. I have listened attentively to speeches from many different men—Statesmen, Legislators, Congressmen—but I failed to find in the institutions which they represented, anything that is an excuse, even, for the grandiloquent laudations that they usually indulged in. On the contrary, I find so much of which to complain, in which not only my own interests, but those of every working man and woman in the country are involved, that I cannot hold my peace and see the impending desolation—which now threatens to bring a period of woe to us all—approach unopposed.

We live in an age of progress. Not any body of whom I know even pretends that our institutions are perfect; although the action of some may seem to assume that they are. Not any body will venture to say we have reached a point in anything beyond which it is impossible to go. Not any body will deny, however, that individual enterprises have outstripped the general institutions by which they are regulated; nor that it has come about that these enterprises control the institutions that created them, and, by so doing, are remanding the country backward from democracy toward despotic control; are increasing the distance between the extremes of wealth and poverty—making the representatives of the former fewer and more powerful, and the victims of the latter more numerous and destitute every year; in a word, are subjugating the "Lower Millions" to the will of the "Upper Ten."

In the early days of the Republic, so called, when simplicity and patriotism were the moving characteristics in the minds of the people; when the wealthiest in the land considered it no dishonor to sit at the dinner-table with the men and women in their employ; when the haughtiest dames put their hands to the spinning-wheel and loom; when persons were elected to the offices on account of their fitness, instead of, as now, by money and the prostitution of the polls; I say when these things existed, it is not to be wondered at that the country, under the then recently constructed government, which was in many respects so great an improvement upon the old, was entitled to be called a republic; or that, having supreme confidence in their own honesty of purpose, its framers did not provide for an opposite order of things; for a time when their places might be filled with persons of different impulses and motives, seeking positions of trust which should offer a price at which they would be willing to part with their honor. In those days there were no Credit Mobilier enterprises, and the danger hidden in the womb of the future was not provided for. They imagined, no doubt, that they had constructed a government for themselves that would meet all demands of posterity.

But they were mistaken. A single century has dissipated the hopes which were built on their work. That which they intended should secure to every person the inalienable rights of the Text of the Constitution, has become a gigantic engine of oppression, grinding to the earth a large proportion of the common people who, all their lives long, tax their strength to the utmost, and die at the end, leaving their families destitute, and without the means to decently bury them, while the results of their toil is being enjoyed by others.

So general and oppressive has this condition become, and its injustice so evident, that on every hand the murmurings of discontent among the masses are breaking out into rebellion, in which the hope for reformation is replaced by the desire for revolution. All up and down this broad country secret meetings are held, in which the most extreme remedies are freely discussed; and yet those to whom the people have intrusted the public interests sleep on peacefully, and dream of the next job, seemingly ignorant that the day of judgment is at hand; while still another class are watching the opportunity, tiger-like, to spring upon the throat of liberty as it struggles in the strife, and strangle it in its despotic grasp, so that they may plant themselves upon its ruins. When we thus pass behind the political scenes and observe what is there going on, the heart that beats with the love of justice and freedom; which cares for its country's welfare; which has a single sentiment of the brotherhood of man born in the soul, may well cry out: Can there be Reformation, or must it be Revolution, before justice shall be done?

But what were the ends to be secured by the establishment of this government, different from those that had resulted from other governments, and wherein has it failed, and of what can it be impeached? Let us go back to the beginning, and by the words of its constructors learn what their intentions were

We can then decide by comparing them with what the results have been, whether their ideas are realized, or whether there is a failure.

I presume you are aware that some of the original proposers of a new government, and prominently among them Benjamin Franklin, entertained apprehensions as to the durability and efficacy of the Constitution as it was finally adopted. On the 17th of September, 1787, this venerable man said : " I confess that there are several parts of this Constitution which I do not approve. I agree to this Constitution, with all its faults, because I believe a general government necessary for us ; and I further believe that this is likely to be well administered for a course of years, and can only end in despotism when the people shall become corrupted. Thus I consent to this Constitution, because I expect no better. The opinions I· have had of its errors I sacrifice to the public good ;" and in speaking thus he undoubtedly expressed, in a very guarded manner, the fears of all who moved originally in the matter.

It may be useful, also, to refer to some eloquent remarks of the late eminent jurist, Judge Story. He said : " Let the American youth never forget that they possess a noble inheritance, capable of transmitting, if wisely improved, to their latest posterity, the peaceful enjoyment of liberty, of property, of religion and of independence. It has been reared for immortality. Its defenses are impregnable from without. It may, nevertheless, perish in an hour, by the folly or corruption or negligence of its only keepers, the people. Republics fall when the wise are banished from the public councils because they dare to be honest, and the profligate are rewarded because they flatter the people in order to betray them."

Now what is the deduction to be drawn from this language, coming from these great men ? Clearly, when carried to the ultimate, that the government is not the Constitution and the laws enacted under it, but really the persons who, for the time, make and administer the laws—a good government when these are good men, a bad government when these are bad men— which amounts in substance, to this : that there is no system of government in existence ; that which is called a system being the will merely of those in power for the time being. And to be convinced that this is really so here, it is necessary to review the political history of the country only as far back as 1860. It would be as safe for the people if there were no Constitution, the government being evolved from year to year, as to depend for political existence upon what is now called a Constitution. Indeed, it is to be questioned if there have not been times when it would have been better for the public welfare had there been no constitutional obligations standing in the way of public opinion ; and whether those obstacles do not oftener prevent the right than the wrong from being done.

Furthermore, a constitution for a republic should contain no provisions that could possibly cause the popular will to be defeated. Constitutions and governments for republics should be framed; first, to protect the inalienable rights of each member of the community, and should declare these rights in language so clear that they could not be mistaken; and second, to administer the popular will, as expressed by the people themselves in their approval of all measures before they take effect. The Declaration of Independence and the text of the Constitution were written evidently with these two ideas prominent, and the reason it was feared by some that the Constitution, as adopted, would prove a failure, was because it was not framed in consonance with these ideas. This Declaration and text were the rule by which the structure should have been erected, and had it so been erected, there would have been no need for, or danger of, revolution to-day; whereas we are standing upon its verge, without the remotest hope that it may be averted, and perhaps when the situation is inspected, it may not appear altogether as if it ought to be averted. There are times in the affairs of nations when revolutions are not only necessary, but obligatory upon a people, and it is an open question if such a time is not now impending over this country. One of two things will surely be: There must be reformation behind the political scenes, or there will be revolution outside of them.

Is it asked of what the people complain that, ignored, should call them to take back the power which the government has smuggled? If so, the reply will come back: Of almost everything that exists to-day as the result of government. There is neither freedom, equality or justice in the land, as I will shortly show. The attempt, by the British Government, to enforce a stamp act, such as the people have endured here, almost without murmur, for the last ten years, was one of the chief causes of disaffection of the colonies; while the further attempt to introduce and tax tea, was sufficiently obnoxious to rouse the people to declare that "The time of destruction, or manly opposition, has now come."

And now mark the result. The action of about fifty men, in destroying a cargo of tea, brought on the revolutionary war. If fifty men, out of three millions of inhabitants at that time, with the limited dissatisfaction that existed against the crown, could bring about a revolution, how many men and women out of forty millions inhabitants are required, with the wide-spread dissatisfaction now existing, to bring about revolution?

Do not misunderstand me. I am not advocating revolution; I am demanding what belongs of right to the people. I am asking for reformation; but if it be denied, I fall back upon the right of revolution, which no freeman will deny, and I will use every effort I have at my command to produce it.

The people all over the country are saying: Give us back

our rights, or we will take them ; and the stupid legislators and blundering officials, with their consciences and perceptions alike blunted by the array of spoils upon which their eyes are fixed, to the exclusion of everything else, don't seem to know that anything is the matter; they act as if everything was calm and quiet. And so it is, but it is the calmness that precedes the earthquake ; and I forewarn them that they are sleeping over what is liable to burst forth any day, and cost them their heads for their stupid blundering.

This may be called seditious ; but would you have me, knowing this, permit it to come upon them unawares ? I speak for the people, the great, honest, industrial masses, who, being obliged to toil every day to obtain barely their needed sustenance, have no time to look after the persons to whom they have intrusted their interests, and who, knowing they are being robbed day after day, year after year, cannot leave their labor to counsel together as to the means of relief. Want stands at their home-door, grinning a ghastly grin at their families, and warning them to waste no time ; they know there is something wrong somewhere, but they have not the opportunity to find it out.

I repeat, I speak for this class, and as against that class which devotes its time and talent to devising means to secure the results which the other class produce. As between these two I demand justice ; and by the God of Justice it shall be rendered, peaceably if it can, forcibly if it must. Hunger, with its long, bony fingers, pinched cheeks and fiery eye, shall not much longer hold horrid revel in hut or hovel, in a land that trembles under the weight of its own productions, and is studded from end to end with palatial homes in which luxury abides. Not much longer shall thousands of men, women and children eke out a miserable life upon what a "sport" would disdain to feed his dogs, while the favored few wallow in superfluities.

GENERAL CHARGES.

But I was about to speak of the causes for dissatisfaction that are driving this country into revolution, and had said that almost everything which exists as a result of government belongs among them. Two years ago, when I was importuning Congress to do political justice to woman, which was denied, I found that the wiser portion of Congressmen feared the country was drifting into revolution. Not less than three, whom I consider the wisest of the whole lot, confessed, when pressed to answer, that they did not believe another administration would pass without tremendous political changes ; and the pulse-beats of the country indicate that they are near at hand. The immediate causes will be, as I shall shortly show, the efforts of those who have monopolized the power, the wealth and the money, to hold them, as against the growing demand for a settlement on the part of the people who have produced them.

Will they who scout the idea of revolution remember that until Fort Sumter was fired upon, there were scarcely a hundred people in the country who believed war possible; and that they were accounted as insane? But it came in spite of the wise ones, and it scourged the country as it was never scourged before. The single question of losing its negroes inspired the South to fight. Shall we repeat the blunder of that time by assuming that the people who hold the political power and the wealth of the country will not fight when they see that they are going to be taken from them?

Do not deceive yourselves. Negro slavery was not so great a cause of dissatisfaction then, as are the more subtle slaveries of to-day, now. Nor were the slave oligarchs any more alarmed about their slaves then, than are the po itical, financial and industrial oligarchs for their possessions, now. The public sentiment, however, had outgrown the institution of slavery, and sealed its doom. So also is the public sentiment outgrowing the despotic rule of the aristocrats of to-day, and it will seal their fate. But the latter, no less than was the former, are a part of our system of government, and as slavery proved a failure, and as such was abolished, so also are the others to follow in the same way.

The developments of the past two years—the corruptions, frauds and failures—are a sweeping condemnation of the system under which they have flourished. From Tammany down to the latest Brooklyn *expose*, first and last, one and all—they speak in unmistakable tones of the approaching culmination of the system. They prove beyond cavil that the government has degenerated into a mere machine, used by the unscrupulous to systematically plunder the people. Look where we may, confirmation stares us in the face. From the head at Washington down to the pettiest public office, it is the same story—fraud, corruption, peculation everywhere

What else is to be expected? If Congress—in league with, probably, the Cabinet, if not the President himself—can be induced to push a Pacific Railroad scheme to obtain stock in a Credit Mobilier, and, being exposed, can whitewash itself by such a farce as was enacted in Congress last winter, why, indeed, should not every official in the country go into the same business, and hope to escape in like manner? Examples like that, set in high places, will be copied in lower grades; and these again are legitimate fruit of our system of government.

Even the highest officials no longer hesitate to openly ally themselves with professional speculators, and this brings the exclamation: Can it be possible that the people's money, paid by them into the public treasury, is being used as a basis for speculation, that officials, even the President himself, should rush frantically to the rescue of the jeopardized market? Can it be true, as hinted by those who ought to know, that the large banking firms, recently suspended, were operating on government funds; and, as has been stated of a case in Washington, that drafts upon the Treasury for large amounts were made recently to bolster up their trembling ventures?

Nothing is more probable. It is a well-known fact that, on the eve of the Pennsylvania election last year, the Secretary of the Treasury went into Wall street, and manipulated the market through his pet bankers. Who that knows anything about that little scheme doubts that the profits were largely used to make that election certain?

' When officials near the head of the government are known to speculate *a la* Credit Mobilier; when jobbing schemes are continually bought through Congress, to say nothing about the needed approval at the White House; when men of highest respectability in the community, and very religious withal—Head-Lights in the Young Men's Christian Assassination Association —warm friends of the administration—by a method that is winked at as a mistake only, accidentally defraud the revenue of a few millions; when bank officials remove from the country and safely carry the people's deposits with them; when a Tammany Ring converts millions of the public money to its own use, for charitable purposes (?), and it is accounted of little significance; when hypocrisy sits enthroned in the most popular churches, and the Christians, in a holy unity that was never known until now, seek to establish a Sectarian God, Christ and Bible in the organic law of the country, and are going to succeed; in a word, when everything that is false, corrupt and damnable runs riot at the expense of the hard-working, industrial masses, and is considered too respectable to be inquired into by anybody who comes out of a Nazareth; when all these things are, is it not time that a change come? is it not time for this Babel (which we call government, and which is growing so high as to put its occupants beyond reach of the people), to topple over and be buried in its own ruins?

I do not war upon the people as individuals who are involved in these things. To put others in their place would be a change of persons merely. It is the system that is at fault. If it were not for its glaring defects, individuals, however badly disposed, could not take advantage of the people, who elevate them to positions of honor and trust. I repeat, again, therefore, that our system of government, after a century's trial, has been proved a failure. It has ultimated in corruption and peculation in all its departments, and is rotten and ready to fall; and it ought to fall, and it will fall.

It is in vain to hope that the tide now rushing on a headlong course can be turned into safer channels. Things are going from bad to worse too fast, and with too great momentum. No mere revulsion can purify them. A system in which disease generates and spreads to involve its every part, coursing with fevered rapidity in all its veins, is as impossible of medication as rottenness itself. These things to which we have referred are the symptoms of the disease, which, itself, lies back in the vital parts of the system out of which they are evolved.

SPECIFICATIONS.

I charge upon this government, in the first instance, that it is not republican in form, and is therefore directly opposed, not only to the spirit of the Declaration of Independence, but also to the letter of the Constitution. The Preamble to the Constitution declares that governments are instituted among men, deriving their just powers from the consent of the governed, to secure the inalienable rights to life, liberty and the pursuit of happiness. Now, if a government be instituted and maintained which does not obtain its powers from the consent of the governed, can it, according to the Constitution itself, and the purposes for which it was adopted, be a just government? and if not a just government, can it be a republican government? Nobody will so pretend. Nevertheless, this government is maintained by the absolute denial of the right to express either consent or dissent of more than one-half of the governed ; what is still more reprehensible, they who are thus excluded are recognized by the Constitution as lawful citizens and entitled to equal civil and political rights with any other class.

A despotic government is one in which people are governed without their consent. As a principle, it does not matter whether the governing power is vested in the hands of one person, as in Russia ; in those of a Parliament and a Queen, as in England, or in those of one-half the people, as in this country. There is no difference at bottom between these several governments. Each is the arbitrary rule of a part of the people over the remainder who have no voice or power in that rule.

For my part (and I speak now for myself only), I deny the right of the men of this country to legislate for me, and I will not submit to any of their laws to which I could not consent if I were permitted to dissent, and that limit my personal rights, declared inalienable by the text of the Constitution ; and more especially will I not conform to those which are made to control my social rights, when everybody knows they are intended for women only, men never even pretending to conform to them. I spit upon such despotism ; and every woman who does not is either a willing or unwilling slave ; and they are rapidly waking up to this fact. The government of this country was instituted and is maintained and administered by men over women who have not consented to it, and many of whom protest against it. It is, therefore, in no sense of the word a Republican government, and upon this count it ought to fall; and it will fall.

Again I charge upon this government that it is a failure, because it has neither secured freedom (and by this I mean the personal rights of individuals), maintained equality nor administered justice to its citizens. These three terms constitute the political Trinity. If it have any existence at all in a government, each of the terms will be present. There can be no such thing as justice unless there are freedom and equal conditions; there can be no such thing as equality unless there is freedom. The Trinity is, therefore, to be expressed thus: There must be equality maintained among a free people, whose intercourse is regulated by justice. Institute that law in any country and there will be perfect government; and so far as it does not exist in this country to-day, so far is the government not republican, and, consequently, a failure.

Moreover, it is evident that the legislation of the country, State and National, tends to defeat equality and justice and to introduce and build up unequal conditions, and unjust relations; while caste and class distinctions are becoming more distinctly marked, every day. How much further this may proceed, depends upon the temper of those upon whom the so-called upper classes are presuming to establish themselves.

These "upper classes" may be variously enumerated. First of all is the Land Oligarchy, and this class probably is the foundation of all the rest, since if it did not exist, the others could never have arisen. Now what is the principle underlying this oligarchy? How did it come about that they own the land? They purchased it, it is replied. Of whom did they purchase it? Of its previous owners—away back to its first occupants. And how did its first occupants obtain it? Oh, they took it. Is it not clear then that all the title any body has to any land, is that which they who "took it" had to convey? And this is no title at all, unless they can show they purchased it from its Maker. For this is to what we are soon come to in property rights. There is but one fact that can give individual title to anything; and that is, the fact of being its maker; or the further fact of equal exchange of things between makers.

Man never made the land, and, therefore, he can never obtain a title that can make it justly his, as against the claim of any other living being. Land, like the water and air, is natural wealth, the use of which belongs of right to all the people; and being a natural right, cannot be alienated or forfeited. There is as much right to bottle up the air and deal it out for pay, as there is to claim the land and sell it for gain.

Man individually has certain demands that require the use of the land to supply; and therefore every man, woman and child has a God-given right to his or her share for this purpose, the withholding of which by any power whatever, is as arbi-

trary an usurpation as it would be to shut them out from breath-
ing the air, or to deprive them of the use of water. You see,
my friends, that it is human justice and human rights, as interpreted by the laws of nature, and governing the existence of
man that I am seeking, and before these all human enactments
must sooner or later fall.

The Land Oligarchy, then, will be compelled to surrender
the land to the people; and the government must institute a
just method of securing its use to them, having a proper regard
to the relations between the mechanic and the farmer. The
difference between that condition and the present, would not be
so great as at first may be supposed; the single exception
would be that no person could control more than his equal proportion, of which he would hold possession so long as he paid
the taxes minus the rentals, now exacted by the oligarchy.

Do you not see how infinitely this would better the condition of every occupant of a small body of land, and especially
the farmers of the great West? It could never be encumbered
by debt or mortgage, and could never be taken away so long as
the small taxes should be paid. But taxes, even, are soon to
be among the things of the past. A government that cannot
support itself ought not to exist. But I will not discuss this
just here. I will repeat, merely for the sake of emphasis, that
a government that cannot support itself without taxing the people, ought not to exist!

But I must pay my parting respects to the Land Oligarchy.
A more unjust, inhuman and unnatural thing does not exist.
A single instance will demonstrate that it is all of these. For
comparatively nothing the ancestry of the present Mr. Astor
obtained possession—I will not say acquired title—of the land
in this city, which, by its increase in value, has made him worth
half a hundred million dollars, and the income from the land
has enabled him to cover it with costly warehouses and dwellings, increasing its money producing capacity at every step.

Now, even admitting that he had a rightful title to it originally, I want to ask who is entitled to the increase? Have the
Astors added to its value? Nobody will pretend it. It was the
general growth and prosperity of the city, which resulted again
from the general growth and prosperity of the country that has
done this.

I cannot pursue this further. I throw out these hints to
direct your attention to this infamous wrong. The principles
underlying them are fundamental, and are as certain to obtain
in practice as is the right to come uppermost; and they who
have rolled in luxuries, without so much as a single day's productive labor in their whole lives, and at the expense of those who
have labored, will be compelled to lay their hands to work, in
order to obtain the means of life. The solution of this question
of Industrial Justice means just this and nothing less, and those

whom it is going to put to work may as well begin to prepare.

Having disposed of the land question, there come the almost equal tyrants, wealth and money to be beheaded. The relations which these terms bear to each other are so little understood, it is necessary, before entering upon their discussion, to point them out. Money is not wealth. Wealth cannot be money. Wealth is whatever there is that can be used to sustain life or add to its comforts, and it consists of two kinds, natural and artificial.

All natural wealth belongs of original right to all the people collectively, for their individual use, and each person is an heir to an equal proportion. All other wealth is produced, and of natural right belongs to the individuals who produce it; or to those who obtain it by an equitable exchange of something they do produce.

To illustrate: a farmer may exchange one-half of the yearly products of his own labor for one-half the yearly products of the labor of a mechanic, and that would be an equitable exchange. What we are seeking is equity, and it would not be equity for the farmer to exchange one-half of his products for one-fourth of the mechanic's products.

This question of justice in industry is a subtle one, and yet it is most simple. The equitable price of anything is determined by its cost; and cost consists of two items only, consumption of time in its production and of material, out of which it is produced, where this is itself a production. The establishment of price by the rule of supply and demand can never be equitable. To demonstrate this unquestionably, we have only to consider that a barrel of flour will sustain the life of a given number of persons a given number of days. It will not do more than this if it cost a thousand dollars; it will not do less if it cost but fifty cents, and so of every other necessary or comfort of life.

The chief cause of the present unequal distributions of wealth, it is clear is this unjust system of exchange, regulated by the ever varying rule of demand and supply, instead of the equitable rule of cost. To show the iniquitous effect of this rule, we have only to imagine a case where a person has a remedy which cannot be obtained elsewhere, in time, which another requires to save his life. By the rule of demand and supply, the price is fixed at a million dollars and paid—while had it been fixed by its cost, it would have been no more than five dollars. Now is not this result the same as it would have been, had the equitable price been asked and paid, and the remaining nine hundred and ninety-nine thousand nine hundred and ninety-five dollars, stolen? The difference is in the manner of its getting, not in the thing done. One is considered legal, while the other is denominated robbery. "A rose by any other name smells as sweet" still holds good.

And it is also clear that, if the system of effecting exchanges of commodities was governed by cost, there could be no such unequal conditions as now obtain, and the system of middlemen, merchants, more properly hucksters, would be abolished.

With the abolition of the system of middlemen, would follow the downfall of its ally—the modern newspapers. As the advertising medium of this class, without the support of which three-fourths of them could not exist, they are conducted specifically in the interest of trade and as against those of labor. This is the reason why the influential papers let the discussion of the labor problem, severely alone. So long as the present systems exist, so long must the interests of these two classes remain in antagonism. One hundred and fifty millions dollars are annually paid by the hucksters in puffing their wares, every one of which is a tax upon labor in the increased cost of what they consume, or else in the decreased cost of what they sell. Remember I do not impeach the Press ; I am questioning the manner of its conduct merely. But this again is another evidence of the fallacies of our system which, when changed to a' correct basis, will rear a Press of its own, dedicated to humanitarian, instead of class interests, upon the latter of which it will not rely for support. More than this ; The inauguration of a system of public markets would return to productive labor one-half the people who are now living by retailing its products, upon the productive class, and thus, by so much, lessen the number of hours for daily labor.

The practice of permitting one class of people to speculate in the products of the laboring class, robs the producer or consumer, or perhaps both. We have prominent examples of this in New York City. The consumers of coal have paid as much as $15 a ton for that which at the mines in Pennsylvania cost a dollar and a half. Now either the producer of the coal received thirteen and a half dollars too little, or the consumer paid that sum too much, less only the actual cost of transportation. Again I repeat, a legal system of robbery not less infamous in its conception than it is cruel in its results.

Furthermore it is to be observed that coal is natural wealth in which no one can have a right to traffic for profit ; and with all other natural wealth obtained from the earth, such as metals, salt, oil and wood, belongs to the people as a whole, and should be produced for their use, by the government, at cost. Whatever objection may be made to these propositions, we can only reply that they are principles existing in nature, for which no one is responsible, and which cannot be diverted from their natural application, except at the cost of injustice to somebody. In a word, there is no escape from them ; and until they are taken up and reduced to a working system of government, the peoples of the earth will continue to suffer from industrial injustice, the ignorant and the weak being subjugated in some way by cultivated talent to the strong.

Now money is the thing invented—not produced—to represent wealth and to facilitate its exchange; and gold being wealth, cannot be money. Gold is natural wealth, and all the gold there is in the world belongs of right to all the people, and may be used but not owned rightfully. True, gold may be coined and called, and used for, money, but it is a costly money; and is more gold, when so used, than Bank-note paper is paper when in the form of money. The reason why gold coin is considered the best money, is because it is something more than money, being wealth, and changes from its character as money into its original properties, whenever that which it is used to represent, as money, is no longer represented by it. But it is no better as money, than something else would be which is only money—a scientific representation of wealth. The excuse for using gold as money may be used with equal force for any other kind of wealth, which is equally as convenient.

A representative of wealth is good so long as that which it represents is commanded by it. A note at hand is one kind of money, and is good so long as its maker is possessed of the wealth with which to redeem it; and of the willingness to redeem it; and this is the test of all personal money. Individuals or companies may part with the wealth which their outstanding notes or money represent, and lose the proceeds, and then the money becomes worthless.

Therefore all individual notes or money, or the notes or money of any company, or bank, under whatever regulations, are liable to become worthless, and consequently are not a safe money.

Bank notes are never perfect money, unless there is dollar for dollar in gold wealth with which to redeem them, and if this were always maintained, there would be no method of profit and consequently no banks. Hence banks are not a legitimate subject for legislation, either for protection or regulation, under a republican government.

A perfect representative of wealth and consequently a safe money, is that which represents wealth that cannot be destroyed, lost, exchanged, sold or carried out of the jurisdiction of the government under which it is issued. A money issued by a government representing the total wealth of the country, therefore is the only safe money that can be made. This, then, is the money which the people of republics should have; and it should be loaned by the government to the people, without interest, upon the deposit of sufficient security. And this should be the only dealings permitted in money under the guarantee of law, dealings between individuals being left to their honor. This would abolish all banks, and all speculative operations, and reduce the business of the country to a legitimate basis, and with cost as the limit of price, fix something like permanent values upon every commodity of exchange.

With such a money as this the government may retire its outstanding obligations including bonds, at par, stopping the interest upon the latter at once, which would inaugurate successfully the new order of things. But this, even, would be an act of injustice, since I shall show you why the Public Debt ought to be repudiated.

The Public Debt was incurred to carry on the war, and was largely, if not wholly, obtained from those who had money in their possession which did not represent any product of labor the result of their own industry ; but which was the result of the industry of others, obtained without equity. Hence if it were given to prosecute the war, it was done in behalf of the whole people, to whom all surplus wealth, over a proportionate amount of the whole, for each individual, of right belongs.

If justice were established in the world, it would be impossible for a few of the people to accumulate all the wealth ; therefore it cannot be unjust to restore to the people that which has been unjustly taken from them. Now consider this question impartially and without prejudice : To whom does the accumulated wealth of this country belong ? To the few who pretend to own it, or those who created it ? Dispense with your legal ideas and preconceived notions of property, and answer this as though necessary for your soul's safety. Again I ask who are the rightful owners of the accumulated wealth of the country ? I say, those who produced the wealth by their labor, for which they could not have been equitably paid, since if they had, they would not be poor to-day. And if this is so, then repudiation is right.

But there is another reason why the bonds' ought not to be paid. In the exigency of the war, many of these bonds were sold at sixty cents on the dollar, which has been almost wholly returned in the shape of interest, and therefore is equitably cancelled. The bondholders, however, want to obtain for the six hundred dollars which these bonds cost, first, twenty years' interest— twelve hundred dollars—and, finally, one thousand dollars on the maturity of the bond ; or, twenty-two hundred dollars for six hundred. And this is called legal honesty ; but justice writes it down as common robbery. It may be urged against repudiation that it would be a breach of faith ; but a sufficient reply to this is, that an unrighteous pledge is better broken than kept. And, finally, the most complimentary light in which the holders of the accumulated wealth of the world can be considered, is that they have it in trust for the whole people, to be returned to them when called for, which it will soon be, and that, too, in unmistakable terms.

Another outrage which is perpetrated upon the productive classes by the government, and which should naturally follow the public debt question for consideration, is that of taxation. Let it appear as preposterous as it may, it is nevertheless true that these classes pay every dollar of taxation—they run the government and pay its debts. No matter in what form the tax is levied and collected, it comes home at last to the door of the daily laborers of the country. To show this conclusively requires scarcely more than a single statement:

Probably the total taxation of the country, for national, State, county and municipal purposes, is not less than a thousand millions dollars. At the end of the fiscal year, has the accumulated wealth in the hands of the few been reduced by this amount? No; it has been increased instead of reduced. How increased? By the addition of more produced wealth. Produced by whom? By the laborers of the country. Therefore, though these taxes have been paid to the Treasury by the holders of wealth, the laborer must have furnished the means, else would their bank accounts have been decreased. Can anything be clearer than this, or anything more monstrous and unjust? And when the industrial classes have taken time to consider these things, they will refuse to submit to it.

Do you ask how this is to be remedied? I will tell you how it may be remedied, and how, if revolution be not precipitated, it can be. If Congress would save the country from temporary anarchy, it ought to pass, immediately it assembles, a general law entirely remodeling the system of taxation, which, if carried out, may safely carry the country over the gulf of revolution.

Every family not having more than a numerical proportion of the entire wealth of the country should be exempt from all taxes, while those possessing more than this average, should be taxed progressively, after the following manner: If ten thousand dollars be exempt, all over that sum should be taxed, say, one-half per cent.; all over fifty thousand, three-fourths per cent.; all over one hundred thousand, one per cent.; all over two hundred thousand, two per cent., and so on up to a million, which should be taxed twenty-five per cent.

This would inaugurate a redistribution to the people of the accumulated wealth, and, in a measure, do justice to labor. In other words, it would put a penalty upon holding more than an average amount of wealth. This, in conjunction with the abolition of the revenue system and the adoption of free money, without which free trade would be destructive to mechanical industry, may be accepted by the industrial interests as a settlement of the now unsolved question between them and capital.

But why do I come before the people with the fundamental principles of scientific organization, at this specific time? Because we are on the verge, if not already in the flood of a financial convulsion that will shake this country from centre to circumference, and, if I mistake not the signs of the times, that will prove a more memorable event than has ever occurred, and in what respect I shall show you hereafter.

What is the financial condition in this city? Complete stagnation; greenbacks at a premium of four per cent. and interest, three per cent. per day on Government Bonds as collaterials. Nothing doing in other securities. Nobody depositing any money in the banks, but everybody becoming his own banker. Merchants doing nothing, are glum and fearful; and manufacturers discharging their employes. Fifty thousand men in the city without work and without money. Such a condition cannot last long. There will soon be a breaking loose somewhere. A month's continued pressure and one-half the firms in the city will fail!

But what has produced this condition? It is the result of the recent panic in Wall street, introduced by the failure of Jay Cooke & Co., and followed by other pet bankers of the government. This involved a sufficient number of professional speculators, who were obliged to realize on their ventures, to cause a fall of from ten to twenty per cent. in all the speculative stocks, and in two days it was found necessary to close the Stock Exchange, shut the doors of the Clearing House (which was virtually the closing of every bank), and to call upon the government in lustiest tones to come forward to avert the threatened disaster.

What was this danger? Simply this: Had not business been stopped by these precautionary measures, every banker and broker involved in stocks and every bank would have failed. Why? Because the banks are loaded up with these railroad stocks, upon which they have loaned up to within ten, and on some to within five, per cent. of their recent market value, and it was impossible for their customers to make good, in money, the shrinkage of ten to twenty per cent. that took place, aggregating perhaps not less than a hundred millions of dollars for the banks of this city alone.

A continuation of sales of stocks under the panic and increasing failures would have pressed them down fifty per cent., broken every bank, and tumbled the whole country into financial dismay and ruin; and more than probably before this time have ultimated in riot and anarchy and the proclamation of martial law, to have been soon followed by the Dictatorship, or perhaps the Empire. But of this more anon.

Now, all this confusion and threatening anarchy was not the result of any want of general productiveness of the industrial classes. No! We are exporting at this special time more than ever before, the balance of trade is largely in our favor, and even in the panic the price of gold is decreasing. It appears, therefore, that this is a purely speculative condition, brought about by a failure of the outside public to go into Wall street, as has been their custom to do, and buy the stocks after the manipulators had worked them up to enormous prices. Finding themselves with the whole list of stocks on their hands, and large interest constantly augmenting their cost and no purchasers, the speculators had at last to begin to throw them over—that is to realize—at a loss.

By such an operation as this, have the commercial and industrial interests of the country been jeopardized. But this is not the end. The grand bursting of the speculative bubble has been put off merely, not prevented. The most extraordinary measures resorted to, re-enforced by the whole power of the government, aided by a systematic attempt on the part of the papers—purchased, no doubt—have been able only to delay the day of reckoning, without in the least restoring confidence or curing the malady.

And now the papers are beginning gradually to break the real condition to the people; to tell them that things have a "fictitious value" and a "false basis," which "must be remedied." That the merchants are getting involved because they cannot obtain their usual accommodations from the banks, which have advanced their deposits on these depreciated stocks.

Thus the money of the business community deposited in banks and of the laboring classes in savings institutions is locked up in stocks at a price greatly above the possibility of present or even future realization. Of course there must be a crash, and no one can tell to what extent the disaster will spread.

Now what shall be the verdict against a system of finance conjoined with that of internal improvements which puts it in the power of a few bold or reckless speculators at any time to entirely unsettle and undermine the industrial interests of the country? For my part I would say, Sink it in everlasting oblivion. I would have the people take possession of the entire railroad system of the country, upon the stocks of which the tendency to speculate has been introduced into the country, and thus destroy the chief means of indulging this mania that is spreading to almost every staple product of the country. It is not uncommon now to hear of "corners" in cotton, pork, wheat, and so on to the end of the list, every one of which is conceived and executed at the expense of the producing classes.

Moreover the railroad system of the country is too extensive and too intimately involved with the general public welfare to be longer trusted in the hands of those who make it the basis of these speculative schemes, and thereby keep the country in a constant turmoil. Sixty thousand miles of railroad, at a cost of three billions dollars, is an immense power, and wielded, as it virtually is, by a half dozen men, is a dangerous power, and is already potent enough to control the legislation of the country in its own interests. A system of watering their capital stocks has also obtained, by which process the industries may be taxed a thousand millions dollars to make the roads earn their eight per cent. dividends.

It is becoming patent, however, even to the railroad kings, that, unless some great national revulsion in favor of despotism is actually accomplished, they will have to give up their roads to the people. Already is the West, which is taxed two bushels of wheat to transport one bushel to New York, up in arms against the oppression, and is moving public opinion in the direction of the remedy, while the "Granges"—the first political organization to which women were ever admitted as equals—are organizing for reformation, or revolution, if it come.

I am aware of the very general prejudice that exists against the management of the railroads by the government; but this is largely due to the prevalent and growing idea that everything with which the government is connected is liable to abuse from official corruption; certainly, however, this could not possibly exceed that which exists in railroads now. This should not, however, be judged from the present government, but from that which is to succeed it. But the experience in the same direction that is furnished by the postal service, indicates that there would be equal improvement in the railroad service over the present, that there is in this over the old method.

And were the same regulations applied to the transportation both of passengers and merchandise that obtain in the mails, there would be a perfect solution of the vexed questions of freight and passenger tariffs. The same principle that transports a letter from New York to San Francisco for three cents, while it costs the same to send one to Philadelphia, would set the wheat of Minnesota down in the New York market costing no more than that grown in the Genesee Valley.

If the postal service is self-supporting, or nearly so, conducted upon this principle, why cannot the entire system of transportation be made the same?

The government being the source of money is its legitimate custodian and carrier. It should prepare methods to receive the people's money and to pay or transmit it from one to another, on demand, but without interest. The post office is the natural channel, and the money-order system the true method of exchange, and by adding to its present functions, the further one as a depository of the people's money, a reliable commercial system, infinitely superior to the present, as the blindest must see, would be the outcome. In such a system there would be no bank suspensions; no worthless or depreciated currency; no protested drafts; no failure of savings banks and robbery of the poor;—in short all the imperfectious and insecurities of the present, would be replaced by regularity and security.

There is no doubt but this will be the future of transportation. Indeed, it is necessary, to establish equal conditions for the people all over the country. The people of the Mississippi Valley are now compelled to pay larger prices for everything they consume, and realize less for all they have to sell, than do the inhabitants not so far removed from the commercial centre of the country. This is an inequality of which they have just cause of complaint, although they do not yet understand the principle upon which it is founded.

SUMMARY OF GENERAL REFORM.

Thus I have rapidly sketched the moving principles upon which any system of general reform, to meet the demands of justice and equity, must be based, and have made hasty reference to the oppressive systems that have been builded, and which subsist upon productive labor; but to bring these pointedly to view, I will briefly restate the three general principles, which, if adopted, will settle the questions at issue between labor and capital and inaugurate industrial justice, and the three methods by which this is now prevented, to wit: The monopoly of land, in defiance of natural right; the monopoly of wealth, through the regulation of prices by the law of demand and supply, in defiance of the law of equity, instead of by that of cost, which is its exemplification, and interest for the use of the mere representative of wealth—money. Abolish these and inaugurate a system of free land by the payment of taxes; of free money, based upon the public faith, and, as a method of transition, or of equalization of the accumulated wealth, of progressive taxation.

The exchange of all commodities, all produced wealth, by the law of equivalents, cost being made the limit of price, would leave in the hands of the producer the entire results of his labor, or their equivalents. Under this law, to possess property a person would have first to produce it, while commercial exchanges should be effected by the paid agents of the people through a general system of public markets.

In addition to this, the abolition of interest, together with the institution of progressive taxation, would quickly compel the bondholders and the money lenders—the leeches now fastened upon the vitals of industry, sucking, sucking, sucking its blood, day after day and year after year—to earn their own food, clothing and shelter, instead of stealing it, legally I admit, from those who do labor.

In this analysis all considerations of policy and expediency, which are ever at war with principles, have been ignored, and an earnest effort made to reach the truth. It may be said that it is impossible to change our systems so that they shall be founded upon these principles; but I affirm that truth and justice are always possible, and it is only the unwillingness of those who are playing the part of the executors of falsehood and injustice that stand in the way. Granted, that the common industrial classes do not understand what is theirs by natural right; it does not follow that they never will, nor that they ought not to enjoy it. The negro slaves did not know their rights until, in many instances, they were actually forced upon them; but the Garrisons and the Douglasses and the Phillipses understood them, and paved the way for them to be obtained. So now shall the Garrisons, the Douglasses and the Phillipses of labor slavery also pave the way for its slaves to obtain their rights, born with them from the very Constitution itself, of their Mother, Nature; and I will never cease the demand or stop agitation until the modern oligarchs shall willingly deliver these slaves to freedom, or else until they are compelled to do so by the stern logic of war.

ERRORS OF OMISSION.

I have thus far discussed chiefly those evils which oppress the people by the commission of errors by the government. There is still another class of crimes, almost equally reprehensible, which may be named *Errors of Omission*. These have special reference to the dependent and unfortunate classes—the women, the children, the criminals, the maimed and the insane, which together make up a sum total of human misery almost too horrible to contemplate, and which fix a stigma of reproach, an indelible blotch of infamy, upon this pretendedly enlightened people which would merit the contempt of the most barbarous nation on the globe. This, at the first glance, may seem to be too severe an indictment of our civilization; but I say it is just, since such things as obtain here would put the savages to shame.

The people have fought for freedom, and become drunk upon the name. They have forgotten that this blessed boon cannot exist unless equality and justice also obtain. They have imprinted the former, omitting the last two, upon their banners, and have first gone mad with enthusiasm, and, secondly, have sunk into a comatose condition, in which they occasionally, when stung into temporary consciousness by some passing event, yelp out Freedom with all their might, without the least idea as to what is really going on about them in the world.

I say the dependent and unfortunate classes, and name women as among them, and they belong to both of them. And when I say they so belong, I mean that the beautiful social system that has been enforced virtually commits every woman to one or the other of these classes. I do not say that there are not any women who rise superior to the condition imposed upon them by the system. No thanks to the system, however, that they do it; but, in spite of it. I say that the present social system, enforced both by law and a falsely educated public opinion, makes every woman dependent for support and comfort upon some man, and it does not give the least consideration as to whether she obtains it or not. It says to her: Here is the theory, live by it if you can; die by it if you must and the devil take the unfortunate. We, the government, we the men to whom belong all the realities of this world, can't do anything more for you except you become a social outcast, as they gracefully call unfortunate women, when we will perhaps patronize you as our demands require. I repeat again, and I wish my voice could reach the ear and the soul of every man and woman in the world, that the theory of our social system is, that women are dependent upon men, and that to secure support they must marry and merge their identity and individuality in some man, and then it leaves her unmindful, and indifferent as to whether she secure it or not.

If she do not do this, however, and, following the male theory, attempts to support herself and to answer the demands of her maternal nature, she is compelled to suffer social death. Hence, I say, woman belongs to the unfortunate as well as to the dependent class. These are facts, and though you may ignore you can't dodge them, however unpalatable they may be. Take them home and think about them, and see if you can come to any just and truthful conclusion except that woman is man's industrial and social slave, dependent upon her ministrations to his demands to obtain a support. Think of it, I repeat, calmly and deliberately, and then condemn those who are demanding social reform, if you can.

So long as men maintain this social theory, and so long as women are its willing slaves, I say change the law, so that they shall be protected in it; so that women shall not be made dependent upon individual men. Make it a duty of the State to see that the theory which it insists on enforcing is carried out to its logical results. Let it see that woman has a support and not compel her to surrender herself to a single person, and to forever after be compelled to rely upon him for life and its comforts, when in so many instances both are denied her.

I want to ask every woman who, under this theory, has secured all the necessities and the comforts of life, how many women would frequent the haunts of vice in the Green streets of the world, if they were placed on an equality with you; and before you come to a conclusion, remember, if you had been situated in the same circumstances that have driven them there, and they in those that have surrounded you, that it is more than probable you would have been where they are while they, perhaps, would have filled your places?

Therefore, society having constructed a social system that makes it impossible that there should not be unfortunately circumstanced women, and as it afterward condemns them to social ostracism and death because they are unfortunate, it is a self-contradiction and stultification and needs to be remodeled to make it consistent with itself. The fashionable women of the day say that outcasts prefer to remain in vice rather than do the menial work they can obtain; but let them ask themselves if they were driven to the acceptance of one or the other of these alternatives, whether they would not choose the comforts that are lavished upon the mistress, with indolence and ease, rather than the drudgery to which the kitchen scrub is subjected?

A beautiful thing, this social system of yours! People sit in judgment over their brothers and sisters, when, if they were to exchange places, they would do the same thing which is condemned. Yea, verily, a beautiful, a just, a righteous system, worthy a so-called Christian civilization, but which would not be tolerated among the heathen. Let the government, let the male lords and rulers provide that women shall not be dependent upon men as individuals. So long as she conforms to the instituted theory and is therefore dependent, make her the ward of the State, of man collectively.

The same principle involved here applies with equal force to children. Under this social system children are born and made dependent upon the individual—the father—for support and proper training, without any provision whatever for a failure. If the father do not or cannot provide for them. what does the State care, except to commit them for vagrancy?

What does the City of New York, this Christian city, with its numerous churches dedicated to God and Christ, care for the thousands of children who live from its slop barrels, or the thousands more who die from partial starvation and neglect! Does your beautiful social system have any place or care whatever for them? No! none at all. The very classes which need its care and protection are utterly ignored in its provisions. Out upon such Christianity as this. It is unworthy of a barbarous age, to say worthy of this professedly Christian time.

I arraign this thing that goes by the name of Christianity, as a fraud; and its so-called teachers as imposters. They profess to be the followers of Jesus of Nazareth, while they neither teach, preach or practice the fundamental principles which He taught and practiced. Poets and seers of all ages, climes and tongues have sung and prophesied of a good time coming, when the lion and the lamb shall lie down together (on earth of course), and a little child shall lead them; when swords shall be beaten into plow-shares, and spears into pruning-hooks (on earth of course), and the nations shall learn war no more (because there shall then be no causes for war, as the people will then have learned that they are all brothers of one common parent, and will no longer be in active competition for everything as they now are); when all shall know the Lord, from the least even unto the greatest, and when the whole race shall be united in one government, as a common human family, owning God as the common parent, and Nature as their common inheritance.

All these are doctrines, fundamental to a religion that has any right to the name of Christian. But do we hear them taught by Christian orators? No! The only good time coming of which they give us any hope, is when the human family is to be divided into two parts; one part of about ninety-nine one-hundredths being in hell, and the one one-hundredth part in heaven rejoicing over their salvation.

This is their future. But what of the practical present! Do they ever preach: Inasmuch as ye gave no meat to him that was an hungered; no drink to him that was a thirst; that ye took not the stranger in; clothed not the naked; ministered not to the sick, and visited not them who were in prison;—I say do they preach that, inasmuch as Christians have done none of these things to the least among you, that they have not done them unto Christ?

When I used to go to their churches I never heard such preaching. They may have varied in the last fifteen years. Still I don't think the leopard has changed his spots very decidedly, although I do hear that it isn't popular to preach up quite so hot a hell as they once did (the stock of brimstone is probably running low); nor quite so horrible a devil as the one that used to beat God whenever he had a tustle with him (perhaps he's growing aged and infirm, and isn't quite so hard to handle as formerly); neither do I hear as much about the gold and silver that was so bountifully provided for the fortunate ones in heaven (which, by the way, had better be sent to earth to relieve the suffering and needy); and I think they have also changed the psalm that was continually sung around the throne;—all these things, I say, may be modified, as rather unpopular just now; but it is after all the same old devil, with his claws where people have nails, and hoofs where the feet ought to be—the same that used to frighten me and my mates from the back seats in the church to the mourners bench; and I denounce them as infamous frauds, palmed off upon a people which will not think for itself, by forty thousand ministers, who, if their devil should accidently get killed, wouldn't know what to do for their bread and butter.

I charge these forty thousand ministers that they are frauds, wantonly ignoring the real doctrines of Jesus, and imposing others upon the people. The fundamental principles to which I have referred are never retailed from Christian pulpits nor practiced by Christian laymen. Therefore, judged by their own standard, they are impostors and Christianity a failure; and it ought to fail; and it will fall.

Jesus frequented the abodes of the lowly and despised of earth. He ate with publicans, sinners and harlots; and of these

last He said to the Scribes of His time, as He wo .ld to the
Scribes of our times, They will enter the kingdom of heaven before you. If Jesus, with His rough-clad disciples, should make
His appearance, some Sunday, near a Fifth-avenue church, and
should offer to heal the sick by the laying on of hands, and to
tell fortunes, as He did, these impostors would have him arrested
as a blasphemer ; or if he were to pass through the country and
break into a field of corn and gather it for Himself and disciples,
He would be charged as a thief and sent to Sing Sing ; or again,
if Paul were to stand up in any of the churches, and discuss the
social question as he did to the Corinthians, the Y. M. C. A.
would have him in Ludlow for obscenity ; and would take care
to fix his bail at so large a sum they would feel sure that none
of his crowd could get him out ;—and this is your boasted
Christianity. How many years longer shall such a disgrace to
an enlightened people rear its head in this land ? I give it until
1900 to die, twenty years for every spire that now points sky-
ward, to be leveled with the ground or changed to other uses.
Remember, I say till 1900.

There are thousands of fathers in New York out of employment and out of money, with wives and from three to ten
children suffering for bread. How are they to get on through
the winter ? Does your boasted system ask or care ? No ! But
if they should steal a loaf of bread to keep the children from
starving, or a basket of coal to keep them from freezing, it
makes ample provision that they shall be sent to Sing Sing.
Isn't this true ? Then never again extol your social system,
until you have swept it of its brutalities ; nor of your beautiful
government and of your Christian institutions, until those who
need their protection are given consideration. I'll none of them
until some of the principles and teachings of Christ are reduced to practice.

The Bible says, "Go to now ye rich men, weep and howl
for the miseries that shall come upon you. Behold the hire of
the laborers who have reaped down your fields, which is kept
back by fraud, crieth, and the cries of them which have reaped,
have entered the ears of the Lord." Do the professed Christians, with their long purses and longer faces, believe this ? Did
the recent Evangelical Alliance have anything to say about it ?
No ! Yet it is in the Bible, by which they profess to govern
their lives ! The judgment day, however, is at hand. The cries
of them that have reaped down the fields of the rich ; that have
builded their houses ; that have produced their wealth, crieth, and
the cries of them have reached the ears of the Lord of Justice,
and woe to the rich men. Let them weep and howl for the miseries that shall come upon them if they harken not to the cries,
while yet there is time of their own accord to do justice to the
classes who have made them what they are.

So long as the government maintains a theory that compels

every man to depend upon his individual exertions for a living for himself, wife and children, it should also guarantee him continuous labor at equitable wages. I said there are thousands whose families are suffering for food who cannot obtain work at any price. What shall they do? Beg, steal or starve? These are their only alternatives, and yet you will curse them if they do either.

Governmental employ for everybody who cannot obtain labor elsewhere; and governmental care for wives and children who need it, must be introduced as a supplement to the present systems. Not to do this is barbarous. Already is our civilization blackened with the disgraceful accounts of the miseries that the omission to do this has caused, and if it be not done, and that at once (I speak it in sorrow, but I know it too well), there will be riot in New York before spring.

Yes, there must be provisions for unprovided wives and uncared-for children by government, that will place them upon an equality with the best classes of society as to food, shelter and clothing, with physical and industrial, as well as intellectual education for the children; and employment must be given to every needy man and woman. Under such regulation only, is there the remotest possibility for a continuation of the present governmental and social systems. In no other way can Reformation prevent Revolution; and it ought not to be prevented by anything less.

Your criminal jurisprudence has also developed another infamous system. Your station-houses and jails are a sickening disgrace; while your prisons and penitentiaries are foul generators of misery and crime. A term in them will harden the best man or woman into confirmed degradation. In your eagerness to punish crime, you destroy the man or woman. You rush them, being merely charged with crime, into your pest-hells, where they lie pent up for months, without even an investigation, and then you hurry them through something called a trial, often without a defense, and if it is possible to fix the act upon them with any degree of certainty, they are hurried to the place which seals their future career, and where they are treated worse than brutes, and as if they were not human. A "States Prison Bird" has little chance in your social system. He can practice only those things for a living which continually return him. And all this is done by your system and its executors, as I said in the case of unfortunate women, never stop to think if they had been placed in the same circumstances as under which the criminal committed his crime, that they would have undoubtedly done the same thing, or perhaps something worse.

You erect and maintain a system one of the legitimate fruits of which is crime, and then you punish the unfortunate individuals who enact the villain character of the drama prepared by you for them. Verily consistency is a jewel that is sadly wanting in all parts of this beautiful system which is palmed off upon the world as the one thing good and true and pure, but in which ignorance too frequently passes for innocence and experience is mistaken for crime.

You must, therefore, change your criminal discipline from the theory of punishment for crime, to that of reform for the man and woman. In the first place, according to your own theory of Christianity, you have no right to punish anybody. "Judge not lest ye be judged," is fundamental to the Christian theory, and how can you punish, unless you first judge? I repeat, then, that you have no right whatever to punish anybody for any crime; but you may protect yourselves from its recurrence. In doing this, however, you should use no means that of themselves will tend to make men and women worse than they are. Your Prisons must be transformed into vast Reformatory Workshops, where men and women can work and be paid equitable wages, having all the common comforts during their restraint.

Sometimes, however, when I see the utter indifference to the horrid barbarities that are practiced under these systems, I almost despair of reform. Indeed, I seem to feel to say to you that there will be no reformation except through bloody revolution. Wrongs have been heaped upon wrongs until they have reached heavenward and moved the avenging angel. Great wrongs have always been washed out by great rivers of blood, and I fear the time for this has not yet passed away from the earth.

Behind the political scenes the actors in the political drama are so busily engaged in their own personal schemes they have no time to listen to the cries that are reaching the ears of the God of Justice, and you, the people, are too much engrossed in your individual money getting, to give the necessary attention to secure any change. For the last three years, in one way and another, I have done everything that lay in my power—I have sacrificed fortune, reputation and friends—in the attempt to rouse the people to a sense of the impending danger. But they will not listen. For my efforts, however, they have branded me all over the world as the vilest of women and the most dangerous of individuals. They have robbed me of everything except my self-respect, which they could not take and with which only remaining I defied them as they made off with the rest; they have locked me up in jail when the officials who made out the order knew there was no law for it, and have pursued me without mercy on every hand.

And why? Simply because, as I told you, I have endeavored to rouse the people to a realization of the impending judgment, for long years of crime which the government has committed against the people. And they knew unless they could shut my mouth that I should succeed and they would be relieved by the people from further official duty. Yes, though I am only a little woman, the political oligarchs who are manipulating this country for a monarchy, fear me. And well they may, for I preach their doom. I sing the battle cry of freedom, equality and justice for the people, and they know that it will be caught up by them and that its re-echo from the pine forests of Maine, from the wheat fields of Minnesota, from the golden mountains of the Pacific slope, from the cotton and rice plantations of the South, will hurl from the places builded by the labors of the masses all who have been false to the trusts reposed in them.

Now to what does all this logically tend? Clearly, if it be correctly understood, To the redistribution among the people of the natural wealth of the world as well as the equal benefits and comforts resulting from its use, and the establishment for the present aristocracies of society, which are the chief aim of almost everybody's life, an aristocracy founded on personal worth, intellectual capacity and moral grandeur, which will become the new incentives or motives of life. *Now*, only man is compelled by the political, industrial and social systems that are enforced, to make wealth or money-getting his chief aim, while every woman's highest aim is to entrap the most successful man into marriage. *Then*, for these will be substituted in the case of both men and women, who will be equal in the wealth plane, the attainment of the highest positions in the community, not for the sake of their emoluments, for these will be equal in all grades, but for the sake of doing the most good to society, and of thus becoming its most honored and beloved members. Can any one think of any really valid objection to such a change? I think not!

A RELIGIOUS AND POLITICAL DESPOTISM.

And now I come to consider the means that are to be used to prevent, if possible, the attainment by the people to what I have shown you is theirs by natural right; to prevent even the peaceable reformation that is sought, and to fasten the present conditions irrevocably on the people. In the first place, it is to be observed that a religious despotism or even a national religion, cannot exist in a politically free country, since in the former instance it would be liable to be overturned at any time by a popular election, nor, in the latter instance, since a free people could not be compelled to support a national religion. Hence it is evident at the outset that they who are moving for a national religion as they term it, know it can be established only when freedom, politically, ceases to exist.

Therefore this God-in-the-Constitution movement means more that the establishment of a formal national religion. Indeed if what is going on behind the political scenes were really made known to the people, the intentions of a grand conspiracy would be exposed, in which the leading spirits of all the monopolies are engaged, but which as yet has existence only in secret conference. The God-in-the-Constitution movement, the gradual concentration of the monopolies, and the consolidation of political power are all parts of a single conspiracy to change this form of government first, probably, to a Dictatorship and then to an Empire.

No movement approaching this in significance and importance was or can ever be sprung upon a nation without a vast deal of previous secret plotting and preparation, and each of the parts of this conspiracy are now driven together to make common cause against a common foe—Progress. As I have already shown, monopoly and the present political strategists are doomed, even in their success, to fall ; but no more certainly than is their near ally in the conspiracy, whose present foundation is being undermined by the rapid spread of what they call the heresy of Spiritualism.

During the last twenty-five years not less than ten millions of people have changed their *belief* of existence in a future state to the *knowledge* of that existence. Millions of people have had communications from their so-called dead friends, denying the truth of the chief doctrines of the so-called Christian religion; and this knowledge and denial have spread into the churches, and are powder-posting their structures with such fearful rapidity that its "pillars" realize unless something can be done at once to relieve the condition—to stop this infidelity, as the Evangelical Alliance recently put it—that the whole Christian structure will crumble to pieces and fall. They also know there is but one way to stop it ; and that is, to crush it out by whatsoever stringent means, directed by the strong arm of the general government.

The bondholders, money-lenders and railroad kings say to the politicians : If you will legislate for our interests, we will retain you in power, and, together (you with the public offices and patronage and we with our immense dependencies and money), we can control the destinies of the country, and change the government to suit ourselves ; and now, finally, come in the threatened church power, and it says: If you will make your government a Christian government, we will bring all the "Faithful" to your support ; and thus united, let me warn you, they constitute the strongest power in the world. It is the government, all the wealth of the country, backed up by the church, against the unorganized mass of reformers, every one of whom is pulling his or her little string in opposing directions.

Now, my friends, do not dismiss this as a matter of imagery conjured up in my mind. I am sorry to affirm to you that there is too much truth in it, the half of which I have not even touched upon. Stop for a moment and consider what God-in-the Constitution, with these hell-fire people as its executors, means. It is nothing less than the substitution of the Bible-God and Christ, as interpreted by the church, for the present rule. Now do not understand me as impeaching the Bible, God or Christ as I understand them, but as objecting to being compelled to accept or give tacit assent to the interpretations of the church.

No one more strenuously than I do, can urge the teachings attributed to Christ. I believe in His law of love, which instructs us to love our neighbors and their children as well as we do ourselves and our children, and in thus loving to care for them as well; I believe in His advice to the rich man, to "go sell all thou hast and give to the poor," and I believe in his judgment of the woman: "Let him that is without sin cast the first stone." I believe that "to the pure in heart all things are pure;" and in its corollary, that to the impure in heart all things are impure; in a word I believe in the beauty and purity of all the teachings of Christ as laid down in the Bible; but I do not happen to believe that they were original with him, since every one of them in some form are found in Christs of earlier origin than Jesus, or that He any more than all other men and women, or in any other sense, was the Son of God.

But I do not believe in the Christian God nor the Christian devil, nor in their heaven or hell; and it is because the facts of Spiritualism have exploded these misinterpreted remnants of mythological figures. It is robbing them of their power over the people, by dispelling the fear of death the devil and hell and they are roused to the necessity of putting down this most dangerous of all humbugs, as it has been denominated by one fully convinced of its facts. I grant that they fully appreciate it, because it is the most dangerous thing to their ridiculous creeds and dogmas and to their power and positions that could arise in the world.

The people, however, do not apprehend any danger, nor will they until it is too late, and they find themselves called upon, under pressure, to be converted. You remember the arguments that Christians used to make in Spain and elsewhere, not to mention the more modern ones of burning witches and hanging Quakers by the Puritans of New England, whose God, Christ and devil was the self-same of which these Christians now desire to become the self-constituted earthly vicegerents.

Don't comfort yourselves with the idea that they will not use equally as persuasive measures as they teach that their God uses to convert you, nor that they think a few turns on "The Wheel" or a few stretches on "The Rack" or a little quiet roasting at "The Stake," at all out of place when the issue is so great as the salvation of your souls from everlasting torments in hell fire; where the worm dieth not and the fire is not quenched, where the pavements are of infants' skulls a span in length and all the other necessary appointments to make the place good and hot. No! Don't mistake people who profess to believe in such an internal monster as they picture their God as being who would torment in ell a child whom he loves and whom, if almighty, he could save, for a single unrepented crime. They will have no more mercy or pity than He has, nor will they leave any means untried to save you from the vengeance of His wrath.

I do not overstate the picture. I take their own words, their own God as interpreted by themselves, and draw the unavoidable conclusion. If their religion is such infernalism, they should not blame me for depicting it to the people. Indeed, if they believe it themselves, they ought rather to thank me for the service I render, in showing the importance of escaping such dreadful things.

I, however, do not fear their God, I am only afraid of them, for I know if they once get the power, I shall be one of the first upon whom they will try their persuasive arguments; there will be need of my immediate conversion.

But, seriously, it will not do to let this thing succeed. It is the last frantic effort of expiring despotism struggling to regain its lost estate; and if it succeed, it will endeavor to crush out the last prospect for progress. It was necessary only to have attended the recent sessions of the Evangelical Alliance in New York, to have comprehended what this means; but if it fail, the last hope of despotism of every kind will sink into merited oblivion, and be buried in the dead past, only thenceforth to be thought of as one of the horrors of antiquity, because of the crimes that belong to its reign on earth.

I have already shown you how all this may be accomplished in the event of a general panic resulting from wide-spread financial and commercial ruin. If this do not come about in the regular order of events, and at the proper time, it can be made to order. Indeed, who can tell but what has already occurred is the initial step in the drama. Does it not seem just the least bit strange that notably among the ruined, are all the houses specially known as Government Bankers; and with them also notably houses supposed to be in the interest of one of the railroad kings of the country and probably the wealthiest of them all? Think of it, and see if by putting this and that together you cannot frame a reasonable theory for all that is passing, as connected with a grand scheme to subvert the government!

But if this is not as I suspect it to be, a genuine panic can be inaugurated any day. There are many millions of gold loaned, on call, in Wall street, mostly from English bankers. If that were to be suddenly "called" it would put gold to two hundred and United States bonds to fifty and speculative stocks to nothing, and ruin every bank, banker, broker, merchant and business in the country, conducted upon accommodation loans as nearly everything is at the present. In such a condition riot would certainly ensue, martial law become a necessity, and the empire a probability, because, as I say, all "the powers that be" are in league to make one.

Who can say that the prominent European powers are not in the secret and that they would not lend it every possible aid? Do you not remember that the most autocratic of all the generals of the army, and the one nearest the President, last year, made the tour of Europe, virtually having conference with every monarch? Wasn't that also just the least bit singular, at such a time and conducted under the circumstances it was? And who shall say that every ambassador to an European court is not secretly committed to such a movement?

The result once accomplished Europe would extend all needed aid, and, though the value of all stocks, banks and property would be, for the time, almost nothing, yet the movers rely upon the general prosperity of the country to advance them again, in the course of time, to their present prices, and being as they would be, securely aggregated in the hands of the few and the despotism firmly established, their end would be accomplished. They would have the government and the wealth safely vested in themselves. This, I have good reason for believing, is the programme already laid out to establish a monarchy on the ruins of this so-called Republic. And what, I ask, have the people with which to oppose it? At most a few liberal leagues and a few secret societies, without either general concert of action or means of any kind to resist anything successfully. You may laugh at it if you will, but the people of this country are to-day powerless as against such a combination, and I fear they will find it out only when too late.

I have thus reviewed the present political situation, and analyzed the principles of Reformation demanded by the times and shown how Revolution may be averted, unless there are movers behind the Political Scenes who intend to force it; in which case there will be a short, sharp, bloody and decisive struggle, that at first will be altogether in favor of the conspiracy, but which will ultimate in the success of the people and the inauguration of a new and higher order of civilization. The Dictatorship, even the Empire, may succeed, and the Christian Bigots be installed as God's vicegerents on Earth, but their reign will be short and bitter, and the more decisive their success at the outset, the more terrible will be their ultimate overthrow. They will go down in a common ruin and there will be no more despots ever again to possess themselves of the rights and liberties of the people.

Let us hope, however, that all this may be averted, at least let us not be guilty of any remissness of duty in endeavoring to avert it; and that the reign of peace on earth and good will among men may come without being preceded by a reign of terror. Let us hope also that the delirium or madness by whicn the despots would retain their power, may give way to the sentiments of humanity and brotherhood, and that the real hrist —the spirit of love—may indeed become an earthly ruler and build up a real Republic in the Earth in the place of this which is one only in name.

Now, as a summary, permit me to present the outlines of a form of government for a Republic : At its base would be all the people of a given age and upward, f the various wards of cities and the school-districts of the country. These would elect their city and county governments from among themselves, which in turn would elect also from among themselves, the governments of the several States. Each of these would form their own organizations and appoint their executive heads, and also, during good behavior, all executive officers of whatever branch of the government having jurisdiction within their several limits. The State governments would also, in turn, elect, from their own members, the national government, which would also appoint its own· executive officers and form itself into the several national executive Bureaus, each having its own executive head ; while all propositions, made by the several governmental bodies, would be legislated upon by the people, by popular vote, before becoming laws.

In such a government as this there would be no political parties. Party strife and the demoralizing effect of general political elections would be abolished, and all the public efforts of the people turned to proper legislation, and the business of the Public Press directed to the advancement of the general welfare and intelligence. In this government every citizen, of a given age, would be a legislator ; and every person elected in any ward or school district, a candidate for the executive head of the nation, each department of the government of which would be a natural outgrowth of the next below it, and all of which together would form a single structure reaching from the base, the people, the legislative power, to the apex—the executive head, administering the will of the people. To the inauguration of such a government for this people is my life dedicated.

But let us now enlarge the range of our speculations. Let us rise from the nation to the world. What is the condition of mankind at large, at this juncture, and with reference to the subjects under consideration ? It is one in some measure of feverish agitation ; but one still more of the symptoms of a world-wide commotion which is suppressed for the moment by the circumstances of the times. It is the partial calm before the storm ; the clearing of the decks for action ; the marshalling of forces—as it presents itself to my mind—for the final and decisive conflict between grand and universal opposing principles. These are, in the main, the principles of arbitrary authority and the principle of freedom.

These two principles have always stood in open or suppressed antagonism to each other; but it has been, so far as manifested, hitherto, within limited areas, or as affecting special questions. To-day, the controversy is being broadened out to the universal arena, and is involving all issues. It is beginning to appear that principles are in their nature universal. There is not one set for politics, another for religion, another for domestic life and so on; but one and the same set of principles for all spheres. It is social, or more strictly universal science which is teaching us these results.

But even in advance of science, the stern logic of events is leading up to the same conclusion. Conservatism and Radical Progression are the same in kind whether they crop out in the church or in the State or elsewhere; and each knows and affinitises with its own in other and whatsoever divine ranges of affairs. The absolute monarch knows, by an unfailing instinct, that the absolute Pope is his friend and natural ally, at bottom; whatsoever minor dissensions may exist between the crown and the tiara; and the most radical progressionist recognizes, by the same instinct, despite all· intense family feuds, the essential affiliation with him or her of the free religionist or the great popular preacher who allies himself in any sense with the spirit of progress.

To superficial observers minor differences are apt to disguise fundamental identities. At bottom, or viewed on the large scale, Protestanism as a whole movement, and the Christian Alliance itself—*in so far as it means Protestantism*—revivalism and the sanctification movement in the churches, are in common cause with Atheism, Infidelity, Spiritualism and Socialism, on the one hand, tending to the freedom of the individual; and Papacy and Despotism or Cæsarism are in common cause with all conservatism and retroactive tendency in society at large, on the other hand. In the big family difference, therefore, even brother Comstock and myself belong to the same wing, are members of the same communion; however distasteful to him may be the affiliation, and I confess that it is with some difficulty that I am philosophical enough to recognize such a sample of fraternity. But such is the fact. In the broadest division there are only those two armies in the field, conservatives and radicals. Conservatism though retroactive ending in despotism; and, radicalism by the way of progression, ending in the sovereignty of the individual, and all the freedoms—free love being merely the logical and legitimate ultimatum of that drift. Mr. Comstock, the Youn Men's Christian Association, the Christian Alliance and Protestantism itself, are therefore illogical as long as they are not free lovers, and conservatives of all schools are illogical while not subscribing to the infallibility of the Pope, or of some supreme potentate or other.

This double universality of the two underlying principles of human society—authority and freedom—is as I have said becoming every day more distinctly pronounced—both actually, or in the logic of events; and theoretically, or in the scientific understanding of the subject. Now it has appeared to me that this national arraying of these great opposite forces must continue to become more and more pronounced; the lines more and more strictly drawn; the antagonism and mutual aggressiveness fiercer and fiercer, until the most tremendous and bloody conflict would inevitably ensue. This reasoning of mine, such as it is, has been continuously reinforced, in my mind, for some years past, by a succession of vived spiritual presentations or visions. I have repeatedly seen, in this way, the streets of this very city drenched in blood, the mobs and armies headed by priests and clergy and even by women, new Amazons and Joans of Arc, mingling in the bloody fray; the stores and warehouses of the great merchants taken for military hospitals and the deposits of arms; and whole quarters of the city desolate—burnt and burning, while the deadly fight was still raging from street to street and from house to house, with hecatombs of victims piled up in the public avenues and crossings. Material-minded men may call all this fancy, imagination, hallucination, what they will; but I know better. I know that these visions, of which I have been a subject from early girlhood to this hour, are something very different from ordinary imagination, and that they are a distinct class of mental phenomena having a quality and a value of their own. Thousands of other intelliment men and woman know the same in their own experiences and by observation in this age. Some hundreds, probably, of this audience, have as I have, more or less of this second sight.

I may not know, however, and indeed I do not profess to know the exact nature and the full value of these extraordinary and exceptional experiences. It seems to me that the priest and the doctor who charge themselves with the care and cure of the souls and bodies of men should have been able to help me to the better understanding of myself in this matter; but whenever I have consulted them I have found them either weakly and confessedly ignorant, or else pompously pretentious and dogmatically ignorant on the whole subject. So I have been left to wend my way unaided through the mazes of an experience so strange that I could not allude to the tithe of it without risking my reputation for decent good sense, if not indeed for sanity. I must be excused, therefore, for any extravagances I may seem to commit, on the ground that even the wisest of the old style teachers, have proved failures whenever they have undertaken to guide me. Left to my own guidance I have simply, done, therefore, the best that I could. I have said what I thought. I have been true to the conviction that was in me. I have said and written that I believed we were on the verge of a great social convulsion. I have seen that it was absolutely essential to the well-being of humanity that freedom should be vindicated. I have committed myself with unstinted earnestness, with the enthusiasm and the daring of an iconoclast, to the destruction of everything which stood in its way. I have established, I believe, the reputation of honest conviction and earnest devotion in that direction. I have not shrunk from contemplating all consequences. I have seen, or supposed I saw, the worst, even, of what I was helping to provoke. I reasoned that to ultimate or drive out to extremities the demand for freedom, would incite a corresponding reaction on the side of conservatism, and the assertion of authority. I expected persecution, a resort to repressive legislation, an alliance of all the conservative forces, a desperate and final struggle in behalf of authority. I expected to see Catholicism and despotism reinforced by accessions from Protestant and republican ranks ; to see the lines more rigorously drawn ; the pressure more earnest to take sides ; a desperate battle inaugurated. Still, with all these prospects, I felt it imperatively laid upon me to proclaim the doctrines of freedom.

I may have been mistaken—not I am certain in the divine origin and the high claims of the doctrine of freedom. But the world may possibly be riper for change than I, possibly riper than my spirit-guides may have thought. I have had at my side, all along, friends who have urged other views. I have been reminded that authority and conservatism have also their true place in the world ; that there must, therefore, be some just ground of reconciliation between these two opposing principles —that in other words Reform could be effected without Revolution, or rather without revolution of the body and physical-force character. I have been told that the time for adjusting opinion by the sound has gone past ; that a positive physical-force tyranny, like slavery or an unbearable oppression of that order, might need still to be disrupted and cast off by a physical-force or uprising, but that nothing whatever would be gained or could be gained, toward settling metaphysical and social problems by any amount of violence. It was suggested to me that my interior views of bloody conflict might be symbolic merely of the great intellectual and moral warfare which is actually transpiring in the world. These and other arguments have been urged by those to whom I most habitually defer in matters of judgment. Especially was it said that in science, of the universe kind, there is steadily arising an umpire to which both and all parties will in the end gladly appeal ; that the great *lis pendens* of humanity will be tried ultimately in that court, and that the verdict and the execution of the decree will be gracefully submitted to on all hands.

I have listened to every statement with an eager ear I have wanted to believe. I, too, have prayed for humanity :

"If it be possible, let this cup pass from us." But I have not been able to believe. My visions and the conviction borne in upon my soul that we are about to fall upon evil days have been too definite and forceful to admit of doubt of their significance. But I dread the truthfulness of my own impressions. I shrink with horror from the reality of bloody strife. And I do not want to be obstinate or perverse. I know that my forebodings and Cassandra-like ratiocinations have a meaning; but I am willing, and more than willing to be convinced that it is other and less fearful, than the interpretation which I have given them.

I come before you, therefore, to-night in a new spirit; not so much to promulgate *my* convictions; not so much as the trumpeter of new truths; as to receive impressions; to feel the pulse of public opinion; to learn of you, more, perhaps, than I shall instruct. I want to know what others think; what is the burden of the mission whispered to their souls for the waiting millions? What is the common message to mankind upon which we can all agree? Clearly to my mind it is either Revolution or Reform—Reform in any event; either with or without Revolution—*Revolution in any event*—but, whether with or without its bloody accompaniments.

To solve this question let us endeavor again to look behind the scenes. I have said that perhaps the world is riper for change than I have apprehended. Perhaps the old style conservative reactionary forces are weaker than I have thought; perhaps the enmity to reform in behalf of freedom is already more exhausted and reduced than I have supposed; perhaps the genial spring-time of humanity's golden age of the future is destined to come in without the common cataclysm of the breaking up of the long hard winter.

> "We sleep and wake and sleep, but all things move;
> The sun flies forward to his brother sun;
> The dark earth follows, wheeled in her eclipse:
> And human things returning on themselves
> Move onward, leading up the golden year.

> "Ah, though the times when some new thought can bud
> Are but as poet's seasons when they flower,
> Yet seas that daily gain upon the shore
> Have ebb and flow conditioning their tides,
> And slow and sure comes up the golden year.

> "When wealth no more shall rest in mounded heaps,
> But smit with freer light shall slowly melt
> In many streams to fatten lower lands,
> And light shall spread, and man be liker man
> Through all the season of the golden year.
> *   *   *   *   *   *

> "But we grow old. Ah! when shall all men's good
> Be each man's rule, and universal peace
> Lie like a shaft of light across the land,
> And like a lane of beams athwart the sea,
> Through all the circle of the golden year?"

Perhaps the aspirations for the golden year is more diffused in men's hearts than I have believed, and that they only wait to discern the signs of its coming. Perhaps the seeming perversity and dulness of mankind is more of the head, and less of the heart. Perhaps science, then, which is the opening of the mind's eye, may show the way and reconcile the most opposite. And perhaps already the anticipation of some such reconciliation is softening asperities and cultivating the sentiment of friendly mutual acceptance.

My mind has taken this turn in consequence of the wonderful change which I have myself experienced within the last few months in the temperature of the social atmosphere. Up to, and subsequent to the time of my imprisonment in this city, for the cause of freedom and free speech, bitterness and hostility towards me personally seemed literally to fill the air. The glacial breezes from the north pole could not be more frigid and unsympathetic than the public sentiment which surrounded me. But of late a wonderful revolution in this particular has taken place. I have of late been basking in the genial rays of public favor. In New Jersey, at the State Convention of Spiritualists, I was received after my release from prison, with an ovation. In Massachusetts, at the great camp meeting at Silver Lake and Harwich, I addressed audiences of from five to fifteen thousand people amidst acclamations of enthusiasm, and the Boston press reported fairly and without slang or abatement the substance of what I said. Now, I have just returned from the three-days' meeting of the National Convention of Spiritualists at Chicago, where, after three days of the most unrestricted discussion and with the whole issue centered on the question of indorsing or repudiating my social doctrines, I was, almost unanimously, elected for the third time President of that Association. And there also at Chicago I was treated with courtesy and high appreciation by almost the entire press. It is not alone Spiritualists, therefore, but the whole public which seems to have quietly and sincerely arrived at the determination that I and the principles which I advocate shall have fair play according to merit, and along with all other things.

It may at first seem arrogant that I should assume, that a change of treatment towards me personally and towards my ideas, indicates any great or wide-spread change in social opinion at large. But if you reflect that I stand representative for the most radical and the most opprobrious of doctrines, and that these very doctrines as I have promulgated them, have just aroused the old and seemingly dead lion of persecution into what, we may now hope, were the final agonies of a feeble death-struggle, it may not seem too much to claim that when *I* am tolerated *everything* is tolerated; and that the extension of courtesy, kindness and fair play to me, anew, and after all that has past, is a solemn reaffirmation of a true Americanism, and perhaps the tocsin of freedom for all opinion actually achieved, and without the bloody catastrophy which my too anxious intuitions have foreseen. I am at least willing and desirous to entertain this hope, and no one will rejoice more than I to have my own prophecies thus happily disappointed.

But, yet, mere toleration is not all that is demanded. A sentimental unity of mankind is inadequate. The Christian Alliance, in agreeing to sink out of sight, in each others presence, their denominational differences, have not in any radical manner solved the doctrinal problems which have divided them. So in society at large, to tolerate, even to defend the expression of all ideas, is not, of itself, an arrival at the truth of ideas. Investigation inaugurated is not investigation accomplished. We have still before us an immense work; the greater work than all that has preceded it.

The career of distruction and merely critical reform ends in a sense when freedom is achieved; but freedom itself *is merely opportunity.* With the opportunity secured, we are prepared to learn the truth, theoretically and experimentally. We must then call in the great teachers, or become great teachers ourselves. After the war came the Freedmen's Bureau, and its educational operations. So now if we have received toleration we must show our competency to improve by its advantages.

Looking again behind the scenes we shall discover, that this age is the interregnum of faith. A disparing cry comes from the Pope in respect to the prospects of the Church. Protestanism is oozing out into infidelity, while, however, infidelity verging into science, is gradually laying the foundations of a new faith. Something grand and novel is about to burst on the earth. Religion, when it becomes practical and humanitarian, will come to mean a hundred times more than it has ever meant yet on the world. Something new and grand is about to occur; which will crystallize anew and consolidate all the elements of the new faith and the new social order.

A new age dates from the present. An old dispensation is closing up. The new element will be something decisive, reconciliative, all-embracing. It will have in it the religious, the scientific and the practical quality—all in one. Is it to be some new opening out of the marvels of Spiritualism? Is it the "Social Palace" and "the Social Solutions" of M. GODIN. Is it the Positivism of AUGUSTE COMTE? Is it the Universology, the Integralism and the Pantarchy of STEPHEN PEARL ANDREWS? Is it the New Jerusalem to be let down out of Heaven? Is it all of these combined and blended into one; or is it some other and unthought of thing which shall be the key to the whole mystery of the past, and the keystone of the arch of the future social structure. I shall be content, for the hour, if I shall have completed the preliminary work of clearing away obstructions, and establishing the habit of fearless and universal investigation and experiment; in social matters as well as in all others.

I cannot rid myself of the impression, however, that we must strike very deep for the true basis of the final solution and reconciliation. Will not Good and Evil, God and the Devil, be somehow and sometime reconciled to the comprehension of man? Is not the seeming evil always the dark background merely of the higher good? And is not the universal scheme of being, broader than we have apprehended? Is not the old Persian faith of two eternally opposite principles, with some modern improvement furnishing their monastic identity, the higher as it is the older doctrine than Christian theology?

Perhaps I can look forward to the cessation at an early day of my duties as an agitator. I have a loving heart for all mankind, and I would far rather be understood and loved than to be misunderstood and hated. I would rather teach and lead into the higher philosophy and the higher life than to break up old foundations, horrifying and disturbing the minds of men. I am tired of fighting. I would rather be Hypasia than Semiramis or Boadecea. I would rather know and make known the highest truth than conquer the whole earth.

Thus much at least I see. Politics and patriotism are falling into the position of relative inferiority as compared with statesmanship and publicism, and statesmanship and publicism are in turn yielding the palm to sociology, as that science which deals with every range of human affairs in their cosmical or planetary amplitude. Sociology must in time have its basis in universal science. Reformers must, therefore, I see, become scientific, when they pass from the destructive to the constructive phase of their work.

I would rather help to form true institutions, and so call down the blessings of this age and of posterity on my head for positive and permanent achievements, than merely to combat old errors, or achieve negative triumphs, ever so many, or ever so brilliant. Sympathize with me my dear sisters, and my true brothers, in the effort to learn, in order that I may teach; and let us all be instant in season and out of season in the good work of the future.

Then, when we shall have accomplished this work, will begin the long-time sung and prophesied millennium, in which love instead of hate, equality in place of aristocracy, and justice where now is cruelty, shall reign with undisturbed and perpetual sway, and peace on earth and good will among men abound. Because I see this for humanity, in the near future, has made me willing and able to endure what its advocacy has cost me of personal discomfort and of public censure. Finally, in conclusion: May the God, Justice; the Christ, Love, and the Holy Ghost, Unity—the Trinity of Humanity,—ascend the Universal Throne, while all nations, in acknowledging their supremacy, shall receive their blessings—their benedictions.

Reprinted in *Woodhull & Claflin's Weekly* (Sept. 13, 1873, pp. 2-7, 14), with the remark: "In view of the increasing importance of the money question as related to the reconstruction of society, we . . . present the principles that underlie it."

A SPEECH

ON

THE PRINCIPLES OF FINANCE,

BY

VICTORIA C. WOODHULL,

DELIVERED AT

COOPER INSTITUTE, NEW YORK CITY,

THURSDAY, AUGUST 3, 1871.

NEW YORK:
WOODHULL, CLAFLIN & CO., No. 44 BROAD STREET.

1871.

PROSPECTUS.

WOODHULL & CLAFLIN'S WEEKLY.

[The only Paper in the World conducted, absolutely, upon the Principles of a Free Press.]

It advocates a new government in which the people will be their own legislators, and the officials the executors of their will.

It advocates, as parts of the new government—

1. A new political system in which all persons of adult age will participate.

2. A new land system in which every individual will be entitled to the free use of a proper proportion of the land.

3. A new industrial system, in which each individual will remain possessed of all his or her productions.

4. A new commercial system in which "cost," instead of "demand and supply," will determine the price of everything and abolish the system of profit-making.

5. A new financial system, in which the government will be the source, custodian and transmitter of   money, and in which usury will have no place.

6. A new sexual system, in which mutual consent, entirely free from money or any inducement other than love, shall be the governing law, individuals being left to make their own regulations; and in which society, when the individual shall fail, shall be responsible for the proper rearing of children.

7. A new educational system, in which all children born shall have the same advantages of physical, industrial, mental and moral culture, and thus be equally prepared at matur· y to enter upon active, responsible and üseful lives.

All of which will constitute the various parts of a new social order, in which all the human rights of the individual will be associated to form the harmonious organization of the peoples into the grand human family, of which every person in the world will be a member.

Criticism and objections specially invited.

The WEEKLY is issued every Saturday.

Subscription price, $3 per year; $1.50 six months; or 10c. single copy, to be had of any Newsdealer in the world, who can order it from the following General Agents:

The American News Co., New York City;

The New York News Co., New York City;

The National News Co., New York City;

The New England News Co., Boston, Mass.

The Central News Co., Philadelphia, Pa.;

The Western News Co., Chicago, Ill.

Sample copies, mailed on application, free.

VICTORIA C. WOODHULL AND TENNIE C. CLAFLIN, Editors and Proprietors.

COL. J. H. BLOOD, Managing Editor.

All communications should be addressed

WOODHULL & CLAFLIN'S WEEKLY,
Box 3,791, New York City.

THE PRINCIPLES OF FINANCE.

MONEY! IS IT A PRINCIPLE OR A PROPERTY?

To the careful student of history, there is a very great deal more to be considered than the mere political facts that stand as land-marks along the path of progress which the nations have traversed since the plains of Iran poured forth their hosts westward. These facts are the mere externals that adorn the pages of historic lore, and embellish the memories of the great men who have lived in and moved the world at various times in various nations, or which clothe the lives of tyrants and usurpers with their just reward.

The superficial student of history cares only for the *results* of the evolution of nations—for the *fact* that Sesostris was the greatest of Egyptian kings; or that Semiramis rose by her military sagacity from the rank of a mean official's wife to be, first, the Queen of Ninas, and afterward to be the Assyrian Queen, who should march an army of three millions men across the Indus to conquer the Indian King. Running down the course of events, he traces the rise and fall of nations—after Assyria then Egypt, next Persia, Greece, Rome and then the Dark Ages, out of whose womb was evolved modern Europe; and, lastly, the birth, development, struggle and recovery of the most remarkable nation which has yet arisen in the world.

Behind these facts, which are but results, lie the real motor powers of history; and they are deeper, broader and more important than is that which *they* evolve. There is an external and an internal phase to everything existent in the world. Up to *this* generation the external has apparently borne the more prominent part in determining what should be next. But *now* the analytic age has begun, wherein facts do not suffice; wherein new systems, new theories, new philosophies and even new religions are constructed, not by an examination of the *errors* of what has been, but by the *discovery* and *application* of the principles, the powers, which underlie those errors.

Heretofore there has been no inquiry made by the rulers of the people into the general principles of government. It was sufficient that there was a government maintained, the governors caring for little but the power to compel the people to do their bidding. But it is beginning to dawn upon the minds of those who have something more than a selfish interest in humanity that there *is* a *science* of government, aye, even that there is a science of society: and such minds are endeavoring by the deepest researches to discover the principles of these sciences.

In our government, the principle of individual rights is theoretically held, though in its application government still interferes with those rights. The legitimate functions of a government, based upon the rights of every individual over whom its power is exercised, are limited to the *duties* that will best *subserve* and *protect* the interests of individuals. The proper understanding and practice of these functions is the most important thing for a people to arrive at, but, having arrived at this as the basis of all the relations of the people, the scientific construction of the various departments of the complete superstructure which is to cover all the public interests of all the people, as well as to maintain their private interests intact, can be begun.

After the general principles of government are properly formulated in Constitutions and vitality given them by laws, a correct, a' scientific financial system stands *next* in importance. If a country have a true system of *government*, and do not have a true system of *finance*, it can never attain to any *permanent* prosperity. Literally speaking, finance is a *part* of government; since, in organizing it, means for its support are among the first considerations. Hence it is plain, if there are principles of government, so must there also be principles of finance.

It has never been pretended, so far as I know, even by the pro foundest political economists, who are sticklers for the gold standard, that any financial systems the world has ever known were developed by the scientific application of self-evident truths, which is the nature of principles.

The various systems of which use has been made were simply *experimental*, devised for *politic* reasons, as the *best* methods to meet the exigencies of the times in which they were required. Instance the Greenback, the necessity for which was such as to shake the nation to its very centre, and to fill the minds of all patriots with a dread foreboding.

If there have been no scientific money systems in vogue, and it now comes out that the world has arrived at that degree of advancement wherein *policy* should give way to *principles*, even in finance, there can be nothing gained by going back to review the errors, failures and fallacies of the past. Nothing valuable can be gained by wading through the almost innumerable statistics which have accumulated to a sufficiently great extent to bewilder the most comprehensive intellects. Having for ten years been deeply engaged in studying the principles of government, I learned that no system of government could be perfect unless its financial department was perfected; therefore I have frequently endeavored to solve the financial problems which statistics propose, but *invariably* failed to learn anything that even promised to look well as a basis for a new and improved system, to say nothing of its promises in operation.

The conclusion was inevitable, that there have been *no* acknowledged or even known, fundamental principles of finance operating in *any* of the many systems of the many nations, and that the so-called money of the world *is not now, nor ever was*, money, in the scientific sense of that term.

All the statistics, failures and errors of the past, with which the history of money abounds, being of no value, must be utterly ignored in any inquiry which proposes to predicate a natural and scientific money, as distinguished from arbitrary inventions, devised to meet the various exigencies of nations in their growth, prime and decay. And *any* person who proposes to teach finance, or a new system, by arraying before you the evidences of the past, contained in figures amounting to billions of dollars, simply proposes to try *another experiment*, to *culminate* in another failure.

Therefore I shall present no principals, per cents. and compounded amounts, except, perhaps, as examples to illustrate the mathematical impossibilities of the fallacious theories by which financiers have attempted to dazzle the world, but who have only succeeded in accumulating in the hands of a very select few that which by an exact justice should belong to, and be distributed among, the people generally.

In order to intelligently discuss and arrive at legitimate conclusions regarding the question of money, it should be *first* determined just what is to be involved in the discussion; for around this, as around all other general things, there has been such a mass of rubbish and extraneous matter aggregated that the main question is always in danger of being lost sight of, unless this be first removed and the real issue left clearly exposed.

Most of the confusion which follows the attempts to solve the money question arises out of the fact that the *same* words in the mouths of *different* people do not mean the *same* things, or that *different* words are used by *different* people to mean the *same* thing. If there are two words in common use to represent similar objects, but which, upon close analysis, *do not* represent precisely the same thing, it is better that *one* of them be discarded. It is necessary, therefore, to settle, prior to the beginning of this argument, *precisely* what the several terms *do* mean which are prominently in use in connection with the money question. It is, perhaps, near the truth to say that this settlement is the argument Very few persons have any well-defined comprehension of what is the *real* significance of the terms *gold, money, currency, intrinsic value* and *wealth.* If these words are analyzed, what do they scientifically represent?

Gold is a product of the earth only to be originally obtained by labor and expense, and both practically and scientifically bears like relations *to* labor that all other things do which are produced *by* labor; and none other. But there has been an importance attached to gold which has not been accorded to *any other* product of labor. It has been coined and called money, because it was coined, and by custom and common acceptance made an *arbitrary* standard of value, which *none* of its qualities warrant when subjected to analysis, as will be shortly shown.

Gold bears the same relation to *real* money that a religious theory bears to *real* religion, which theory, when comprehended by the intellect of the people, loses its value as a substitute for real religion; but which, until comprehension comes, it is better to have than to have none at all. So also with gold. It has in *theory* been considered as *money;* but when a *true* money comes to be comprehended, it will lose its value as a substitute therefor, and sink to its proper sphere among the other products of labor.

It is altogether probable that gold was the very best substitute for money during that part of the world's evolution wherein people were guided and controlled by policy and before principles were recognized as that which should govern, let their action lead where it might. As the world is now beginning to act from *principle,* for the sake of the *truth,* so also must they now begin to formulate the principle of money for the sake of the principle.

Wealth is whatever is produced by labor which adds to the *comforts,* the *happiness* or the *life* of man; and everything that does this, either directly or indirectly, has intrinsic value—that is, has the capacity to bless mankind.

Wealth may, and should, be divided into two kinds, namely, *permanent* wealth and *transitory* wealth.

Permanent wealth consists of all those products of labor which are not themselves *transferable* into life, comfort or happiness, but which may at all times be *exchanged* for that which is thus transferable into that which can be used to continue life. Gold, silver and precious stones are among the best illustrations there are of permanent wealth.

Transitory wealth consists of all those products of labor of which *direct* use is made to maintain life or to add to its comforts and happiness, and which, *by* such process, are absorbed *into* and become *a part of* the life of humanity. Transitory wealth, it will be seen, is much the more important of the two, since, if people only possessed permanent wealth, their life could not be continued an hour by it, unless there were a possibility of exchanging it for the necessities of life.

It would seem that *all* kinds of wealth are intrinsically valuable, since its various kinds may be either *directly* used to maintain life or may be *exchanged* for those which will maintain life. Wealth and intrinsic value, then, mean the same thing.

But what does the term *money* mean: or has it no necessary significance in the inquiry?

There was a time when there was no such *thing* or *word* as money; but at that time there was life to continue, for which wealth was necessary. It seems that *wealth* had existence before *money* was thought of. Wealth is substance, of which money is the principle or representative, but which, in itself, has no intrinsic value.

Money is an invention made to *represent* wealth, or value, in order that its various kinds may be exchanged with facility, or that they may be exchanged without the absolute and direct and immediate receipt and delivery of one product of labor for another product of labor. All the products of labor may be exchanged *directly*, and without the use of any representative or go-between, which for the time being stands representative of the one or the other, but *not so well* at all times and under all circumstances. Money is *anything* which stands representative of any product of labor; that is, that can be made use of to facilitate the exchange of any of the results of labor, which are wealth. A representative of anything cannot be the thing itself, therefore, if money is a representative of wealth it is not itself wealth. Were A, B and C to at all times exchange their products between themselves by *direct transfer*, they would have *no use* for money; they would exchange —deliver and receive—*actual* values. But when A desires from B some of his products, himself not having on hand any of his products which B desires, he receives from B his value and gives him his representative of value—his note—promising that at a future time he will deliver B the *actual* value which he desires.

Currency is only a *form* of money, the same as *gold* is only a form of wealth; and in the same manner that gold is wealth, is currency money. Money being the principle of representation in exchange, everything of which use is made to facilitate exchange in the form of representative value is money. Anything which can be transferred from one party to another, anything that is negotiable which is not actual value of itself, is money. This includes not only all currency, bank notes, but also bills of exchange, the ledger and bonds. These are *all* representatives of wealth, *all* demands for payment at a future time of a certain specified sum, and consequently are money. It is quite evident that, with the terms *wealth* and *money*, we have all the necessary distinctions which should enter into the abstract question of finance. All other terms are but names for separate kinds or forms of these terms, to be made use of when they respectively arise in making exchanges.

Now, every one must at once concede that that which best represents all of the products of labor will also best *exchange* them, and is therefore the *best* money. It is *equally clear* that gold in *no way* represents *any* labor but that which produces it. If gold were a true representative of the results of *all* other labor, except that which produces it, would it not also be apparent that *such* labor must be *equal* to *all* other labor. Were gold a thousand times more valuable than it is held to be, it would not *even then* be able to represent all other values. Therefore, gold is a *false* standard of value, a *false* representative of wealth.

Many people think and speak as if gold would be of no use to this country if it were to come into disuse as *money;* that we should entirely lose it as *wealth;* the very reverse is really true, since we should have just the same quantity of gold that we *now* have, to be used for the *same* purposes for which it is now required, to wit: to export to other countries in exchange for imports.

Suppose our imports to amount to a thousand millions dollars per annum, and that we export cotton, corn and pork to that amount, what use would we have for gold except to loan other countries, and could we not *loan* it as *gold*, taking their representatives of value for it equally as well as though it were coined into money, having the seal and stamp of the government ? It is well known that we do not export gold to Europe as so many American dollars, but as so much gold, by weight of a certain degree of fineness, the stamp of the government attesting to that degree.

Again : Suppose that we had no cotton, corn or pork to give in exchange for our imports, and that we produced a thousand millions dollars' worth of gold per annum, should we not be *equally* well conditioned to trade with Europe ?

It is seen that the real character and qualities of gold are the same as are those of any other product of labor, which we can exchange direct, for other products of labor which we want more than we do the gold. If at any time the balance of trade is *against* us, and we have *no* cotton, corn, pork, gold or *anything* *else* to make it good, we must then make it good by our representatives of value—our bonds—to be converted when we shall have these products. This process has been actually going on ever since we began to export bonds, either national, state, county, city, railroad or bonds of other incorporated companies.

Now, is it not *perfectly* evident that we have not only produced by labor what we have exported, which we have been pleased to denominate merchandise, but also that we have produced all the gold that has been exported ; and in this connection is it not just as much an article of merchandise as is either cotton or corn ? Gold cannot at *one* and the *same* time be both *money* and *merchandise*. If *gold* is money, so also is *wheat, cotton* and *corn* money, since they perform the same *services* and possess the same *qualities* as merchandise that gold does.

To be perfectly clear in our conclusions, money must be resolved into its *uses*, and entirely divested of all its *fictitious* and *irrelevant* relations. The fact that money is that thing which is made use of to exchange real values must be the initial starting-point, of which sight must never be lost until it is *definitely* settled what will *best* perform this service. Anything which can be made use of for *any other purpose whatever*, is *not* the *best* thing to be made use of as money ; because the demand for such a thing for such other purposes destroys its positive value as money by causing fluctuations in its exchanging power.

It is a grave financial error for this country to endeavor to return to gold as money. All the practices under the gold standard have been positive and ample refutations of the arbitrary value accorded to gold. A *dollar* in gold can only exchange a *dollar* in value in any other substance; and the practice of issuing a greater amount of bank notes than the bank has gold dollars to redeem them by, is a *legalized* system to *rob* the people; since it is *evident* that a bank having three hundred thousand dollars in notes in circulation, and only one hundred thousand dollars in gold in its vaults, can redeem but *one-third* of its circulation if it be all presented at once for redemption. All the other securities of a bank, such as its discounts, personal property and real estate, may become of no value, or may be placed out of reach of the holders of its circulation, so that the only *real* security for its circulation is what it may have in gold in its vaults. Beside, what right has a bank to receive legal interest on three times the amount of its real security? Is not this a most *transparent* method of *swindling* the people? Hence I assert that the use of gold as money *always* results disastrously to the producers of wealth, and *always* beneficially to those who are permitted to absorb all their productions.

Another unanswerable reason why gold cannot answer the requirements of money is found in the *degrees of value* which belong to different products of labor, and which are *universally* determined by the sacrifice required to produce them. That is to say, all other things being equal, the *relative* value of products is determined by the *time* and *labor* required to produce them. The increase in the value of manufactured material is in *exact* proportion to the *time* required and *wealth* consumed in their manufacture. The value of gold is determined in *precisely* the same manner; and it is simply foolishness to assert that the value of gold never changes, or that it has the same purchasing power at all times.

Suppose there should be immense fields of gold suddenly developed all over the country, so that it would become as common and plentiful as iron or coal, would it not decrease in value in comparison with other products? That is to say, would an ounce of gold then possess as great a proportionate value to other products as it now does? No one will pretend it. Then gold is just as much the subject of fluctuation as is any other product of labor, and for *just the same* reasons—demand and supply—which are the great arbitrators of values in all parts of the world.

Everybody knows that for a certain quantity of gold a certain quantity of cotton may be obtained, and for a certain quantity of corn a horse. The fact that the horse is obtainable by the corn does not convert the corn into money, neither does gold any more than the corn become money because the cotton is obtained thereby. The gold for the time is equal in value to the cotton, and so is the corn to the horse. Now. what is required of money is this: Suppose the gold, cotton, corn and the horse to be of equal value, a person possessing an amount of money representing the value of either of the four can, at his discretion, purchase whichever he may choose; since the money would equally represent the gold, cotton, corn and the horse. Anything that may be used for money that will not do the same thing for any variety of the products of labor, values being equal, is not money in any sense of that term.

Incidentally in this connection, because it has an indirect bearing upon the question under consideration, I wish to call attention to a mistake that has been productive of more financial ills and consequent injustice to a large proportion of the people, who are the wealth producers, than any other single cause, and that is the fundamental error of making land, wealth, which it is no more entitled to be, scientifically, than gold is to be called money. Wealth is that which is produced. Land exists. All improvements made upon land are wealth; *but the land proper, never.*

In this almost fatal mistake—almost fatal to the humanitarian interests of the so-called common people—which is fundamental in its nature, is found the *basis* upon which rest the vast disparities in the distributions of wealth, and which gives to certain favored individuals the means of realizing vast fortunes without ever resorting to the production of wealth, or of even accumulating it by trafficking in the different kinds of wealth.

There are numerous examples of this manner of becoming possessed of riches. People acquire title to lands which, by favorable .....ation, come into great demand and consequently rise in value from *one dollar per acre to hundreds of thousands of dollars per acre.* By what principle of *equity* and *right* should *any* person be entitled to such vast increases in capital invested in land, when it is entirely attributable to the movements of the community which produce it, and in no single particular to the individual? To be so entitled is for the individual to possess advantages over others to which no just communal government should for a moment consent—is to have the right to appropriate to self the results of labor which belong in common to all the people. Such results are against *all* principles of equity and justice, and is one of the *greatest,* if not *the* greatest error of the present, regarding the equities of property, and is the foundation and prophecy of all other kinds of monopoly.

It occurs to me that an objection may be raised to my argument classing gold as wealth, and defining wealth to be that which can be made use of to minister to life, comfort and happiness; or perhaps to the distinction of permanent and transitory wealth. Gold, as permanent wealth, can only minister to man through its exchange for other valuables of which direct use can be made. It may be said that in *that* sense gold can legitimately be money.

But if there are objectors to this argument, I beg to call their attention to the conclusive fact that gold *can never* be representative of all other kinds of wealth. It is just as impossible that it should be, as it is that a bridge *one* hundred feet in length should span a river *five* hundred feet in width. It must further be remembered that the uses for which money is required demand an invention which can be made use of for *no other* purpose whatever, and that money is the name of an invention *demanded* and made for the purpose of *facilitating* exchanges— for making them easy, *convenient* and *adaptable* to *all* conditions of *all* persons.

Every attempt ever made to compel gold to answer the demands of money has been a disastrous failure. So long as a country enjoys continuous prosperity under a gold standard of value, it is all well enough. The people make use of an expanded volume of currency in the full faith that prosperity will continue and everything be smooth and right.

But anon a *change* comes, the nation is precipitated into conditions which require *more* than its accumulations of gold to meet. *That* being exhausted, it is *inevitable* that representation be resorted to. The wealth in the form of gold not being adequate, and other wealth not having been used or accepted as money, paper representatives of it are the *only* resort. So it appears that when an *emergency* arises the people are *involuntarily* pressed to the use of the principle of representation, which is the *only* scientific thing that can be called money. So that while a paper representative of wealth is, *with everything else*, a product of labor, it is more than that; it is the embodiment and application of a principle, which other products of labor are not;. and all principles are fundamental; are the basis of all permanent and all purely scientific things and truths, while wealth is the realized product of the outworking of principles, directed and appropriated by man for his use and convenience.

The direct inquiry can now be made as to *what* will *best perform* what the people require of money; and money is that which can be used to *represent* real values without an absolute *transfer* of such values. The basis of all value of this country is our *present* accumulated *real* wealth and our *capacity* to increase it, and this accumulation and the prospective increase may be *wholly* represented by money and the nation never become bankrupt.

A person may possess wealth to the amount of ten thousand dollars upon which he may issue his representatives of value, or promises to pay that value. These representatives of value would circulate among those who believe in the capacity and intention of the utterer to give *up* to them, *when* demanded, that which they represent. Everybody by his individual right has the authority to issue such representatives of value, and no government has any right to prohibit their circulation; because the people, as individuals, have the right to take or refuse them. The issue of bank notes is upon the same principle, and so long as the government does not in substance *indorse* these issues, the people have the *perfect* right to deal in them—to receive and deliver them.

But there is an insuperable objection—one which cannot be overcome by any governmental requirements—to these representatives being called the real money of the people, since circumstances over which *neither* their utterers nor receivers can have *any* control may render them valueless—may make it impossible for those who uttered them to redeem them—and their holders find themselves with *bits of paper* representing *nothing;* but for which they parted with real value.

So far as this condition is confined to individuals who had no other reason for receiving them, and no other assurance of their real value than the supposed *capacity* and *intention* of the uttering person or persons, it is *strictly* a legitimate condition ; and one with which the sufferers can find *no* fault ; since of their own free will and choice they received the utterer's assurances that his representatives were of real value. An individual upon his personal judgment, without undue persuasion, accepts another's representative ; if it prove *bad* he has *himself only* to blame for the loss, as coming from an error of judgment ; and *no power* or *authority* has any right to step in to compel the making of amends for this error. *This* is the simple doctrine of the *rights* of *individuals,* with which *no third party* has any right to interfere after the occurrence of the fact. But when banks are organized under certain formula of law, framed by the people or their representatives through government, the people receive and pay out their issues—representatives of their value—*not* because they have special confidence in the capacity and intention of the individuals who compose the management, *but* because they *suppose* the management has conformed to *those certain forms of law* which are *intended* to render them safe. In this way the government, at least indirectly, gives *credit* to the bank, and *currency* to its issues, and the people accept them *simply* because the government has done so.

But if these banks are mismanaged either ignorantly or intentionally, or managed by designing men, as often they are, who make use of the governmental sanction to swindle the people, as many times they have, *where* can the people look for redress ; *where should* they look for redress? The government is justly responsible to the people for all such issues, since it did not require real security from the banks, and government should make reparation therefor.

This is precisely our objection to *any* and *all* forms of bank issues. There can be *no* arrangement made so *perfect* in security to her people as to *guarantee* them *absolutely* against all hazard, that will permit the banks to make the profits which they seem to think they are entitled to make from the people. In *absolute* security there can be *no* profit. Bank profits demand the circulation of more notes than they have *real* value to represent. Profits come only from speculating either upon the *confidence* or the *money* of the people, and government has *no* right to *protect* such *illegitimate* and *unjust* practices.

Our present system of banking is a *swindle* upon the people, which it is simply surprising that they endure as they have and do. For the banks to be permitted to filch from the people twenty-four million dollars per annum is an *outrageous villainy* which, if comprehended by the people in its *true light*, could not exist *another year*. 'Tis true these banks complied with the law passed in a time of dire necessity, and that through them the government acquired the means to conduct the war. But did not the people themselves do even *more* than furnish money, which was promised to be returned; did they not freely give their *lives*, which can never be returned, and which the government never thought of promising to either return or guarantee, and that, too, for the pitiful sum of thirteen dollars per month? What comparison is there between the sacrifices made by the two classes of people, the capitalists who have absorbed the wealth of the country and the laborers who still continue to give life, property and vitality *to* the country. There is absolutely *no* chance for a comparison; the distinction is *too* great.

It seems to me that if either class is entitled to superior consideration—to receive millions of the people's money—it is the common people who so freely offered their *lives* to save their country, instead of those who simply *loaned* their money at enormous rates of interest, with the certain knowledge that it would be repaid. The present claims are too preposterous, and deceptive, and too unjust to be long continued.

All bank notes in their ultimate effects are frauds upon the people, and their continuation as a circulating medium is only possible because that part of the people who suffer from them have not yet risen into a proper understanding of the question. The time is, however, near at hand when those who have reveled in the result, of the wear and tear of the muscle, and the sweat of the brow, of the common laborer, will be compelled to produce honestly and equitably everything they would enjoy.

The substitute for all kinds of bank notes as the money for the people should be a *purely people's money*—a *national currency* whose basis of value would be the accumulated wealth of the country, and also its capacity for regularly increasing such wealth. Is there any reliance to be placed in a currency issued by an individual or a number of individuals through an incorporated bank, based upon his or their wealth, which is at all times liable to pass into the hands of other individuals? Yes, there is a presumptive reliance—an indefinite security—but the security is not perfect. In comparison with this security place that of a currency issued by the government, based upon the *entire* wealth of the *whole* country, which, no matter how much it might be changed about among the different persons comprising the nation by various contingencies, could never depart from the country; which fact would render it safe under any and all contingencies that could possibly arise, excepting alone the entire destruction of the country and its government by a foreign power; which contingency is not sufficiently imminent to cause any present alarm.

A national currency *thus* based would have not only *all the gold* of the country as a basis, but also *all other kinds of wealth.* Is it not perfectly plain that such a money would be just so much better than common bank notes, with a one-third gold basis, as the total amount of the wealth of the country is greater than such amount of gold? It would be in the most complete sense the people's money. It would be a system of mutual banking wherein every individual of the country would have an interest, instead of there being a vast number of mutual banking institutions, such as has been proposed by a person of profound financial ideas.

As before stated, my objection to all systems of individual banking is that the *basis* of their issues is at all times *liable* to pass from the possession of such individuals; whereas, in a national currency—the *money* of the people, *themselves* in the aggregate the basis and security—there could be *no such* liability; since, if *parts* of the security pass from original to secondary hands, it is *still* the basis of the currency, and could never be transferred beyond the jurisdiction of security by the operations of designing or incapable persons. By no possibility could there ever a loss occur to the holder of such a currency, except it be destroyed in his hands.

Undoubtedly the *greenback* was the *nearest* approach to a *real* money that any people of the earth ever made. We have only to observe how *admirably* it has answered nearly all the purposes for which people require money, to be convinced that it has the very best—the most secure—basis that it is possible for a money to have. It stands representative of the capacity and willingness of the government—the representative of all the people—to pay.

But it is one of the most *difficult* of things for the people to divorce their minds from the idea that gold is the only possible, real money. Yet the *facts* attaching to the greenback stand out in bold and indisputable relief, perfectly and entirely dispelling all basis for the idea. Because the greenback was the *first* step toward a real money that the country ever took, which left gold entirely out of the question, the impression still remains with the people that a *return* must be made to a gold basis; never stopping to observe how vastly superior the wealth basis is to what the gold basis would be.

Bank note currency, or a currency issued by an individual or by a class of individuals, always carries along with itself the *idea* and *need* of redeemability. If, however, there is any thought among the people that the utterers cannot meet their *promises* of redemption, at that *very* time when, of *all* others, *confidence* is necessary to avoid *ruin*, they rush to prove the suspected incapacity; and generally they do prove it.

The idea of, and necessity for, redeemability, is that which *most* requires to be *divorced* from money. Money—real money—should never require to be redeemed. It should always be just as valuable to retain possession of as anything could be into which it may be converted. Anything that requires to be redeemed in order to make it *permanently* valuable or a representative of value is utterly unworthy the name of

money, because it does not truly represent *real* wealth. It is that currency of which there is doubt about the real wealth it pretends to represent which requires to be made redeemable before it will circulate;
and *this* fact proves *most* conclusively that it is *not* money in any true
sense of that term: that is to say, it is not that which requires to be
converted into substance.

It is readily perceivable that a national currency having continually
all the nation's wealth, accumulated and prospective, as its basis, never
need to be redeemed. This *single* consideration is of quite sufficient
importance to *alone* warrant its immediate adoption and use upon the
standard of wealth. The gold standard is the flimsiest deception of
which it is possible to imagine. The people's talk of approaching a gold
standard as the ultimate of appreciation is the *merest jeu d'esprit.* Gold
is now selling at say 113. Suppose that during the next year its price
should gradually decline to par, or, in the phraseology of the goldites,
their country's general credit should appreciate to par, would the process
of appreciation *necessarily* stop just at *that* point? Why should it not
just as reasonably *continue* to appreciate, so that in another year
gold would be below the par of the country's credit? This simple
analysis proves beyond *all* cavil the arbitrariness of the gold standard
of value.

The credit of a country increases or diminishes without *any* regard
whatever to its gold producing or paying capacity. It is governed
by its capacity for the *general* production of *all* kinds of wealth over
and above its average consumption. It is just the same with a country
as it is with an individual; the individual, to become wealthy and to
have a good credit, must not necessarily ever have *any* gold; but he must
be able to produce or acquire more than he consumes by his general
expenses. A country must proceed by the same process to become
wealthy, and it is simply an *absurdity* for people to talk of the *prosperity*
of the country when *high prices* for *everything* are induced and fostered
by a system which restricts *general* production in order that *special* production may flourish. Individuals cannot get rich by rading among
themselves, *no matter if they increase the price* of their *wares ten per cent
every year.* Neither can all the individuals of a country do the same

thing. What is required by both is increase in the quantity of what they trade in.

It is not the price of what a people *have* that constitutes their true wealth, but it is the *quantity* of their commodities. A barrel of flour is possessed of no more real value if it cost twenty dollars instead of five. It will not maintain life a day longer, let the price even be a thousand dollars. Thus we arrive at the real basis of values—the real wealth—and I have introduced this, precisely for the purpose of showing the high-priced protectionists that they know nothing about *true* values or *true* economy, as well as to also show that there is *no* real wealth except that which conduces to higher ends than its simple acquisition. Wealth as an end is despotism. Wealth as a means is humanitarianism.

But to return from this departure to the main subject. For the idea of redeemability for money there should be substituted that of convertibility. A real money should at *all times* be capable of being converted into *that* of which it stands *representative*. And here we arrive at the last analysis of a real money. It will be readily seen how completely a national currency meets this requirement. It would be representative of the productive capacity of the country, and could always be converted into whatever portion or kind of its products might be required; or into the products of other countries which may be acquired by the direct exchange of our own products.

What more than this can be demanded of money; or what better thing invented as money; or what more capable of inspiring and maintaining an even and legitimate confidence?

National currency being the very best possible money, because it is not only the most convenient but also the most secure, there remains *nothing* to be done but to *continue* to so *acquaint the people*, until they become *convinced* of the rapaciousness of those systems by which the *large* majority are compelled to labor *all their lives* for the *very select few*. There is no difficulty in arriving at all the initial points necessary to determine the amount required, how it should be distributed and kept in circulation, or how its circulation should be regulated. These are all practicalities of finance.

But there is *one thing* which has never yet received consideration, which is *absolutely necessary* to make money meet *all* the requirements of money, and at the same time to maintain a *fixed* and *absolute* value at all times and under all circumstances, which money never has had. From its lacking, have come all the various financial convulsions. And *this is*, an absolute measure of value.

Can money be measured so that the same fixedness shall attach to it that attaches to everything else with which we have to do? Money itself has always been considered a measure of value; and it is this false stoppage and foundationless position that has made possible all financial discords, irregularities and inconsistencies. Does it appear to be a strange proposition that money should be measured? Why should not a dollar be just as absolute as a dollar as a pound is as a pound; or as a foot is as a foot; or as a gallon is as a gallon? A cord of wood contains one hundred and twenty-eight solid feet, or eight cord feet. It must *always* be *eight* feet in length, *four* feet in height and *four* feet in width, or some other multiples of one hundred and twenty-eight. A cord can *never* be any more, *never* any less than just that measurement. And the same rule holds of everything else with which we have to do; with quantity, time, space and motion.- All these have fixed and unvarying modes of measurement. But money, the lever by which all these are moved, has been left to fluctuate as it would—to be moved by every different influence, so that in *many instances* what should have brought contentment, peace and continuous prosperity, has bequeathed the direct reverse.

It does not concern us that there are *more yards of cloth* at one time than another, provided that *yard-sticks* are all of the same length. But what *would* concern us would be this: That if with increase of the *quantity* of cloth the *length* of the yard-sticks should increase proportionately; or with the *decrease* of the quantity of flour the *pound* should decrease in like proportion therewith. Now this is just what has always been true of money; its *real* value *increases* and *decreases*, just in proportion as those things which it professes to measure have increased or decreased in quantity. Instead of these things being exchanged or converted into something measured by as *fixed* a *standard* as they are, the attempt is made to measure them by *something* which *constantly in-*

creases and *decreases* in representative capacity. In other words, a dollar is not at all times one and the same thing. Sometimes it is but seventy-five cents. and sometimes a dollar and a half. That is to say that seventy five cents at one time possess the same representative power that a dollar and a half does at another time, which is in substance to say that money has no measure.

Now what is desirable and indispensable is to give money a *fixed measurement*, which shall be *just* as absolute in its measure of the value of money as the pound is in its measure of weight, or as the yard-stick is in its measure of distance. There never is any more cloth, though there be a thousand more yard-sticks. Nor is a yard-stick ever any longer or shorter, if the quantity to be measured is increased or decreased a thousand-fold. Now just to such a fixedness must money be reduced before it will subserve its best purposes and uses, and the only way this can be done is by that method which will also remove the *only possible* objection there can be brought against such a national currency as is proposed. This objection is that by over-issues of currency its value would or might be depreciated.

Let it be supposed that the country's extremest need to meet the demands of the greatest amount of trade is a *billion dollars* currency. At certain times there are greater and less demands for money, which, under our present practices, make a dollar, to-day, worth *four per cent. per annum* interest, and to-morrow increase it to *ten per cent.* It must be remembered that we are now speaking of an *irredeemable currency*, the *representative* of the *wealth* of the nation : that the *government* representing the nation has *uttered* it, in behalf of *the people*, upon the *soundest* and, in reality, the *only* sure basis of value *any* money *can have*—the productive power and capacity of the nation.

An over-issue is the only thing to be guarded against. The government must be prohibited by some *absolute law* from resorting to the process so well known in railroad management as the " *watering process.*" And this is to be accomplished in the following manner : This currency—this money—must be made convertible into a national bond, bearing such a rate of interest while in the hands of the people as shall be determined upon as " the true measure of value"—say three or four per cent.—which experience would necessarily determine as the true point of balance; and the bond also convertible into currency at the option of the holder.

In other words, the people should demand that the Government issue one thousand **million** dollars in bonds, bearing three per cent. interest, payable in currency, and that it issue one thousand million dollars of circulating medium or money to be loaned to whomsoever deposits the bonds as collateral; all loans to be made at three per cent. per annum; to be for six months, with two renewals of three months each, one-half payable on each renewal. The principle underlying the time being that all credits should be settled with each year's products.

The operation of such a system can be very easily traced. Whenever there should be so much currency in circulation that it would be worth *less* than four per cent., the surplus would at once be invested in the four per cent. interest-bearing national bond; and when business should revive and the demand for money to transact it should make money worth *more* than four per cent., then bonds would be converted into currency again until the equilibrium should be re-established. And whenever the demand should be such that all the money would be converted, and money still be worth more than four per cent., then the government should issue enough to produce the equilibrium.

Thus it is seen that the four per cent. or the three per cent. interest-bearing national bond becomes the *fixed measure* of value for money. It would always be worth *just that amount—never* any more; *never* any less. The gallon measure always gives just the same quantity of molasses. The yard-stick always gives just the same quantity of cloth. The pound weight always gives just the same quantity of sugar. So, too, would this measure of money always give just the same amount of real wealth, or its representative, every day, week, month or year, whether applied to wealth in business, to bonds, or to money at interest. An oscillation would be perpetually maintained; first, conversion of currency into bonds; next, conversion of bonds into currency; and whenever the supply of currency should be deficient, *then the issue of more by the government to meet it.* Thus there would be a *people's*

money regulated to *financial* equilibrium, which is the *ultima thule* of convenience for exchanging the products of industry.

It may be remarked, parenthetically, here, that even three per cent. per annum interest is altogether too greatly in favor of capital. A careful calculation of interests and general increase of the nation's wealth discovers that less than a two per cent. interest is required to make the capitalist and the laborer stand upon an equality. Had I the time I would be glad to present you some figures to show to what condition we are tending. I will simply remark, however, if capital continue o receive the present rates of interest for the next thirty-five years, at the end of that time it will have absorbed all the wealth of the country. That is to say, that interest compounded at the rate of 6 per cent. upon the present Banking Capital will amount to a sum larger than the present aggregate of wealth together with the same rate of increase which has governed it during the past, added thereto. Is not this a sufficiently alarming fact to cause people to stop and consider the despotism into which they are rapidly merging?

Everybody who knows anything about the relations of money to the people must prefer such a money as we have indicated to any other kind. It is really the greenback system extended to *all uses* for which money is required, and to which is given a *fixed measure* of value. All people at present interested in national banks and high interest-paying bonds are constitutionally opposed to such a change in our money system. This, however, should not deter its introduction and use. The people's welfare is what should be consulted, and made *the test* of all propositions that are to become theirs to practice. National banks and all banks of issue, with their drain. upon the people to make their immense profits, must be done away, and banks simply as depositories for the accommodation of the people, alone exist.

The national bank and other currency would be gradually called in at the rate of, say ten per cent. a month.

I may add in justification of this plan, that if the Government can loan three hundred millions to the banks for nothing, it can loan to the people for three per cent. ; if at the same time it can pay three per cent. on its bonds and in currency, instead of six per cent. and in gold, it secures a new-found advantage.

But one of the *chief* benefits which would come to the people from the proposed currency would be the *interest* which would accrue to the government—all the people—for the use of this money In other words, *all* the interest now paid to *banks of issue* for *loans*, for the same convenience should be paid to the government. A *part* of the people, for the *use* of money belonging to *all* the people, themselves inclusive, would pay *interest* to the government therefor And what more legitimate method of governmenta. support than this, if by it all other means of taxation could be annulled? The interest now paid by the people of the country to the Banks and Capitalists would, twice over, pay all costs of maintaining the government. A three-per-cent. interest paid to the government or al. loans the people required would not only relieve the people who produce wealth of one-half the interest they now pay, but also of all taxes of all kinds. Is not this a matter to be looked into in the most serious manner ?

With such a currency system *once* inaugurated, the country would begin a gradual process of general prosperity. Wealth, insteac of accumulating in a *few* hands, would continually tend to an *equal* distribution among *all* producing people. A large part of the speculative mania would be rendered futile, and those now devoting all their time to *hatching schemes* by which to defraud the producing classes of their wealth would be *compelled* to turn producers themselves. It is calculated that one-tenth of the male population of this country is engaged in speculative pursuits. In other words, they ' live and grow fat' from those who are engaged in production. And that is our boasted equity our equality.

It should be the object of all reform to make a *nearer* approach to a system of *complete* justice and a *perfect* equity. Any reform tha* does not base itself upon *such* a proposition and whose outlook is not in this direction *is no reform*, and does no* deserve the serious attention of any. There is scarcely an idea prevalent in the community of what true justice and equity consist. But it may be stated as follows : *No person has any just claim to the ownership of anything which he did not produce or which he did not acquire by an equitable exchange of something which he did produce.* Tested by *this* rule, the accumulated wealth of the world is in unjust hands; it is held by those who have *a no better title* thereto than if they had actually stolen it. It has been fraudulently acquired, and that is the word which best expresses the manner of its obtainment. And one of the most effective methods of remedying this growing evil is to attain to a true money system—one founded in the requirements to be met and based upon that which it is to represent—that which it is to be used to exchange. Anything that *departs* from these standards is *not* scientific money. That which *has* these for its standards *is* a scientific money.

Aside from all that has been said, there is a general principle rising into the comprehension of humanity which *must of necessity* dethrone that which has so long been worshiped as the money god. The day for arbitrary rule and standards is drawing to a close, whether they be standards of materiality or spirituality; of morals or intellect; of despotism or democracy. Gold *is* an arbitrary money standard, and with all others of like character *must* fall. The tendency of the world is *against it*, and its doom is *already* sealed. It has been *weighed* in the balance and found wanting.

The interest of the common people, who should always hear every new Christ, demands a reform in our monetary and financial systems. We are aware, however, that there is a great deal of prejudice in their minds in favor of "hard money," and they must be awakened to the fact that hard money is a myth—a play upon words—a deception practiced upon them by those who have played the part of "the appropriators of wealth" lo! these many years, and who would continue to filch *year* after *year* all that the "toiling millions" can compel nature to yield up to them. In this process the laboring classes are the mere avenues through which the earth pours its wealth into the coffers of the capitalists.

Some object that the very numerous and intricate methods to which resort would be required would prove *unmanageable*, and that *corruption* would *inevitably* creep in and undermine its usefulness. Let such consider our almost perfect postal system, and how *well balanced* are all its movements and checks, and find therein their answer. Would there be more intricacy in the proposed system than there now is in the present? Do not all national banks, though nominally distinct, *really* have a common fountain head in government? Does not all their currency come from government? Suppose all these banks, instead of being independent institutions, were an organized system, having a common head, as the banks of New York City virtually have in the Clearing House, would not that be a condition so nearly related to the system which would be required as to show its entire practicability?

Indeed, there is scarcely need that there should be a new department inaugurated to bring such a currency home to the people. Perhaps there never was a system operated in which there was *less* proportionate loss through its executive officers than in our postal system. And this is because the *responsibility* comes *home* to the people. The postmaster is always a resident of the *place* in which he officiates, and, either with or without a civil service law, should be the *appointee* of the citizens whom he is to serve; and, of course, would be a person possessing their special confidence. To such persons might the *care* of the public money well be intrusted; and in *all places* except cities a *single* person could perform both the services of postmaster and of United States financial agent.

Means can be easily devised to make all post offices offices for loaning, as they now sell post office stamps and money orders.

In all that I have said my only purpose has been to endeavor to arrive at a proper understanding of the most important feature of governmental justice and uniform equity among all the people. All past systems have failed to secure this. The world has constantly witnessed the proceeds of the labors of the millions *aggregated* in the hands of the few. This advantage which one class has possessed over another cannot long exist under the rapid spread of intelligence, which marks the present generation; and it behooves *this* people to give *due* consideration to *any* scheme which proposes to lessen this advantage. And *most especially* does it become the duty of the people, if there be such a thing as *principles* of *finance*, to *find* them out and cause them to be practically applied.

In fine, and to resume, the idea of money must first be **separated** from that of the intrinsic value of gold, or any other commodity, and confined to the mere capacity of representing all commodities, and so of facilitating the exchanges of wealth. This, it has been abundantly demonstrated, can be as well, and for various reasons, better done by strips of paper, properly stamped and signed, than by gold or any other metal.

In the next place, these strips of paper, signed by the Government, with the credit and wealth of the whole country, are better than individual promises; though the issuance of individual promises should not and need not be prohibited, as we do not now prohibit anybody from making or receiving private notes, drafts and checks.

Again, the Government Money need not be redeemable, but only convertible into new strips of paper when the old ones are worn out, and into commodies when they are used in trade, and into other Government Securities bearing interest, as I have pointed out.

Still again, money has also been held to be a correct measure of values. This it ought to be, indeed, but has never been so, because it has never been measured itself. Of what use would yard-sticks be, used for measuring cloth, but which had never themselves been measured by anything? The system which I have stated for measuring money itself is believed to be perfect. It is not the individual dollar, relatively to the half dollar or the hundred dollars, that has failed to be measured or fixed; but the rate of increase relatively to other values, of all the Government currency afloat. By the convertibility of any excess of issue sinking its value below a certain standard into interest-paying bonds, any over-issue is immediately absorbed, while a deficiency of issue will be revealed by the fact that absolutely no bonds will be sold. In this manner the whole operation will be self-adjusting from day to day; the value of the aggregate of Government money will be accurately measured and kept uniform; and any interest or temptation which the Government might have to an over-issue would be immediately neutralized by the absorption of such surplus into bonds, upon which the Government itself would be paying interest; or, in other words, assuming an unnecessary and useless burden, in the face of the people and of its own economies. Can anything more perfect be devised ? If so, let us have it by all means ; if not, let this device **be** adopted. A self adjusting, self-regulating admeasurement of the **value** of money would make it a true measure of other values, and is a **sugges-** tion which, if it can be secured, is of unequaled importance.

Another somewhat similar idea was glanced at in passing—that of **a** definite method of determining scientifically the equitable rate **of** interest. This I cannot stop now to explain. It will, however, only be when we come quite down to that basis, that the full value of this financial system will be experienced.

Finally, in its basis, this system of Government money is money issued at the mere cost of printing and circulating; but by adjoining with it the idea of a complete, simple and exceedingly economical means of raising the revenue of the country, the three or four **per** cent. is paid to the treasury ; that is to say, by the people individually to the same people in their collective capacity. Under this system all the various revenue officials and tax assessors and gatherers **would** be dispensed with, and a vast system of economy inaugurated, **which,** in a few years, would transpose us from a borrowing to a loaning **nation,** making us the financial example for all the world. This it also **seems** to me is another invaluable feature of the system, all of which I, **how-** ever, respectfully submit to the decision of the people.

The interests of humanity which are involved in this question **are** greater than are the interests of those who have assumed to *rule* **the** world, and who are endeavoring to *fasten* upon the people *despotism,* **to** escape from which would require the shedding of whole rivers of human blood and the destruction of the best evidences of our civilization., **for** which we have a perfect right to feel the greatest admiration.

A *timely* understanding of the money question would guarantee precisely the reverse of *all* this, and cause humanity to take still *greater* and more rapid *strides* toward that perfect enlightenment which **can** alone thoroughly recognize the common brotherhood of the human **race,** toward which end all reform should be directed.

ECONOMICS

(5)

Humanitarian Money. The Unsolved Riddle . . . 1892.

Humanitarian Money.

THE UNSOLVED RIDDLE.

BY

VICTORIA WOODHULL

(Mrs. JOHN BIDDULPH MARTIN).

LONDON:
1892.

"The two greatest events that have occurred in the history of mankind have been directly brought about by a contraction and, on the other hand, an expansion of the circulating medium of society. The fall of the Roman Empire, so long ascribed, in ignorance, to slavery, heathenism, and moral corruption, was in reality brought about by a decline in the silver and gold mines of Spain and Greece. And, as if Providence had intended to reveal in the clearest manner the influence of this mighty agent on human affairs, the resurrection of mankind from the ruin which those causes had produced was owing to a directly opposite set of agencies being put in operation. Columbus led the way in the career of renovation; when he spread his sails across the Atlantic, he bore mankind and its fortunes in his barque. The annual supply of the precious metals for the use of the globe was tripled; before a century had expired the prices of every species of produce was quadrupled. The weight of debt and taxes insensibly wore off under the influence of that prodigious increase. In the renovation of industry the relations of society were changed, the weight of feudalism cast off, the rights of man established. Among the many concurring causes which conspired to bring about this mighty consummation, the most important, though hitherto the least observed, was the discovery of Mexico and Peru. If the circulating medium of the globe had remained stationary, or declining, as it was from 1815 to 1849, from the effects of the South American revolution and from English legislation, the necessary result must have been that it would have become altogether inadequate to the wants of man: and not only would industry have been everywhere cramped, but the price of produce would have universally and constantly fallen. Money would have every day become more valuable: all other articles measured in money less so; debt and taxes would have been constantly increasing in weight and oppression. The fate which crushed Rome in ancient, and has all but crushed Great Britain in modern times, would have been that of the whole family of mankind. All these evils have been entirely obviated, and the opposite set of blessings introduced, by the opening of the great treasures of Nature in California and Australia."

ALISON : *History of Europe.*

𝔥umanitarian 𝔐oney.

THE UNSOLVED RIDDLE.

BY

VICTORIA WOODHULL

(Mrs. JOHN BIDDULPH MARTIN).

LONDON:
1892.

PRINTED BY

BLADES, EAST AND BLADES. 23. ABCHURCH LANE,

LONDON, E.C.

THE UNSOLVED RIDDLE.

THE enigma propounded by the Sphinx of our day is that of the equitable division, enjoyment, and consumption of wealth ; it is not too much to say that its solution is demanded under pain of death.

Very much more of the people's common happiness depends upon money than even political economists generally suppose. Happiness is very closely allied to prosperity, and general prosperity in a country can never obtain unless it be under a sound financial system. Very few people understand what general prosperity means. It does not mean vast sums of gold in the hands of a few of the inhabitants of the country, while the great majority struggle, month after month, for the absolute necessities of life. There may be a great deal of money in a country and still be very little general prosperity with the common people.

Our methods of producing wealth are undergoing improvement every day. Facilities for the transportation and distribution of products have been increased to an extent undreamed of by earlier economists. But the equitable division and consumption of wealth— who shall solve this riddle.

It has been said that the thing most to be feared is ignorance. And yet it is argued that to call in question the currency of a nation, a subject on which profound ignorance and misapprehension exist ; or worse still, to propose to amend its conditions, would endanger the whole industrial structure, and cause wide-spread distress. We are therefore bidden to hold our peace, lest ignorance should give way to knowledge, and vested interests should suffer. Hasty legislation on, or tinkering with, the finances of a nation may bring on a more acute phase of the social problem ; but there are forces at work which are sure, if not dealt with in time, to culminate in a desperate struggle preceding the reconstruction of the monetary systems of the world. The gradual but sure inroads which interest and rent are making on the sum total of wealth produced, give to the social scientist ample material for reflection.

Money is subject to evolution no less than any other product, be it artificial or natural. To maintain that because a thing has been useful in the past it will always be useful, is to deny the possibility of progress. The system of little gold and a great deal of credit has served a very important function in the rapid creation of wealth. Instead of condemning the whole system, when we are ready to give due credit to what credit has accomplished, we shall understand what credit is.

Commerce consists of the exchanges of wealth; and these exchanges are accomplished by the instruments generally known as money and credit. The redundant or reduced supply of one commodity should not affect the exchanges of all the other commodities of the world, nor should all the exchanges of the world be restricted or limited to the supply of one commodity. If money is to facilitate the exchanges of wealth, it should be based upon all wealth, not upon one form of wealth. When, in 1870, I advocated such a humanitarian money, I was asked, what is wealth? What constitutes it? What is its nature? How can money be based on something about which we have no clear conception? A clever writer on currency questions took issue with the theory advocated in a speech on " The Principles of Finance," which I delivered in New York City, 1871, that labour is the creator of wealth and value. Labour is not wealth, he said, nor does it give value; wealth is a desire. A superficial economist would scoff at the idea that wealth is a desire; the uninformed man or woman would simply say that to be wealthy is to have plenty of money. It is not necessary to tell any one that; even the most ordinary tradesman will know when trade is dull, when customers are falling off; but of what causes these effects he is entirely ignorant. Yet the answer to this one question of what constitutes wealth comprises the art and science of social well being.

Credit does not, as many suppose, increase or add to the actual volume of metallic money, sometimes called hard cash. Credit increases the function of money as a medium of exchange. It is difficult to grasp the full import of this without understanding that money does not represent wealth, it only facilitates the exchanges of wealth. Suppose the aggregate wealth of a nation were computed at a certain sum, money could be issued to that amount to represent that wealth if it were used in only one transaction. In the ordinary way, commodities do not change hands more than half a dozen times. A particular sum of money however can liquidate a hundred debts, the same pieces of coin can be used for the transfer of thousands of various commodities, they can pass through a hundred different hands in one day. It would be curious to estimate how many different exchanges a single shilling or sovereign has effected. It is stated that credit adds about nine times the volume of money to the existing metallic money; now as credit does not add one gold sovereign to the existing stock of gold, this statement appears like a paradox. In what way can credit add to the volume of money which is on a gold basis? If in course of time one hundred sovereigns, or a hundred pound note has liquidated ten debts of that amount, it represents the purchasing power of a thousand pounds. When the money which passes through the Clearing House during the year is computed at billions, it means that billions of purchasing power have exchanged billions of wealth. The sum does not represent actual money amounting to billions, for, the same money may have passed through a thousand hands to make up this total at the end of the year. As it has been maintained that each credit created on a debt adds to the volume of money, it is necessary to illustrate this point. For herein lies the subtle fallacy of estimating the purchasing power *per capita* of a nation by computing the volume of money and the number of the population. For with the same volume of money and total population in two different nations, the purchasing power may vary widely according to the standard of living and the methods of doing business.

For example, if we take the population of the United Kingdom at thirty millions, and the gold sovereigns at ninety, it would give a *per capita* purchasing power to each individual of three pounds, if it were equally divided and changed hands during the week. As the bulk of wages is paid weekly, this would be a fair estimate; if this amount changed hands daily it would be equal to twenty-one pounds *per capita*; if it changed hands once during the month, it would be purchasing power to the amount of only fifteen shillings *per capita*. A man who earns two pounds a week is able to consume or exchange wealth to the amount of only two pounds, provided his standard of living is up to his wages. If his standard is only up to one pound and he hoards one, wealth will be exchanged or consumed to the amount of only one pound, and the full amount of purchasing power in existence will not be utilised.

One man may have purchasing power to the amount of £2,000 a week, and his standard of living for the year may only be up to his income of a week; hence if he kept his money in a strong box in his own house, purchasing power to the extent of £102,000 would be locked up. Another man may have a debt of £10,000 due to him which he cannot collect for a year, he has so much capital locked up, he goes to his banker, gets his bill discounted, pays the money away, and it continues to be circulated until at the end of the year it may represent £200,000 in purchasing power. Taking into consideration the great inequality in the distribution of money, there are over a million tramps in the United States, and several million unemployed, we can imagine what frightful misery would prevail if this money were withdrawn from circulation and locked up by its possessors. When individuals hoard during a panic this is just what happens. Recent writers on currency, in attempting to prove the insufficiency of the volume of money in the United States for the demands of business, draw attention to the fact that with a population which has more than doubled within the last thirty years, the money in circulation *per capita* has diminished by almost half. The wealth of the United States which was estimated about thirty years ago at sixteen billions, has to-day increased to sixty billions. In reality these figures are not conclusive evidence to prove or to disprove the insufficiency of the present volume of money for the demands of business in the United States. The failure to comprehend that a mass of bullion exchanged once in six months, and a small quantity of gold exchanged frequently during the same time, represent the same purchasing power at the end of the half-year, leads to endless confusion.

A sovereign which changes hands a hundred times a week, and a hundred pound note once, represent the same quantity of wealth exchanged during the week; thus the purchasing power of the sovereign and the hundred pound note are made equal. To ascertain the volume of money required to carry on the business of a nation, full weight must be given to the increase of purchasing power which the rapid circulation of money gives, whether simple paper, credit, or gold. The quantity of gold in relation to purchasing power is like one cup and a dozen men who desire a drink of water; each can be accommodated if he waits his turn; if all should demand and insist on being served at the same time, they would find that there were not enough cups, and then a general scrimmage might ensue to be first served. How long each could wait his turn would depend upon the time he had to spare. All obligations or debts are expressed in terms of money, a definite time is given within which they must be met, the law requires debts to be paid in the legal tender, gold; credit being so much in excess of gold it necessarily follows that if the demand for gold is all at the same time, a general scrimmage and severe monetary pressure is the result. And this is why the expansive theory has been found so efficacious in a panic. As time waits for no one, and as the standard of living of the individuals composing a nation determine the circulation of money, the extended purchasing power which increased circulation gives to money is limited by them.

To the student of finance two questions present themselves, the first, whether if a universal system of cash payments prevailed, would such phenomena as commercial crises, financial panics, hard times, be unknown? The second, whether it be possible for consumption to overtake production by falling prices alone, in order that the majority whose purchasing power is so limited, shall enjoy the advantages of civilisation?

Sir Dudley North in 1691 said: "It is the poverty of consumers which causes a glutted market and depression in trade;" this shows that glutted markets and depression in trade are not a nineteenth century phenomenon. The fact that Sir Dudley North could have made such an observation before credit had assumed anything like the gigantic proportions of to-day, shows that a commercial crisis is not to be attributed alone to the expansion of credit in the commercial world. Under a system of cash payments, it is true there would not be the losses from bad debts, and there would not be the uneasiness that is engendered by the fear that debtors will fail to meet their obligations, which, when it becomes general, produces a panic. Further, there would not be the inducement to speculate without a due consideration of possible adverse consequences which a system of credit fosters.

The causes which make a retail dealer unable to pay his debts may be potent even under a system of cash payments; he may be overstocked, or fashions change, or for some other reason buyers fall off. The loss, of course, would fall on him alone as far as the failure to sell his goods went; and his profits have to cover these contingencies. The wholesale dealer and the manufacturer having received cash would not lose, as far as this single transaction is concerned, but they would probably have a larger stock of goods on hand, and if they did not find a market for their goods, these would become so much dead capital. The interests of the manufacturers and the wholesale dealers, therefore, are as much dependent on the would-be purchaser, as the retail dealers are dependent on their customers. Whether the manufacturer converted his raw material into economic goods by means of credit or cash, whether the wholesale dealer sell these finished products to retail dealers on so much credit or for so much gold, does not matter provided these articles are sold to consumers, because each individual engaged in attaining the final result—"consumption"—will be able to meet his liabilities. Whenever consumption is restricted, from whatever cause, we have a glutted market, depression in trade and apparent over-production. The would-be consumer is the pivot of the whole problem. Whatever deters or restrains the would-be purchaser from buying, prevents consumption from overtaking production, and commercial ruin is the result.

It has been argued that these periodic cataclysms are the result of our competitive system. It is true that we do not have a glut in the market of postage stamps, because they are produced according to demand. It is contended that when prices are high in certain industries, capitalists rush in, employ labour, set machinery going until there is over-production ; and when the market is glutted with certain commodities, labourers are discharged, machinery shut down, and depression in trade continues until the surplus is absorbed. There is a large measure of truth in this argument, though over-production in one or two branches of industry would not cause general depression in trade. These discharged labourers are consumers, and when they are idle, these would-be buyers lessen the demand for other goods said to be over-produced ; and not only this, they lower the standard of living of those still in work by being consumers only. If a business man does not make enough during the prosperous season to carry him through a period of depression, how can it be expected that the employé from his scanty wages could have saved enough to carry him through a long period of being out of employment ? He will not be able to consume on credit, and it is just here that the inadequacy of the credit system comes in. If the standard of living of the working man as represented by purchasing power were high enough to enable him to pass through a period of depression until it were really ascertained how far production had exceeded demand, and had time to re-adjust itself, the terrible evils resulting from a system of credit would be averted.

Supply will be only to the one and not to the nine hundred and ninety-nine, if the one have the wherewithal to purchase, and the nine hundred and ninety-nine have not this purchasing power. On the one hand, there is over-production ; on the other, a vast army of unemployed who are in want of the things which are said to be over-produced. So little is this fact understood, that it has even been maintained by many clever business men that low prices and no profits are the results of over-production. If all were in a position to purchase commodities or not, as they felt inclined, then such a statement might be correct. The cause of these economic conditions is not over-production so long as there are wants left unsatisfied ; and therefore to adjust supply to a diminishing demand caused by the poverty of consumers, is not the remedy. Nor does the remedy lie in controlling the output by having a monopoly of such commodity, nor by labour and capital combining to limit the output, so as to adjust supply and demand. The remedy lies in a more equitable and increased purchasing power. For production will be increased, not restricted, side by side with the increase of the purchasing power of the masses.

We must never lose sight of the fact that distribution and consumption depend upon purchasing power. If prices of commodities fall to any great extent because of restricted purchasing power, employers cannot continue to pay the same wages with their diminishing incomes ; wages are lowered in order to leave the necessary margin of profits to continue business. Labourers strike against this reduction in wages, but their efforts will be unavailing until the root of the evil is attacked. It might be supposed that the labourer is benefited by a fall in prices of commodities because the purchasing power of his wages would become so much greater. Cheapness of commodities produced by improved machinery, or better organisation of labour, is one thing, but cheapness brought about by lowering profits to undersell competitors is another. If the prices of commodities fall, the profits of the manufacturer or producer must also fall, and wages must be reduced so as to leave the necessary margin of profit to continue business. Moreover, labourers working for a bare-subsistence wage will lessen the demand for the commodities which other labourers are engaged in producing.

Real wealth and real prosperity do not consist in high prices for everything, but in the quantity which is actually possessed. The point to be attained is the employment of the industry of a country in those directions wherein the most can be produced at the least cost, rather than the other extreme of the least production at the greatest cost. If commodities can be obtained at low prices, and the rate of the working man's wages be increased, then his material condition is improved ; but if low prices involve a reduction of wages, then there is no advantage gained, and his standard of living is lowered. Prices will not be steadied by any amount of combination of labour and capital while the medium of exchange is left to fluctuate as it does. And it is sheer nonsense to talk of a fair return to capital and labour, or fair profits, until we have a fixed standard of value. I said in a

B

lecture published in the *Boston Times*, October 22nd, 1876 : " Every day that any labourer is idle is a loss to the prospective wealth of the country." This fact is the condemnation of the policy of throwing men out of employment whenever business is depressed through vicious speculation. Every labourer thus made idle adds to the general distress, because, from being a producer and a consumer, he becomes a consumer only. If money be loaned for building houses, manufactories, constructing bridges, railroads, and so forth, the money paid away in wages stimulates production in other directions. Unemployed labour lessens the demand for different commodities.

If money be to facilitate the exchanges of wealth, and if production increase a hundredfold, and the population double, while gold increases very little, we shall continue to have glutted markets and depression in trade, more especially if this purchasing power be controlled by the few. Every idle man decreases demand in some direction. It is not demand alone which determines production, but demand and purchasing power. The poverty of consumers only permits them to demand inferior articles. When a person goes into a shop to buy, he does not ask for the best article, but the cheapest that will answer his purpose. What then must be the effect on production if the majority of the population be poor? Though production may be a question of supply and demand, demand is regulated by purchasing power. A man may desire the best quality of goods and yet be forced to buy inferior goods, hence the inferior survives. These conditions react upon the minds of the buyers, and their appreciation of quality deteriorates.

Thus we find that our shops are overloaded with cheap inferior goods. Tradesmen have told me that they cannot now sell the same quality of goods which they used to sell even five or six years ago. It does not pay them to make the superior article for one—the millionaire—while the demand of the nine hundred and ninety-nine is for cheap goods. A merchant prince, who supplies cheap goods for the million, once told me that he never makes up first-class articles, it would not pay him to do so. Of course, as I have said before, the more restricted the purchasing power of the majority, the greater the demand for cheap inferior goods.

Why do we speak of first quality, second quality, third quality, if there be no intrinsic value in goods except that which demand gives? Herbert Spencer has said that self-interest will lead individuals to reject the inferior and choose the superior article, but I have found that the more over-worked, devitalised, or degraded persons are, the less able they are to appreciate real value. Consider how much taste requires to be educated, and how little time outside his particular profession or trade an individual has to learn to appreciate value, especially since work is becoming more and more specialised and sub-divided. A labourer working ten or twelve hours a day at the construction of some special constituent part of a machine, will not have taste sufficiently educated to demand the best, and moreover his wages will not permit him, even if he be clever enough to know or desire the best, to purchase it.

Whether the better drives out the inferior article has a most important bearing upon the production of wealth. It demonstrates the progress or decline in the character of the material wealth that is being produced. Two factors determine the survival of the fittest in the production of wealth, one, the faculty to judge or appreciate the superior quality, the other, the purchasing power to buy or demand the superior article. Without these two factors combined the superior article will not drive out the inferior, and consequently will not survive.

Why is it that unequal distribution of wealth produces luxury and encouragement of the fine arts? It is because one having more than he requires for his actual material wants can devote the surplus wealth to satisfy his æsthetic taste. For instance a man leaves a million dollars to be divided among ten children; he also leaves an estate; he leaves to the oldest son nine hundred thousand dollars with the estate, and only one hundred thousand to be divided equally among the other nine children. The eldest son having more than he requires for his material wants, fosters art by buying beautiful pictures and statues for his gallery, collects other *objets d'art*, becomes an amateur horticulturist and has lovely greenhouses; or an amateur breeder of choice animals, he improves the estate by laying out new roads and other improvements. The other children with their small legacies compete in the industrial or professional ranks, emigrate, or they marry fortunes or mayhap succumb in the struggle for existence.

The one who gets the lion's share (he may not be in any way the superior from the standpoint of the breeder), has all the advantages that wealth and society can give him; the others will be the majority, subjected to the stress of poverty and unfavourable environment. It is not that they would not like to have many of the comforts that their brother has, but it is their poverty which debars them; they have not the purchasing power. The demand for the superior article will be as one to nine; the demand for cheap inferior articles will be as nine to one, and the greater the inequality the greater the demand for cheap inferior articles. There is an intimate relation between centralization of wealth and restricted consumption of commodities. The more the purchasing power gets into the hands of the few the more restricted consumption will become. How much purchasing power has the girl working for a dollar-and-a-half a week? She does not stay in the garret because she prefers it to a nice comfortable room ; she does not go dinnerless from choice. It is because her poverty debars her from purchasing her dinner. On the other hand over-production brings disaster to the producer, and this will continue to be so as long as the masses are too poor to purchase.

The last half-century has seen, by the aid of machinery, an enormous increase in our powers of production. Commodities which were considered luxuries at the beginning of the century, have now come within the reach of all. With this unparalleled increase in the wealth-producing power, purchasing power should have increased in a corresponding ratio, so that all could avail themselves of the increased advantages of civilisation. But instead of this, we find that production and distribution are not adjusted because of the purchasing power.

Political economists hold that men labour to satisfy their desires and physical needs. The great difference between backward races and highly cultivated ones is, that the former have fewer wants. It is necessary to stimulate and increase the wants and needs of working men and women, and to strengthen their self-reliance and responsibility by the power to gratify these wants through their own exertions. When the standard of living is such that the higher faculties fail to be developed, when it has a tendency to keep them at the vegetative stage of existence, it is necessary to encourage discontent.

That the standard of living among the very poor is not what it should be, no one will deny. As the social mal-adjustments become greater, it becomes more difficult every day for the poor to maintain a decent standard. Unless the concentration of capital, brought about by granting special privileges to individuals, be counteracted, the standard of living of the masses must fall still further, and in its train, the standard of civilization. It is evident that if ten thousand a year were equally distributed among twenty families, that the standard of living of the twenty families would be higher than if one family has eight thousand a year, and the nineteen families have about one hundred each to live upon.

In larger figures, if in a population of sixty millions about thirty thousand men control half, or two-thirds, of the wealth of the nation, the standard of living of the remainder must be correspondingly lowered ; must even, in the majority of cases, fall below the margin of decent living. It therefore stands to reason, that the greater these inequalities, the more the standard of civilization must be lowered.

It is acknowledged that the higher the standard of living among the working men and women the greater the efficiency and skill of labour. Shorter hours, better food, good sanitary conditions, conduce to a higher physical and mental standard. When wages fall below the minimum necessary to maintain a healthy manhood and womanhood, it indicates a diseased condition of society.

It is a significant fact that individuals who have been accustomed to a high standard of living are those who make the most strenuous efforts to maintain it. When returning from America a few weeks ago, I was discussing some social questions with a gentleman who had been on a tour of inspection among the steerage passengers. "How terrible to be in that condition," he said to me, "it makes me ill even to go among them. There is a man down there who is going to South Africa on the same business as I am. Who can tell, the wheel of fortune may turn in the future, and he may be here and I in the steerage? No! never that, for I would kill myself first." Why was the idea insufferable to this man that he might possibly have to sink to the degraded state we were discussing? Because he had known the benefits of a higher standard both to his physical and mental nature. A professional man once said to me that he was almost worn out with the struggle to keep his wife and family up to a respectable standard of living, but that he would rather that they should all die together than sink any lower in the scale of existence. It is not the rich man, content even if his neighbour be starving, who raises the level of humanity, but the man and woman with aspirations towards a higher and better life for humanity, with discontent in their hearts at anything which degrades. If we wish to advance, we must stimulate our desire for everything which conduces to a higher and better manhood and womanhood.

Instead of making us dissatisfied with anything which stultifies or suppresses the God in us, the tendency of the social mal-adjustments of the last half-century has been to discourage higher wants and desires. Parsimony has been held to be commendable. We can so economize that we may stultify our intellectual, æsthetic and emotional natures. The standard of living can be so lowered, and people can become so thrifty and economical, that everything which does not contribute to the bare necessities of life can be suppressed. Yet the very pain and repulsion which a highly organised individual feels when thrown into squalid, degrading surroundings, are the outcome of the development and gratification of these higher desires.

Think of the difference in value a sum of money is to a man who hasn't anything to eat, or any place to sleep, and the same sum of money to one who has a superfluity. Twenty-five cents to the starving man or woman represents that which will keep soul and body together for the time; a few dollars to another means genteel poverty; a few hundreds to another represents certain luxuries; a few hundred thousands, more or less, to the millionaire may or may not have exceeded its usefulness. What a wide gulf separates the first and the last.

Unequal distribution of wealth connotes that some have more and others have less. There is a limit to the quantity of gold in the world; if one nation gets more, other nations will get proportionately less. The land of a nation is limited, and if this land becomes the property of the few, the rest of the population will get proportionately less. If one man has all the benefits accruing from supplying certain necessaries to the public, the rest of mankind will be excluded from sharing his profits, or if to one individual the largest share of any trade is given, the less there remains to divide among other individuals pursuing the same trade, and the more numerous the latter, the portion each receives is proportionately smaller. How is centralization of wealth accomplished? By big firms or monopolies absorbing the little ones, individuals co-operating together to get a monopoly; monopolies co-operate together to form trusts. Capitalists by co-operating have made themselves so powerful that they can crush out all small competitors. To-day vast fortunes are an accomplished fact. The power of the few over the many is becoming patent. The case stands to-day as it did when Solon found the wealth and property of Athens had become the property of the few, while the many were poor and miserable; and Plutarch tells us that Lycurgus found the same condition of affairs in Lacedemonia.

The industrial world is fast becoming a series of circles, each narrowing in circumference until the centre is reached; as these circles contract there is an augmentation of purchasing power. The inner circles are able to buy and consume wealth which the outer circles may help to produce, but may not taste the pleasures thereof. How does consumption overtake production by falling prices? The manager of a large business who is receiving fifteen per cent. profits on goods from the hundred buyers at a high price, may find it more advantageous to meet the purchasing power of the five hundred buyers at a lower price, and receive only ten per cent. profits, or to receive five per cent. from the thousand buyers. Should prices fall still lower from some untoward event, there would be no margin of profit, all the calculations of the business men are upset and ruin follows. Commodities as they become cheaper come within the purchasing power of a larger number of buyers, the limit to this factor being the necessary margin of profit, failing which, production will cease altogether; a man of enterprise will not continue to produce at a loss or to give his goods away.

The most important agent which enables consumption to overtake production is increased purchasing power. By this, I do not mean the enhancement of the value of money as compared with other commodities, I mean an actual increase in available cash for everyday use. Through the desire to economise the precious metals we are fast reaching a system of perfected barter in all the larger transactions of business. The addition of every new comfort and luxury which raises the standard of living of the masses, though, makes a further demand upon available cash. To take his seat at a theatre, or ride in the "'bus," or to buy his morning paper and the like, the artisan must have some form of money; the exchange of goods for goods, or service for service, will not enable him to gratify these wants during the present transitional period. There is a growing feeling among the poorer classes of tradesmen that the cash system is the safest, and wherever this feeling predominates, it increases the demand for cash. The addition of every individual in a nation sub-divides the existing quantity of money should there be no increase.

The growing instability of the money market, the recurring panics, the commercial crises, the universal uneasiness, all tend to show the insecurity of the foundation of our present financial system. To any one who probes beneath the surface of these recurring economic convulsions, it must become evident as greater pressure is brought to bear on the existing stock of gold, and a greater and greater commerce is carried on by the expansion of credit, that the sensitiveness of the money market must increase until it becomes acute. If the whole secret of the growing instability of the money market, as the late Professor Jevons stated, is due to the fact that gold does not increase in anything like the same proportion to trade, it proves that gold is not the most stable basis for money. Moreover, if the mere fact of an unusual exportation of gold is liable at any moment to precipitate a monetary crisis, it more than ever proves, not the stability, but the instability of the gold basis. Any untoward circumstance, anything which contracts credit unduly, increases the demand for gold, and may cause a panic. The apprehensions of well-informed persons are so well founded that the most enlightened are in favour of the entire reconstruction of the monetary system.

If the stability of the money markets of the world rests upon so slight a foundation as the ebb and flow of bullion from a nation, and that upon the chances that an unusual number of persons will not demand gold at the same time, the whole ingenuity of statesmen henceforth must be directed towards devising means to prevent the exportation of bullion, and to encourage its importation. To secure this end, we are told, that we must have low prices for everything, the lower the better ; high prices for commodities are sure to cause a drain of bullion from the country. Those manufacturers and merchants who place obstacles in the way of intelligent legislation on this subject cannot see beyond their day, their hour I am inclined to say.

Because there is a large amount of loanable capital to be had at a low discount it is said that the present volume of money in Great Britain is more than enough to meet the demands of business. As an offset against such an argument, it is forgotten that there is a general feeling of distrust and unwillingness to embark in new enterprises. When trade is most stagnant, and everything comparatively at a standstill, there is a diminished demand for money, consequently a larger amount of money-seeking buyers. How absurd it is though to assert upon such evidence that the volume of money is sufficient. After a storm then comes a lull.

Henry D. Macleod strongly insists on the classical theory that demand is the origin and cause of value, and exchangeability the sole essence and principle of wealth. " The most common term in Greek for wealth means simply anything that is wanted and demanded ; when that thing is not in demand it ceases to be wealth. If a person should bring a cargo of wine among a nation of total abstainers, no one would desire or demand the wine : among such a people it would have no value. So among a nation of non-smokers tobacco would have no value ; among a nation of vegetarians beef and mutton would have no value. However much a person might wish to sell his product, if no one would buy it, it would have no value. There must be reciprocal desire and demand."

In a system of barter we can talk of reciprocal demand, but in an industrial system wherein to grow rich is an end and not a means, wealth will be limited not by demand but by purchasing power. To illustrate this theory of wealth : In the suburbs of Rome and Florence an immense number of houses were recently built ; land, labour and material commodities were employed, and according to the theory that labour is the source of all value, wealth was created. Why did these houses become valueless and ruin those who built them ? Because there was no demand for them, and according to the theory that demand, not labour, is the cause and origin of value, these houses were not wealth, nor is that wealth which exceeds demand. Over-production is not wealth, nor does the labour that induces over-production create wealth.

When improved dwellings were constructed some years ago for working men and women, complaints were made that they did not want them ; that they preferred the squalid surroundings, and that when placed in these buildings they would drift back again into their old conditions. If these buildings had been constructed for speculative purposes the same argument would be used—there was no desire or demand for them—hence they were not wealth. There was a demand for the miserable squalid surroundings, however, and they were wealth. This short-sighted aspect of wealth and value is the one which appeals most forcibly to the practical business man of to-day. When these houses were built in the suburbs of Florence and Rome a value was created, wealth was created ; but this wealth, the product of misapplied labour, not being utilised was wasted. Their actual value is not irretrievably lost until the houses fall into decay, but their present value, depending upon demand, which in its turn is determined by purchasing power, may be nil. Speculators who did not take into consideration demand and limited purchasing power did not succeed.

Many ridicule the idea that labour is the cause of value. " Now it is utterly impossible to stir a single step on this subject until this contradiction is cleared up, and we determine whether labour or exchangeability, *i.e.*, demand, is the cause of value. . . . Land in the same localities has very different values : a frontage in a main thoroughfare like Regent Street, Fleet Street, Cheapside, or Cornhill, is of much greater value than an equal space of ground in a back street. How are these different values due to differences of labour when, as we have seen, there has been no labour at all bestowed upon the land ? "

I take it that cost of construction, materials and labour, determines the actual value of both houses alike, the one on the side street and the one on the main. The enhanced value of the one on the main street is relative value, dependent upon the condition that many persons pass up and down or some other external circumstance, which if removed, the relative value would disappear. If labour were paid more highly in the construction of the one house than the other, or if one builder acquired his materials at lower prices than did another, it would make a difference in the cost of construction or selling values of the two houses ; but given the same labour and the same material the actual value would be the same, whereas the relative value would differ widely. Fashion is an important factor in relative value, a change of fashion will often cause a commodity to be a drug in the market.

It is necessary to make a distinction between actual value, relative value and fictitious value, even if it is difficult to draw the lines between the three, or impossible to reconcile the theories that labour is the creator of all wealth and value; or that demand or exchangeability is the essence of wealth ; or that all value is external or relative, and that no value is intrinsic. If a beautiful vase valued at five pounds be accidentally cracked or chipped, its actual value is lessened ; the value of goods which become damaged in carriage is diminished, or lost. This value is not due to the relation of supply and demand, to the fact that too much has been produced, or that there are fewer buyers, or because the currency has contracted and gold has appreciated ; this is a labour value, for it requires just so much labour to replace this form of value. Cost of transportation gives an enhanced value called place value. These goods may possibly not be sold, hence the place value is lost, as was shown to be the case with the form value referred to. The finished product is more valuable than the raw material, and the added value becomes intrinsic. It may be lost or wasted, still it is a value distinct from relative value. In the case of a beautiful landscape garden, the owner ceases to care for it, or desire it, and abandons it, the relative value diminishes : but the actual value of the garden still remains, another man can still enjoy it, though the value of labour being no longer expended upon it, the garden falls into neglect and loses its present value. A genius sits down and writes an exquisite poem on a bit of paper, another bit of paper is a cheque for a hundred thousand pounds : these two bits of paper are destroyed, is there no intrinsic value lost ? The cheque represented value which is not lost, the actual value of the other is lost. Set a stonemason and a great sculptor to work on two blocks of marble, and the finished products will have different intrinsic values. Had the manuscripts of

Virgil, Plato, Aristotle, been lost as the Alexandrian Library was lost, intrinsic value would have been lost to the world. Has the Rosetta stone in the British Museum no intrinsic value?

A find of pre-historic implements, an exhumed mosaic, a bust of Hermes, a frieze by Pheidias, a picture by Rembrandt, have they no intrinsic value? If not, why is an original work more valuable than a copy? A popular novel runs through twenty or more editions, and brings to its author a large income. Its value in money, therefore, is great. An original scientific work may not sell a thousand copies ; it may represent the labour of a lifetime, the author may die in penury and want. A generation hence the novel is forgotten, the scientific work has lightened toil or elevated thought or increased our powers of production a hundred fold. Had the one not an intrinsic value which neither was, nor can be estimated in money. This wealth estimated from the commercial point of view by demand was only the sale of a thousand copies.

In commenting on the death of Professor Romanes, the remark was made to me, "He died poor I suppose?" I could only reply that I did not know, that he may have considered himself rich. If the wealth that he has bequeathed to humanity be assessed and valued by thinkers, it might be accounted fabulous. Nevertheless, we should probably be told that such wealth is incapable of being measured by any economic standard. It is true that from the commercial point of view the value is small.

A colonizing party may go to the interior of Africa, build houses, and have sent to them linen, glass, plate, kitchen utensils, pictures, bric-à-brac, pianos, violins, harps, in fact all those objects which go to make up the *entourage* of wealthy cultured persons. Suddenly a horde of savages overrun the place and drives out or destroys the civilised individuals and remains in possession of all their effects. To the invaders musical instruments have no value, they do not know how to draw forth from them divine strains of harmony. The cooking utensils have no value, they do not know how to use them, their taste has not been educated to the thousand and one delicate confections of our modern *cordon bleu*. The glass, the plate, the damask linen, the pictures, the bric-à-brac give no satisfaction in the absence of asthetic cravings. These things are all useless and valueless to them, they are not wanted or demanded, their value cannot be measured in money, they cannot be exchanged. Do these objects cease to be wealth since desire or demand is not there? No, they do not cease to be wealth, it is wealth wasted or diverted from the proper channel.

The actual value of cost of production is there, the relative value conditioned by demand is nil. In the case of a cargo of fruit taken to an island where there is abundant fruit, there would be no demand for it, but it does not cease to be wealth, for if taken where there is no fruit, there would be a demand. It would be misplaced wealth in the first instance. Barbarians may be living near a gold mine, they know the gold is there, but it is not appreciated, it has no exchange value. Are we therefore to assume that gold is not wealth and is valueless, or that it has no relative value for the time being, the actual value being there, but that it is misplaced or lost value which ultimately may be found? Again, if gold itself were superseded as a medium of exchange by a humanitarian money, and all desire to use it for ornaments should cease, it would have no value now, or in the future, so we come back again to desire or demand as the principle of wealth. Thus we are driven into the two horns of a dilemma, either labour is the creator of value and wealth, or the man or woman who creates a new want, a new need, a desire, creates wealth, or increases desires and demands and so increases wealth.

Taking for granted that material commodities are actual tangible wealth, there is not less of this actual tangible wealth to-day. Accepting the fact that labour is potential, if not actual wealth, until a service is rendered, there is not less but more labour to be commanded. Our powers of production have never in the world's history been so great as at the present time, yet natural resources are undeveloped and men and women idle. When the possibilities of increasing the fertility of the soil by the aid of chemicals and bacteria were never so promising we are suffering most from industrial depression, and men, women and children are hungry and devitalised from lack of proper food.

To what, then, is the stagnation or depression in trade to be attributed?—to the assumption that credit is wealth. The misapprehension with regard to the true causes of industrial depressions will never be cleared up as long as it is assumed that credit is wealth and that it has the same purchasing power as money. Trade is stimulated when money circulates freely—is easy, or plentiful, when credit is good. Financial panics, industrial depressions, are due to the fact that when confidence is shaken, this purchasing power based on credit fades into thin air. Hence demand diminishes, bullion and sovereigns are required to liquidate debts, the man of enterprise is driven to the wall and trade is paralysed. It has been remarked that as commodities become cheaper demand increases; demand is not free then, it is restrained by something behind it. Demand decreases in hard times, contraction of the currency influences exchanges of wealth and over-production is the striking feature.

Tradesmen are desirous of selling their commodities, individuals are in want of them, and yet an exchange cannot be effected because the purchasing power based on credit has disappeared like the mist before the morning sun.

A value may be assigned to a great many comforts essential to physical well-being, without taking into consideration those essential to mental well-being, but no matter what value be assigned to them, or to whatever extent they may become objects of desire or demand, they will be unattainable if the purchasing power be wanting. The power of obtaining wealth is distinct from the creation of wealth. This difference must be clearly understood, because this power of purchasing wealth may be a mortgage on future production. If a man receive a pension from the Government, its value can be measured in money and he can sell it. Is this right therefore wealth, or does it merely represent a claim upon the wealth produced by others? If a young man who is heir to an entailed estate should borrow money on his credit, some would assume that this credit is an increase of wealth, others would assume that it was a consumption of future wealth. It is neither ; in the case of the young man doing no work himself, it is a claim on the wealth to be produced by others in the future.

The study of rapidly accumulated fortunes affords abundant material for the study of wealth. To infer the average wealth of a nation by computing fictitious or inflated valuations, cannot help us to form a correct opinion of its actual wealth. Stock capitalised at far beyond its real value may represent relative, but not actual wealth. When confidence is shaken the value of stocks goes down ; it is, however, difficult to understand how actual or tangible wealth has been increased or diminished. A financier once remarked that he was astonished that so many persons would invest their money in a certain American railroad to far beyond its real value, simply because the family controlling it are reputed to be extremely rich. On the supposition that credit is wealth, when the credit of this family fails shares would go down ; inflated or fictitious value disappears, but actual value is not lessened.

Inflated values and doubtful security are at last reaping their harvest of distrust and financial ruin. The present financial depression in America is not alone due to the repeal of the Silver Purchase Bill, nor to the uncertainty about tariff legislation by the democratic party; it is in large measure the consequence of antecedent events.

The methods by which certain large fortunes have been accumulated have produced a growing feeling of distrust in foreign investors, and this lack of confidence is also felt by Americans. Most of the modern gigantic successful enterprises have become possible, not by means of past savings, but by means of credit on the expectation of future profits.

Although equal division of wealth increases individual purchasing power and demand, it is doubtful whether many, or even any, of the great enterprises would have been carried through if existing purchasing power or the power to command the services of others had not been concentrated. Small sums in individual hands would not have been productive capital. Individuals realising this have incorporated themselves in order to supply public necessities from which are derived such large revenues. If by the credit of the government individuals were to set to work, wealth would be created no less than by the credit of an individual. For instance, all those enterprises or improvements from which no surplus over expenses incurred is expected, the government is obliged to undertake, while such enterprises as municipal lighting, water works, and so forth are undertaken by individuals, because they anticipate future profits.

The sum of money required to facilitate the production and exchanges of wealth for a stationary nation could be ascertained with almost mathematical precision. The sum of money required for a progressive nation must depend upon the extent to which the standard of living is improving.

The rehabilitation of silver to its former position would, I think, only prolong the present system of capitalistic production and competition. The single gold standard has the merit of hastening a system of perfected barter.

We cannot tell to what extent we are going forward or falling back, until fictitious values give way to actual values. To give an example of what I mean by fictitious values : it was suggested some time since that it would be advisable to affix the price to the Blenheim Raphael in the National Gallery. It was said that many persons were so ignorant that they did not know the value of this addition to the national collection. The value of this picture to the ignorant would have been price £70,000. In times when there is a contraction of the currency, the purchasing power of money becoming greater, the value of the picture measured by this standard would go up. If gold should become very plentiful by the discovery of numerous mines, the value of the picture according to this standard would again vary. This would be an example of fictitious value. In a degenerate age fictitious values take the place of actual values. To appreciate true values indicates capacity in the individual, and as this capacity in the majority is developed or lost, a nation is progressing or retrograding. In contrast to the modern spirit of valuing works of art by the sum of money paid out, is the Greeks' love of the beautiful. The story is told which I give without alteration: Praxiteles, one of the most distinguished artists of ancient Greece, was both a statuary in bronze and a sculptor in marble. He was unsurpassed in the delineation of the softer beauties of the human form, especially in the female figure. His most celebrated work was his marble statue of Aphrodité, which was placed in her temple at Cnidus. It was esteemed the most perfectly beautiful of the statues of the goddess, and travellers from all parts of the civilised world went to see it. So highly did the Cnidians themselves esteem their treasure that when Nicomedes, King of Bithynia, offered them, as the price of it, to pay off the whole of their heavy public debt, they preferred to endure any suffering rather than part with it.

The factors which are producing the extremes of wealth and poverty and their attendant evils are not confined to one race, but are at work in every civilised nation. Riches and poverty are producing wider differences between individuals than the mere accident of birthplace. Slum children are much the same all over the world, there may be differences in the complexion of their skins, but not much in the complexion of their minds. In the same way individuals of the various races who hold the highest social positions, are kin in feeling, culture, and education. The slight differences of habits, of temperament, of features, of language, are as nothing compared to the differences which separate the highly-cultured intellectual man from a depraved, defective individual of his own race. It is said that science has no nationality ; science tells us of what marble is composed, where it is to be found, what chemicals will dissolve it, and such knowledge becomes the property of Jew, Christian, Mohammedan, irrespective of creed ; or of the Turk, the Indian, the German, the American, irrespective of race. When this marble is wrought into a David or a Moses, it is the soul of a Michael Angelo in like manner which adds to the wealth of mankind regardless of creeds, race, or national prejudices. A better method of instilling knowledge into the young by an improved kinder-garten system may originate in the brain of a German pastor, but as soon as its value becomes known, it is adopted in England, France and other countries, and the English, French and German children are alike benefited by it. Improved methods of sanitation, of lighting, of transportation, of building, of carrying on business, as soon as they become known, are utilised to perfect the conditions of town dwellers without racial prejudice. Some are slower to avail themselves of scientific discoveries and improvements, but they are available to all. It is only ignorance which blocks the way.

Scarcely anyone comprehends the full import of what cutting down expenses entails. Society is so interdependent to-day, and the interaction of relative forces so great, and what is real economy so little understood, that retrenching or economising during a period of hard times not only lowers the general standard of living, but may have other disastrous effects. Those who are best informed on the subject of charity organisations, assert that three months out of work may not turn the balance in favour of the pauper or tramp, but six months or a year's cessation from regular work is almost sure to do it. Had periodic commercial crises no other effect than a temporary derangement of the money market, the question of a sound financial system would not be such a burning issue.

Every well organised government should be able to tell how many men and women are out of employment, and should discriminate between those who are capable and willing to work, and the physically and mentally incapable of sustained or efficient effort.

In a financial crisis, in hard times, in depression of trade, the nervous system of men thrown out of work may break down through worry, or the fear of starvation, or their blood may become deteriorated from not having sufficient or proper food. I read a few weeks ago an obituary notice of the late Prince Alexander of Battenberg, who died at the early age of thirty-six. In referring to the cause of his death it was stated that the disease first manifested itself soon after the battle of Slivnitza, and was attributable to the hardships to which he was then exposed. We feel pity for this brilliant life cut short at such an early age, but there are many brilliant lives in the industrial army cut short from a similar cause. Men and women thrown out of work are often compelled to endure hardships which are the beginning of physical and mental troubles from which they may never recover. The instability of the money market in one great commercial centre may have as a remote result disastrous physical effects. One nation does not wish to burden itself with a foreign pauper, and yet, without knowing it, may have been the direct cause of that individual's wreckage.

In the "Twenty-third Annual Report of Charities of the State of New York" there is a report on the removal of alien paupers, showing how much money would be saved by the State if a certain number of alien paupers were returned to their homes, and giving the condition of those persons who were found in the various poorhouses, almshouses, hospitals, and charitable institutions of this state. It says :—

"The saving of future expenditure to the State by these modest annual ones is so enormous that it almost passes the belief of those not familiar with the subject. It amounts in economy to millions, as can be proved by estimating the cost of supporting in institutions 1,391 persons at only two dollars per week (making no estimate of the cost of the added 'plant' or buildings necessary to contain them), a total of nearly $2,800 per week, and of $145,600 per annum for the whole number.

"Estimating the duration of life of this class of dependents, had they been allowed to remain in the country, at the minimum average of fifteen years, the result of the wise forethought of the State in annually appropriating the small sums used since 1880 to return foreign paupers found in it—an ultimate saving of $2,184,000, independent of the expense of housing them and providing salaried officers for their care-taking for that period of time, fifteen years—is definitely proved, and an illegitimate burden on our people thrown back where it originated, and where it justly and naturally belongs.

"Obviously no measure can be more prudent for the State than to protect itself, as far as it can, from the noisome sediment that forced pauper immigration from all Europe deposits, almost immediately upon arrival, in its institutions, supported by taxation, and also in those of its counties, cities, and towns, locally supported in like manner."

The question agitating the scientific sociologists of to-day is not whether the pauper who is destined to be a burden to the State be a Pole, an Italian, a German, a Swede, or of any other nationality, but what produces the pauper who is liable to be a burden to any State. If it be breeding, then we must spread the necessary knowledge on this vital subject; if it be the environment, then we must do away with the economic condition which has, as a result, this human wreckage. They are either human failures or they are human wreckage.

In the mad struggle to become rich, very few, I am sure, ever stop to consider what money is, or what power it wields for so much good or evil to the human race. Purchasing power determines the character of the environment, and the environment determines our character. A man or woman, who through poverty cannot buy sufficient nourishing food, or command lodgings with good pure air, is an example of the purchasing power determining the environment ; insufficent food and vitiated atmosphere, causing a deterioration of the blood and nervous system, which produces the pauper, the drunkard, the criminal, and other human failures, are examples of the environment determining the character.

Every individual, worthy or unworthy, is the product of breeding and environment. The worse the breeding, the less provocation is required by the environment to develop inherent defects; the more perfect the breeding, the better able is the individual to resist and overcome adverse conditions, but even he or she will succumb, provided sufficient strain is brought to bear.

We shall have made a marked advance in civilization when the ideal standard of living is established, as well as the ideal standard of breeding. With increased facilities for production, the standard of living of the workers should have risen in proportion. A Humanitarian government would first of all determine what the standard of minimum comfort should be for a respectable family; it would then study the influences at work which lower this standard, or prevent individuals from maintaining it; then it would legislate to remove these evils. But it is much better that the standard of living in any society should be raised by increased individual responsibility and self-reliance than by State interference. It is much better to increase wages by a more just and equitable distribution of wealth, than to increase them by providing food and clothing, as well as schooling, for the children of the very poor by the State, although true statesmen will recognize that hungry and half-starved children are more injured than benefited by compulsory education. All such aids would not advance the material well-being of workers under our present competitive system. Wages would still be at the subsistence line, with the expense of feeding and clothing of children deducted.

The unsettling of values, the dislocation of industries, the loss of confidence are terrible things to contemplate, no doubt, but they are like a grave malady which becomes more dangerous the longer the surgeon's knife is withheld.

ECONOMICS

(6)

The Financial Crisis in America . . . 1896.

Reproduced from *The Humanitarian* (Nov. 1896, pp. 330-339).

THE FINANCIAL CRISIS IN AMERICA.

BY THE EDITOR.

IN ordinary times the election of a President of the United States can be of very little interest to foreigners except as news of passing events. An election having grave economic issues at stake, like the approaching one, cannot but have consequences which will be felt, if not already appreciably felt, all over the civilised globe. So interdependent are the business interests of all nations to-day, that any doubt as to whether an existing monetary system is going to be maintained has far-reaching results in all large commercial centres. Other nations cannot stand aloof and view the situation as mere onlookers having no vital interest in the issues.

It is said that if the citizens of the United States choose to be Quixotic enough to commit financial suicide in order to give an object lesson to other nations, it is they who will suffer. Even those who are most anxious to see silver rehabilitated as full legal tender, think it a suicidal policy for the United States to attempt to do so alone. By eminent bimetallists it is thought that conjoint action of some, if not all the leading nations of the world is necessary to reinstate silver in the interests of a stable financial system. In the forthcoming Presidential election in the United States, each party is confident of success. One curious feature of the campaign is that among the republicans there are many staunch bimetallists from conviction, and among the democrats many strong monometallists equally decided as to the soundness of their views. Even among those who are opposed to the free silver men, there are many who cannot but feel that protection is a retrograde policy, a temporary measure at best, that while on the one hand protection with high tariff will cause a further disorganisation of trade, free coinage of silver will cause a general unsettling of existing values on the other. Thus we have men pledged to support their party in opposition to their own personal convictions. Neither candidates nor policies seem to carry with them the ungrudging approbation of the general public. The possible political issue, therefore, while it will undoubtedly have far-reaching results from which, if it be unwise, it may take years to recover, cannot be regarded as the verdict of the nation when party interests dominate principles. Though appeals to individual self interest, and purely personal motives may decide the ultimate result of the election, a reform in the currency is a problem of the immediate future. That there is a grave crisis before the Americans no one with ordinary foresight can doubt.

The money agitation only assumed an active form when the large purchases of silver with the diminishing gold reserve in the Treasury made it doubtful whether the United States would be able to maintain the gold standard. It was the consequent financial panic which made the money question such a burning issue. It was the repeated bond issues to maintain the gold reserve which enabled the populists and others to make a plea for a reformed currency such as was never made before in the history of America. The ignorance of the masses on currency questions was depicted in lurid colours and contrasted with the knowledge of financial experts. As it is supposed by so many that the mere agitation for silver is without other foundation than the desire to have cheap money, it is well to follow some of the arguments.

It was said that these large withdrawals of gold from the Treasury, and consequent issues of bonds, were deals on the part of Wall Street to make large profits without much risk, owing to the character of the securities. In other words, it was maintained that the panic was organised and manipulated, that sixteen millions in unnecessary interest on a single bond issue, were foisted on the people, without future benefit to the nation. As soon as another bond issue was imminent, in speeches and the editorial columns of leading daily papers, such arguments as this were used by some of the most conservative men having no monetary theories.

"It would be an outrage to make even one more issue of these bonds, which are out of the reach of the people, and which yield an enormous profit to bankers, who, directly they have paid the gold into the Treasury, proceed to pull it out again by presenting legal tenders (greenbacks) for redemption."

During the Venezuelan scare another bond issue became necessary, plunging the nation further into debt without future benefit.

It is scarcely surprising that the public mind is in a ferment over the currency question, when those who recognise the necessity for reform state as did a well-known financier, in reference to the last bond issue :

" If the hundred million loan is successfully placed, it will, like its predecessors, be only a temporary expedient, but will undoubtedly create an improved sentiment and give time to continue the campaign of education. . . . . One of the errors prevalent in the United States is that ' there is lots of money in the country.' Lots of conventional money, if you please—paper money—but very little of the real money that is current throughout the civilised world, and that is gold. What there is of this is held on the Pacific Coast, and is owned by banks and trust companies in other parts of the country. It is not in circulation."

Such statements made by men supposed to have authority to speak on the subject, only serve as powerful weapons in the hands of those who are agitating for a re-adjustment of the monetary system. The feeling of insecurity imparted to business, together with a general lack of confidence, have become chronic. That it will become acute under present conditions is only a question of time. The feeling of distrust is still further accelerated, because the impression is being conveyed to the masses that moneyed interests are combining to prevent gold from being exported, pending the election, to prevent a further bond issue, and that the same money power which could prevent it, could make these bond issues necessary when it suited their purpose. To show that this view is not alone held by the United States, I quote a few lines from an editorial in the *Times* of Friday, September 11th last.

" We are satisfied, however, that the present bullion movement is a ' natural ' one—that is, that it is the result of indebtedness of Europe to the United States, brought about by ordinary commercial operations, and not, as is still alleged in some quarters, by the artificial creation of finance paper drawn in America. That in certain contingencies the leading New York bankers intended to create finance paper in order to obtain gold is admitted, and, in our opinion, their resolution to do so was wise. It was wise, and in the true sense patriotic, to take measures to prevent any possibility of the United States Treasury being exhausted of gold during the turmoil and alarm which the present Presidential election is inevitably producing."

The belief is becoming widespread that a few bullionists have the power to manipulate the money market, and bring pressure to bear in a given direction whenever they deem it expedient. Such arguments prove most effective weapons in an effort to stir up a revolt against an existing monetary system.

Mr. Carlisle, Secretary of the Treasury, from whom most of the arguments on the soundness of the present system have been derived, fails to realize the real point of the whole controversy. Referring to the absurdity of the demonetization of silver affecting prices, Mr. Carlisle in one of his speeches states :—

" Substantially the whole argument for free coinage, so far as it is addressed to the honest people of the country, is based upon this flimsy foundation, upon an erroneous principle and a false assumption of facts. That the amount of money in circulation, or available for circulation, has more or less influence upon the prices of commodities is not disputed by anybody; but it is not the amount of metallic or redemption money alone that exerts this influence. If all other conditions remain the same, if the relations between supply and demand are unchanged, if the cost of production, transportation, and financial exchanges are stable, an increase or decrease of the currency in circulation, or available for circulation, will to a certain extent increase or decrease prices, as the case may be; but by the terms 'money' and 'currency' in this connection, I mean every element that enters into and is utilised in the complicated processes of buying and selling in the markets for products and in the mercantile exchanges, whether it be gold, silver, bank notes, United States notes, cheques, bills, or other forms of credit, written or unwritten. Credit or confidence is an element of far greater importance in fixing or upholding prices than the mere amount of actual money in use, or available for use, and in fact 95 per cent. of the entire business of the country is transacted without the actual use of metallic money, or its paper representatives; and as to metallic money itself, whether in gold or silver, it is not used to the extent of more than 1 per cent. in our business transactions. In view of these facts, which are as well established as any other facts relating to our commercial and financial operations, how absurd it is to contend that prices are fixed by the amount of that particular kind of currency which does not constitute more than one-hundredth part of the whole. In the broadest and most comprehensive sense the business capacity and personal integrity of each individual constitute a part of the effective currency of the community in which he lives, because these characteristics enable him to become a purchaser of the commodities he has to sell, although at the time he may have neither money nor property. Credit is a purchasing power, and the man who possesses it competes in the markets with the men who possess actual money, and contributes as much as they to the maintenance of prices. To assert that prices are fixed by the amount of redemption money alone is equivalent to the assertion that if all the silver dollars, subsidiary silver coin, silver certificates, United States notes, Treasury notes, National Bank notes, and every other form of credit were destroyed, leaving nothing but the gold, prices would remain the same as they are now—a proposition so preposterous on its face that I presume no man with any regard for his reputation would venture to make it except in a disguised form."

What is the need of coin at all if ninety-five per cent. of the entire business of the country is transacted without the actual use of metallic money? Mr. Carlisle's argument is a mis-statement of facts; it is only necessary to study money movements, and the ebb and flow of bullion, to fully realise the fallacy. Industrial activity varies even in ordinary business years, and there is greater or less demand for the medium of exchange to facilitate transfers of commodities. In business transactions there is a go-between sometimes having as a result most serious consequences. Business is carried on in terms of money, and actual sums of money are supposed to change hands. A man is not able to say I will pay you with so much goods, he promises to pay in so much money, and when there is a severe monetary pressure he may not be able to sell his goods, nor procure money. Commodities cannot pay debts, they must first be converted into money, and when the extinguished credit is a severe contraction of the volume of money, this may spell ruin. In such times, this business capacity and personal integrity which constitute effective currency, according to Mr. Carlisle, cannot save a man from bankruptcy. Mr. Carlisle himself states what would be the effect on prices if nothing were left in circulation but gold, and it is because the contraction of credit money has such disastrous effects on prices of commodities that it has been erroneously assumed by some that an industrial crisis is simply an acute phase of falling prices. Whereas forced sales alone to meet liabilities in actual money is sufficient to unsettle values. Property must be sold at a sacrifice, and investors are told now is the time to purchase.

Never in the history of the United States have we heard so much about good money, honest money, as we have heard in the last three or four years. I have asked able men, presumably well informed on this subject, to give me a definition of sound money and the answer has generally been that it is money received in every market of the world. I have found that the public generally, regarding money as a mere medium of exchange, have accepted depreciated paper money as well as depreciated coins if habit made them accustomed to exchange those tokens as possessing so much value. In fact it is only a small class of persons who make it their business to mark these differences in depreciation and appreciation, and gain a living thereby, who really know what honest money is, if by that we mean a certain weight of bullion. A student of monetary science might consider honest or sound money an ideal standard by which the mutual indebtedness and obligations of society are reckoned. It does not matter whether you reckon this mutual indebtedness in dollars, shillings or francs; it signifies that a service has been rendered to society for which a service is due by society.

Bastiat, who is so often quoted on this subject, argues :—

"You have a crown piece. What does it mean in your hands? It is, as it were, the witness and the proof that you have at some time done some work which, instead of profiting by, you have allowed Society to enjoy in the person of your client. This crown piece witnesses that you have rendered a service to Society, and, moreover, states the value of it. It witnesses, besides, that you have not received back from Society a real equivalent service, as was your right."

It is all very well to attribute the financial upheaval in the United States to ignorant backwoodsmen not having proper banking facilities, but such statements no more enlighten us as to the real situation than a man living in a small country town all his life is able to sum up the various economic movements of the world. The advanced money men attribute their zeal for a reformed currency to the fact that the supply of gold is too limited to be a stable basis for the immense superstructure of credit erected thereon. The mere fact that an extraordinary demand for gold, or unusual exportation is at any time liable to precipitate a monetary crisis, is worth taking into consideration. A growing sensitiveness of the money market, engendered by the apprehension of a recurrence of one of those periodic crises which so shake the stability of a nation, becomes more and more apparent. In a system of trade largely carried on with borrowed capital, bullion movements are regarded with ever-increasing anxiety. Whenever the state of the reserve has reached danger point, a wave of apprehension becomes apparent in the stringency of the loan market, too often paralysing trade and dislocating industries. Those financiers who can directly influence these bullion movements will be more and more held responsible.

The greatest evil of our present monetary system is not so much the appreciation of gold, not so much the fluctuations in value, it is the fear that the gold will not be forthcoming when an unusual demand is made upon it. A collapse of credit is a contraction of the volume of money under our present system—the difficulty of raising money with ordinary security, and at times with even extraordinary security, the impossibility of converting property into money to meet liabilities, the apparent over-production and glutted markets which follow leave various evil consequences.

There was a time when there was no such thing as money; who is daring enough to prophesy what signification will be given to the term a century hence? The mere study of the various commodities that have been used as money within historic times, how other commodities came to be valued in terms of one commodity, the convenience which this system gave for the exchanges of unequal values of wealth, is not sufficient to give us a clear conception of its use or service to mankind. The most instructive part of a historical review of the function and use of money would be an exposition of the power which it has acquired outside and above the individual; the power which a man has by virtue of money in his own possession, the absolute power which money in the hands of others has over him.

Were there no money in the world, and were anyone to propose its creation and use to facilitate the exchanges of wealth to-day, I have no doubt he or she would be laughed at, if not persecuted, for daring to suggest the establishing of a system which would place power and wealth in the hands of the few. Without hesitation I am ready to assert that it would be impossible, with our present economic knowledge, to inaugurate the present monetary system.

Without money in the world, what would be our present state of civilization? The influence that money has had in the marvellous development and the rapid accumulation of wealth is not in the satisfaction of personal wants. Ninety-nine individuals are satisfied with things as they are, the hundredth desires something better, higher, different, if to this one is given the power to satisfy the simple wants of the ninety-nine, and they in turn are obliged to work to produce that which will satisfy a superior need, an advance in civilization is made. In the theocracies of antiquity, magnificent monumental works were produced—temples, pagodas, palaces, without money in the world. There is reason for believing that pre-historic nations evolved a literature, a philosophy, a *moral* which in many respects we might envy, without money in the world. The system which absolutely placed the services of the slave at the command of a master, and that which compels the wage-slave by necessity to satisfy other wants than his own differ in degree only, not in kind. Were there no such thing as money in the world, men and women would continue to work to satisfy their wants, but as the general tendency of human nature is to let well enough alone—to fight against change, to avail themselves slowly of improvements—in our consideration of the influence that money has had in evolution, we must take into account these human characteristics.

Postponing a present satisfaction, the labourer deposits a few shillings weekly in the savings bank. These accumulated savings which enable him to command something solid furnish on a small scale an example of the immense influence which concentrated capital has had in the creation of wealth. The accumulation of something not perishable which enables the individual to command something substantial is a great advance over primitive barter. The full advantage of this system is not only in enabling the individual to accumulate a sufficient sum to become productive capital, but these accumulations of deposits in the meantime enable others to create or produce wealth in the shape of a loanable fund, as Mr. Bagehot so ably indicated. This loanable fund has been a tremendous factor for progress in the power it gave to create new industries, and in its power to disrupt old stagnating conditions. Probably, when we have superseded the present monetary system by perfected barter, capital seeking investment, to which I have so often referred, will be regarded as the great disruptive factor of progress. If a commercial enterprise requires a million capital to carry it through successfully, it need not wait till the millionaire decides to take the initiative; the man of enterprise can command this loanable fund often with the anticipation of future profits, and not as the result of past savings, perhaps in direct conflict with those who profit by an old method.

A law when it is first framed, except in autocracies or absolute monarchies, is supposed to be the expression of the wishes of the people or at least is made with their sanction. After a time in succeeding generations this law has assumed the power to control and check the actions of individuals who had nothing to do with its origin, and may even be bitterly opposed to it. Similarly, the power and influence that money has assumed to control the actions and even the destinies of individuals and nations, is most instructive. The power it has to command the services of others, and whether this power be legitimate and justifiable or even a necessity of a higher evolution of Society, is being brought home to the masses at the close of the nineteenth century as it has never been before in the history of the world. An army is of immense service in defence against foreign invasions, or aggressive warfare against enemies, but it can also be used as a powerful factor in putting down civil dissatisfaction and crushing out any internal desire for change or better economic conditions which run counter to the established order of those having power to command this army. So it is with money.

So many, so various, so contradictory are the statements and arguments made by serious, right-meaning persons, on the question of money, that the confusion with regard to the subject cannot be wondered at. Obviously, with two diametrically opposed views, both cannot be right. There can be, though, different aspects of the same problem, containing a measure of truth in all. As a rule, the attempt has been made only to point out the fallacies contained within the various arguments for one system or the other, without giving due consideration to the evidence which proves their plea to be right under certain conditions. It is too late in the day to reject our opponents' views as false and misleading simply because they do not agree with ours. If we are really in earnest in our desire to solve the money problem, we shall endeavour to understand the point of view which led up to such conflicting statements.

Able economists have stated that it is advantageous for a country to have very little money, for then a premium on production is established, and export trade is developed by the low prices, which follow as a necessary consequence. Others, no less eminent, state that trade is stimulated when money is easy and circulates freely. Others again tell us that—

"Every purposed increase of the money supply by act of government, having for its object the raising of prices and the scaling down of debts, is subject to the gravest impeachment on the grounds, not only of morality, but also of economic expediency. It carries with it the sting of fraud ; and it leaves behind it a retribution swift, sure and terrible. A metallic inflation, however, due to the discovery of new resources in nature, or to improvements in the arts, is subject to no such objection. Hume, McCulloch, Chevalier and Cairnes support the proposition that a considerable increase of the money supply from such a source, if not too rapid, may, by reducing the burden of existing taxes, debts and fixed charges, and by setting a premium on business enterprise in the shape of enhanced profits, greatly promote current industry. This beneficial influence may be carried so far as to appear to constitute a creative force."

With such contradictory and irreconcilable statements as that low prices for commodities alone will benefit the nation, and raising the prices will alone stimulate industrial activity, there must be some radical misapprehension of facts.

A rise or fall in prices of commodities can only be attributed to inflation or contraction of the volume of money where there is a general rise or fall in prices of all commodities. In such a general rise or fall, neither producer nor consumer can be said to benefit, for if a man receives more for what he sells, he must pay more for what he buys. The theory that it is the falling prices in a contraction of the volume of money which checks industry, is equally fallacious. Where falling prices are due to money, general cost of production would decrease, leaving the margin of profits the same. In like manner the assumption that an increase in the volume of money by raising prices stimulates industry is wrong, because a general rise in price would involve so much more added cost to production, thus balancing profits.

It cannot be denied that inflation or contraction of the volume of money has weighty consequences in other ways. An increase in the volume of money, by stimulating fresh industries, by increasing the loanable fund to men of enterprise, by increasing demand in other directions, has a beneficial effect. Sudden contraction of the currency caused by the shrinkage of credit, has most disastrous effects in diminishing demand, which has, as a result, apparent over-production. The theory that a natural increase in the volume of the currency reduces the burden of existing taxes, debts and fixed charges, and a contraction of the currency increases these burdens, is correct. Here it is a question of robbing Peter to pay Paul ; if money appreciates, the debtor suffers, if money depreciates in value, the creditor. We see the application of this theory in the view held that if the free coinage of silver be adopted in America, all the gold will be drained away. Apart from the so much talked about Gresham law there is the theory that cheap, that is plentiful, money, would enhance the prices of our commodities, and our creditors would demand gold in liquidation of their debts. Since the United States have to pay some three or four hundred millions a year to European nations in balancing their claims, this would be a serious matter. In reality the first effect that the free coinage of silver would have would be to decrease the volume of money ; the violent contraction of credit money which would follow, would have a marked effect on prices.

In the argument that scarcity of money and consequent low prices promote industry and foreign trade, thus securing to a nation general prosperity, lies the root of the evil, because the root is the insufficiency of the gold basis to maintain with security the immense superstructure of credit. The foundation for such a statement is that the United States must pay our foreign indebtedness in gold when prices are high. They can only pay them with commodities when they undersell their markets. Practically, prosperity becomes identified with the amount of the gold reserve to maintain the gold standard. The means by which this reserve can best be protected, and the best methods to prevent its leaving the country, become the most serious problems of practical statesmanship.

It is imperative that the campaign of education on the money question should be continued, and, after the excitement of the election is over, the necessity for a Currency Commission to investigate the best methods for a re-construction of the whole system, will every day become more and more apparent. The present situation is attributed to doubtful legislation with regard to silver, and to currency cranks acting from interested motives. Various articles on the subject convey the impression that the working man is very obtuse on money questions, and is completely carried away by any wild-cat scheme, or irresponsible promises for a cheap and inflated currency. Anything further from the truth can scarcely be imagined. He is open to conviction, and is really desirous of arriving at the truth on the subject, being deeply impressed with the economic necessity for a stable currency. The wage-earning class, if anything, more than others read with avidity the numberless contributions which have flooded the United States on the subject for the last four or five years. Try as each side may to misrepresent facts, to mislead the public during a Presidential election, our legislators will not be able to burke the real financial issue.

Victoria Woodhull Martin.

ECONOMICS

(7)

What of the Future? . . . 1896.

Reproduced from *The Humanitarian* (Feb. 1896, pp. 90-96).

WHAT OF THE FUTURE?
BY THE EDITOR.

NEVER in the history of our civilisation has there been a time
when the actions of persons in authority have been submitted
to such keen and searching criticism as at present.   During the
last half of this century, science has made so many startling discoveries in every direction, that we are no longer satisfied with mere
statements of governmental policy ; we demand motives and causes.
If our boasted civilisation is to stand the test of time and be a guide
and light to future generations, we cannot afford to have our stability
disturbed by what the next century may term a spasm of intellectual
flatulency exhibited by those in power.   The questions are being
asked on every hand :—What is their state of health?   What are their
antecedents?   These questions being answered favourably or unfavourably, no matter whether the person be president or emperor, his
conduct is analysed, and given importance or treated with indifference.

The occurrences of the last few weeks have taught a lesson in
finance as well as in diplomacy.   They have also shown how easy it is
to excite the ignorant or the unbalanced by appeals to their passions
and prejudices, and how dangerous it is to have a political organisation
which makes it to the interest of any one individual or party to play
upon these very weaknesses of the human animal for their benefit.   In
marked contrast to the warlike spirit evoked by ill-advised speeches
and inflammatory articles, have been the temperate and judicious
criticisms in different quarters with the object of determining what
justification might exist for such utterances.   There was a time when
to question the infallibility of the Church was a heinous crime ; to
doubt the divine guidance of the State was treason, and often dire
consequences were the result.   Blind faith, blind obedience was
exacted, no matter where it led or what the consequences might be.
To augment spiritual and temporal power, it was probably necessary
to endow with super-human attributes those in authority in nation-
making.   Stability was further insured by making this authority
hereditary.

The scientific statesman does not overlook, nor does he fail to give due weight to any factor which has had an influence in nation-making. The divine right of kings and the infallibility of the Church, or spiritual and temporal power combined, have exercised an important part in the past in developing and civilising the human animal. It would be folly to under-estimate the value of fostering and strengthening patriotism in the past by celebrating victorious wars, by honouring heroes, by commemorating events which have been influential in augmenting temporal power; in like manner as the Church, following the precedent of Paganism, appointed saints' days and holy days in order to augment spiritual power.

Recent events and their consequent arousing of national animosities have awakened a desire in our minds to know of what national pride is composed. Whence is its origin? Had primitive village communities national pride? It is well to analyse the origin and use of patriotism, when a slighter provocation than that which would incite individuals to quarrel may suffice to plunge nations into war. Let us take the United States as an example. The national life extends only a little over a century. Two years ago I was asked to give my views on Independence Day, and my expression of them was published widely in the United States. I then referred to Independence Day as a political holiday which celebrates an epoch in nation-making. I also said: "At the time when the revolted Colonies were not yet united, and the strength and success of the young Republics depended upon concerted action, to develop a new-born patriotism was of paramount importance." The celebration of Independence Day was a bond of union, keeping fresh in the mind what had been fought for and won by collective action. As the sound of the drum arouses the old war-horse, and brings into play early training or experiences, so the fireworks and other demonstrations revive recollections and scenes which played so important a part in the history of the United States. Every day in the year could represent some event in history, but in that case the national holidays would fail to serve any purpose by becoming too common.

This difficulty, however, is obviated by the fact that as time creeps on the enthusiasm aroused by particular events commences to wane. Generation succeeds generation, and the immediate persons who have been actors in a particular drama, or who have been directly interested, pass away. More especially is this true in the instance of Independence Day. It appeals particularly to Americans of three or more generations, and most of all to those thirteen States which fought for independence from the arbitrary demands of George III. It was not a desire simply on the part of the Americans to emancipate themselves from the protection of the Mother Country which brought on the war, but a protest and revolt of the American colonies against unjust taxation. A proposition to tax the American colonies to raise revenues in George II's time was dismissed as impracticable, as the Americans were unrepresented in Parliament. "George III," says Buckle, "having a most exalted opinion of his own authority, and being entirely ignorant of public affairs, thought that to tax the Americans for the benefit of the English would be a masterpiece of policy." The thirteen colonies, however, did not see the question in the same light, and the result we know. To-day the thirteen States have become forty-four; the population of the United States of America during the last generation has been constantly recruited by foreigners from every nation of Europe; in New York alone, there are about 350,000 Germans, 400,000 Irish, 120,000 Italians, and other nationalities going to make up the population called American. These can have no interest in nursing or keeping up national or State prejudices. To them Independence Day is a mere word, and each State is simply a geographical area of the United States.

It has, in the past, been vitally essential to inspire pride in national institutions, traditions, and customs, in order to bring about the solidarity of cohering groups by causing them to have an identity of interests. But as a nation became powerful it was less and less necessary to celebrate national holidays.

The economic problem which led to the War of Independence may no less conceivably lead to civil wars or revolutions to-day. The correct adjustment of taxation for raising necessary revenue is a living issue at the present time. The new generation is interested in the course of events of the immediate present; there are problems to-day as vital for the social well-being as those which have preceded them. The demands of the present over-shadow those of the past, and displace the outworn symbol of Independence Day by the new enthusiasm for the economic independence of our wage-slaves; a new revolt against unjust taxation is an issue of the immediate future. An equitable re-adjustment of taxation, not only as between class and class, but as between sex and sex, will give to Independence Day in the coming century a significance entirely different from that which it has borne in the first century of the national life of the United States.

Growing commercial interests, rapid transit, the almost instantaneous communication between nation and nation, have served to break down barriers and to soften prejudices. There are other forces modifying differences and uniting nations, such as international congresses, science, and art. Science knows no nationality. Correct observation of phenomena, some grand generalisation derived therefrom, far-reaching inventions, are heirlooms to humanity. Who questions the nationality of a Raphael, of a Beethoven, of a Shakespeare, of a Darwin, of a Pasteur? Humanity claims them. Are the hasty utterances of an august personage the voice of the nation that gave birth to a Goethe and a Helmholtz? How many have toiled long and ceaselessly never to receive in their lives the crown of their desires, leaving other nations to perfect and reap the glory! How many have suffered even unto martyrdom for some truth which returns after centuries, as bread cast upon the waters, to bless other nations.

Capital seeking investment is the great disruptor of modern times; it is as ruthless as war in breaking up old conditions and making them give way to the new. As once tribe combined with tribe for mutual protection or to overcome some common foe, so is labour now forced to combine with labour in self-defence. Commercial enterprise is dissolving old stagnating conditions, everywhere forcing one and all into competition for the markets of the world. The immense superstructure of credit which has reinforced the limited medium of exchange, is doing as much to unite nations by making them feel an identity of interest, as was done by those forces which compelled isolated groups to unite for mutual benefit in nation-making. The very possibility of a one thousand million dollar shrinkage in values in America by the recent war-scare, and the damage inflicted on German trade in England by the Emperor's action, demonstrates how opposed are commercial interests and military action. The development of the resources of other countries through the anticipation of future profits has made the financial interests of nations so interdependent, that the disturbance of credit in any one country is felt in every monetary centre.

Every economist well knows that the greatest evil a nation has to fear is not so much war, as the importation of immigrants satisfied with a lower standard of living than its own wage-slaves are willing to accept. In the history of civilisation, if there is one thing more apparent than another, it is that as commerce was extended, as the population gave up agricultural pursuits and their occupations became more diversified ; as their wants increased and their demands became more difficult to satisfy,—they grew rich and prosperous. Civilisation was developed and spread. Where individuals returned to agricultural pursuits, where their life was simplified, where they were easily satisfied and content with little, their civilisation was arrested, the onward march of progress turned back. A vegetative pastoral life may be beautiful to contemplate from the poet's standpoint, but the contentment of the sage who nibbles a crust in a state of philosophic abstraction, the hermit content to dwell in a cave, are not the real benefactors of mankind. There is nothing too good for me, there is not a loom which can spin anything fine enough, there is not a creation of art which is wasted while I live. It is my misfortune if I cannot possess what the divine spark of genius has endowed with life; I can appreciate, if I cannot enjoy. Is there a soul so refined, so exalted, as to be alive to all the marvellous creations which the mind, impressing itself upon the raw material of nature has been able to evolve, then that soul is the real benefactor, the real propelling force of a higher type of civilisation.

A clever artificer must be encouraged by appreciation and a demand for his work, otherwise his labour is in vain. The decadence of civilisation is not alone due to the unequal distribution of wealth, any more than are the shortcomings of democracy to the freedom of the franchise. Decay commences when the mal-adjustment of wealth is so great that production takes the form of supplying the extravagant and wasteful wants of the few, while the majority are kept at the bare subsistence line, or are reduced to pauperism. Taking a cursory review of the growth and spread of civilisation, it will be found that perfect equality is almost as powerful an obstruction to progress as the extremes of inequality. In the survival of village communities we find generations of economic stagnation. They supply each other's or their own simple wants, and are perfectly satisfied. They have provided sufficient safeguards against internal decay, as for instance a provision that any one leaving the community shall not derive benefits from the community, his share becoming the property of those who helped to make the value; if succession fails, the proceeds revert to the public fund. These communities, unless broken up by pressure from outside, have continued for hundreds of years in a self-satisfied condition of well-being at a low level. Did the mere fact of survival indicate the fittest? Communities or nations representing generations of stagnant survival might be cited as other examples. Do these represent the highest civilisation? Human beings are dissatisfied with a lower standard of life when they have known a higher, but if economic conditions are such that callous indifference and hopeless despair crushes out all desire, then it is that nations are menaced by more destructive foes than wars or international differences.

To catch the popular vote, and in order to retain office, politicians have resorted to insincere promises, tricks and artifices of every description, until the free institutions which they profess to represent are pronounced a failure. When in power, legislators must practise procrastination until it becomes a fine art, until the people no longer desire or have forgotten that for which they clamoured.

We cannot arrive at any logical conclusions with regard to the evils or blessings of popular government so long as the relations of fertility to greater or less mental capacity are not taken into consideration, together with conditions which have a prejudicial influence on the individuals who as voters are to carry on the government of their country by the agency of their representatives. Although Macaulay did not take into consideration the conditions which make our human failures or insure their survival, he foresaw the evils resulting from the rapid multiplication of the unfit. Writing to Henry S. Randall in 1857, he said :—

"I never uttered a word nor wrote a line indicating an opinion that the supreme authority in a State ought to be entrusted to the majority of citizens told by the head. I have long been convinced that institutions, purely democratic, must, sooner or later, destroy liberty or civilisation, or both. Your Constitution is all sail and no anchor. Either some Cæsar or Napoleon will seize the reins of government with a strong hand, or your Republic will be as fearfully plundered and laid waste by barbarians in the twentieth century as the Roman Empire was in the fifth, with this difference—that the Huns and Vandals, who ravaged the Roman Empire, came from without, and that your Huns and Vandals will have been engendered within your own country, by your own institutions."

The twentieth century will not close without seeing the readjustment of social conditions or social ruin. In such a social reconstruction Huns and Vandals will no longer be bred. There are already indications that augur well for mankind in the growth of humanitarianism, which is making itself manifest in altruism. The "Economic Man" of Adam Smith, and of John Stuart Mill, is giving place, under the influence of legislation, dictated by popular sentiment, to the "Sympathetic Man" of the future.

History is a continuous record of the inevitable advance from the family to the tribe, the tribe to the nation, the nation to the empire. China, Chaldea, Persia, bear evidence in this direction. Rome and Carthage contended in a death-struggle for the empire of the world ; Greece, distracted by tribal jealousies, went down before the power, imperial *de jure*, if not *de facto*, of Rome. The feudal Duchies of France, the legacy of Merovingian and Carlovingian kings, the Heptarchy of England, the detached kingdoms of Leon, Aragon and Castile have been merged in the suzerainties of France, England and

Spain. Germany and Italy are the most recent instances of this inevitable centralising process.

Trade and commerce have been subject to the same law ; fiscal regulations have submitted to similar necessities. When turnpike roads were established in England, the home counties petitioned Parliament for protection against the rural districts, whose produce they deemed to be thus brought into an unfair competition with their own. When the enterprise of the United States, already protected each against the others by tariffs, was directed towards the Central (then the Far-Western) States, the older colonies sought for individual advantage by further measures of protection. All these barriers, under the stress of war with the mother-country, were swept away for ever, and the United States of America were welded into what is now the largest area in the world in which a free nation enjoys the advantages of free trade.

In the meantime, the British Empire has stamped the old world as the indubitable heritage of the Anglo-Saxon race ; her colonies have more than once, and notably in the last few weeks, shown that they are not merely held together by a nominal allegiance, but that in time of peril the Empire is as one country. Imperial federation is still in the future ; the federation of the Anglo-Saxon race may not be much more remote. It is not too much to say that if recent events have shown that racial jealousies, and even antipathies, must be admitted to exist among the unthinking, open discord between its two great branches is admitted to be impossible by those in whom reason controls passion.

Who will be the men by whom this great step towards the amalgamation of mankind in an harmonious whole will be brought about ? Not those, surely, such as we see swarming in our centres of population to-day, absorbed in the struggle for life, with no care beyond the morrow, with no interest save in the preservation of self. The future, said the Greek poet of old, lies in the lap of the Gods ; but, in this respect the future is in our own hands. It is to the children of the present generation that we entrust the heritage that we have received from the past. It is for us to see that this trust is placed in no ignoble hands ; that those who succeed us be—

"Stronger ever born of weaker, lustier body, larger mind,"

that our descendents shall be able to repeat, without fear of contradiction, the proud claim of the Homeric warrior, "we boast that we are far better than our sires."

Victoria Woodhull Martin.

REFERENCES

The writings reprinted in *The Woodhull Reader* were found in the Miriam Y. Holden Library of Books by and about Women, New York City, and in the New York Public Library. A special debt of gratitude is owed to Mrs. Holden for her generous co-operation. The editor also wishes to thank Mr. Lewis C. Koch for his perceptive reading and constructive suggestions.

For those who wish to study the life and career of Victoria Woodhull in greater depth, the following references are provided:

ADDITIONAL WORKS BY VICTORIA WOODHULL

The Alchemy of Maternity. [Cheltenham: N. Sawyer & Co., 1889]. (Leaflet No. 3 of the Manor House Club, Norton Park, near Tewkesbury).

The Argument for Woman's Electoral Rights, Under Amendments XIV. and XV. of The Constitution of the United States: A Review of My Work at Washington, D.C., in 1870-1871. (London: Norman, 1887).

Breaking the Seals; or, The Key to the Hidden Mystery. (New York: Woodhull & Claflin, 1875).

The Elixir of Life; or, Why Do We Die? (New York: Woodhull & Claflin, 1873).

A Fragmentary Record of Public Work Done in America, 1871-1877. (London: Norman, 1887).

The Garden of Eden: The Allegorical Meaning Revealed. (London 1890). Revised.

Goethe's Elective Affinities: With an Introduction by Victoria C. Woodhull (Boston 1872).

The Human Body The Temple of God; or, The Philosophy of Sociology [Written with Tennessee Claflin]. (London 1890).

The Humanitarian (London) July 1892 - December 1901 (monthly).

Humanitarian Government. (London 1890).

A New Constitution for the United States of the World Proposed for the Consideration of the Constructors of Our Future Government. (New York: Woodhull, Claflin & Co., 1872). [Substantially the same as *A Page of American History. Constitution of the United States of the World* (N.p. [1870]).

The Origin, Tendencies and Principles of Government: or, A Review of the Rise and Fall of Nations from Early Historic Time to the Present; with Special Considerations Regarding the Future of the United States as the Representative Government of the World. (New York: Woodhull, Claflin & Co., 1871).

Paradise Found. (London: Culliford, n.d.).

The Scientific Propagation of the Human Race or, Humanitarian Aspects of Finance and Marriage. ([New York] 1893).

A Speech on the Garden of Eden; or, Paradise Lost and Found. (New York: Woodhull & Claflin, 1876).

Woodhull & Claflin's Weekly (New York) May 14, 1870 - June 10, 1876 (weekly). Among the interesting articles by Victoria Woodhull are "The Religion of Humanity" (November 2, 1872); "Moral Cowardice & Modern Hypocrisy" (December 28, 1872); "The Scare-Crows of Sexual Slavery" (September 27, 1873).

WORKS ABOUT VICTORIA WOODHULL

Becker, Beril. *Whirlwind in Petticoats.* (Garden City, N.Y., 1947). (Fictionalized).

Brief Sketches of The Life of Victoria Woodhull (Mrs. John Biddulph Martin). (N.p., n.d.).

Darewin, G. S. *Synopsis of the Lives of Victoria C. Woodhull, (now Mrs. John Biddulph Martin) and Tennessee Claflin (now Lady Cook).* (London [1891]).

[Darwin, M. F.] *One Moral Standard for All.* (N.p., n.d.).

Davenport, Walter and Derieux, James C. *Ladies, Gentlemen and Editors.* (Garden City, N.Y., 1960).

Davis, Paulina Wright. *A History of the National Woman's Rights Movement, for Twenty Years.* (New York: Journeymen Printers, Co-Operative Association, 1871).

Holbrook, Stewart H. *Dreamers of The American Dream.* (New York 1957).

Johnson, Gerald W. *The Lunatic Fringe.* (Philadelphia & New York [1957]).

Johnston, Johanna. *Mrs. Satan: The Incredible Saga of Victoria C. Woodhull.* (New York [1967]).

Legge, Madeleine. *"Two Noble Women, Nobly Planned."* [London 1893].

Marberry, M. Marion. *Vicky; a Biography of Victoria C. Woodhull.* (New York [1967]).

Mott, Frank Luther. *A History of American Magazines.* (Cambridge, Mass., 1938). Vol. III.

Nelson, James M. "America's Victoria," *Bulletin of the Historical and Philosophical Society of Ohio* (October 1958).

Sachs, Emanie. *"The Terrible Siren" Victoria Woodhull (1838-1927).* (New York 1928).

Shaplen, Robert. *Free Love and Heavenly Sinners.* (New York [1954]).

Stern, Madeleine B. *We the Women: Career Firsts of Nineteenth-Century America.* (New York 1963, reprinted New York: Lenox Hill Publishing Corp., 1974).

Tilton, Theodore. *Victoria C. Woodhull. A Biographical Sketch.* (New York 1871). (The Golden Age Tracts, No. 3).

[Treat, Joseph]. *Beecher, Tilton, Woodhull, The Creation of Society.* (New York 1874).

Wallace, Irving. *The Square Pegs: Some Americans Who Dared To Be Different.* (New York 1957).